VOLUME 64

SCREEN WORLD™

The Films of 2012

BARRY MONUSH

SCREEN WORLD
Volume 64 Copyright © 2013 by Barry Monush
Executive publisher, Ben Hodges

Published in 2013 by Theatre World Media
Distributed by Applause Theatre & Cinema Books
An Imprint of Hal Leonard Corporation
7777 West Bluemound Road
Milwaukee, WI 53213

Trade Book Division Editorial Offices
33 Plymouth Street, Montclair, NJ 07042

Printed in the United States of America
Book design by Tony Meisel

ISBN 978-1-48034-253-8
ISSN 1545–9020

theatreworld.com

To CHRISTOPHER WALKEN

Whose incomparable screen presence, enigmatic line-readings, idiosyncratic characterizations, and mesmerizing style of acting have made him one of the most treasured, applauded, and excitingly unpredictable actors in film.

SCREEN (theatrical releases only): 1969: *Me and My Brother*, **1971:** *The Anderson Tapes*, **1972:** *The Happiness Cage*, **1976:** *Next Stop, Greenwich Village*, **1977:** *The Sentinel*; *Annie Hall*; *Roseland*; **1978:** *The Deer Hunter* (Academy Award Winner for Best Supporting Actor); **1979:** *Last Embrace*; **1980:** *Heaven's Gate*, **1981:** *The Dogs of War*, *Pennies from Heaven*; **1983:** *Brainstorm*; *The Dead Zone*; **1985:** *A View to a Kill*; **1986:** *At Close Range*; **1987:** *Deadline/Witness in the War Zone*; **1988:** *The Milagro Beanfield War*, *Biloxi Blues*; *Homeboy*; **1989:** *Communion*; **1990:** *King of New York*; **1991:** *The Comfort of Strangers*; **1992:** *Mistress*; *Batman Returns*; **1993:** *True Romance*; *Wayne's World 2*; **1994:** *Pulp Fiction*; **1995:** *Wild Side*; *Search and Destroy*; *The Prophecy*; *The Addiction*; *Nick of Time*; *Things to Do in Denver When You're Dead*; **1996:** *The Funeral*; *Basquiat*; *Last Man Standing*; **1997:** *Touch*; *Suicide Kings*; *Excess Baggage*; *Mousehunt*; **1988:** *Illuminata*; *New Rose Hotel*; *Antz* (voice); **1999:** *Blast from the Past*; *Sleepy Hollow*; **2000:** *The Opportunists*; **2001:** *Joe Dirt*; *America's Sweethearts*; *The Affair of the Necklace*; **2002:** *Scotland, Pa.*; *Poolhall Junkies*; *The Country Bears*; *Catch Me if You Can* (Oscar nomination as Supporting Actor); **2003:** *Kangaroo Jack*; *Gigli*; *The Rundown*; **2004:** *Envy*; *Man on Fire*; *The Stepford Wives*; *Around the Bend*; **2005:** *Wedding Crashers*; *Undertaking Betty/Plots with a View*; *Domino*; **2006:** *Click*; *Man of the Year*; **2007:** *Hairspray*, *Balls of Fury*, *Romance & Cigarettes*; **2011:** *Kill the Irishman*; **2012:** *Dark Horse*; *Seven Psychopaths*; *A Late Quartet*; *Stand Up Guys*; **2013:** *The Power of Few*.

CONTENTS

In Praise of the Not-so-Misérables

I guess there's hope yet for movie audiences when *Lincoln*, a stirring slice of history on an important topic, ends up making a hell of a lot more money than the CGI-overloaded, horror mash-up *Abraham Lincoln: Vampire Hunter*. Audiences were transfixed by Daniel Day-Lewis' mesmerizing portrayal of our 16th President, reinforcing Abe's image as an American icon of inestimable admiration to an even greater degree than I would have thought possible, with a worthy, Steven Spielberg-directed movie now forever attached to the Lincoln name. And there were other signs of hope … *Les Misérables* came to the screen after a long wait and proved to be not only a rousing adaptation of the stage smash but a musical of tremendous box office drawing power, with, among its many highlights, a jaw-dropping one-take rendition of "I Dreamed a Dream" by Oscar-winning Anne Hathaway; Ben Affleck's exciting dramatization of one of history's most fascinating, little-known events, *Argo*, was not only a moneymaker but elevated the actor into the position as one of our most interesting current directors, bringing him the Academy Award for Best Picture as the icing on the cake (even if the Academy didn't see fit to give him so much as a mention in the director's category); *Life of Pi* took a novel nearly everyone declared "un-filmable" and thanks to masterful (Oscar-winning) direction by Ang Lee kept audiences enthralled with a story set mostly on a lifeboat, with one human and a tiger for the leads; *Silver Linings Playbook* was a superbly written and directed (by David O. Russell) mix of angst and humor, showcasing some fine actors, chief among them Jennifer Lawrence in an Academy Award-winning performance; and *Django Unchained* proved that there is no filmmaker like Quentin Tarantino when it comes to reinventing history with a button-pushing flourish, a streak of stylized violence, and quotably good dialogue, delivered by a topnotch cast (everyone from the slyly engaging, Oscar-winning Christoph Waltz to Don Johnson, Leonardo DiCaprio, Samuel L. Jackson, and Dennis Christopher) with flair.

These were all in that exalted realm I had started to worry was a thing of the past, movies that are both award season-favorites and very popular at the box office. You didn't necessarily have to qualify for either, however, in order to be a stand-out entry in the year, because there was also much to praise about: *Bernie*, a quirky, disturbing true story about the sweetest murderer you'd ever want to know, played to perfection by Jack Black; *The Grey*, a tense and terrifying pursuit of the "and you think *your* day was bad" sort, with Liam Neeson at his determined best; *Flight,* which put dependable Denzel Washington into the pilot's seat for a seering portrait of one troubled soul; the sublime acting ensemble of Kevin Kline, Diane Keaton, Dianne Wiest, and others in the gentle *Darling Companion*; another bit of demented originality from the too-long-away Whit Stillman, *Damsels in Distress*; an impressive adaptation of the red-hot best seller *The Hunger Games*; *Celeste & Jesse Forever*, which rose above rom-com clichés thanks chiefly to a terrific Rashida Jones; a bittersweet and underrated high school reunion ensemble, *10 Years*; *Jeff, Who Lives at Home*, which gave Jason Siegel and Ed Helms their most challenging roles yet, not to mention reminding us once again of the outstanding talents of Susan Sarandon; the spot-on and frequently hilarious homage to everybody's favorite lowbrow comedians, *The Three Stooges*; the third and in many ways most exemplary of the complex and exciting Batman features directed by Chris Nolan, *The Dark Knight Rises*; an all-too-realistic glimpse into the hell of fighting crime in modern-day L.A. in *End of Watch*; the time-bending *Looper*, a superior sci-fi and one of several movies to showcase the increasingly excellent Joseph Gordon-Levitt; *The Campaign*, which gleefully sent up electoral mudslinging and the unethical corporate control of politics; *The Best Exotic Marigold Hotel*, which took full advantage of a UK dream cast, with Judi Dench at another peak; the tricky *Thin Ice*, which pulled the rug out from under viewers more than once, most effectively; *Skyfall*, certainly the most multi-faceted and surprising of the Daniel Craig 007 adventures to date; *Moonrise Kingdom*, which presented just the right balance of Wes Anderson's patented weirdness and genuine heart; *To Rome with Love*, a pleasurable anthology from the great Woody Allen; *Promised Land*, the sort of finely wrought, issue-driven drama that was once the norm in Hollywood films; *The Woman in the Fifth*, a fascinating puzzle with top notch work by Ethan Hawke as a writer on a mental descent; *Magic Mike*, which took the potentially trashy topic of male strippers and made it something deeper and more thought-provoking than could be imagined; the satirical and sad *Seeking a Friend for the End of the World*, which for once delivered the apocalypse with grace rather than GCI-onslaught; *Killer Joe*, presenting a mostly riveting batch of lowlife cinematic scum with Matthew McConaughey at the forefront; a smart look at the delicate balance required to endure families in Julie Delpy's *2 Days in New York*, certainly the best use on screen so far of Chris Rock; *The Perks of Being a Wallflower*, which featured some three-dimensional teenagers you actually wanted to spend time with, as played by Logan Lerman, Emma Watson, and most outstandingly, Ezra Miller; *The Sessions*, a moving and honest exploration of sexuality, with 2012's most surprising Oscar omission, John Hawkes; a deliberately theatrical take on *Anna Karenina* that somehow worked against all odds, containing an incisive, unjustly unsung turn by Jude Law; and *The Impossible*, a startling recreation of a horrific real-life Tsunami, with exemplary work by Ewan McGregor, Naomi Watts, and young Tom Holland.

As always you couldn't depend on audiences to take to everything of quality; while animation continues to have an amazingly dependable track record at U.S. box offices, the two most original and charming of them, *Frankeweenie* (give me the weird and wonderful Edgar "E" Gore over the *Madagascar* menagerie any day!) and *The Pirates! Band of Misfits* (a perfect use of Hugh Grant's droll delivery), were among the weaker performers at the turnstiles where this genre was concerned. And the trend towards too many ticket buyers choosing sequels over original presentations remains a depressing reality that doesn't promise to change any time soon. But you can't admonish the industry and exhibitors for not providing enough choices. Believe it or not, by *Screen World*'s count, far as we could tell, there were 872 new releases in 2012, which is probably about 800 more than most folks are even aware of. What's the point, I wonder, of continually saturating the market until even the most interesting titles float away in a flood towards oblivion, probably never to be discovered, even down the line on DVD or streaming or whatever next week's latest technological innovation might be? It's great to create, but it's even better to achieve impact and resonance, is it not?

— Barry Monush

ACKNOWLEDGMENTS

Abramorama, Anchor Bay, Anthology Film Archives, The Cinema Guild, Cinema Libre, Columbia Pictures, DreamWorks, Brian Durnin, E1 Entertainment, Film Forum, First Independent Pictures, First Run Features, Focus Features, Fox Searchlight, Freestyle Releasing, Ben Hodges, IFC Films, International Film Circuit, Tim Johnson, Marybeth Keating, Kino International, Koch Lorber Films, Lionsgate, Tom Lynch, MGM, Magnolia Films, Tony Meisel, Miramax Films, Music Box Films, New Line Cinema, New Yorker Films, Oscilloscope, Paladin, Paramount Pictures, Paramount Vantage, Roadside Attractions, Screen Gems, Screen Media, Seventh Art Releasing, Samuel Goldwyn Films, James Sheridan, Sony Pictures Classics, Strand Releasing, Summit Entertainment, TLA Releasing, TriStar, Truly Indie, Twentieth Century Fox, United Artists, Universal Pictures, Variance Films, Walt Disney Pictures, Warner Bros., The Weinstein Company

DOMESTIC FILMS A

2012 Releases / January 1–December 31

THE DEVIL INSIDE

(PARAMOUNT) Producers, Matthew Peterman, Morris Paulson; Executive Producers, Lorenzo di Bonaventura, Steven Schneider, Mark Vahradian, Erik Howsam; Director, William Brent Bell; Screenplay, William Brent Bell, Matthew Peterman; Photography, Gonzalo Amat; Designer, Tony DeMille; Costumes, Terri Prescott; Music, Brett Detar, Ben Romans; Editors, Timothy Mirkovich, William Brent Bell; Special Effects Makeup, Leigh Hudgens; Visual Effects, Skulley Effects; Casting, Kelly Wagner, Dominika Posseren; an Insurge Pictures presentation of a Prototype production; Dolby; HD Widescreen; Deluxe color; Rated R; 83 minutes; Release date: January 6, 2012

CAST

Isabella Rossi	**Fernanda Andrade**
Father Ben Rawlings	**Simon Quarterman**
Father David Keane	**Evan Helmuth**
Michael Schaefer	**Ionut Grama**
Maria Rossi	**Suzan Crowley**
Rosa Sorlini	**Bonnie Morgan**
Lt. Dreyfus	**Brian Johnson**

Dr. Jeff Victoroff, Pamela Davis (Themselves), John Prosky (Father Christopher Aimes), Claudiu Isotodor (Dr. Antonio Costa), Toma Danila (Marco), Claudiu Trandafir (Father Robert Gallo), Maria Junghietu (Mrs. Sorlini), Ilinca Harnut (Italian Nurse), Corneliu Ulici (Romanian Priest), Andrei Aradits (Hopper), Sorin Cocis (Italian Doctor), Lelia Goldoni (Susan Meadows), Suzanne Freeman (Reporter), Greg Wolf (News Anchor), Kana Kashimoto (Asian Student), Ed Zabel (Dead Priest), Jonathan Salkind (Dead Assisting Priest), Cole Godvin (Dead Nun)

Twenty years after her mother killed three would-be exorcists, Isabella Rossi decides to find out why she has been incarcerated in a mental institution in close proximity to Vatican City.

Simon Quarterman © Paramount Pictures

Ron Eldard, Jill Hennessy, Bobby Cannavale

Ron Eldard, Bobby Cannavale © Magnolia Films

ROADIE

(MAGNOLIA) Producers, Mike Downey, Sirad Balducci; Executive Producers, Christen B.J. & Jamie Lewis, Ian M. Stratford, James Quinlan; Director, Michael Cuesta; Screenplay, Gerald Cuesta, Michael Cuesta; Photography, Andy Lilien; Designer, John El Manahi; Costumes, Manuela Harding; Music, Chris Seefried; Editor, Kane Platt; a Hero Content presentation; Dolby; Color; HD; Rated R; 95 minutes; Release date: January 6, 2012

CAST

Jimmy	**Ron Eldard**
Nikki	**Jill Hennessy**
Randy Stevens	**Bobby Cannavale**
Mom	**Lois Smith**
Don Muller	**David Margulies**
Marilyn Muller	**Catherine Wolf**
Lizette	**Suzette "Azariah"Gunn**

Gary Cruz (Hispanic Store Owner), Anthony Mangano, Lourdes Martin (Cops), Jarlath Conroy (Wes, Motel Clerk), Lynne Lipton (Waitress), Arian Moayed (Irfan), Diana Ravelo (Yopi), Darrell Vanterpool (Teen), Sammy Rhee (Korean Man in Liquor Store), Obaid Kadwani (Taxi Driver), Brandon Reilly (Young Jimmy), K.C. Hughes (Young Nikki)

Fired after working for 20 years as a roadie for Blue Oyster Cult, a devastated Jimmy returns to his home town wondering just where his life is now heading.

Mark Wahlberg, Ben Foster

Mark Wahlberg, Kate Beckinsale, Connor Hill

Lukas Haas, Mark Wahlberg, Caleb Landry Jones

Giovanni Ribisi, Mark Wahlberg © Universal Studios

CONTRABAND

(UNIVERSAL) Producers, Tim Bevan, Eric Fellner, Baltasar Kormákur, Stephen Levinson, Mark Wahlberg; Executive Producers, Liza Chasin, Evan Hayes, Bill Johnson; Director, Baltasar Kormákur; Screenplay, Aaron Guzikowski; Based upon the 2008 film *Reykjavik Rotterdam* written by Arnaldur Inribason and Óskar Jónasson; Photography, Barry Ackroyd; Designer, Tony Fanning; Costumes, Jenny Eagan; Music, Clinton Shorter; Editor, Elísabet Ronalds; Special Effects Coordinator, William Casey Pritchett; Casting, Sheila Jaffe; a Working Title production in association with Blueeyes/Leverage/Closest to the Hole productions, presented in association with Relativity Media; Dolby; Super 35 Widescreen; Color; Rated R; 110 minutes; Release date: January 13, 2012

CAST

Chris Farraday	**Mark Wahlberg**
Kate Farraday	**Kate Beckinsale**
Sebastian Abney	**Ben Foster**
Tim Briggs	**Giovanni Ribisi**
Andy	**Caleb Landry Jones**
Gonzalo	**Diego Luna**
Captain Camp	**J.K. Simmons**
Danny Raymer	**Lukas Haas**
Jim Church	**David O'Hara**
Bud Farraday	**William Lucking**
Tarik	**Kevin "Lucky" Johnson**
Olaf	**Ólafur Darri Ólafsson**

Robert Wahlberg (John Bryce), Jason Mitchell (Walter), Paul LeBlanc (CBP Official), Amber Gaiennie (Danny's Bride), Kent Jude Bernard (Tommy Raymer), Jackson Beals (Desmond), Jaqueline Fleming (Jeanie), Connor Hill (Michael Farraday), Bryce McDaniel (Eddie), John Wilmot (House Owner), Dane Rhodes (AA Guy), Juliette Marie Enright (Sadie), Ritchie Montgomery (Sebastian's Cousin), Viktor Hernandez (Edwin), Shannon Maris (Interviewer), J. Omar Castro (Benito), Michael L. Nesbitt (Chief Mate), Jack Landry (Second Mate), Carlos Compean (Port Pilot), Kirk Bovill (Crew Member), Rose Bianco (Superintendent), Brian Nguyen (Taxi Driver), Roland Ruiz (Kid), Ian Casselberry (Kinkos), Victor Lopez (Skinny Kid), Laura Bergeron-Iglesias (Rosa), Eddie Fiola, Max Daniels (Armored Truck Drivers), Joshua Teixidor (Boss), Randy Austin (Deckhand), Anthony Frederick (CBP Officer), Michael Beaseley (Davis), Turner Crumbley (Laird), Lance E. Nichols (CBP Agent), Anthony "Ace" Thomas (Construction Worker), Eric Weinstein (Trucker)

When his brother-in-law finds himself threatened with death after running afoul of a drug dealer, former smuggler Chris Farraday pulls together a gang of thieves to score the needed cash by way of a Panamanian counterfeiting operation. Remake of the 2008 Icelandic film *Reykjavik-Rotterdam* (no U.S. theatrical release), which starred the director of this film.

Jeremy Jordan, Keke Palmer

Dolly Parton, Queen Latifah

Jesse L. Martin, Queen Latifah, Keke Palmer © Warner Bros.

JOYFUL NOISE

(WARNER BROS.) Producers, Michael Nathanson, Joseph Farrell, Catherine Paura, Broderick Johnson, Andrew A. Kosove; Executive Producers, Timothy M. Bourne, Queen Latifah, Shakim Compere; Co-Producers, Yolanda T. Cochran, Steven P. Wegner; Director/Screenplay, Todd Graff; Photography, David Boyd; Designer, Jeff Knipp; Costumes, Tom Broecker; Music, Mervyn Warren; Music Supervisor, Linda Cohen; Editor, Kathryn Himoff; Choreographer, Michele Lynch; Casting, Mark Fincannon; an Alcon Entertainment presentation of a Farrell Paura Prods./O.N.C. Entertainment production; Dolby; Super 35 Widescreen; Technicolor; Rated PG-13; 118 minutes; Release date: January 13, 2012

CAST
Vi Rose Hill	**Queen Latifah**
G.G. Sparrow	**Dolly Parton**
Olivia Hill	**Keke Palmer**
Randy Garrity	**Jeremy Jordan**
Walter Hill	**Dexter Darden**
Pastor Dale	**Courtney B. Vance**
Marcus Hill	**Jesse L. Martin**
Baylor Sykes	**Kirk Franklin**
Earla	**Angela Grovey**
Caleb	**Andy Karl**
Bernard Sparrow	**Kris Kristofferson**

Dequina Moore (Devonne), Paul Woolfolk (Manny), Francis Jue (Mr. Hsu), Roy Huang (Justin), Judd Derek Lomand (Officer Darrell Lino), Karen Peck ("Mighty High" Soloist), Ivan Kelley Jr. (Our Lady of Perpetual Tears Soloist), David Dwyer (Caleb's Dad), Stevie Ray Dallimore (Restaurant Manager), Kevin Bulla (Stage Manager), Ziah Colon (Club Girl), Hajji Golightly (Man at Table), Rana Kirkland, Bruce Williamson (Church Kitchen Patrons), Maurice Johnson (Man with Cellphone), Ceasar Davis, Michelle Kabashinski, Promise Ramsey (Pacashuau Sacred Divinity Choir Members), Takara Clark, Dixie Light, Shari Dyon Perry, Brian Ashton Smith (Holy Vision Church of Detroit Choir Members), Karen Beyer, Whitney Christopher, David Faust, Jyn Hall, Katie Kneeland, Craig A. Meyer ("Mighty High" Choir Members), Shameik Moore, Isabella Amara, Chloe Bailey, Valencia Barnes, Trey Best, Nia Imani (Our Lady of Perpetual Tears Choir Members), Todd Graff (Man in Audience)

After Vi Rose Hill is appointed the new choir director of the Pacashau Sacred Divinity Choir, the previous choirmaster's widow's anger at being bypassed for the position is exacerbated when her grandson falls in love with Vi's daughter.

Queen Latifah, Courtney B. Vance

HAYWIRE

(RELATIVITY MEDIA) Producer, Gregory Jacobs; Executive Producers, Ryan Kavanaugh, Tucker Tooley, Michael Polaire; Co-Executive Producer, Alan Moloney; Co-Producer, Kenneth Halsband; Director, Steven Soderbergh; Screenplay, Lem Dobbs; Photography, Peter Andrews (Steven Soderbergh); Designer, Howard Cummings; Costumes, Shoshana Rubin; Music, David Holmes; Editor, Mary Ann Bernard (Steven Soderbergh); Special Effects Coordinator, Kevin Hannigan; Stunts, R.A. Rondell; Fight Choreographer, J.J. Perry; Casting, Carmen Cuba; a Relativity Media presentation with the participation of the Bord Scannán na hÉireann/the Irish Film Board; American-Irish; Dolby; Hawk Scope Widescreen; Technicolor; HD; Rated R; 92 minutes; Release date: January 20, 2012

CAST

Mallory Kane	**Gina Carano**
Paul	**Michael Fassbender**
Kenneth	**Ewan McGregor**
John Kane	**Bill Paxton**
Aaron	**Channing Tatum**
Studer	**Mathieu Kassovitz**
Scott	**Michael Angarano**
Rodrigo	**Antonio Banderas**
Alex Coblenz	**Michael Douglas**
Jiang	**Anthony Brandon Wong**

Debby Ross Rondell (Diner Waitress), Julian Alcaraz (Victor), Eddie J. Fernandez (Barroso), Lluís Botella (Helpful Guy), Aaron Cohen (Jamie), Maximino Arciniega (Gomez), James Flynn (Hotel Clerk), Karl Shiels (Goatee), Bobby Andrew Burns, Al Goto (Sheriffs), R.A. Rondell, John Wylie, Todd Thacher Cash (State Troopers), Edward A. Duran, Derik Pritchard (Armed Men), J.J. Perry, Tim Connolly (Kenneth's Henchmen), Natascha Berg (Rodrigo's New Wife)

When a highly skilled assassin realizes she has been targeted by the government for extermination, she sets out to take revenge on those who ordered her dead.

Gina Carano, Channing Tatum

Michael Fassbender, Gina Carano

Ewan McGregor, Gina Carano © Relativity Media

Michael Douglas, Gina Carano

Tristan Wilds

RED TAILS

(20TH CENTURY FOX) Producers, Rick McCallum, Charles Floyd Johnson; Executive Producer, George Lucas; Director, Anthony Hemingway; Screenplay, John Ridley, Aaron McGruder; Story, John Ridley; Photography, John B. Aronson; Designer, Nicholas Palmer; Costumes, Alison Mitchell; Music, Terence Blanchard; Editors, Michael O'Halloran, Ben Burtt; Visual Effects Animation, Industrial Light & Magic; Special Effects Supervisors, Kamil Jaffar, Roman Tudzaroff; Visual Effects Supervisor, Craig Hammack; Stunts, Pavel Bezdek; Casting, Alexa L. Fogel, Christine Kromer; a Lucasfilm Ltd. production; Dolby; HD Widescreen; Color; Rated PG-13; 125 minutes; Release date: January 20, 2012

CAST

Col. A.J. Bullard	**Terrence Howard**
Maj. Emmanuel Stance	**Cuba Gooding, Jr.**
Marty "Easy" Julian	**Nate Parker**
Joe "Lightning" Little	**David Oyelowo**
Ray "Junior" Gannon	**Tristan Wilds**

Ne-Yo (Andrew "Smokey" Salem), Elijah Kelley (Samuel "Joker" George), Marcus T. Paulk (David "Deke" Watkins), Leslie Odom Jr. (Declan "Winky" Hall), Michael B. Jordan (Maurice Wilson), Kevin Phillips (Leon "Neon" Edwards), Andre Royo (Antwan "Coffee" Coleman), Cliff Smith (Sticks), Bryan Cranston (Col. William Mortamus), Lee Tergesen (Col. Jack Tomlinson), Gerald McRaney (Maj. Gen. Luntz), Daniela Ruah (Sofia), Lars van Riesen (Pretty Boy), Matthew Marsh (Brig. Gen. Hauser), Barnaby Kay (Cmdg. Gen. Westlake), Joshua Dallas (Ryan), Michael Lindley (Kellison), Okezie Morro (Jammer), Mark Bowen, Andrew Flach (R&R Crewmen), Aml Ameen (Bg 'O Bones), Anthony Welsh (St. Lou), Rick Otto (Flynt), Rupert Penry-Jones (Campbell), Todd Detwiler (Campbell's Bombardier), Ryan Early (Bryce), Ciarán McMenamin (Lowe), Mike Bautista (Campbell's Gunner), Michael Dixon (Lead Bomber Gunner), Leon Ockenden (Co-Pilot), Adam Gold (German Spotter), Richard Conti (German Guard), Philip Bulcock (Mission Captain), Robert Kazinsky (Chester), Justin Irving (Air Controller), Ben Steel (Luntz's Lieutenant), Paul Fox (Miller), David Gyasi (Corporal), Nathaniel Martello-White (Command Officer), Henry Garrett (Hart), Matt McEnerney (Lt. Mikey), Gabriel Fleary (2nd Air Traffic Controller), Jiri Kohout (German Pilot ME262), Byron Asher (Campbell's Navigator), Brian Gross (Lt. White), Matthew Alan (Pool Player), Jeremy Kocal, Paul Hampshire, Dan Hirst (German Ground Soldiers), Mark Doerr (German POW Camp Commander), Blake Ellis (German POW Camp Guard), Dave Power (Prisoner #1), Sam Daly (Mikey), Chris Riedell (Bomber Navigator), Jesse Caldwell (General), Tina D'Marco (Sofia's Mother), Jaime King (Voice of Axis Mary), Sam Kennard (Pilot Ben), Nick Hendix (Co-Pilot Al), Richard Fiala (Bomber Pilot C), Radim Jira (Bomber Co-Pilot D), Tim Day (Side Gunner H), Daniel Cerv (Side Gunner J), Jakub Smid (Side Gunner G), Max Selim (Bouncing Betty Co-Pilot), Michal Kern (Navigator J)

The true story of the ground-breaking World War II African-American fighter pilot squadron known as the Tuskegee Airmen.

Cuba Gooding Jr., Terrence Howard

Nate Parker © Lucasfilm Ltd.

David Oyelowo

UNDERWORLD: AWAKENING

(SCREEN GEMS) Producers, Tom Rosenberg, Gary Lucchesi, Len Wiseman, Richard Wright; Executive Producers, David Kern, James McQuaide, David Coatsworth, Eric Reid, Skip Williamson, Henry Winterstern; Directors, Mårlind & Stein; Screenplay, Len Wiseman, John Hlavin, J. Michael Straczynski, Allison Burnett; Story, Len Wiseman, John Hlavin; Based on characters created by Kevin Grevioux, Len Wiseman, Danny McBride; Photography, Scott Kevan; Designer, Claude Paré; Costumes, Monique Prudhomme; Music, Paul Haslinger; Editor, Jeff McEvoy; Casting, Tricia Wood, Deborah Aquila; Stunts, Brad Martin; Special Effects Coordinator, Joel Whist; a Lakeshore Entertainment production in association with Sketch Films; Dolby; HD Widescreen; Deluxe color; 3D; Rated R; 88 minutes; Release date: January 20, 2012

CAST
Selene	**Kate Beckinsale**
Dr. Jacob Lane	**Stephen Rea**
Detective Sebastian	**Michael Ealy**
David	**Theo James**
Eve	**India Eisley**
Lida	**Sandrine Holt**
Thomas	**Charles Dance**

Kris Holden-Reid (Quint), Jacob Blair (Officer Kolb), Adam Greydon Reid (Med Tech #1), Catlin Adams (Olivia), Robert Lawrenson (Waterfront Cop), Lee Majdoub (Desk Guard #1), John Innes (Medical Supervisor), Tyler McClendon (Scientist), Panou, Ian Rozylo (Old City Cops), Benita Ha (Surgical Nurse), Christian Tessier (Security Guard #1), Kurt Max Runte (Troop Leader), Mark Gibbon (Announcing Guard), Richard Cetrone, Dan Payne (Lycan Creatures), Wes Bentley (Antigen Scientist)

Vampire warrioress Selena escapes imprisonment, only to discover that humans are now aware of the existence of her breed and are hell-bent on wiping them out.

Fourth entry in the Screen Gems series following *Underworld* (2003), *Underworld: Evolution* (2006), and *Underworld: Rise of the Lycans* (2009).

Kate Beckinsale © Lakeshore Entertainment

Harry Kullijian, Carol Channing

Carol Channing © Entertainment One

CAROL CHANNING: LARGER THAN LIFE

(ENTERTAINMENT ONE) Producer/Director, Dori Berinstein; Screenplay, Dori Berinstein, Adam Zucker; Photography, Rob Van Alkemade; Music, Craig Sharmat; *Hello, Dolly!* and *La Cage aux Folles* music, Jerry Herman; Animation, Asterisk Animation, based on original drawings by Al Hirschfeld; Co-Producer, B. Harlan Boll; a Dramatic Force production; Color; Rated PG; 87 minutes; Release date: January 20, 2012; Documentary on performer Carol Channing.

WITH
Carol Channing, Harry Kullijian, Loni Anderson, Mary Jo Catlett, Marge Champion, Tyne Daly, Phyllis Diller, Betty Garrett, Tippi Hedren, Jerry Herman, Angela Lansbury, Rich Little, Bob Mackie, Jimmy Nederlander Sr., Debbie Reynolds, Chita Rivera, Harvey Sabinson, George Schlatter, Richard Skipper, Lily Tomlin, Tommy Tune, Bruce Vilanch, Barbara Walters, JoAnne Worley; *The 'Dolly' Boys*: Bill Bateman, Julian Brightman, Kevin Burrows, James Darrah, Halden Michaels, Bobby Randall, Randy Slovacek, Matthew Sipress; *The 'Gypsy of the Year' Dancers*: John Bantay, Ward Billeison, Jonathan Day, James Harkness, Michael Quinn, George Smallwood, Jonathan Stahl, Will Taylor; *The Kennedy Center Honors Rehearsal*: Rob Ashford, David Chase, Chris Bailey, Nathan Balser, Spencer Liff, Michaeljon Slinger, Alex Stoll, Ephraim M. Sykes, Ryan Watkinson, Charlie Williams; *'Memphis' Cast Members*: Tyrone A. Jackson, Paul McGill, John Eric Parker.

Dallas Roberts, Dermot Mulroney, Liam Neeson, Nonso Anozie

Liam Neeson © Open Road Films

Frank Grillo, Dallas Roberts, Dermot Mulroney, Joe Anderson, Nonso Anozie, Liam Neeson

THE GREY

(OPEN ROAD FILMS) Producers, Jules Daly, Joe Carnahan, Ridley Scott, Mickey Liddell; Executive Producers, Jim Seibel, Bill Johnson, Tony Scott, Jennifer Hilton Monroe, Spencer Silna, Adi Shankar, Ross T. Fanger; Co-Producer, Douglas Saylor Jr.; Director, Joe Carnahan; Screenplay, Joe Carnahan, Ian Mackenzie Jeffers; Based on the story *Ghost Walker* by Ian Mackenzie Jeffers; Photography, Masanobu Takayanagi; Designer, John Willett; Costumes, Courtney Daniel; Music, Marc Streitenfeld; Editors, Roger Barton, Jason Hellmann; Special Makeup and Animatronics Effects, Greg Nicotero, Howard Berger; Special Effects Coordinator, James Paradis; Casting, John Papsidera; Presented in association with Inferno in association with LD Entertainment of a Scott Free/Chambara Pictures production in association with 1984 Private Defense Contractors; Dolby; Super 35 Widescreen; Deluxe color; Rated R; 117 minutes; Release date: January 27, 2012

CAST

John Ottway	**Liam Neeson**
Diaz	**Frank Grillo**
Talget	**Dermot Mulroney**
Hendrick	**Dallas Roberts**
Flannery	**Joe Anderson**
Burke	**Nonso Anozie**
Hernandez	**Ben Hernandez Bray**
Lewenden	**James Badge Dale**
Ottway's Wife	**Anne Openshaw**

Peter Girges (Company Clerk), Jonathan James Bitonti (Ottway, 5 years old), James Bitonti (Ottway's Father), Ella Kosor (Talget's Little Girl), Jacob Blair (Cimoski), Lani Gelera, Larissa Stadnichuk (Flight Attendants)

After their plane crashes in the wilderness a group of oil refinery workers must depend upon the quick thinking of hired sharpshooter John Ottway to help save them from a pack of ferocious wolves.

Liam Neeson

MAN ON A LEDGE

(SUMMIT) Producers, Lorenzo di Bonaventura, Mark Vahradian; Executive Producers, Jake Myers, David Ready; Director, Asger Leth; Screenplay, Pablo F. Fenjves; Photography, Paul Cameron; Designer, Alec Hammond; Costumes, Susan Lyall; Music, Henry Jackman; Editor, Kevin Stitt; Special Effects Coordinator, Conrad Brinks Jr.; Stunts, Stephen Pope; Casting, Deborah Aquila, Tricia Wood, Julie Tucker, Ross Meyerson; a di Bonaventura Pictures production; Dolby; Panavision; Color; Rated PG-13; 102 minutes; Release date: January 27, 2012

CAST

Nick Cassidy	**Sam Worthington**
Lydia Mercer	**Elizabeth Banks**
Joey Cassidy	**Jamie Bell**
Mike Ackerman	**Anthony Mackie**
Jack Dougherty	**Edward Burns**
Suzie Morales	**Kyra Sedgwick**
David Englander	**Ed Harris**
Angie	**Genesis Rodriguez**
Dante Marcus	**Titus Welliver**

Mandy Gonzalez (Manager), William Sadler (Valet), Barbara Marineau (Screaming Woman), J. Smith-Cameron (Psychiatrist), Patrick Collins (Father Leo), Afton Williamson (Janice Ackerman), Robert Clohessy (Prison Guard), Joe Lisi (Desk Sergeant), Candice McKoy (Cop – Bullhorn), John Solo (Cop – Room), James Yaegashi, Daniel Sauli (Police Technicians), Frank Pando (Cameraman), Jason Kolotouros (ESU), Michael Lee Laurence (Bearded Guy), Don Castro (CSI Tech), Pooja Kumar (Englander's Assistant), John Dossett (Ted Henry), Sylvia Kauders (Angry Traffic Woman), Felix Solis (Nestor), Jabari Gray, James Andrew O'Connor (Brooklyn Cops), Anna Arvia, Jonathan Walker (Investors), Liz Holtan (Lady), Jason Furlani (Cop), Terry Serpico (Lutz), Erin Quill (Cop – File), Arthur Nascarella (Construction Worker), Jimmy Palumbo, J. Bernard Calloway (Detectives), Gerry Vichi (Older Orthodox Man), Geoffrey Cantor (Gordon Evans), Brett Smith (Tactical Leader), John Comer (Correction Officer)

A former cop's threat to jump off the ledge of a Manhattan hotel turns out to be an elaborate diversion involving the stolen diamond that had landed him in prison.

Jamie Bell, Genesis Rodriguez © Summit Entertainment

Elizabeth Banks, Sam Worthington

Anthony Mackie

Ed Harris

ONE FOR THE MONEY

(LIONSGATE) Producers, Tom Rosenberg, Gary Lucchesi, Wendy Finerman, Sidney Kimmel; Executive Producers, Eric Reid, Andre Lamal, Bruce Toll, Katherine Heigl, Nancy Heigl; Co-Producer, Zane Weiner; Director, Jullie Ann Robinson; Screenplay, Stacy Sherman, Karen Ray, Liz Brixius; Based on the 1994 novel by Janet Evanovich; Photography, James Whitaker; Designer, Franco-Giacomo Carbone; Costumes, Michael Dennison; Music, Deborah Lurie; Editor, Lisa Zeno Churgin; Casting, Deborah Aquila, Tricia Wood, Julie Tucker, Ross Meyerson; a Lakeshore Entertainment, Lionsgate, Wendy Finerman production in association with Sidney Kimmel Entertainment, Abishag Prods.; Dolby; Super 35 Widescreen; Deluxe color; Rated PG-13; 91 minutes; Release date: January 27, 2012

CAST

Stephanie Plum	**Katherine Heigl**
Joe Morelli	**Jason O'Mara**
Ranger	**Daniel Sunjata**
Jimmy Alpha	**John Leguizamo**
Lula	**Sherri Shepherd**
Grandma Mazur	**Debbie Reynolds**

Debra Monk (Mrs. Plum), Nate Mooney (Eddie Gazarra), Adam Paul (Bernie Kuntz), Fisher Stevens (Morty Beyers), Ana Reeder (Connie), Patrick Fischler (Vinnie Plum), Ryan Michelle Bathe (Jackie), Leonardo Nam (John Cho), Annie Parisse (Mary Lou), Danny Mastrogiorgio (Lenny), Gavin-Keith Umeh (Benito Ramirez), Louis Mustillo (Mr. Plum), Harry O'Toole (William Earling), Rex the Hamster (Rex), John Joseph Williams (Mooch Morelli), Jennifer Vos (Waitress), Marla Sucharetza (Sunny), Angela Pietropinto (Mama Morelli), Alexis Treadwell Murray (Carmen), Jack Erdie (Flat Nose Louis), Jake Andolina, Joshua Elijah Reese (Cops), Tommy Lafitte (Locksmith), David Early (Carmen's Neighbor), Robert Oppel (Shaw Street Thug), Bo Graham (Old Man on Street), Carnel McMorris Jr. (Grandson), Olga Merediz (Rosa Gomez), Michael Laurence (Lonnie Dodd), Jared Burke (Struggling FTA), Lisa Ann Goldsmith (Police Woman), Jarrod DiGiorgi (Ziggy Kuleska), David Flick (Sal), Jared Pfennigwerth (Darren), Alexis Ferrante, Alana Hixson (Jersey Girls), Kathleen Murray (Noisy Neighbor)

Stephanie Plum accepts a position hunting down bail jumpers when she finds out that her ex-boyfriend is among those being sought.

Debbie Reynolds, Katherine Heigl © Lionsgate

Kelly McGillis © Magnet Releasing

Sara Paxton, Pat Healy

THE INNKEEPERS

(MAGNET) Producers, Peter Phok, Larry Fessenden, Derek Curl; Executive Producers, Malik B. Ali, Badie Ali, Hamza Ali, Greg Newman; Director/Screenplay/Editor, Ti West; Photography, Eliot Rockett; Designer, Jade Healy; Costumes, Elisabeth Vastola; Music, Jeff Grace; Special Effects Makeup, Brian Spears; Casting, Lisa Fields; a Dark Sky Films & Glass Eye Pix presentation; Dolby; Super 35 Widescreen; Color; Rated R; 102 minutes; Release date: February 3, 2012

CAST

Claire	**Sara Paxton**
Luke	**Pat Healy**
Gayle, The Angry Mom	**Alison Bartlett**
Young Boy	**Jake Schlueter**
Leanne Rease-Jones	**Kelly McGillis**

Lena Dunham (Barista), George Riddle (Old Man), Brenda Cooney (Madeline O'Malley), John Speredakos (Officer Mitchell), Sean Reid, Kurt Venghaus, Thomas Mahoney, Michael Martin, Michael P. Castelli (Medics)

On the eve of shuttering the Yankee Pedlar Inn after a century of service, the last remaining employees decided to find out if the place is genuinely haunted as legend has told.

Dermot Mulroney, Ted Danson © Universal Studios

John Krasinski, Drew Barrymore

Ahmaogak Sweeney,
John Pingayak

BIG MIRACLE

(UNIVERSAL) Producers, Steve Golin, Michael Sugar, Tim Bevan, Eric Fellner; Executive Producers, Liza Chasin, Debra Hayward, Stuart Besser, Paul Green; Director, Ken Kwapis; Screenplay, Jack Amiel, Michael Begler; Based on the 1989 book *Freeing the Whales: How the Media Created the World's Greatest Non-Event* by Tom Rose; Photography, John Bailey; Designer, Nelson Coates; Costumes, Shay Cunliffe; Music, Cliff Eidelman; Editor, Cara Silverman; American-British; Casting, Mary Gail Artz, Shani Ginsberg; an Anonymous Content/Working Title production; Dolby; Super 35 Widescreen; Technicolor; Rated PG; 107 minutes; Release date: February 3, 2012

CAST

Rachel Kramer	**Drew Barrymore**
Adam Carlson	**John Krasinski**
Jill Jerard	**Kristen Bell**
Col. Scott Boyer	**Dermot Mulroney**
Pat Lafayette	**Tim Blake Nelson**
Kelly Meyers	**Vinessa Shaw**
J.W. McGraw	**Ted Danson**
Nathan	**Ahmaogak Sweeney**
Malik	**John Pingayak**

Stephen Root (Governor Haskell), James LeGros (Karl Hootkin), Kathy Baker (Ruth McGraw), John Michael Higgins (Wes Handrick), Rob Riggle (Dean Glowacki), John Chase (Roy), Ishmael Angalook Hope (Bud), Othneil 'Anaqulutuq' Oomittuk Jr. (Inupiat Whaler), Andrew Daly (Don Davis), Thomas R. Daly (Frank), Maliaq Kairaiuak (Dana), Jeffrey Evan (Arnold), Randy Eledge (Oil Man), Thom Van Dorp (Don Carr), Maury Ginsberg, Kelly Lee Wiliams, Megan Baldino, Wayne Mitchell (News Producers), Maeve Blake (Shayna Dobler), Krista Schwarting (Diane Dobler), Liam Boles (Cooper Dobler), Opal Sidon (Darcy), Michael Gaston (Porter Beckford), Ken Smith (Stu), Tim Palmer (Lloyd Dobler), Gregory Jbara (Gen. Stanton), Princess Lucaj, Mary Rock (Hotel Clerks), Jason Martin (Rich), Jessica Tiihonen, Christine Kim, Robert Forgit (Prudhoe Bay Reporters), Bruce Altman (Chief of Staff), Anthony Fryer (National Guard Co-Pilot), Brady Ingledue (Alaskan Northern Oil Worker), Hillarie Putnam (Minneapolis Reporter), Brett Baker (Barrow Street Reporter), Shea Whigham (SAR Pilot Conrad), Kathryn Harris (Teacher), R.F. Daley (Chariman of the Joint Chiefs of Staff), Stefan Kapicic (Yuri), Jackie Purcell (Icebreaker Reporter), Mark Ivanir (Dimitri), Quinn Redeker (President Reagan), Beth Beardsley, Anju Bhargava, Robertus A. Schaaper (Foreign Reporters), Michael Miller, Andrey Nikolaev (Russians), Teresa Pingayak (Malik's Wife), Jeff Bergman (Reagan's Voice)

When a family of whales becomes trapped in the frozen waters off Barrow, Alaska, an environmentalist rallies the citizens to help free them before time runs out.

James LeGros, Rob Riggle

Alex Russell

Dane DeHaan

Dane DeHaan, Michael B. Jordan, Alex Russell

CHRONICLE

(20TH CENTURY FOX) Producers, John Davis, Adam Schroeder; Executive Producer, James Dodson; Director, Josh Trank; Screenplay, Max Landis; Story, Max Landis, Josh Trank; Photography, Matthew Jensen; Designer, Stephen Altman; Costumes, Diana Cilliers; Music Supervisor, Andrew von Foerster; Editor, Elliot Greenberg; Special Effects Supervisor, Mickey Kirsten; Visual Effects Supervisor, Simon Hansen; Stunts, Kerry Gregg; Casting, Ronna Kress; a Davis Entertainment Co. production in association with Dune Entertainment; Dolby; Deluxe Color; HD; Rated PG-13; 84 minutes; Release date: February 3, 2012

CAST

Andrew Detmer	**Dane DeHaan**
Matt Garretty	**Alex Russell**
Steve Montgomery	**Michael B. Jordan**
Richard Detmer	**Michael Kelly**
Casey Letter	**Ashley Hinshaw**
Karen Detmer	**Bo Petersen**
Monica	**Anna Wood**
Wayne	**Rudi Malcolm**
Sean	**Luke Tyler**
Samantha	**Crystal Donna Roberts**
Costly	**Adrian Collins**
Howard	**Grant Powell**
Austin	**Armand Aucamp**
Cala	**Nicole Bailey**

Lynita Crofford (Casey's Mom), Royston Stoffels (Pharmacist), Patrick Walton Jr. (Park Ranger), Lance Elliot (Police Officer), Nadine Suliaman (School Flyer Girl), Pierre Malherbe (Police Detective), Joe Vaz (Michael Ernesto), Matthew Dylan Roberts (Ernesto's Neighbor), Allen Irwin (Redneck Trucker), Chelsea Nortje (Girl in Window), Francois Coetzee (Thug #3), Hendrik Kotze (Priest), Matt Adler, Robert Clotworthy (Newscasters), Daisy Tormé (Karen Detmer's Voice)

A bullied teen and his friends stumble upon a mysterious hole which bestows upon them telekinetic powers.

Alex Russell © 20th Century Fox

SAFE HOUSE

(UNIVERSAL) Producer, Scott Stuber; Executive Producers, Denzel Washington, Scott Aversano, Adam Merims, Alexa Faigen, Trevor Macy, Marc D. Evans; Director, Daniel Espinosa; Screenplay, David Guggenheim; Photography, Oliver Wood; Designer, Brigitte Broch; Costumes, Susan Matheson; Music, Ramin Djawadi; Editor, Richard Pearson; Casting, Sarah Halley Finn; a Bluegrass Films production, presented in association with Relativity Media; Dolby; Panavision; Deluxe color; Rated R; 115 minutes; Release date: February 10, 2012

Vera Farmiga, Sam Shepard © Universal Studios

CAST

Tobin Frost	**Denzel Washington**
Matt Weston	**Ryan Reynolds**
Catherine Linklater	**Vera Farmiga**
David Barlow	**Brendan Gleeson**
Harlan Whitford	**Sam Shepard**
Carlos Villar	**Ruben Blades**
Ana Moreau	**Nora Arnezeder**
Daniel Kiefer	**Robert Patrick**
Alec Wade	**Liam Cunningham**

Joel Kinnaman (Keller), Fares Fares (Vargas), Jena Dover, Stephen Rider, Daniel Fox, Tracie Thoms, Sara Arrington, Kenneth Folk (CIA Analysts), Bryan Van Niekerk (Linklater's Assistant), Nicole Sherwin (Whitford's Assistant), Pope Jerrod (Beck), Allen Irwin (Greer), Jake McLaughlin (Miller), Aidan Bennetts (Ericksson), Vernon Willemse (Velez), Traian Milenov, Dumani Mtya, Thembaletu Tyutu, Oliver Bailey, Roy Taylor (Vargas Lieutenants), Boris Martinez (Strip Club Mercenary), Stephen Bishop, Scott Sparrow (Marine Guards), Justin Shaw (Private Security Guard), Fana Mokoena (Officer-in-Charge), Jody J. Abrahams, Dirk Stoltz, Craig Palm, Craig Hawks, Tyrone Dadd (Stadium Cops), Tilly Powell (Woman Trampled), Lynita Crofford (Reporter at Stadium), Tanit Phoenix (Hostess), Abdul Ntotera (Businessman), Ayabonga Mtekeli (Boy), Nambitha Mpumlwana (Illana), Lelethu Nongalaza (Ernestine), Namhla Tshuka (Villar Daughter), Simphiwe Mabuya (Villar Son-in-Law), Louis Gouws (BMW Driver), Jerry Mofokeng (Man at Mint), Robert Hobbs (Morgan), John C. King (CNN Reporter, Himself), Bruce Young, Aidan Whytock, Geon Nel (CIA Aides – S.A.)

When the safe house he is assigned to guard is attacked by mercenaries, CIA agent Matt Weston takes off with his prisoner, traitorous agent Tobin Frost, in hopes of keeping him one step ahead of those out to eliminate him.

Ryan Reynolds, Nora Arnezeder

Ryan Reynolds

Denzel Washington

JOURNEY 2:THE MYSTERIOUS ISLAND

(NEW LINE CINEMA/WB) Producers, Beau Flynn, Tripp Vinson, Charlotte Huggins; Executive Producers, Richard Brener, Michael Disco, Samuel J. Brown, Marcus Viscidi, Michael Bostock, Evan Turner; Director, Brad Peyton; Screenplay, Brian Gunn, Mark Gunn; Story, Richard Outten, Brian Gunn, Mark Gunn; Photography, David Tattersall; Designer, Bill Boes; Music, Andrew Lockington; Editor, David Rennie; Special Effects Supervisor, Peter Chesney; Visual Effects Supervisor, Boyd Shermis; Stunt Coordinator, Alex Daniels; a Contrafilm production Dolby; Deluxe color; 3D; Rated PG; 94 minutes; Release date: February 10, 2012

CAST

Hank	**Dwayne Johnson**
Alexander	**Michael Caine**
Sean Anderson	**Josh Hutcherson**
Kailani	**Vanessa Hudgens**
Gabato	**Luis Guzmán**
Liz	**Kristin Davis**
Jessica	**Anna Colwell**
Cop	**Stephen Caudill**
Tour Guide	**Branscombe Richmond**
Hockey Player	**Walter Bankson**

Sean Anderson and his stepdad team up to find Sean's grandfather who has gone missing on a mysterious island. Sequel to the 2008 film *Journey to the Center of the Earth* (New Line) with Josh Hutcherson repeating his role.

Michael Caine, Josh Hutcherson

Josh Hutcherson, Luis Guzmán, Vanessa Hudgens, Dwayne Johnson
© New Line Cinema

Dwayne Johnson

Luis Guzmán, Vanessa Hudgens, Michael Caine, Dwayne Johnson, Josh Hutcherson

Linda Cardellini, Michael Shannon

Linda Cardellini, John Slattery © Dada Films

RETURN

(DADA FILMS) Producers, Noah Harlan, Ben Howe, Liza Johnson; Executive Producers, Abigail Disney, Meredith Vieira, Amy Rapp; Associate Producer, Charlie Birns; Co-Producer, Aaron Levine; Director/Screenplay, Liza Johnson; Photography, Anne Etheridge; Music, T. Griffin; Editor, Paul Zucker; Casting, Kerry Barden, Paul Schnee; a Fork Films presentation of a 2.1 Films/True Enough production in association with Meredith Vieira Productions; Dolby; Deluxe color; Not rated; 97 minutes; Release date: February 10, 2012

CAST
Kelli	**Linda Cardellini**
Mike	**Michael Shannon**
Bud	**John Slattery**
Julie	**Talia Balsam**
Ed	**Paul Sparks**
Shannon	**Louisa Krause**
Jackie	**Emma Lyle**

Rosie Benton (Brooke), James Murtaugh (Mr. Miller), Rutanya Alda (Mrs. Miller), Bonnie Swencionis (Cara Lee), Tabitha Depew, Victoria Depew (Bree), Wayne Pyle (Franklin), Roetta Collins (Clerk), Edward Crawford (Travis), Cheyenne Ruggiero (Girl #1), Dannah Chaifetz (Avinelle), Daniel Breen, Chris Sager (Cops), Linda Kutrubes (Mom), Robin Taylor (Vonnie)

Kelli returns from her tour of duty, anxious to continue her small town life, only feel more like an outsider than she could have imagined.

PRIVATE ROMEO

(WOLFE) Producers, Agathe David-Weill, Kevin Ginty; Co-Producer, Alli Maxwell; Director/Screenplay, Alan Brown; Based on the 1597 play *Romeo and Juliet* by William Shakespeare; Photography, Derek McKane; Designer, Maki Takenouchi; Music, Nicholas Wright; Music Supervisor, Sara Matarazzo; Editor, Craig Weiseman; Casting, Stephanie Holbrook; Color; HD; Not rated; 98 minutes; Release date: February 10, 2012.

CAST
Sam Singleton	**Seth Numrich**
Glenn Mangan	**Matt Doyle**
Josh Neff	**Hale Appleman**
Carlos Moreno	**Bobby Moreno**
Omar Madsen	**Chris Bresky**

Charlie Barnett (Ken Lee), Adam Barrie (Adam Hersh), Sean Hudock (Gus Sanchez)

At a military academy, a group of cadets rehearsing *Romeo and Juliet* find themselves living a parallel story of Shakespeare's tragedy.

Sean Hudock, Seth Numrich, Bobby Moreno © Wolfe Video

Matt Doyle

Channing Tatum, Rachel McAdams

Channing Tatum, Rachel McAdams

Scott Speedman © Spyglass Entertainment

Channing Tatum, Rachel McAdams

THE VOW

(SCREEN GEMS) Producers, Roger Birnbaum, Gary Barber, Jonathan Glickman, Paul Taublier; Executive Producers, J. Miles Dale, Austin Hearst, Susan Cooper; Co-Producers, Cassidy Lange, Rebekah Rudd; Director, Michael Sucsy; Screenplay, Abby Kohn, Marc Silverstein, Jason Katims; Story, Stuart Sender; Photography, Rogier Stoffers; Designer, Kalina Ivanov; Costumes, Alex Kavanagh; Music, Rachel Portman, Michael Brook; Music Supervisor, Randall Poster; Editors, Nancy Richardson, Melissa Kent; Casting, Cathy Sandrich Gelfond, Amanda Mackey; a Spyglass Entertainment presentation of a Birnbaum/Barber production; Dolby; Super 35 Widescreen; Deluxe color; Rated PG-13; 104 minutes; Release date: February 10, 2012

CAST
Paige	**Rachel McAdams**
Leo	**Channing Tatum**
Rita Thornton	**Jessica Lange**
Bill Thornton	**Sam Neill**
Gwen	**Jessica McNamee**
Dr. Fishman	**Wendy Crewson**
Lily	**Tatiana Maslany**
Kyle	**Lucas Bryant**
Jeremy	**Scott Speedman**
Josh	**Joey Klein**
Jim	**Joe Cobden**

Jeananne Goossen (Sonia), Dillon Casey (Ryan), Shannon Barnett (Carrie), Lindsay Ames (Shana), Kristina Pesic (Lizbet), Britt Irvin (Lina), Sarah Carter (Diane), Angela Vint (Nurse), Rachel Skarsten (Rose), Bill Turnbull (Funky Clerk), Dharini Woollcombe (Receptionist), Rosalba Martinni (Bakery Lady), Jeff Authors (Professor), Roland Rothchild (DMV Worker), Jonathan Psaila (Mikey)

After a car accident causes Paige to lose her memory, her husband Leo must start from scratch and woo her back to him.

Greg Kinnear, Alan Arkin

Greg Kinnear © ATO Pictures

THIN ICE

(ATO PICTURES) formerly *The Convincer*; Producers, Mary Frances Budig, Elizabeth Redleaf, Christine Kunewa Walker; Executive Producer, Alan Arkin; Co-Producers, Andrew Peterson, Mark Steele; Line Producer, Julie Hartley; Director, Jill Sprecher; Screenplay, Jill Sprecher, Karen Sprecher; Photography, Dick Pope; Designer, Jeff Schoen; Costumes, Tere Duncan; Music, Jeff Danna; Casting, Jeanne McCarthy, Lynn Blumenthal; a Werc Werk Works production in association with Spare Room Productions; Dolby; Super 35 Widescreen; Deluxe Color; Rated R; 93 minutes; Release date: February 17, 2012

Greg Kinnear, Billy Crudup

CAST
Mickey Prohaska	**Greg Kinnear**
Gorvy Hauer	**Alan Arkin**
Randy	**Billy Crudup**
Bob Egan	**David Harbour**
Karla Gruenke	**Michelle Arthur**
Jo Ann Prohaska	**Lea Thompson**
Leonard Dahl	**Bob Balaban**
Sherri	**Jennifer M. Edwards**
Phil Peters	**Peter Moore**
Judy Vandenhoevel	**Michelle Hutchison**
Glen Vandenhoevel	**James Detmar**

John Paul Gamoke (Man at Coffee Shop), Scott Crouch (Casino Emcee), Michael Paul Levin (Chuck Stankel), Kathryn Lawrey (Hotel Clerk), Joe Minjares (Hotel Manager), Peter Thoemke (Frank Richie), Alan Johnson (Bill Morton), Alec George (Shane), Tony Papenfuss (Buckhorn Bartender), Sue Scott (Bank Teller), Terry Hempleman (Dick Zimmer), Chris Carlson (Don Schmidt), John Elsen (Patrol Cop), Gary Groomes (Traveler), Isabell O'Connor (Samaritan), Mike Hagerty (Jerry), Wayne Morton (The Real Gorvy), Peggy O'Connell (The Real Gorvy's Wife), Johnny Hagen (Buckhorn Bar Patron), Didja, Gibson (Pete the Dog)

Greg Kinnear, Billy Crudup

An insurance agent, desperate to move from the frigid Wisconsin climate and reunite with his estranged wife, hopes to earn the necessary cash by swindling a retired farmer.

UNDEFEATED

(WEINSTEIN CO.) Producers, Rich Middlemass, Dan Lindsay, Seth Gordon, Ed Cunningham, Glen Zipper; Executive Producers, Ralph Zipper, Nigel Sinclair, Guy East, Chris Miller, Sean Combs, Paolo Coppola, Meeraj Kohli, Michele Farinola, Jillian Longnecker; Directors/Photography/Editors, Dan Lindsay, TJ Martin; Music, Michael Brook; an Exclusive Media Group and Zipper Bros. Films presentation of a Spitfire Pictures Production in association with Level 22 and Five Smooth Stones Productions; Color; Rated PG-13; 113 minutes; Release date: February 17, 2012. Documentary on how the Manassas Tigers, an underprivileged football team, became a success through the coaching of Bill Courtney.

WITH
Montrail "Money" Brown, O.C. Brown, Bill Courtney, Chavis Daniels

2011 Academy Award Winner for Best Documentary Feature.

Idris Elba © Columbia Pictures

GHOST RIDER: SPIRIT OF VENGEANCE

(COLUMBIA) Producers, Steven Paul, Ashok Amritraj, Michael De Luca, Avi Arad, Ari Arad; Executive Producers, E. Bennett Walsh, David S. Goyer, Stan Lee, Mark Steven Johnson; Directors, Mark Neveldine, Brian Taylor; Screenplay, Scott M. Gimple, Seth Hoffman, David S. Goyer; Story, David S. Goyer; Based on the Marvel comic; Photography, Brandon Trost; Designer, Kevin Phipps; Costumes, Bojana Nikitovic; Music, David Sardy; Music Supervisor, Kier Lehman; Editor, Brian Berdan; Special Effects Supervisor, Nick Allder; Visual Effects Supervisor, Eric Durst; a Hyde Park Entertainment presentation in association with Imagenation Abu Dhabi, a Marvel Entertainment/Crystal Sky Pictures/Ashok Amritraj/Michael De Luca/Arad Production; Dolby; Deluxe color; 3D; Rated PG-13; 95 minutes; Release date: February 17, 2012

CAST

Johnny Blaze/Ghost Rider	**Nicolas Cage**
Nadya	**Violante Placido**
Rourke	**Ciarán Hinds**
Moreau	**Idris Elba**
Ray Carrigan	**Johnny Whitworth**
Fanny	**Fergus Riordan**
Grannik	**Spencer Wilding**

Sorin Tofan (Kurdish), Jacek Koman (Terrokov), Anthony Head (Benedict), Cristian Iacob (Vasil), Christopher Lambert (Methodius), Jai Stefan (Krakchev), Vincent Regan (Toma Nikasevic), Ionut Cristian Lefter (Young Johnny Blaze), Will Ashcroft (Grey Suited Man), Sabina Branduse (Nurse), Tobias Öjerfalk (Dude, Forest), Adina Galupa (Girl, Forest), Alin Panc (EMT Worker)

A motorcyclist, cursed to transform into a demonic biker, is told he will be relieved of his torment if he can help track down a young boy who might be the spawn of Satan. Sequel to the 2007 film *Ghost Rider*, with Cage repeating his role.

© Weinstein Co

Chris Pine, Reese Witherspoon, Tom Hardy

Chris Pine, Tom Hardy, Angela Bassett © 20th Century Fox

Chelsea Handler

THIS MEANS WAR

(20TH CENTURY FOX) Producers, Robert Simonds, James Lassiter, Will Smith, Simon Kinberg; Executive Producers, Michael Green, Jeffrey Evan Kwatinetz, Brent O'Connor; Director, McG; Screenplay, Timothy Dowling, Simon Kinberg; Story, Timothy Dowling, Marcus Gautesen; Photography, Russell Carpenter; Designer, Martin Laing; Costumes, Sophie de Rakoff; Music, Christophe Beck; Editor, Nicolas de Toth; Special Effects Coordinator, Alex Burdett; Stunts, Jeff Habberstad, Joey Box; Casting, Kim Davis-Wagner, Justine Baddeley; an Overbrook Entertainment/Robert Simonds Company production; Dolby; Super 35 Widescreen; Deluxe color; Rated PG-13; 97 minutes; Release date: February 17, 2012

CAST

Lauren	**Reese Witherspoon**
FDR Foster	**Chris Pine**
Tuck	**Tom Hardy**
Heinrich	**Til Schweiger**
Trish	**Chelsea Handler**
Joe	**John Paul Ruttan**

Abigail Leigh Spencer (Katie), Angela Bassett (Collins), Rosemary Harris (Nana Foster), George Touliatos (Grandpa Foster), Clint Carleton (Jonas), Warren Christie (Steve), Leela Savasta (Kelly), Natassia Malthe (Xenia), Laura Vandervoort (Britta), Dominique Bourassa Brownes (Hong Kong Beauty), Paul Wu (Korean Leader), Daren A. Herbert (Agent Bothwick), Kevin O'Grady (Agent Boyles), Jesse Reid (Agent Dickerman), Viv Leacock (Agent Downing), Jenny Slate (Emily), Kasey Ryne Mazak (Ken, Sushi Chef), Kevan Ohtsji (Sushi Chef), Baline Patry (Bucket Head Kid), Aleks Paunovic (Karate Dad), Joey Forfellow (Karate Kid), Jakob Davies (Boy with Glasses), Patrick Monroe (Tuck Sparring Partner), Elizabeth Weinstein (Smart Consumer Receptionist, Ella), Ash Lee (Smart Consumer Employee), Conrad Coates (Smart Consumer Guard, Hudson), Lauren Dowe (Sweater Set Girl), Lee Razavai (Goth Girl), Affion Crockett (Video Clerk), Jennifer Kitchen, Lossen Chambers (Focus Group Women), John Stewart (Trish's Husband), Jill Teed, Patrick Sabongui (CIA Agents), Graeme Goodhall, Alex Pesusich, Ché Pritchard (Dancers, Waiters), Louise Hradsky, Kirstyn Konig, Tyrell Witherspoon, Richard O'Sullivan, Jennifer Oleksiuk (Dancers), Paul Becker (Choreographer), Allan Gray (Tailor), Dariusz Slowik (Strip Club Bouncer), Mike Dopud (Ivan), Klodyne Rodney (Dog Shelter Worker, Betty), Mason Brown (Dog Shelter Kid, Nick), Thomas Potter (CIA Clerk, Jenkins), Desiree Zurowski, Fred Henderson (Older Family Friends), Mamie Laverock (Mamie), Gretal Montgomery (Flight Attendant, Maya), Michael Papajohn (German Goon), Arien Boey (Trish's Kid), Derek Waters (Valet), Mike Johnson (Heinrich's Driver), Panou (CIA Helicopter Handler)

Discovering that they are both dating the same woman, CIA agents Tuck and Foster decide to make each other's lives a living hell by using their trained skills to sabotage one another's efforts to woo and win Lauren.

Tom Hardy, Chris Pine

Kerri Kennedy-Silver, Paul Rudd, Jennifer Aniston, Justin Theroux, Malin Akerman

Alan Alda © Universal Studios

Paul Rudd, Joe Lo Truglio

WANDERLUST

(UNIVERSAL) Producers, Judd Apatow, Ken Marino, Paul Rudd, David Wain; Executive Producer, Richard Vane; Director, David Wain; Screenplay, Ken Marino, David Wain; Photography, Michael Bonvillain; Designer, Aaron Osborne; Costumes, Debra McGuire; Music, Craig Wedren; Music Supervisor, Jonathan Karp; Editors, David Moritz, Robert Nassau; an Apatow production in association with A Hot Dog, presented in association with Relativity Media; Dolby; Color; Rated R; 98 minutes; Release date: February 24, 2012

CAST

George Gergenblatt	**Paul Rudd**
Linda Gergenblatt	**Jennifer Aniston**
Seth	**Justin Theroux**
Carvin Waggie	**Alan Alda**
Eva	**Malin Akerman**
Rick	**Ken Marino**
Wayne	**Joe Lo Truglio**
Karen	**Kathryn Kahn**
Kathy	**Kerri Kenney-Silver**
Almond	**Lauren Ambrose**

Michaela Watkins (Marissa), Jordan Peele (Rodney), Linda Lavin (Shari), Jessica St. Clair (Deena Schuster), Todd Barry (Sherm), Martin Thompson (Dale), Ian Patrick (Grisham), John D'Leo (Tanner), David Wain, Michael Showalter, Michael Ian Black (Themselves), Zandy Hartig (Marcy), Keegan Michael Key (Marcy's Flunkie), Mather Zickel (Jim Stansel), Juan Piedrahita (Paco), Peter Salett (Manfreddie), Patricia French (Beverly), Nina Hellman (Protester), Richard Jones (Jerry Beaver), Juana Samayoa (Stephanie Davis), David Cardenas (Ronny Shames), Sharon Lubin (Danielle Melster), Vester Grayson (Janie Brody), Ronald McFarlin (Billy Marcus), Roger Parham-Brown (Glen Stover), Jim Moffatt (Tony Piloski), Sung-Suk Garber (Janice Woo), Craig Wedren, Amy Miles, Charles Gansa, Roberto Zincone, Fran Capitanelli (The Elysium Band), Ray Liotta (Himself)

With no prospects left in New York after he is fired, George and his wife hightail it south with the intention of crashing at his brother's place but instead wind up living on a commune, where they hope to come to peace with themselves.

Paul Rudd, Jennifer Aniston

GOOD DEEDS

(LIONSGATE) Producers, Tyler Perry, Ozzie Areu, Paul Hall; Executive Producers, Joseph P. Genier, Michael Paseornek; Co-Producer, H.H. Cooper; Director/Screenplay, Tyler Perry; Photography, Alexander Gruszynski; Designer, Ina Mayhew; Costumes, Johnetta Boone; Music, Aaron Zigman; Music Supervisor, Joel C. High; Editor, Maysie Hoy; Casting, Kim Taylor-Coleman; a Tyler Perry Studios/Lionsgate production; Dolby; Deluxe color; Rated PG-13; 110 minutes; Release date: February 24, 2012

Tyler Perry, Thandie Newton

CAST

Wesley Deeds	**Tyler Perry**
Lindsey Wakefield	**Thandie Newton**
Natalie	**Gabrielle Union**
John	**Eddie Cibrian**
Walt Deeds	**Brian White**
Ariel	**Jordenn Thompson**
Wilimena	**Phylicia Rashad**
Brenda	**Beverly Johnson**
Heidi	**Rebecca Romijn**
Mark Freeze	**Jamie Kennedy**
Mr. Brunson	**Andrew Hyatt Masset**
Mrs. Bunson	**Victoria Loving**

Tom Thon (Milton), Susan Shalhoub Larkin (Margaret), Nevaina (Teacher), Jennifer Van Horn (Principal), Karenlie Riddering (Child Care Worker), Clay Adams (Security Guard), Daniel Orellana (Tow Truck Driver), Divakar Shukla (Clerk), Jessica Stamper (Woman #1), Mark E. Swinton, Brenda Porter, Bob Lanoue (Shelter Workers), Gordon Price (Homeless Man), Crystle Stewart (Secretary), Ashley LeConte Campbell (Social Worker), Brenda Sharman (Gate Attendant)

A wealthy businessman, about to reluctantly wed, meets an Iraq War widow struggling to make ends meet by working as a cleaner at his office and decides to help improve her life.

Beverly Johnson, Phylicia Rashad, Gabrielle Union

Thandie Newton, Jordenn Thompson

Brian White, Eddie Cibrian © Lionsgate

ACT OF VALOR

(RELATIVITY) Producers, Mouse McCoy, Scott Waugh; Executive Producers, Michael Mailis, Bert Ellis, Benjamin Statler, Lance Sloane, Ryan Kavanaugh, Tucker Tooley, Jason Colbeck, Jason Clark, Jay Pollak, Max Leitman; Directors, Scott Waugh, Mouse McCoy; Screenplay, Kurt Johnstad; Photography, Shane Hurlbut; Designer, John Zachary; Music, Nathan Furst; Music Supervisors, Peter Afterman, Alison Litton; Editors, Scott Waugh, Michael Tronick; Casting, Nancy Nayor; a Bandito Brothers film, presented in association with Tom Clancy; Dolby; Panavision; Technicolor; HD; Rated R; 110 minutes; Release date; February 24, 2012

CAST

Lisa Morales	**Roselyn Sanchez**
Abu Shabal	**Jason Cottle**
Christo	**Alex Veadov**
Walter Ross	**Nestor Serrano**
Lt. Rorke's Wife	**Alisa Marshall**

LCDR Rorke, SOC Dave, SOC Sonny, SOC Weimy, SO1 Ray, SO1 Ajay, SOC Mikey, SOCS Van D, Katelyn, Admiral Callaghan, Capt. Duncan Smith, SOCS Billy (Themselves), Gonzalo Menendez (Cmdr. Pedros), Emilio Rivera (Sanchez), Dimiter Marinov (Kerimov), Alexander Asefa, Kenny Calderon, Sam Cespedes, Nick Gomez, Victor Palacios, Jeymi Ramos, Sebastian Rey, Gilbert Rosales (Christo's Thugs), Jeffrey Barnachea, Drea Castro, Jimmy Chiu, Craig H. Davidson, Aurelius DiBarsanti, Conrad Garcia, Marissa Labog, Reginald Long, Christian Mante, Henry Pinpin, Ernie Reyes Jr., Fred Sabado, Sarifa Salanga, Sonny Sison, Philip Un (Recruits), Raul Canizales II, Juan Diaz, Pedro Sergio Esobedo, Richie Gaona, Dorian Kingi, Francisco Lopez, Gilbert Mares, Marco Morales, Sam Pascua, Mario Perez, Oscar Pesqueira, Shawn Robinson, Alfredo Sanchez, Jesús Fernández (Cartel & Mexican SOFs), Tommy Rosales Jr. (Christo's RHM), Charles Chiyangwa, Jesse Cotton, Colin Fleming, Dyonte Griffin, Charles Mathers, Zakaria Sall, Ray Shirley, Odain Watson (Somalians), Antoni Corone (Yacht Henchman), Carla Jimenez (Screaming Mom), Maria Juani, Aspen Widowson, Lydia Lane (Yacht Girls), Artie Malesci (Surveillance Boat Driver), Marc Margulies (US Ambassador), Angela Mora (Sleeping Wife), Ed Abel Pineda (Sleeping Husband), Sopheakna Ngourn (Ice Cream Truck Girl), Thomas Rosales Jr. (Christo's Thug), Dan Southworth (News Reporter)

A team of Navy SEALs is assigned the task of extracting a CIA agent who has been abducted by a Costa Rican smuggling kingpin.

Lt. Rorke © Relativity Media

Once-ler, Lorax and the Bar-ba-luts

Lorax

Mr. O'Hare

Grammy Norma, Audrey, Ted

Humming Fish © Universal Studios

Dr. Seuss' THE LORAX

(UNIVERSAL) Producers, Chris Meledandri, Janet Healy; Executive Producers, Audrey Geisel, Ken Daurio, Cinco Paul; Director, Chris Renaud; Co-Director, Kyle Balda; Screenplay, Cinco Paul, Ken Daurio; Based on the 1971 book by Dr. Seuss; Designer, Yarrow Cheney; Art Director, Eric Guillon; Music, John Powell; Editors, Ken Scretzmann, Claire Dodgson, Steven Liu; Songs, John Powell, Cinco Paul; Animation Director, Lionel Gallat; Character Designer, Jérémie Moreau; an Illumination Entertainment production; Dolby; Color; 3D; Rated PG; 101 minutes; Release date: March 2, 2012

VOICE CAST

The Lorax	**Danny DeVito**
The Once-ler	**Ed Helms**
Ted	**Zac Efron**
Audrey	**Taylor Swift**
Mr. O'Hare	**Rob Riggle**
Ted's Mom	**Jenny Slate**
Grammy Norma	**Betty White**
Uncle Ubb	**Stephen Tobolowsky**
Aunt Grizelda	**Elmarie Wendel**
Brett/Chet	**Danny Cooksey**

Nasim Pedrad (Once-ler's Mom), Joel Swetow, Michael Beattie (Marketing Guys), Dave B. Mitchell, Dempsey Pappion (Commercial Guys), Chris Renaud (Forest Animals); Jack Angel, Bob Bergen, John Cygan, Debi Derryberry, Bill Farmer, Jess Harnell, Sherry Lynn, Danny Mann, Mona Marshall, Mickie McGowan, Laraine Newman, Jan Rabson, Claira Nicole Titman, Jim Ward (Additional Voices)

The Once-ler tells the story of how he foolishly ruined the environment by chopping down all the Truffula Trees, despite protestations and warnings of a bleak future from a creature called the Lorax.

Robert De Niro, Julianne Moore © Focus Features

Robert De Niro, Paul Dano

Robert De Niro

BEING FLYNN

(FOCUS) Producers, Paul Weitz, Andrew Miano, Michael Costigan; Executive Producers, Jane Rosenthal, Meghan Lyvers, Kerry Kohansky, Caroline Baron, Nick Flynn; Director/Screenplay, Paul Weitz; Based on the 2004 memoir *Another Bullshit Night in Suck City* by Nick Flynn; Photography, Declan Quinn; Designer, Sarah Knowles; Costumes, Aude Bronson-Howard; Music, Badly Drawn Boy; Music Supervisor, Linda Cohen; Editor, Joan Sobel; Casting, Joseph Middleton; a Depth of Field/Corduroy Films/Tribeca production; Dolby; Super 35 Widescreen; Color; Rated R; 102 minutes; Release date: March 2, 2012

CAST

Jonathan Flynn	**Robert De Niro**
Nick Flynn	**Paul Dano**
Jody Flynn	**Julianne Moore**
Denise	**Olivia Thirlby**
Carlos	**Eddie Rouse**
Jeff	**Steve Cirbus**
Joy	**Lili Taylor**
Gabriel	**Victor Rasuk**

Liam Broggy (Young Nick), Chris Chalk (Ivan), Wes Studi (Captain), Michael Gibson (Sgt. Bob), Thomas Middleditch (Richard), Sarah Quinn (Religious Girl), Ben Foronda (Punky Guy), Dale Dickey (Marie), Joshua Alscher (Crack Smoker), Dawn McGee (Waitress), Billy Wirth (Travis), Kelly McCreary (Inez), Deidre O'Connell (Frowzy Woman), Katherine Waterston (Sarah), Robert Andrews, Roy Milton Davis (Homeless Men), Michael Genadry (Young Counselor), Kelli Crump (Desk Clerk), Dara Tomanovich (Beautiful Woman), Jane Lee (Laura), Evan Wadle (Young Guy), Victor Pagan (Beady-Eyed Bill), Rony Clanton (Skid), Michael Buscemi (Dennis), Lorenzo Murphy (Morphine Addict), William Sadler (Ray), Joseph Prioleau (George), Lee Stringer (Homeless Man in Line), John O'Brien (Airline Pilot), Joey Boots (NA Guy), Luis Moco (Punk Rocker), Marilyn Torres (Little Girl's Mother), Stephen Williams, Carlton Bembry (Counselors), Rufino Colion (Shelter Guest #1), Jeff Ware (Jerry), Samira Wiley (Asha), Stuart Rudin (Moses), Gabriel Millman (Housing Counselor), Thomas Hoffman (Barlow), Joyce Myricks (Nurse/Counselor), Dwight Folsom (Isaac Clegg), George Astarian, Anthony Piccolo (Beating Teens), Kevin Keels (Banker at Party)

A young man trying to come to grips with his own restless existence must now cope with his long-absent father, an angry, half-deluded vagrant who swears he has written a great, unpublished novel.

Lili Taylor, Paul Dano

PROJECT X

(WARNER BROS.) Producer, Todd Phillips; Executive Producers, Joel Silver, Scott Budnick, Andrew Rona, Alex Heineman, Marty P. Ewing; Director, Nima Nourizadeh; Screenplay, Matt Drake, Michael Bacall; Story, Michael Bacall; Photography, Ken Seng; Designer, Bill Brzeski; Costumes, Alison McCosh; Music Supervisor, Gabe Hilfer; Editor, Jeff Groth; Casting, Juel Bestrop, Seth Yanklewitz; Stunts, Allan Graf; a Silver Pictures production, a Green Hat Films production; Dolby; Technicolor; Rated R; 88 minutes; Release date: March 2, 2012

CAST

Thomas	**Thomas Mann**
Costa	**Oliver Cooper**
JB	**Jonathan Daniel Brown**
Dax	**Dax Flame**
Kirby	**Kirby Bliss Blanton**
Everett	**Brady Hender**
Tyler	**Nick Nervies**
Alexis	**Alexis Knapp**
Miles	**Miles Teller**
Dad	**Peter Mackenzie**
Mom	**Caitlin Dulany**

Rob Evors (Rob), Rick Shapiro (T-Rick), Martin Klebba (Angry Little Person), Pete Gardner (Older Guy), Nichole Bloom (JB's Girl), Sam Lant, Henry Michaelson (Freshman Party Crashers), Brendan Miller (Brendan), Brent Tarnol, Kyle Kwasnick (Locker Room Guys), David Sanchez, Ayydé Vargas, Chelsea Carbaugh-Rutland, Zach Lasry, Michael C. Stretton, Andrew Harbour, Allan Chanes, Holden Morse (High School Students), Raz Mataz, Briana Mari Wilde, Jarod Einsohn, Chet Hanks, Julian Evens (Party Goers), Jesse Marco (DJ), Chic Daniel, Kevin Dunigan (Police Officers), Colleen Flynn (Mrs. Stillson), Sophia Santi (Hispanic Neighbor), Jodi Harris (Older Guy's Wife), Frank Buckley (Channel 6 Reporter), Serene Branson (Channel 8 Reporter), Robb Reesman (Police Captain), Kevin Ryder (Kevin), Bean Baxter (Bean), Big Boy, Jimmy Kimmel, Jillian Barberie (Themselves)

Thomas reluctantly allows his obnoxious friend Costa to throw him a birthday party, which turns into an apocalyptic nightmare as the festivities get entirely out of hand.

© Warner Bros.

Nick Nervies, Brady Hender

Oliver Cooper, Jonathan Daniel Brown, Dax Flame, Thomas Mann

JOHN CARTER

(WALT DISNEY STUDIOS) Producers, Jim Morris, Lindsey Collins, Colin Wilson; Director, Andrew Stanton; Screenplay, Andrew Stanton, Mark Andrews, Michael Chabon; based on the 1917 story *A Princess of Mars* by Edgar Rice Burroughs; Photography, Dan Mindel; Designer, Nathan Crowley; Costumes, Mayes C. Rubeo; Music, Michael Giacchino; Editor, Eric Zumbrunnen; Special Effects Supervisor, Chris Corbould; Special Effects Coordinator, Scott R. Fisher; Animation Supervisor, Eamonn Butler; Stunts, Tom Struthers; Casting, Marcia Ross; a Disney presentation; Dolby; Deluxe color; Panavision; 3D; Rated PG-13; 132 minutes; Release date: March 9, 2012

Woola, Taylor Kitsch © Walt Disney Studios

CAST

John Carter	**Taylor Kitsch**
Dejah Thoris	**Lynn Collins**
Sola	**Samantha Morton**
Tars Tarkas	**Willem Dafoe**
Tal Hajus	**Thomas Haden Church**
Matai Shang	**Mark Strong**
Tardos Mors	**Ciaran Hinds**

Dominic West (Sab Than), James Purefoy (Kantos Kan), Bryan Cranston (Powell), Polly Walker (Sarkoja), Daryl Sabara (Edgar Rice Burroughs), Arkie Reece (Stayman #1, Helm), Davood Ghadami (Stayman #3), Pippa Nixon (Lightmaster), James Embree, Philip Philmar (Therns), Figs Jackman (Man in the Bowler), Emily Tierney (Pretty Woman in NYC Doorway), Edmund Kente (Telegraph Clerk), Rupert Frazer (Thompson), Nicholas Woodeson (Dalton), Kyle Agnew (Stable Boy), Don Stark (Dix the Storekeeper), Josh Daugherty, Jared Cyr (Rowdies), Sean Carrigan (Cavalryman), Dusty Sorg (Twitchy Corporal), Christopher Goodman (Stockade Guard), Amanda Clayton (Sarah Carter), Akima Castaneda (Apache Leader), Joseph Billingiere, Alderd Westley Montoya (Apaches), Phil Cheadle (Thern in Cave), David Schwimmer (Young Thark Warrior), Arnie Alpert, Ian Ray, Peggy Clements, Evelyn Dubuc, Connie Jhil McEntyre (Council Members), Daniel O'Meara (Vas Kor), Emma Clifford (Lightman, Helm), Oliver Boot (Bodyguard, Matai), Rebecca Starker (Stayman #1, Navigator), Philip Arditti (Spotter #2), Jon Favreau (Thark Bookie), Art Malik (Zodangan General), Holly Weston (Carter's Wife), Gary Milner (Zodangan Guard), Cate Fowler (Matron of Chamber, Matai), Darwin Shaw (Zodangan Officer, Matai), Eileen Page (Elderly Woman, Matai), Simon Evans (Zodangan Guard), Myriam Acharki (Priestess), Steven Cree (Humble Guard), Garry Tubbs (Orkney Dig Worker), Jeremy Booth (Doctor)

Lynn Collins, Taylor Kitsch

A confederate soldier is mysteriously transported to Mars where he finds himself in the midst of a war between the planet's inhabitants.

White Apes, Taylor Kitsch

Dominic West

JIRO DREAMS OF SUSHI

(MAGNOLIA) Producers, David Gelb, Kevin Iwashina, Tom Pellegrini; Executive Producers, Matthew Weaver, Joey Carey, Stefan Nowicki, Ed Ojdana, Chris Kelly, Jennifer Carrico Kelly, Jeffrey C. Norman, Ross M. Dinerstein; Director/Photography, David Gelb; Editor, Brandon Driscoll-Luttringer; a City Room Films presentation of a Weaver/Pellegrini, Preferred Content production in association with Sundial Pictures presentation; Dolby; Color; HD; Rated PG; 81 minutes; Release date: March 9, 2012. Documentary on 85-year-old Jiro Ono, owner of the 10-seat Tokyo restaurant Sukiyabashi Jiro

WITH

Jiro Ono, Yamamoto Masuhiro, Takashi Ono, Yoshikazu Ono

Jiro Ono

A THOUSAND WORDS

(DREAMWORKS) Producers, Alain Chabat, Stephanie Danan, Nicolas Cage, Norm Golightly, Brian Robbins, Sharla Sumpter Bridgett; Executive Producer, Jane Bartelme; Director, Brian Robbins; Screenplay, Steve Koren; Photography, Clark Mathis; Designer, Clay A. Griffith; Costumes, Mary Vogt; Music, John Debney; Editor, Ned Bastille; Co-Producers, Lars Winther, Marc Haimes; a Work After Midnight Films/Saturn Films production; Distributed by Paramount Pictures; Dolby; Super 35 Widescreen; Technicolor; Rated PG-13; 91 minutes; Release date: March 9, 2012

CAST

Jack McCall	**Eddie Murphy**
Caroline McCall	**Kerry Washington**
Dr. Sinja	**Cliff Curtis**
Aaron Wiseberger	**Clark Duke**
Annie McCall	**Ruby Dee**
Samantha Davis	**Allison Janney**
Tyler McCall	**Emanuel Ragsdale**

Jill Basey (Woman in Starbucks), Greg Collins (Construction Worker), Robert LeQuang, Michael G. Wilkinson, Lyndsey Nelson, Michael Cody Gilbert (Starbucks Customers), Lou Saliba (Shrink), Mitchell Fink, Edi Patterson (Agents), Emily A. Burton (Crying Student), Tracy Mulholland (Young Student), Brad Keimach, Dilip Jha (Sinja Aides), Jorge A. Alvarez (Mariachi Band Leader), Kayla Blake (Emily), Leonard Earl Howze (Orderly), Winston J. Rocha (Gaudencio), Jack McBrayer (Starbucks Barista), John Witherspoon (Blind Man), Bethany Dwyer (Mary), Alain Chabat (Christian Léger de la Touffe), Thierry Segall, Noel Courteblenche (French Businessmen), Sara Holden (Hostess), Lennie Loftin (Robert Gilmore), David Burke (Gil Reed), Jeff Kahn (Waiter), Matt Winston (Kid Space Teacher), Daniel Hepner, Eric Archibald (Sensitive Dads), Philip Pavel (Overly Enthused Dad), Raquel Bell (Kid Space Mom), Kamala Jones (Hotel Employee), Kharrison Sweeney (Rotund Man), Brian Gallivan (Tony), Steven M. Gagnon (Ira), Daniel Saltos (Gaudencio Assistant), Lauren Schuchman (Waitress), Ted Kennedy (Homeless Man), Jane Bartelme (Nun), Darcy Rose Byrnes (10 Year Old Girl), Eshaya Draper (Young Jack), Sarah Scott Davis (Young Annie), Skip Crank (Ice Cream Vendor), Justin Soul Robbins, Miles Robbins (Boys), Floyd Levine (Man on Pier), Bunny Levine (Woman on Pier), Brian Norris (Steven)

Eddie Murphy, Clark Duke © DreamWorks Pictures

Eddie Murphy, Kerry Washington

A magical tree appears in the yard of a self-centered, fast-talking literary agent who soon realizes that every time he speaks the tree looses a leaf. Worried that this means when all the branches are empty, he will die, he tries to go through the day without speaking a word.

Chris O'Dowd, Kristen Wiig, Maya Rudolph, Jon Hamm

Adam Scott, Megan Fox

Edward Burns, Kristen Wiig © Roadside Attractions

FRIENDS WITH KIDS

(ROADSIDE ATTRACTIONS/LIONSGATE) Producers, Jon Hamm, Jennifer Westfeldt, Joshua Astrachan, Jake Kasdan, Riza Aziz, Joey McFarland; Executive Producers, Mike Nichols, John Sloss, Lucy Barzun Donnelly, Joe Gatta; Co-Producer, Kathryn Dean; Director/Screenplay, Jennifer Westfeldt; Photography, William Rexer II; Designer, Ray Kluga; Costumes, Melissa Bruning; Music, Marcelo Zarvos; Music Supervisors, Randall Poster, Stephanie Diaz-Matos; Editor, Tara Timpone; a Red Granite Pictures presentation of a Points West Pictures and Locomotive production; Dolby; Color; HD; Rated R; 100 minutes; Release date: March 9, 2012

CAST

Jason Fryman	**Adam Scott**
Julie Keller	**Jennifer Westfeldt**
Ben	**Jon Hamm**
Missy	**Kristen Wiig**
Leslie	**Maya Rudolph**
Alex	**Chris O'Dowd**
Mary Jane	**Megan Fox**
Kurt	**Edward Burns**
Elaine Keller	**Lee Bryant**
Marcy Fryman	**Kelly Bishop**
Phil Fryman	**Cotter Smith**

Owen Bento (Troy), Derek Cecil (Pete), Brian d'Arcy James (Husband in Restaurant), Ilana Levine (Mom in Restaurant), Georgia Levi Fumusa (Daughter in Restaurant), Rekha Luther (Life Coach), Loulou Sloss (Girl Acting Up in Restaurant), Katie Foster (Julie's Assistant), Robert Halpern, Daniel Halpern (Cole), Peter K. Hirsch (Doctor in Delivery Room), John Lutz (Jason's Colleague at Work), Nina Lafarga (Penelope), Summer Perry, Ryann Egnel (Kate), Theo Mitchell (Joe at 12 months), Vince Vappo (Julie's Date, Businessman), Ken Barnett (Stage Manager, Chicago), Ryann Pacheco, Jacob Pacheco (Twins in Restaurant), Jim McMillan (Missy's New Boyfriend), Brody Frederick (Joe, 2 ½ years)

Worried that having children has ruined the romantic lives of their friends, Julie and Adam decide to have a kid together while continuing to date others.

Adam Scott, Jennifer Westfeldt

SILENT HOUSE

(LD/OPEN ROAD) Producers, Agnes Mentre, Laura Lau; Executive Producers, Mickey Liddell, Jennifer Hilton Monroe, Danny Perkins, Adeline Fontan Tessaur, Eva Diederix, George Paaswell; Directors, Chris Kentis, Laura Lau; Screenplay, Laura Lau; Based on the 2011 Gustavo Hernández film *La casa muda,* written by Oscar Estevez; Photography, Igor Martinovic; Designer, Roshelle Berliner; Costumes, Lynn Falconer; Music, Nathan Larson; Visual Effects Supervisor, Sasa Jokic; Special Effects Coordinator, Drew Jiritano; Casting, Kerry Barden, Paul Schnee; an Elle Driver presentation in association with Silverwood Films; Dolby; Color; Rated R; 86 minutes; Release date: March 9, 2012

CAST
Sarah	**Elizabeth Olsen**
John	**Adam Trese**
Peter	**Eric Sheffer Stevens**
Sophia	**Julia Taylor Ross**
Stalking Man	**Adam Barnett**
Little Girl	**Haley Murphy**

While helping her father and her uncle prepare the family's lakeside house for sale, Sarah begins to suspect that a deadly intruder has entered the premises.

Elizabeth Olsen © LD/Open Road

Eric Sheffer Stevens, Elizabeth Olsen, Adam Trese

Frank Stennett, Tyler Ross, Stephen Cone © Wolfe Video

Tyler Ross, Jacob Leinbach

THE WISE KIDS

(WOLFE) Producers, Sue Redman, Laura Klein, Stephen Cone; Co-Producers, Monte Redman, Carolyn Redman, Tim Whitfield, Mitchell Crosby; Director/Screenplay/Editor, Stephen Cone; Photography, Stephanie Dufford; Designer, Caity Birmingham; Costumes, Erin Amelia White; Music, Mikhail Fiksel; Casting, Matthew Miller, Mlckie Paskal, Jennifer Rudnicke; a Cone Arts presentation; Stereo; Technicolor; HD; Not rated; 95 minutes; Release date: March 16, 2012

CAST
Brea	**Molly Kunz**
Tim	**Tyler Ross**
Laura	**Allison Torem**
Jerry	**Matt DeCaro**
Elizabeth	**Sadieh Rifai**
Austin	**Stephen Cone**

Cliff Chamberlain (Dylan), Sadie Rogers (Cheryl), Ann Whitney (Ms. Powell), Rodney Lee Rogers (Pastor Jim), Jacob Leinbach (Brad), Lee Armstrong (Harry), Addison Quilla Dent (Stephen), Sharon Graci (Kathy), Sullivan Hamilton (Haley), Kendall Hinson (Keri), Danielle Howle (Paige), Eric Hulsebos (Ryan), Justin Johnson (Patrick), Jonathan Jones (Josh), Will Kinnear (Adam), Tessa Nicole (Savannah), Alyssa Puckett (April), Cynthia Pulsifer (Cynthia), Laurel Schroeder (Erin), Porter Spicer (Matthew), Frank Stennett (Frank), Kendra Gaige, Melanie Gaige (Church Members), Sue Redman (Club Woman), Braxton Williams (Braxton), Joe Debney (Man at Party), Luca del Puppo (Jogger), Sue Redman (Club Woman), Bryan Basque (Club Boy), Haley Sirisky, Khaleil Burden, Hannah Reynolds (Youth Group)

A group of Christian teens finds their beliefs put to the test when one of their circle begins to embrace the fact that he is gay, thereby accepting a life that goes against all they have been taught.

JEFF, WHO LIVES AT HOME

(PARAMOUNT VANTAGE) Producers, Lianne Halfon, Russell Smith, Jason Reitman; Executive Producers, Steven Rales, Helen Estabrook; Line Producer, Robert J. Dohrmann; Directors/Screenplay, Jay Duplass, Mark Duplass; Photography, Jas Shelton; Designer, Chris Spellman; Costumes, Meagan McLaughlin; Music, Michael Andrews; Editor, Jay Deuby; Casting, Terri Taylor; an Indian Paintbrush presentation of a Right of Way production in association with Mr. Mudd; Dolby; Deluxe color; Rated R; 83 minutes; Release date: March 16, 2012

Jason Segel, Ed Helms

CAST

Jeff	**Jason Segel**
Pat	**Ed Helms**
Sharon	**Susan Sarandon**
Linda	**Judy Greer**
Carol	**Rae Dawn Chong**
Steve	**Steve Zissis**
Kevin	**Evan Ross**
TV Pitchman	**Benjamin Brant Bickham**
Clerk	**Lee Nguyen**
Paul	**Joe Chrest**

Tim J. Smith, Ernest James (Guards), David Kency (Teammate), Raion Hill (Thug), Zac Cino (Gil), Lance E. Nichols (Elderly Man, Phone), Carol Sutton (Elderly Woman), Katie Aselton (Hostess), J.D. Evermore (Waiter), John Neisler (Kevin Kandy Employee), Matt Malloy (Barry), Ian Hoch (Bartender), Robert Larriviere (Manager), Jesse Moore (Taxi Driver), Scotty Whitehurst (Teen Driver), Wally Crowder (Fisherman), Carol Wells (Younger Girl), Savanna Kinchen (Older Girl), Eddie Matthews (Father), Jennifer Lafleur (TV Announcer), Deneen D. Tyler (Woman Calling the Police), Randall Kamm (Field Reporter)

An affable stoner, certain that a cryptic phone call has some deeper meaning, inadvertently hooks up with his estranged brother, who is devastated to discover that his wife is having an affair.

Judy Greer © Paramount Vantage

Susan Sarandon

Rae Dawn Chong

Genesis Rodriguez,
Will Ferrell © Pantelion

CASA DE MI PADRE

(PANTELION) Producers, Will Ferrell, Adam McKay, Emilio Diez Barroso, Darlene Caamaño Loquet, Andrew Steele; Executive Producers, Kevin Messick, Scott Lumpkin, Jessica Elbaum, Billy Rovzar, Fernando Rovzar, Alex Garcia; Co-Producer, Rudy Scalese; Director, Matt Piedmont; Screenplay, Andrew Steele; Photography, Ramsey Nickell; Designer, Kevin Kavanaugh; Costumes, Trayce Gigi Field, Marylou Lim; Music, Andrew Feltenstein, John Nau; Music Supervisor, Hal Willner; Editor, David Trachtenberg; Casting, Allison Jones; a Nala, Pantelion Films, Televisia Films and Lionsgate presentation of a Gary Sanchez production, a Nala Films production; Dolby; Panavision; Deluxe color; Rated R; 84 minutes; Release date: March 16, 2012

CAST
Armando	**Will Ferrell**
Onza	**Gael García Bernal**
Raul	**Diego Luna**
Sonia	**Genesis Rodriguez**
Miguel Ernesto	**Pedro Armendáriz Jr.**
DEA Agent Parker	**Nick Offerman**

Efren Ramirez (Esteban), Adrian Martinez (Manuel), Manuel Urrego (Officer Blancardo), Louis Carazo (Young Miguel), Elijah Velarde (Young Armando), Alejandro Patino (Hector), Jerry Collins (DEA Agent #2), Sandra Echeverría (Miguel Ernesto's Wife), Eduardo Ricard, Pedro Lopez, James Victor (Old Friends), William Marquez (Doctor), Dan Haggerty (Himself), José Luis Rodríguez 'El Puma' (Wedding Singer), Eric Leiderman, Patricia Guggenheim, Bob Dassie (Band Members), Mariann Gavelo (Esmeralda), Molly Shannon (Sheila), Gayle Sherman (Margarite), Thomas Rosales Jr. (Friend George), Armando Guerrero (Father Guizman)

The ineffectual son of a Mexican rancher falls for his brother's beautiful fiancée as the family becomes embroiled in a battle with a deadly crime lord. This send-up of Telemundos is spoken in Spanish.

DETACHMENT

(TRIBECA) Producers, Austin Stark, Benji Kohn, Chris Papavasiliou, Bingo Gubelmann, Greg Shapiro, Carl Lund; Executive Producers, Adrien Brody, Peter Sterling Andre Laport; Co-Executive Producer, Marco Frigeri; Director/Photography, Tony Kaye; Screenplay, Carl Lund; Designer, Jade Healy; Costumes, Wendy Schecter; Music, The Newton Brothers; Music Supervisor, Andy Gowan; Editors, Barry Alexander Brown, Geoffrey Richman; Casting, Beth Melsky; a Paper Street Films in association with Kingsgate Films and Appian Way production; Dolby; Color; HD; Not rated; 97 minutes; Release date: March 16, 2012

CAST
Henry Barthes	**Adrien Brody**
Principal Carol Dearden	**Marcia Gay Harden**
Mr. Charles Seaboldt	**James Caan**
Ms. Sarah Madison	**Christina Hendricks**
Dr. Doris Parker	**Lucy Liu**
Ms. Perkins	**Blythe Danner**

Tim Blake Nelson (Mr. Wiatt), William Petersen (Mr. Sarge Kepler), Bryan Cranston (Mr. Dearden), Sami Gayle (Erica), Betty Kaye (Meredith), Louis Zorich (Grampa), Isiah Whitlock Jr.(Mr. Mathias), Chris Papavasiliou (Dr. Hart), Kwoade Cross (Andy), David Hausen (Angry Dad), Roslyn Ruff (Angry Mother), Jerry Walsh (Cafeteria Worker), John Cenatiempo, Brenda Pressley (Child Services Officers), Tiffani Holland (Cindy), Lucian Maisel (David), Alex Boniello (Dennis), Sze Ming Au (Ellen), Mary Joy, Justin Campbell (Orderlies), Michael Hammond (Frank), Ronen Rubenstein (Gangsta), Al Calderon (George), Brennan Brown (Greg Raymond), Celia Schaefer (Gretchen from the Free Clinic), Reagan Leonard (Henry's Mother), Tarikk Mudu (Jerry), Kevin T. Collins (John in Apartment), Stephen Payne (John on Bus), James Hosey (Kenny), Michael Kaufman (Kid in Henry's Class), Nancy Rodriguez (Lupe), Aaron Sauter (Marcus), Josh Pais (Meredith's Father), Renée Felice Smith (Missy), Doug E. Doug (Mr. Norris), Rebecka Ray (Mrs. Wiatt), Patricia Rae (Ms. Estrada), Mama Kohn (Prep Club Girl #1), Corwin Tuggles (Ricky), Lonon Jay Wilson (School Cop), Samantha Jade Logan (Spitting Daughter), Ralph Rodriguez (Student #23), Annabel Barrett (Student #4), April Maxey (Tanya), Amber Vanterpool (Tina), Eli Massilon (Tony), Alsharik Sejour (Tutored Kid), Jonathan Hudson (Wiatt's Son), Elvis Muccino (Young Henry)

A troubled substitute teacher, who hopes to keep his distance by floating from school to school, finds himself unexpectedly involved when he shelters a 15-year-old girl from repeated abuse.

Sami Gayle, Adrien Brody © Tribeca Film

Channing Tatum, Jonah Hill, Dave Franco

Channing Tatum, Jonah Hill

Jonah Hill, Brie Larson

21 JUMP STREET

(COLUMBIA/MGM) Producers, Neal H. Moritz, Stephen J. Cannell; Executive Producers, Jonah Hill, Channing Tatum, Ezra Swerdlow, Tania Landau; Directors, Phil Lord, Christopher Miller; Screenplay, Michael Bacall; Story, Michael Bacall, Jonah Hill; based on the television series created by Patrick Hasburgh and Stephen J. Cannell; Photography, Barry Peterson; Designer, Peter Wenham; Costumes, Leah Katznelson; Music, Mark Mothersbaugh; Editor, Joel Negron; Casting, Jeanne McCarthy, Nicole Abellera; Stunts, Jeffrey Gibson; an Original Film, SJC Studios Produciton, presented in association with Relativity Media; Dolby; Super 35 Widescreen; Deluxe color; Rated R; 108 minutes; Release date: March 16, 2012

CAST

Schmidt ("Doug McQuaid")	**Jonah Hill**
Jenko ("Brad McQuaid")	**Channing Tatum**
Molly Tracey	**Brie Larson**
Eric Molson	**Dave Franco**
Mr. Walters	**Rob Riggle**
Domingo	**DeRay Davis**
Captain Dickson	**Ice Cube**
Zack	**Dax Flame**
Mr. Gordon	**Chris Parnell**
Ms. Griggs	**Ellie Kemper**
Principal Dadier	**Jake Johnson**
Deputy Chief Hardy	**Nick Offerman**
Officer Judy Hoffs	**Holly Robinson Peete**
Delroy	**Johnny Pemberton**
Roman	**Stanley Wong**
Juario	**Justin Hires**
Amir	**Brett Lapeyrouse**
Lisa	**Lindsey Broad**
Annie Schmidt	**Caroline Aaron**
David Schmidt	**Joe Chrest**
Phyllis	**Geraldine Singer**
Fugazy	**Dakota Johnson**
Jr. Jr.	**Rye Rye**
Burns	**Valerie Tian**
Sanders	**Jaren Mitchell**
Billiam Willingham	**Johnny Simmons**

Keith Kurtz (DJ Ay Papi), Randal Reeder (Karl), Peter Epstein, Anthony Molinari (One-Percenters), Luis Da Silva (Luis, One-Percenter #3), Dominic Alexander (Lukas, One-Percenter #4), Mike Seal (Ed, One-Percenter #5), Spencer Boldman (French Samuels), Joe Nin Williams (Scott), Chad Hessler, Kevin Murphy, Victor Paguia (Crazies), Chanel Celaya (Melodie), Carol Sutton (Hamilton Principal), Andrea Frankle (Cinnamon), Tiffney Wagoner, Andrea Madison (Prostitutes), Hristo Birbochukov (Accompanist), Candi Brooks (VW Bug Driver), Turner Crumbley (EMT), Harley Elizabeth Farris, Brittany Alger (Eric's Friends), Joshua Nelms, Courtney Jarrell, Melissa Cordero (Naked Drama Threesome), Beau DeLatte (Adorable Boy), Charles Ferrara (Janitor), Mark Adams (Police Chief), Brian Heath Rossitto (Instructor), Johnny Depp (Officer Tom Hanson), Peter DeLuise (Officer Doug Penhall)

Two new police recruits are sent to participate in an undercover program that will allow them to pass themselves off as high school students while trying to find out who is dealing a dangerous new drug. Based on the FOX series (1987-1990), with original cast members Johnny Depp, Peter DeLuise, and Holly Robinson (Peete) making cameo appearances here.

Ice Cube

Dave Franco © Columbia Pictures

Dax Flame, Ellie Kemper, Channing Tatum

Channing Tatum

Channing Tatum, Jonah Hill

Channing Tatum, Jonah Hill

THE HUNGER GAMES

(LIONSGATE) Producers, Nina Jacobson, Jon Kilik; Executive Producers, Robin Bissell, Suzanne Collins, Louise Rosner-Meyer; Director, Gary Ross; Screenplay, Gary Ross, Suzanne Collins, Billy Ray; Based on the 2008 novel by Suzanne Collins; Photography, Tom Stern; Designer, Philip Messina; Costumes, Judianna Makovsky; Music, James Newton Howard; Editors, Stephen Mirrione, Juliette Welfling; Visual Effects Supervisor, Sheena Duggal; Casting, Debra Zane; a Color Force/Lionsgate production; Dolby; Arri Widescreen; Technicolor; Rated PG-13; 142 minutes; Release date: March 23, 2012

CAST

Katniss Everdeen	**Jennifer Lawrence**
Peeta Meelark	**Josh Hutcherson**
Gale Hawthorne	**Liam Hemsworth**
Haymitch Abernaty	**Woody Harrelson**
Effie Trinket	**Elizabeth Banks**
Cinna	**Lenny Kravitz**
Caesar Flickerman	**Stanley Tucci**
President Snow	**Donald Sutherland**
Seneca Crane	**Wes Bentley**
Claudius Templesmith	**Toby Jones**
Cato	**Alexander Ludwig**
Clove	**Isabelle Fuhrman**
Rue	**Amandla Stenberg**
Marvel	**Jack Quaid**
Thresh	**Dayo Okeniyi**
Glimmer	**Leven Rambin**
Primrose Everdeen	**Willow Shields**
Katniss' Mother	**Paula Malcomson**
Venia	**Kimiko Gelman**
Flavius	**Nelson Ascencio**
Octavia	**Brooke Bundy**
Portia	**Latarsha Rose**
Foxface	**Jacqueline Emerson**
Atala	**Karan Kendrick**
Tribute Boy District 3	**Ian Nelson**
Tribute Girl District 3	**Kalia Prescott**
Tribute Boy District 4	**Ethan Jamieson**
Tribute Girl District 8	**Mackenzie Lintz**
Tribute Boy District 9	**Imanol Yepez-Frias**
Tribute Girl District 9	**Annie Thurman**
Tribute Girl District 10	**Dakota Hood**
Hob Vendor	**Sandra Lafferty**
Registration Woman	**Rhoda Griffis**
Propaganda Film Tribute	**Sandino Moya-Smith**
Peeta's Mother	**Raiko Bowman**

Dwayne Boyd, Anthony Reynolds, Judd Lormand (Peacekepeers), Amber Chaney (Avox Girl), Shane Bissell (Birthday Boy), Katie Kneeland (Hovercraft Tech), Steve Coulter, Sharon Morris, Tim Taylor, Jack Ross (Game Center Techs), Phillip Troy Linger (Katniss' Father)

In the future, when children of those responsible for an unsuccessful uprising against the government are forced to participate in a kill or be killed sport, young Katniss Everdeen volunteers to join the deadly Hunger Games so that her sister may be spared.

Jennifer Lawrence, Liam Hemsworth

Isabelle Fuhrman, Alexander Ludwig, Jack Quaid, Leven Rambin

Jennifer Lawrence, Josh Hutcherson

Donald Sutherland, Wes Bentley

Amandla Stenberg

Elizabeth Banks, Jennifer Lawrence

Lenny Kravitz, Woody Harrelson, Josh Hutcherson

Stanley Tucci, Jennifer Lawrence

Jennifer Lawrence © Lionsgate

Willem Dafoe, Shanyn Leigh

4:44 LAST DAY ON EARTH

(IFC FILMS) Producers, Juan De Dios Larrain, Pablo Larrain, Peter Danner, Vincent Maraval, Brahim Chioua; Line Producer, Adam Folk; Director/Screenplay, Abel Ferrara; Photography, Ken Kelsch; Designer, Frank De Curtis; Music, Francis Kuipers; Editor, Anthony Redman; a Fabula/Funny Balloons/Wild Bunch production in association with Bullet Pictures; Dolby; Color; Not rated; 85 minutes; Release date: March 23, 2012

CAST
Cisco	**Willem Dafoe**
Skye	**Shanyn Leigh**
Tina	**Natasha Lyonne**
Noah	**Paul Hipp**
Cisco's Ex	**Dierdra McDowell**

Triana Jackson (JJ, Cisco's Daughter), Trung Nguyen (Li, Delivery Boy), Anita Pallenberg (Diana, Sky's Mother), Trung Nguyen (Delivery Boy), José Solano (Javi, Drug Dealer), Judith Salazar (Carmen, Friend of Dealer), Jimmy Valentino (Karaoke Singer), Paz de la Huerta (Woman on Street), Pat Kiernan (News Anchor), Tony Redman (Voice on Phone), Francis Kuipers (Teddy), Selena Mars (Skye Dancer), Justin Restivo (Suicide Victim), Bojana Vasik (Woman with Coat), Frank Aquilino (Man outside Bar), Maria Schirripa (Wailing Woman), Muriel Sprissler Dafoe (Cisco's Mother), Nicholas Deceolia (Man in Window), Andy Akka (The Inebriated Drunk), Phil Akka (The Money Man)

A painter and an actor face Earth's final hours before the designated time of destruction arrives.

GOON

(MAGNET) Producers, Don Carmody, David Gross, André Rouleau, Jay Baruchel, Ian Dimerman; Executive Producers, Jesse Shapira, Mark Slone; Director, Michael Dowse; Screenplay, Jay Baruchel, Evan Goldberg; Based on the 2002 book *Goon: The True Story of an Unlikely Journey into Minor League Hockey* by Adam Frattasio and Doug Smith; Photography, Bobby Shore; Designer, Gord Wilding; Costumes, Heather Neale; Music, Ramachandra Borcar; Editor, Reginald Harkema; Casting, Lori Stefaniuk; a Myriad Pictures & Alliance Films presentation; American-Canadian; Dolby; Color; Rated; R; 92 minutes; Release date: March 30, 2012

CAST
Doug Glatt	**Seann William Scott**
Pat	**Jay Baruchel**
Eva	**Alison Pill**
Ross Rhea	**Liev Schreiber**
Dr. Glatt	**Eugene Levy**

Marc-André Grondin (Xavier Laflamme), Kim Coates (Ronnie Hortense), Nicholas Campbell (Rollie Hortense), Richard Clarkin (Gord Ogilvey), Jonathan Cherry (Marco Belchier), Ricky Mabe (John Stevenson), George Tchortov (Evgeni), Karl Graboshas (Oleg), Larry Woo (Park Kim), Stephen Sim (Backup Goalie), Ellen David (Mrs. Glatt), David Paetkau (Ira Glatt), Mike Bell (Donovan), Jeff Strome (Oldfield), Jeff Scott Wahl (Reg), Dave Wheeler (Sportscaster), Bryan Clark (Bartender), David Duncan (Darren), Patricia Edgar (Elderly Waitress), James Durham (Customer), Jeff Bromley (Guy), Don Carmody (Guy in Leather Jacket), Kalyn Bomback (Kelly), Dominick Blais (O'Sullivan), Curt Keilback (Rod McCaudry), James Knight (Ref), Tom Anniko (Shamrock's Coach), Amy Groening (Teenage Singer), Ali Hassan (Uncle Stevie), Sean Skene (Assassin #1/Concord Player #2), Gabriel Daniels (Blanko), Ken St. Mars (Hamilton Defenseman), Derrick Poplawski (Lowell Kings Opponent), Tim Kiriluk, Lance Cartwright (Mirimachi Opponents), George Larague (Huntington), Andrew Degryse, Jay Roberts (MTL Tomahawk Players), Veronica Malinowski (Paris Hilton Lookalike), Geoff Banjavich (Brandon), Mark Olafson (Flannerty), Dave Lawrence (Richard), Jim Toth (Reporter), Marc Joyal (Quebec Fab), Brandy Jaques (Stripper), Howard Jerome (Albee Cohen), Aron Tager (Mr. Goldsmith), Sidney Leeder (Young Woman), Sarah Scheffer (Barbara Cohen), Darren Ross (Lineman #1)

A slow-witted bouncer gets his chance to fulfill his dreams when his fighting skills land him a spot on a minor league hockey team.

Jay Baruchel, Seann William Scott © Magnet Releasing

Alex Hopkins

Alex Hopkins © Weinstein Co.

BULLY

(WEINSTEIN CO.) formerly *The Bully Project*; Producers/Screenplay, Lee Hirsch, Cynthia Lowen: Executive Producer, Cindy Waitt; Director/Photography, Lee Hirsch; Music, Ion Furjanic, Justin Rice, Christian Rudder; Music, Ion Furjanic, Bishop Allen; Music Supervisor, Brooke Wentz; Editors, Lindsay Utz, Jenny Golden; a Where We Live Films production; Dolby; Color; Rated PG-13; 98 minutes; Release date: March 30, 2012. Documentary on the continuing problem of kids being bullied in school;

WITH

Ja'Meya Jackson, Kelby Johnson, Londa Johnson, Bob Johnson, Alex Libby, Jackie Libby, Philip Libby, Maya Libby, Jada Libby, Ethan Libby, Logan Libby, Kim Lockwood, David Long, Tina Long, Teryn Long, Troy Long, Devon Matthews, Barbara Primer, Kirk Smalley, Laura Smalley, Trey Wallace

Julia Roberts © Relativity Media

MIRROR MIRROR

(RELATIVITY MEDIA) Producers, Bernie Goldmann, Ryan Kavanaugh, Brett Ratner; Executive Producers, Tucker Tooley, Kevin Misher, Jeff Waxman, Robbie Brenner, Jamie Marshall, Jason Colbeck, Tommy Turtle, Josh Pate, John Cheng; Co-Producers, Kenneth Halsband, Nico Soultanakis, Agit Singh; Director, Tarsem Singh Dhandwar; Screenplay, Melisa Wallack, Jason Keller; Photography, Brendan Galvin; Designer, Tom Foden; Costumes, Eiko Ishioka; Music, Alan Menken; Music Supervisors, Happy Walters, Bob Bowen; Editors, Nick Moore, Robert Duffy; Visual Effects Supervisor, Tom Wood; Casting, Kerry Barden, Paul Schnee; a Goldmann Pictures, Relativity Media, Rat Entertainment, Misher Films production, presented in association with Yuk Films; Dolby; Technicolor; Rated PG; 106 minutes; Release date: March 30, 2012

CAST
The Queen	**Julia Roberts**
Snow White	**Lily Collins**
Prince Alcott	**Armie Hammer**
Brighton	**Nathan Lane**
Napoleon	**Jordan Prentice**
Half Pint	**Mark Povinelli**
Grub	**Joey Gnoffo**
Grimm	**Danny Woodburn**
Wolf	**Sebastian Saraceno**
Butcher	**Martin Klebba**
Chuckles	**Ronald Lee Clark**

Robert Emms (Charles Renbock), Mare Winningham (Baker Margaret), Michael Lerner (Baron), Sean Bean (King), Bonnie Bentley (Caroline, Poor Woman), Arthur Holden, Kwasi Songui, Eric Davis, Kathleen Fee (Nobles), Nadia Verrucci, Adam Butcher (Servants), Dawn Ford (Townswoman, Old Lady), Alex Ivanovici (Town Magistrate), Richard Jutras (Townsman), Mélodie Simard (Child), Kimberly-Sue Murray (Villager), André Lanthier (Lord Waverly), Lisa Noto (Magical Cottage Queen), William Calvert, Nicholas Guest (Door Guards), Frank Welker (Voices of Mannequins and Beast)

When Snow White attracts the attention of a wealthy prince, her stepmother, the Queen, has her banished to the forest where she befriends a band of dwarfs who help her save the kingdom.

This film received an Oscar nomination for costume design.

Lily Collins, Armie Hammer

Joey Gnoffo, Sebastian Saraceno, Ronald Lee Clark, Mark Povinelli, Danny Woodburn, Martin Klebba, Jordan Prentice, Armie Hammer

Armie Hammer, Sean Bean, Mare Winningham, Nathan Lane

WRATH OF THE TITANS

(WARNER BROS.) Producers, Basil Iwanyk, Polly Johnsen; Executive Producers, Thomas Tull, Jon Jashni, Callum McDougall, Kevin De La Noy, Louis Leterrier; Director, Jonathan Liebesman; Screenplay, Dan Mazeau, David Leslie Johnson; Story, Greg Berlanti, David Leslie Johnson, Dan Mazeau; Photography, Ben Davis; Designer, Charles Wood; Music, Javier Navarrete; Editor, Martin Walsh; Special Effects Supervisor, Neil Corbould; Visual Effects Supervisor, Nick Davis; Casting, Jina Jay; a Thunder Road Film production, presented in association with Legendary Pictures; Dolby; Super 35 Widescreen; Technicolor; 3D; Rated PG-13; 98 minutes; Release date: March 30, 2012

Danny Huston, Sam Worthington

CAST

Perseus	**Sam Worthington**
Zeus	**Liam Neeson**
Hades	**Ralph Fiennes**
Ares	**Edgar Ramirez**
Agenor	**Toby Kebbell**
Andromeda	**Rosamund Pike**
Hephaestus	**Bill Nighy**
Poseidon	**Danny Huston**
Helius	**John Bell**
Korrina	**Lily James**

Alejandro Naranjo (Mantius), Freddy Drabble (Apollo), Kathryn Carpenter (Athena), Matt Milne, Kett Turton (Elite Guards), Sinéad Cusack (Clea), Spencer Wilding (Minotaur), Juan Reyes (Prison Warden), Jorge Guimerá (Theodulus), Asier Macazaga (Theron), Daniel Galindo Rojas (Eustachius), Lamberto Guerra (Timon), George Blagden, Killian Burke (Soldiers), Alastair Cording (Villager #1), Caoilfhionn Dunne (Woman #1), Martin Bayfield (Cyclops)

Perseus enlists the aide of Andromeda and Agenor to help him rescue Zeus, who has been imprisoned in the underworld by Hades, who hopes to gain power over the gods. Sequel to the 2010 WB film *Clash of the Titans*.

Rosamund Pike, Toby Kebbell, Lily James, Sam Worthington

Bill Nighy

Spencer Wilding © Warner Bros.

AMERICAN REUNION

(UNIVERSAL) Producers, Craig Perry, Warren Zide, Chris Moore, Adam Herz; Executive Producers, Louis G. Friedman, Paul Weitz, Chris Weitz, Seann William Scott, Jason Biggs; Directors/Screenplay, Jon Hurwitz, Hayden Schlossberg; based on characters created by Adam Herz; Photography, Daryn Okada; Designer, William Arnold; Costumes, Mona May; Music, Lyle Workman; Music Supervisor, Jojo Villanueva; Editor, Jeff Betancourt; Casting, Jay Scully; a Practical Pictures/Zide Pictures production, presented in association with Relativity Media; Dolby; Super 35 Widescreen; Technicolor; Rated R; 113 minutes; Release date: April 6, 2012

CAST

Jim Levenstein	**Jason Biggs**
Michelle	**Alyson Hannigan**
Oz	**Chris Klein**
Kevin	**Thomas Ian Nicholas**
Vicky	**Tara Reid**
Steve Stifler	**Seann William Scott**
Heather	**Mena Suvari**
Finch	**Eddie Kaye Thomas**

Justin Isfeld, John Cho (MILF Guys), Jennifer Coolidge (Stifler's Mom), Eugene Levy (Jim's Dad), Natasha Lyonne (Jessica), Dania Ramirez (Selena), Katrina Bowden (Mia), Jay Harrington (Dr. Ron), Ali Cobrin (Kara), Chuck Hittinger (AJ), Shannon Elizabeth (Nadia), Chris Owen (Sherman), Charlene Amoia (Ellie), Jesse Malinowski (Kyle), Robert Hayes (Bo), Vik Sahay (Prateek Duraiswamy), Stevie Ray Dallimore (Kara's Dad), Kim Wall (Kara's Mom), Neil Patrick Harris (Celebrity Dance-Off Host), George Christopher Bianchi (Evan), Jennifer Sun Bell (Madison), Autumn Dial (Alexa), Rebecca Field (Loni), Vince Pisani, Terri James (Alums), Jen Kober (Ingrid), Raheem Babalola (Deshaun), Valarie Kobrovsky (Prateek's Hot Girlfriend), Benjamin G. Arthur (Chester), Hart Turner (Reed), Matt Mangum (Adam), Molly Cheek (Jim's Mom), Brian Mahoney (Police Officer), Chad Ochocinco (Himself), Zane Wind (Mitch), Randy Hurwitz (Mom at Party), Helenna Santos Levy (Oz Fan), Michael Beasley (Reggie), Pam Green (Ali), Joseph Kaiser (Jim, 13 yrs.), Michael May (Stifler, 13 yrs.), Logan Van Sickle (Oz, 13 yrs.), Chase Krepp (Kevin, 13 yrs.), Maximiliano Wissinger (Finch, 13 yrs.), John Jason Bailey (Random Alumni), Elizabeth Shea Hurwitz (Baby at Party), Rod C. Rich (Bar Mitzvah Dad), Jenna Willis (Computer Voice), Rebecca De Mornay (Finch's Mom)

Jim Levenstein and his best buds reunite for their high school reunion and take stock in the direction their lives have gone. Previous theatrically released entries in the Universal series are *American Pie* (1999), *American Pie 2* (2001), and *American Wedding* (2003).

Alyson Hannigan, Dania Ramirez © Universal Studios

Chris Klein, Jason Biggs, Eddie Kaye Thomas, Thomas Ian Nicholas

Jennifer Coolidge, Eugene Levy

Thomas Ian Nicholas, Tara Reid

DAMSELS IN DISTRESS

(SONY CLASSICS) Producers, Whit Stillman, Martin Shafer, Liz Glotzer; Director/Screenplay, Whit Stillman; Co-Producer, Charlie Dibe; Line Producer, Jakob Jaffke; Photography, Doug Emmett; Designer, Elizabeth J. Jones; Costumes, Ciera Wells; Music, Mark Suozzo, Adam Schlesinger; Choreographer, Justin Ceme; Editor, Andrew Hafitz; Casting, Kerry Barden, Paul Schnee, Amy McIntyre Britt/Anya Colloff; a Westerly Films presentation of a Steeplechase-Analytic production; Dolby; Color; Rated PG-13; 99 minutes; Release date: April 6, 2012

CAST

Violet Wister	**Greta Gerwig**
Lily	**Analeigh Tipton**
Rose	**Megalyn Echikunwoke**
Heather	**Carrie MacLemore**
Fred Packenstacker/Charlie Walker	**Adam Brody**
Xavier	**Hugo Becker**
Frank	**Ryan Metcalf**
Thor	**Billy Magnussen**
Priss	**Caitlin Fitzgerald**
Jimbo	**Jermaine Crawford**
Depressed Debbie	**Aubrey Plaza**
Rick DeWolfe	**Zach Woods**
Mad Madge	**Alia Shawkat**
Freak Astaire	**Nick Blaemire**

Taylor Nichols (Professor Black), Aja Naomi King (Positive Polly), Carolyn Farina (Carolina Antonucci), Domenico D'Ippolito (Complainer Student), Meredith Hagner (Alice), Joe Coots (Barman), Cortez Nance Jr. (Groundskeeper), Jordanna Drazin (Emily Tweeter), Madison Cerniglia, Veronica Mu (Classmates), Laila Drew (Young Rose), Shinnerrie Jackson (Sharise), Gerron Atkinson (Sincere Highway Worker), Jonnie Louis Brown (Fresh Highway Worker), Shawn Williams (Campus Cop), Doug Yasuda (Professor Ryan), Todd Bartels, Edward J. Martin (Charlie's Friends), Max Lodge (ALA Pamphlet Guy), Bryce Burke (Gladitaor), Jared Burke (Cary, Jumper), Clare Halpine (Cary's Girlfriend), Colleen Dengel (Seminar Cynthia), Will Storie (D.U. Brother, Hygiene), Christopher Angerman (D.U. Brother, Boots)

Transfer student Lily joins a group of unorthodox college girls who have made it their mission to revolutionize life at East Coast College.

Caitlin Fitzgerald, Billy Magnussen

Hugo Becker, Analeigh Tipton

Greta Gerwig, Ryan Metcalf © Sony Pictures Classics

Greta Gerwig, Adam Brody

THE THREE STOOGES

(20TH CENTURY FOX) Producers, Bradley Thomas, Charles B. Wessler, Bobby Farrelly, Peter Farrelly; Executive Producers, Earl M. Benjamin, Robert N. Benjamin, Marc S. Fischer; Co-Producers, J.B. Rogers, Adam McCarthy, Mark Charpentier, Kris Meyer; Directors, Peter Farrelly, Bobby Farrelly; Screenplay, Mike Cerrone, Bobby Farrelly, Peter Farrelly; Photography, Matthew F. Leonetti; Designer, Arlan Jay Vetter; Costumes, Denise Wingate; Music, John Debney; Music Supervisors, Tom Wolfe, Manish Raval; Editor, Sam Seig; Special Effects Coordinator, Robert Vazquez; Special Makeup Designer, Tony Gardner; Stunts, Tierre Turner; a Conundrum Entertainment/Charles B. Wessler Entertainment production in association with C3 Entertainment; Dolby; Deluxe color; HD; Rated PG; 92 minutes; Release date: April 13, 2012

CAST

Larry	**Sean Hayes**
Curly	**Will Sasso**
Moe	**Chris Diamantopoulos**
Mother Superior	**Jane Lynch**
Lydia	**Sophia Vergara**
Sister Rosemary	**Jennifer Hudson**
Mac	**Craig Bierko**
Mr. Harter	**Stephen Collins**
Sister Mary-Mengele	**Larry David**
Teddy	**Kirby Heyborne**
Mrs. Harter	**Carly Craig**
Sister Bernice	**Kate Upton**
Sister Ricarda	**Marianne Leone**
Monsignor Ratliffe	**Brian Doyle-Murray**
Young Moe	**Skyler Gisondo**
Young Larry	**Lance Chantiles-Wertz**
Young Curly	**Robert Capron**
The Situation	**Michael Sorrentino**
Snooki	**Nicole Polizzi**
JWoww	**Jenni "JWoww" Farley**
Ronnie	**Ronnie Magro**
Sammi	**Samantha Giancola**
Murph	**Avalon Robbins**
Peezer	**Max Charles**
Young Teddy	**Jake Peck**
Head Nurse	**Patty Ross**
Officer Armstrong	**Lee Armstrong**
Ling	**Emy Coligado**
Carbunkle	**Ray Collins**
Baby Moe	**Carter Hayden**
Baby Curly	**Cooper Callihan**
Baby Larry	**Kieran Vine**
Moe's Hip Executive	**Isaiah Mustafa**
Executive	**Mark Kogan**

Michael D'Allessio, Donna D'Allessio (Moe's Audition Staff), Bob Kocsis, Apple Kocsis (Children), Jackie Flynn (Golf Superintendent Dave Lamson), Sandra Dorsey (Heavyset Woman), Vince Canlas (Japanese Chef), Ric Reitz (Jon Hamm), Caryl West (Maid), Sayed Badreya (Orderly), Johnny Seal (Production Security Guard), Debbie Walker (Terrified Nun), Michael L. Kuhn (Tour Guide), Pamela Smith (Reporter), Lucy Thomas (Orphan Brady), Charlie Thomas (Young Boy at Party), Danny Smith (French Chef), Kyla Kennedy White (Balloon Girl), Erin Allin O'Reilly, Caitlin Colford, Caroline Scott, Mariann Neary (Nuns), Jesse Farrelly, Jerod Mayo, Troy Brown (Gang Bangers), Patricia French (Laundry Worker), Roy Jenkins (Office Maycroft), Barry Guy (Staple in Hat Guy), Matthew L. Collins (Policemen #3), William F. Scannell (Handsome Security Guard), Jonathan S. Kennedy (Party Security), Lin Shaye (Nurse Crochet), Steve Tyler (Camera Man), Myron Parker Jr., J.R. Fondessy (Orphans), Robert Benjamin (Hipster Orphan), Reid Meadows (Weezer), Dwight Howard (Himself), Dallas Hobbs (Basketball Player), Antonio Sabato, Jr., Justin Lopez (Handsome Guys)

Moe, Larry and Curly set out to make the $830,000 needed to help save the orphanage where they were raised.

Carter Hayden, Kieran Vine, Cooper Callihan

Will Sasso, Chris Diamantopoulos, Sean Hayes

Chris Diamantopoulos, Sean Hayes, Will Sasso © 20th Century Fox

Chris Diamantopoulos, Will Sasso, Sean Hayes

Jennifer Hudson, Sean Hayes, Chris Diamantopoulos, Will Sasso

Larry David, Will Sasso, Sean Hayes, Chris Diamantopoulos

Kate Upton, Will Sasso, Chris Diamantopoulos, Sean Hayes

Kate Upton, Jane Lynch, Jennifer Hudson, Larry David

Sofia Vergara, Will Sasso, Chris Diamantopoulos, Sean Hayes

Sean Hayes

Fran Kranz, Chris Hemsworth, Anna Hutchison © Lionsgate

Richard Jenkins, Amy Acker, Bradley Whitford

Kristen Connolly

Fran Kranz

THE CABIN THE WOODS

(LIONSGATE) Producer, Joss Whedon, Executive Producer, Jason Clark; Co-Producer, John Swallow; Director, Drew Goddard; Screenplay, Joss Whedon, Drew Goddard; Photography, Peter Deming; Designer, Martin Whist; Music, David Julyan; Music Supervisor, Dan Sano; Editor, Lisa Lassek; Visual Effects Supervisor, Todd Shifflett; Casting, Amy McIntyre Britt, Anya Colloff; a Mutant Enemy production; Dolby; Super 35 Widescreen; Color; Rated R; 95 minutes; Release date: April 13, 2012

CAST

Dana	**Kristen Connolly**
Curt	**Chris Hemsworth**
Jules	**Anna Hutchison**
Marty	**Fran Kranz**
Holden	**Jesse Williams**
Sitterson	**Richard Jenkins**
Hadley	**Bradley Whitford**
Truman	**Brian White**
Lin	**Amy Acker**
Mordecai	**Tim DeZarn**
Ronald the Intern	**Tom Lenk**

Dan Payne (Matthew Buckner), Jodelle Ferland (Patience Buckner), Dan Shea (Father Buckner), Maya Massar (Mother Buckner), Matt Drake (Judah Buckner), Nels Lennarson (Clean Man), Rukiya Bernard (Labcoat Girl), Peter Kelamis, Adrian Holmes (Demo Guys), Chelah Horsdal (Demo Girl), Terry Chen (Operations Guy), Heather Doerksen (Accountant), Patrick Sabongui (Elevator Guard), Phillip Mitchell (Lead Guard), Naomi Dane (Japanese Floaty Girl), Ellie Harvie (Military Liaison), Patrick Gilmore (Werewolf Wrangler), Brad Dryborough (Chem Department Guy), Emili Kawashima (Japanese Frog Girl), Aya Furukawa, Maria Go, Serena Akane Chi, Abbey Imai, Marina Ishibashi, Miku Katsuura, Alicia Takase Lui, Jodi Tabuchi, Sara Taira, Alyssandra Yamamoto (Japanese School Girls), Richard Cetrone (Werewolf/Merman), Phoebe Galvan (Sugarplum Fairy), Simon Pidgeon, Matt Phillips (Dismemberment Goblins), Lori Stewart (Floating Witch), Gregory Zach (Fornicus, Lord of Bondage and Pain), Sigourney Weaver (The Director)

Five friends arrive at a remote cabin in the woods, unaware that their every move is being watched by a mysterious group of technicians who are there to unleash horror.

Zac Efron

Jay R. Ferguson, Taylor Schilling

THE LUCKY ONE

(WARNER BROS.) Producers, Denise Di Novi, Kevin McCormick; Executive Producers, Ravi Mehta, Alison Greenspan, Bruce Berman; Co-Producer, Kerry Heysen; Director, Scott Hicks; Screenplay, Will Fetters; Based on the 2008 novel by Nicholas Sparks; Photography, Alar Kivilo; Designer, Barbara Lang; Music, Mark Isham; Music Supevisor, John Bissell; Editor, Scott Gray; Casting, Ronna Kress; a Di Novi Pictures production, presented in association with Village Roadshow Pictures; Dolby; Super 35 Wdescreen; Color; Rated PG-13; 101 minutes; Release date: April 20, 2012

CAST

Logan	**Zac Efron**
Beth	**Taylor Schilling**
Ellie	**Blythe Danner**
Ben	**Riley Thomas Stewart**
Keith Clayton	**Jay R. Ferguson**
Judge Clayton	**Adam LeFevre**
Victor	**Robert Terrell Hayes**
Deputy Moore	**Joe Chrest**
Roger Lyle	**Russ Comegys**

Sharon Morris (Principal Miller), Ann McKenzie (Charlotte Clayton), Kendal Tuttle (Aces), Cameron Banfield (Young Marine), Ritchie Montgomery (Cottage Owner), Courtney J. Clark (Logan's Sister), Trey Burvant (Logan's Brother in Law), Gavin Reyna (Logan's Nephew), Matthew Michaud (Logan's Nephew), Reverend Dustin Bergene (Pastor), Ned Yousef (Iraqi Translator), Naim Alherimi (Cursing Old Man), Jillian Batherson (Amanda), Dorian Jamal Davis, Cole Jackson (Teasing Boys), Douglas M. Griffin (Bartender), Donna Heckel-Reno (Dog Owner), Hunter Reno (Dog Owner's Son), Amanda Fetters (Grace), Calvin Quatroy (Hamden Fisherman), Marcie Antony Courtney, Michael A. Cowan, Deborah Denise Graves, Gary Harris, Melba Marie Harris, Consuella Johnson Lumas, Tina Marie Lumas, Gregory J. Probst, Valerie Diane Vaughn (Choir Members), Mayfield, Zigg West, Sam Knight, Jett (Rock Band)

While serving in Iraq, a soldier credits a photo of a young girl for saving his life, so he decides to track her down once he returns to the States.

Zac Efron, Taylor Schilling

Blythe Danner © Warner Bros. Pictures

DARLING COMPANION

(SONY CLASSICS) Producers, Anthony Bregman, Lawrence Kasan, Elizabeth Redleaf; Executive Producers, Meg Kasdan, John J. Kelly, Christine Kinewa Walker; Co-Producers, Stefanie Azpiazu, Andrew Peterson, Mark Steele; Director, Lawrence Kasdan; Screenplay, Meg Kasdan, Lawrence Kasdan; Photography, Michael McDonough; Designer, Dina Goldman; Costumes, Molly Maginnis; Music, James Newton Howard; Editor, Carol Littleton; Casting, Ronna Kress; a Werc Werk Works/Likely Story/Kasdan Pictures production; Dolby; Color; Rated PG-13; 103 minutes; Release date: April 20, 2012

CAST

Bryan	**Mark Duplass**
Russell	**Richard Jenkins**
Beth	**Diane Keaton**
Joseph	**Kevin Kline**
Grace	**Elisabeth Moss**
Sheriff Morris	**Sam Shepard**
Penny	**Dianne Wiest**
Carmen	**Ayelet Zurer**
Christus	**Charles Halford**
Ellie	**Lindsay Sloane**
Sam	**Jay Ali**

Robert Bear (Possum), Casey (Freeway), Paul Kiernan (Patient), Jericho Watson (Ethan), Yolanda Wood (Cop), D.L. Walker (Burly Cop), Dina Goldman (Caterer), Ruben Barboza, Aline Andrade (Waiters), Jon Kasdan (Officiant), Mark Robinette (Bandleader), Craig Miner, Ryan Shupe (Band Members), Anne Cullimore Decker (Muriel), Anthony Bregman (Jeff), Tod Huntington (Deputy Chas), Jason Jensen (Ponytailed Runner), Christina Thurmond (Redhead), Lorry Houston (Co-Pilot), Jon Florence (Pilot), Jan Broberg (Hysterical Wife), Zack Phifer (Comforting Husband), Lawrence Kasdan (Man on Street)

Joseph and Beth's relationship is put to the test when he becomes responsible for losing the new dog she has found and become so attached to.

Kevin Kline

Diane Keaton, Elizabeth Moss, Casey

Mark Duplass, Richard Jenkins

Dianne Wiest © Sony Pictures Classics

Meagan Good, Romany Malco, Regina Hall, Gary Owen, Terrence J, Kevin Hart

Jerry Ferrara, Terrence J

THINK LIKE A MAN

(SCREEN GEMS) Producer, Will Packer; Executive Producers, Steve Harvey, Rushion McDonald, Rob Hardy, Glenn S. Gainor; Director, Tim Story; Screenplay, Keith Merryman, David A. Newman; Based upon the 2009 book *Act Like a Lady, Think Like a Man* by Steve Harvey; Photography, Larry Blanford; Designer, Chris Cornwell; Costumes, Salvador Pérez, Jr.; Music, Christopher Lennertz; Editor, Peter S. Elliot; Casting, Kim Hardin; a Rainforest Films production; Dolby; Deluxe color; Rated PG-13; 122 minutes; Release date: April 20, 2012

CAST

Dominic	**Michael Ealy**
Jeremy	**Jerry Ferrara**
Mya	**Meagan Good**
Candace	**Regina Hall**
Cedric	**Kevin Hart**
Lauren	**Taraji P. Henson**
Michael	**Terrence J**
Loretta	**Jenifer Lewis**
Zeke	**Romany Malco**

Gary Owen (Bennett), Gabrielle Union (Kristen), La La Anthony (Sonia), Chris Brown (Alex), Wendy Williams (Gail), Sherri Shepherd (Vicki), Caleel Harris (Duke), Arielle Kebbel (Gina), Steve Harvey (Himself), J. Anthony Brown (Mr. Johnson), Tommy Miles (Dominique), Sharon Brathwaite-Sanders (Nija), Angela Gibbs (Candace's Mom), Tony Rock (Xavier), Bruce Bruce (Chubby Man), Tika Sumpter (Dominic's Girlfriend), Brent Bailey (Waiter), Matt Hish (Restaurant Chef Owner), Omar Leyva (Sal), Dennis Nollette (Business Man), Chrisanne Eastwood (Shayla), Jessica Camacho (Melissa), J.B. Smoove (Bartender), Luenell (Aunt Winnie), Melyssa Ford (Sleepy Girl), Gwen Yeager (Dramatic Woman), Andrew Roffe (Frat Guy), Keri Hilson (Heather), Noah Longo (Enthusiastic Man), Bunnie Rivera (Latina Soccer Mom), Teria Birlon (Cashier), Peter Arpesella (Francois Designer), Kelly Rowland (Brenda), Danny Vola (Coffee Shop Singer), Jamie Foster Brown (Aunt Winnie's Friend), William Packer (Man in Bathroom), Austin MacKinnon (Bookstore Patron), Ron Artest, Matt Barnes, Shannon Brown, Rashad Butler, Darren Collison, Lisa Leslie (Themselves), Grace Baine (Soccer Mom), Tara Beaulieu (Sally), Morris Chestnut (James), Claude Knowlton (Nico)

Four guys vow to take revenge when they discover that their girlfriends have been basing their relationships on a self-help book.

Romany Malco, Meagan Good © Screen Gems

Michael Ealy, Taraji P. Henson

Bob Marley © Magnolia Films

MARLEY

(MAGNOLIA) Producers, Steve Bing, Charles Steel; Executive Producers, Ziggy Marley, Chris Blackwell; Co-Producer, Zach Schwartz; Line Producer, Geraldine Hawkins; Director, Kevin Macdonald; Photography, Alwin Küchler, Mike Eley; Editor, Dan Glendenning; a Shangri-La Entertainment presentation of a Tuff Gong Pictures production in association with Cowboy Films; American-British; Dolby; Color; Rated PG-13; 145 minutes; Release date: April 20, 2012. Documentary on legendary musician Bob Marley

WITH

Ziggy Marley, Jimmy Cliff, Cedella Marley, Rita Marley, Cindy Breakspeare, Lee Perry, Lee Jaffe, Chris Blackwell, Neville Bunny Wailer Livingston, Constance Marley, Danny Sims, Peter Marley, The Wailers, Diane Jobson, Neville Garrick, Judy Mowatt, Dr. Carlton Pee-Wee Fraser, Pascaline Bongo Ondimba, Aston Family Man Barrett, Evelyn Dotty Higgin, Ibis Pitts, Junior Marvin, Mrs. Margaret James, Nancy Burke, Marcia Griffiths, Donald Kinsey, Hugh Creek Sledgo Peart, Lloyd Bread McDonald, Alvin Seeco Patterson, Dudley Sibley, Clive Chin, Allan Skill Cole, Desmond Desi Smith, Eddie Sims, Imogene Aunt Amy Wallace, Dr. Conroy Cooper, Carlton Santa Davis, Waltraud Ullrich, Tony Welch, Dennis Thompson, Derek Higgin

THE GIANT MECHANICAL MAN

(TRIBECA) Producers, Molly Hassell, Jenna Fischer, Michael Nardelli; Executive Producers, Brent Stiefel, Michael Cowan, Michael Gallant, Tim Nardelli, Mike Ilitch Jr., Glenn P. Murray; Director/Screenplay, Lee Kirk; Photography, Doug Emmett; Designer, Paulette Georges; Costumes, Mona May; Music, Rich Ragsdale; Music Supervisors, Patrick Belton, Sanaz Lavaedian; Editor, Robert Komatsu; a Stealth Media Group presentation in association with Votiv Films, a Taggart Productions production an Andycat Production; Dolby; Color; Rated PG-13; 94 minutes; Release date: April 27, 2012.

CAST

Janice	**Jenna Fischer**
Tim	**Chris Messina**
Jill	**Malin Akerman**
Doug	**Topher Grace**
Pauline	**Lucy Punch**
Brian	**Rich Sommer**
Mark	**Bob Odenkirk**

Travis Schuldt (Hal Baker), Valentine Miele (Mahoney), Sean Gunn (George), Greg Trzaskoma (Craig), Eddie Ebell (Mitch), Chase Kim (Mitch's Sidekick), Sarab Kamoo (Sonia), John Cabrera (Toby), Jennifer O'Kain (Camilla), Nick Holmes (Wesley), Matt Champagne (Juice Dad), Ella Anderson (Daughter), Robert Maffia (Monkey Man), Marty Bufalini (Newscaster John), Rachel Avery (Newscaster), Amy Julia Cheyfitz (Usher), Steffen Dziczek (Habitat Coordinator)

Forced to move in with her sister and facing an uncertain future, Janice is drawn to a similar lost soul who tries to make a living as a silver-painted street performer.

Chris Messina, Bob Odenkirk

Jenna Fischer, Topher Grace © Tribeca Film

Mindy Kaling, Randall Park, Kevin Hart, Emily Blunt, Rhys Ifans

Chris Pratt

Jason Segel, Emily Blunt © Universal Studios

Jason Segel, Brian Posehn

THE FIVE-YEAR ENGAGEMENT

(UNIVERSAL) Producers, Judd Apatow, Nicholas Stoller, Rodney Rothman; Executive Producers, Richard Vane, Jason Segel; Director, Nicholas Stoller; Screenplay, Jason Segel, Nicholas Stoller; Photography, Javier Aguirresarobe; Designer, Julie Berghoff; Costumes, Leesa Evans; Music, Michael Andrews; Music Supervisor, Jonathan Karp; Editors, William Kerr, Peck Prior; an Apatow/Stoller Global Solutions production, presented in association with Relativity Media; Dolby; Deluxe color; Rated R; 124 minutes; Release date: April 27, 2012

CAST

Tom Solomon	**Jason Segel**
Violet Barnes	**Emily Blunt**
Alex Eilhauer	**Chris Pratt**
Suzie Barnes-Eilhauer	**Alison Brie**
Winton Childs	**Rhys Ifans**
Chef Sally	**Lauren Weedman**
Carol Solomon	**Mimi Kennedy**
Pete Solomon	**David Paymer**
Sylvia Dickerson-Barnes	**Jacki Weaver**

Jim Piddock (George Barnes), Eric Scott Cooper (B&B Manager), Dakota Johnson (Audrey), Jane Carr (Grandma Katherine), Clement von Franckenstein (Grandpa Baba), Michael Ensign (Grandpa Harold), Madge Levinson (Grandma Leonora), Murray Miller (SF Wedding Barn Manager), Eileen Grubba (Botanical Garden Manager), Mark Rademacher (Priest), Kevin Yon (Rabbi), Heather Mathieson (Justice of the Peace), Mindy Kaling (Vaneetha), Randall Park (Ming), Kevin Hart (Doug), Kumail Nanjiani, Wajid, Gerry Bednob (Pakistani Chefs), Tim Heidecker (Negotiating Chef), Molly Shannon (Onion Chef), Brian Posehn (Tarquin), Suzie Kluce (Deli Customer), Tracee Chimo (Margaret), Chris Parnell (Bill), Gina Ragnone (Ashley), Kenneth Small (Not Zach), Francesca DelBanco (Cake Shop Owner), Stephanie Faracy (Florist), Zoe Niemkiewicz (Vanessa), Tyler Hamway (Vaneetha's Date in Bar), Michele Messmer (Band Manager), Fred Lindholm (Bingo Caller), Richard Rector (Randy), Aaron Lustig (Michigan Rabbi), Chris Newman (Used Car Lot Guy), Da'Vone McDonald (Taco Customer), Laurie Brown (Prof. Walch), Nicholas Delbanco (Prof. Delbanco), Corey Fischer (Justice of the Peace), Nicholas Totis (Vaneetha's Boyfriend), Adam Campbell (Gideon)

Tom and Violet's efforts to get married are constantly thwarted by changes in their lives, stretching their "engagement" over a five year period and threatening the stability of their relationship.

BERNIE

(MILLENNIUM) Producers, Ginger Sledge, Richard Linklater, Celine Rattray, Martin Shafer, Liz Glotzer, Matt Williams, David McFadzean, Judd Payne, Dete Meserve; Executive Producers, Donald Fox, Darby Parker, Jack Gilardi Jr., Johnny Lin, William T. Conway, John Paul DeJoria, Jack R. Selby, Duncan Montgomery, John Sloss, Alex Gudim, Lisa Collins-Gudim; Director, Richard Linklater; Screenplay, Richard Linklater, Skip Hollandsworth; Based on the 1998 article "Midnight in the Garden of East Texas" in *Texas Monthly* by Skip Hollandsworth; Photography, Dick Pope; Designer, Bruce Curtis; Costumes, Kari Perkins; Music, Graham Reynolds; Music Supervisor, Lisa Brown Leopold; Editor, Sandra Adair; Casting, Beth Sepko, Sheila Steele; a Mandalay Vision and Wind Dancer Films presentation of a Detour Filmproduction; Dolby; Deluxe color; Rated PG-13; 99 minutes; Release date: April 27, 2012

CAST

Bernie Tiede	**Jack Black**
Marjorie Nugent	**Shirley MacLaine**
Danny Buck	**Matthew McConaughey**
Scrappy Holmes	**Brady Coleman**
Lloyd Hornbuckle	**Richard Robichaux**
Don Leggett	**Rick Dial**
Sheriff Huckabee	**Brandon Smith**
Reverend Woodard	**Larry Jack Dotson**
Molly	**Merrilee McCommas**
Carl	**Mathew Greer**
Larry Brumley	**Tommy G. Kendrick**
Prof. Fleming	**Richard Jones**
Friend of Deceased	**Charles Bailey**
Mrs. Pebworth	**Suzi McLaughlin**
Mrs. Estes	**Juli Erickson**
Mr. Estes	**Grant James**
Dwayne Nugent	**J.D. Young**
Dwayne Jr.	**Charlie Stewart**
Lewie	**Joe Stevens**
Esmeralda	**Raquel Gavia**
Mel	**David Blackwell**
Kevin	**Gabriel Luna**
Truck Driver	**Christian Stokes**
Cashier	**Mona Lee Fultz**
Lonnie	**Sonny Carl Davis**
Jerry	**Dale Dudley**
The Judge	**Jerry Biggs**

Wray Crawford (Sheriff's Deputy #2), Margaret Hoard (Café Waitress), Quita Culpepper, Angela McClure (Reporters), Chris Humphrey (Roselyn), Amparo Garcia-Crow (Lenora), Valerie Frazee (Robin), Joe Leroy Reynolds (Deputy Sheriff), Marjoie Dome, Tim Cariker, Fern Luker, Jack Payne, Anne Reeeves, Kay Epperson, Ira Bounds, James Baker, Kay McConaughey, Kristi Youngblood, Kenny Brevard, Margaret Bowman, Mollie Fuller, Tanja Givens, Glenda Jones, Travis Blevins, Sylvia Froman, Martha Long, Jo Perkins, Reba Tarjick, James Wilson, Teresa Edwards, Billy Vaticalos, Rob Anthony, Pam McDonald, Kathy Gollmitzer, Cozette McNeely (Townspersons), Chris Barfield, Taylor Bryant, Colin Bevis, Jacqui Bloom, Joshua Denning, Ellie Edwards, Alaina Flores, Jennifer Foster, Leslie Hethcox, Jordan Hill, Berkley Jones, Trevor McGinnis, Mika Odom, Chell Parkins, David Ponton, Gray Randolph, Rachel Hull-Ryde, Ian Saunders, Madelyn Shaffer, Larissa Slota, Daniel Rae Srivastava, Ellen Stader, Lara Wright (Community Theater Group), Betty Andrews, Marcia Bailey, Umpy Bechtol, Nita Bouldin, Nellie Hickerson, Jeanetta Kloppe, Geraldine Miller, Sharon Rugsbee, Debbie Shaw, Flo Weiershausen, Gina Wooten (Mrs. Senior Carthage Pageant Contestant), Gary Askins, Benjamin Bachelder, Meredith Beal, Stacey Bruck, Michelle Briscoe, Lesa Brooks, Gayla Bruce, Brenda Bunton, Kristi Copeland, Jeff Davis, Orion Gallagher, Kenneth Liverman, Linda Rudwick, Mary Stifflemire (Jurors)

The true story of how a beloved funeral director befriended a much-hated widow in a small Texas town, eventually leading to tragedy.

Shirley MacLaine, Jack Black

Matthew McConaughey, Larry Jack Dotson

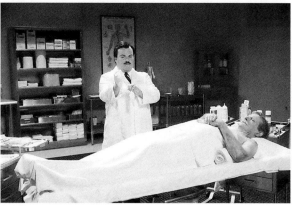

Jack Black

Jack Black

Shirley MacLaine, Jack Black

Jack Black (center)

Matthew McConaughey © Millennium Films

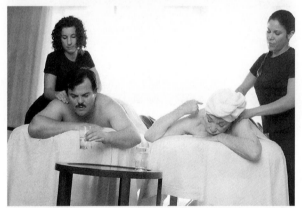

Jack Black, Shirley MacLaine

Brady Coleman, Jack Black

Alice Eve

Luke Evans

John Cusack © Relativity Media

THE RAVEN

(RELATIVITY MEDIA) Producers, Aaron Ryder, Marc D. Evans, Trevor Macy; Executive Producers, Glen Basner, Jesús Martínez Asencio, James D. Stern; Co-Producer, Richard Sharkey; Director, James McTeigue; Screenplay, Hannah Shakespeare, Ben Livingston; Photography, Danny Ruhlmann; Designer, Roger Ford; Costumes, Carlo Poggioli; Music, Lucas Vidal; Editor, Niven Howie; Makeup, Hair and Prosthetics Designer, Daniel Parker; Special Effects Coordinator, Szilvia Paros; Visual Effects Supervisor, Marcus Hindborg; Casting, Lucinda Syson; an Intrepid Pictures presentation in association with Galavis Film of an Intrepid Pictures/Filmnation production; American-Hungarian-Spanish; Dolby; Super 35 Widescreen; Technicolor; Rated R; 111 minutes; Release date: April 27, 2012

CAST

Edgar Allan Poe	**John Cusack**
Detective Fields	**Luke Evans**
Emily Hamilton	**Alice Eve**
Capt. Charles Hamilton	**Brendan Gleeson**
Maddux	**Kevin McNally**
John Cantrell	**Oliver Jackson-Cohen**
Capt. Eldridge	**Jimmy Yuill**
Ivan	**Sam Hazeldine**
Mrs. Bradley	**Pam Ferris**
Reagan	**Brendan Coyle**

Adrian Rawlins (Doc Clements), Aidan Feore (Stage Manager), Dave Legeno (Percy), Michael Cronin (Old Gentleman), Michael Poole (Professor), Michael Shannon (Dr. Morgan), Charity Wakefield (Field's Maid), John Warnaby (Griswold), Matt Slack (Sailor), Ian Virgo (Fire Marshal), Michael J. Fourticq (Bookseller), Jasmina Ilic (Older Tenement Woman, Dead), Teodora Uveric (Young Tenement Woman, Dead), Kristof Farkas (Wretching Student), Luka Mijatovic (Small Boy), József Tálos (Sherry Merchant), Matt Devere (Hamilton's Security Guard), Sergej Trifunovic (Salty Sailor), Milos Djuricic (Porter – Paris), Bojan Peric (Officer at Precinct), Ana Sofrenovic (Lady Macbeth), Steve Agnew (Doctor in *Macbeth*), Malina Nikolic (Gentlewoman in *Macbeth*), Miklós Kapácsy, Andrew Hefler (Headline Men), Pierre Boris Jaurdin (French Officer), Tamara Krcunovic (Doc Clements' Maid), Jason M. Ryan (Crew Member), Antal Publik (Cardinal), László Konter (Breathless Tenement Man), Mark Phelan, Krisztián Peer (Barflies), Annamaria Ordog (Actress), Ádám Földi (Church Secretary), Dejan Cubrilov (Maurice Robichaux), Máté Haumann (Uniformed Guard), Péter Fancsikai (Young Man Skeleton), Sava Rapic (Servant)

When a serial murder in Baltimore begins executing his victims using the stories of Edgar Allan Poe as his basis, the great writer himself is enlisted to help the police solve the crimes.

John Cusack, Brendan Gleeson

SAFE

(LIONSGATE) Producers, Lawrence Bender, Dana Brunetti; Executive Producers, Stuart Ford, Brian Kavanaugh-Jones, Kevin Spacey, Deepak Nayar; Co-Producer, Joseph N. Zolfo; Director/Screenplay, Boaz Yakin; Photography, Stefan Czapsky; Designer, Joseph Nemec III; Costumes, Ann Roth; Music, Mark Mothersbaugh; Music Supervisor, Liz Gallacher; Editor, Frederic Thoraval; Action Choreographer, Chad Stahleski; Casting, Douglas Aibel; an IM Global presentation in association with Automatik of a Lawrence Bender production in association with Trigger Street Productions; Dolby; Super 35 Widescreen; Deluxe color; Rated R; 95 minutes; Release date: April 27, 2012

CAST

Luke Wright	**Jason Statham**
Mei	**Catherine Chan**
Captain Wolf	**Robert John Burke**
Han Jiao	**James Hong**
Alex Rosen	**Anson Mount**
Mayor Tramello	**Chris Sarandon**

Sándor Técsy (Emile Docheski), Joseph Sikora (Vassily Docheski), Igor Jijikine (Chemaykin), Reggie Lee (Quan Chang), James Colby (Det. Mears), Matt O'Toole (Det. Lasky), Jack Gwaltney (Det. Reddick), Barry Bradford (Det. Benoit), Jay Giannone (Det. Kolfax), James Tolbert III (Crazy Guy), Danni Lang (Ling), Julian Marzal (Lt. Teague), Scott Nicholson (Sgt. Mackelvane), Kathy Ann Zhang (Kake), Byron Zheng (Feng), Lyman Chen (Principal), Howie Brown (Mayor's Aide), Nicolas Martí Salgado (Teenager), Danny Hoch (Julius Barkow), Suzanne Savoy (Furious Woman), Dan McCabe (Young Homeless Man), John Wooten, Brian Anthony Wilson (Shelter Security), Victor Pagan (Wild-Eyed Man), Henry Kwan (Korean Grocer), Marvina Vinique (Sales Girl), Jennifer Skyler (Hotel Receptionist), Kate Rogal (Hooker), Tony Cheng (Disco Triad), Dmitriy Kojevnikov (Mamoschka's Chef), Oksana Lada (Mamoschka's Hostess), Al Kao (Asian Patrolman), John Cenatiempo (Russian Gangster), Dan Shea (Police Tech), George Colucci (Middle-Aged Man), Matt Dellapina (Uniformed Cop), Stephen Oyoung (Triad Laptop Soldier), Tim Carr (Young Aide), Daoud Heidami (Taxi Driver), Ben Sinclair (Angry Man), Oleg Ivanov (Russian Mobster), Zun Lin (Triad with Duffel), Alexander Kogan (Russian Singer), Laurence Covington (Irate Homeless Man)

A former, down-on-his-luck martial arts fighter rescues a 12-year-old Chinese girl from the same men who killed his wife, only to discover that she is a math prodigy in possession of a valuable numerical code wanted by the Russian mob.

Catherine Chan, Jason Statham © Lionsgate

Christopher Denham, Brit Marling

Kandice Stroh, Nicole Vicius © Fox Searchlight

SOUND OF MY VOICE

(FOX SEARCHLIGHT) Producers, Hans Ritter, Brit Marling, Shelley Surpin; Executive Producers, Eric Richter, Victoria Guenier; Director, Zal Batmanglij; Screenplay, Zal Batmanglij, Brit Marling; Photography, Rachel Morrison; Designer, Scott Enge; Costumes, Sarah de Sa Rego; Music, Rostam Batmanglij; Editor, Tamara Meem; Casting, Danielle Aufiero, Amber Horn; Presented in association with 1737 Films/Skyscraper; Dolby; Color; HD; Rated R; 85 minutes; Release date: April 27, 2012

CAST

Peter Aitken	**Christopher Denham**
Lorna Michaelson	**Nicole Vicius**
Maggie	**Brit Marling**
Carol Briggs	**Davenia McFadden**
Joanne	**Kandice Stroh**

Richard Wharton (Klaus), Christy Meyers (Mel), Alvin Lam (Lam), Constance Wu (Christine), Matthew Carey (Lyle), Jacob Price (PJ), David Haley (O'Shea), James Urbaniak (Mr. Pritchett), Annie O'Donnell (Mrs. Dewitt), Laura Leyva (Principal Garner), Travis Johns (Timothy), Ben Carroll, Edgar Martin (Officers), Piper Mackenzie Harris (Heidi), Tonita Castro (Lumala), Virginia Montero (Motel House Keeper), Amber Horn (Museum Guide), Sean Mandell (Street Kid), Sam Tiger (Partygoer), Jack Griffo (Young Peter), Kyle Hacker (Lucas), Sasha Wexler (Waitress), Samantha Garcia, Alia Kahn, Kristina Marie Ortiz, Ema Li Vo, Marisa Imbroane, Tiffany Martinez, Gabrielle Pastore (School Girls), Hannah Johnson (Narrator), Avery Pohl (Abigail Pritchett)

A Los Angeles couple infiltrates a San Fernando Valley-based cult to expose their practices, but find themselves in deeper danger than they could possibly have anticipated.

Chris Evans, Robert Downey Jr.

Robert Downey Jr.

Scarlett Johansson © Marvel Studios

Chris Hemsworth, Chris Evans

Samuel L. Jackson

Marvel's THE AVENGERS

(MARVEL STUDIOS/PARAMOUNT) Producer, Kevin Feige; Executive Producers, Louis Desposito, Patricia Whitcher, Victoria Alonso, Jeremy Latcham, Alan Fine, Jon Favreau, Stan Lee; Director/Screenplay, Joss Whedon; Story, Zak Penn, Joss Whedon; Photography, Seamus McGarvey; Designer, James Chinlund; Costumes, Alexandra Byrne; Music, Alan Silverstri; Music Supervisor, Dave Jordan; Visual Effects Supervisor, Janek Sirrs; Visual Effects & Animation, Industrial Light & Magic; a Marvel Studios presentation in association with Paramount Pictures of a Marvel Studios production; Dolby; Color; 3D; Rated PG-13; 143 minutes; Release date: May 4, 2012

Mark Ruffalo, Robert Downey Jr.

CAST

Tony Stark (Iron Man)	**Robert Downey, Jr.**
Steve Rogers (Captain America)	**Chris Evans**
Bruce Banner (The Hulk)	**Mark Ruffalo**
Thor	**Chris Hemsworth**
Natasha Romanoff (Black Widow)	**Scarlett Johansson**
Clint Barton (Hawkeye)	**Jeremy Renner**
Loki	**Tom Hiddleston**
Nick Fury	**Samuel L. Jackson**
Agent Phil Coulson	**Clark Gregg**
Agent Maria Hill	**Cobie Smulders**
Selvig	**Stellan Skarsgård**
Pepper Potts	**Gwyneth Paltrow**
Voice of Jarvis	**Paul Bettany**
The Other	**Alexis Denisof**
NASA Scientist	**Tina Benko**
Georgi Luchkov	**Jerzy Skolimowski**
Weaselly Thug	**Kirill Nikiforov**
Tall Thug	**Jeff Wolfe**
Young Girl	**M'laah Kaur Singh**
Calcutta Woman	**Rashmi Rustagi**
World Security Council	**Powers Boothe, Jenny Agutter, Arthur Darbinyan, Donald Li**
Carrier Bridge Techs	**Warren Kole, Alicia Sixtos, Jesse Garcia**
Agent Jasper Sitwell	**Maximilliano Hernández**
Gala Scientist	**Dieter Riesle**
German Old Man	**Kenneth Tigar**
Young Shield Pilot	**Walter Perez**
Security Guard	**Harry Dean Stanton**
Maintenance Guy	**Josh Cowdery**
Waitress	**Ashley Johnson**

Katsumi Komatsu, Yumiko Komatsu, Momoko Komatsu (Japanese Family), Robert Clohessy (Police Sergeant), Enver Gjokaj (Young Cop), Fernanda Toker (Office Woman), Andrea Vecchio, Robin Swoboda (News Reporters), Brent McGee (Faceless Pilot), Jamie McShane, Michael Zhang, William Christopher Stevens, Kelley Robins Hicks (Celebration Montage Interviewees), Romy Rosemont (Shawna Lynde), James Eckhouse (Senator Boynton), Stan Lee, Thomas Roberts, Pat Kiernan (Themselves), Damion Poitier (Man #1), Lou Ferrigno (Voice of the Hulk)

Tom Hiddleston

Nick Fury brings together a team of super heroes to save the world from the vengeful Loki. Previous related films in the Marvel series were *Iron Man* (2008), *The Incredible Hulk* (2008), *Iron Man 2* (2010), *Thor* (2011), and *Captain America* (2011).

This film received an Oscar nomination for visual effects.

Jeremy Renner, Scarlett Johansson

Bella Heathcote, Michelle Pfeiffer, Jackie Earle Haley, Johnny Depp,
Chloë Grace Moretz, Jonny Lee Miller, Gulliver McGrath

Johnny Depp, Jonny Lee Miller, Charlotte Spencer

Helena Bonham Carter, Bella Heathcote

Bella Heathcote

Johnny Depp, Eva Green

Johnny Depp

Michelle Pfeiffer

Johnny Depp

DARK SHADOWS

(WARNER BROS.) Producers, Richard D. Zanuck, Graham King, Johnny Depp, Christi Demrowski, David Kennedy; Executive Producers, Chris Lebenzon, Tim Headington, Bruce Berman; Co-Producer, Katterli Frauenfelder; Director, Tim Burton; Screenplay, Seth Grahame-Smith; Story, John August, Seth Grahame-Smith; Based on the television series created by Dan Curtis; Photography, Bruno Delbonnel; Designer, Rick Heinrichs; Costumes, Colleen Atwood; Music, Danny Elfman; Editor, Chris Lebenzon; Special Effects Supervisor, Joss Williams; Visual Effects Supervisor, Angus Bickerton; Fight Choreographer, James Grogan; Casting, Susie Figgis; an Infinitum Nihil/GK Films/Zanuck Company production, presented in association with Village Roadshow Pictures; Dolby; Technicolor; Rated PG-13; 114 minutes; Release date: May 11, 2012

CAST

Barnabas Collins	**Johnny Depp**
Elizabeth Collins Stoddard	**Michelle Pfeiffer**
Dr. Julia Hoffman	**Helena Bonham Carter**
Angelique Bouchard	**Eva Green**
Roger Collins	**Jonny Lee Miller**
Carolyn Stoddard	**Chloë Grace Moretz**
Willie Loomis	**Jackie Earle Haley**
Victoria Winters/Josette DuPres	**Bella Heathcote**
David Collins	**Gulliver McGrath**
Mrs. Johnson	**Ray Shirley**
Clarney	**Christopher Lee**
Himself	**Alice Cooper**
Joshua Collins	**Ivan Kaye**
Naomi Collins	**Susanna Cappellaro**
David's Mother	**Josephine Butler**
Sheriff	**William Hope**
Board Members	**Shane Rimmer, Michael J. Shannon**
Henchman	**Harry Taylor**
Captain Rubberpants	**Glen Mexted**
Bearded Hippie	**Guy Flanagan**
Hard Hats	**Nigel Whitmey, Philip Bulcock**
Collinsport Cop	**Sean Mahon**
Young Victoria	**Alexia Osborne**
Vicky's Father	**Richard Hollis**
Vicky's Mother	**Felicity Brangan**
Windcliff Doctor	**Michael Anthony Brown**
Guests	**Jonathan Frid, Kathryn Leigh Scott, Lara Parker, David Selby**

Sophie Kennedy Clark, Hannah Murray, Victoria Bewick (Hippie Chicks), Charlotte Spencer (Coat Check Girl), Gabriel Freilich (Hippie #3), Justin Tracy (Young Barnabas – age 6), Thomas Grube, Jeff Mash (Construction Workers), Raffey Cassidy (Young Angelique), Janine Craig, Adelle Young, Dominica Van Santen, Josephine McGrail (Go Go Dancers)

200-year-old vampire Barnabas Collins awakens in 1972 where he once again meets up with the jealous witch who had cursed him to his blood-sucking fate. Based on the ABC daytime serial (1966-71), with four of the original cast members (Jonathan Frid, Kathryn Leigh Scott, Lara Parker, David Selby) making guest appearances here.

GIRL IN PROGRESS

(PANTELION) Producers, Benjamin Odell, John Fiedler; Executive Producers, Jeffrey H. Rosen, Barry Rosen, Fernando Perez Gavilan, Greg Coote, James McNamara, Robert Lundberg; Co-Producer, Christopher Dalton; Director, Patricia Riggen; Screenplay, Hiram Martinez; Photography, Checco Varese; Designers, Richard Paris, Linda Del Rosario; Music, Christopher Lennertz; Music Supervisor, Howard Paar; Editor, Dan Schalk; Casting, Kerry Barden, Paul Schnee, Rich Delia; a Lionsgate presentation in association with Pantelion Films and Televisa Films of a Latitude Entertainment/Panamax Films/Oriole Leaf Films/Dilettante production in association with Triangle Financial Services; Dolby; Color; Rated PG-13; 92 minutes; Release date: May 11, 2012

CAST
Grace	**Eva Mendes**
Ansiedad	**Cierra Ramirez**
Ms. Armstrong	**Patricia Arquette**
Dr. Harford	**Matthew Modine**
Mission Impossible	**Eugenio Derbez**
Emile	**Russell Peters**

Landon Liboiron (Trevor), Richard Harmon (Bad Boy), Raini Rodriguez (Tavita), Brenna O'Brien (Valerie), Tiere Skovkye (Jezabel), Kendall Cross (Alice Harford), Margot Brenner (Chloe), Michael P. Northey (Alpha Male), Jocelyne Loewen (Becky), Bernadette Beck (Shannon), Rady Panov (Mike Ferguson), Sean Mathieson (George), June B. Wilde (Dream Teacher), Robin Douglas (Olga), Dana Michael Woods (Gilliam), Blu Mankuma (Principal), Doreen Ramus (Maude), Elizabeth McLaughlin (Teacher), Colin Foo (Lo Mein), Lesley Ewen (Nurse), Patti Allan (Woman), Sean Campbell (Uniformed Officer), Sean Michael Kyser (Harford's Son), Lossen Chambers (Lady Customer), Kathryn Kirkpatrick (Maid), Madison Desjarlais (Girl), Mario Casoria (Gardener), Espinoza Paz (Himself)

A hard working single mom tries to keep herself afloat, leaving very little time for her increasingly rebellious teenage daughter.

Eva Mendes, Cierra Ramirez © Pantelion

Joel Murray, Tara Lynne Barr © Magnet Releasing

GOD BLESS AMERICA

(MAGNET) Producers, Sean McKittrick, Jeff Culotta; Executive Producer, Edward H. Hamm Jr.; Co-Producers, Jim Goldthwait, Jason Stewart; Director/Screenplay, Bobcat Goldthwait; Photography, Bradley Stonesifer; Designer, Natalie Sanfilippo; Costumes, Sara de Sa Rego; Music, Matt Kollar; Music Supervisor, Linda Cohen; Editors, Jason Stewart, David Hopper; Casting, Ruth Lambert, Robert McGee; a Darko Entertainment presentation in association with Jerkschool Productions; Dolby; Color; HD; Rated R; 105 minutes; Release date: May 11, 2012

CAST
Frank	**Joel Murray**
Roxy	**Tara Lynne Barr**
Alison	**Melinda Page Hamilton**
Ava	**Mackenzie Brooke Smith**
Brad	**Rich McDonald**

Maddie Hasson (Chloe), Larry Miller (Chloe's Dad), Dorie Barton (Chloe's Mom), Travis Wester (Ed), Lauren Phillips (Donna), Guerrin Gardner (Tampon-Throwing Tuff Gurl), Kellie Marie Ramdhanie (Melissa, Tuff Gurl), Aris Alvarado (Steven Clark), Romeo Brown (John Tyler), Sandra Vergara, Jamie Harris (American Superstarz Hosts), Alexie Gilmore, James McAndrew (Morning Show Hosts), Brendalyn Richard (Karen), Geoff Peirson (Frank's Boss), Tom Kenny, Eliza Coyle, Jill Talley, Joe Liss (Office Staff), Bryce Johnson (Co-Worker), Cameron Denny (Office Worker), Scot Zeller (Ronald), Danny Geter (Mutual of Onodaga Security Guard), Dan Spencer (Doctor), Leslie Noble (Medical Building Woman), Regan Burns (Michael Fuller), Bruce Nozick (TMI Host), Orson Oblowitz (TMI Flunky), Frank Conniff (Stan Kurtz), Tom Lenk, Jack Plotnick (Party Planners), Morgan Murphy (Fast Food Employee), Gilland Jones (Girl Who Gets Shot in Movie Theater), Naomi Glick (Kimberly Black), Jacob Demonte-Finn, Carson Aune (Boys Who Get Shot in Movie Theater), Toby Huss (Man with Cell Phone Who Gets Shot), Christopher Allen Nelson (Trooper), Iris Almario (Sophia Milo), Tony V (Pancake Eating Pedophile), Mo Gaffney (Singing Waitress), Andrea Squibb "Harper" (Roxy's Mother), David Mendenhall (Roxy's Father), Steve Agee (American Superstarz Crew Member), Chris Doyle (American Superstarz Security Guard Who Gets Shot), Kirk Bovill (Police Captain), Michael Carbonaro (Robbie Barkley), Philip Anthony Traylor (American Superstarz Backdoor Security Guard), Paul Eliopoulos (Rev. Goran), Mike Tristano (Shady Gun Dealer), Lon Gowan (Guy Who Runs in the Audience and Gets Shot), Daniel Everson (Audience Member Who Runs and Gets Shot), Samantha Droke, James Rustin (Chloe's BFFs), Nathan Kim, Zuzana Humplova, Hunter Hamilton, Suzanne "Suze-Q" Pirnat (Dancer), Brad Rowe (Angry Tea Bagger), Nate Scholz (Paparazzi)

A terminally ill man, fed up with America's cultural decline, teams up with a high school girl who shares his rage and decides to eliminate the country's most irritating celebrities.

Sacha Baron Cohen, Anna Faris

Ben Kingsley, Sacha Baron Cohen © Paramount Pictures

Sacha Baron Cohen

THE DICTATOR

(PARAMOUNT) Producers, Sacha Baron Cohen, Alec Berg, David Mandel, Jeff Schaffer, Anthony Hines, Scott Rudin; Executive Producers, Peter Baynham, Mario Jo Winkler-Iofrreda, Dan Mazer; Director, Larry Charles; Screenplay, Sacha Baron Cohen, Alec Berg, David Mandel, Jeff Schaffer; Photography, Lawrence Sher; Designer, Victor Kempster; Costumes, Jeffrey Kurland; Music, Erran Baron Cohen; Editors, Greg Hayden, Eric Kissack; Stunts, Alex Daniels; Special Effects Coordinators, Drew Jiritano, Fred Buchholz; Casting, Allison Jones; a Four by Two Films/Berg Mandel Schaffer/Scott Rudin production; Dolby; HD Widescreen; Color; Rated R; 83 minutes; Release date: May 16, 2012

CAST

Aladeen/Efawadh	**Sacha Baron Cohen**
Zoey	**Anna Faris**
Tamir	**Ben Kingsley**
Nadal	**Jason Mantzoukas**
Slade	**Kevin Corrigan**

Megan Fox, Edward Norton (Themselves), Sayed Badreya (Omar), Rocky Citron (Baby Aladeen), Liam Campora (Aladeen age 6), Aasif Mandvi (Doctor), Rizwan Manji (Patient), Rick Chambers (Newscaster Voiceover), Elsayed Mohamed (Wadiyan Olympic Official), Adeel Akhtar (Maroush), Fred Armisen (Waiter/Minister), Bobby Lee (Mr. Lao), Chris Parnell (News Anchor), Jessica St. Clair (Denise), Horatio Sanz (Aide on Balcony), Elena Goode, Naz Homa, Dawn Zimniak, Victoria Beltran, Danielle Burgio, Dominique DiCaprio, Aja Frary (Virgin Guards), Fred Melamed (Head Nuclear Scientist), Justo Usin (Assassin), Joey Slotnick (Homeless Man), Ian Roberts (NYC Cop), David Fonteno (Secretary General), Anna Katarina (Angela Merkel), Michael Delaney, William Fowle (Delegates), Olek Krupa (Gazprom Executive), Alan Cox (BP Executive), Mitchell Green (Joteph), Jenny L. Saldaña (Hannah), George Bartenieff (Romanian Accountant), Chris Gethard (Clark), Sean T. Krishnan (Waiter/Cereal Loving Soldier), Eliyas Qureshi (Angry Wadiyan Diner), Chris Elliott (Mr. Ogden), Jon Glaser (Obnoxious Customer), Daniel Burress (Customer in Bathroom), Pete Wiggins (Bratty Kid Customer), Adam LeFevre (Man in Helicopter), Marceline Hugot (Woman in Helicopter), Anthony Mangano (Arresting Officer), Melissa Francis (Local News Reporter), Tim J. Ellis (Offended Customer), Michael Hardart (Store Customer), Miriam Tolan (Health Inspector's Wife), Zachary Mackiewicz (Health Inspector's Son), J.B. Smoove (Funeral Usher), Hollis Granville (Eldridge Douglas), Ann Dev'Unay (Mourner), Sondra James (Friendly Customer), Tara Copeland (Mom Shopping with Toddler), Sydney Berry (Toddler), Kathryn Hahn (Pregnant Woman), Seth Morris (Pregnant Woman's Husband), Kate Pak (Mrs. Lao), Regina Anne Rizzo (Puppeteer), Tracey Ruggiero (Mugging Victim), Karl Marcia DeBonis (Woman in Hotel Window), Nasim Pedrad (GMW Host), Garry Shandling (Inspector), John C. Reilly (Clayton), Mousa Kraish, Neimah Djourbachi, Sevan Greene, Nadav Malamud (Wadiyan Soldiers)

A megolamaniacal Middle Eastern dictator ends up adrift in New York after his country's rightful air successfully carries out a scheme to have the ruler replaced by a look-alike.

Adeel Akhtar, Ben Kingsley, Sacha Baron Cohen

BATTLESHIP

(UNIVERSAL) Producers, Brian Goldner, Scott Stuber, Peter Berg, Sarah Aubrey, Duncan Henderson, Bennett Schneir; Executive Producers, Jonathan Mone, Braden Aftergood; Director, Peter Berg; Screenplay, Jon Hoeber, Erich Hoeber; Based on Hasbro's *Battleship* game; Photography, Tobias Schliessler; Designer, Neil Spisak; Costumes, Louise Mingenbach; Music, Steve Jablonsky; Executive Music Producer, Rick Rubin; Editors, Colby Parker Jr., Billy Rich, Paul Rubell; Special Effects Supervisor, Burt Dalton; Visual Effects Supervisor, Grady Cofer; Casting, Lindy Lowy, John Brace; a Bluegrass films/Film 44 production, presented in association with Hasbro; Dolby; Super 35 Widescreen; Deluxe color; Rated PG-13; 131 minutes; Release date: May 18, 2012

CAST
Lt. Alex Hopper	**Taylor Kitsch**
Cmmdr. Stone Hopper	**Alexander Skarsgård**
Petty Officer Cora "Weps" Raikes	**Rihanna**
Samantha Shane	**Brooklyn Decker**
Captain Yugi Nagata	**Tadanobu Asano**
Cal Zapata	**Hamish Linklater**
Admiral Shane	**Liam Neeson**
Secretary of Defense	**Peter MacNicol**

John Tui (Chief Petty Officer Walter "The Beast" Lynch), Jesse Plemons (Boatswain Mate Seaman Jimmy "Ordy" Ord), Gregory D. Gadson (Lt. Col. Mick Canales), Jerry Ferrara (Sampson JOOD Strodell), Adam Godley (Dr. Nogrady), Rico McClinton (Capt. Browley), Joji Yoshida (Chief Engineer Hiroki), Louis Lombardi (Bartender), Norman Vincent McLafferty (Old Salt), Stephen C. Bishop (JPJ OOD), Dante Jimenez (JPJ XO Mullenaro), Daven Arce (JPJ Helmsman), Ralph Richardson (JPJ Starboard Gunner), Biunca Love (JPJ BMOW), Michael Sherman (JPJ JOOD), Austin Naulty, Patricia Brown, Gregory Harvey (JPJ Firemen), James Rawlings (JPJ Scat), Andrew Serpas (JPJ Armorer), Damien Seanard Parker (JPJ Helibay Sailor), Carson Aune (CIC Gunner), Doug Penty (CIC Watch Supervisor), Josh Pence (Combat Systems Coordinator), Jason Henderson (Radar System Controller), Brint Terrell (Chart Table Plotter), Brad Faucheux (Chart Table Log Keeper), Dustin J. Reno (Electronic Warfare Supervisor), John Schmotzer (CIC Watch Officer), Peter W. Berg (JPJ 2nd Gunner), Jonathan Groves, Lloyd Pitts (JPJ Port Gunners), Ryan Tinio (JPJ Radar Op), Allie Sillah (JPJ Lead Helmsman), John Santiago (JPJ Switchboard Operator), Kiley Margeson (Gun Console Operator), Jeffrey Johns (Surface Warfare Coordinator), Esther Solomon (JPJ CIWS Operator), Kevin Garlington (JPJ Air Warfare Coordinator), Anthony Czumalowski, James Hadde, Pat Lancaster, Jordan Kirkwood, Jane Dubiel, John Weaver, Mark Lindquist, Philip Cody Neilson (JPJ Sailors), Dane Justman (Sampson OOD), Dustin Watchman (Sampson Helmsman), Drew Rausch (Sampson XO), Ryland Reamy (Sampson CIC TAO), Donald Willcutt (Sampson Starboard Lookout), Eli Miranda (Sampson Boatswain), Josh Demuth (Sampson Port Lookout), Thomas Grieser (Sampson Watch Officer), Chris Darling (Sampson OS DA), Tyrone Gregg (Sampson Gunner), Brian Hirono (Myoko OOD), Yutaka Takeuchi (Myoko XO), Nobuharu Harada (Myoko JOOD), Masaomi Uchida (Myoko Helmsman), Kyle Ken Shimabukuro (Myoko Radar Operator), Masashi Takekawa (Myoko Starboard Lookout), Hyoe Joe Takahashi (Myoko BMOW), Rick Hoffman (Chairman, Joint Chiefs of Staff), Stephen Baldini (State Dept. Official), Bill Stinchcomb (Marine Commandant), Bruce Mandell (Army Chief of Staff), Gary Grubbs (Air Force Chief of Staff), David Jensen (NASA Director), Mike Meldman (Commander Meldman), Hunter Meldman (Ensign), George Arine (Japanese Vice Admiral), Bill McMullen (JPL Supervisor), Joe Chrest (JPL Controller), Benjamin Lloyd (Officer Blake), Billy Slaughter (BIP Technician), Griff Furst (BIP HQ Controller #2), Terri Battee, Angelo Denova (BIP Journalists), Colby Parker Jr., Geoff Clayton, David Kors (BIP Scientists), Christopher McGahan (Cal's Jr. Tech), Kerry Cahill (Cal's Colleague), Liz Wicker, Michelle Arthur, Natalia Castellanos, Dan Cooke, Leni Ito, Jay Jackson (Newscasters), Jackie Johnson (Herself), Frank Cassavetes (Grizzled Gunner), Tom McCurdy (Adm. Shane's Aide), Rami Malek (Watch Officer)

An alien invasion requires quick thinking by a maverick Navy team to save the world from destruction.

© Universal Studios

Taylor Kitsch, Rihanna

Liam Neeson

Chris Rock, Tom Lennon © Lionsgate

Matthew Morrison, Cameron Diaz

Jennifer Lopez, Rodrigo Santoro

WHAT TO EXPECT WHEN YOU'RE EXPECTING

(LIONSGATE) Producers, Mike Medavoy, Arnold W. Messer, David Thwaites; Executive Producers, Mark Bakshi, Heidi Murkoff, Erik Murkoff, Allison Shearmur, Jim Miller; Director, Kirk Jones; Screenplay, Shauna Cross, Heather Hach; Inspired by the 1984 book by Heidi Murkoff; Photography, Xavier Grobet; Designer, Andrew Laws; Costumes, Karen Patch; Music, Mark Mothersbaugh; Music Supervisors, PJ Bloom, John Houlihan; Editor, Michael Berenbaum; Casting, Deborah Aquila, Tricia Wood; a Phoenix Pictures production/a Lionsgate production, presented in association with Alcon Entertainment; Dolby; Deluxe color; Rated PG-13; 110 minutes; Release date: May 18, 2012

CAST

Jules	**Cameron Diaz**
Holly	**Jennifer Lopez**
Wendy	**Elizabeth Banks**
Marco	**Chace Crawford**
Skyler	**Brooklyn Decker**
Gary	**Ben Falcone**
Rosie	**Anna Kendrick**
Evan	**Matthew Morrison**
Ramsey	**Dennis Quaid**
Vic	**Chris Rock**
Alex	**Rodrigo Santoro**
Davis	**Joe Manganiello**
Gabe	**Rob Huebel**
Craig	**Tom Lennon**

Amir Talai (Patel), Rebel Wilson (Janice), Wendi McLendon-Covey (Kara), Dwayne Wade, Whitney Port, Megan Mullally, Cheryl Cole, Tyce Diorio, Taboo (Themselves), Kim Fields (Social Worker), Jesse Burch (Hutch Davidson), Mimi Gianopulos (Molly), Genesis Rodriguez (Courtney), Tom Clark (Lose It & Weep Host), Taylor Kowalski (J.J.), Aerli Austen (Co-Worker), Kate Kneeland (Hotel Doctor), Bree Dawn Shannon (Holly's Client), Kelley Hinman, Jon Stafford (Ramsey's Friends), Rhoda Griffis (Convention Organizer), Elizabeth Becka (Agency Official), Catherine Dyer (Adoption Mom), Brian Bascle (Adoption Dad), Sharon Morris (Jules' Obstetrician), Eric Mendenhall (Wendy's Doctor), Maria Howell (Jules' Doctor), Sharon Gee (Skyler's Doctor), Scott Poythress (Anesthesiologist), Nico Ward (Jules' Nurse), Cynthia Evans (Wendy's Nurse), Pam Smith (Skyler's Nurse), Jimi Kocina (Lab Tech), Jasmine Kaur (Nurse), Valerie Payton (Hospital Receptionist), Andrew Arthur Medlin (Magazine Editor), Andrew Laws (Photographer), Richard Mitchell (Stakehouse Waiter), Jessie Ward (Cute Girl), Hannah Kasulka (Pretty Girl), Wilbur Fitzgerald (Elderly Swimmer), J. Todd Smith (Interpreter), Africa Miranda (Adina), Tegga Lendado (Ethiopian Priest), Matthew Lintz (Disruptive Kid), Emily Westergreen (Young Pregnant Wife), Reginald Womack, Resean Womack (Jordan), David Thwaites (Ad Guy), Veronica Yung (Food Truck Girl), Steve Coulter (Rosie's Doctor), Cornelia Brianna Moreland (Vic's Wife), Heena Sabnani (Patel's Wife), Charles David McDonald, Richard Meeder Jr., Nico Gutierrez, William Wayne Viar, Anthony J. Carrozza, Lewis Jeffrey Pike (A1A Band), Kristy Foggitt, Becky Simmons (A1A Band Dancers), Macsen Lintz (Young Boy), Adam Baaklini (BBQ Waiter), Chelsea Cardwell, Catherine Barrow (BBQ Waitresses), Tricia Miranda, Ryan DiLello (Dance Partners), Bart Hansard (Marco's Boss), Dougie Jones (Teenager at Food Truck), Zenia Boyd, Michael H. Cole (Contestants), Megan Hayes, Julie Ivey (Convention Attendees)

A diverse collection of women and men experience a variety of reactions and situations as they are expecting babies.

Harrison Gilbertson,
Jennifer Connelly

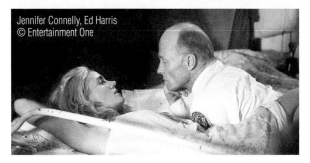

Jennifer Connelly, Ed Harris
© Entertainment One

VIRGINIA

(ENTERTAINMENT ONE) formerly *What's Wrong with Virginia*; Producers, Christine Vachon, Hopwood Depree XIV, Scott J. Brooks; Executive Producers, Gus Van Sant, Yeardley Smith, Jay Froberg, Greg Suess; Director/Screenplay, Dustin Lance Black; Co-Producers, Matthew Myers, Ellen Wander; Photography, Eric Edwards; Designer, Laura Fox; Costumes, Danny Glicker; Music, Nick Urata; Music Supervisor, Mary Ramos; Editors, John David Allen, Beatrice Sisul; Casting, Kerry Barden, Paul Schnee; a Ticktock Studios, Killer Films and Crabcake Entertainment production; Deluxe color; Rated R; 116 minutes; Release date: May 18, 2012

CAST
Virginia	**Jennifer Connelly**
Richard Tipton	**Ed Harris**
Jessie Tipton	**Emma Roberts**
Betty	**Carrie Preston**
Willie	**Barry Shabaka Henley**
Emmett	**Harrison Gilbertson**
Roseanna Tipton	**Amy Madigan**

Kevin Patrick Brown (Jerry), Tom Van Howe (Sheriff's Patrol Host), Ward Burton (Ward), Paul Walter Hauser (Dale), Paul Boocock (Teacher), Yeardley Smith (Mrs. Whitaker), Toby Jones (Max), Michele DeSelms (Local Newscaster), Dennis Rauss (Governor), Alex Frost (Josh Tipton), Penny Slusher (Mrs. Tyler), Will Zahrn (Barry), Meighan Gerachis (Secretary Dawn), Drew Kuhse (Pizza Delivery Man), Rocky Rector (Mailman), Kathy Ruark (Cashier), Jo Yang (Shin-Lee), Derek Minter (Delivery Man), Elic Bramlett (Bank Manager), Jack Rutledge (Bank Security Guard), Tristan Peach (Elder Gelernter), Lucas Grabeel (Elder Jones), Bradley Matthys (Justice of the Peace), Audrey Morgan (Nurse), Dan Krauth, Linsay Kus (Field Reporters), Joanie Tourison (Stage Announcer), Dan Waterhouse (Officer Lee), Dan Schippers, Gary Clayton (Mormon Boys)

A schizophrenic woman's relationship with her son is challenged when the teen pursues an affair with the daughter of the married local sheriff with whom his mother has been carrying on for years.

MEN IN BLACK 3

(COLUMBIA) Producers, Walter F. Parkes, Laurie MacDonald; Executive Producers, Steven Spielberg, G. Mac Brown; Director, Barry Sonnenfeld; Screenplay, Etan Cohen; Based on the Malibu Comic by Lowell Cunningham; Photography, Bill Pope; Designer, Bo Welch; Costumes, Mary Vogt; Music, Danny Elfman; Editor, Don Zimmerman; Visual Effects Supervisors, Ken Ralston, Jay Redd; Alien Make-up Effects, Rick Baker; Casting, Ellen Chenoweth; an Amblin Entertainment production in association with Parkes+MacDonald Imagenation, presented in association with Hemisphere Media Capital; Dolby; 3D; Super 35 Widescreen; Deluxe color; Rated PG-13; 103 minutes; Release date: May 25, 2012

CAST
Agent J	**Will Smith**
Agent K	**Tommy Lee Jones**
Young Agent K	**Josh Brolin**
Boris the Animal	**Jemaine Clement**
Agent O	**Emma Thompson**
Griffin	**Michael Stuhlbarg**

Mike Colter (Colonel), Nicole Scherzinger (Boris's Girlfriend), Michael Chernus (Jeffrey Price), Alice Eve (Young Agent O), David Rasche (Agent X), Keone Young (Mr. Wu), Bill Hader (Andy Warhol), Cayen Martin (Colonel's Son), Clarke Thorell, Adam Mucci, Tom McComas, Douglas Crosby (Prison Guards), Woodie King, Jr. (2012 MIB HQ Guard), Jack O'Connell (1969 MIB HQ Guard), Tobias Segal, Jon Shaver, Geritt Vandermeer (1969 MIB Agents), Alexandra O'Hara (Mom), Violet O'Hara (Little Chocolate Milk Girl), Valence Thomas (Coney Island Hippie), Chloe Sonnenfeld (Coney Island Flower Child), Lanny Flaherty (Obadiah Price), Jonathan O'Hara (MIB Desk Agent), Rick Baker (Brain Alien), Joseph D'Onofrio, Joseph R. Gannascoli (NY Mets Fans), Katy Frame (Diner Waitress), Kevin Townley (Funky 60's Dude), Stephen Brian Jones (Guru), Tyler Johnson (Muscle Boy at Happening), Kati Rediger (Muscle Boy's Girlfriend), Victor Joel Ortiz, Charlie Barnett (Air Force MP's), Ian Blackman (Car Theft Victim), Jeremy Beiler (Hotel Doorman), Liliane Klein (Screaming Lady on Ferris Wheel), Britt Johnson (Detained Teenage Alien), Jared Johnston (Neil Armstrong), Ken Arnold (Buzz Aldrin), Jonathan Drew (Michael Collins), Joel Brady (1969 Man in Elevator), David Pittu (Roman the Fabulist), Lenny Venito (Bowling Ball Head), Anthony J. Gallo (Four-Armed Alien), James Martin Kelly, Will McLaughlin (1969 NYPD Cops), Kimmy Suzuki (Mr. Wu's Bartender), Kirk Larsen (Dead Zed), Javier Jose Rivera Nieves (Transvestite at Happening), Barry Sonnenfeld (Husband Watching Launch), Susan Ringo (Wife Watching Launch), Stephanie Ellis, Amy Erwitt (Young Wives Watching Launch), Ben Brown (Young Husband Watching Launch), Will Arnett (Agent AA), Rip Torn (Large-Headed Alien at Funeral), Justin Bieber, Tim Burton, Lady Gaga (Aliens on Monitors)

Agent J travels back to 1969 in order to prevent his partner Agent K's younger self from being assassinated by a nefarious alien bent on destroying the world. Previous entries in the Columbia series starring Will Smith and Tommy Lee Jones: *Men in Black* (1997) and *Men in Black II* (2002).

Michael Stuhlbarg, Will Smith, Josh Brolin © Columbia Pictures

Jonathan Sadowski, Olivia Taylor Dudley, Devin Kelley, Jesse McCartney, Ingrid Bolsø Berdal © Warner Bros. Pictures

Devin Kelley, Jonathan Sadowski, Nathan Phillips

Ingrid Bolsø Berdal, Nathan Phillips, Jonathan Sadowski, Dimitri Diatchenko, Devin Kelley, Olivia Taylor Dudley, Jesse McCartney

Olivia Taylor Dudley, Jesse McCartney, Ingrid Bolsø Berdal, Nathan Phillips, Jonathan Sadowski, Devin Kelley, Dimitri Diatchenko

CHERNOBYL DIARIES

(WARNER BROS.) Producers, Oren Peli, Brian Witten; Executive Producers, Richard Sharkey, Rob Cowan, Andrew A. Kosove, Broderick Johnson, Allison Silver, Milan Popelka, Alison Cohen; Director, Brad Parker; Screenplay, Oren Peli, Carey Van Dyke, Shane Van Dyke; Story, Oren Peli; Photography, Morten Søborg; Designer, Aleksandar Denic; Costumes, Momirka Bailovic; Music, Diego Stocco; Editor, Stan Salfas; Special Effects Supervisor, Mark Forker; Casting, Terri Taylor; an Alcon Entertainment, Filmnation Entertainment and Oren Peli/Brian Witten Pictures presentation; Dolby; Color; Rated R; 85 minutes; Release date: May 25, 2012

CAST
Amanda	**Devin Kelley**
Paul	**Jonathan Sadowski**
Chris	**Jesse McCartney**
Natalie	**Olivia Taylor Dudley**
Michael	**Nathan Phillips**
Zoe	**Ingrid Bolsø Berdal**
Uri	**Dimitri Diatchenko**
Russian Checkpoint Guard	**Milos Timotijevic**
Restaurant Owner	**Zinaida Dedakin**
Little Girl	**Ivana Milutinovic**

Milutin Milosevic, Ivan Djordjevic, Ivan Jovic (Ukranian Thugs), Alex Feldman (Medic Goldshmidt), Kristof Konrad (Medic Grotzky), Pasha Lynchnikoff (Doctor), Jay Kash (Humanoid)

A trip to an abandoned town near the site of the Chernobyl nuclear plant disaster turns into a nightmare for a group of thrill seeking tourists when their van breaks down and they find themselves being terrorized by unexpected inhabitants.

Gabriel Rush, Edward Norton, Chandler Frantz

Frances McDormand, Bruce Willis

Jared Gilman

MOONRISE KINGDOM

(FOCUS) Producers, Wes Anderson, Scott Rudin, Steven Rales, Jeremy Dawson; Executive Producers, Sam Hoffman, Mark Roybal; Director, Wes Anderson; Screenplay, Wes Anderson, Roman Coppola; Photography, Robert Yeoman; Designer, Adam Stockhausen; Costumes, Kasia Walicka Maimone; Music, Alexandre Desplat; Music Supervisor, Randall Poster; Editor, Andrew Weisblum; Co-Producers, Molly Cooper, Lila Yacoub; Casting, Douglas Aibel; an Indian Paintbrush presentation of an American Empirical picture; Dolby; Technicolor; Rated PG-13; 94 minutes; Release date: May 25, 2012

CAST

Captain Sharp	**Bruce Willis**
Scout Master Ward	**Edward Norton**
Walt Bishop	**Bill Murray**
Laura Bishop	**Frances McDormand**
Social Services	**Tilda Swinton**
Cousin Ben	**Jason Schwartzman**
Sam	**Jared Gilman**
Suzy Bishop	**Kara Hayward**
The Narrator	**Bob Balaban**
Commander Pierce	**Harvey Keitel**
Izod	**L.J. Foley**
Roosevelt	**Seamus Davey-Fitzpatrick**
Lionel Bishop	**Jake Ryan**
Lazy Eye	**Charlie Kilgore**
Jed	**Neal Huff**
Skotak	**Gabriel Rush**
Redford	**Lucas Hedges**
Gadge	**Chandler Frantz**
Nickleby	**Tommy Nelson**
Murray Bishop	**Tanner Flood**
Rudy Bishop	**Wyatt Ralff**
Panagle	**Andreas Sheikh**
Deluca	**Rob H. Campbell**
Mr. Billingsley	**Larry Pine**
Becky	**Marianna Bassham**
Secretary McIntiro	**Eric Anderson**
Chef	**Max Derderian**
Edgar	**Hugo DeAscentis**
Mrs. Billingsley	**Liz Callahan**

James Demler (Noah), Christine Noel (Noah's Wife), Jean-Michael Pion (Ham), John Peet (Junior Khaki Scout Master), Carolyn Pickman (Mrs. Lynn), Ada-Nicole Sanger (Sparrow), Isabella Guinness (Owl), Violet Guinness (Bittern), Caris Yeoman (Curlew), Lily Tiger McEnerney (Dove), Kevin DeCoste (Morse Code Khaki Scout), Tyler Metivier (Bugler Boy Scout), Cooper Murray (Indian Chief Khaki Scout), Coledyn Garrow (Trampoline Khaki Scout), Ben Haffner (Archery Khaki Scout), Michael Malvesti (B-B-Q Khaki Scout), Richie Conant, Johnathon Deneault, Jack TeJean Hartman, Preston Hatch, Alex Milne, Jordan Puzzo (For Lebanon Khaki Scouts), Steve Smith (Voice of Weather Man), Dakota Pimentel (Acolyte), Roman Keitel (Acolyte's Assistant), Derek Sardella (Pigeon Scout)

A young scout escapes from camp in order to run away with the girl of his dreams.

This film received an Oscar nomination for original screenplay.

Chandler Frantz, Edward Norton

Kara Hayward © Focus Features

Jason Schwartzman, Jared Gilman, Kara Hayward

Kara Hayward, Jared Gilman, Jason Schwartzman

Bill Murray

Jared Gilman

Kristen Stewart

Charlize Theron

Sam Claflin

Chris Hemsworth, Kristen Stewart

Ian McShane, Chris Hemsworth, Brian Gleeson, Bob Hoskins, Johnny Harris

Charlize Theron, Christopher Obi

Kristen Stewart

SNOW WHITE AND THE HUNTSMAN

(UNIVERSAL) Producers, Joe Roth, Sam Mercer; Executive Producers, Palak Patel, Gloria Borders; Director, Rupert Sanders; Screenplay, Evan Daugherty, John Lee Hancock, Hossein Amini; Screen Story, Evan Dougherty; Photography, Greig Fraser; Designer, Dominic Watkins; Costumes, Colleen Atwood; Music, James Newton Howard; Editors, Conrad Buff, Neil Smith; Special Effects Supervisors, Neil Corbould, Michael Dawson; Visual Effects Supervisors, Cedric Nicolas-Troyan, Philip Brennan; Stunts, Steve Dent, Ben Cooke; Prosthetics Makeup Designer, David White; Casting, Lucy Bevan; a Roth Films production; Dolby; Panavision; Deluxe color; Rated PG-13; 127 minutes; Release date: June 1, 2012

CAST

Snow White	**Kristen Stewart**
The Huntsman	**Chris Hemsworth**
Ravenna	**Charlize Theron**
William	**Sam Claflin**
Finn	**Sam Spruell**
Beith	**Ian McShane**
Muir	**Bob Hoskins**
Gort	**Ray Winstone**
Nio	**Nick Frost**
Duir	**Eddie Marsan**
Coll	**Toby Jones**
Quert	**Johnny Harris**
Gus	**Brian Gleeson**
Duke Hammond	**Vincent Regan**
King Magnus	**Noah Huntley**
Queen Eleanor	**Liberty Ross**
Mirror Man	**Christopher Obi**
Greta	**Lily Cole**
Anna	**Rachael Stirling**
Lily	**Hattie Gotobed**
Young Snow White	**Raffey Cassidy**
Young William	**Xavier Atkins**
Young Ravenna	**Izzy Meikle-Small**
Ravenna's Mother	**Anastasia Hille**
Young Finn	**Elliot Reeve**
Thomas	**Mark Wingett**
Iain	**Jamie Blackley**
Broch	**Dave Legeno**
Percy	**Matt Berry**
Black Knight General	**Greg Hicks**
Black Knight	**Peter Ferdinando**
Guard on Duty	**Andrew Hawley**
Aldan	**Joey Ansah**
Duke's Commander	**Gregor Truter**
Soldier	**Tom Mullion**

Imprisoned by her wicked stepmother, Snow White escapes into the Black Forest where she enlists the aide of a huntsman and some dwarves to help her raise an army and vanquish evil.

This film received Oscar nominations for costume design and visual effects.

Chris Hemsworth © Universal Studios

PROMETHEUS

(20TH CENTURY FOX) Producers, Ridley Scott, David Giler, Walter Hill; Executive Producers, Michael Costigan, Mark Huffam, Michael Ellenberg, Damon Lindelof; Director, Ridley Scott; Screenplay, Jon Spaihts, Damon Lindelof; Based on elements created by Dan O'Bannon, Ronald Shusett, and on original design elements by H.R. Giger; Photography, Dariusz Wolski; Designer, Arthur Max; Costumes, Janty Yates; Music, Mark Streitenfeld; Editor, Pietro Scalia; Visual Effects Supervisor, Richard Stammers; Visual Effects Producer, Allen Maris; a Scott Free/Brandywine production; Dolby; Panavision; Deluxe color; 3D; Rated R; 123 minutes; Release date: June 8, 2012

CAST

Elizabeth Shaw	**Noomi Rapace**
David	**Michael Fassbender**
Meredith Vickers	**Charlize Theron**
Janek	**Idris Elba**
Peter Weyland	**Guy Pearce**
Charlie Holloway	**Logan Marshall-Green**
Fifield	**Sean Harris**
Millburn	**Rafe Spall**
Chance	**Emun Elliott**
Ravel	**Benedict Wong**
Ford	**Kate Dickie**

Logan Marshall-Green, Noomi Rapace, Michael Fassbender

Branwell Donaghey, Vladimir Furdik, C.C. Smiff, Shane Steyn (Mercenaries), Ian Whyte (Last Engineer), John Lebar (Ghost Engineer), Daniel James (Sacrifice Engineer), Patrick Wilson (Shaw's Father), Lucy Hutchinson (Young Shaw), Giannina Facio (Shaw's Mother), Anil Biltoo (Linguist Teacher), Louisa Staples (Greeting Message Violinist), James Embree, Florian Robin, Matthew Burgess, Eugene O'Hare (Mechanics), Richard Thomson, Jenny Rainsford, Philip McGinley, Rhona Croker (Archaeological Assistants)

In the year 2093, a group of scientists journeys to a distant planet in hopes of making contact with aliens they believe were responsible for initiating life on Earth. Previous related 20th Century Fox entries: *Alien* (1979), *Aliens* (1986), *Alien³* (1992), *Alien Resurrection* (1997), and *Alien vs. Predator* (2007).

This film received an Oscar nomination for visual effects.

Charlize Theron, Idris Elba

Michael Fassbender © 20th Century Fox

Elizabeth Olsen, Jane Fonda, Catherine Keener © IFC Films

Jeffrey Dean Morgan, Catherine Keener, Jane Fonda

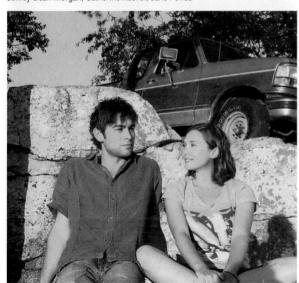

Chace Crawford, Elizabeth Olsen

PEACE, LOVE, & MISUNDERSTANDING

(IFC FILMS) Producers, Claude Dal Farra, Brice Dal Farra, Lauren Munsch, Jonathan Burkhart; Executive Producers/Screenplay, Christina Mengert, Joseph Muszynski; Co-Executive Producers, Peter Graham, Stephen Hays; Director, Bruce Beresford; Photography, Andre Fleuren; Designer, Carl Sprague; Costumes, Johann Stegmeir; Music, Spencer David Hutchings; Editor, John David Allen; Casting, Kerry Barden, Paul Schnee; a Strategic Motion Ventures presentation of a BCDF Pictures production; Dolby; HD Widescreen; Deluxe color; Rated R; 96 minutes; Release date: June 8, 2012

CAST

Grace	**Jane Fonda**
Diane	**Catherine Keener**
Jude	**Jeffrey Dean Morgan**
Cole	**Chace Crawford**
Zoe	**Elizabeth Olsen**
Jake	**Nat Wolff**
Darcy	**Rosanna Arquette**
Mark	**Kyle MacLachlan**
Mariam	**Joyce Van Patten**
Carole	**Maddie Corman**
Sara	**Katharine McPhee**
Richard	**Joseph Dunn**
Cindy	**Ann Osmond**
Tara	**Marissa O'Donnell**

Teri Gibson (Elaine), Robert Bowen Jr. (Robert), Wayne Pyle, Alison Ball (Party Guests), Laurent Rejto (Thumbs Up Cyclist), Edward Morgan (Finger Driver), Denise Burse (Angel), Poorna Jagannathan (Mira), Terry McKenna (Jasper), Kai Beck (Tara's Friend), Dannah Chaifetz (Astrologer), Joe "Jaz" Scaifari (Nude Biker), April Crisafulli (Tara's Mom), Michael Patrick Burke (Film Festival Organizer), Don Stitt (Customer)

An uptight Manhattan lawyer reluctantly journeys with her children to Woodstock to spend time with her long-estranged mother, a hippie whose loose lifestyle she opposes.

Jane Fonda

Aubrey Plaza, Karan Soni, Jake Johnson © FilmDistrict

Aubrey Plaza, Mark Duplass

SAFETY NOT GUARANTEED

(FILMDISTRICT) Producers, Marc Turtletaub, Peter Saraf, Stephanie Langhoff, Derek Connolly, Colin Trevorrow; Executive Producers, Mark Duplass, Jay Duplass, John Hodges, Michael B. Clark; Director, Colin Trevorrow; Screenplay, Derek Connolly; Photography, Benjamin Kasulke; Designer, Ben Blankenship; Costumes, Rebecca Luke; Music, Ryan Miller; Music Supervisor, Marguerite Phillips; a Big Beach and Duplass Brothers production; Dolby; Super 35 Widescreen; Color; Rated R; 86 minutes; Release date: June 8, 2012

CAST

Darius	**Aubrey Plaza**
Kenneth	**Mark Duplass**
Jeff	**Jake Johnson**
Arnau	**Karan Soni**
Liz	**Jenica Bergere**
Belinda	**Kristen Bell**

Jeff Garlin (Mr. Britt), Mary Lynn Rajskub (Bridget), Basil Harris (Restaurant Manager), David Leo Schultz (Coworker), William Hall, Jr. (Shannon), Alice Hung (Shift Manager), Hassan "Cristos" Messiah, Keli Schurman-Darby (Couple in Car), Lynn Shelton (Uptight Mom), Peter Jacobs (Deputy Sheriff), Tony Doupé (Smith), Xola Malik (Jones), Grace Arends (Darcy), Lauren Carlos (Young Darius), Tom Ricciardelli (Security Guard), Kimberly Durham (Linsey), Scott Swan (Halloween)

Three reporters from a Seattle magazine investigate the story behind a bizarre classified ad looking for a partner to travel through time.

LOLA VERSUS

(FOX SEARCHLIGHT) Producers, Michael London, Jocelyn Hayes Simpson, Janice Williams; Executive Producers/Screenplay, Zoe Lister-Jones, Daryl Wein; Co-Producer, Matthew Myers; Director, Daryl Wein; Photography, Jakob Ihre; Designer, Teresa Mastropierro; Costumes, Jenny Gering; Music, Fall on Your Sword; Music Supervisor, Jim Black; Editors, Suzy Elmiger, Susan Littenberg; Casting, Suzanna Smith Crowley, Jessica Kelly; Presented in association with Groundswell Productions; Dolby; Color; Rated R; 86 minutes; Release date: June 8, 2012

CAST

Lola	**Greta Gerwig**
Luke	**Joel Kinnaman**
Alice	**Zoe Lister-Jones**
Henry	**Hamish Linklater**
Lenny	**Bill Pullman**
Robin	**Debra Winger**

Ebon Moss-Bacharach (Nick), Jay Pharoah (Randy), Maria Dizzia (Subletter), Jonathan Sale (Fantasy Bar Guy), Adriane Leonx (Professor), Ray Iannicelli, Kathryn Kates (People at Restaurant), Cheyenne Jackson (Roger), Kena Onyenjekwe, Jeanine Moss, Micah Parker (Henry's Band), Parisa Fitz-Henley (Peggy), Bill Kocis (Hypnotist), Izzy Ruiz, John Tobias (Strip Club Men), Victor Cruz (Bodega Owner), Sandor Técsy (Plaza Man), Rob Yang (Student), Nikki Casseri (Jamie Dahl), Stefano Da Fre (Joshua)

Dumped by her fiancée weeks before their wedding, 29-year-old Lola ends up back in the New York dating scene, receiving advice from her loyal friend Alice.

Hamish Linklater, Greta Gerwig

Zoe Lister-Jones, Greta Gerwig, Bill Pullman © Fox Searchlight

MADAGASCAR 3: EUROPE'S MOST WANTED

(DREAMWORKS/PARAMOUNT) Producers, Mireille Soria, Mark Swift; Directors, Eric Darnell, Tom McGrath, Conrad Vernon; Screenplay, Eric Darnell, Noah Baumbach; Designer, Kendal Cronkite-Schaindlin; Music, Hans Zimmer; Editor, Nick Fletcher; Supervising Animators, Cassidy Curtis, Mark Donald, Carlos Fernandez Puertolas, David Torres; Casting, Leslee Feldman, Christi Soper Hilt; a DreamWorks Animation production; Dolby; Color; 3D; Rated PG; 85 minutes; Release date: June 8, 2012

VOICE CAST

Alex	**Ben Stiller**
Marty	**Chris Rock**
Melman	**David Schwimmer**
Gloria	**Jada Pinkett Smith**
Julien	**Sacha Baron Cohen**
Maurice	**Cedric the Entertainer**

Andy Richter (Mort), Tom McGrath (Skipper/1st Policeman), Frances McDormand (Capt. Chantel DuBois), Jessica Chastain (Gia), Bryan Cranston (Vitaly), Martin Short (Stefano), Chris Miller (Kowalski), Christopher Knights (Private), Conrad Vernon (Mason/2nd Policeman), Vinnie Jones (Freddie the Dog), Steve Jones (Jonesy the Dog), Nick Fletcher (Frankie the Dog), Paz Vega (Horses), Frank Welker (Sonya), Danny Jacobs (Croupier/Circus Master), Dan O'Connor (Casino Security/Mayor of New York City), Eric Darnell (Comandante/Zoo Official/Zoo Announcer), Stephen Kearin (4th Policeman), Emily Nordwind (Zoo Official), Asucena Jimenez (Kid in Crowd)

In their efforts to return home to the Central Park Zoo, Alex the lion and his friends join a European circus, with a relentless animal control officer in hot pursuit. Third installment in the DreamWorks series following *Madagascar* (2005) and *Madagascar: Escape 2 Africa* (2008).

Gloria, Melman, Marty

Alex © DreamWorks Animation

Selma Blair, Jordan Gelber © Brainstorm Media

Jordan Gelber, Mia Farrow

DARK HORSE

(BRAINSTORM MEDIA) Producers, Ted Hope, Derrick Tseng; Executive Producer, Nick Quested; Director/Screenplay, Todd Solondz; Photography, Andrij Parekh; Designer, Alex DiGerlando; Costumes, Kurt and Bart; Music Supervisor, Michael Hill; Editor, Kevin Messman; Visual Effects Supervisor, Louis Morin; Casting, Ann Goulder, Gayle Keller; a Goldcrest Films presentation of a Double Hope production; Dolby; Color; Not rated; 86 minutes; Release date: June 8, 2012

CAST

Richard	**Justin Bartha**
Miranda (formerly "Vi")	**Selma Blair**
Justin	**Zachary Booth**
Phyllis	**Mia Farrow**
Abe	**Jordan Gelber**
Mahmoud	**Aasfi Mandvi**
Jiminy	**Tyler Maynard**
Marie	**Donna Murphy**
Jackie	**Christopher Walken**
Phil	**Lee Wilkof**

Peter McRobbie (Arnie), Mary Joy (Lori), Di Quon (Waitress), Melisa Young (Wedding Singer), Abe Mendel (Accountant), Tara-Lee Pollin, Keith Kuhl (Dancing Bride and Groom), Laurena Baros, Courtney Cooper, Daniel Genalo, Nicole Guidetti, Brian Henninger, Graham Kurtz, Leah O'Donnell, Cody Rigsby, Steven Rosa (Dancers)

A socially inept, overweight man with seemingly no ambitions in life, reaches out to a seriously depressed woman he has met at a wedding, thinking there might be a chance that they can somehow become a couple.

YOUR SISTER'S SISTER

(IFC FILMS) Producer, Steven Schardt; Executive Producers, Vallejo & Dashiell Gantner, Jennifer Roth, Mark Duplass, Lynn Shelton; Co-Executive Producers, Dave Nakayama, Lance Rosen; Co-Producers, Mel Eslyn, Megan Griffiths; Associate Producers, Jennifer Maas, Kate Bayley; Director/Screenplay, Lynn Shelton; Photography, Benjamin Kasulke; Designer, John Lavin; Music, Vinny Smith; Music Supervisors, Mel Eslyn, Sandy Wilson; Editor, Nat Sanders; an Ada Films production; Color; HD; Rated R; 90 minutes; Release date: June 15, 2012

CAST
Iris	**Emily Blunt**
Jack	**Mark Duplass**
Hannah	**Rosemarie DeWitt**
Al	**Mike Birbiglia**
Waitress	**Kate Bayley**

Jeanette Maus, Jennifer Maas, Dori Hana-Scherer, Evan Mosher, Steve Snoey, Jason Dodson, Pete Erickson, Kathryn Lebo, Seth Warren, Dusty Warren (Tom's Friends), Mel Eslyn, Jeremy Mackie, Norman Tumolva, Kate Jarvis, Nathan M. Miller (Photography Studio Crew), Kimberly Chin (Mother), Kohen Chin, Beckett Chin (Young Boys), Jason Braggs, John Lavin, Lee Luna, Petra Kjorsvik (Diner Patrons)

After the death of his brother, Jack is invited by his friend Iris to stay at her father's cabin, where her sister Hannah has suddenly shown up after a recent break-up.

Mark Duplass © IFC Films

Emily Blunt, Rosemarie DeWitt

PAUL WILLIAMS STILL ALIVE

(ABRAMORAMA) Producers, Jim Czarnecki, Stephen Kessler, Mike Wilkins, David Zieff; Co-Producer, Alicia Van Couvering; Co-Executive Producers, Robert Cohen, Lesa Lakin; Director/ Screenplay, Stephen Kessler; Photography, Vern Nobles; Designer, Perry Andelin Blake; Editor, David Zieff; a 3W Films presentation; Color; Rated PG-13; 87 minutes; Release date: June 8, 2012. Documentary about the rollercoaster career of songwriter-performer Paul Williams

WITH
Paul Williams, Stephen Kessler

Paul Williams © Abramorama Entertainment

Vanilla Ice, Adam Sandler

Andy Samberg, Leighton Meester

Tony Orlando, Adam Sandler

Adam Sandler, Andy Samberg © Columbia Pictures

THAT'S MY BOY

(COLUMBIA) Producers, Adam Sandler, Jack Giarraputo, Heather Parry, Allen Covert; Executive Producers, Barry Bernardi, John Morris, Dennis Dugan, Tim Herlihy; Director, Sean Anders; Screenplay, David Caspe; Photography, Brandon Trost; Designer, Aaron Osborne; Costumes, Ellen Lutter; Music, Rupert Gregson-Williams; Music Supervisors, Michael Dilbeck, Brooks Arthur, Kevin Grady; Editor, Tom Costain; Casting, Rachel Tenner; a Happy Madison production, presented in association with Relativity Media; Dolby; HD Widescreen; FotoKem color; Rated R; 116 minutes; Release date: June 15, 2012

CAST

Donny Berger	**Adam Sandler**
Todd	**Andy Samberg**
Jamie	**Leighton Meester**
Father McNally	**James Caan**
Chad	**Milo Ventimiglia**
Gerald	**Blake Clark**
Helen	**Meagen Fay**

Vanilla Ice, Todd Bridges (Themselves), Tony Orlando (Steve Spirou), Will Forte (Phil), Rachel Dratch (Phil's Wife), Nick Swardson (Kenny), Peggy Stewart (Grandma Delores), Luenell (Champale), Ciara (Brie), Ana Gasteyer (Mrs. Ravensdale), Eva Amurri Martino (Younger Mary McGarricle), Justin Weaver (Young Donny), Susan Sarandon (Present Day Mary McGarricle), Dan Patrick (Randall Morgan), Rex Ryan (Jim Nance), Dana Min Goodman, Julia Lea Wolov, Rebecca Marshall, Abigail Klein, Carrie Wiita (Bridesmaids), Jackie Sandler (Masseuse), Erin Andrews (Randall Morgan's Receptionist), Sam Kaufman, Danny Mendelson (School Buddies), Colin Quinn (Strip Club DJ), Peter Dante (Dante Spirou), Rao Rampilla (Convenience Store Owner), Patty Ross (Judge), Chris Titone, J.D. Donaruma (Hotel Desk Clerks), Alan Thicke (TV Version of Donny's Dad), Ian Ziering (TV Version of Donny), Mike Sandler (Rabbi), Sadie Sandler, Sunny Sandler (Lemonade Stand Kids), Abdoulaye NGom (Father Shakalu), Baron Davis (Gym Coach), Amber Paul (Halo Stripper), Brad Grunberg (Tubby Tuke), Dennis Dugan (School Janitor), Allen Zwolle (Principal), Nancy Yee (Maid), Koji Kataoka (Butler), Jason Venezia, Kristen Valinch (Naked Couple in Car), Sheriden Thomas (Gym Teacher), Claude Tondreau (Class President Candidate), Michael J. Cammilleri, Scott T. Beardsley, Christian E. Boeger (Jazz Trio at Party), Sue Lee (Makeup Girl), Robert Harvey (Cocktail Party Guest), Paul E. Pabst (Producer Tom Kleinschmidt), Todd J. Fritz (Joey the Cameraman), Patrick S. O'Connor (Cameraman Charles Hornbeam Jr.), Andrew J. Perloff (Lou "Boom Mic" Giammona), Rich Eisen (Marathon Race Announcer)

Having fathered a child while he was a 13-year-old student, dead beat dad Donny Berger re-enters the life of his now-grown son, much to the young man's displeasure.

ROCK OF AGES

(NEW LINE CINEMA/WB) Producers, Matthew Weaver, Scott Prisand, Carl Levin, Tobey Maguire, Garrett Grant, Jennifer Gibgot; Executive Producers, Toby Emmerich, Richard Brener, Michael Disco, Samuel J. Brown, Hilary Butorac Weaver, Janet Billig Rich, Adam Shankman, Chris D'Arienzo; Director, Adam Shankman; Screenplay, Justin Theroux, Chris D'Arienzo, Allan Loeb; Based on the 2005 stage musical written by Chris D'Arienzo; Photography, Bojan Bazelli; Designer, Jon Hutman; Costumes, Rita Ryack; Original Score, Adam Anders, Peer Astrom; Music Supervisor, Matt Sullivan; Choreographer, Mia Michaels; Editor, Emma E. Hickox; Casting, Juel Bestrop, Seth Yanklewitz; a Corner Store Entertainment production in association with Material Pictures in association with Offspring Entertainment; Dolby; HD Widescreen; Technicolor; Rated PG-13; 123 minutes; Release date: June 15, 2012

CAST

Sherrie Christian	**Julianne Hough**
Drew Boley	**Diego Boneta**
Lonny	**Russell Brand**
Paul Gill	**Paul Giamatti**
Patricia Whitmore	**Catherine Zeta-Jones**
Constance Sack	**Malin Akerman**
Justice	**Mary J. Blige**
Dennis Dupree	**Alec Baldwin**
Stacee Jaxx	**Tom Cruise**
Mike Whitmore	**Bryan Cranston**
Mitch Miley	**Will Forte**
Stefano	**Eli Roth**

Dakota Sage Grant (Little Girl on Bus), Matt Rush Sullivan (Random Guy), Erica Frene (Beth), Michael Olusczak (Crook), Anthony Bellisimo (Rocker Thief), Alan Shane Hartline (Bartender Jimmy), James Martin Kelly (Doug Flintrock), Celina Beach (Mayor's Secretary), Angelo Donato Valderrama (Chico), Dan Finnerty (Tour Manager – Stacee), Kevin Nash, Jeff Chase (Stacee's Bodyguards), Chantal Gonsalves, Tyne Stecklein, Hanna Lee Sakakibara, Jaimie Goodwin (Stacee Groupies), Anne Fletcher (Church Horse Mother), Denise Faye, Marriann Nelson (Protest Mothers), Porcelain Black (Singer), Christopher J. Tywoniak, Maxwell F. Terlecki, Robert Reef, Marcus Johns (Drew's Band), Vivi Pineda, Aniela McGuinness, Elvire Emanuelle (Waitresses), David Gibbs, Mark Dzier, Brev Sullivan, Daniel Wills (Arsenal Band), Prince Shah (Store Manager), Benjamin Malone (Motel Manager), Arielle Reitsma (Slutty Girl), Anya Garnis (Destiny), Barry Habib, Constantine Maroulis (Record Executives), Heather Leigh Davis (Clothes Stylist), Josh Randall (Z-Guyeezz #1, Danny), Jack Mountford (Z-Guyeezz #2, Joey), Elgin Kos Aponte (Z-Guyeezz #3, Kevy), Veronica Berry (Louise, Assistant #2), Karelix Alicea (Sinnamon), T.J. Miller (Rolling Stone Receptionist), Nuno Bettencourt, Joel Hoekstra, Debbie Gibson, Sebastian Bach, Kevin Cronin, Misterwill, Jack Desroches (Rockers), Choice Gray (Kissing Girl), Sophie Cook (Fan); *Dancers*: Twani Edwards, Natalia Gonzalez, Tara Nicole Hughes, Kesley Lack, Mary Ann Lamb, Isis Masoud, Jill Nicklaus, Maria Ines Serritella, Jenni Lynn Thomasson, Kelly Truzzolino (Protesting Mothers); Shana Burns, Eric Gil, Digo Padovan, Ian Paget, Jonathan Prater, Shekitra Starke (Bourbon Workers); Alexis Adler, Leo Chavez, Danielle Core, Chelsea Corp, Chriz Embroz, Lina Ferrera, Sebastian Garcia, Susie Garcia, Tony Gonzalez, Michelle Griffith, Milena Hale, Ann Lewin, Marissa Alma Nick, Javier Perez, Hector Silva, Katrina Rose Tandy (Bourbon Patrons), Katherine Akra, Bill Angell, Alethea Austin, Michael Balderrama, Janeth Briceño, Jeyne Butterfly, Bubba Carr, Lisa Marie Cordoba, Jocelyn Dowling, Jennifer Fain, Marlowe Fisken, Scott Fowler, Tony Francisco, Courtney Gallano, Brittany Grimsley, Neil Haskell, Michael Higgins, Scott Alan Hislop, Grace Jones, Cris Judd, Keith Kuhl, Brooke Lipton, Tiffany Paige Maher, Tiger Martina, Angelique Martinez, Mark Myars, Frank Meli, Carolyn Pace, Chris Pederson, Nathan Prevost, Danielle Rueda-Watts, Julie Wiesman, Tovaris Wilson, Will B. Wingfield (Venus Gentleman's Club)

Two young singers arrive in L.A. hoping to make it big in the 1980s music scene, while a struggling club pins its hopes on the appearance of legendary rock star Stacee Jaxx.

Julianne Hough, Mary J. Blige

Julianne Hough, Diego Boneta

Tom Cruise

Julianne Hough

Alec Baldwin, Russell Brand

Tom Cruise, Paul Giamatti © New Line Cinema

Malin Akerman, Tom Cruise

Alec Baldwin, Tom Cruise

Julianne Hough, Diego Boneta

Catherine Zeta-Jones

Tyler Ross, Natalie West

Tyler Ross © Breaking Glass

NATE & MARGARET

(BREAKING GLASS) Producers, Ash Christian, Nathan Adloff; Executive Producers, Brian Baker, Charles Solomon Jr.; Director, Nathan Adloff; Screenplay, Justin D.M. Palmer, Nathan Adloff; Photography/Editor, Brian Levin; Designer, Chelsea Warren; Costumes, Gwen Smuda; Music, Kevin O'Donnell; a Cranium Entertainment presentation; Color; HD; Not rated; 79 minutes; Release date: June 22, 2012

CAST
Margaret	**Natalie West**
Nate	**Tyler Ross**
James	**Conor McCahill**
Darla	**Gaby Hoffmann**
Gregory Maddock	**Charles Solomon Jr.**
Jeffrey Tomlinson	**Cliff Chamberlain**

Danny Rhodes (Matthew), Allison Latta (Rebecca), Sadieh Rifai (Danielle), Shawn Ryan (Joey), John Ainsworth (Officer Martin), Angela LaRocca (Mary), Kathryn Hribar (Emmi), Brian Levin (Brian), Kristen Toomey (Stand-Up Comedian), Scott Miller (Comic Wars Producer), Michael Kutza (Heckler), Michael Emery (Chad), Holly Martin Baker (Cassie), Billy Baker (Timmy), Shannon Edwards (Bored Club Patron)

An unlikely friendship develops between a cheerful, 19-year-old gay film student and his cranky neighbor, a 52-year-old waitress aspiring to be a standup comic.

THE INVISIBLE WAR

(CINEDIGM) Producers, Amy Ziering, Tanner King Barlow; Executive Producers, Regina Kulik Scully, Jennifer Siebel Newsom, Geralyn Dreyfous, Abigail Disney, Maria Cuomo Cole, Sarah Johnson Redlich, Women Donors Newtwork, Sally Jo Fifer, Teddy Leifer, Nicole Boxer-Keegan; Co-Executive Producer, Kimball Stroud; Director/ Screenplay, Kirby Dick; Photography, Thaddeus Waddleigh, Kirsten Johnson; Music, Mary J. Blige; Editors, Doug Blush, Derek Boonstra; Design & Animation, Bil White; a Chain Camera Pictures and Regina Kulik Scully & Jennifer Siebel Newsom presentation in association with ITVS, Fork Films, Cuomo Cole productions, Rise Films and Canal Plus; Color; HD; Not rated; 93 minutes; Release date: June 22, 2012. Documentary on sexual abuse in the U.S. military.

WITH

Sarah Alberson, Jeremiah Arbogast, Susan Avila-Smith, Teah Bedney, Helen Benedict, Anu Bhagwati, Jessica Brakey, Susan Burke, Rebecca Catagnus, Tia Christopher, Kori Cioca, Paula Coughlin, Susan Davis, Ayana Defour, Valine DeMos, Debra Dickerson, Tandy Fink, Allison Gill, Mya Haider, Elle Helmer, Amy Herdy, Mary Kay Hertog, Jessica Hinves, Amando Javier, Christina Jones, Claudia Kennedy, Rob Khale, Ariana Klay, Anthony Kurta, Dennis Laich, Robin Lynne Lafayette, Lee Le Teff, Brian Lewis, Carolyn Maloney, Geri Lynn Matthews, Michael Matthews, Donna McAleer, Rob McDonald, Trina McDonald, Kristen Miller, Stace Nelson, Chellie Pingree, Greg Rinckey, Mitch Rosaaen, Amy Rosaaen-McDonald, Loretta Sanchez, Hannah Sewell, Jerry Sewell, Louise Slaughter, Jackie Speier, Russell Strand, Loree Sutton, Niki Tsongas, Mike Turner, Wilma Vaught, Theresa Verderber-Phillips, Regina Vasquez, Katie Weber, Miette Wells, Andrea Werner, Kaye Whitley, Amy Ziering, Kirby Dick

This film received an Oscar nomination for documentary feature.

Kori Cioca, Rob Cioca © Cinedigm

Elle Helmer

Benjamin Walker

Benjamin Walker

Benjamin Walker, Dominic Cooper

Anthony Mackie, Rufus Sewell, Erin Wasson © 20ᵗʰ Century Fox

ABRAHAM LINCOLN, VAMPIRE HUNTER

(20ᵀᴴ CENTURY FOX) Producers, Tim Burton, Timur Bekmambetov, Jim Lemley; Executive Producers, Michele Wolkoff, John J. Kelly, Simon Kinberg, Seth Grahame-Smith; Director, Timur Bekmambetov; Screenplay, Seth Grahame-Smith, Simon Kinberg; Based on the 2010 novel by Seth Grahame-Smith; Photography, Caleb Deschanel; Designer, François Audouy; Costumes, Carlo Poggioli, Varvara Avdyushko; Music, Henry Jackman; Editor, William Hoy; Visual Effects Supervisors, Michael Owens, Craig Lyn; Visual Effects Producer, Kendrick Wallace; Special Makeup Creator, Greg Cannom; Stunts, Mic Rodgers; Fight Choreographer, Tsay Igor; Casting, Mindy Marin; a Burton/Bekmambetov/Lemley production; Dolby; Super 35 Widescreen; Deluxe color; 3D; Rated R; 105 minutes; Release date: June 22, 2012

CAST

Abraham Lincoln	**Benjamin Walker**
Henry Sturges	**Dominic Cooper**
Will Johnson	**Anthony Mackie**
Mary Todd Lincoln	**Mary Elizabeth Winstead**
Adam	**Rufus Sewell**
Jack Barts	**Marton Csokas**
Joshua Speed	**Jimmi Simpson**
Thomas Lincoln	**Joseph Mawle**
Nancy Lincoln	**Robin McLeavy**
Vadoma	**Erin Wasson**
Jefferson Davis	**John Rothman**
Willie Lincoln	**Cameron M. Brown**

Frank Brennan (Senator Jeb Nolan), Lux Haney-Jardine (Young Abraham Lincoln), Curtis Harris (Young Will), Bill Martin Williams (RR Pastor), Alex Lombard (Gabrielle), Raevin Stinson (Prostitute), Jacqueline Fleming (Harriet Tubman), John Neisler (Rev. Dresser), Aaron Toney (Will's Brother), Meade Patton (Doctor), Teri Wyble (Henry's Wife), Lawrence Turner (Pharmacist), Jake La Botz (Bull Run Private), Dane Rhodes (Captain Slash), Earl Maddox (Angry Resident), John McConnell (Scroll Official), Bernard Hocke (White House Doctor), Alan Tudyk (Stephen A. Douglas), Ritchie Montgomery, Scott Michael Jefferson (Guests), Pierre Pichon (Meditation Bartender), Maya M. Marshall (Slave Ball Dancer), Michael Madary (General), Alex Bulat (Typographer), Jillian Batherson, Casey Lane Bundick, Chelsea Bruland, Edward R. Cox, Kristin Daniel, Brian Paul Falgoust, Tara Francis, Sean Glazebrook, Lauren Hammond, Kelly Hasandras, Brent Henry, Rianne Herron, Kyle Khan, Erin Mallory, Laura B. Manning, Jennifer Schemke, Francis Scully, Elsie Semmes, Simeon Sjöberg, Mark C. Stevens, Aaron Thacker-Woodruff (Dancers)

The death of his beloved mother by a vampire sets Abraham Lincoln on a life-long, all-consuming mission to destroy all bloodsuckers he encounters on his path to the White House.

Derek Luke, Keira Knightley, Steve Carell

Patton Oswalt, Steve Carell © Focus Features

Keira Knightley, Gillian Jacobs, T.J. Miller, Steve Carell

SEEKING A FRIEND FOR THE END OF THE WORLD

(FOCUS) Producers, Steve Golin, Joy Gorman Wettels, Steven Rales, Mark Roybal; Executive Producers, Nathan Kahane, Nicole Brown; Co-Producers, Kelli Konop, Jeff Sommerville; Director/Screenplay, Lorene Scafaria; Photography, Tim Orr; Designer, Chris Spellman; Costumes, Kristin M. Burke; Music, Rob Simonsen, Jonathan Sadoff; Music Supervisor, Linda Cohen; Editor, Zene Baker; Special Effects Coordinator, Donald Frazee; Casting, Jeanne McCarthy, Nicole Abellera; a Mandate Pictures and Indian Paintbrush presentation of an Anonymous Content production; Dolby; HD Widescreen; Color; Rated R; 101 minutes; Release date: June 22, 2012

CAST

Dodge	**Steve Carell**
Penny	**Keira Knightley**
Owen	**Adam Brody**
Speck	**Derek Luke**
Frank	**Martin Sheen**
Anchorman	**Mark Moses**
Diane	**Connie Britton**
Warren	**Rob Corddry**
Karen	**Melanie Lynskey**
Trucker	**William Petersen**
Roache	**Patton Oswalt**
Darcy, Chipper Host	**T.J. Miller**
Katie, Waitress	**Gillian Jacobs**

Brad Morris (Radio Announcer), Nancy Carell (Linda), Roger Aaron Brown (Alfred), Rob Huebel (Jeremy), Trisha Gorman (Crying Woman), Tonita Castro (Elsa), Leslie Murphy (Amy), Vince Grant (Man #1, Chip), Amy Schumer (Woman #1, Lacey), Marshall Manesh (Indian Man), Aleister (Sorry), Bob Stephenson (Officer Wally Johnson), Rene Gube (Cell-Mate), Jim O'Heir (Cop #2), Daniel Maurio (Toilet Guy), Melinda Dillon (Rose)

As the end of the world nears, two people who have been abruptly abandoned by their partners, end up falling in love.

Adam Brody

BEASTS OF THE SOUTHERN WILD

(FOX SEARCHLIGHT) Producers, Michael Gottwald, Dan Janvey, Josh Penn; Executive Producers, Philipp Englehorn, Paul Mezey, Michael Raisler; Co-Producers, Matthew Parker, Chris Carroll; Director, Benh Zeitlin; Screenplay, Lucy Alibar, Benh Zeitlin; Based on the 2007 stage play *Juicy and Delicious* by Lucy Alibar; Photography, Ben Richardson; Designer, Alex DiGerlando; Costumes, Stephani Lewis; Music, Dan Romer, Benh Zeitlin; Editors, Crockett Doob, Affonso Goncalves; Special Effects Producer, Lucas Joaquin; a Cinereach presentation of a Cinereach and Court 13 production in association with Journeyman Pictures; Dolby; Color; HD; Rated PG-13; 93 minutes; Release date: June 27, 2012

Quvenzhané Wallis

CAST

Hushpuppy	**Quvenzhané Wallis**
Wink	**Dwight Henry**
Jean Battiste	**Levy Easterly**
Walrus	**Lowell Landes**
Little Jo	**Pamela Harper**
Miss Bathsheba	**Gina Montana**
LZA	**Amber Henry**
Joy Strong	**Jonshel Alexander**
Boy with Bell	**Nicholas Clark**
Winston	**Joseph Brown**
Peter T	**Henry D. Coleman**
T-Lou	**Kaliana Brower**

Philip Lawrence (Dr. Maloney), Hannah Holby (Open Arms Babysitter), Jimmy Lee Moore (Sgt. Major), Jovan Hathaway (The Cook), Kendra Harris (Baby Hushpuppy), Windle Bourg (Herself)

In a backwards swamp area called the Bathtub, 6-year-old Hushpuppy defends herself and her father against the threat of flooding and the onslaught of giant aurochs.

This film received Oscar nominations for picture, actress (Wallis), director, and adapted screenplay.

Quvenzhané Wallis © Fox Searchlight

Quvenzhané Wallis

Dwight Henry

TED

(UNIVERSAL) Producers, Scott Stuber, Seth MacFarlane, John Jacobs, Jason Clark; Executive Producer, Jonathan Mone; Director/Story, Seth MacFarlane; Screenplay, Seth MacFarlane, Alec Sulkin, Wellesley Wild; Photography, Michael Barrett; Designer, Stephen Lineweaver; Costumes, Debra McGuire; Music, Walter Murphy; Song: "Everybody Needs a Best Friend" by Walter Murphy (music) and Seth MacFarlane (lyrics)/performed by Norah Jones; Editor, Jeff Freeman; Special Effects Coordinator, Judson Bell; Visual Effects Supervisor, Blair Clark; Character Animation and Visual Effects, Tippet Studio, Iloura; Casting, Sheila Jaffe; a Media Rights Capital presentation of a Fuzzy Door production, a Bluegrass Films production, a Smart Entertainment production; Dolby; Deluxe color; Rated R; 106 minutes; Release date: June 29, 2012

CAST

John Bennett	**Mark Wahlberg**
Lori Collins	**Mila Kunis**
Voice of Ted	**Seth MacFarlane**
Rex	**Joel McHale**
Donny	**Giovanni Ribisi**
Guy	**Patrick Warburton**
Thomas	**Matt Walsh**
Tami-Lynn	**Jessica Barth**
Robert	**Aedin Mincks**
Frank	**Bill Smitrovich**
Narrator	**Patrick Stewart**
Young John	**Brett Manley**

Norah Jones, Sam J. Jones, Tom Skerritt, Ted Danson, Ray Romano (Themselves), Ralph Garman (John's Dad), Alex Borstein (John's Mom), John Viener (Alix), Laura Vandervoort (Tanya), Robert Wu (Mr. Ming), Ginger Gonzaga (Gina), Jessica Stroup (Tracy), Melissa Ordway (Michelle), Max Harris (Greenbaum Kid), Zane Cowans (Kid #1/Young Ted's Voice), T.J. Hourigan, Owen Clarke (Kids), Kristina Ellery (Heavenly), Katelyn Lorren (Cherene), Chanty Sok (Angelique), Sarah Fischer (Sauvignon Blanc), Cassie Djerf (Waitress), Joe Sirani, Pat Shea (Guys at Table), Paul Campbell (Guy in Line), Josh Duvendeck, Chris Cox (Guys), Henry Penzi (Partygoer, Ted's Buddy), Talía Cabrera (Girl at Party), Colton Shires (Teenage John), Viera Andrea Moya (Plymouth PR Worker), Heajee Kim (Club Girl), Lydia Hannibal (Ellen), Shawn Thornton (Crazy Guy), Eric Weinstein (Stagehand), Danny Smith (Waiter), Mike Nikitas, Robin Hamilton (Newscasters), Mike Henry (Southern Newscaster), Johnny Lee Davenport (Husband), Christina Everett (Wife), Ryan Reynolds (Jared)

35-year-old John Barrett must make the decision to part with his living, foul-mouthed teddy bear so that he can marry his increasingly impatient girlfriend and move on with his life.

This film received an Oscar nomination for original song ("Everybody Needs a Best Friend").

Sarah Fischer, Chanty Sok, Ted, Kristina Ellery, Katelyn Lorren

Laura Vandervoort © Universal Studios

Ted, Sam J. Jones
Mark Wahlberg, Ted, Mena Suvari

Olivia Wilde, Chris Pine

Chris Pine, Elizabeth Banks © DreamWorks Pictures

Michelle Pfeiffer

PEOPLE LIKE US

(DREAMWORKS/TOUCHSTONE) Producers, Roberto Orci, Bobby Cohen, Clayton Townsend; Executive Producer/Director, Alex Kurtzman; Screenplay, Alex Kurtzman, Roberto Orci, Jody Lambert; Photography, Salvatore Totino; Designer, Ida Random; Costumes, Mary Zophres; Music, A.R. Rahman; Music Supervisor, Liza Richardson; Editor, Robert Leighton; Casting, Denise Chamian; a DreamWorks Pictures and Reliance Entertainment presentation of a K/O Paper Products production; Dolby; Syper 35 Widescreen; Deluxe color; Rated PG-13; 114 minutes; Release date: June 29, 2012

CAST

Sam	**Chris Pine**
Frankie	**Elizabeth Banks**
Josh	**Michael Hall D'Addario**
Lillian	**Michelle Pfeiffer**
Hannah	**Olivia Wilde**
Ted	**Mark Duplass**
Dr. Amanda	**Sara Mornell**
Ike Rafferty	**Philip Baker Hall**
Jerry	**Dean Chekvala**

Barbara Eve Harris (Mrs. Haney), David Burrus (Derek), Joseph Wise (Danny), Devin Brochu (Simon), Gabriela Milla (Lucy), Abhi Sinha (Manager), Jon Favreau (Richards), Rob Brownstein (Sales VP Ben), Christiann Castellanos (Secretary), Darren O'Hare, Maximilian Osinski (Telemarketers), Leshay Tomlinson Boyce (Attendant), Paul Sanchez (AA Group Leader), Ken Barnett, Stephanie Bast, Shaughn Buchholz, Pippa Hinchley, David Kelsey, LeRoy S. Mobley, Nick Smoke, Amanda Young (AA Members), Scott Weintraub (Teacher), Aaron Farb (Lab Teacher), Sonya Leslie (Nurse), Alexander Leeb (German Guy), Katie Sigismund, Sheila Shaw, Katy Boyer (Lillian's Friends), Peggy Lynn Moore (Waitress), Liza Del Mundo (Receptionist), Michael D. Parr (Sleazy Par Patron), Omar Vega (Taco Stand Worker), Tara Inden (LAX Flight Attendant), James Hosney (Minister), Dave Zyler, Moosie Drier, Rif Hutton, Steve Alterman (70's Studio Techs), Liza Richardson (CD Narrator)

Called on to settle his father's estate, Sam is shocked to discover that he has a 30-year-old sister whom he was never told about.

Chris Pine, Elizabeth Banks, Michael Hall D'Addario

Matthew McConaughey

Adam Rodriguez, Kevin Nash, Channing Tatum, Matt Bomer, Joe Manganiello

Adam Rodriguez © Warner Bros,

Alex Pettyfer, Matthew McConaughey

Channing Tatum, Cody Horn, Olivia Munn

Channing Tatum

MAGIC MIKE

(WARNER BROS.) Producers, Nick Wechsler, Gregory Jacobs, Channing Tatum, Reid Carolin; Director, Steven Soderbergh; Screenplay, Reid Carolin; Photography, Peter Andrews (Steven Soderbergh); Designer, Howard Cummings; Costumes, Christopher Peterson; Music Supervisor, Frankie Pine; Editor, Mary Ann Bernard; Choreographer, Alison Faulk; Casting, Carmen Cuba; a Nick Wechsler/Gregory Jacobs production of an Iron Horse/Extention 765 enterprise; Dolby; Hawk Scope Widescreen; Technicolor; HD; Rated R; 109 minutes; Release date: June 29, 2012

CAST

Magic Mike	**Channing Tatum**
Adam	**Alex Pettyfer**
Dallas	**Matthew McConaughey**
Brooke	**Cody Horn**
Joanna	**Olivia Munn**
Ken	**Matt Bomer**
Nora	**Riley Keough**
Big Dick Richie	**Joe Manganiello**
Tarzan	**Kevin Nash**
Tito	**Adam Rodriguez**
Tobias	**Gabriel Iglesias**
Sal	**James Martin Kelly**
George	**George Sack**
Portia	**Micaela Johnson**
Ruby	**Denise Vasi**
Paul	**Reid Carolin**
Birthday Girl	**Camryn Grimes**
Liz	**Kate Easton**
Banker	**Betsy Brandt**
Ken's Wife	**Mircea Monroe**
Kim	**Caitlin Gerard**
Ryan	**Michael Roark**
Girl in Line	**Avery Camp**
Obnoxious Bar Guy	**Asher Wallis**
Havana Nights Girl	**Alison Faulk**
Blonde Bachelorette	**Catherine Lynn Stone**
Silhouette Girl	**Jennifer A. Skinner**
Cowboy Lap Dance Girl	**Vanessa Ryan**
Pony Girl	**Teresa Espinoza**
Dr. Love Girl	**Monica Garcia**
Tarzan's Girl	**Annette Houlihan Verdolino**
Boxing Girl	**Candace Marie Celmer**
Girl Richie Lifts	**Lyss Remaly**
Tito's Girl	**Jannel Diaz**
Herman the Pig	**Maynard the Pig**
Sorority Girl	**Yari De Leon**
Kim's Boyfriend	**Cameron Banfield**
Thugs	**Keith Kurtz, Marland Burke**
Raver Girl	**Ashley Hayes**

Hoping to start his own business, Mike juggles three jobs, including that of the star attraction at a Florida strip club.

Joe Manganiello

Alex Pettyfer, Channing Tatum

Matt Bomer

Tyler Perry's MADEA'S WITNESS PROTECTION

(LIONSGATE) Producers, Tyler Perry, Ozzie Areau, Paul Hall; Executive Producers, Michael Paseornek, John J. Kelly; Director/Screenplay, Tyler Perry, based on his characters; Photography, Alexander Gruszynski; Designer, Eloise C. Stammerjohn; Costumes, Carol Oditz; Music, Aaron Zigman; Music Supervisor, Joel C. High; Editor, Maysie Hoy; Casting, Kim Taylor-Coleman; a TPS/Lionsgate production; Dolby; Deluxe color; Rated PG-13; 114 minutes; Release date: June 29, 2012

CAST

Madea/Joe/Brian	**Tyler Perry**
George Needleman	**Eugene Levy**
Kate Needleman	**Denise Richards**
Barbara Needleman	**Doris Roberts**
Jake	**Romeo Miller**
Walter	**Tom Arnold**
Pastor Nelson	**John Amos**
Hattie	**Marla Gibbs**
Cindy Needleman	**Danielle Campbell**
Howie Needleman	**Devan Leos**

Shayne Anderson (TSA Agent), Dean Balkwill (Attendant), Nelson Bonilla (Agent Mulligan), Frank Brennan (Jack Goldberg), Eric Brooks, Jonny Clemson (Bellmen), Daniel Brule (Bike Messenger), John Paul George (John Paul), Meg Gillentine (Flight Attendant), John Joslin (Lucas), Andy Koehler (Pilot), Arin Logan (Bank Receptionist), Eaddy Mays (Agent Thomas), Shane Partlow (FBI Agent), Wanda Smith (Security Guard), Kathleen J. Bertrand, Colette L. Coward, Tiffany Davis, Darren Ellis, Alfreda Gerald, Betsy Christian Gerald-Randolph, Patricia Elaine Grigsby, Eric Bernard Jackson, Theresa Hightower, Sheneca Holmes, Kipper Jones, John Madgett, Latrice Pace, Penny Yvette Ray, Frederick Sawyers, Myra Walker, Erika Ware, Delrick O. White (Choir) , Charlie Sheen (himself)

Realizing he has been set up to take the fall for a shady mob-backed Ponzi scheme, Wall Street investment banker George Needleman and his family are put under witness protection at the Southern home of the overbearing Madea.

Eugene Levy, Doris Roberts © Lionsgate

Denise Richards, Tyler Perry

John Amos, Romeo Miller

Tyler Perry, Eugene Levy

Andrew Garfield

Martin Sheen, Sally Field, Andrew Garfield

Rhys Ifans © Columbia Pictures

THE AMAZING SPIDER-MAN

(COLUMBIA) Producers, Laura Ziskin, Avi Arad, Matt Tolmach; Executive Producers, Stan Lee, Kevin Feige, Michael Grillo; Director, Marc Webb; Screenplay, James Vanderbilt, Alvin Sargent, Steve Kloves; Story, James Vanderbilt; Based on the Marvel comicbook by Stan Lee and Steve Ditko; Photography, John Schwartzman; Designer, J. Michael Riva; Costumes, Kym Barrett; Music, James Horner; Editors, Alan Edward Bell, Pietro Scalia; Visual Effects Supervisor, Jerome Chen; Special Visual Effects, Sony Pictures Imageworks Inc.; 3D Visual Effects Supervisor, Rob Engle; Stunts; Andy Armstrong, James Armstrong; Fight Coordinator, Gary Ray Stearns; Casting, Francine Maisler; a Marvel Entertainment/ Laura Ziskin/Avi Arad/ Matt Tolmach production; Dolby; HD Widescreen; Color; HD; 3D; Rated PG-13; 136 minutes; Release date: July 3, 2012

CAST

Peter Parker (Spider-Man)	**Andrew Garfield**
Gwen Stacy	**Emma Stone**
Dr. Curt Connors (The Lizard)	**Rhys Ifans**
Captain Stacy	**Denis Leary**
Uncle Ben	**Martin Sheen**
Aunt May	**Sally Field**
Rajit Ratha	**Irrfan Khan**
Richard Parker	**Campbell Scott**
Mary Parker	**Embeth Davidtz**
Flash Thompson	**Chris Zylka**
Peter Parker (age 4)	**Max Charles**
Jack's Father	**C. Thomas Howell**
Jack	**Jake Ryan Keiffer**

Kari Coleman (Helen Stacy), Michael Barra (Store Clerk), Leif Gantvoort (Cash Register Thief), Andy Pessoa (Gordon), Hannah Marks (Missy Kallenback), Kelsey Chow (Hot Girl), Kevin McCorkle (Mr. Cramer), Andy Gladbach, Ring Hendricks-Tellefsen (Physics Nerds), Barbara Eve Harris (Miss Ritter), Stan Lee (School Librarian), Danielle Burgio (Nicky's Girlfriend), Tom Waite (Nicky), Keith Campbell (Car Thief), Steve DeCastro (Car Thief Cop), Jill Flint (Receptionist), Mark Daugherty (OsCorp Intern), Milton González (Rodrigo Guevara), Skyler Gisondo (Howard Stacy), Charlie DePew (Philip Stacy), Jacob Rodier (Simon Stacy), Vincent Laresca (Construction Worker), Damien Lemon (Taxi Driver), Ty Upshaw (Police Officer with Sketch), James Chen (Police Officer), Alexander Bedria (Officer, SWAT), Tia Texada (Sheila, Subway), Jay Caputo (Subway Guy), John Burke (Newscaster, News Chopper), Terry Bozeman (Principal), Jennifer Lyons (Second Girl, Subway), Michael Massee (Man in the Shadows), Amber Stevens (Ariel)

Bitten by a genetically altered spider, a teen is given remarkable powers that enable him to track down the killer of his beloved uncle and fight a crazed scientist bent on death and destruction.
Previous films in the Columbia series, with Tobey Maguire as Peter Parker, were *Spider-Man* (2002), *Spider-Man 2* (2004) and *Spider-Man 3* (2007).

Emma Stone, Andrew Garfield

John Travolta, Taylor Kitsch

SAVAGES

(UNIVERSAL) Producers, Moritz Borman, Eric Kopeloff; Executive Producers, Fernando Sulichin, Shane Salerno, Todd Arnow; Director, Oliver Stone; Screenplay, Shane Salerno, Don Winslow, Oliver Stone; Based on the 2010 novel by Don Winslow; Photography, Dan Mindel; Designer, Tomás Voth; Costumes, Cindy Evans; Music, Adam Peters; Editors, Joe Hutshing, Stuart Levy, Alex Marquez; Visual Effects Supervisor, Paul Graff; Stunts, Keith Woulard; Casting, Sarah Halley Finn; a Moritz Borman production, presented in association with Relativity Media; Dolby; Panavision; Deluxe color; Rated R; 130 minutes; Release date: July 6, 2012

CAST

Chon	**Taylor Kitsch**
O (Ophelia Sage)	**Blake Lively**
Ben	**Aaron Johnson**
Dennis	**John Travolta**
Lado	**Benicio Del Toro**
Elena	**Salma Hayek**
Spin	**Emile Hirsch**
Alex	**Demián Bichir**
Esteban	**Diego Cataño**
Chad	**Shea Whigham**

Joaquín Cosio (El Azul), Antonio Jaramillo (Jaime), Jake McLaughlin (Doc, Sniper), Alexander Wraith (Sam, Sniper), Antony Cutolo (Billy, Sniper), Leonard Roberts (Hayes, O's Security), Joel David Moore (Craig), Ali Wong (Claire), Sandra Echeverría (Magda), Sean Stone (Eric, Marijuana Grower), Lucinda Serrano (Myrna, DEA Translator), Jana Banker (Volleyball Girl), Candra Docherty (Grow House Girl), Nana Agyapong (Bicycle Delivery Girl), Gary Stretch (Badass Biker), Karishma Ahluwalia (Chad's Girlfriend), Jonathan Carr (Valet), Kurt Collins (Waiter), Amber Dixon (Sophia, Cartel Girl), Sala Baker (Motorcycle Cop), Tara Stone (Mall Shopper), Matthew Saldivar (Cartel Technician), Wilfredo Lopez, Marco Morales (Cartel Enforcers), Charles Haugk (DEA Agent), Sam Medina (Cartel Heist Driver), Ben Bray (Cartel Heist Passenger), Gonzalo Menendez (Hernando, Cartel Associate), Maya Merker (Elena's Maid), Donnabella Mortel (TV News Reporter), Trevor Donovan (Matt, Magda's Boyfriend), Leana Chavez (Gloria, Mexican Girlfriend), Gillian Zinser, Florine Deplazes (Beach Girls), Kaj Mollenhauer (Sarah, Dennis' Daughter), Alexandra Gold Jourden (Hannah, Dennis' Daughter), Charles Ingram (Cartel Sniper), Akima (Indian Chief), Dennis Garcia (Tribal Cop), Eddie Follis, Holly Follis (DEA Agents), Mía Maestro (Dolores, Lado's Wife), Schae Harrison (Dennis' Wife)

A team of successful pot growers faces danger when a powerful and vicious Mexican cartel insists on going into business with them.

Taylor Kitsch, Blake Lively, Aaron Johnson

Blake Lively, Benicio Del Toro

Benicio Del Toro, Salma Hayek © Universal Studios

KATY PERRY: PART OF ME

(PARAMOUNT) Producers, Brian Grazer, Katy Perry, Bradford Cobb, Steve Jensen; Executive Producers, Craig Brewer, Randy Phillips, Michael Rosenberg, Eric Huggins, Edward Lovelace, James Hall; Directors, Dan Cutforth, Jane Lipsitz; Costumes, Johnny Wujek; Music, Deborah Lurie; Editor, Scott Richter; Stereographer, Brian Taber; an Insurge Pictures presentation of an Imagine Entertainment/Perry/ Direct Management Group production in association with AEG Live and EMI Music North America; Dolby; Deluxe color; 3D; Rated PG; 94 minutes; Release date: July 5, 2012. Documentary on pop singer Katy Perry's transcontinental concert tour

WITH

Katy Perry, Adele, Angelica Cob-Baehler, Glen Ballard, Justin Bieber, Russell Brand, Bradford Cobb, Todd Delano, Jason Flom, Lady Gaga, Whoopi Goldberg, Angela Hudson, Ann Hudson, David Hudson, Keith Hudson, Mary Hudson, Mark Hunter, Jessie J, Steve Jensen, Lucas Kerr, Mia Moretti, Tamra Natisin, Rihanna, Shannon Woodward, Johnny Wujek; *Band:* Adam Marcello (Drums), Casey Hooper (Guitar), Patrick Matera (Guitar), Max Hart (Keys), Joshua Moreau (Bass); *Background Vocals:* Lauren Allison Ball, Tasha Layton; *Dancers:* Leah Adler, Lockhart Brownlie, Anthony Burrell, Lexie Contursi, Ashley Ashida Dixon, Brandee Evans, Bryan Gaw, Malik LeNost, Rachael Markarian, Scott Myrick, Cassidy Noblett.

Katy Perry

Katy Perry © Paramount Pictures

Tammy Blanchard, Mira Sorvino

Tammy Blanchard, Mike Doyle © Dada Films

UNION SQUARE

(DADA FILMS) Producers, Richard Guay, Neda Armian; Co-Producers, Glenn Trotiner, Peter Bobrow; Director, Nancy Savoca; Screenplay, Mary Tobler, Nancy Savoca; Photography, Lisa Leone; Designer, Sarah Frank; Costumes, Liz Prince; Editor, Jennifer Lee; Casting, Sig de Miguel, Steve Vincent; an Armian Pictures and Cine-Si presentation; Color; Rated R; 80 minutes; Release date: July 13, 2012

CAST
Lucy	**Mira Sorvino**
Jenny	**Tammy Blanchard**
Nick	**Michael Rispoli**
Andy	**Christopher Backus**
Bill	**Mike Doyle**
Lucia	**Patti LuPone**

Daphne Rubin-Vega (Sara), Harper Dill (Trish), Michael Sirow (Voice of Jay), Holden Backus (Mike)

Just as she's about to commit to her fiancé, Jenny receives an unwanted extended visit from her estranged sister Lucy.

Morgan Freeman, Virginia Madsen

Emma Fuhrmann, Morgan Freeman

Morgan Freeman

THE MAGIC OF BELLE ISLE

(MAGNOLIA) Producers, Rob Reiner, Alan Greisman, Lori McCreary, David Valdes, Salli Newman; Executive Producers, Martin Schafer, Liz Glotzer, Jared Ian Goldman; Director, Rob Reiner; Screenplay, Guy Thomas; Photography, Reed Morano; Designer, Tom Lisowski; Costumes, Shawn-Holly Cookson; Music, Marc Shaiman; Editor, Dorian Harris; Casting, Susan Shopmaker; a Castle Rock Entertainment, Revelations Entertainment and a Summer Magic/Firebrand production; Dolby; Color; Rated PG; 109 minutes; Release date: July 6, 2012

CAST

Monte Wildhorn	**Morgan Freeman**
Charlotte O'Neil	**Virginia Madsen**
Willow O'Neil	**Madeline Carroll**
Finnegan O'Neil	**Emma Fuhrmann**
Flora O'Neil	**Nicolette Pierini**
Henry	**Kenan Thompson**
Al Kaiser	**Fred Willard**
Joe Viola	**Kevin Pollak**
Carl Loop	**Ash Christian**
Fire Captain	**C.J. Wilson**
Mahmoud	**Debargo Sanyal**
Karen Loop	**Jessica Hecht**
Bookstore Owner	**Christopher McCann**
Clown	**Lucas Rooney**
Luke Ford	**Boyd Holbrook**

A once prominent author, battling writer's block and alcoholism, takes a lakeside cabin on Belle Isle, where he befriends a single mother and her young daughters.

Virginia Madsen © Magnolia Films

ICE AGE: CONTINENTAL DRIFT

(20th CENTURY FOX) Producers, Lori Forte, John C. Donkin; Executive Producers, Chris Wedge, Carlos Saldanha; Directors, Steve Martino, Michael Thurmeier; Screenplay, Michael Berg, Jason Fuchs; Story, Michael Berg, Lori Forte; Photography, Renato Falcao; Art Director, Nash Dunnigan; Music, John Powell; Editors, James M. Palumbo, David Ian Salter; Supervising Animators, James Bresnahan, Nick Bruno; Stereoscopic Supervisor, Daniel Abramovich; Casting, Christian Kaplan; a 20th Century Fox Animation presentation of a Blue Sky Studios production; Dolby; Widescreen; Deluxe Color; 3D; Rated PG; 87 minutes; Release date: July 13, 2012.

VOICES

Manny	**Ray Romano**
Sid	**John Leguizamo**
Diego	**Denis Leary**
Crash	**Seann William Scott**
Eddie	**Josh Peck**

Peter Dinklage (Captain Gutt), Wanda Sykes (Granny), Jennifer Lopez (Shira), Queen Latifah (Ellie), Aziz Ansari (Squint), Joy Behar (Eunice), Christopher Campbell (Creature Siren/Various Voices), Alain Chabat (Silas), Ester Dean (Siren), Drake (Ethan), Jason Fricchione (Dumb Mammoth/Various Voices), Nick Frost (Flynn), Josh Gad (Louis), Ben Gleib (Marshall), George Jacobs (Beaver), Nick Minaj (Steffie), Heather Morris (Katie), Kunal Nayyar (Gupta), Keke Palmer (Peaches), James Palumbo (Panicked Start), Simon Pegg (Buck), Alexandra Romano (Meghan), Matthew Simmons (Teen Elk), Eddie "Piolin' Sotelo (Uncle Fungus), Patrick Stewart (Ariscratle), Meghan Thurmeier (Baby Bird), Alan Tudyk (Milton/Hunky Siren), Chris Wedge (Scrat), Rebel Wilson (Raz), Alexa Kahn (Hyrax)

A massive earthquake separates Manny and his friends from Manny's family. Fourth in the 20th Century Fox series following *Ice Age* (2002), *Ice Age: The Meltdown* (2006), and *Ice Age: Dawn of the Dinosaurs* (2009).

Diego, Shira © 20th Century Fox Animation

Silas, Raz, Flynn Gutt, Squint, Dobson, Scrat, Diego, Manny, Sid

Jackie Siegel © Magnolia Films

David Siegel, Jackie Siegel

THE QUEEN OF VERSAILLES

(MAGNOLIA) Producers, Lauren Greenfield, Danielle Renfrew Behrens; Executive Producers, Frank Evers, Dan Cogan; Co-Producer, Rebecca Horn Black; Co-Executive Producers, Allison Amon, Julie Parker Benello, Abigail Disney, Patricia Greenfield, Gerry Grossman, Lilly Hartley, Pierre Hauser, Mette Heide, Patricia Lambrecht, Lisa Mehling, Jeffrey Tarrant; Director, Lauren Greenfield; Photography, Tom Hurwitz; Music, Jeff Beal; Editor, Victor Livingston; an Evergreen Pictures presentation in association with Impact Partners and Candescent Films; American-Dutch-British-Danish; Dolby; Color; Rated PG; 100 minutes; Release date: July 20, 2012. Documentary on 74-year-old Florida billionaire David Siegel, his 43-year-old wife, Jackie, and their appallingly opulent lifestyle;

WITH

David Siegel, Jackie Siegel, Virginia Nebab, Alyse Zwick.

THE DARK KNIGHT RISES

(WARNER BROS.) Producers, Emma Thomas, Christopher Nolan, Charles Roven; Executive Producers, Benjamin Melniker, Michael E. Uslan, Kevin de la Noy, Thomas Tull; Co-Producer, Jordan Goldberg; Director, Christopher Nolan; Screenplay, Jonathan Nolan, Christopher Nolan; Story, Christopher Nolan, David S. Goyer; Based upon *Batman* characters created by Bob Kane and published by DC Comics; Photography, Wally Pfister; Designers, Nathan Crowley, Kevin Kavanaugh; Costumes, Lindy Hemming; Music, Hans Zimmer; Editor, Lee Smith; Special Effects Supervisor, Chris Corbould; Special Effects Coordinator, Scott Fisher; Stunts, Tom Struthers; Casting, John Papsidera; a Syncopy production, presented in association with Legendary Pictures; Dolby; Panavision; Technicolor; Rated PG-13; 164 minutes; Release date: July 20, 2012

CAST

Bruce Wayne (Batman)	**Christian Bale**
Alfred	**Michael Caine**
Commissioner Gordon	**Gary Oldman**
Selina Kyle	**Anne Hathaway**
Bane	**Tom Hardy**
Miranda Tate	**Marion Cotillard**
John Blake	**Joseph Gordon-Levitt**
Lucius Fox	**Morgan Freeman**
Foley	**Matthew Modine**
Dr. Pavel	**Alon Moni Aboutboul**
Daggett	**Ben Mendelsohn**
Stryver	**Burn Gorman**
Captain Jones	**Daniel Sunjata**
CIA Op	**Aidan Gillen**
Mayor	**Nestor Carbonell**
Jen	**Juno Temple**
Congressman	**Brett Cullen**

Sam Kennard (Special Ops Sergeant), Aliasha Tepina (Hooded Man #2), Nick Julian (Caterer), Miranda Nolan, Claire Julien (Maids), Reggie Lee (Ross), Joseph Lyle Taylor (DWP Man), Chris Ellis (Fr. Reilly), Tyler Dean Flores (Mark), Duane Henry (SWAT in Dive Bar), James Harvey Ward (SWAT in Alley), Gonzalo Menendez (Cop in Manhole), Cameron Jack, Lex Daniel (Sewer Thugs), Thomas Lennon (Doctor), Trevor White (Yuppie), Rob Brown (Allen), Fredric Lehne (Exchange Security Chief), Courtney Munch (Security Guard), Chris Hill, Travis Guba (Paparazzi), Jay Benedict (Rich Twit), Will Estes (Officer Simon Jansen), David Dayan Fisher (Shoe Shine Man at GSE), P.J. Griffith (Sniper at Exchange), Glen Powell, Ben Cornish, Russ Fega (Traders), Andres Perez-Molina (Valet at Museum), Brent Briscoe (Veteran Cop), John Nolan (Fredericks), Oliver Cotton (2 Star Air Force General), Mark Kileen (Airport Cop), Sarah Goldberg, John Macmillan (Analysts), Robert Wisdom (Army Captain at Bridge), Ronnie Gene Blevins (Cement Truck Driver), John Hollingsworth (CIA Analyst), Ian Bohen (Cop with Gordon), Uri Gavriel (Blind Prisoner), Noel G. (Ex-Prisoner at River), Max Schuler (Foley's Kid), Daina Griffith (Foley's Wife), Hector Atreyu Reuiz (Gangbanger), Patrick Cox (Huge Inmate), Aramis Knight (Kid with Apple), Josh Stewart (Barsad), William Devane (President), Harry Coles (Younger Prison Child), Joey King (Older Prison Child), Liam Neeson (Ra's Al Ghul), Julie Mun (Reporter at Stadium), Cillian Murphy (Dr. Jonathan Crane, "Scarecrow"), David Gyasi (Skinny Prisoner), Patrick Jordan (Special Forces #2), Tom Conti (Prisoner), Joshua Elijah Reese (Mercenary at City Hall), Desmond Harrington (Uniform), Mychael Bates (Bomb Truck Driver), Rory Nolan (Little Boy at Bridge), Tomas Arana (Wayne's Lawyer), Peter Holden, David Monahan (Applied Sciences Techs), Jillian Armenante (Lawyer's Clerk), Aja Evans (Greeter at Museum), Aldous Davidson (Valet at Wayne Enterprises), Michael James Faradie (Guard at Blackgate), Wade Williams (Warden at Blackgate), Antwan Lewis (Reporter at Wayne Enterprises), Jake Canuso (Waiter in Florence Café), Josh Pence (Young Ra's Al Ghul), India Wadsworth (Warlord's Daughter), Kevin Kiely, Daniel Newman (Thugs in Basement), Massi Furlan (Janitor at GSE), Warren Brown, Luke Rutherford, Phillip Browne, Christopher Judge (Mercenary

Security), Aldo Bigante (2nd Cop with Gordon), Charles Jackson Coyne (Anthem Singer), Patrick Leahy (Board Member #2), Todd Gearhart (Uniform #2)

After eight years in seclusion, during which he had been treated as an outlawed vigilante, billionaire Bruce Wayne resumes the crime fighting guise of Batman in order to stop the psychopathic Bane from turning Gotham City into a terrorist stronghold and causing untold destruction. Third in Warner Bros.' Christian Bale/Christopher Nolan *Batman* series, following *Batman Begins* (2005) and *The Dark Knight* (2008).

Christian Bale

Anne Hathaway

Christian Bale © Warner Bros. Pictures

Morgan Freeman, Marion Cotillard

Matthew Modine

Tom Hardy

Christian Bale, Michael Caine

Tom Hardy, Christian Bale

Christian Bale

Annette Bening, Antonio Banderas

Zoe Kazan, Paul Dano, Chris Messina

RUBY SPARKS

(FOX SEARCHLIGHT) Producers, Albert Berger, Ron Yerxa; Executive Producers, Robert Graf, Zoe Kazan, Paul Dano; Directors, Jonathan Dayton, Valerie Faris; Screenplay, Zoe Kazan; Photography, Matthew Libatique; Designer, Judy Becker; Costumes, Nancy Steiner; Music, Nick Urata; Music Supervisor, Dan Wilcox; Editor, Pamela Martin; Casting, Kim Davis-Wagner, Justine Baddeley; a Bona Fide production; Dolby; Deluxe color; Rated R; 104 minutes; Release date: July 25, 2012

CAST
Calvin Weir-Fields	**Paul Dano**
Ruby Sparks	**Zoe Kazan**
Harry	**Chris Messina**
Gertrude	**Annette Bening**
Mort	**Antonio Banderas**
Cyrus Modi	**Aasif Mandvi**
Langdon Tharp	**Steve Coogan**
Susie	**Toni Trucks**
Lila	**Deborah Ann Woll**
Dr. Rosenthal	**Elliott Gould**
Mabel	**Alia Shawkat**
Saskia	**Jane Anne Thomas**
Adam	**John F. Beach**
Mandi	**Eleanor Seigler**

Emma Julia Jacobs (Party Goer at Langdon's), Wallace Langham (Warren), Rightor Doyle, Eden Brolin (Part Goers – Hammer), Michael Silverblatt (Himself), Mary Jo Deschanel (Professor), Kai Lennox (Sort of Weird Guy), Ole Olofson (Older Dude), Jack Levinson, China Shavers (Party Goers – Book Release), Casey Genton (Busboy), Michael Berry Jr. (Silverlake Passerby), Lindsay Fishkin (Box Office Teller), Claudia Bestor (Lecture Curator), Oscar (Scotty the Dog)

Struggling to complete another novel, author Calvin Weir-Fields conjures up a real woman from the character he is creating and discovers that she will do anything or behave in any way according to whatever he decides to write.

Paul Dano © Fox Searchlight

Zoe Kazan, Paul Dano

KILLER JOE

(LD ENTERTAINMENT) Producers, Nicolas Chartier, Scott Einbinder; Executive Producers, Zev Foreman, Roman Viaris, Christopher Woodrow, Molly Conners, Vicki Cherkas; Co-Producer, Patrick Newall; Director, William Friedkin; Screenplay, Tracy Letts, based on his 1993 play; Photography, Caleb Deschanel; Designer, Franco-Giacomo Carbone; Costumes, Peggy Schnitzer; Music, Tyler Bates; Editor, Darrin Navarro; Casting, Denise Chamian; a Voltage Pictures and PPC presentation in association with Worldview Entertainment, a Voltage Pictures/Ana Media production; Dolby; Deluxe color; Rated NC-17; 102 minutes; Release date: July 27, 2012

CAST
Killer Joe Cooper	**Matthew McConaughey**
Chris Smith	**Emile Hirsch**
Dottie Smith	**Juno Temple**
Sharla Smith	**Gina Gershon**
Ansel Smith	**Thomas Haden Church**
Digger Soames	**Marc Macaulay**
Pizza Manager	**Scott Martin**
Saleslady	**Carol Sutton**
G-Man	**Danny Epper**
Biker Thug	**Jeff Galpin**
Filpatrick	**Gregory C. Bachaud**
Preacher	**Charley Vance**
Adele	**Julia Adams**
Rex	**Sean O'Hara**
Waitress	**Lynette Zumo**
Pizza Patrons	**Graylen Banks, Geraldine Glenn, Tony Severio**

Badly in need of money to pay off a debt, Chris Smith hires hitman Joe Cooper to bump off his stepmother, believing he will be able to collect on the insurance.

Emile Hirsch, Matthew McConaughey © LD Entertainment

Gina Gershon, Thomas Haden Church

Emile Hirsch, Gina Gershon, Thomas Haden Church, Juno Temple

Matthew McConaughey

Kathryn McCormick

Ryan Guzman © Lionsgate

STEP UP REVOLUTION

(LIONSGATE/SUMMIT) Producers, Adam Shankman, Jennifer Gibgot, Patrick Wachsberger, Erik Feig; Executive Producers, Bob Hayward, David Garrett, Meredith Milton, Jon M. Chu, Matthew Smith, Nan Morales; Director, Scott Speer; Screenplay, Amanda Brody; Based on characters created by Duane Adler; Photography, Crash; Designer, Carlos A. Menéndez; Costumes, Rebecca Hofherr; Music, Aaron Zigman; Music Supervisor, Buck Damon; Editor, Matthew Friedman; Choreographer, Jamal Sims; Stereographer, Nick Brown; Casting, Joanna Colbert, Richard Mento; a Summit Entertainment presentation of an Offspring Entertainment production; Dolby; HD Widescreen; Deluxe color; 3D; Rated PG-13; 98 minutes; Release date: July 27, 2012

Kathryn McCormick, Ryan Guzman

CAST
Sean	**Ryan Guzman**
Emily	**Kathryn McCormick**
Eddy	**Misha Gabriel**
Penelope	**Cleopatra Coleman**
Jason	**Stephen "tWitch" Boss**
Trip	**Tommy Dewey**
Mr. Anderson	**Peter Gallagher**

Michael "Xeno" Langebeck (Mercury), Claudio Pinto (Francisco), Nicole Dabeau (Newscaster), Chris Charles (Lamborghini Driver), Katie Peterson, Alejandro Posada (People by the Ocean), Marc Macaulay (Uniformed Cop), Mario Ernesto Sánchez (Ricky), Sabina V. Gomez (Ricky's Mother), Dominique Bell (Sarah), Megan Boone (Claire), Mia Michaels (Olivia), Tangi Colombel (Tommy), Claudia Rocafort (Curator), Jordana DePaula (Cute Salesperson), Tiger Kirchharz (Curator), Kevin Anthony (Bob Cooper), Steve Zurk (Councilman Casey), Chadd Smith (Vladd), Mari Koda (Jenny Kido), Adam Sevani (Moose), Danielle Dominiquez (Vera), Brandy Lamkin (Brittany), Celestina, Justin "Jet Li" Valles, Phillip Assaad Chbeeb, Angeline Appel, Daniel Graham, Brittny Sugarman (Mob Dancers), Patrick Fox, Juan Gamero (Businessmen), Robb Ross (Bartender), Ron Shimshilashvili (Super Model) , Emiliano Díez (Mayor Fernandez), Karelix Alicea, Tallie Brinson III, Angela Randle Elgani, Giovanni Velazquez (Dancers), Sheri Shea (Commissioner's Trophy Wife)

Sean and his gang of flash-mob dancers use their street moves to protest the efforts of a resort tycoon to raze their neighborhood. Fourth in the series following: *Step Up* (Touchstone, 2006), *Step Up 2 the Streets* (Touchstone, 2008), and *Step Up 3D* (Touchstone/Summit, 2010).

Ryan Guzman (front)

THE WATCH

(20ᵗʰ CENTURY FOX) Producer, Shawn Levy; Executive Producers, Dan Levine, Monica Levinson; Director, Akiva Schaffer; Screenplay, Jared Stern, Seth Rogen, Evan Goldberg; Photography, Barry Peterson; Designer, Doug Meerdink; Costumes, Wendy Chuck; Music, Christophe Beck; Music Supervisor, George Drakoulias; Editor, Dean Zimmerman; Special Effects Supervisor, Steve Riley; Casting, Alyssa Weisberg; a 21 Laps production; Dolby; HD Widescreen; Deluxe color; Rated R; 102 minutes; Release date: July 27, 2012

CAST

Evan	**Ben Stiller**
Bob	**Vince Vaughn**
Franklin	**Jonah Hill**
Jamarcus	**Richard Ayoade**
Abby	**Rosemarie DeWitt**
Sgt. Bressman	**Will Forte**

Mel Rodriguez (Chucho), Doug Jones (Hero Alien), Erin Moriarty (Chelsea), Nicholas Braun (Jason), R. Lee Ermey (Manfred), Joe Nunez (Antonio Guzman), Liz Cackowski (Carla), Johnny Pemberton (Skater Kid), Sharon Gee (Mrs. Kim), Eric Goins (Random Jogger – Jared), Robert C. Sibley, Grace Fronebarger, Bonnie Silver (Retirees), Jill Jane Clements, Paul Barlow Jr. (City Council Members), Thomas Elliott (Hooters Volunteer), Sean Robert Goulding (Costco Employee – TV), Amy Napier Viteri (Reporter), Dax Flame (Teenage Announcer), Ryan Girard, Katie Kneeland (Paul's Guests), Ted Huckabee, Jeremiah Williams, Ethan Shapanka, Marla Malcolm, Lindsey Coley, LaDona Allison (Orgy People), Andy Samberg, Jorma Taccone, Akiva Schaffer (Casual Wankers), Cathy Shim (Asian Housewife), Carissa Capobianco (Mandy), Kelsey Talley, Melia Talley (Twins), Patricia French (Franklin's Mom), Erinn Hayes (Bob's Wife), Zack Mines (Prom Date), Emilee Yuye Sikes (Evan's Daughter), Billy Crudup (Neighbor)

Four men who form a neighborhood watch group uncover evidence of an alien invasion.

Ben Stiller, Johnny Pemberton, Jonah Hill © 20ᵗʰ Century Fox

Richard Ayoade, Vince Vaughn, Ben Stiller, Jonah Hill

Ai Weiwei

Ai Weiwei © Sundance Selects

AI WEIWEI: NEVER SORRY

(SUNDANCE SELECTS) Producers, Alison Klayman, Adam Schlesinger; Executive Producers, Andrew Cohen, Julie Goldman, Karl Katz; Director/ Photography, Alison Klayman; Music, Ilan Isakov; Editor, Jennifer Fineran; a United Expression Media presentation in association with Muse Film & Television of a Never Sorry production; Color; Not rated; 91 minutes; Release date: July 27, 2012. Documentary on Chinese artist and activist Ai Weiwei

WITH

Ai Dan, Gao Ying, Lu Qing, Wang Fen, Chen Danqing, Feng Boyi, Gu Changwei, He Yunchang, Hsieh "Sam" Teching, Hung Huang, Rong Rong, Zhang Hongtu, Zuoxiao Zuzhou

TOTAL RECALL

(COLUMBIA) Producers, Neal H. Moritz, Toby Jaffe; Executive Producers, Ric Kidney, Len Wiseman; Director, Len Wiseman; Screenplay, Kurt Wimmer, Mark Bomback; Screen Story, Ronald Shusett, Dan O'Bannon, Jon Povill, Kurt Wimmer; Inspired by the 1966 short story *We Can Remember it for You Wholesale* by Philip K. Dick; Photography, Paul Cameron; Designer, Patrick Tatopoulos; Costumes, Sanja Milkovi Hays; Music, Harry Gregson-Williams; Editor, Christian Wagner; Visual Effects Supervisor, Peter Chiang; Casting, Debra Zane; Stunts, Andy Gill; Fight Coordinators, Jeff Imada, Brad Martin; an Original Film production; Dolby; Super 35 Widescreen; Color; Rated PG-13; 118 minutes; Release date: August 3, 2012

Colin Farrell

CAST

Douglas Quaid/Carl Hauser	**Colin Farrell**
Lori Quaid	**Kate Beckinsale**
Melina	**Jessica Biel**
Cohaagen	**Bryan Cranston**
Harry	**Bokeem Woodbine**
Matthias	**Bill Nighy**
McClane	**John Cho**
Marek	**Will Yun Lee**
Reisistance Fighter	**Milton Barnes**

James McGowan (Military Adjutant), Natalie Lisinska (Bohemian Nurse), Michael Therriault (Bank Clerk), Stephen MacDonald (Slacker), Mishael Morgan (Rekall Receptionist), LinLyn Lue (Resistance Woman), Dylan Scott Smith (Hammond), Andrew Moodie (Factory Foreman), Kaitlyn Leeb (Three-Breasted Woman), Leo Guiyab, Nykeem Provo, Steve Byers (Hauser Cover Indentities), Danny Waugh (Officer), Geoffrey Pounsett (Sentry Lieutenant), Jesse Bond (Lead Sentry), Warren Belle (Security Sentry), Vincent Rother, Matthew Nette, Brooks Darnell (Sentries), Brett Donahue (Sentry Trooper), James Downing (Synth Captain), Simon Sinn (Murray), Lisa Chandler (Prostitute), Miranda Jade Fratton (Girl on Balcony), Shereen J. Airth (Red-Headed Lady), Phillip Moran (Immigration Officer), Clive Ashborn, Emily Chang, Bill Coulter, Merella Fernandez, Alicia-Kay Markson, Brian C. Rodriguez (Newscasters), Leigh Folsom (The Fall Announcer Voice), Brian T. Delaney (ATC Dispatcher Voice), Cam Clarke (Terminal Announcer Voice), Bridget Hoffman (Chopper Voice)

Jessica Biel, Colin Farrell

After a failed attempt to submit himself to a secret program that allows people to experience alternate lives, Douglas Quaid becomes a hunted man, told by pursuing authorities that he is not who he has assumed he is all along.
Remake of the 1990 TriStar film that starred Arnold Schwarzenegger, Rachel Ticotin, and Sharon Stone.

Kate Beckinsale

Kate Beckinsale, Bryan Cranston © Columbia Pictures

Robert Capron, Zachary Gordon, Peyton List

Robert Capron, Zachary Gordon © 20th Century Fox

DIARY OF A WIMPY KID: DOG DAYS

(20TH CENTURY FOX) Producers, Nina Jacobson, Brad Simpson; Executive Producers, Jeff Kinney, Jeremiah Samuels; Director, David Bowers; Screenplay, Maya Forbes, Wallace Wolodarsky; Based upon the 2009 book by Jeff Kinney; Photography, Anthony B. Richmond; Designer, Brent Thomas; Costumes, Monique Prudhomme; Music, Edward Shearmur; Music Supervisor, Julia Michels; Editor, Troy Takaki; a Fox 2000 Pictures presentation of a Color Force production; Dolby; Super 35 Widescreen; Color; Rated PG; 94 minutes; Release date: August 3, 2012

CAST

Greg Heffley	**Zachary Gordon**
Frank Heffley	**Steve Zahn**
Rowley Jefferson	**Robert Capron**
Rodrick Heffley	**Devon Bostick**
Susan Heffley	**Rachael Harris**
Holly Hills	**Peyton List**
Fregley	**Grayson Russell**
Chirag Gupta	**Karan Brar**
Patty Farrell	**Laine MacNeil**

Connor Fielding, Owen Fielding (Manny Heffley), Melissa Roxburgh (Heather Hills), Philip Maurice Hayes (Stan Warren), Terence Kelly (Grandpa Heffley), Bronwen Smith (Mrs. Jefferson), Alfred E. Humphreys (Mr. Jefferson), Elise Gatien (Madison), John Shaw (Mr. Draybick), Andrew McNee (Coach Malone), Tom Stevens (Lenwood Heath), Bryce Hodgson (Ben Segal), Christopher Thorgard DeSchuster (Chris the Bass Player), Dalila Bela (Taylor Pringle), Frank C. Turner (Troop Master Barrett), Emily Holmes (Mrs. Hills), Jeff Kinney (Mr. Hills), Amitai Marmorstein (Cranium Shaker Operator), Roan Curtis, Sydney Wong (Girls at Cranium Shaker), Reese Alexander (Cop), Cameron Mitchell, Jr. (Country Club Manager), Latonya Williams (Receptionist Amy), Nicole Fraissinet (Receptionist Julie), Doug Abrahams (Rodrick's Rescuer), Melody B. Choi (Snack Bar Girl), Wanda Ayala (High Diving Fan), Kyle Cassie (Country Club Waiter), Kevin James (Country Club Pool Guy), Amy Esterle (Country Club Waitress), Gerry Durand (Country Club Valet), Joshua Ballard (Spag Union Math Boy), Matt Mazur (Spag Union Tracking Device Boy), Jared Abrahamson (Tim Warren), Matteo Stefan (Biff Warren), Colin MacKechnie (Chip Warren), Sofia Bowers (Li'l Cutie), Dawn Chubai (Newscaster), Anne Openshaw (Mrs. Warren), Keith MacKechnie (Man in Kitchen), Simon Chin (Restaurant Owner), BJ Harrison (Dry Cleaner), Russell Roberts (Confederate Soldier), Paul Fisher (Spag Union Announcer), David Palacio (Spag Union Boy), Oliver (Sweetie the Dog), Hero (The Warren's Dog)

When his father insists he must work for the summer, Greg Heffley pretends that he has already gotten a job at a posh country club, allowing him to hang out with his friend Rowley and the girl he's crushing on. Third in the 20th Century Fox series following *Diary of a Wimpy Kid* (2010) and *Diary of a Wimpy Kid: Rodrick Rules* (2011).

Laine MacNeil, Robert Capron, Zachary Gordon, Peyton List

Steve Zahn, Zachary Gordon, Robert Capron, Frank C. Turner

Rashida Jones, Andy Samberg

Ari Graynor, Eric Christian Olsen

Emma Roberts © Sony Classics

Elijah Wood

CELESTE & JESSE FOREVER

(SONY CLASSICS) Producers, Lee Nelson, Jennifer Todd, Suzanne Todd; Director, Lee Toland Krieger; Executive Producers/Screenplay, Rashida Jones, Will McCormack; Photography, David Lanzenberg; Designer, Ian Phillips; Costumes, Julia Caston; Music, Sunny Levine, Zach Cowie, for Biggest Crush; Editor, Yana Gorskaya; Casting, Angela Demo, Barbara J. McCarthy; an Envision Media Arts and Team Todd production; Dolby; HD Widescreen; Color; Rated R; 91 minutes; Release date: August 3, 2012

CAST

Celeste	**Rashida Jones**
Jesse	**Andy Samberg**
Paul	**Chris Messina**
Beth	**Ari Graynor**
Tucker	**Eric Christian Olsen**
Skillz	**Will McCormack**
Riley Banks	**Emma Roberts**
Scott	**Elijah Wood**
Veronica	**Rebecca Dayan**
Max	**Rich Sommer**
Nick	**Matthew Del Negro**
Rupert	**Rafi Gavron**

Rob Huebel (Business Man Cutting in Line), Shira Lazar, Matthias Steiner (Themselves), Kate Krieger (Yogurt Girl), Andreas Beckett (German Announcer), Janel Parrish (Savannah), Jessica Joffe (Saleswoman), Chris Pine (Mystery Buddy), Zoë Hall (Waitress), Lenny Jacobson (Peter Pan), Chris D'Elia (Snow White), Sarah Haskins (Parent), Lauren Sanchez (News Reporter), Ashli Dowling (Bartender), Willy Mac (Bear), Robert Kya-Hill (Priest), Amanda MacLachlan, Sarah Wright, Jordan Reid (Bridesmaids), Joel Michaely, Philip Pavel (Gay Men), Louisa Kendrick (Celeste's Lawyer), Jason Antoon (Young Man)

On the verge of divorcing, Celeste and Jesse still come across as the perfect couple, even while making the effort to move on and find new partners in their lives.

Meryl Streep, Tommy Lee Jones

Tommy Lee Jones, Meryl Streep, Steve Carell

Meryl Streep, Jean Smart

HOPE SPRINGS

(COLUMBIA) Producers, Todd Black, Guymon Casady; Executive Producers, Steve Tisch, Jason Blumenthal, Nathan Kahane, Jessie Nelson; Co-Producers, Kelli Konop, Brian Bell, Lawrence Grey; Director, David Frankel; Screenplay, Vanessa Taylor; Photography, Florian Ballhaus; Designer, Stuart Wurtzel; Costumes, Ann Roth; Music, Theodore Shapiro; Editor, Steven Weisberg; Casting, Margery Simkin; a Columbia Pictures, Mandate Pictures, Metro-Goldwyn-Mayer Pictures presentation of a Film 360/Escape Artists production; Dolby; HD Widescreen; Deluxe color; Rated PG-13; 100 minutes; Release date: August 8, 2012

CAST

Kay	**Meryl Streep**
Arnold	**Tommy Lee Jones**
Dr. Feld	**Steve Carell**
Eileen, Kay's Friend	**Jean Smart**
Brad, Their Son	**Ben Rappaport**
Molly, Their Daughter	**Marin Ireland**
Mark, Their Son-in-Law	**Patch Darragh**
Vince, Arnold's Friend	**Brett Rice**
Cora, the Waitress	**Becky Ann Baker**
Karen, the Bartender	**Elisabeth Shue**
Charlie, the Docent	**Charles Techman**
Danny, the Bookstore Clerk	**Daniel J. Flaherty**
Mike, the Innkeeper	**Damian Young**
Carol, the Neighbor	**Mimi Rogers**

Ann Harada (Ann, the Happy Wife), Jack Haley (Jack, the Happy Husband), Susan Misner (Dana, Dr. Feld's Wife), Rony Clanton (Ronnie, the Taxi Driver), John Srednicki (John, the Waiter), Madeline Ruskin (Maddie, Brad's Girlfriend), Lee Cunningham (Lee, the Unhappy Wife), Paul J. Letersky (Paul, the Unhappy Husband), Rogina Bedell-O'Brien (Rogina, the Exiting Patient), Stephen Lee Davis (Steve, the Grocery Shopper)

Meryl Streep, Elisabeth Shue © Columbia Pictures

Frustrated by the increasing lack of physical intimacy in their lives, Kay signs herself and her reluctant husband Arnold up for a series of counseling sessions she hopes will bring them closer together once again.

THE BOURNE LEGACY

(UNIVERSAL) Producers, Frank Marshall, Patrick Crowley, Jeffrey M. Weiner, Ben Smith; Executive Producers, Henry Morrison, Jennifer Fox; Director/Story, Tony Gilroy; Screenplay, Tony Gilroy, Dan Gilroy; Inspired by the *Bourne* series of books created by Robert Ludlum; Photography, Robert Elswit; Designer, Kevin Thompson; Costumes, Shay Cunliffe; Music, James Newton Howard; Editor, John Gilroy; Special Effects Supervisors, Garry Elmendorf, Steven Kirshoff; Stunts, Chris O'Hara; Casting, Ellen Chenoweth; a Kennedy/Marshall production in association with Captivate Entertainment, presented in association with Relativity Media; Dolby; Panavision; Deluxe color; Rated PG-13; 135 minutes; Release date: August 10, 2012

CAST

Aaron Cross	**Jeremy Renner**
Dr. Marta Shearing	**Rachel Weisz**
Ret. Col. Eric Byer, USAF	**Edward Norton**
Ret. Adm. Mark Turso, USN	**Stacy Keach**
Terrence Ward	**Dennis Boutsikaris**
Outcome #3	**Oscar Isaac**
Pam Landy	**Joan Allen**
Dr. Albert Hirsch	**Albert Finney**
Noah Vosen	**David Strathairn**
Ezra Kramer	**Scott Glenn**
Dita Mandy	**Donna Murphy**
Arthur Ingram	**Michael Chernus**
Zev Vendel	**Corey Stoll**
Dr. Benezara	**Tony Guida**
Dr. Lieberburg	**Sonnie Brown**
Dr. Dan Hillcott	**Neil Brooks Cunningham**
Dr. Donald Foite	**Zeljko Ivanek**
Lean Forward MSNBC Anchor	**Alice Gainer**
CNN Reporter	**Prue Lewarne**
MSNBC Man Analyst	**Howard Leader**
Sterisyn-Morlanta Gateman	**James Joseph O'Neil**

Rob Riley (Outcome #6), Noel Wilson (Neuro Luncheon MC), Corey Johnson (Ray Wills), Jennifer Kim (Outcome #4), Page Leong (Mrs. Yun), John Douglas Thompson (Lt. Gen. Paulsen), Adi Hanash (Outcome #1), Robert Prescott (Air Force Officer), David Wilson Barnes (Drone Spec), Don Guillory (Drone Pilot), Patrick Vincent Marro (Drone Command Guard), Ali Reza (Dr. Talwar), Gita Redd (Dr. Chandra), Tom Riis Farrell, Steve Routman, Peter Lewis, Anitha Gandhi, Heather Rasche, Natalie Bird, Nilaja Sun (Blue Lab Doctors), Christopher Mann, Billy Smith (Lab Guards), Murray Knudsen (Alaska Airport Guard), Susan Egbert (DIA Attorney), Tim Devitt (FBI Honcho), Brian Poteat (State Investigator), Clayton Barber (Gene), Elizabeth Marvel (Dr. Connie Dowd), Michael Papajohn (Larry), David Leitch (The Driver), Michael Berresse (Leonard), Deidre Goodwin (Candent Spokesperson), Laura Spaeth (Walking Woman), Sam Gilroy, Rachel Black, Sharon Washington, Frank Deal, Rob Yang, Catherine Curtin, Matt Oberg, Gary Lee Mahmoud (C-Team), Faye Yvette McQueen (TSA Guard), Pat Battle (MSNBC Anchor), Nico Bernuth, Jane Jameston (Flight Attendants), Roland Manansala (Steri-M Guard), John Arcilla (Joseph), Josh Banks (Mackie's Assistant), Shane Jacobson (Mackie), Allen Jo, Jonathan Eusebio, Jon Valera (Guards), Carl Villa Roman (Sterival Catwalk Guard), Louis Ozawa Changchien (LARX #3), Madeleine Nicolas (Landlady), Ruby Ruiz (Philippine Pharmacist), Cherry Devera (Crisis Translator), Julienne Orindain (TV Girl), Antonette Garcia (TV Mom), Sonny Tuazon, Normandy Bacaltos, Edgar Letran, Alvin Zalamea, Spencer Sano (Manila Cops), Julie Ysla (Woman with the Bag), Joel Torre (Citrus Samaritan), Hermie Concepcion (Pissed-Off Guy), Arthur Acuña (Manila Driver), Adrian Talinga (Captain's Son), Lou Veloso (Captain), Ian Blackman (Landy's Attorney), Jodie Applegate Kay, Tony Carlin, Karen Pittman, Ana Berry, Matthew J. Walters, Brian O'Neill (Landy Reporters)

Under investigation for their unorthodox black ops programs, the CIA decides to eliminate all trained agents from Operation Outcome, only to have one these targeted men, Aaron Cross, escape assassination. Fourth in the *Bourne* Universal series following: *The Bourne Identity* (2002), *The Bourne Supremacy* (2004), and *The Bourne Ultimatum* (2007), all of which starred Matt Damon. Joan Allen repeats her role from the 2nd and 3rd films; Albert Finney and David Strathairn from *Ultimatum*.

Edward Norton

Jeremy Renner, Rachel Weisz

Rachel Weisz, Jeremy Renner © Universal Studios

Clarke Peters

Clarke Peters, Thomas Jefferson Byrd

RED HOOK SUMMER

(VARIANCE) Producer/Director, Spike Lee; Screenplay, James McBride, Spike Lee; Co-Producer, James McBride; Photography, Kerwin Devonish; Designer, Sarah Frank; Costumes, Emilio Sosa; Music, Bruce Hornsby; Songs, Judith Hill; Editor, Hye Mee Na; a 40 Acres and a Mule Filmworks in association with Variance Films presentation; Dolby; Technicolor; Rated R; 121 minutes; Release date: August 10, 2012

CAST

Da Good Bishop Enoch Rouse	**Clarke Peters**
Flik Royale	**Jules Brown**
Chazz Morningstar	**Toni Lysaith**
Box	**Nate Parker**
Deacon Zee	**Thomas Jefferson Byrd**
Sister Sharon Morningstar	**Heather Alicia Simms**
Blessing Rowe	**Colman Domingo**
Kevin	**James Ransone**
Colleen Royale	**De'Andre Aziza**
Sister Sweet	**Kimberly Hébert-Gregory**
Mother Darling	**Tracy Camilla Johns**
Mr. Mookie	**Spike Lee**
Cliff	**Daniel Breaker**

Stephen Henderson (Deacon Yancy), Jonathan Batiste (Da Organist TK Hazelton), Samantha Ivers (Patty), Kofi Alleyne (Butter Turron), Fred Tolliver Jr. (Born Knowledge), Lillie Marshall (Miss Marshall), Arthur French (Mr. Curtis), Quincy Tyler Bernstine (Hazel), Sincere Peters (Blessing Rowe – 12 Yrs Old), Isiah Whitlock Jr. (Det. Flood), Al Palagonia (Det. Haggerty), Eve Lora (Box's Lady), Louanne Harris (Donna, Kayak Instructor), Kalon Jackson (Husband/Father), Jackson Lee, Tyheim Smith (Kayak Kids), Nesean Smith (Lil' Budda), Jim Davis (Choir Director), Sumayya Ali, Charles Anthony Bryant, Janinah Burnett, Courtney D. Carey, Shani Foster, Kevin D. Johnson, Brian K. Major, Sakura Myers, Mari-Yan L. Pringle, Gregory A. Robinson, Moriah Scott, Charlotte Small, Briana Swann, Brandon Waddles (Lil' Peace of Heaven Baptist Church of Red Hook Choir)

Sent from his middle-class home in Atlanta to spend the summer in Brooklyn with his deeply religious grandfather, young Flik Royale faces not only the shock of inner city living but the Bishop's efforts to coax the boy into following Jesus.

Jules Brown, Toni Lysaith © Variance Films

Toni Lysaith, Clarke Peters, Jules Brown

John Lithgow, Dan Aykroyd

Zach Galifianakis

Zach Galifianakis, Dylan McDermott

THE CAMPAIGN

(WARNER BROS.) Producers, Will Ferrell, Adam McKay, Jay Roach, Zach Galifianakis; Executive Producers, Amy Sayres, Jon Poll, Chris Henchy; Director, Jay Roach; Screenplay, Chris Henchy, Shawn Harwell; Story, Adam McKay, Chris Henchy, Shawn Harwell; Photography, Jim Denault; Designer, Michael Corenblith; Costumes, Daniel Orlandi; Music, Theodore Shapiro; Editors, Craig Alpert, Jon Poll; Casting, Allison Jones; a Gary Sanchez/Everyman Pictures production; Dolby; Technicolor; Rated R; 85 minutes; Release date: August 10, 2012

CAST

Cam Brady	**Will Ferrell**
Marty Huggins	**Zach Galifianakis**
Mitch	**Jason Sudeikis**
Tim Wattley	**Dylan McDermott**
Rose Brady	**Katherine LaNasa**
Mitzi Huggins	**Sarah Baker**
Glenn Motch	**John Lithgow**
Wade Motch	**Dan Aykroyd**
Raymond Huggins	**Brian Cox**
Mrs. Yao	**Karen Maruyama**
Clay Huggins	**Grant Goodman**
Dylan Huggins	**Kya Haywood**
Cam Jr.	**Randall Cunningham**
Jessica Brady	**Madison Wolfe**
Travis	**Thomas Middleditch**
Tripp	**Josh Lawson**
Diane	**Heather Lawless**
Mr. Mendenhall	**Jack McBrayer**
Mrs. Mendenhall	**Elizabeth Wells Berkes**
Dermot	**Billy Slaughter**
Intern Jason	**Aaron Jay Rome**
Shana	**Kate Lang Johnson**
Becky	**Amelia Jackson-Gray**

Bobby Tisdale (Huggins Supporter), Wolf Blitzer, Piers Morgan, Bill Maher, Chris Matthews, Dennis Miller, Lawrence O'Donnell, Joe Scarborough, Mika Brzezinski, Willie Geist, Ed Schultz, Uggie (Themselves), P.J. Byrne (Rick – Ad Agency Guy), Patrick Weathers (Old Councilman), Gerry May (Carter Baines), Tzi Ma (Mr. Zheng), Bill Martin Williams (Senator Lloyd), Danny Vinson (Elder Dan), John D. Reaves (Banker), Scott A. Martin (Wes – Cam Brady Supporter), Rob Mariano (Boston Rob), Mike "The Miz" Mizanin (The Miz), Randy Bachman, Mick Dalla-Vee, Marc Lafrance, Brent Howard Knudsen, Charles Frederick Turner (Bachman & Turner), Danny Hanemann, Jason Kirkpatrick (Hunters), Taryn Terrell (Janette), J.D. Evermore (State Official), Matt Borel (Rainbowland Moderator), Millard Darden (Moderator Carl Terry), Mikki Val (Town Hall Moderator), Ramona Tyler (Reporter Brenda Britton), Steve Wilkins (Reporter Darren), Rowan Joseph (Reporter Gary), Dane Rhodes (Working-Class Man), Trey Burvant (Man at Debate), Joe Chrest (Rainbowland Audience), Cranston Clements, John Vidacovich, Tommy Malone (Pentecostal Band), Sion Daneshrad (Rabbi), Peaches Davis (Mrs. Cutler), George Young (Choir Director), Stephanie Dotson (Choir Soloist), Dylan DePaula (Young Cam), Seth Morris (Confession Husband), Tara Copeland (Confession Wife), Frank Drank, Luka Jones, Paul Zies (Biker Guys), Early Whitesides (Elderly Man), Leslea Fisher (Election Night Girl), Steve Tom (Congressman), Catherine Shreves (Anchor Rachel), Amber Dawn Landrum (Punched Baby's Mother), Dustan Costine (Police Officer), Tim Hickey (Patriotic Passerby), Loriel Hennington, Tyne Stecklein, Krystal Ellsworth, Kayla Radomski, Brittany Perry-Russell, Colleen Craig (Dancers)

Mudslinging escalates when long-term Congressional candidate Cam Brady, believing he is running unopposed, suddenly must go head to head with genteel, naive Marty Huggins who has been selected to run for office by a pair of corrupt power brokers.

Will Ferrell, Jason Sudeikis

Kya Haywood, Grant Goodman, Zach Galifianakis, Sarah Baker

Will Ferrell

Katherine LaNasa, Madison Wolfe, Randall Cunningham

Karen Maruyama, Zach Galifianakis © Warner Bros. Pictures

Dan Aykroyd, John Lithgow, Brian Cox, Josh Lawson

TWIXT

(PATHÉ/AMERICAN ZOETROPE) Producer/Director/Screenplay, Francis Ford Coppola; Executive Producers, Fred Ross, Anahid Nazarian; Photography, Mihai Malaimare Jr.; Art Director, Jimmy DiMarcellis; Costumes, Marjorie Bowers; Music, Dan Deacon, Osvaldo Golijov; Editors, Robert Schafer, Glen Scantelbury, Kevin Bailey; Special Makeup Effects, Aurora Bergere; Special Effects Coordinator, Doug E. Williams; an American Zoetrope production; Dolby; Color/black and white; 3D; Not rated; 90 minutes; Release date: August 10, 2012

CAST
Hall Baltimore	**Val Kilmer**
V	**Elle Fanning**
Denise	**Joanne Whalley**
Sheriff Bobby LaGrange	**Bruce Dern**
Edgar Allan Poe	**Ben Chaplin**
Sam Malkin	**David Paymer**
Flamingo	**Alden Ehrenreich**

Don Novello (Melvin), Lisa Biales (Ruth), Anthony Fusco (Pastor Allan Floyd), Ryan Simpkins (Carolyne), Lucas Rice Jordan (P.J.), Bruce A. Miroglio (Deputy Arbus), Fiona Medaris (Vicky), Katie Crom (Circe), Lucy Bunter (Library Assistant), Dorothy Tchelistcheff (Miss Gladys), Lorraine Gaudet (Operator), Stacey Mattina (Woman in Store), Marissa Lenhardt (Opera Singer), Tom Waits (The Narrator)

A down-on-his-luck writer becomes involved in the long-unsolved mystery surrounding the deaths of several children when he is contacted by the ghost of a girl who may be connected with the crime.

Val Kilmer, Elle Fanning

Val Kilmer, Bruce Dern © American Zoetrope

Yu Nan, Terry Crews, Sylvester Stallone, Randy Couture, Dolph Lundgren
© Lionsgate

THE EXPENDABLES 2

(LIONSGATE) Producers, Avi Lerner, Kevin King-Templeton, Danny Lerner, Les Weldon; Executive Producers, Jon Feltheimer, Jason Constantine, Eda Kowan, Basil Iwanyk, Guymon Casady, Danny Dimbort, Boaz Davidson, Trevor Short; Co-Producers, Robert Earl, Jib Polhemus, Matt O'Toole, Guy Ayshalom, Zygi Kamasa; Director, Simon West; Screenplay, Richard Wenk, Sylvester Stallone; Story, Ken Kaufman, David Agosto, Richard Wenk; Based on characters created by David Callaham; Photography, Shelly Johnson; Designer, Paul Cross; Costumes, Lizz Wolf; Music, Brian Tyler; Editor, Todd E. Miller; Casting, Kate Dowd; a Millennium Films presentation of a Nu Image production; Dolby; Super 35 Widescreen; Deluxe color; Rated R; 103 minutes; Release date: August 17, 2012

CAST
Barney Ross	**Sylvester Stallone**
Lee Christmas	**Jason Statham**
Yin Yang	**Jet Li**
Gunnar Jensen	**Dolph Lundgren**
Booker	**Chuck Norris**
Vilain	**Jean-Claude Van Damme**
Church	**Bruce Willis**
Trench	**Arnold Schwarzenegger**

Terry Crews (Hale Caesar), Randi Couture (Toll Road), Liam Hemsworth (Billy the Kid), Scott Adkins (Hector), Yu Nan (Maggie), Amanda Ooms (Pilar), Charisma Carpenter (Lacy), Nikolette Noel (Billy's Wife), Georgi Zlatarev (Bojan), Alexander Moskov (Stephan), Denis Vasilev (Jarek), Nikola Dodov (Sick Man), Wenbo Li (Hostage – Dr. Zhou), Borislav Zahariev (Sang Leader), Penka Kodova (Bartender), Arkanay Boonsong (Rebel Leader), Dimo Alexiev (Sang Soldier), Velislav Pavlov (Sang), Liubo Simeonov (Talking Sang), Anton Trendafilov, Marii Rosen, Julian Stanishkov, Velimir Velev (Miners), Irina Krichely, Lyudmila Slaneva, Silvia Petkova, Alexandra Spasova, Juliana Saiska, Sanya Borisova, Biliana Petrinska, Diana Dobreva (Village Women), Liubomir Simeonov (Giant Sang)

When one of their colleagues is brutally killed during a mission, Barney Ross and his team of mercenaries seek revenge on the crimelord responsible. Sequel to the 2010 Lionsgate film, with most of the principals returning to their roles.

CJ Adams, Jennifer Garner, Lin-Manuel Miranda, Joel Edgerton

Jennifer Garner, CJ Adams, Joel Edgerton © Walt Disney Studios

CJ Adams, Jennifer Garner

THE ODD LIFE OF TIMOTHY GREEN

(WALT DISNEY STUDIOS) Producers, Scott Sanders, Ahmet Zappa, Jim Whitaker; Executive Producers, John Cameron, Mara Jacobs; Director/Screenplay, Peter Hedges; Story, Ahmet Zappa; Photography, John Toll; Designer, Wynn Thomas; Costumes, Susie DeSanto; Music, Geoff Zanelli; Music Supervisor, Dana Sano; Editor, Andrew Mondshein; Special Makeup Effects Supervisor, Greg Nicotero, KNB EFX Group; Casting, Bernard Telsey; a Disney presentation of a Scott Sanders production; Dolby; Deluxe color; Rated PG; 104 minutes; Release date: August 15, 2012

CAST

Cindy Green	**Jennifer Garner**
Jim Green	**Joel Edgerton**
Timothy Green	**CJ Adams**
Joni Jerome	**Odeya Rush**
Evette Onat	**Shohreh Aghdashloo**
Brenda Best	**Rosemarie DeWitt**
James Green Sr.	**David Morse**
Uncle Bub	**M. Emmet Walsh**
Aunt Mel	**Lois Smith**
Reggie	**Lin-Manuel Miranda**
Ms. Bernice Crudstaff	**Dianne Wiest**
Franklin Crudstaff	**Ron Livingston**

James Rebhorn (Joseph Crudstaff), Common (Coach Cal), Michael Arden (Doug Wert), Rhoda Griffis (Dr. Lesley Hunt), Karan Kendrick (Mother at Doctor's Office), Shimei Bailey (Little Boy in Elevator), Judy Langford (Ms. Crudstaff's Assistant), Michael Beasley, Cullen Moss (Cops), Gene Jones (Neighbor), Jason Davis (Bart Best), Patrick Brouder (Dash Best), Kendall Sanders (Rod Best), Lucy Gebhardt (Bethany Best), Sharon Morris (Principal Morrison), Dorothy Macdonald (Trixie Crudstaff), Chan Creswell (Billy Crudstaff), William Harrison (Bobby Crudstaff), Dwayne Boyd (Ref), Mattie Liptak (#8), Jay Freer (Coach Bob Francesconi), Tim Ware (Mayor Handelman), Steve Coulter (Charlie Frohn), Susan Bruce (Molly Frohn), Josey Cuthrell Tuttleman (Lily), Tara Lee (Nurse), Joe Crosson (Factory Worker), Tim Guinee (Voice of Marty Rader), Shaun O'Banion (Voice of Alan Rust),

A couple unable to conceive a child, bury their hopes in the backyard and are shocked when a little boy suddenly appears to fulfill the vacancy in their lives.

CJ Adams, Odeya Rush

Frank Langella, Liv Tyler

Susan Sarandon, Frank Langella

Frank Langella, Robot

Jeremy Sisto © Samuel Goldwyn Films

ROBOT & FRANK

(GOLDWYN) Producers, Galt Niederhoffer, Sam Bisbee, Jackie Kelman Bisbee, Lance Acord; Executive Producers, Danny Rifkin, Bob Kelman, Tom Valerio, Jenna Schultz, Delaney Schultz, Bill Perry, Jeremy Bailer, Ann Porter; Co-Producers, Erika Hampson, Cody Ryder; Director, Jake Schreier; Screenplay, Christopher Ford; Photography, Matthew J. Lloyd; Designer, Sharon Lomofsky; Costumes, Erika Munro; Music, Francis and the Lights; Editor, Jacob Craycroft; a Stage 6 Films presentation of a Park Pictures film in association with White Hat Entertainment and Dog Run Pictures; Dolby; HD Widescreen; Color; Rated PG-13; 90 minutes; Release date: August 17, 2012

CAST

Frank	**Frank Langella**
Hunter	**James Marsden**
Madison	**Liv Tyler**
Jennifer	**Susan Sarandon**
Voice of Robot	**Peter Sarsgaard**
Jake	**Jeremy Strong**
Sheriff Rowlings	**Jeremy Sisto**
Robot	**Rachael Ma**

Dario Barosso (Freckles), Bonnie Bentley (Ava), Ana Gasteyer (Shoplady), Joshua Ormond (Flattop), Katherine Waterston (Shopgirl), James D. Compton (Skinny Sheriff)

Over his objections, an aging, one-time thief is given a robot by his children to assist him through his daily duties, so the old man decides to use the appliance for his own illegal means.

Mike Epps, Carmen Ejogo

Tika Sumpter, Carmen Ejogo, Jordin Sparks

SPARKLE

(TRISTAR) Producers, Debra Martin Chase, T.D. Jakes, Salim Akil, Mara Brock Akil, Curtis Wallace; Executive Producers, Whitney Houston, Howard Rosenman, Gaylyn Fraiche, Avram Buch Kaplan; Director, Salim Akil; Screenplay, Mara Brock Akil; Story, Joel Schumacher, Howard Rosenman; Photography, Anastas Michos; Designer, Gary Frutkoff; Costumes, Ruth E. Carter; Music, Salaam Remi; Executive Music Consultant, R. Kelly; Choreographer, Fatima Robinson; Editor, Terilyn A. Shropshire; Casting, Tracy "Twinkie" Byrd; a Debra Martin Chase/T.D. Jakes/Akil Productions production, presented in association with Stage 6 Films; Dolby; HD Widescreen; Deluxe color; Rated PG-13; 116 minutes; Release date: August 17, 2012

CAST

Sparkle	**Jordin Sparks**
Emma	**Whitney Houston**
Stix	**Derek Luke**
Satin	**Mike Epps**
Sister	**Carmen Ejogo**
Dolores	**Tika Sumpter**
Levi	**Omari Hardwick**
Black	**Cee-Lo Green**
Larry	**Curtis Armstrong**
Red	**Terrence J**

Tamela Mann (Ms. Sara Waters), Michael Beach (Rev. Bryce), Bre'ly Evans (Tune Ann), Linda Boston (Sister Clora), Sidi Henderson (Mr. Bell), Erika Hoveland (Larry's Secretary), Debra Port (Receptionist), Kem L. Owens (Buddy), Sarah Hansen (Heckler), Doug Mingo (Goofy Guy), Mark Rademacher (Filmore Manager), David Regal (Stage Manager), Cory Pritchett (Ham), Howard Rosenman (Landlord), Robert Forte Shannon (Stix's Opponent), Margaret Scott (Church Saint), Goapele Mohlabane (Girl Group – Lead Singer), Fatima Morris, Keeley Morris (Girl Group – Backup Singers), Britanny Perry Russell, Charmaine Jordan (Sparkle's Backup Singer), Dalibor Stolevski (TV Host), Tiffany Alexander (Prison Guard), Stephanie Moseley, Temecha Myers (Rehearsal Dancers), Ruth E. Carter (Sugar), Melora Rivera (Hussy)

In 1968 Detroit, three sisters dream of taking their successful music act into the big time.
Remake of the 1976 film that starred Irene Cara, Philip Michael Thomas, Lonette McKee, and Dwan Smith.

Whitney Houston

Derek Luke, Omari Hardwick © TriStar

PARANORMAN

(FOCUS) Producers, Arianne Sutner, Travis Knight; Directors, Sam Fell, Chris Butler; Screenplay, Chris Butler; Photography, Tristan Oliver; Designer, Nelson Lowry; Costumes, Deborah Cook; Music, Jon Brion; Editor, Christopher Murrie; Lead Animators, Travis Knight, Jeff Riley, Payton Curtis; Animation Supervisor, Brad Schiff; Character Designer, Heidi Smith; Visual Effects Supervisor, Brian Van't Hul; Casting, Allison Jones; a LAIKA production; Dolby; Color; Widescreen; 3D; Rated PG; 92 minutes; Release date: August 17, 2012

Courtney, Norman, Alvin, Neil, Mitch © Focus Features

VOICE CAST

Norman Babcock	**Kodi Smit-McPhee**
Neil	**Tucker Albrizzi**
Courtney Babcock	**Anna Kendrick**
Mitch	**Casey Affleck**
Alvin	**Christopher Mintz-Plasse**
Sandra Babcock	**Leslie Mann**
Perry Babcock	**Jeff Garlin**
Grandma	**Elaine Stritch**
Mr. Prenderghast	**John Goodman**

Bernard Hill (The Judge), Jodelle Ferland (Aggie), Tempestt Bledsoe (Sheriff Hooper), Alex Borstein (Mrs. Henscher), Hannah Noyes (Salma), Jack Blessing (Slob Guy/Civil War Ghost), Ranjani Brow (Movie Lady), Michael Corbett (Movie Zombie), David Cowgill (Greaser Ghost), Nicholas Guest (Hippie Ghost/Mobster Ghost), Emily Hahn (Sweet Girl), Bridget Hoffman (Crystal/Parachutist Ghost/Librarian), Wendy Hoffman (Gucci Lady), Holly Klein (Hair Dryer Ghost), Alicia Lagano (Tourist), Scott Menville (Deputy Dwayne/Rapper Guy), Nick Petok, Ariel Winter (Blithe Hollow Kids), Jeremy Shada (Pug), Steve Alterman, Kirk Baily, Jacob Bertrand, Liz Bolton, Ava Benavente, Cam Clarke, Lara Cody, Caitlin Cutt, Susan Dudeck, Denis Faye, Eddie Frierson, Matthew Ford Holt, Rif Hutton, David Joliff, Ashley Lambert, Donna Lynn Leavy, Evan R. Mehta, Edie Mirman, Juan Pacheco, Kelsey Rootenberg, Joshua Stern, David Zyler (Blithe Hollow Townspersons)

An adolescent misfit, scorned by his town because he claims he can speak with ghosts, tries to stop an ancient witch's curse that has unleashed zombies upon the populace.

This film received an Oscar nomination for animated feature.

Alvin, Courtney, Mitch, Neil Norman

Norman

Norman, Neil

Ann Dowd

Dreama Walker © Magnolia Films

COMPLIANCE

(MAGNOLIA) Producers, Sophia Lin, Lisa Muskat, Tyler Davidson, Theo Sena, Craig Zobel; Executive Producers, James Belfer, Carina Alves, David Gordon Green; Director/Screenplay, Craig Zobel; Photography, Adam Stone; Designer, Matthew Munn; Costumes, Karen Malecki; Music, Heather McIntosh; Editor, Jane Rizzo; Casting, Kerry Barden, Paul Schnee; a Dogfish Pictures in association with Muskat Filmed Properties and Low Spark Films presentation of a Bad Cop/Bad Cop production; Dolby; HD Widescreen; Color; HD; Rated R; 90 minutes; Release date: August 17, 2012

CAST

Sandra	**Ann Dowd**
Becky	**Dreama Walker**
Officer Daniels	**Pat Healy**
Van	**Bill Camp**
Kevin	**Philip Ettinger**
Detective Neals	**James McCaffrey**

Matt Servitto (Supplier), Ashlie Atkinson (Marti), Nikiya Mathis (Connie), Ralph Rodriguez (Julio), Stephen Payne (Harold), Amelia Fowler (Brie), John Merolla (Customer), Desmin Borges (Officer Morris), Matt Skibiak (Robert Gilmour), Maren McKee (Daughter), Raymond McAnally (Portland Detective), George Asatrian (Convenience Store Clerk), Rebecca Henderson (Lawyer), Jeffrey Grover (Television Journalist)

The manager of a convenience store is contacted by phone by a man claiming to be a police officer who insists that one of her employees has been stealing from the business.

HIT AND RUN

(OPEN ROAD) Producers, Andrew Panay, Nat Tuck, Kim Waltrip; Executive Producers, Jim Casey, Erica Murray, Tobin Armbrust, Guy East, Nigel Sinclair; Directors, Dax Shepard, David Palmer; Screenplay, Dax Shepard; Photography, Bradley Stonesker; Designer, Emily Bloom; Costumes, Brooke Dulien; Music, Julian Wass; Editor, Keith Croket; a Panay Films and Primate production in association with Kim and Jim Productions, presented in association with Exclusive Media; Dolby; HD Widescreen; Deluxe color; Rated R; 100 minutes; Release date: August 22, 2012

CAST

Yul Perrkins (Charles Bronson)	**Dax Shepard**
Annie Bean	**Kristen Bell**
Alex Dmitri	**Bradley Cooper**
Randy Anderson	**Tom Arnold**
Debby Kreeger	**Kristin Chenoweth**
Gil Rathbinn	**Michael Rosenbaum**
Neve	**Joy Bryant**
Allen	**Ryan Hansen**
Clint Perrkins	**Beau Bridges**

Jess Rowland (Terry Rathbinn), Carly Hatter (Angella Roth), Steve Agee (Dude #1), Kal Bennett (Cashier Mary Ann), John Duff (Body Builder Catalyst), David Koechner (Sanders), Jason Bateman (Keith Yert), Nate Tuck (Pat Rickman), Matt Mosher (Student #1), Sean Hayes (Sandy Osterman), Kyla Snodgrass, Shea Snodgrass (Kids in Yard), Jamie Snodgrass (Mother in Yard), Laura Labo (Farmhouse Woman), Graham Mackie, Todd Conant, Valentina Arizo, Virginia Briscoe, Gloria Sue Holmes, Bob Noss (Naked Motel Guests)

A former criminal in the witness protection program must high-tail it out of town with his shocked girlfriend when his whereabouts are revealed to the bank robber he helped put in jail.

Joy Bryant, Bradley Cooper, Ryan Hansen © Open Road Films

Beau Bridges, Kristen Bell, Dax Shepard

Wolé Parks

PREMIUM RUSH

(COLUMBIA) Producer, Gavin Polone; Executive Producer, Mari Jo Winkler-Ioffreda; Director, David Koepp; Screenplay, David Koepp, John Kamps; Photography, Mitchell Amundsen; Designer, Thérèse DePrez; Costumes, Luca Mosca; Music, David Sardy; Editors, Jill Savitt, Derek Ambrosi; Stunts, Stephen Pope; Casting, John Papsidera, Pat McCorkle; a Pariah production; Dolby; Super 35 Widescreen; Deluxe color; Rated PG-13; 91 minutes; Release date: August 24, 2012

CAST
Wilee	**Joseph Gordon-Levitt**
Bobby Monday	**Michael Shannon**
Vanessa	**Dania Ramirez**
Nima	**Jamie Chung**
Manny	**Wolé Parks**
Raj	**Aasif Mandvi**
Mr. Leung	**Henry O**
Bike Cop	**Christopher Place**

Sean Kennedy (Marco), Kymberly Perfetto (Polo), Anthony Chisholm (Tito), Ashley Austin Morris (Receptionist), Kevin Bolger (Squid), Lauren Ashley Carter (Phoebe), Charles Borland (Campus Guard), Aaron Tveit (Kyle, Student), Amy Hohn (Upper West Side Lady), Doug Williams (Desk Officer), Sebastian La Cause, Nick Damici (Detectives), Kelvin Whui (Dealer), Henry Kwan, Keenan Leung, Wally Ng, Nancy Eng, Zhao Mao Chen (Lin's Pai Gow Players), Brian Koppleman (Loan Shark), Hoon Lee, Lyman Chen (Floor Managers), Boyce Wong (Mr. Lin), Jimmy P. Wong (Enormous Asian Man), Kenny Wong (2nd Asian Man), Jade Wu (Bingo Caller), Huang Gian Jin, Tony Cheng, Li Jing Xian, Lam Yung, Hui Yuk Lung (Basement Pai Gow Players), Darlene Violette (Debra), Kin Shing Wong (Sodoku Man), Jason A. Iannacone (21st Precinct Cop), Ted Sod (Worker), Alexis Krauss, Derek Miller (Sleigh Bells), Carsey Walker Jr. (Dread), Matthew Rauch (Paramedic), Michael Leon-Wooley (NYPD Tow Truck Driver), Victor Chan (Squad Cop), PJ Sosko, Jerry Walsh (Uniformed Cops – Impound Lot), Ruth Zhang (Nima's Mom), Bojun Wang (Nima's Son), Richard Hsu (Clipboard Guy – China), Mario D'Leon (Moosey), Kate Manning (Bike Chick), Fernando Rivera (Cyclehawk Guy), Djani Johnson (Johnny), Wai Ching Ho (Sister Chen)

A Manhattan bicycle messenger is pursued by a dangerous and determined cop when he is asked to deliver a valuable ticket that will benefit whoever is in possession of it.

Joseph Gordon-Levitt, Dania Ramirez

Joseph Gordon-Levitt

Joseph Gordon-Levitt, Michael Shannon © Columbia Pictures

SLEEPWALK WITH ME

(IFC FILMS) Producers, Ira Glass, Jacob Jaffke; Executive Producers, Brian Bedol, Ken Lerer, Alissa Shipp; Co-Executive Producer, Mike Lavoie; Director, Mike Birbiglia; Co-Director, Seth Barrish; Screenplay, Mike Birbiglia, Ira Glass, Joe Birbiglia, Seth Barrish; Based on the 2008 play by Mike Birbiglia; Photography, Adam Beckman; Designer, Tania Bijlani; Costumes, Ciera Wells; Music, Andrew Hollander; Music Supervisor, Anthony Roman, Lilah Wilson; Editor, Geoffrey Richman; Casting, Jennifer Euston; a Bedrocket Entertainment and Official Comedy presentation in association with WBEX Chicago's This American Life and Secret Public Productions; Color; Rated PG-13; 90 minutes; Release date: August 24, 2012

CAST

Matt Pandamiglio	**Mike Birbiglia**
Abby	**Lauren Ambrose**
Janet	**Cristin Milioti**
Frank	**James Rebhorn**
Linda	**Carol Kane**
Aunt Lucille	**Marylouise Burke**
Uncle Max	**Loudon Wainwright III**

Kevin Barnett (Comic #2), Alice Blythe, Ludwig Persik, James Head, Davlyn Grant (A Cappelas), Alberto Bonilla (Wedding Coordinator), Danny Borbon (Tommy), Hannibal Buress (Hannibal), Christopher Cantwell (Overzealous Student), Aya Cash (Hannah), Teddy Cañez (Pedro), Wyatt Cenac (Chris), James Creque (Interviewer), Romeo D'Costa (Sleep Technician), William C. Dement (Dr. Dement), Lucy DeVito (Hilary), Phillip Ettinger (Doug), James Fauvell (The Pool Guy), Marcia M. Francis (College Student), Ira Glass (Wedding Photographer), Justin Harris (Groomsman), Edward James Hyland (General), Sondra James (Colleen), Chike Johnson (Lieutenant), Alex Karpovsky (Ian Gilmore), Maggie Kemper (The Mother), Azhar Khan (Tow Truck Driver), Jessi Klein (Lynn), Ben Levin (Phillip), John Lutz (Chip), Marc Maron (Marc Mulheren), Emily Meade (Samantha), Santos Morales (Large Adult Man), Ron Nakahara (Ron), Mena Nerurkar (The Realtor), Amanda Perez (Tammy), Henry Phillips (Henry), Chavez Ravine (Cleaning Lady), Anderson Chan (Groom's Friend), Kristen Schaal (Cynthia), Amy Schumer (Amy), Jason Selvig (Dave), Nate Steinwachs (College Student), Ray Thomas (Dr. Regan), David Wain (Pete), Alan Wilkis (Guitar Strumming Emcee), Angelic Zambrana (Melissa)

A struggling stand-up comedian must also cope with a stagnant relationship and insomnia.

Mike Birbiglia, Lauren Ambrose, Carol Kane, James Rebhorn

Mike Birbiglia, Danny Borbon, Amanda Perez © IFC Films

© Oscilloscope Laboratories

SAMSARA

(OSCILLOSCOPE) Producer, Mark Magidson; Director/Photography, Ron Fricke; Concept and Treatment, Ron Fricke, Mark Magidson; Music, Michael Stearns, Lisa Gerrard, Marcello de Francisi; Line Producer, Myles Connolly; a Magidson Films presentation; Dolby; Color; Super Panavision 70; Not rated; 99 minutes; Release date: August 24, 2012. A plotless travelogue of various stunning images throughout the world.

Gary Oldman

Shia LaBeouf, Mia Wasikowska

LAWLESS

(WEINSTEIN CO.) Producers, Douglas Wick, Lucy Fisher, Megan Ellison, Michael Benaroya; Executive Producers, Dany Wolf, Rachel Shane, Jason Blum, Scott Hanson, Cassian Elwes, Laura Rister, Robert Ogden Barnum, Ted Schipper, Randy Manis, Ben Sachs; Co-Producers, John Allen, Matthew Budman; Co-Executive Producers, Clayton Young, James Lejsek; Director, John Hillcoat; Screenplay, Nick Cave; Based on the 2008 book *The Wettest County in the World* by Matt Bondurant; Photography, Benoit Delhomme; Designer, Chris Kennedy; Costumes, Margot Wilson; Music, Nick Cave, Warren Ellis; Editor, Dylan Tichenor; Visual Effects Supervisors, Bill Taylor, Mark Stetson, Dick Edwards, Mark O. Forker; Casting, Francine Maisler, Kathleen Driscoll-Mohler; a Benaroya Pictures and Filmnation Entertainment presentation in association with Annapurna Pictures of a Douglas Wick/Lucy Fisher production, a Blumhansonallen Films production,; Dolby; HD Widescreen; Technicolor; HD; Rated R; 115 minutes; Release date: August 29, 2012

CAST
Jack Bondurant	**Shia LaBeouf**
Forrest Bondurant	**Tom Hardy**
Howard Bondurant	**Jason Clarke**
Charlie Rakes	**Guy Pearce**
Maggie Beauford	**Jessica Chastain**
Bertha Minnix	**Mia Wasikowska**
Cricket Pate	**Dane DeHaan**
Danny	**Chris McGarry**
Mason Wardell	**Tim Tolin**
Floyd Banner	**Gary Oldman**

Lew Temple (Deputy Henry Abshire), Marcus Hester (Deputy Jeff Richards), Bill Camp (Sheriff Hodges), Alex Van (Tizwell Minnix), Noah Taylor (Gummy Walsh), Mark Ashworth, Tom Proctor (Hopheads), Bruce McKinnon (Jimmy Turner), Eric Mendenhall (Spoons Rivard), Toni Byrd (Ida Belle), Robert T. Smith (Young Jack), Jake Nash (Young Forrest), William J. Harrison (Young Howard), Joyce Baxter (Aunt Winnie), Jeff Braun (Doctor), Malinda Baker (Young Black Girl), Tom Turbiville (Goon #1), Chad Randall, Terry Keasler (Muggers), Duncan Nicholson (Junior), Ron Clinton Smith, Ricky Muse (Bootleggers), Anna House (Old Mountain Woman), Peter Krulewitch (Stogie Pete)

After years of running a successful bootlegging trade in Franklin County, Virginia, the Bondurant Brothers business is threatened by the appearance of a ruthless special deputy dead-set on destroying their operations

Tom Hardy, Jessica Chastain © Weinstein Company

Dane DeHaan, Guy Pearce

Lauren Anne Miller, Ari Graynor

Lauren Anne Miller

Justin Long © Focus Features

FOR A GOOD TIME, CALL …

(FOCUS) Producers, Katie Anne Naylon, Lauren Anne Miller, Josh Kesselman, Jen Weinbaum, Jenny Hinkey; Executive Producers, Daniel M. Miller, Ari Graynor, Joe Nasser, Jack Nasser; Director, Jamie Travis; Screenplay, Katie Anne Naylon, Lauren Anne Miller; Photography, James Laxton; Designer, Sue Tebbutt; Costumes, Maya Lieberman; Music, John Swihart; Editor, Evan Henke; Casting, Angela Demo, Barbara J. McCarthy; an AdScott Pictures production in association with Anne in the Middle, Principal Entertainment, Nasser Entertainment Group; Dolby; HD Widescreen; Color; Rated R; 85 minutes; Release date: August 31, 2012

CAST

Katie Steele	**Ari Graynor**
Lauren Powell	**Lauren Anne Miller**
Jesse	**Justin Long**
Sean	**Mark Webber**
Charlie	**James Wolk**
Rachel Rodman	**Nia Vardalos**
Adele Powell	**Mimi Rogers**
Scott Powell	**Don McManus**
Krissy	**Sugar Lyn Beard**
Morty	**Steven Shaw**
Jerry	**Seth Rogen**
Harold	**Ken Marino**
Cabbie	**Kevin Smith**

Lawrence Mandley (Henry), Eddie Geller (Drunk Guy), Josh Ruben (Lamp Guy), Martha MacIsaac (Inmate), The Legend of Zelda Miller-Rogen (Zelda), Kimberly Cossette (Pole Dancing Instructor)

In need of a roommate, Katie Steele ends up reluctantly sharing her apartment with a once-hated rival whom she convinces to join her in running a phone sex hotline in order to pay the bills.

Ari Graynor, Justin Long, Lauren Anne Miller

THE GOOD DOCTOR

(MAGNOLIA) Producers, Jonathan King, Dan Etheridge, Orlando Bloom; Executive Producers, Leonid Lebedev, Sharon Miller; Co-Producer, Julia Lebedev; Line Producer, Samson Mucke; Director, Lance Daly; Screenplay, John Enbom; Photography, Yaron Orbach; Designer, Eve Cauley Turner; Costumes, Jill Newell; Editor, Emer Reynolds; Casting, Jeanne McCarthy, Nicole Abellera; a Code Red Productions presentation of a King/Etheridge Production in association with Viddywell; Dolby; HD Widescreen; Color; Rated PG-13; 90 minutes; Release date: August 31, 2012

CAST

Dr. Martin Blake	**Orlando Bloom**
Diane Nixon	**Riley Keough**
Nurse Theresa	**Taraji P. Henson**
Dr. Waylans	**Rob Morrow**
Jimmy	**Michael Peña**
Dan	**Troy Garity**
Detective Krauss	**J.K. Simmons**

Molly Price (Mrs. Nixon), Wade Williams (Mr. Nixon), Sorel Carradine (Valerie), Gary Cervantes (Mr. Sanchez), Monique Gabriela Curnen (Nurse Maryanne), Jean St. James (Nurse Carol), David Clennon (Dr. Harbison), Courtney Ford (Stephanie), Marin Hinkle (Dr. Sayler), Rick Irwin (Dr. Alex Schwartz), Nathan Keyes (Rich), Noel Thurman (Mandy Claypool), Jason Axinn, Kenneth Mark Bhan, Izumi, Elizabeth Saydah (Resident Doctors), Michelle Cates (ICU Nurse), James Kimball (Anesthesiologist), Tina Martin, Julie McKinnon (Nurses), Randall Park (Clerk), Gary Slevers (Patient), Alex Zubarev (Little Boy)

An ambitious young doctor becomes so obsessed with a young girl who has been admitted to the hospital for a kidney infection that he stoops to unethical means to keep her there.

Orlando Bloom, Riley Keough

Taraji P. Henson, Orlando Bloom © Magnolia Films

Matisyahu, Natasha Calis © Lionsgate

Madison Davenport, Kyra Sedgwick

THE POSSESSION

(LIONSGATE) Producers, Sam Raimi, Robert Tapert, J.R. Young; Executive Producers, Stan Wertlieb, Peter Schlessel, John Sacchi, Nathan Kahane, Joe Drake, Michael Paseornek, Nicole Brown; Line Producer, Shawn Williamson; Director, Ole Bornedal; Screenplay, Juliet Snowden, Stiles White; Photography, Dan Laustsen; Designer, Rachel O'Toole; Costumes, Carla Hetland; Music, Anton Sanko; Music Supervisor, Linda Cohen; Editor, Eric L. Beason; Casting, Nancy Nayor; a Ghost House Pictures presentation; Dolby; Super 35 Widescreen; echnicolor; Rated PG-13; 91 minutes; Release date: August 31, 2012

CAST

Clyde	**Jeffrey Dean Morgan**
Stephanie	**Kyra Sedgwick**
Em	**Natasha Calis**
Professor McMannis	**Jay Brazeau**
Hannah	**Madison Davenport**
Brett	**Grant Show**
Tzadok	**Matisyahu**

Rob LaBelle (Russell), Nana Gbewonyo (Darius), Anna Hagan (Eleanor), Brenda Crichlow (Miss Shandy), Iris Quinn (Doctor), Graeme Duffy (Lab Tech), David Hovan (Adan), Chris Shields (Assistant Coach), Adam Young (Preston), Jim Thorburn (First Responder), Quinn Lord (Student), Nimet Kanji (Nurse Patty), James O'Sullivan (Pest Control Guy), Marilyn Norry (Principal), Armin Chaim Konfeld (Rebbe Shah), John Cassini (Stephanie's Attorney), Josh Whyte (Player), Greg Rogers (Dr. Walterson), Agam Darshi (Court Representative), Jarett John (Moss), Timothy Paul Perez (Officer), Cameron Sprague (Abyzou), Jordan Stein (Hasidic Teen), Charles Siegel, Ari Solomon, Alex Bruhanski, Richard Newman, Robert Morrissette (Hasidim), Sol Pavony (Hasidic Rabbi), Erin Simms (Possessed Italian Girl), Frank Ferrucci (Italian Priest), Sharmaine Yeoh (Possessed Islamic Girl), Antoine Safi (Islamic Exorcist), Ned Bellamy (Trevor)

A teenager purchases a strange box, unaware that it contains a deadly spirit that quickly takes possession of the unwitting girl.

Zoe Saldana, Bradley Cooper

Nora Arnezeder, Ben Barnes

Bradley Cooper, Michael McKean

THE WORDS

(CBS FILMS) Producers, Jim Young, Tatiana Kelly, Michael Benaroya; Executive Producers, Laura Rister, Cassian Elwes, Lisa Wilson, Bradley Cooper; Co-Producers, Ben Sachs, James Lejsek, Rose Ganguzza; Directors/Screenplay, Brian Klugman, Lee Sternthal; Photography, Antonio Calvache; Designer, Michèle LaLiberté; Costumes, Simonetta Mariano; Music, Marcelo Zarvos; Music Supervisor, Laura Katz; Editor, Leslie Jones; Casting, Eyde Belasco; a Benaroya Pictures presentation in association with Parlay Films and Waterfall Media of an Animus Films and Serena Films production; Dolby; Super 35 Widescreen; Color; Rated PG-13; 97 minutes; Release date: September 7, 2012

CAST

Rory Jansen	**Bradley Cooper**
The Old Man	**Jeremy Irons**
Clay Hammond	**Dennis Quaid**
Daniella	**Olivia Wilde**
Dora Jansen	**Zoe Saldana**
Celia	**Nora Arnezeder**
Rory's Father	**J.K. Simmons**
Nelson Wylie	**Michael McKean**
Timothy Epstein	**Ron Rifkin**
Young Man	**Ben Barnes**

John Hannah (Richard Ford), Zeljko Ivanek (Joseph Cutler), Vito DeFilippo (New York Apartment Doorman), Lucinda Davis (Vendor), James Babson (Dam Zuckerman), Kevin Desfosses (Rory's Assistant), Brian Klugman (Jason Rosen), Elizabeth Stauber (Carny Rosen), Gianpaolo Venuta (Dave Farber), Raphael Grosz-Harvey, Brent Skagford, Andrew MacKay (Soldiers), Gloria Cooper (Rory's Mother), Weston Middleton (Nick Weinstein), Lee Sternthal (Brett Cropsey), Holden Wong, Daniel Gervais (Fordham's Assistants), Anders Yates (Clay Hammond's Assistant), Jean-Marie Montarbut (Paris Doctor), Robert Paul Chauvelot (Conductor), Leni Parker (Journalist), Sebastien Pilotte (Celia's Husband), Emile Rivard (Celia's Child), David Gow (Hotel Desk Clerk), Kathleen Fee (Woman on the Bus), Keeva Lynk (Cynthia), Jeanie Hackett (Joyce Weinstein), Gordon Masten (Elderly Man), Jude Beny (Elderly Woman), Mark Camacho (Fan)

A struggling writer seizes his chance at success when he stumbles upon a decades old manuscript and decides to pass the book off as his own.

Bradley Cooper, Jeremy Irons © CBS Films

Christopher Abbott, Melanie Lynskey

Blythe Danner © Oscilloscope Laboratories

HELLO I MUST BE GOING

(OSCILLOSCOPE) Producers, Mary Jane Skalski, Hans Ritter; Co-Producer, Susan Leber; Director, Todd Louiso; Screenplay, Sara Koskoff; Photography, Julie Kirkwood; Designer, Russell Barnes; Costumes, Bobby Frederick Tilley II; Music, Laura Veirs; Editor, Tom McArdle; Casting, Kerry Barden, Paul Schnee, Allison Estrin; an Enjoy Your Gum Pictures presentation of a Next Weeekend/Skyscraper Films production of a Momus & Klamm film; Dolby; Color; Rated R; 95 minutes; Release date: September 7, 2012

CAST
Amy	**Melanie Lynskey**
Ruth	**Blythe Danner**
Stan	**John Rubinstein**
Jeremy	**Christopher Abbott**
David	**Dan Futterman**
Gwen	**Julie White**

Sara Chase (Missy), Daniel Eric Gold (Noah), Damian Young (Larry Hammer), David T. Koenig (Gary), Meera Simhan (Karen), Jimmi Simpson (Phil), Andrea Bordeaux (Hostess), Tori Feinstein (Caley), Eli Koskoff (Teenager), Kate Arrington (Courtney), Darcy Hicks (Stacia), Greta Lee (Gap Girl), Andreina Sosa-Keifer (Private Caterer)

Following her divorce, Amy moves back in with her parents to start life anew, which includes having an affair with a 19-year-old actor.

BACHELORETTE

(RADiUS-TWC) Producers, Jessica Elbaum, Will Ferrell, Adam McKay, Brice Dal Farra, Claude Dal Farra, Lauren Munsch; Executive Producers, Chris Henchy, Paul Prokop, Jason Janego, Tom Quinn; Co-Producers, Leslye Headland, Carly Hugo, Matt Parker; Director/Screenplay, Leslye Headland, based on her 2010 play; Photography, Doug Emmett; Designer, Richard Hoover; Costumes, Anna Bingemann; Music, Andrew Feltenstein, John Nau; Music Supervisors, Jim Black, Dana Sano, Libby Umstead; Editor, Jeffrey Wolf; Casting, Jennifer Euston; a Strategic Motion Ventures presentation of a BCDF Pictures and Gary Sanchez Productions production; Dolby; HD Widescreen; Color; Rated R; 87 minutes; Release date: September 7, 2012

CAST
Regan	**Kirsten Dunst**
Katie	**Isla Fisher**
Gena	**Lizzy Caplan**
Trevor	**James Marsden**
Joe	**Kyle Bornheimer**
Becky	**Rebel Wilson**

Adam Scott (Clyde), Ann Dowd (Victoria), Hayes MacArthur (Dale), Andrew Rannells (Manny), Ella Rae Peck (Stefanie), Paul Corning (Jack Johnson Guy), Anna Rose Hopkins (Club Monaco Customer), Sue Jean Kim (Wedding Planner), Horatio Sanz (Barely Attractive Guy), Megan Neuringer, Leslie Meisel (Singing Cousins), Jenn Schatz (Geeky Bridesmaid), Beth Hoyt (Anorexic Bridesmaid), Shauna Miles (Theresa), Arden Myrin (Melissa), Melissa Stephens (Wasted Stripper), Chris Cardona (Scores Bouncer), June Diane Raphael (Cool Stripper), Candy Buckley (Sheila), Alden Ford (Photographer), Erik Parian (Band Singer)

Self-involved Regan and her two, equally shallow friends, Gena and Katie, are horrified to discover that plain, overweight Becky will be the first of their high school friends to get married.

Isla Fisher, Lizzay Caplan, Kirsten Dunst © Weinstein Company

Zachary Booth, Thure Lindhadt

Thure Lindhardt, Zachary Booth

Thure Lindhardt, Zachary Booth

Thure Lindhardt © Music Box Films

KEEP THE LIGHTS ON

(MUSIC BOX FILMS) Producers, Marie Therese Guirgis, Lucas Joaquin, Ira Sachs; Executive Producers, Ali Betil, Jawal Nga, Adam Hohenberg, Lars Knudsen, Jay Van Joy; Associate Producers, Iddo Patt, Alex Scharfman; Director, Ira Sachs; Screenplay, Ira Sachs, Mauricio Zacharias; Photography, Thimios Bakatakis; Designer, Amy Williams; Costumes, Elisabeth Vastola; Music, Arthur Russell; Editor, Affonso Gonçalves; Music Supervisor, Susan Jacobs; Casting, Avy Kaufman; a Parts and Labor, Post FactoryNY Films, Alarum Pictures and Film 50 presentation; Color; Not rated; 102 minutes; Release date: September 7, 2012

CAST

Erik Rothman	**Thure Lindhardt**
Paul Lucy	**Zachary Booth**
Herself	**Marilyn Neimark**
Karen	**Paprika Steen**
Russ	**Sebastian La Cause**
Claire	**Julianne Nicholson**
Katie	**Sarah Hess**
Katie's Mom	**Roberta Kirshbaum**
Katie's Cousin	**Jamie Petrone**
Vivian	**Maria Dizzia**
Esther	**Stella Schnabel**
Jill	**Jodie Markell**
Dan	**Justin Reinsilber**
Alassane	**Souléymane Sy Savané**

James Bidgood, John Michael Cox Jr., Henry Arango, Agosto Machado (Themselves), Ed Vassallo (Thomas), Miguel del Toro (Igor), Calder Kusmierski Singer (Club Kid), Shane Stackpole (Luca), Chris Lenk (Hustler)

Erik's nearly decade-long relationship with Paul is constantly challenged by the latter's drug dependency.

Laetitia Casta, Richard Gere

Brit Marling, Richard Gere

Susan Sarandon, Richard Gere © Roadside Attractions

ARBITRAGE

(ROADSIDE ATTRACTIONS/LIONSGATE) Producers, Laura Bickford, Kevin Turen, Justin Nappi, Robert Salerno; Executive Producers, Brian Young, Mohammaed Al Turki, Lisa Wilson, Stanislaw Tyczynski, Lauren Versel, Maria Teresea Arida, Ron Curtis; Director/Screenplay, Nicholas Jarecki; Photography, Yorick Le Saux; Designer, Beth Mickle; Costumes, Joseph G. Aulisi; Music, Cliff Martinez; Music Supervisor, Michael Perlmutter; Editor, Douglas Crise; Casting, Laura Rosenthal; a Green Room Films and TreeHouse Pictures presentation of a co-production of Parlay Films, LB Productions, Artina Films in association with Alvernia Studios, Lucky Monkey Pictures; Dolby; Super 35 Widescreen; Deluxe color; Rated R; 107 minutes; Release date: September 14, 2012

CAST

Robert Miller	**Richard Gere**
Ellen Miller	**Susan Sarandon**
Det. Michael Bryer	**Tim Roth**
Brooke Miller	**Brit Marling**
Julie Côte	**Laetitia Casta**
Jimmy Grant	**Nate Parker**
Syd Felder	**Stuart Margolin**
Gavin Briar	**Chris Eigeman**
James Mayfield	**Graydon Carter**
Chris Vogler	**Bruce Altman**
Jeffrey Greenberg	**Larry Pine**

Curtiss Cook (Det. Mills), Reg E. Cathey (Earl Monroe), Felix Solis (A.D.A. Deferlito), Tibor Feldman (Judge Rittenband), Austin Lysy (Peter Miller), Monica Raymund (Reina), Gabrielle Lazure (Sandrine Côte), Shawn Elliott (Flores), Sophie Curtis (Ava Stanton), Ted Neustadt (Ben), Maria Bartiromo (Herself), David Faber (CNBC Newscaster), Josh Pais (John Aimes), Paul Fitzgerald (Paul Barnes), Julian Niccolini (Four Seasons Maitre'd), Evelina Oboza (Julie's Assistant), Alyssa Sutherland (Jeffrey's Receptionist), Paula Devicq (Cindy), Io Bottoms (Mae), Zack Robidas (Tom), Betsy Aidem (Vogler's Secretary), Sam Kitchin (Brent), Glen Lee (Robert's Houseman), Jennifer Lee Crowl (Receptionist), Quinn Friedman, Olivia Salerno, Tyler Turen (Grandchildren), Michael Leif O'Brien (Painter), Angel Picard-Ami (Woman in Gallery), Jamie Johnson (Julie's Suitor)

A hedge fund billionaire trying to unload his company and its debts on an unsuspecting buyer ends up having to pull off an even greater deception following an accident that puts the police on his trail.

Nate Parker

10 YEARS

(ANCHOR BAY) Producers, Marty Bowen, Wyck Godfrey, Channing Tatum, Reid Carolin; Executive Producers, Scott Lumpkin, Frank Mancuso Jr., Eric Gores; Co-Producer, Adam Londy; Director/Screenplay, Jamie Linden; Photography, Steve Fierberg; Designer, Kara Lindstrom; Costumes, Trayce Field; Music, Chad Fischer; Music Supervisor, Season Kent; Editor, Jake Pushinsky; a Boss Media presentation of a Temple Hill/Iron Horse production; Dolby; Color; Rated PG-13; 100 minutes; Release date: September 14, 2012

Channing Tatum, Rosario Dawson

CAST

Anna	**Lynn Collins**
Mary	**Rosario Dawson**
Jess	**Jenna Dewan-Tatum**
Garrity	**Brian Geraghty**
Sam	**Ari Graynor**
Reeves	**Oscar Isaac**
Paul	**Ron Livingston**
Marty	**Justin Long**
Andre	**Anthony Mackie**
Elise	**Kate Mara**
AJ	**Max Minghella**
Olivia	**Aubrey Plaza**
Scott	**Scott Porter**
Cully	**Chris Pratt**
Jake	**Channing Tatum**

Eiko Nijo (Suki), Kelly Noonan (Julie), Aaron Yoo (Peter Jung), Daniel Scott Lumpkin Jr. (Daniel), Lily Lumpkin (Lilly), Mike Miller (Photographer), Nick Zano (Nick Vanillo), Isaac Kappy (Gutterball), Sara A. Emami (Sara), Bryce Hayes (Pushy Classmate), Marie A. Kohl (Pushy Classmate's Wife), Brady Kephart (Hair Gel Guy), Kenneth McGlothin (Taller Geek), Todd Malta (Todd), Lauren Poole (Todd's Wife), Cat Stone (Cat), Alex Knight (Band Geek), Frantz Durand (Frantz), Michelle Griego (Amber Lynn), Lava Buckley (Pushy Classmate's Wife), Monique Candelaria (Amy Lee), Juliet Lopez (Becky), Rebekah Wiggins (Mona), Ivan Martin (Bartender Jerry), Antonio Spirovski (Dancer), Jack Nation (Anna's 6-year-old)

A group of friends gathers for their ten year high school reunion, where a number of unresolved issues and feelings are confronted.

Jenna Dewan Tatum, Channing Tatum © Anchor Bay

Ari Graynor, Chris Pratt

Max Minghella, Justin Long

THE MASTER

(WEINSTEIN CO.) Producers, Joanne Sellar, Daniel Lupi, Paul Thomas Anderson, Megan Ellison; Executive Producers, Adam Somner, Ted Schipper; Director/Screenplay, Paul Thomas Anderson; Photography, Mihai Malaimare Jr.; Designers, Jack Fisk, David Crank; Costumes, Mark Bridges; Music, Jonny Greenwood; Editors, Leslie Jones, Peter McNulty; Special Effects Coordinator, Michael Lantieri; Casting, Cassandra Kulukundis; a Joanne Sellar/Ghoulardi Film Company/Annapurna Pictures production; Dolby; Panavision Super 70; Deluxe color; Rated R; 136 minutes; Release date: September 14, 2012

CAST

Freddie Quell	**Joaquin Phoenix**
Lancaster Dodd	**Philip Seymour Hoffman**
Peggy Dodd	**Amy Adams**
Helen Sullivan	**Laura Dern**
Elizabeth Dodd	**Ambyr Childers**
Val Dodd	**Jesse Plemons**
Bill William	**Kevin J. O'Connor**
John Moore	**Christopher Evan Welch**
Doris Solstad	**Madisen Beaty**
Frank	**Frank Bettag**
Norman Conrad	**Martin Dew**
Wayne Gregory	**Joshua Close**
Susan Gregory	**Jillian Bell**
Cliff Boyd	**Kevin J. Walsh**
Mrs. Solstad	**Lena Endre**
Mildred Drummond	**Patty McCormack**
Margaret O'Brien	**Barbara Brownell**
Michelle Mortimer	**Brady Rubin**
Beatrice Campbell	**Jill Andre**
James Sullivan	**Barlow Jacobs**
Chi Chi Crawford	**Mimi Cozzens**
Clark	**Rami Malek**
V.A. Doctor	**Price Carson**
Rorschach Doctor	**Mike Howard**
V.A. Nurse	**Sarah Shoshana David**

Bruce Goodchild (V.A. Doctor, Interview), Matt Hering, Dan Anderson, Andrew Koponen, Jeffrey W. Jenkins, Patrick Biggs, Ryan Curtis, Jay Laurence, Abraxas Adams (V.A. Patients), Tina Bruna, Kevin Hudnell, Hunter Craig, Ryder Craig, Rodion Salnikov, Emily Gilliam, Kody Klein (Portrait Customers), Amy Ferguson (Martha the Salesgirl), W. Earl Brown (Fighting Businessman), Ariel Felix, Vladimir Velasco, John Mark Reyes, Brian Fong (Filipino Workers), Diane Cortejo (Young Filipino Woman), Leonida A. Bautista (Nana), Myrna De Dios (Angry Filipino Woman), Katie Boland (Young Woman), Lorelai Hoey (Baby), William O'Brien (Hiring Hall Voice), Zan Overall (Bartender), Brigitte Hagerman (New York Party Girl), Charley Morgan (New York Lawyer), Gigi Benson, Liz Clare, Fiona Dourif, Audrey Finer, Rose Fox, Baily Hopkins, Mari Kearney, Sarah Klaren, Ally Johnson, Brittany Kilcoyne McGregor, LaRain Ring (Dancers), David Warshofsky (Philadelphia Police), Kimberly Ables Jindra (Processing Patient), Theo Crisell (Jail Bird), Thomas Knickerbocker (Judge Phoenix), Eban Schletter (Pianist), Scott Rodgers (Drummer), Melora Walters (Vocalist), Emily Jordan, Amanda Caryn Jobbins (British Receptionists), Olivia Rosemarie Barham, Napoleon Ryan (Pub Customers), Jennifer Neala Page (Winn Manchester), Olesya Grushko (Bikini Girl)

Freddie Quell, a deeply troubled, alcoholic World War II vet, is taken under the wing of the Cause, a mysterious cult run by the charismatic Lancaster Dodd, who assures Freddie that they will be able to rid him of his demons.

This film received Oscar nominations for actor (Phoenix), supporting actor (Hoffman), and supporting actress (Adams).

Ambyr Childers, Philip Seymour Hoffman, Rami Malek

Amy Adams, Philip Seymour Hoffman, Ambyr Childers

Ambyr Childers, Rami Malek, Philip Seymour Hoffman

Madisen Beaty, Joaquin Phoenix

Joaquin Phoenix

Joaquin Phoenix

Joaquin Phoenix

Joaquin Phoenix, Philip Seymour Hoffman

Joaquin Phoenix © Weinstein Company

Jay Galloway

Amy Adams, Justin Timberlake

Clint Eastwood

John Goodman, Amy Adams, Clint Eastwood © Warner Bros. Pictures

TROUBLE WITH THE CURVE

(WARNER BROS.) Producers, Clint Eastwood, Robert Lorenz, Michele Weisler; Executive Producer, Tim Moore; Director, Robert Lorenz; Screenplay, Randy Brown; Photography, Tom Stern; Designer, James J. Murakami; Costumes, Deborah Hopper; Music, Marco Beltrami; Editor, Gary D. Roach, Joel Cox; Casting, Geoffrey Miclat; a Malpaso production; Dolby; Panavision; Technicolor; Rated PG-13; 111 minutes; Release date: September 21, 2012

CAST

Gus Lobel	**Clint Eastwood**
Mickey Lobel	**Amy Adams**
Johnny Flanagan	**Justin Timberlake**
Pete Klein	**John Goodman**
Phillip Sanderson	**Matthew Lillard**
Smitty	**Chelcie Ross**
Lucious	**Raymond Anthony Thomas**
Max	**Ed Lauter**
Neil	**Clifton Guterman**
Rosenbloom	**George Wyner**

Bob Gunton (Watson), Jack Gilpin (Schwartz), Robert Patrick (Vince), Scott Eastwood (Billy Clark), Matt Bush (Danny), Louis Fox (Lloyd), Ricky Muse (Jimmy), Tom Dreesen (Rock), James Patrick Freetly (Todd), Joe Massingill (Bo Gentry), Julia Walters (Young Mickey), Carla Fisher (Law Receptionist), Nathan Wright (Drunk Fan), Sam Collins, Chandler George Brown (Kids), Don Young, Leon Lamar (Regulars), Peter Hermann (Greg), Dane Davenport, Eric Mendenhall (Waiters), Norma Alvarez (Grace Sanchez), Tyler Silva (Carlos Sanchez), Jay Galloway (Rigo Sanchez), Melissa Lorenz (Mom in Diner), Jack Lorenz (Boy in Diner), Rory Lorenz (Girl in Diner), Dave Cohen, Rhubarb Jones (Announcers), Seth Meriwether (Wilson), Kenny Alfonso (Umpire), Josh Warren (Pitcher), Clayton Landey (Manager), Matt Brady (Swannanoa Manager), Bart Hansard (Bo's Father), Ryan Patrick Willliams, Xavier Floyd (Grizzly Players), Rus Blackwell (Rick), Brian F. Durkin (Matt Nelson), Darren Le Gallo (Nurse), Sammy Blue (Musician), Patricia French (Diner Waitress), Jackie Prucha (Secretary), Scott Estep (Umpire), Tom Nowicki (Red Sox GM), Jason Gondek (Red Sox Exec), Bud Selig (Himself), Mark Thomason (Braves Official), Cara Mantella (Assistant)

An aging baseball scout whose eyes are failing is joined by his daughter on his latest scouting trip, where she makes an effort to patch up their past differences.

DIANA VREELAND: THE EYE HAS TO TRAVEL

(GOLDWYN/EPIX) Producer/Director, Lisa Immordino Vreeland; Co-Directors/ Editors, Bent –Jorgen Perlmutt, Frederic Tcheng; Executive Producer, Jonathan Gray; Co-Executive Producer, Mark Lee; Photography, Cristobal Zanartu; Music Supervisor, Susan Jacobs; a Gloss presentation of a Mago Media production; Color; Rated PG-13; 86 minutes; Release date: September 21, 2012. Documentary on Diana Vreeland's 50-year reign as the "Empress of Fashion"

WITH

Richard Avedon, David Bailey, Lillian Bassman, Marisa Berenson, Pierre Bergé, Manolo Blahnik, June Burns Bove, Felicity Clark, Bob Colacello, Rae Crespin, Jeff Daly, Hubert de Givenchy, Oscar de la Renta, Philippe de Montebello, Polly Devlin, Simon Doonan, John Fairchild, Tonne Goodman, Carolina Herrera, Reinaldo Herrera, Anjelica Huston, Lauren Hutton, Calvin Klein, Harold Koda, Kenneth Jay Lane, Katell le Bourhis, Ali MacGraw, China Machado, Tai Missoni, Rosita Missoni, Ingrid Sischy, Barbara Slifka, Anna Sui, Joel Schumacher, Diane von Furstenberg, Veruschka von Lehndorff, Susan Train, Penelope Tree, Alexander Vreeland, Frecky Vreeland, Olivia Vreeland, Nicky Vreeland, Tim Vreeland; VOICES: Annette Miller, Jonathan Epstein.

Diana Vreeland

Diana Vreeland © Samuel Goldwyn Films

Jennifer Lawrence, Max Thieriot

Elisabeth Shue, Jennifer Lawrence © Relativity Media

HOUSE AT THE END OF THE STREET

(RELATIVITY MEDIA) Producers, Aaron Ryder, Peter Block, Hal Lieberman; Executive Producers, Steve Samuels, Anthony Visconsi II, Dominic Visconsi Jr., Allison Silver, Sonny Mallhi, Ryan Kavanaugh, Tucker Tooley; Director, Mark Tonderai; Screenplay, David Loucka; Story, Jonathan Mostow; Photography, Mirlosaw Baszak; Designer, Lisa Soper; Costumes, Susan Fijalkowska; Music, Theo Green; Music Supervisor, Steve Lindsey; Editor, Steven Mirkovich; Visual Effects Supervisors, Linus Lindblak, Tim Carras; Stunts, Laylton Morrison; Casting, John Papsidera; a FilmNation Entertainment and a Bigger Boat production; American-Canadian; Dolby; Techniscope; Deluxe color; Rated PG-13; 101 minutes; Release date: September 21, 2012

CAST

Elissa	**Jennifer Lawrence**
Ryan	**Max Thieriot**
Sarah	**Elisabeth Shue**
Weaver	**Gil Bellows**
Carrie Anne	**Eva Link**
Tyler	**Nolan Gerard Funk**

Allie MacDonald (Jillian), Jordan Hayes (Penn State Carrie Anne), Krista Bridges (Mary Jacobson), James Thomas (Ben Reynolds), Hailee Sisera (Caitlin), Craig Eldridge (Dan Gifford), Jonathan Higgins (Dr. Kohler), Olivier Surprenant (Jake), Lori Alter (Jenny Gifford), Joy Tanner (Bonnie Reynolds), Bobby Osborne (Young Ryan), Gracie Tucker (Young Carrie Anne), Will Bowes (Robbie), Jon McLaren (Zak), John Healy (John Jacobson), Jasmine Chan (Alice), Jonathan Malen (Ray), Claudia Jurt (Dr. Marianna Harrison)

After Elissa moves into a new home with her mom, she befriends Ryan, whose sister had murdered her parents four years earlier in the house next door.

Reece Thompson, Emma Watson, Logan Lerman, Mae Whitman

Logan Lerman

Logan Lerman, Ezra Miller

Emma Watson

Erin Wilhelmi, Adam Hagenbuch, Logan Lerman, Mae Whitman, Ezra Miller, Emma Watson

Erin Wilhelmi, Logan Lerman, Mae Whitman © Summit Entertainment

THE PERKS OF BEING A WALLFLOWER

(SUMMIT) Producers, Lianne Halfon, Russell Smith, John Malkovich; Executive Producers, James Powers, Stephen Chbosky; Director/Screenplay, Stephen Chbosky, based on his 1999 novel; Photography, Andrew Dunn; Designer, Inbal Weinberg; Costumes, David C. Robinson; Music, Michael Brook; Music Supervisor, Alexandra Patsavas; Editor, Mary Jo Markey; Casting, Mary Vernieu, Venus Kanani; a Mr. Mudd production; Dolby; Deluxe color; Rated PG-13; 102 minutes; Release date: September 21, 2012

Logan Lerman, Mae Whitman, Ezra Miller, Erin Wilhelmi

CAST

Charlie	**Logan Lerman**
Sam	**Emma Watson**
Patrick	**Ezra Miller**
Mary Elizabeth	**Mae Whitman**
Charlie's Mother	**Kate Walsh**
Charlie's Father	**Dylan McDermott**
Aunt Helen	**Melanie Lynskey**
Mr. Anderson	**Paul Rudd**
Brad	**Johnny Simmons**
Candace	**Nina Dobrev**
Ponytail Derek	**Nicholas Braun**
Craig	**Reece Thompson**
Dr. Burton	**Joan Cusack**
Senior Bully	**Patrick de Ledebur**
Linebacker	**Brian Balzerini**
Nose Tackle	**Tom Kruszewski**
Susan	**Julia Garner**
Mr. Callahan	**Tom Savini**
Mean Freshman Girl	**Emily Callaway**
Shakespeare Girl	**Chelsea Zhang**
Freshman Boy	**Jesse Scheirer**
Twins	**Justine Schaefer, Julie Schaefer**
7-Year-Old Charlie	**Leo Miles Farmerie**
9-Year-Old Candace	**Isabel Muschweck**
Bob	**Adam Hagenbuch**
Alice	**Erin Wilhelmi**
Rocky MC	**Jordan Paley**
Chris	**Zane Holtz**
Policeman	**Timothy J. Breslin**
Emergency Room Officer	**Mark McClain Wilson**
Emergency Room Doctor	**Atticus Cain**
Young Mom	**Stacy Chbosky**
Priest	**Dihlon McManne**
School Principal	**Laurie Klatscher**
Peter	**Landon Pigg**
Sam's Mom	**Jennifer Enskat**
Patrick's Dad	**William L. Thomas**
Candace's Friend	**Morgan Wolk**

Ezra Miller, Emma Watson

A shy freshman, troubled by past events, is taken under the wing of extroverted Patrick and his half sister Sam who try their best to coax the boy out of his shell and particate in life.

Logan Lerman, Emma Watson, Ezra Milller, Mae Whitman, Erin Wilhelmi

END OF WATCH

(OPEN ROAD) Producers, John Lesher, David Ayer, Nigel Sinclair, Matt Jackson; Executive Producers, Randall Emmett, Stepan Martirosyan, Remington Chase, Adam Kassan, Chrisann Verges, Guy East, Tobin Armbrust, Jake Gyllenhaal; Co-Producers, Alex Ott, Ian Watermeier, Julian Longnecker; Director/Screenplay, David Ayer; Photography, Roman Vasyanov; Designer, Devorah Herbert; Costumes, Mary Claire Hannan; Music, David Sardy; Music Supervisors, Season Kent, Gabe Hilfer; Casting, Mary Vernieu, Lindsay Graham; an Exclusive Media presentation in association with Emmett/Furla Films, a Le Grisbi Production in association with Crave Films; Dolby; Color; Rated R; 109 minutes; Release date: September 21, 2012

CAST

Brian Taylor	**Jake Gyllenhaal**
Miguel "Mike" Zavala	**Michael Peña**
Gabby Zavala	**Natalie Martinez**
Janet	**Anna Kendrick**
Van Hauser	**David Harbour**
Sarge	**Frank Grillo**
Orozco	**America Ferrera**
Mr. Tre	**Cle Sloan**
Captain Reese	**Jaime FitzSimons**
Davis	**Cody Horn**
Bonita	**Shondrella Avery**

Cody Horn

Everton Lawrence (Man Friend), Leequwid "Devil" Wilkins (CK), James "Pistol" McNeal (DJ), Zone (Too Tall), Alvin Norman (Peanut), Richard Cabral (Demon), Diamonique (Wicked), Maurice Compte (Big Evil), Yahira "Flakiss" Garcia (La La), Manny Jimenez Jr. (Casper), Nicholle Barreras (Cindy), Michael Monks, Hugh Daly (Homicide Detectives), Kristy Wu (Sook), David Castañeda Jr. (Mexican Cowboy), Candace Smith (Sharice), Serene Branson, Eric Garcetti (Themselves), Ramon Camacho (Tall Cowboy), Kevin Vance (Ice Agent), Corina Calderon (Jazmine), David Fernandez Jr. (Spooky), Nelly Castillo (Young Mother), McKinley Freeman (Williams), John A. Russo (LAPD Honor Guard), Tom Spencer (LAPD Chief of Police)

Jake Gyllenhaal, Anna Kendrick

Two police officers are plunged even deeper into the crime-ridden hell of South Central L.A. when they invoke the wrath of members of a dangerous drug cartel.

Michael Peña, Jake Gyllenhaal

Michael Peña, Jake Gyllenhaal © Open Road Entertainment

© Public Square Films

Peter Staley

HOW TO SURVIVE A PLAGUE

(PUBLIC SQUARE FILMS) Executive Producers, Joy Tomchin, Dan Cogan; Producers, Howard Gertler, David France; Director, David France; Screenplay, David France, T. Woody Richman, Tyler H. Walk; Photography, Derek Wiesehahn; Music, Stuart Bogie; Editors, Tyler H. Walk, T. Woody Richman; a Public Square Films presentation of a France/Tomchin film, in association with Ford Foundation/Justfilms, Impact Partners and Little Punk; 120 minutes; Color; Not Rated; Release date: September 21, 2012. Documentary on how two coalitions, ACT UP and TAG (Treatment Action Group), were instrumental in bringing attention to the AIDS crisis and getting the government agencies to develop compounds for treatment.

WITH
Bill Bahlman, David Barr, Gregg Bordowitz, Jim Eigo, Susan Ellenberg, Mark Harrington, Larry Kramer, Iris Long, Ray Navarro, Bob Rafsky, Peter Staley

This film received an Oscar nomination for documentary feature.

WON'T BACK DOWN

(20TH CENTURY FOX) Producer, Mark Johnson; Executive Producers, Ron Schmidt, Tom Williams, Michael Flaherty; Director, Daniel Barnz; Screenplay, Brin Hill, Daniel Barnz; Photography, Roman Osin; Designer, Rusty Smith; Costumes, Luca Mosca; Music, Marcelo Zarvos; Editor, Kristina Boden; Casting, Laura Rosenthal, Julie Madison, Nadia Lubbe Simon; a Walden Media presentation of a Gran Via production; Dolby; Super 35 Widescreen; Deluxe color; Rated PG; 121 minutes; Release date: September 28, 2012.

CAST

Jamie Fitzpatrick	**Maggie Gyllenhaal**
Nona Alberts	**Viola Davis**
Michael Perry	**Oscar Isaac**
Evelyn Riske	**Holly Hunter**
Breena Harper	**Rosie Perez**
Principal Thompson	**Ving Rhames**

Emily Alyn Lind (Malia Fitzpatrick), Dante Brown (Cody Alberts), Lance Reddick (Charles Alberts), Bill Nunn (Principal Holland), Ned Eisenberg (Arthur Gould), Marianne Jean-Baptiste (Olivia Lopez), Liza Colón-Zayas (Yvonne), Nancy Bach (Deborah), Keith Flippen (Ben), Robert Haley (Tim), Lucia Forte (District Receptionist), Sarab Kamoo (Principal Chamudes), Teri Clark (Cody's Teacher), Joe Coyle (Clay Bathgate), Jennifer Massey (Valerie Bathgate), Jane Mowder (Jan), Reavis Graham (Hank Hart), Anthony Marino, Jr. (Tyler), Richard Barlow (Mr. Brandt), Rebecca Harris (Ms. Southwick), Kevin Jiggetts (Mr. Mannis), Patricia Cray (Ms. Schwartz), Juan Veza (Mr. Parrish), Franklin Ojeda Smith (Mr. King), Sara Lindsey (Thompson's Assistant), Sue Jin Song, Ted Russell, Carmella Gioio (Bureaucrats), Kurt Yue (Daddy Drop-Off), Gabrielle McClinton (Babysitter), Elisa Perry (Rhonda), Dionne Audain (Adam's Parent), Becky Meister, Toni Romano (Teachers), Stephen Weigand (Riske's Assistant), Landri Shannan (Landri), Paige Nelson (Dana), Kyle Norton (Nintendo Kid), Jack Walz, Ivanna Eubanks (Kids at Lottery), Rick Applegate (School Superintendent), Julius Tennon (Thomas)

A concerned mother and a beleaguered teacher take advantage of the "parent trigger" law and decide to oust the administration from their underperforming school and take charge.

Maggie Gyllenhaal, Rosie Perez, Viola Davis © 20th Century Fox

Quasimodo, Jonathan, Dracula

Eunice, Mavis, Dracula

Mariachi Band © Sony Pictures Animation

HOTEL TRANSYLVANIA

(COLUMBIA) Producer, Michelle Murdocca; Executive Producers, Adam Sandler, Robert Smigel, Allen Covert; Co-Producer, Lydia Bottegoni; Director, Genndy Tartakovsky; Screenplay, Peter Baynham, Robert Smigel; Story, Todd Durham, Dan Hageman, Kevin Hageman; Designer, Marcelo Vignali; Art Directors, Ron Lukas, Noelle Triaureau; Character Designers, Carter Goodrich, Carlos Grangel, Craig D. Kellman; Music, Mark Mothersbaugh; Music Supervisor, Liza Richardson; Head of Layout, James C.J. Williams; Senior Animation Supervisor, James Crossley; Editor, Catherine Apple; Visual Effects Supervisor, Daniel Kramer; Casting, Mary Hidalgo; a Sony Pictures Animation film; Dolby; 3D; Deluxe color; Rated PG; 91 minutes; Release date: September 28, 2012

VOICE CAST

Dracula	**Adam Sandler**
Jonathan	**Andy Samberg**
Mavis	**Selena Gomez**
Frankenstein	**Kevin James**
Eunice	**Fran Drescher**
Wayne	**Steve Buscemi**
Wanda	**Molly Shannon**
Griffin	**David Spade**
Murray	**CeeLo Green**
Quasimodo	**Jon Lovitz**
Suit of Armor	**Brian George**

Luenell (Shrunken Heads), Brian Stack (Pilot), Chris Parnell (Fly), Jackie Sandler (Martha), Sadie Sandler (Winnie/Young Mavis), Robert Smigel (Fake Dracula/Marty), Rob Riggle (Skeleton Husband), Paul Brittain (Zombie/Hydra), Jonny Solomon (Gremlin Man/Hydra), Jim Wise (Shrunken Head/Hydra), Craig Kellman (Guy in Crowd/Hydra), Brian McCann (Hairy Monster/Hydra), James C.J. Wiliams (Foreman)

Dracula's worries about his daughter Mavis leaving the nest are compounded by the appearance at the family's hotel of a mortal lad who takes a fancy to the girl.

PITCH PERFECT

(UNIVERSAL) Producers, Paul Brooks, Max Handelman, Elizabeth Banks; Executive Producer, Scott Niemeyer; Co-Producer, Jeff Levine; Director, Jason Moore; Screenplay, Kay Cannon; Based on the 2008 book *Pitch Perfect: The Quest for Collegiate A Cappella Glory* by Mickey Rapkin; Photography, Julio Macat; Designer, Barry Robison; Costumes, Salvador Perez; Music, Christophe Beck, Mark Kilian; Executive Music Producers, Julianne Jordan, Julia Michels; Music Supervisor, Sarah Webster; Editor, Lisa Zeno Churgin; Choreographer, Aakomon "AJ" Jones; Casting, Kerry Barden, Paul Schnee; a Gold Circle Films/Brownstone production; Dolby; Color; Rated PG-13; 112 minutes; Release date: September 28, 2012

CAST

Beca	**Anna Kendrick**
Jesse	**Skylar Astin**
Fat Amy	**Rebel Wilson**
Bumper	**Adam DeVine**
Aubrey	**Anna Camp**
Chloe	**Brittany Snow**
John	**John Michael Higgins**
Gail	**Elizabeth Banks**
Benji	**Ben Platt**
Stacie	**Alexis Knapp**
Cynthia Rose	**Ester Dean**
Lilly	**Hana Mae Lee**
Jessica	**Kelley Jackle**
Denise	**Wanetah Walmsley**
Ashley	**Shelley Regner**
Mary Elise	**Caroline Fourmy**
Kori	**Nicole Lovince**

Utkarsh Ambudkar (Donald), Michael Viruet (Unicycle), David Del Rio (Kolio), John Benjamin Hickey (Dr. Mitchell), Freddie Stroma (Luke), Jinhee Joung (Kimmy Jin), Jacob Wysocki (Justin), Jawan Harris (Timothy), Richard Kohnke (Football Player – ATO), Scott Shilstone (Frat Boy – ATO), Brock Kelly (Howie – ATO), Drew Battles (Emcee at Regionals), Katrina Despain (UMass Greeter), Cameron Stewart (Tom), Kether Donahue (Alice), Karen Gonzalez (Barb), Lauren Gros, Alex Biglane (RIAC Representatives), Michael Alexander (Jewish Student), Tyler Forrest (High Note #1), Joe Lo Truglio, Har Mar Superstar, Jason Jones, Donald Faison (Clefs), Jabari Thomas (Emcee – Opening), Judd Lormand (Emcee at Semi-Finals), Christopher Mintz-Plasse (Tommy), Steven Bailey, Michael Anaya, Greg Gorenc, Brian Silver, Wes Lagarde (Trebles), Jonathan Brannan, Donald Watkins (Opening Trebles), Jessica Jain, Nate Howard (High Notes), Ben Haist, Rose Davis, Chiara Pittman, Emilia Graves, Emily Rodriguez, Sawyer McLeod, Chase Cooksey, Adam Gilbert (BU Harmonics), Megan Dupre, Brittney Alger, Monika Guiberteau, Jessica Poumaroux, Jackie Tuttle, Elizabeth Chance, Margo Melancon, Brooke Fontenot (Opening Bellas), C.J. Perry (Opening Bellas #9/Footnote #5), Maya Estephanos, Brian Mason, Xavier Joe Wilcher, Julia Friedman, Esther Long, Aakomon Jones (Sockapellas), Sora Connor, Elise Wilson, Sean Bankhead, Matthew Laraway, Madison Benson, Kenneth Tipton, Jeremy Strong, Dylan Cheek, Naeemah McCowan, Allison Sahonic, Codie L. Wiggins (Footnotes), Kelly Snow, Nathan Swedberg, Matthew Savarese, Sanford Williams, Charles Miller, Brandon Borror-Chappel, Sean McDonald, Nicholas Cafero, Alexander Fabian, Paul Ruess, Andrew O'Shanick, Samuel Brennan, Thaddeus Potter, Jacob Mainwaring, Alexander Sneider, William Laverack (Hullabaloos), Renaldo McClinton (Rapper #1), Richard Coleman, Margaret Osburn, Dan Iwrey, Ali Bloomston, Shawn Barry, Alexandra Weinroth, Ciera Dawn Washington, Felipe Fuentes (ND Auditoners), Glen Aucion (Beatboxer), Deke Sharon, Ed Boyer, Brandon Kitchel, Jasper Randall, Drew Seeley, Jeff Lewis (Male Voices), Laura Dickinson, Candice Helfand, Windy Wagner, Jessica Rotter, Kari Kimmel, Kala Blach, Emily Benford (Female Voices), Timothy Wyant (Judge)

The Barden Bellas, a college a cappella group, gathers together a group of misfit singers in hopes of dethroning the reigning champions, the Treblemakers.

Hana Mae Lee, Rebel Wilson, Ester Dean, Anna Kendrick, Alexis Knapp

Adam DeVine, Utkarsh Ambudkar, Skylar Astin, Michael Viruet

Rebel Wilson, Anna Camp © Universal Pictures

Joseph Gordon-Levitt, Noah Segan

Paul Dano, Joseph Gordon-Levitt

Joseph Gordon-Levitt, Bruce Willis

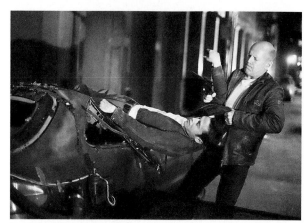

Joseph Gordon-Levitt, Bruce Willis

Jeff Daniels, Noah Segan

Joseph Gordon-Levitt, Bruce Willis

Summer Qing, Bruce Willis

Emily Blunt

LOOPER

(TRISTAR) Producer, Ram Bergman, James D. Stern; Executive Producers, Douglas E. Hansen, Julie Goldstein, Peter Schlessel, Joseph Gordon-Levitt, Dan Mintz; Co-Producers, Dave Pomier, Eleanor Nett, Lucas Smith, Christopher C. Chen; Director/Screenplay, Rian Johnson; Photography, Steve Yedlin; Designer, Ed Verreaux; Costumes, Sharen Davis; Music, Nathan Johnson; Editor, Bob Ducsay; Prosthetic Makeup Artist for Joseph Gordon-Levitt, Jamie Kelman; Visual Effects Supervisor, Karen Goulekas; Casting, Mary Vernieu; a FilmDistrict, Endgame Entertainment presentation in association with DMG Entertainment of a Ram Bergman production; Dolby; Panavision; Deluxe color; Rated R; 118 minutes; Release date: September 28, 2012

CAST

Joe	**Joseph Gordon-Levitt**
Old Joe	**Bruce Willis**
Sara	**Emily Blunt**
Seth	**Paul Dano**
Kid Blue	**Noah Segan**
Suzie	**Piper Perabo**
Abe	**Jeff Daniels**
Cid	**Pierce Gagnon**
Old Joe's Wife	**Summer Qing**
Beatrix	**Tracie Thoms**
Old Seth	**Frank Brennan**
Jesse	**Garret Dillahunt**
Dale	**Nick Gomez**
Zach	**Marcus Hester**
Gat Men	**Jon Eyez, Kevin Stillwell, Thirl Haston**
Loopers	**James Hebert, Kenneth Brown Jr., Cody Wood**
Tye	**Adam Scott Boyer**
Tall Gat Man	**Jeff Chase**
Bodega Owner	**Ritchie Montgomery**
Apt Super	**David Jensen**
Daniel	**Kamden Beauchamp**
Farm Vagrant	**Josh "The Ponceman" Perry**
Old Dale	**David Martinez**
Seth Vagrant	**Wayne Dehart**
Beggar Kid	**Ian Patrick**
Big Craig	**Craig Johnson**
Parking Attendant	**Robert Harvey**

In the future when time travel has been outlawed, Joe, a hired gun, becomes a "looper" for the mob, traveling into the past in order to exterminate his targets, until he realizes that he is the next mark ordered to be killed.

Joseph Gordon-Levitt © TriStar

FRANKENWEENIE

(WALT DISNEY PICTURES) Producers, Tim Burton, Allison Abbate; Executive Producer, Don Hahn; Director, Tim Burton; Screenplay, John August; Based on a 1984 screenplay by Lenny Ripps, based on an original idea by Tim Burton; Photography, Peter Sorg; Designer, Rick Heinrichs; Editors, Chris Lebenzon, Mark Solomon; Animation Director, Trey Thomas; Puppet Characters Designers and Creators, MacKinnon & Saunders; Music, Danny Elfman; Animation Supervisor, Mark Waring; Visual Effects Supervisor, Tim Ledbury; Casting, Ronna Kress; Dolby; Deluxe color; 3D; Rated PG; 88 minutes; Release date: October 5, 2012

VOICE CAST

Mrs. Frankenstein/Weird Girl/ Gym Teacher	**Catherine O'Hara**
Mr. Frankenstein/Mr. Burgemeister/Nassor	**Martin Short**
Mr. Rzykruski	**Martin Landau**
Victor Frankenstein	**Charlie Tahan**
Edgar "E" Gore	**Atticus Shaffer**
Elsa Van Helsing	**Winona Ryder**
Bob	**Robert Capron**
Toshiaki	**James Hiroyuki Liao**
Bob's Mom	**Conchata Ferrell**
New Holland Townsfolk	**Tom Kenny**

Persephone van Helsing/Shelly/
    Were-Rat/Colossus/Mr.
    Whiskers/Driver
	Dee Bradley Baker

Giant Sea Monkeys	**Jeff Bennett**
Sparky	**Frank Welker**

Distraught over the death of his beloved dog, Sparky, young Victor Frankenstein decides to bring the pet back to life using the power of electricity. Expanded version of Tim Burton's 1984 live-action short film of the same name.

This film received an Oscar nomination for animated feature.

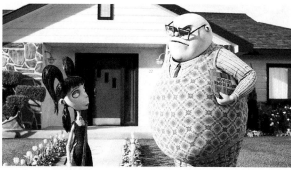
Elsa Van Helsing, Mr. Burgemeister

Sea Monkeys, Bob © Walt Disney Pictures

Mr. Rzykruski

Edgar "E" Gore

Weird Girl

Toshiaki

Mr. Frankenstein, Victor, Sparky, Mrs. Frankenstein

Victor, Sparky

Nassor

Edgar "E" Gore, Elsa Van Helsing, Were-Rat

Persephone

Matthew McConaughey, Zac Efron

John Cusack, Matthew McConaughey © Millennium Films

Macy Gray

Nicole Kidman

THE PAPERBOY

(MILLENNIUM) Producers, Avi Lerner, Ed Cathell III, Cassian Elwes, Hilary Shor, Lee Daniels; Executive Producers, Danny Dimbort, Trevor Short, John Thompson, Boaz Davidson, Mark Gill, Jan De Bont; Director, Lee Daniels; Screenplay, Pete Dexter, Lee Daniels; Based on the 1995 novel by Pete Dexter; Photography, Roberto Schaeffer; Designer, Daniel T. Dorrance; Costumes, Caroline Eselin-Schaeffer; Music, Mario Grigorov; Editor, Joe Klotz; Casting, Billy Hopkins, Leah Daniels-Butler; a Nu Image and a Lee Daniels Entertainment Production; Dolby; Widescreen; Color; Rated R; 107 minutes; Release date: October 5, 2012

CAST

Jack Jansen	**Zac Efron**
Ward Jansen	**Matthew McConaughey**
Charlotte Bless	**Nicole Kidman**
Hillary Van Wetter	**John Cusack**
Yardley Acheman	**David Oyelowo**
W.W. Jansen	**Scott Glenn**
Tyree Van Wetter	**Ned Bellamy**
Ellen Guthrie	**Nealla Gordon**
Anita Chester	**Macy Gray**
Hustler #1	**Edrick Browne**
Victim	**Kevin Waterman**
Sheriff Thurmond Call	**Danny Hanemann**

Peter Murnik (Death Row Guard), John Fertitta (Sam Ellison), James Oliver (Mr. Guthrie, Wedding Guest), Gary Clarke (Weldon Pine), Ava Bogle (Renee, Nail Biter), Adam Sibley (Eugene), J.D. Evermore (Gate Guard), Rene' J.F. Piazza (Kitchen Supervisor), Phyllis Montana LeBlanc (Bartender), Paul Michael Fisher (Wedding Photographer), Lydia Rooks, Nicole Barré (Charlotte Girlfriends), Camille Balsamo (Pam, Beach Girl), Leslie Hippensteel (Kim, Beach Girl), Grace Hightower (Yardley's Girlfriend), Lorrie Chilcoat (Wedding Singer), Stephanie Jordan, Carmen Barika, Nicole Porche (Singers), Faizon Love (Comedian), Stiggidy Steve (Hustler #3), Rahsaana Ison (Lady in Bar), Katarzyna Wolejnio (Jennifer), Nikolette Noel (Nancy), Corrina Lyons (Cousin Alice), John Thompson (Interviewer)

Charlotte Bless asks reporter Ward Jansen to re-investigate the facts behind Hillary Van Wetter being placed on death row for murder, in hopes that she will be able to wed the prisoner.

Leighton Meester © ATO

Allison Janney, Oliver Platt, Hugh Laurie, Alia Shawkat

THE ORANGES

(ATO) Producers, Anthony Bregman, Leslie Urdang, Dean Vanech; Executive Producers, Ian Helfer, Jay Reiss, Stefanie Azpiazu, Sam Hoffman, Dan Revers; Co-Producers, Geoff Linville; Director, Julian Farino; Screenplay, Ian Helfer, Jay Reiss; Photography, Steven Fierberg; Designer, Dan Davis; Costumes, David Robinson; Music, Klaus Badelt, Andrew Raiher; Music Supervisor, Robin Urdang; Editor, Jeffrey M. Werner; Casting, Jeanne McCarthy; an Olympus Pictures production, a Likely Story production in association with Filmnation Entertainment; Dolby; Color; Rated R; 90 minutes; Release date: October 5, 2012

CAST

Nina Ostroff	**Leighton Meester**
David Walling	**Hugh Laurie**
Paige Walling	**Catherine Keener**
Vanessa Walling	**Alia Shawkat**
Toby Walling	**Adam Brody**
Circle	**Boyd Holbrook**
Carol Ostroff	**Allison Janney**
Terry Ostroff	**Oliver Platt**

Tim Guinee (Roger), Lucas Papaelias (Mikhalay), Hoon Lee (Henry Chart), Aya Cash (Maya), Sam Rosen (Ethan), Cassidy Gard (Samantha), Heidi Kristoffer (Meredith), Laura Flanagan (Diane), Stephen Badalamenti (Taxi Driver), John Srednicki (Waiter), Jennifer Bronstein (Amy)

Two suburban families find their friendship put to the test when patriarch David Walling has an affair with the Ostroffs' teenage daughter, who has returned home for the holidays after a 5-year absence.

THE HOUSE I LIVE IN

(ABRAMORAMA) Producers, Eugene Jarecki, Melinda Shopsin; Co-Producer, Christopher St. John; Executive Producers, David Alcaro, Joslyn Barnes, Sally Jofifer, Nick Fraser, Danny Glover, John Legend, Russell Simmons; Director/Screenplay, Eugene Jarecki; Photography, Sam Cullman, Derek Hallquist; Editor, Paul Frost; Music, Robert Miller; a Charlotte Street Films presentation of an Edgewood Way production, a BBC/ITVS/ZDF co-production; American-Dutch-British-German-Japanese-Australian; Color; HD; Not rated; 108 minutes; American release date: October 5, 2012

WITH

Michelle Alexander, Shanequa Benitez, Mark Bennett, Mike Carpenter, Larry Cearly, Eric Franklin, Maurice Haltiwanger, Carl Hart, Nannie Jeter, Anthony Johnson, Gabor Maté, Mark Mauer, Richard Lawrence Miller, Charles Ogletree, Kevin Ott, Susan Randall, David Simon, Julie Stewart, Dennis Whidbee

Documentary on the injustices committed as part of America's losing battle with the war on drugs.

Shanequa Benitez © Abramorama Entertainment

Maurice Haltiwanger

Charice, Kevin James

Salma Hayek, Kevin James

HERE COMES THE BOOM

(COLUMBIA) Producers, Todd Garner, Kevin James; Executive Producers, Adam Sandler, Jack Giarraputo, Jeff Sussman, Marty P. Ewing; Director, Frank Coraci; Screenplay, Allan Loeb, Kevin James; Photography, Phil Méheux; Designer, Perry Andelin Blake; Costumes, Hope Hanafin; Music, Rupert Gregson-Williams; Editor, Scott Hill; a Hey Eddie/Broken Road/Happy Madison production; Dolby; Color; Rated PG; 105 minutes; Release date: October 12, 2012

CAST
Scott Voss	**Kevin James**
Bella Flores	**Salma Hayek**
Marty Streb	**Henry Winkler**
Principal Betcher	**Greg Germann**
Themselves	**Joe Rogan, Mark DellaGrotte**
Eric Voss	**Gary Valentine**
Malia	**Charice**
Niko	**Bas Rutten**

Reggie Lee (Mr. De La Cruz), Mookie Barker (Asst. Principal Elkins), Jackie Flynn (Joe Duffy), Nikki Tyler-Flynn (Molie Streb), Melissa Peterman (Lauren Voss), Thomas C. Gallagher (Peter Voss), Blaine Stevens (Mary Shannon Voss), Jonathan Michael Trautmann (Derrick), Germaine De Leon (Martinez), Steven Ritchie (Brian), Shelly Desai (Miguel), Earnestine Phillips (Muba), Richard Arum (French Man), Nils Veenstra (Nard), Philippe Stella Jan Cornelis (Koen), John C. Blenn (Bearded Board Member), Gabriel Ricker (Student in Stairwell), Evan Reuben (Student Bassist), Krzysztof Soszynski (Ken Dietrich), Mike Goldberg, Bruce Buffer, Herb Dean, Jacob "Stitch" Duran, Wanderlei Silva, Marie DellaGrotte (Themselves), Lenny Clarke (Loud Dietrich Fan), Ryan Parsons (Dietrich's Cornerman), Jason Miller ("Lucky" Patrick Murphy), Jeff Sussman (Ref at College Gymnasium), Scott Voss (Tattooed Man at Factory), James Robinson (Fighter at Factory), Justin McKinney (Ref at Factory), Richie Minervini (Announcer at Factory), Rafael Cordeiro (Fighter at Pier), Nicholas Turturro (Ref at Pier), Craig Minervini (Announcer at Pier), Satoshi Ishii (Fighter at Fairgrounds), Michael Burton (Ref at Fairgrounds), Mark Muñoz (Fighter at Lombardo's), George Klein (Ref at Lombardo's), Romulo Barral (Fighter at Horse Arena), Gino Falsetto (Ref at Horse Arena), Chael Sonnen (Arguing Fighter), Natalie Boss (Health Club Receptionist), Daniel Guire (Yoga Student), Frank Coraci (Disoriented Gym Patron), Joseph Anderson (Man with Guitar), Odis Spencer Jr. (Citizenship Official), Melchor Menor, Daniel Perez, Neil LeGallo (Sityodtong Gym Fighters)

Told that extra-curricular activies will be cut unless his school can raise some extra cash, biology teacher Scott Voss attempts to raise the required amount by becoming a mixed martial-arts fighter.

Kevin James, Henry Winkler

Bas Rutten, Henry Winkler, Mark DellaGrotte, Kevin James © Columbia Pictures

Michael Hall D'Addario

Ethan Hawke, Juliet Rylance

Ethan Hawke © Summit Entertainment

Clare Foley

SINISTER

(SUMMIT) Producers, Jason Blum, Brian Kavanaugh-Jones; Executive Producers, Scott Derrickson, Charles Layton; Director, Scott Derrickson; Screenplay, Scott Derrickson, C. Robert Cargill; Photography, Christopher Norr; Designer, David Brisbin; Costumes, Abby O'Sullivan; Music, Christopher Young; Editor, Frédéric Thoraval; Casting, Sheila Jaffe, Ruth Salen; a Blumhouse and Automatik Production, Alliance Films presentation in association with IM Global; Dolby; HD Widescreen; Technicolor; Rated R; 110 minutes; Release date: October 12, 2012

CAST

Ellison Oswald	**Ethan Hawke**
Tracy Oswald	**Juliet Rylance**
Sheriff	**Fred Dalton Thompson**
Deputy	**James Ransone**
Trevor Oswald	**Michael Hall D'Addario**
Ashley Oswald	**Clare Foley**
E.M.T.	**Rob Riley**
Anchor	**Tavis Smiley**
Reporter	**Janet Zappala**
Stephanie	**Victoria Leigh**
BBQ Boy	**Cameron Ocasio**
Pool Party Boy	**Ethan Haberfield**
Lawn Work Girl	**Danielle Kotch**
Sleepy Time Boy	**Blake Mizrahi**
Bughuul/Mr. Boogie	**Nick King**
Professor Jonas	**Vincent D'Onofrio**

Hoping to replicate a previous publishing success, author Ellison Oswald moves his family into a house where the previous residents had been brutally murdered and uncovers a horrific mystery in a cache of home movies left behind.

SMASHED

(SONY CLASSICS) Producers, Jonathan Schwartz, Andrea Sperling, Jennifer Cochis; Executive Producers, Audrey Wilf, Zygi Wilf; Co-Producers, Stephen Ricci, Elise Salomon, Stephanie Meurer; Director, James Ponsoldt; Screenplay, James Ponsoldt, Susan Burke; Photography, Tobias Datum; Designer, Linda Sena; Costumes, Diaz Jacobs; Music, Eric D. Johnson, Andy Cabic; Editor, Suzanne Spangler; Casting, Avy Kaufman, Kim Coleman; a Super Crispy Entertainment presentation of a Jonathan Schwartz/Andrea Sperling production; Dolby; Color; Rated R; 83 minutes; Release date: October 12, 2012

CAST

Kate Hannah	**Mary Elizabeth Winstead**
Charlie Hannah	**Aaron Paul**
Dave Davies	**Nick Offerman**
Principal Barnes	**Megan Mullally**
Jenny	**Octavia Spencer**
Rochelle	**Mary Kay Place**

Kyle Gallner (Owen Hannah), Mackenzie Davies (Millie), Bree Turner (Freda), Brad Carter (Felix), Barrett Shuler (Greg), Rene Rivera (Rico), Richmond Arquette (Arlo), David Grammer (Junior), Ron Lynch (Chuck), Elise Salomon (Tina), Anjini Taneja Azhar (Winnie), Aileen Davila (Hillary), Silas Agape Garcia (Ramon), Wilson Schwartz (Toby), Haley Brooke Walker (Isabel), Lisa Yamada (Angela), Murray Gershenz (Ted), Jane Noltemeyer (Susan), Brian Haynes (DJ Supa Crispy)

Realizing that her drinking has gotten out of hand and her job as a teacher is in jeopardy, Kate Hannah joins AA, which causes her to question her marriage and her troubled relationship with her mother.

Aaron Paul, Mary Elizabeth Winstead

Mary Elizabeth Winstead, Octavia Spencer © Sony Classics

Esai Morales, Jason Beghe © Atlas Distribution Co.

ATLAS SHRUGGED II: THE STRIKE

(ATLAS DISTRIBUTION CO.) Producers, Jeff Freilich, Harmon Kaslow, John Aglialoro; Executive Producer, William A. Dunn; Co-Producer, Bernie Laramie; Director, John Putch; Screenplay, Duke Sandefur, Brian Patrick O'Toole, Duncan Scott; Based on the 1957 novel *Atlas Shrugged* by Ayn Rand; Photography, Ross Berryman; Designer, Roland Rosenkranz; Costumes, Bonnie Stauch; Music, Chris Bacon; Editor, John Gilbert; Casting, Jeff Gerrard DiGerolamo; a Harmon Kaslow & John Aglialoro Prods. production; Dolby; Widescreen; HD; Color; Rated PG-13; 111 minutes; Release date: October 12, 2012

CAST

Dagny Taggart	**Samantha Mathis**
Henry Rearden	**Jason Beghe**
Francisco d'Anconia	**Esai Morales**
James Taggart	**Patrick Fabian**
Lillian Rearden	**Kim Rhodes**
Eddie Willers	**Richard T. Jones**
John Galt	**D.B. Sweeney**

Paul McCrane (Wesley Mouch), John Rubinstein (Dr. Floyd Ferris), Robert Picardo (Dr. Robert Stadler), Ray Wise (Head of State Thompson), Diedrich Bader (Quentin Daniels), Bug Hall (Leonard Small), Arye Gross (Ken Danagger), Rex Linn (Kip Chalmers), Larisa Oleynik (Cherryl Brooks), Jeff Yagher (Jeff Allen), Michael Gross (Ted "Buzz" Killman), Stephen Macht (Clem Weatherby), Thomas F. Wilson (Robert Collins), Jordana Capra (Judge Griffin), Jennifer Cortese (Gwen Ives), Rebecca Dunn (Lillian's Friend), Mel Fair (Luke Stone), Kip Gilman (Judge Beckstrom), Martin Grey, Dana Sparks (Reception Guests), Amy Hedrick (Laura Bradford), Kevin M. Horton (Dave Mitchum), Gildart Jackson (Gilbert Keith Worthing), James Jordan (Operator), Jamie Rose (Sara Connelly), Patricia Tallman (Holly), Teller (Laughlin), Alexa Hamilton (Giselle), Darren Server (Richard Halley), Michael James Spall (Orren Boyle), Bruce Van Patten (Board Member)

With the economy facing collapse, business magnate Dagny Taggart pins her hopes for rescue on developing an electromagnetic motor. Sequel to the 2011 film *Atlas Shrugged Part 1*, with an all-new cast.

Emayatzy Corinealdi, David Oyelowo

Omari Hardwick, Emayatzy Corinealdi © AAFFRM

MIDDLE OF NOWHERE

(AAFFRM) Producers, Howard Barish, Ava DuVernay, Paul Garnes; Co-Producer, Tilane Jones; Director/Screenplay, Ava DuVernay; Photography, Bradford Young; Costumes, Stacy Beverly; Music, Kathryn Bostic; Music Supervisor, Morgan Rhodes; Editor, Spencer Averick; Casting, Aisha Coley; a Participant Media and AaFFRM presentation of a Kandoo Films and Forward Movement production; Dolby; Color; Rated R; 99 minutes; Release date: October 12, 2012

CAST
Ruby	**Emayatzy Corinealdi**
Brian	**David Oyelowo**
Derek	**Omari Hardwick**
Rosie	**Edwina Findley**
Fraine	**Sharon Lawrence**
Ruth	**Lorraine Toussaint**

Dondre Whitfield (Littleton), Maya Gilbert (Gina), Andy Spencer (Bus Hustler), Amber Sharae Topsy (Bus Passenger), Sancho Martin (Juju Club Lead Dancer), Craig Cole (Prison Guard), William "Bill" Connor (ATF Agent), René Mena, Tommy Shayne Manfredi, Claude Bragg, Dario A. Lee, Joshua S. Patterson (Inmates), Bruce Katzman (Averick), Troy Curvey III (Rashad), Ellen Baker, Nick Mazzone, Alexandria Tyson, Calen Moore (Prison Visitors), Samba Schutte, Monet Ravenell (JuJu Club Dancers), Yvette Cason (Mrs. Hastings), Vera R. Taylor (Probation Board Member), Nisa Ward (Fraine's Assistant), Nehemiah Sutton (Nickie), Kayleh Brown (DeeDee), Romann Aric (Jordann)

With her husband living out his 8-year prison sentence, Ruby drops out of medical school with the intention of focusing on her spouse, only to find solace with a bus driver.

BROOKLYN CASTLE

(PRODUCERS DISTRIBUTION AGENCY) Producers, Katie Dellamaggiore, Nelson Dellamaggiore, Brian Schulz; Executive Producers, Geoff Gibson, Robert McClellan, Julie Parker Benello, Wendy Ettinger, Judith Helfand; Co-Executive Producers, Neal Flaherty, Le Castle Film Works; Director/Screenplay, Katie Dellamaggiore; Photography, Brian Schulz; Music, B. Satz; Editor, Nelson Dellamaggiore; a Rescued Media production in association with Indelible Marks and Chicken and Egg Pictures; Color; Rated PG; 101 minutes; Release date: October 19, 2012. Documentary about five members of a chess team from an inner city Brooklyn junior high school

WITH
Justus Williams, Rochelle Ballantyne, Pobo Efekoro, Alexis Paredes, Patrick Johnston , Elizabeth Spiegel, John Galvin, Fred Rubino, James Black, Michelle Braithwaite, Christina Inuwere, Lisa Johnston, Viviana Paredes Toledo, Latisha Williams

Alexis Paredes

© Producers Distribution Agency

John Hawkes

Helen Hunt, John Hawkes

Moon Bloodgood

THE SESSIONS

(FOX SEARCHLIGHT) formerly *The Surrogate*; Producers, Judi Levine, Stephen Nemeth, Ben Lewin; Executive Producers, Maurice Silman, Julius Colman, Douglas Blake; Director/ Screenplay, Ben Lewin; Photography, Geoffrey Simpson; Designer, John Mott; Costumes, Justine Seymour; Music, Marco Beltrami; Editor, Lisa Bromwell; Casting, Ronnie Yeskel; Presented in association with Such Much Films and Rhino Films; Dolby; Color; Rated R; 95 minutes; Release date: October 19, 2012

CAST

Mark O'Brien	**John Hawkes**
Cheryl Cohen-Greene	**Helen Hunt**
Father Brendan	**William H. Macy**
Vera	**Moon Bloodgood**
Amanda	**Annika Marks**
Josh	**Adam Arkin**
Mikvah Lady	**Rhea Perlman**
Rod	**W. Earl Brown**
Susan	**Robin Weigert**
Dr. Laura White	**Blake Lindsley**
Clerk	**Ming Lo**
Joan	**Rusty Schwimmer**
Carmen	**Jennifer Kumiyama**
Greg	**Tobias Forrest**
Tony	**Jarrod Bailey**
Matt	**James Martinez**
Young Mark	**Paul Maclean**
Girl on Beach	**Phoebe Lewin**
Unicyclist	**Jonathan Hanrahan**
Waiter	**Jason Jack Edwards**
Man in Elevator	**J. Teddy Garces**
E.R. Doctor	**Daniel Quinn**
Ambulance Driver	**B.J. Clinkscales**
Cat	**Terry**

Determined to lose his virginity, a 38-year-old man who has lived most of his life in an iron lung hires a sex surrogate to help him accomplish the goal.

This film received an Oscar nomination for supporting actress (Hunt).

William H. Macy

William H. Macy

Helen Hunt

Helen Hunt, John Hawkes

John Hawkes, Helen Hunt

John Hawkes, Annika Marks © Fox Searchlight

Edward Burns, Tyler Perry

Carmen Ejogo, Tyler Perry © Summit Entertainment

ALEX CROSS

(SUMMIT) Producers, Bill Block, Paul Hanson, James Patterson, Steve Bowen, Randall Emmett, Leopoldo Gout; Executive Producers, George Furla, Stepan Martirosyan, Remington Chase, Jeff Rice, Ethan Smith, John Friedberg, Christopher Corabi; Director, Rob Cohen; Screenplay, Marc Moss, Kerry Williamson; Based on the 2006 novel *Cross* by James Patterson; Photography, Ricardo Della Rosa; Designer, Laura Fox; Costumes, Abigail Murray; Music, John Debney; Editors, Thom Noble, Matt Diezel; Stunts, Gary Hymes, Tom McComas; Casting, Ronna Kress; a Block/Hanson and James Patterson Entertainment production, an Emmett/Furla Films production in association with Envision Entertainment; Dolby; Super 35 Widescreen; Deluxe color; Rated PG-13; 102 minutes; Release date: October 18, 2012

CAST

Alex Cross	**Tyler Perry**
Thomas Kane	**Edward Burns**
Picasso	**Matthew Fox**
Leon Mercier	**Jean Reno**
Maria Cross	**Carmen Ejogo**
Nana Mama	**Cicely Tyson**
Monica Ashe	**Rachel Nichols**
Capt. Richard Brookwell	**John C. McGinley**

Werner Daehn (Erich Nunemacher), Yara Shahidi (Janelle Cross), Sayeed Shahidi (Damon Cross), Bonnie Bentley (Det. Jody Klebanoff), Stephanie Jacobsen (Fan Yau Lee), Giancarlo Esposito (Daramus Holiday), Chad Lindberg (Chemist), Simenona Martinez (Pop Pop Jones), Jessalyn Wanlim (Paramita Megawati), Christian Mathis (Fight Manager), Ingo Rademacher (Ingo Sacks), Tiren Jhames (Guard, Manning Station), Sonny Surowiec (Hans Friedlich), Darcy Leutzinger (Bomb Squad Head), Brian Jackson (Bomb Squad Member), Christopher Stadulis, Timtohy Richardson, Steffen Dziczek (Soon to Be Dead Men), Ideene Dehdashti (Screaming Girl), David Bender (Lt. Max), Chris Wallis, Matt Frieden (Computer Techs), Barbara Cashulin (Hostess), Peter Lawson Jones (Minister), Marcelo Tubert (Cloche), Alexandra Ruddy (Brookwell Aide), Keith Cameron (Bodyguard), Rory Markham (Nenad Stanisic), Timothy Sitarz (Packard Plant Rapist), E. Ray Goodwin Jr., Dan Wynands, Simon Rhee (Fan Yau Bodyguards), Andrew Comrie-Picard (Mercier's Driver), I. Ketut Resi Yogi (Bali Houseboy), I. Wayan Suwita, I. Ketut Arya Wijaya (Bali Police Captains)

Detective-psychologist Alex Cross engages in a deadly game of cat and mouse with a serial killer whose ultimate target is a Detroit-based industrialist.

Cicely Tyson

Matthew Fox

THE LONELIEST PLANET

(SUNDANCE SELECTS) Producers, Lars Knudsen, Jay Van Joy, Helge Albers, Marie Therese Guirgis; Executive Producers, Hunter Gray, Dallas M. Brennan, Rabinder Sira, Chris Gilligan, Shelby Alan Brown, Gregory Shockro; Director/ Screenplay, Julia Loktev; Based on the 2005 short story *Expensive Trips Nowhere* by Tom Bissell; Photography, Inti Briones; Designer/Costumes, Rabiah Troncelliti; Music, Richard Skelton; Editors, Michael Taylor, Julia Loktev; a Parts and Labor, and Flying Moon production in association with Wild Invention in co-production with ZDF Das Kleine Fernsephspiel, in cooperation with Arte with support from Hessen Invest Film; American-German; Color; HD; Not rated; 113 minutes; American release date: October 26, 2012

CAST

Alex	**Gael García Bernal**
Nica	**Hani Furstenberg**
Dato	**Bidzina Gujabidze**

The tight relationship between Alex and Nica is put to the test when they take a guided camping expedition through the Caucasus Mountains.

Gael García Bernal, Bidzina Gujabidze, Hani Furstenberg

Hani Furstenberg, Gael García Bernal © Sundance Selects

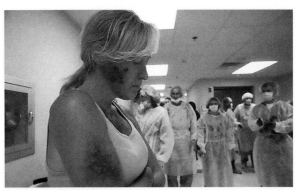

Jane McNeill © Roadside Attractions

THE BAY

(LIONSGATE/ROADSIDE ATTRACTIONS) Producers, Barry Levinson, Jason Blum, Steven Schneider, Oren Peli; Executive Producers, Brian Kavanaugh-Jones, Jason Sosnoff, Colin Strause, Greg Strause; Co-Producer, Liam O'Donnell; Director, Barry Levinson; Screenplay, Michael Wallach; Story, Barry Levinson, Michael Wallach; Photography, Josh Nussbaum; Designer, Lee Bonner; Costumes, Emmie Holmes; Music, Marcelo Zarvos; Editor, Aaron Yanes; Visual Effects, Hydraulx; Casting, Ellen Chenoweth; a Lionsgate and Alliance Films in association with IM Global, Hydraulx Entertainment and Automatik presentation of a Baltimore Pictures/ Haunted Movies production; Dolby; Color; Rated R; 85 minutes; Release date: November 2, 2012

CAST

Alex	**Will Rogers**
Stephanie	**Kristen Connolly**
Donna Thompson	**Kether Donohue**
Mayor John Stockman	**Frank Deal**
Dr. Jack Abrams	**Stephen Kunken**

Nansi Aluka (Jacqueline), Christopher Denham (Sam), Kimberly Campbell (Nurse Rebecca), Beckett Clayton-Luce (Charles), Dave Hager (Jerry), Tara Polhemus, Sean Johnson, Madison Nulty (Teenagers at Bay), Murat "Murf Dawg" Erdan (Mike- Radio Host), Lamya Jezek (Layma), Anthony Reynolds (Steve Slattery), Lauren Cohn (Marsha Rosenblatt), Lucia Forte (Marla Spatafora), Stacy Rabon (Middle Age Woman), Charles Weaver (Water Rescue Worker), Keyla S. Childs (Ms. Crustacean), Justin Welborn (Activist), Rick Benjamin (News Anchor Bernie), Christi Lowe (News Anchor Marsha), Jack Landry (Larry), Holly Allen (Sally), Robert Treveiler (Dr. Williams), Brandon Hanson (Camerman Jim), Michael Beasley (Officer Jimson), Heidi Lawson (Nurse Jessica), Kenny Alfonso (Dr. Michaels), Jody Thompson (Officer Paul), Andrew Stahl (Sheriff Lee Roberts), Zoe Clark, Wyatt Hays (Children at Party), Brandon O'Dell (Bill), John Harrington Bland (Man attacking Dr. Abrams), James Patrick Freetly (Bob – Fishing), Alisa Harris (Mom at Fair), Truman Brothers (Tim), Tim Parati (Fair Man), Bridget Gethins (Fat Lady), Sue Plassmann (Woman with Boils), Chris Walters (Harvey), Nan Stephenson (Harvey's Wife), Kenya N. Phifer (Woman Calling 911), Tim Ross (Reporter, Brian Berger), Jonathan "Lund" Maverick (George Khouri), Jane McNeill (Victim One), Ken Moran (Chicken Feeder), Rasool Jahan (Dr. Nu), CDC Divakar Shukla (Dr. Sacredoti), Zach Hanner (EPA Staffer), Troy Rodeseal (Man with Belly), Jennifer Burch (Teen with Infested Arm), Sarah Jordan Levin (Jennifer's Friend), Rachel Eddy (Girl Texting), Jason Sosnoff (Marine Biologist), Toni Sosnoff (Stephanie's Mother), David Andalman (Officer Don Donaldson), Sharon McHenry Power (Sandra)

A reporter arrives in Claridge, Maryland to find the truth behind the mysterious deaths of hundreds of people three years prior.

Don Cheadle, John Goodman

James Badge Dale

Melissa Leo

Nadine Velazquez, Tamara Tunie

Denzel Washington, Don Cheadle

Denzel Washington, Kelly Reilly

FLIGHT

(PARAMOUNT) Producers, Walter F. Parkes, Laurie MacDonald, Steve Starkey, Robert Zemeckis, Jack Rapke; Executive Producers, Cherylanne Martin; Director, Robert Zemeckis; Screenplay, John Gatins; Photography, Don Burgess; Designer, Nelson Coates; Costumes, Louise Frogley; Music, Alan Silvestri; Editor, Jeremiah O'Driscoll; Special Effects Supervisor, Michael Lantieri; Visual Effects Supervisor, Kevin Baillie; Stunts, Charles Croughwell; Casting, Victoria Burrows; an Imagemovers/Parkes/MacDonald production; Dolby; HD Widescreen; Deluxe color; Rated R; 138 minutes; Release date: November 2, 2012

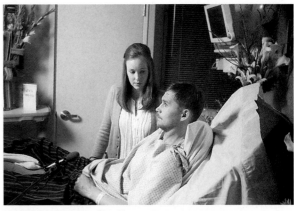

Bethany Anne Lind, Brian Geraghty

CAST

Capt. William "Whip" Whitaker	**Denzel Washington**
Hugh Lang	**Don Cheadle**
Nicole	**Kelly Reilly**
Harling Mays	**John Goodman**
Charlie Anderson	**Bruce Greenwood**
Ken Evans	**Brian Geraghty**
Margaret Thomason	**Tamara Tunie**
Ellen Block	**Melissa Leo**
Katerina Marquez	**Nadine Velazquez**
Gaunt Young Man	**James Badge Dale**
Avington Carr	**Peter Gerety**
Vicky Evans	**Bethany Anne Lind**
Deana	**Garcelle Beauvais**
Will	**Justin Martin**
Kip	**Conor O'Neill**
Tiki Pot	**Charlie E. Schmidt**
Schecter	**Will Sherrod**
Camelia Satou	**Boni Yanagisawa**
Fran	**Adam Tomei**
Derek Hogue	**Dane Davenport**
Craig Matson	**E. Roger Mitchell**
Dr. Kenan	**Ravi Kapoor**
Mark Mellon	**Tommy Kane**
Len Caldwell	**Tom Nowicki**
Trevor	**Ron Caldwell**
Whip's Dad	**Timothy Adams**
Young Will	**Darius Woods**
Two Beer Barry	**Dylan Kussman**
Son on Plane	**Carter Cabassa**
Father on Plane	**Adam Ciesielski**

Denzel Washington, Don Cheadle, Bruce Greenwood

John Crow (Field Reporter), Jill Jane Clements (Morning Nurse), Susie Spear Purcell (Waitress), Philip Pavel (Bartender), Piers Morgan, Jim Tilmon (Themselves), Reverend Charles Z. Gardner (Pentecostal Minister), Jason Benjamin (Carr's Business Guy), Ric Reitz (Carr's Attorney), Janet Metzger (Sheila), Sharon Blackwood, Pam Smith (Peach Tree Employees), Shannon Walshe (Tilda Banden), Rhoda Griffis (Amanda Anderson), Michael Beasley (Officer Edmonds), Ted Hall (TV Reporter), Laila Pruitt (Girl on Elevator), Precious Bright (Mom on Elevator), Steve Coulter (NTSB Officer at Hearing), Ted Buckabee (Prison Guard)

After pilot Whip Whittaker manages to land a troubled plane with most of the lives on board saved, he must face the fact that his out-of-control drinking means that the toxology report has found alcohol in his system at the time of the deed.

This film received Oscar nominations for actor (Washington) and original screenplay.

Denzel Washington © Paramount Pictures

A LATE QUARTET

(ENTERTAINMENT ONE/RKO PICTURES) Producers, Tamar Sela, Yaron Zilberman, Vanessa Coifman, David Faigenblum, Emmanuel Michael, Mandy Tagger Brockey; Executive Producers, Adi Ezroni, Ted Hartley, Peter Pastorelli, Cassandra Kulukundis; Director, Yaron Zilberman; Screenplay, Yaron Zilberman, Seth Grossman; Photography, Frederick Elmes; Designer, John Kasarda; Costumes, Joseph G. Aulisi; Music, Angelo Badalamenti; Music Supervisor, Maureen Crowe; Editor, Yuval Shar; Casting, Cassandra Kulukundis; an Opening Night Productions production in association with Concept Entertainment, Spring Pictures and Unison Films; Dolby; Hawk Scope; Color; Rated R; 105 minutes; Release date: November 2, 2012

Mark Ivanir, Philip Seymour Hoffman, Christopher Walken, Catherine Keener

CAST

Robert Gelbart	**Philip Seymour Hoffman**
Juliette Gelbart	**Catherine Keener**
Peter Mitchell	**Christopher Walken**
Daniel Lerner	**Mark Ivanir**
Alexandra Gelbart	**Imogen Poots**
Pilar	**Liraz Charhi**
Gideon Rosen	**Wallace Shawn**
Dr. Nadir	**Madhur Jaffrey**
Brenda	**Megan McQuillan**
Miriam Mitchell	**Anne Sofie von Otter**

Marty Krzywonos (Cab Driver), Nina Lee (Herself), Jasmine Hope Bloch (Cello Student), Rebeca Tomas (Flamenco Dancer), Cristian Puig (Flamenco Singer), Pamela Quinn (Parkinson's Class Instructor), Kevin Cannon (Actor), Keiko Tokunaga, Luke Fleming (Student Violinists), Andrew Yee (Steve the Cellist), Amy Schroeder (Julliard Classroom Student), Alyssa Lewis (Little Girl)

The future of a string quartet is threatened when its oldest member realizes he is suffering from Parkinson's disease and will have to soon retire.

Imogen Poots © RKO Pictures

Mark Ivanir, Catherine Keener

Liraz Charhi

RZA

Russell Crowe

Cung Le, Byron Mann

THE MAN WITH THE IRON FISTS

(UNIVERSAL) Producers, Marc Abraham, Eric Newman, Eli Roth: Executive Producers, Tom Karnowski, Thomas A. Bliss, Kristel Laiblin; Director, RZA; Screenplay, RZA, Eli Roth; Based on a story by RZA; Photography, Chi Ying Chan; Designer, Drew Boughton; Costumes, Thomas Chong; Music, RZA, Howard Drossin; Editor, Joe D'Augustine; Action Coordinator, Corey Yuen; a Quentin Tarantino presentation of a Strike Entertainment/Arcade Pictures production; American-Hong Kong; Dolby; HD Widescreen; Color; Rated R; 95 minutes; Release date: November 2, 2012

CAST

Blacksmith	**RZA**
Zeni Yi, The X-Blade	**Rick Yune**
Jack Knife	**Russell Crowe**
Bronze Lion	**Cung Le**
Madam Blossom	**Lucy Liu**
Brass Body	**Dave Bautista**

Jamie Chung (Lady Silk), Byron Mann (Silver Lion), Daniel Wu (Poison Dagger), Zhu Zhu (Chi Chi), Gordon Liu (Abbott), Andrew Ng (Senior Monk), Kuan Tai Chen (Gold Lion), Xue Jing Yao (Copper Lion), Telly Liu (Iron Lion), Dong Wen-Jun (White Lion), Zhan De Re (Lion Clan Messenger), Lu Kai (Lion Clan Servant), MC Jin (Chan), Leung Ka-Yan (Hyena Chief), Liu Chang Jiang (Grey Hyena), Brian Yang (Blue Hyena), Hu Minnow (Yellow Hyena), Masanobu Otsuka (Red Hyena), Grace Huang, Andrew Lin (Gemini), Ren Luomin (Wolf Clan Leader), Eli Roth (Wolf Clan #2), Darren Scott (Rodent Chief), Hong Jia (Jackal Captain), Liu Yindi (Jackal Lieutenant), Didi Qian (Lady Tagmata), Lu Wei (Crazy Hippo's Widow), Yuchen Du, Betty Zhou (Jack Knife's Widows), Pam Grier (Jane), Jon Benn (Master John), Jake Garber (Jake), Beau van Erven Dorens (Bo), Dennis Chan (Dragon Innkeeper), Osric Chau (Blacksmith's Assistant), Gang Zhou (Crazy Hippo), Celina Jade (Dragon Inn Singer), Isabella Qian (Urchin Girl), Lian Shuliang (Rodent Innkeeper), Terence Yin (Governor), Mary Christina Brown (Jasmine)

Three men band together to stop sadistic militia leader Silver Lion and his deadly horde from taking over Jungle Village.

Lucy Liu © Universal Pictures

Vanellope, Ralph © Walt Disney Studios

Ralph

WRECK-IT RALPH

(WALT DISNEY STUDIOS) Producer, Clark Spencer; Executive Producer, John Lasseter; Director, Rich Moore; Screenplay, Phil Johnston, Jennifer Lee; Story, Rich Moore, Phil Johnston, Jim Reardon; Additional Story Material, Sam Levine, John C. Reilly, Jared Stern; Music, Henry Jackman; Editor, Tim Mertens; Visual Effects Superisor, Scott Kersavage; Animation Supervisor, Renato Dos Anjos; Character Designer, Andre Medina; Casting, Jamie Sparer Roberts; a Walt Disney Animation Studios production; Dolby; Deluxe color; 3D; Rated PG; 101 minutes; Release date: November 2, 2012

VOICE CAST

Ralph	**John C. Reilly**
Vanellope	**Sarah Silverman**
Felix	**Jack McBrayer**
Calhoun	**Jane Lynch**
King Candy	**Alan Tudyk**
Taffyta Muttonfudge	**Mindy Kaling**
Markowski	**Joe Lo Truglio**
Mr. Litwak	**Ed O'Neill**
General Hologram	**Dennis Haysbert**
Mary	**Edie McClurg**
Gene/Zombie	**Raymond S. Persi**
Don	**Jess Harnell**

Rachael Harris (Deanna), Skylar Astin (Roy), Adam Carolla (Wynnchel), Horatio Sanz (Duncan), Maurice LaMarche (Root Beer Tapper), Stefanie Scott (Moppet Girl), John DiMaggio (Beard Papa), Rich Moore (Sour Bill/Zangrief), Katie Lowes (Candlehead), Jamie Elman (Rancis Fluggerbutter), Josie Trinidad (Jubileena Bing Bing), Cymbre Walk (Crumbelina De Caramello), Tucker Gilmore (Sugar Rush Announcer/Turtle), Brandon Scott (Kohut), Tim Mertens (Brad), Kevin Deters (Clyde), Gerald C. Rivers (M. Bison), Martin Jarvis (Saitine), Brian Kesinger (Cyborg), Roger Craig Smith (Sonic the Hedgehog), Phil Johnston (Surge Protector), Reuben Langdon (Ken), Kyle Hebert (Ruy), Jamie Sparer Roberts (Yuni Verse)

Tired of having to play a villain, a video game character named "Wreck-It Ralph" abandons his job and goes in search of another game hoping to earn a medal and thereby prove himself a good-guy.

This film received an Oscar nomination for animated feature.

Top right: Ralph (center) and Video Game Bad Guys

Bottom right : Fix it Felix and the Nicelanders

THE DETAILS

(RADIUS TWC) Producers, Mark Gordon, Hagai Shaham, Bryan Zuriff; Executive Producers, Mickey Liddell, Jennifer Hilton; Director/Screenplay, Jacob Aaron Estes; Photography, Sharone Meir; Designer, Toby Corbett; Costumes, Christie Wittenborn; Music, Tomandandy; Music Supervisor, Chris Douridas; Editor, Madeleine Gavin; Line Producer, Eugene Mazzola; Casting, John Papsidera; an LD Entertainment presentation of a Mark Gordon Company, Estes Shaham Entity presentation; Dolby; Color; Rated R; 91 minutes; Release date: November 2, 2012

CAST
Dr. Jeff Lang	**Tobey Maguire**
Nealy Lang	**Elizabeth Banks**
Lincoln	**Dennis Haysbert**
Peter Mazzoni	**Ray Liotta**
Rebecca Mazzoni	**Kerry Washington**
Lila	**Laura Linney**
José	**José Gandara**
Miles Lang	**Miles Ellenwood**
Alma	**Rose Cano**
Angela	**Marlette Buchanan**

Gary Schwartz (Plans Inspector), Traci Crouch (Pregnant Traci), Cathy Vu (Fantasy Fruit Girl), Gretchen Liebrum (Great Internet Boobs), James Kruk (Wine and Cheese Man), Lucas Steel Estes (Ultrasound Child), Sam Trammell (Chris)

Dr. Jeff Lang's seemingly idyllic middle-class life is sent spiraling out of control when a series of unfortunate choices backfire and he must deal with their unpleasant consequences.

Elizabeth Banks, Tobey Maguire, Miles Ellenwood

Ray Liotta, Kerry Washington © Radius TWC

Dennis Haysbert

Laura Linney, Tobey Maguire

VAMPS

(ANCHOR BAY) Producers, Lauren Versel, Molly Hassell, Stuart Cornfeld, Maria Teresa Arida, Adam Brightman; Executive Producers, Stanislaw Tycznyski, Julie Kroll, Kamal Nahas, John Jencks, Lisa Wilson, Stephen Hays, Peter Graham; Co-Executive Producer, Kevin Ragsdale; Director/Screenplay, Amy Heckerling; Photography, Tim Suhrstedtasc; Designer, Dan Leigh; Costumes, Mona May; Music, David Kitaygorodsky; Music Supervisor, Elliot Lurie; Editor, Debra Chiate; Casting, Amanda Mackey, Cathy Sandrich Gelfond; a Lucky Monkey Pictures & Red Hour Films presentation in association with Parlay Films, Alvernia Studios, 120 DB Films and Electric Shadow USA; Dolby; Color; Rated PG-13; 92 minutes; Release date: November 2, 2012

CAST

Goody	**Alicia Silverstone**
Stacy	**Krysten Ritter**
Joey	**Dan Stevens**
Danny	**Richard Lewis**
Cisserus	**Sigourney Weaver**
Dr. Van Helsing	**Wallace Shawn**

Justin Kirk (Vadim), Kristen Johnston (Mrs. Van Helsing), Malcolm McDowell (Vlad Tepish), Zak Orth (Renfield), Marilu Henner (Angela), Scott Thomson (Erik), Todd Barry (Ivan), Natalie Gal (Eesa), Meredith Scott Lynn (Rita), Amir Arison (Derek), Larry Wilmore (Prof. Quincy), Joel Michaely (Peter, Nerdy Sales Guy), Bettina Bresnan (Mary Anne Cachillo), Gael Garcia Bernal (Diego Bardem), Leisa Pulido (Landlady), Glen Trotiner (Leather Guy), Olivia Walby (Baby Goody), Taylor Negron (Pizza Guy), Emily Goldwyn (Juicy Girl), Ivan Sergei (Detective), Johanna Went (Rat Eating Woman), Dan Stevens (Joey), Rhonda English (Nurse #1), Eshaq Michael (Gunman), Annie Kitral (Elderly Woman), Thomas Mahard (Elderly Man), Christopher Jarecki (Legal Clerk), Brian Backer (Dentist)

A pair of Manhattan vampires' comfortable existence is threatened when one of the girls falls in love with a young man who happens to be a member of the Van Helsing family of vampire hunters.

Scott Thomson, Alicia Silverstone, Kristen Ritter © Anchor Bay

Besedka Johnson, Dree Hemingway © Music Box Films

STARLET

(MUSIC BOX FILMS) Producers, Blake Ashman-Kipervaser, Kevin Chinoy, Francesca Silvestri, Patrick Cunningham, Chris Maybach; Executive Producers, Ted Hope, Giancarlo Canavesio, Sol Tryon, Shih-Ching Tsou, Saerom Kim, Saemi Kim; Director/Editor, Sean Baker; Screenplay, Sean Baker, Chris Bergoch; Photography, Radium Cheung; Designer, Mari Yui; Costumes, Tsou Shih-Ching; Music, Manual; Music Supervisor, Stephanie Diaz-Matos; Casting, Julia Kim; a Maybach Cunningham presentation of a Freestyle Picture Company and Cre Film production in association with Mangusta Productions; HD Widescreen; Color; Not rated; 104 minutes; Release date: November 9, 2012

CAST

Jane	**Dree Hemingway**
Sadie	**Besedka Johnson**
Melissa	**Stella Maeve**
Mikey	**James Ransome**
Arash	**Karren Karagulian**

Boonee (Startlet), Justin Boyd, Tracy Correll (Yard Sale People), Zoe Voss (Waiting Room Girl), Krystle Alexander (Nurse), Jessica Pak (Manicurist), Jackie J. Lee (Nail Salon Attendant), Dean Andre (Taxi Driver), Rony (Weed Buyer), Dawn Bianchini (Bingo Hall Attendant), Edmund C. Pokrzywnicki (Bingo Caller), Dave Bean, Eliezer Ortiz (Police Officers), Andy Mardiroson (Car Salesman), Cesar Garcia (Repo Man), Heather Wang, Helen Yeotis (Diner Waitresses), Dale Tanguay, Patrick Cunningham (Coffee Shop Gawkers), Jonathan Stromberg (Camera Phone Guy), Jamie Lynn Perritt (Renegade Receptionist), Christine Nelson (Renegade Worker), Michael O'Hagan (Janice), Chris Bergoch (Poor Schlub), Adam Kolkman (Renegade Worker), Manuel Ferrara, Asa Akira, Jules Jordan, Kristina Rose (Themselves), Amin Joseph (Shadow), Cammeron Ellis (Cammie), James Frey (Renegade PA), Nick Santoro (Director F.J. Sloan), Paul H. Kim (Renegade Set Photographer), Joey Rubina (Joey), Josh Sussman (Zana Fan), Weldon "Red" Johnson (POV Sound Person), Kaci Starr, Lily Labeau (POV Performers), Nicole Barseghian, George Barseghian (Arash's Children), Hend Baghdady (Arash's Wife), Jessi Palmer, Cassandra Nix (Model House Tenants), Liz Beebe (Gracie), Tracey Sweet (Webcame Teen)

An irresponsible, aspiring young actress makes an effort to bond with the elderly widow living next door after she discovers an unexpected relic from the older woman's past.

James Balog

Jeff Orlowski

Adam Lee Winter

CHASING ICE

(SUBMARINE DELUXE/DOGWOOF) Producers, Paula DuPré Pesmen, Jerry Aronson; Associate Producers, Stacy Sherman, Billy Ray; Director/Photography, Jeff Orlowski; Screenplay, Mark Monroe; Photography, James Balog; Music, J. Ralph; Song: "Before My Time" by J. Ralph/performed by Scarlett Johansson and Joshua Bell; Editor, Davis Coombe; an Exposure Production in association with Diamond Docs; Dolby; Color; Rated PG-13; 80 minutes; Release date: November 9, 2012. Documentary on how environmental photographer James Balog became aware of the effects of rapid climate change when he was sent to the Arctic to capture images for *National Geographic*;

WITH

James Balog, Svavar Jónatansson, Louie Psihoyos, Kitty Boone, Sylvia Earle, Dennis Dimick, Adam LeWinter, Jason Box, Tad Pfeffer, Suzanne Balog, Jeff Orlowski, Synte Peacock, Terry Root, Thomas Swetnam, Peter Hoeppe, Gerald Meehl, Emily Balog, Martin Nørgaard, Simone Balog, James Woolsey, Martin Sharp, Richard Warp

This film received an Oscar nomination for original song ("Before My Time").

James Balog © Submarine Deluxe

LINCOLN

(WALT DISNEY STUDIOS) Producers, Steven Spielberg, Kathleen Kennedy; Executive Producers, Daniel Lupi, Jeff Skoll, Jonathan King; Co-Producers, Adam Somner, Kristie Macosko Krieger; Director, Steven Spielberg; Screenplay, Tony Kushner; Based in part on the 2005 book *Team of Rivals: The Political Genius of Abraham Lincoln* by Doris Kearns Goodwin; Photography, Janusz Kaminski; Designer, Rick Carter; Costumes, Joanna Johnston; Music, John Williams; Editor, Michael Kahn; Casting, Avy Kaufman; a DreamWorks Pictures, 20th Century Fox and Reliance Entertainment presentation in association with Participant Media of an Amblin Entertainment/Kennedy/Marshall Company production; Dolby; Super 35 Widescreen; Deluxe color; Rated PG-13; 149 minutes; Release date: November 9, 2012

CAST

Abraham Lincoln	**Daniel Day-Lewis**
Mary Todd Lincoln	**Sally Field**
William Seward	**David Strathairn**
Robert Todd Lincoln	**Joseph Gordon-Levitt**
W.N. Bilbo	**James Spader**
Preston Blair	**Hal Holbrook**
Thaddeus Stevens	**Tommy Lee Jones**
Fernando Wood	**Lee Pace**
George Yeaman	**Michael Stuhlbarg**
James Ashley	**David Costabile**
Alexander Stephens	**Jackie Earle Haley**
Ulysses S. Grant	**Jared Harris**
Robert Latham	**John Hawkes**
Edwin Stanton	**Bruce McGill**
Richard Schell	**Tim Blake Nelson**
John Hay	**Joseph Cross**
George Pendleton	**Peter McRobbie**
Tad Lincoln	**Gulliver McGrath**
Elizabeth Keckley	**Gloria Reuben**
John Nicolay	**Jeremy Strong**
William Slade	**Stephen McKinley Henderson**
Alexander Coffroth	**Boris McGiver**
Asa Vintner Litton	**Stephen Spinella**
Clay Hawkins	**Walton Goggins**
William Hutton	**David Warshofsky**
Private Harold Green	**Colman Domingo**
Corporal Ira Clark	**David Oyelowo**
Lydia Smith	**S. Epatha Merkerson**
White Soldiers	**Lukas Haas, Dane DeHaan**

Carlos Thompson (Navy Yard – Shouting Soldier), Bill Camp (Mr. Jolly), Elizabeth Marvel (Mrs. Jolly), Byron Jennings (Montgomery Blair), Julie White (Elizabeth Blair Lee), Charmaine Crowell-White (Minerva – Blair's Servant), Ralph D. Edlow (Leo – Blair's Servant), Grainger Hines (Gideon Welles), Richard Topol (James Speed), Walt Smith (William Fessenden), Dakin Matthews (John Usher), James Ike Eichling (William Dennison), Wayne Duvall (Senator Bluff Wade), Bill Raymond (Schuyler Colfax), Michael Stanton Kennedy (Hiram Price), Ford Flannagan (White House Doorkeeper – Tom Pendel), Bob Ayers (White House Petitioner), Robert Peters (Jacob Graylor), John Moon (Edwin LeClerk), Kevin Lawrence O'Donnell (Charles Hanson), Jamie Horton (Giles Stuart), Joseph Dellinger (Nelson Merrick), Richard Warner (Homer Benson), Elijah Chester (Union Army Officer), Dave Hager (Capt. Nathan Saunders – *River Queen*), Sean Haggerty (Officer in Peace Commissioners Exchange), Michael Shiflett (Senator R.M.T. Hunter), Gregory Itzin (Judge John A. Campbell), Stephen Dunn (Petersburg Siege Lines – Confederate Officer), Chase Edmunds (Willie Lincoln), John Hutton (Senator Charles Sumner), Robert Ruffin (Major Thompson Eckert), Drew Sease (David Homer Bates), John Lescault (Gustavus Fox), Scott Wichmann (Charles Benjamin), Adam Driver (Samuel Beckwith), Jean Kennedy Smith, Shirley Augustine, Sarah Wylie, Margaret Ann McGowan, Hilary Montgomery (House of Representatives Shouters), Asa-Like Twocrow (Ely Parker), Lancer Dean Shull (Union Soldier – Bodyguard), Robert Wilharm, Kevin Kline, Sgt. John Jones, Paul Gowans, Joseph Miller (Wounded Soldiers), John Bellemer (Faust), Mary Dunleavy (Marguerite), Christopher Evan Welch (Clerk – Edward McPherson), Alan Sader (Sergeant at Arms), Gannon McHale (Aaron Haddam), Ken Lambert (Augustus Benjamin), Tom Belgrey (Arthur Bentleigh), Ted Johnson (John Ellis), Don Henderson Baker (Walter Appleton), Raynor Scheine (Josiah S. "Beanpole" Burton), Armistead Nelson Wellford (Nehemiah Cleary), Michael Ruff (Harold Hollister), Rich Willis, Stephen Bozzo (House of Representatives Soldiers), Christopher Alan Stewart (Sergeant – Grant's HQ), Teddy Eck (Corporal – Grant's HQ), Todd Fletcher (Walter H. Washburn), Charles Kinney (Myer Strauss), Joseph Carlson (Joseph Marstern), Michael Goodwin (Chilton A. Elliot), Edward McDonald (Daniel G. Stuart), James Batchelder (Howard Guillefoyle), Gregory Hosaflook (John F. McKenzie), Joe Kerkes (Andrew E. Finck), William Kaffenberger (John A. Casson), Larry Van Hoose (Avon Hanready), C. Brandon Marshall (Rufus Warren), David Graham, Benjamin Shirley, Henry Kidd, Joseph Frances Filipowski (Rebel Shouters – House of Representatives), Tom Aldridge, Sidney Blackmer, Billy Caldwell, Glenn Crone, Martin Dew, Theodore Ewald, Todd Hunter, Joe Inscoe, Raymond Johnson, Gary Keener, Randolph Meekins, Frank Moran, Charley Morgan, Chad Pettit, Barry Privett, Leslie Rogers, Marcello Rollando, Keith Tyree, Kevin J. Walsh, Robert Wray (House of Representatives), Christopher Boyer (Gen. Robert E. Lee), Stephen Dunford (Actor Swordsman), David Doersch (Actor Demon Affrit), Christopher Carmill (Leonard Grover), Robert Shepherd (Dr. Joseph K. Barnes)

In the final months of the Civil War, President Abraham Lincoln fights to establish a Constitutional Ammendant to abolish slavery.

2012 Academy Award Winner for Best Actor (Daniel Day-Lewis) and Best Production Design.

This film received additional Oscar nominations for picture, supporting actor (Tommy Lee Jones), supporting actress (Sally Field), director, adapted screenplay, cinematography, costume design, film editing, original score, and sound mixing.

Daniel Day-Lewis

Sally Field

Lee Pace © Walt Disney Studios

Jared Harris

David Strathairn, Tim Blake Nelson, John Hawkes, James Spader

Daniel Day-Lewis

Byron Jennings, Joseph Cross, Hal Holbrook, Daniel Day-Lewis, David
Strathairn, Jeremy Strong, David Costabile

Sally Field, Wayne Duvall, John Hutton, Tommy Lee Jones, David Costabile

Jackie Earle Haley

Right: Daniel Day-Lewis,
Stephen McKinley Henderson,
Joseph Gordon-Levitt,
Gulliver McGrath

Tracey Heggins, Judi Shekoni

Taylor Lautner, Kristen Stewart

BREAKING DAWN - PART 2

(SUMMIT) Producers, Wick Godfrey, Karen Rosenfelt, Stephenie Meyer; Executive Producers, Marty Bowen, Greg Mooradian, Mark Morgan, Guy Oseary; Co-Producer, Bill Bannerman; Director, Bill Condon; Screenplay, Melissa Rosenberg; Based on the 2008 novel *Breaking Dawn* by Stephenie Meyer; Photography, Guillermo Navarro; Designer, Richard Sherman; Costumes, Michael Wilkinson; Music, Carter Burwell; Music Supervisor, Alexandra Patsavas; Editor, Virginia Katz; Makeup Designer, Jean Ann Black; Visual Effects Supervisor, Terry Windell; Casting, Debra Zane; a Temple Hill production in association with Sunswept Entertainment; Dolby; Super 35 Widescreen; Color; Rated PG-13; 115 minutes; Release date: November 16, 2012

CAST

Bella Swan	**Kristen Stewart**
Edward Cullen	**Robert Pattinson**
Jacob Black	**Taylor Lautner**
Dr. Carlisle Cullen	**Peter Facinelli**
Esme Cullen	**Elizabeth Reaser**
Alice Cullen	**Ashley Greene**
Jasper Hale	**Jackson Rathbone**
Emmett Cullen	**Kellan Lutz**
Rosalie Hale	**Nikki Reed**
Charlie Swan	**Billy Burke**
Sam Uley	**Chaske Spencer**
Renesmee	**Mackenize Foy**
Irina	**Maggie Grace**
Caius	**Jamie Campbell Bower**
Marcus	**Christopher Heyerdahl**
Aro	**Michael Sheen**
Santiago	**Lateef Crowder**
Felix	**Daniel Cudmore**
Demetri	**Charlie Bewley**
Vasilii	**Billy Wagenseller**
Jane	**Dakota Fanning**
Alec	**Cameron Bright**
Sasha	**Andrea Powell**
Tanya	**MyAnna Buring**
Kate	**Casey LaBow**
Carmen	**Mia Maestro**
Eleazar	**Christian Camargo**
Amun	**Omar Metwally**
Kebi	**Andrea Gabriel**
Tia	**Angela Sarafyan**
Benjamin	**Rami Malek**
Senna	**Tracey Heggins**
Zafrina	**Judi Shekoni**
Garrett	**Lee Pace**

John Edward Lee (English Punk), Patrick Brennan (Liam), Lisa Howard (Siobhan), Marlane Barnes (Maggie), Bill Tangardi (Randall), Toni Trucks (Mary), Erik Odom (Peter), Valorie Curry (Charlotte), Joe Anderson (Alistair), Pacey Gillespie, Brayden Jimmie, Swo Wo Gabriel (Young Quileutes), Guri Weinberg (Stefan), Noel Fisher (Vladimir), Amadou Ly (Henri), Janelle Froehlich (Yvette), Masami Kosaka (Toshiro), Alex Rice (Sue Clearwater), Tony Bentley (Maitre D'), Wendell Pierce (J. Jenks), Julia Jones (Leah Clearwater), Booboo Stewart (Seth Clearwater), JD Pardo (Nahuel), Marisa Quinn (Hullen), Christie Burke (Renesmee – Young Woman), Angelo Renai (Minister Weber), Abigail Cornell, Isabella Iannuzzi, Milli Wilkinson, Eliza Faria (Renesmee – 4 years), Tate Clemons, Taylor Diane Robinson, Kailyn Stratton, Rachel St. Gelais (Renesmee – 5 years), Blythe Barrington-Hughes (Renesmee – 7 years)

Ashley Greene, Jackson Rathbone

After becoming a vampire and giving birth to a daughter, Bella finds her happiness with Edward threatened by the Volturi, who are intent of destroying the "immortal child" whom they deem a threat to all vampires.

Final chapter in the Summit series following *Twilight* (2008), *New Moon* (2009), *Eclipse* (2010), and *Breaking Dawn – Part 1* (2011).

Robert Pattinson, Kristen Stewart

Taylor Lautner, Mackenzie Foy, Kristen Stewart

Kellan Lutz, Kristen Stewart

Christian Camargo, Mia Maestro

Dakota Fanning, Cameron Bright

Billy Burke, Mackenzie Foy, Alex Rice © Summit Entertainment

SILVER LININGS PLAYBOOOK

(WEINSTEIN CO.) Producers, Donna Gigliotti, Bruce Cohen, Jonathan Gordon; Executive Producers, Bob Weinstein, Harvey Weinstein, George Parra, Michelle Raimo Kouyate, Bradley Cooper; Co-Executive Producer, Renee Witt; Director/ Screenplay, David O. Russell; Based upon the 2010 novel *The Silver Linings Playbook* by Matthew Quick; Photography, Masanobu Takayanagi; Designer, Judy Becker; Costumes, Mark Bridges; Music, Danny Elfman; Music Supervisor, Susan Jacobs; Editor, Jay Cassidy; Casting, Mary Vernieu; Dolby; Color; Rated R; 122 minutes; Release date: November 16, 2012

Jennifer Lawrence, Bradley Cooper

CAST

Pat Solatano	**Bradley Cooper**
Tiffany Maxwell	**Jennifer Lawrence**
Pat Solatano, Sr.	**Robert De Niro**
Dolores Solatano	**Jacki Weaver**
Danny	**Chris Tucker**
Dr. Cliff Patel	**Anupam Kher**
Ronnie	**John Ortiz**
Jake Solatano	**Shea Whigham**
Veronica	**Julia Stiles**
Randy	**Paul Herman**
Officer Keogh	**Dash Mihok**
Ricky D'Angelo	**Matthew Russell**
Tiffany's Mother	**Cheryl Williams**
Tiffany's Father	**Patrick McDade**
Nikki	**Brea Bee**
Regina	**Regency Boies**
Jordie	**Phillip Chorba**
Dr. Timbers	**Anthony Lawton**
Nancy (High School Principal)	**Patsy Meck**
Older Waitress	**Maureen Torsney Weir**
Jeffrey	**Jeff Reim**
Fritzy	**Fritz Blanchette**
Dance Competition Announcer	**Rick Foster**
Ricky D'Angelo's Mother	**Bonnie Aarons**
Doug Culpepper	**Ted Barba**
Ricky D'Angelo's Friends	**Elias Birnbaum, Matthew Michaels**
Lawyer at Bar	**Peter Postiglione**
Fighting Eagle Fan	**Richard Eklund III**
Indian Invasion	**Sanjay Shende, Mihir Pathak, Ibrahim Syed**
Dr. Patel's Wife	**Madhu Narula**
Jake's Fiancée	**Samantha Gelnaw**
Tanya	**Tiffany Green**
Dancer Santos	**Tal Livshitz**
Dancer Aguilar	**Vlada Semenova**
Dancer Makarov	**Zhan Paulovich**
Dancer Tretiak	**Svetlana Roosiparg**

Bradley Cooper, Jennifer Lawrence

Pat Solatano returns home after spending 8 months in a state institution, hoping to rebuild his life by re-establishing relations with his estranged wife, but instead is drawn to an outspoken young woman with her own set of problems.

2012 Academy Award Winner for Best Actress (Jennifer Lawrence).

This film received Oscar nominations for picture, actor (Cooper), supporting actor (De Niro), supporting actress (Weaver), director, adapted screenplay, and film editing.

Jacki Weaver, Robert De Niro

Bradley Cooper, Jennifer Lawnrece

Jennifer Lawrence, Bradley Cooper

Chris Tucker © Weinstein Company

Bradley Cooper, Jacki Weaver, Chris Tucker

Robert De Niro, Bradley Cooper

Bradley Cooper

Suraj Sharma, Richard Parker

Suraj Sharma, Richard Parker

Richard Parker, Suraj Sharma

Suraj Sharma

Suraj Sharma

Suraj Sharma © 20th Century Fox

Richard Parker

Richard Parker

Suraj Sharma

LIFE OF PI

(20TH CENTURY FOX) Producers, Gil Netter, Ang Lee, David Womark; Executive Producer, Dean Georgaris; Co-Producer, David Lee; Director, Ang Lee; Screenplay, David Magee; Based on the 2001 novel by Yann Martel; Photography, Claudio Miranda; Designer, David Gropman; Costumes, Arjun Bhasin; Music, Mychael Danna; Editor, Tim Squyres; Visual Effects Producer, Susan MacLeod; Visual Effects, Rhythm & Hues Studios, MPC, BUF Compagnie, Crazy Horse Effects, Lola VFX; Tiger Trainer/Consultant, Thierry Le Portier; Stunts, Charlie Croughwell; Casting, Avy Kaufman; a Fox 2000 Pictures presentation in association with Dune Entertainment and Ingenious Media of a Haishang Films/Gil Netter production in association with Big Screen Prods. and Ingenious Film Partners; Dolby; Deluxe color; 3D; Rated PG; 126 minutes; Release date: November 21, 2012

CAST

Pi Patel	**Suraj Sharma**
Adult Pi Patel	**Irrfan Khan**
Gita Patel	**Tabu**
The Writer	**Rafe Spall**
Cook	**Gérard Depardieu**
Santosh Patel	**Adil Hussain**
Young Pi	**Ayush Tandon**
5-year-old Pi	**Gautam Belur**
Anandi, Pi's Girlfriend	**Shravanthi Sainath**
The Priest	**Andrea Di Stefano**
Pi's Younger Brother Ravi at 7	**Ayran Kahn**
Ravi Patel at 18/19	**Vibish Sivakumar**
Ravi Patel at 13/14	**Mohd. Abbas Khaleeli**
Older Insurance Investigator	**James Saito**
Younger Insurance Investigator	**Jun Naito**
Mamaji	**Elie Alouf**
Dance Master	**Padmini Ramachandran**
Science Teacher	**T.M. Karthik**
Indian History Teacher	**Amarendran Ramanan**
Librarian	**Hari Mina Bala**
Buddhist Sailor	**Wang Bo-Chieh**
Tsimtsum Captain	**Ko Yi-Cheng**
Sailor	**Huang Jian-Wei**
Selvam	**Ravi Natesan**
Anandi's Friends	**Swati Van Rijswijk, M. Keerthana**
Pi's Wife	**Mythili Prakash**
Pi's Son	**Raj Patel**
Pi's Daughter	**Hadiqa Hamid**
Muslim Worshipper	**Iswar Srikumar**
Bullies	**Adyant Balaji, Chirag Agarwal, Ahan André Kamath, Om Kamath, Srilekh Katta**
Dancers	**Indumohan Poornima, Josephine Nithya B., Samyuktha S., A. Deiva Sundari, G. Vasantakumary, A. Vithya**

When the Patel family decides to move their zoo from India to Canada, the freighter carrying their menagerie capsizes during a storm leaving their 17-year-old son Pi adrift for 227 days with only a tiger as his companion.

2012 Academy Award Winner for Best Director, Best Cinematography, Best Visual Effects, and Best Original Score.

This film received additional Oscar nominations for picture, adapted screenplay, film editing, original song ("Pi's Lullaby"), production design, sound editing, and sound mixing.

RISE OF THE GUARDIANS

(DREAMWORKS/PARAMOUNT) Producers, Christina Steinberg, Nancy Bernstein; Executive Producers, Guillermo del Toro, William Joyce, Michael Siegel; Director, Peter Ramsey; Screenplay, David Lindsay-Abaire; Based on *The Guardians of Childhood* series of books by William Joyce and the 2005 short film *The Man in the Moon* directed by William Joyce; Designer, Patrick Marc Hanenberger; Music, Alexandre Desplat; Editor, Joyce Arrastia; Visual Consultant, Roger Deakins; Visual Effects Supervisor, David Prescott; a DreamWorks Animation SKG production; Dolby; Deluxe color; 3D; Rated PG; 97 minutes; Release date: November 21, 2012.

VOICE CAST

North	Alec Baldwin
Pitch	Jude Law
E. Aster Bunnymund	Hugh Jackman
Jack Frost	Chris Pine
Tooth Fairy	Isla Fisher
Jamie Bennett	Dakota Goyo
Caleb	Khamani Griffin
Claude	Kamil McFadden
Sophie Bennett	Georgie Grieve
Jamie's Mom/Jack's Mother	Emily Nordwind
Monty	Jacob Bertrand
Pippa/Jack's Sister	Olivia Mattingly
Cupcake	Dominique Grund

Ryan Crego (Burgess Dog Walker), April Lawrence, Peter Ramsey (Burgess Pedestrians), Isabella Blake-Thomas (British Girl), Stuart Allan Bertman (British Boy), Rich Dietl (Yeti)

Jack Frost is enlisted by North and his team of mythical characters to save the Earth from the dreaded Pitch.

Pitch

Bunnymund, Sandman, North, Tooth Fairy, Jack Frost

Elves

Yeti, Bunnymund, North, Yeti, Tooth Fairy © DreamWorks

Jack Frost, Tooth Fairy

Standing: Chris Hemsworth, Adrianne Palicki, Josh Peck, Isabel Lucas, Luian Alcaraz, Alyssa Diaz, Edwin Hodge; Seated: Josh Hutcherson, Connor Cruise

RED DAWN

(FILMDISTRICT) Producers, Beau Flynn, Tripp Vinson; Executive Producers, Vincent Newman, Kevin Halloran; Co-Producer, John Swallow; Director, Dan Bradley; Screenplay, Carl Ellsworth, Jeremy Passmore, based on the 1984 motion picture *Red Dawn* written by Kevin Reynolds and John Milius from a story by Kevin Reynolds; Photography, Mitchell Amundsen; Designer, Dominic Watkins; Costumes, Catherine George; Music, Ramin Djawadi; Music Supervisor, Dana Sano; Editor, Richard Pearson; Visual Effects Producer, Liz Ralston; Stunts, Darrin Prescott; Casting, Deborah Aquilla, Tricia Wood; a Contrafilm production; Dolby; Panavision; Deluxe color; Rated PG-13; 93 minutes; Release date: November 21, 2012

CAST

Jed Eckert	**Chris Hemsworth**
Matt Eckert	**Josh Peck**
Robert Kitner	**Josh Hutcherson**
Toni Walsh	**Adrianne Palicki**
Erin Martin	**Isabel Lucas**
Daryl Jenkins	**Connor Cruise**

Edwin Hodge (Danny), Brett Cullen (Tom Eckert), Alyssa Diaz (Julie), Julian Alcaraz (Greg), Will Yun Lee (Capt. Cho), Jeffrey Dean Morgan (Tanner), Fernando Chien (Lt. Pak), Kenneth Choi (Smith), Matt Gerald (Hodges), Michael A. Knight (Col. Ivanov), Steve Lenz (Pete), Noah Smith (Joe), Michael Beach (Mayor Jenkins), Lucas Kerr (#53, Razner), Linda Boston (Older Woman), Nicholas Yu (Korean Delegate), Spencer Strong Smith (Jim), Rusty Mewha (Brian), Brian D. Thibault (Cashier), Mark Schlereth (Coach Dolen), Dan Lewis (News Anchor), Choau Kue, Sam Looc (Soldiers), Zachary Schafer (Officer), Steven Chan (Korean Official), Dwight Sora (Drunk Officer), Cindy Chu (Clerk), Matthew Yang King (Korean Soldier), Boyuen (Korean General)

A group of teens become heroic resistance fighters when their town is invaded by North Korean soldiers. Remake of the 1984 MGM film of the stame name that starred Patrick Swayze, C. Thomas Howell, Lea Thompson, and Charlie Sheen.

THE CENTRAL PARK FIVE

(SUNDANCE SELECTS) Producers/Directors/Screenplay, Sarah Burns, David McMahon, Ken Burns; Photography, Buddy Squires, Anthony Savini; Music, Doug Wamble; Editor, Michael Levine; Dolby; a production of Florentine Films & WETA Television; Color; Not rated; 119 minutes; Release date: November 23, 2012. Documentary on how five black and Latino teenagers from Harlem were unjustly convicted of raping a woman in NY's Central Park in 1989.

WITH

Angela Black, Calvin O. Butts III, Natalie Byfield, David Dinkins, Jim Dwyer, Ronald Gold, LynNell Hancock, Michael Joseph, Saul Kassin, Ed Koch, Antron McCray, Kevin Richardson, Yusef Salaam, Raymond Santana Sr., Raymond Santana, Michael Warren, Craig Steven Wilder, Korey Wise.

Colin Moore, Korey Wise © Sundance Selects

Yusef Salaam

Toni Collette, Anthony Hopkins, Helen Mirren

Scarlett Johansson, Jessica Biel

Anthony Hopkins, Scarlett Johansson, James D'Arcy © Fox Searchlight

HITCHCOCK

(FOX SEARCHLIGHT) Producers, Ivan Reitman, Tom Pollock, Joe Medjuck, Tom Thayer, Alan Barnette; Executive Producers, Ali Bell, Richard Middleton; Director, Sacha Gervasi; Screenplay, John J. McLaughlin; based on the 1990 book *Alfred Hitchcock and the Making of 'Psycho'* by Stephen Rebello; Photography, Jeff Cronenweth; Designer, Judy Becker; Costumes, Julie Weiss; Music, Danny Elfman; Music Supervisor, David Norland; Special Makeup Effects, Howard Berger, Gregory Nicotero; Editor, Pamela Martin; Casting, Terri Taylor; a Montecito Picture Company/Barnette/Thayer production, presented in association with Cold Spring Pictures; Dolby; Deluxe color; HD Widescreen; Rated PG-13; 98 minutes; Release date: November 23, 2012

CAST

Alfred Hitchcock	**Anthony Hopkins**
Alma Reville Hitchcock	**Helen Mirren**
Janet Leigh	**Scarlett Johansson**
Peggy Robertson	**Toni Collette**
Whitfield Cook	**Danny Huston**
Vera Miles	**Jessica Biel**
Lew Wasserman	**Michael Stuhlbarg**
Anthony Perkins	**James D'Arcy**
Ed Gein	**Michael Wincott**
Geoffrey Shurlock	**Kurtwood Smith**
Barney Balaban	**Richard Portnow**
Joseph Stefano	**Ralph Macchio**
Saul Bass	**Wallace Langham**

Judith Hoag (Lillian), Tara Summers (Rita Riggs), Danielle Burgio (Dead Woman in Tub), Currie Graham (PR Flack), Frank Collison (Henry Gein), Kai Lennox (Hilton Green), Spencer Garrett (George Tomasini), Jon Abrahams, Gil McKinney (Reporters), Terry Rhoads (Jack Russell), Tom Virtue (NY Theater Manager), Karina Deyko (Pretty Secretary), John Lacy (First Guard), Emma Julia Jacobs (Blonde Fan), Lindsey Ginter (Propmaster), Mary Anne McGarry (Hedda Hopper Type), Gina Fricchione (Hairstylist), Josh Yeo (John Gavin), Richard Chassler (Martin Balsam), Paul Schackman (Bernard Herrmann), David Hill (Leonard J. South, Camera Operator), Melinda Chilton (Margo Epper, Perkins' Double), Cynthia Youngblood (June Gleason), John Faircrest (Lighting Crew), Howard Gibson, Lorie Stewart, Howard Gibson, Josette Prevost, Jaehne Moebius (Party Guests), Ana Matallana (Prop Assistant), Paul Henderson, Kay Henderson (Beach Walkers), Spencer Leigh (Nunzio), Sean MacPherson (Waiter), Gerald Casale (David Kirkpatrick), Tara Arroyave (Woman Waiting in Line), Lisa Marie Boiko, Richard Burns, Meredith Claire, Alexia DuBasso, James R. Gavio, James Henderson, Bruce Holman, Dion W.H. Holt, Jeremiah Hundley, Sebastian Vale, Michael Kurtz, Joseph Martino, Jeremy S. Miles, Jon Renfield, Linda Sans, Jammes Tappan, Jon Thibault, Jason Wingo, Cynthia Youngblood (Film Crew)

Director Alfred Hitchcock puts his reputation on the line when he decides to turn the sordid novel *Pscyho* into his next film.

This film received an Oscar nomination for makeup & hairstyling.

Anthony Hopkins

KILLING THEM SOFTLY

(WEINSTEIN CO.) Producers, Brad Pitt, Dede Gardner, Steve Schwartz, Paula Mae Schwartz, Anthony Katagas; Executive Producers, Megan Ellison, Marc Butan, Bill Johnson, Jim Seibel, Bob Weinstein, Harvey Weinstein, Adi Shankar, Spencer Silna; Co-Producers, Roger Schwartz, Matthew Budman, Will French, Douglas Saylor Jr.; Director/Screenplay, Andrew Dominik; Based on the 1974 novel *Cogan's Trade* by George V. Higgins; Photography, Greig Fraser; Designer/Costumes, Patricia Norris; Editor, Brian A. Kates; Casting, Francine Maisler; an Inferno presentation in association with Annapurna Pictures and 1984 Private Defense Contractors of a Plan B Entertainment production, a Chockstone Pictures production; Dolby; Panavision; Deluxe color; Rated R; 97 minutes; Release date: November 30, 2012.

Brad Pitt, James Gandolfini

CAST

Jackie Cogan	**Brad Pitt**
Frankie	**Scoot McNairy**
Russell	**Ben Mendelsohn**
Mickey	**James Gandolfini**
Driver	**Richard Jenkins**
Johnny Amato	**Vincent Curatola**
Markie Trattman	**Ray Liotta**
Steve Caprio	**Trevor Long**
Barry Caprio	**Max Casella**
Dillon	**Sam Shepard**
Slaine	**Kenny Gill**

Linara Washington (Hooker), Ross Brodar (Poker Guy), Wade Allen, Joe Chrest (Business Suit Agents), Christopher Berry (Cab Driver Agent), Kenneth Brown, Jr. (Security Force Agent), Mustafa Harris, John McConnell (Bartenders), Dared Wright (Waiter), Bryan Billingsley, Shannon Brewer, Roger L. Pfeiffer (Bar Patrons)

The mob hires hit man Jackie Cogan to find out the truth behind a heist at a mob-protected card game.

Ray Liotta

Scoot McNairy © Weinstein Company

Richard Jenkins

Catherine Zeta-Jones, Gerard Butler © FilmDistrict

PLAYING FOR KEEPS

(FILMDISTRICT) Producers, Jonathan Mostow, Kevin Misher, Gerard Butler, Alan Siegel, Heidi Jo Markel, John Thompson; Executive Producers, Avi Lerner, Danny Dimbort, Trevor Short, Ed Cathell III, Boaz Davidson, Peter Schlessel; Co-Producers, Andrea Leone, Raffaella Leone; Co-Executive Producer, Diego Martinez; Director, Gabriele Muccino; Screenplay, Robbie Fox; Photography, Peter Menzies; Designer, Daniel T. Dorrance; Costumes, Angelica Russo; Music, Andrea Guerra; Editor, Padraic McKinley; Casting, Denise Chamian; a Misher Films/York Square Prods./Eclectic Pictures/Gerard Butler-Alan Siegel Entertainment/Nu Image in association with Millennium Films; American-Italian; Dolby; Super 35 Widescreen; Technicolor; Rated PG-13; 105 minutes; Release date: December 7, 2012

CAST
George Dryer	**Gerard Butler**
Stacie	**Jessica Biel**
Lewis	**Noah Lomax**
Carl	**Dennis Quaid**
Patti	**Uma Thurman**
Denise	**Catherine Zeta-Jones**
Matt	**James Tupper**
Barb	**Judy Greer**

Abella Wyss (Ally), Grant Goodman (Billy), Grant Collins (Griffin), Aidan Potter (Hunter), Marlena Rayne Lerner (Samantha), Iqbal Theba (Param), Sean O'Bryan (Assistant Coach Jacob), Mike Martindale (Coach Len), Jason George (Chip Johnston), Emily Somers (Dawn), Gerry May (Sports Anchor), Katia Gomez (Lupe), Gisella Marengo, Cindy Creekmore, Nicky Buggs (Moms), Ritchie Montgomery (The Owner, Sports Shop), Jon Mack (Connie), Jesse De Luna (Desk Sergeant), Soumaya Akaaboune (Aracelli), Parker Eppes (Joel), Joe Chrest (Referee), Shanna Forrestall (Clerk), Aisha Kabia, Jody Lambert (ESPN Executives), Adam Kulbersh (ESPN Studio Technician), Kim Hawthorne (ESPN Receptionist), Stan Verrett (Himself), Liann Pattison (Shop Lady), Linda Kay Leonard (Another Mom), Stephanie Swart (Kylie)

An aging, down-on-his-luck soccer player attempts to reconcile with his ex-wife and their young son.

DEADFALL

(MAGNOLIA) Producers, Gary Levinsohn, Shelly Clippard, Ben Cosgrove, Todd Wagner; Executive Producers, Mark Cuban, Josette Perrotta, Adam Kolbrenner, Winifried Hammacher; Director, Stefan Ruzowitzky; Screenplay, Zach Dean; Photography, Shane Hurlburt; Designer, Paul Denham Austerberry; Costumes, Odette Gadoury; Music, Marco Beltrami; Editors, Arthur Tarnowski, Dan Zimmerman; Casting, Randi Hiller; a Studiocanal and 2929 Productions presentation of a Mutual Film Company production; Dolby; Super 35 Widescreen; Color; Rated R; 95 minutes; Release date: December 7, 2012

CAST
Addison	**Eric Bana**
Liza	**Olivia Wilde**
Jay	**Charlie Hunnam**
Hanna	**Kate Mara**
Sheriff Marshall T. Becker	**Treat Williams**
June Mills	**Sissy Spacek**
Chet Mills	**Kris Kristofferson**

Jason Cavalier (Deputy Travis), Patrick Kerton (State Trooper), Alain Goulem (Bobby), Allison Graham (Mandy), Kwasi Songui (Corrections Officer), John Robinson (Ronnie), Job Daniel (Young Boxer), Jocelyne Zucco (Doris), Maxime Savaria (Deputy Brice), Kyle Gatehouse (Deputy Bill), Tom Jackson (Old Indian Hunter), Tomomi Morimoto (Suki), Nobuya Shimamoto (Hiro), Cheryl Diabo (Ottawa Indian Mother), André Kasper Kolstad (Ottawa Indian Child), Anie Pascale (Tricia), Andrew Johnston (Marvin), Sarah Hansen (Amy), Teale Hansen (Lisa), Victor Cornfoot (Snowplow Driver), Warona Setshewaelo (Paramedic)

Following a casino robbery, a brother and sister split up in their trek towards the Canadian border, leading her to link up with an ex-con on his way home for Thanksgiving dinner.

Charlie Hunnam, Olivia Wilde

Sissy Spacek © Magnolia Films

LAY THE FAVORITE

(RADiUS-TWC) Producers, Anthony Bregman, Randall Emmett, George Furla, D.V. DeVincentis, Paul Trijbits; Executive Producers, Agnès Mentre, Vincent Maraval, Richard Jackson, Curtis Jackson, Brandt Andersen, Brandon Grimes, Peter Hampden, James Gibb, James W. Skotchdopole; Director, Stephen Frears; Screenplay, D.V. DeVincentis; Based on the 2010 book *Lay the Favorite: A Memoir of Gambling* by Beth Raymer; Photography, Michael McDonough; Designer, Dan Davis; Costumes, Christopher Peterson; Music, James Seymour Brett; Editor, Mick Audsley; Casting, Victoria Thomas; an Emmett/Furla Films and Wild Bunch presentation of a Likely Story/Emmett/Furla Films/Ruby Films production in association with Jackson Investment Group/Lipsync/Random House Films; American-British; Dolby; Technicolor; Rated R; 94 minutes; Release date: December 7, 2012

CAST
Dirk Heimowitz	**Bruce Willis**
Beth Raymer	**Rebecca Hall**
Rosie	**Vince Vaughn**
Tulip Heimowitz	**Catherine Zeta-Jones**
Jeremy	**Joshua Jackson**
Holly	**Laura Prepon**

Frank Grillo (Frankie), Joel Murray (Darren), Corbin Bernsen (Jerry), Wendell Pierce (Dave the Rave), John Carroll Lynch (Dave Greenberg), Andrea Frankle (Marcia Greenberg), Dominique DuVernay, Darcel White Moreno (Curacao Hookers), Jo Newman (Darcy), Lara Grice (Waitress), Ritchie Montgomery (Jackie), Wayne Péré (Scott), Rio Hackford (Magic), Al Brown (Old Gambler), Adam Kozlowski, Rusty Meyers (Rio Gamblers), Rob Steinberg (Doctor), Hugo Armstrong (Customer), Tracy Miller (Guy), Earl Maddox (Manager), B.J. Parker (Casino Security Guard), Errol Suleyman (Bet Taker), Adruitha Lee (Cashier), Regina Prokop (Sportsbook Gambler), Deven May (Bah Bah), John Salvatore (Gids), Thom Sesma (Young Guy), Matt Pebler (Angelo), Jerome Katz (Some Guy), Yolanda Windsay (Singer), Robert Hoerner (Backup Singer), John Mourain (Herbie, Plane Crash), Rene J.F. Piazza (Fat Guy), Ambyr Childers (Receptionist), William Sabourin, Alexey Marti, Lázaro R.Gutíerrez (ASAP Crew)

A former stripper arrives in Las Vegas seeking work as a cocktail waitress, but discovers that her keen memory and knack for numbers makes her a very desirable mark for the city's top gamblers.

Joshua Jackson, Rebecca Hall © RADiUS TWC

Christopher Walken, Alan Arkin, Al Pacino

Christopher Walken, Al Pacino © Lionsgate

STAND UP GUYS

(LIONSGATE) Producers, Sidney Kimmel, Tom Rosenberg, Gary Lucchesi, Jim Tauber; Executive Producers, Eric Reid, Ted Gidlow, Bruce Toll, Bingham Ray, Matt Berenson; Director, Fisher Stevens; Screenplay, Noah Haidle; Photography, Michael Grady; Designer, Maher Ahmad; Costumes, Lindsay Ann McKay; Music, Lyle Workman; Editor, Mark Livolsi; Casting, Tricia Wood, Deborah Aquila; a Lionsgate/Sidney Kimmel Entertainment/Lakeshore Entertainment production; Dolby; HD Widescreen; Color; Rated R; 95 minutes; Release date: December 14, 2012

CAST
Val	**Al Pacino**
Doc	**Christopher Walken**
Hirsch	**Alan Arkin**
Nina Hirsch	**Julianna Margulies**
Claphands	**Mark Margolis**
Wendy	**Lucy Punch**

Addison Timlin (Alex), Vanessa Ferlito (Sylvia), Katheryn Winnick (Oxana), Bill Burr (Larry), Craig Sheffer, Jay Bulger, Donnie Smith, Buster Reeves (Jargonviews), Yorgo Constantine (Paul), Weronika Rosati (Irena), Courtney Galiano (Lisa), Lauriane Gilliéron (Allison), Arjun Gupta (DJ), Aliya Astaphan (Stephanie), Brandon Scott (Doctor), Roland Feliciano (Orderly), Andrew Staes (Hospital Doctor), Jeffrey Cole (Patient), Eric Etebari (Bartender), Susann Fletcher (Sheila), Earl Carroll (Cook), Eve Brenner (Anita), Sam Upton (Jargonview on Couch), Rick Gomez (Priest), Sami Samvod (Guy at Bar), Keone Young (Song)

Released from prison after a twenty-eight year stretch, a gangster reteams with two of his old cronies, unaware that he has been targeted for a hit.

THE HOBBIT: AN UNEXPECTED JOURNEY

(WARNER BROS.) Producers, Carolynne Cunningham, Zane Weiner, Fran Walsh, Peter Jackson; Executive Producers, Alan Horn, Toby Emmerich, Ken Kamins, Carolyn Blackwood; Co-Producers, Philippa Boyens, Eileen Moran; Director, Peter Jackson; Screenplay, Fran Walsh, Philippa Boyens, Peter Jackson, Guillermo del Toro; Based on the 1937 novel *The Hobbit* by J.R.R. Tolkien; Photography, Andrew Lesnie; Designer, Dan Hennah; Costumes, Ann Maskrey, Richard Taylor, Bob Buck; Music, Howard Shore; Editor, Jabez Olssen; Stunts, Glenn Boswell; Armour, Weapons, Creatures and Special Makeup, Weta Workshop Ltd.; Senior Visual Effects Supervisor, Joe Letteri; Visual Effects Supervisor, Eric Saindon; Visual Effects and Animation, Wet Digital; Casting, Amy Hubbard, John Hubbard, Victoria Burrows, Scot Boland, Liz Mullane, Ann Robinson; a New Line Cinema and Metro-Goldwyn-Mayer Pictures presentation of a Wingnut Films production; Dolby; Color; Widescreen; HD; 3D; Rated PG-13; 169 minutes; Release date: December 14, 2012

CAST

Gandalf	**Ian McKellen**
Bilbo Baggins	**Martin Freeman**
Thorin	**Richard Armitage**
Balin	**Ken Stott**
Dwalin	**Graham McTavish**
Bifur/Tom Troll	**William Kircher**
Bofur	**James Nesbitt**
Bombur	**Stephen Hunter**
Fili	**Dean O'Gorman**
Kili	**Aidan Turner**
Oin	**John Callen**
Gloin/William Troll	**Peter Hambleton**
Nori	**Jed Brophy**
Dori/Bert Troll	**Mark Hadlow**
Ori	**Adam Brown**
Old Bilbo	**Ian Holm**
Frodo	**Elijah Wood**
Elrond	**Hugo Weaving**
Galadriel	**Cate Blanchett**
Saruman	**Christopher Lee**
Gollum	**Andy Serkis**
Radagast	**Sylvester McCoy**
Great Goblin	**Barry Humphries**
Thror	**Jeffrey Thomas**
Thrain	**Mike Mizrahi**
Thranduil	**Lee Pace**
Azog	**Manu Bennett**
Bolg	**Conan Stevens**
Necromancer	**Benedict Cumberbatch**
Yazneg	**John Rawls**
Fimbul/Grinnah	**Stephen Ure**
Master Worrywort	**Timothy Bartlett**
Lindir	**Bret McKenzie**
Goblin Scribe	**Kiran Shah**
Dwarf Miner	**Glenn Boswell**
Young Thrain	**Thomas Robins**

A Hobbit named Bilbo Baggins is enlisted by wizard Gandalf to join a group of dwarves to battle a dragon and retrieve a powerful ring. First of a three-part trilogy.

This film received Oscar nominations for visual effects, makeup & hairstyling, and production design.

William Kircher, Graham McTavish, Martin Freeman, James Nesbitt, John Callen

Graham McTavish, Ken Stott, Martin Freeman

Gollum

Ian McKellen, Hugo Weaving

Elijah Wood, Ian Holm

Dean O'Gorman

Christopher Lee

Ian McKellen, Sylvester McCoy

Cate Blanchett © New Line Cinema

James Gandolfini

Jessica Chastain

Jessica Chastain, Mark Strong

ZERO DARK THIRTY

(COLUMBIA) Producers, Mark Boal, Kathryn Bigelow, Megan Ellison; Executive Producers, Colin Wilson, Ted Schipper, Greg Shapiro; Director, Kathryn Bigelow; Screenplay, Mark Boal; Photography, Greig Fraser; Designer, Jeremy Hindle; Costumes, George L. Little; Music, Alexandre Desplat; Editors, Dylan Tichenor, William Goldenberg; Stunts, Stuart Thorp; Special Effects Supervisor, Richard Stutsman; Visual Effects Supervisor, Chris Harvey; Casting, Mark Bennett, Richard Hicks, Gail Stevens; a Mark Boal production, a First Light production, an Annapurna Pictures production; Dolby; Deluxe color; Rated R; 157 minutes; Release date: December 19, 2012

CAST

Maya	**Jessica Chastain**
Dan	**Jason Clarke**
Patrick, Squadron Team Leader	**Joel Edgerton**
Jessica	**Jennifer Ehle**
George	**Mark Strong**
Joseph Bradley	**Kyle Chandler**
Larry from Ground Branch	**Edgar Ramirez**
C.I.A. Director	**James Gandolfini**
Justin – DEVGRU	**Chris Pratt**
Saber – DEVGRU	**Callan Mulvey**
Hakim	**Fares Fares**
Ammar	**Reda Kateb**
Jack	**Harold Perrineau**
National Security Advisor	**Stephen Dillane**
Thomas	**Jeremy Strong**
J.J.	**J.J. Kandel**
John	**Scott Adkins**
The Wolf	**Fredric Lehne**
Steve	**Mark Duplass**
Jeremy	**John Barrowman**
Jared – DEVGRU	**Taylor Kinney**
Cargo Ship Detainee	**Mohammad K.**
Bagram Guard	**Henry Garrett**
Hassan Ghul	**Homayoun Ershadi**
Pakistani Detention Center Guard	**Darshan Aulakh**
Faraj Courier	**Navdeep Singh**
Human Khalil Al-Balawi	**Musa Sattari**
Case Officer	**David Menkin**
Zied	**Eyad Zoubi**

Julian Lewis Jones (Blackwater Guard), Christian Contreras (C.I.A. Security), Lauren Shaw (Lauren), Zachary Becker (Embassy Tech), John Antonini (Analyst at Embassy), Jessica Collins (Debbie), Christopher Stanley (Admiral Bill McCraven), Wahab Sheikh, Alexander Karim, Nabil Elouahabi, Aymen Hamdouchi, Simon Abkarian (Detainees on Monitor), Ali Marhyar, Parker Sawyers, Akin Gazi, Derek Siow (Interrogators on Monitor), Ashraf Telfah (Kuwait Businessman), Jonathan Olley (Tech from Ground Branch), Ben Lambert (N.S.A. Tech), Manraaj Singh (Rawal Caller), Tushaar Mehra (Abu Ahmed), Daniel Lapaine (Tim, Station Chief), Udayan Baijal (Guard at Maya's Apartment), John Schwab (Deputy National Security Advisor), Martin Delameny (Assistant to National Security Advisor), Nabil Koni (Pakistani Doctor), Anthony Edridge (General in Hangar), Jeff Mash (Deputy Director of C.I.A.), Siaosi Fonua (Henry – DEVGRU), Phil Somerville (Phil – DEVGRU), Nash Edgerton (Nate – DEVGRU EOD), Mike Colter (Mike – DEVGRU), Frank Grillo (Squadron Commanding Officer), Brett Praed, Aron Eastwood, Heemi Browstow, Chris Scarf, Barrie Rice, Rob Young, Spencer Coursen, Chris Perry, Alex Corbet Burcher, Robert G. Eastman, Tim Martin, Mitchell Hall, P.t. (DEVGRU Operators), Alan Pietruszewski, Kevin La Rosa II, Michael David Selig, Ben Parillo (Pilots), Hadeel Shqair (Abu Ahmed's Wife), Noureddine Hajjoujou (Abrar), Nour Alkawaja (Abrar's Wife), Malika Sayd, Siham Rida, Moula Mounia, Zalfa Seurat (UBL Wives), Tarik Haddouch (Khalid), Ricky Sekhon (UBL), Mark Valley (C-130 Pilot)

The true story of the tactics used to track down and eliminate terrorist Al Qaeda leader Osama Bin Laden in May of 2011.

2012 Academy Award Winner for Best Sound Editing (tied with *Skyfall*).

This film received additional Oscar nominations for picture, actress (Chastain), original screenplay, and film editing.

Kyle Chandler, Jason Clarke

Chris Pratt, Joel Edgerton

© Columbia Pictures

Christopher Stanley, Jessica Chastain, Alex Corbet Burcher

Jennifer Ehle

THE GUILT TRIP

(PARAMOUNT) Producers, Lorne Michaels, John Goldwyn, Evan Goldberg; Executive Producers, Seth Rogen, Barbra Streisand, Mary McLaglen, Dan Fogelman, David Ellison, Dana Goldberg, Paul Schwake; Director, Anne Fletcher; Screenplay, Dan Fogelman; Photography, Oliver Stapleton; Designer, Nelson Coates; Costumes, Danny Glicker; Music, Christophe Beck; Editors, Priscilla Ned Friendly, Dana E. Glauberman; Casting, Cathy Sandrich, Jorina King; a Skydance Productions presentation of a Michaels/Goldwyn production; Dolby; Hawk Scope Widescreen; Deluxe Color; Rated PG-13; 95 minutes; Release date: December 19, 2012

CAST

Joyce Brewster	**Barbra Streisand**
Andy Brewster	**Seth Rogen**
Gayle	**Kathy Najimy**
Rob	**Colin Hanks**
Andrew Margolis, Jr.	**Adam Scott**
Ben Graw	**Brett Cullen**
Ryan Mcfee	**Brandon Keener**
Anita	**Miriam Margolyes**
Diana	**Rose Abdoo**
Jessica	**Yvonne Strahovski**

Nora Dunn (Amy), Pedro Lopez (Hitchhiker), Julene Renee-Preciado (Kmart Receptionist), Zabryna Guevara, John Funk, Robert Curtis Brown (Kmart Executives), Tom Virtue, Vivian Vanderwerd (Mature Singles), Worth Howe (Bob), Vicki Goldsmith (Young Joyce), Matthew Levinson, Joseph Levinson (Toddler Andy), Kevin O'Keefe (Budget Car Renter), Rick Gonzalez (Mark), Jeff Witzke (Middlesex Voice Over), Casey Wilson (Amands), Steve Tom (OSH Executive), David Boller (Virginia Hotel Clerk), Ari Graynor (Joyce Margolis), Gabrielle Gumbs (Stripper), Dale Dickey (Tammy), Analeis Lorig (Moonlight), Jeff Kober (Jimmy), Lorna Scott, Kathleen Fletcher (Waitresses), Jen Zaborowski (Caesar's Check-In Clerk), Fred Fletcher (Slots Player), Darryl Sivad (HSN Producer), Davis Neves (HSN Makeup Artist), Jackson Douglas, Constance Esposito (HSN Executives), Shirley Charles (Frantic Mom), Dewain Robinson (Lost Son)

Thinking he might be able to hook her up with a past love, Andy Brewster invites his widowed mother on a 3,000 mile, 8 day road trip during which he also hopes to sell his new cleaning product.

Barbra Streisand, Seth Rogen © Paramount Pictures

Yvonne Strahovski, Colin Hanks

Brett Cullen, Barbra Streisand

Seth Rogen, Barbra Streisand, Brandon Keener

Tom Cruise, Robert Duvall

Tom Cruise, Richard Jenkins, David Oyelowo © Paramount Pictures

JACK REACHER

(PARAMOUNT) Producers, Tom Cruise, Don Granger, Paula Wagner, Gary Levinsohn; Executive Producers, Jake Meyers, Ken Kamins, Kevin Messick, David Ellison, Dana Goldberg, Paul Schwake; Director/Screenplay, Christopher McQuarrie; Based on the 2005 novel *One Shot* by Lee Child; Photography, Caleb Deschanel; Designer, Jim Bissell; Costumes, Susan Matheson; Music, Joe Kraemer; Editor, Kevin Stitt; Special Effects Coordinator, Kevin Hannigan; Stunts/2nd Unit Director, Paul Jennings; Casting, Mindy Marin; a Tom Cruise production, presented with Skydance Productions; Dolby; Panavision; Deluxe color; Rated PG-13; 130 minutes; Release date: December 21, 2012

CAST

Jack Reacher	**Tom Cruise**
Helen Rodin	**Rosamund Pike**
District Attorney Rodin	**Richard Jenkins**
Emerson	**David Oyelowo**
The Zec	**Werner Herzog**
Charlie	**Jai Courtney**
Cash	**Robert Duvall**
Vlad	**Vladimir Sizov**
James Barr	**Joseph Sikora**
Linsky	**Michael Raymond-James**

Alexia Fast (Sandy), Josh Helman (Jeb), James Martin Kelly (Rob Farrior), Dylan Kussman (Gary), Denver Milord (Punk), Susan Angelo (Oline Archer), Julia Yorks (Chrissie Farrior), Nicole Forester (Nancy Holt), Delilah Picart (Rita Coronado), Joe Coyle (Darren Sawyer), Alicia Murton (Mrs. Sawyer), Peter Gannon (Mr. Archer), David Whalen (Mr. Holt), Tristan Elma (Macos Coronado), Sophie Guest (Little Girl), Michael Minro (Eyewitness), Scott A. Martin (Wesley), CJ Ramirez (Secretary), Teri Clark Linden (Night Manager), Jarid Faubel (Man on Bus), Sara Lindsey (Woman on Bus), Jace Jeanes, Andrei Runtso, Efka Kvareciejus (Zec's Thugs), Lee Child (Desk Sergeant), Tommy Lafitte (Man with Ballcap), Kristen Dalton (Mindy), Jordan Trovillion (Goodwill Cashier), Annie Kitral (Pawn Shop Cashier), Lissy Gulick (Diner Waitress), Catherine L. Albers (Jeb's Mom), Larissa S. Emanuele (Sportsbar Waitress), Jason McCune (Construction Foreman), Shane Callahan, Joshua Elijah Reese (SWAT Guys), Nathan Hollabaugh, Christopher Stadulis (Cops)

Convinced that murder suspect James Barr is innocent, an attorney seeks the help of hired killer Jack Reacher to find the men behind a public shooting.

Jai Courtney

John Magaro, Bella Heathcote

Will Brill, Brahm Vaccarella, John Magaro, Jack Huston

Jack Huston © Paramount Vantage

NOT FADE AWAY

(PARAMOUNT VANTAGE) Producers, Mark Johnson, David Chase; Executive Producers, Steven Rales, Mark Roybal, Steven Van Zandt, Kerry Orent; Director/Screenplay, David Chase; Photography, Eigil Bryld; Designer, Ford Wheeler; Costumes, Catherine Marie Thomas; Music Supervisor, Steven Van Zandt; Editor, Sidney Wolinsky; Casting, Meredith Tucker; an Indian Paintbrush presentation in association with the Weinstein Company of a Gran Via/Chase Films production; Dolby; Deluxe color; Rated R; 112 minutes; Release date: December 21, 2012

CAST

Douglas	**John Magaro**
Eugene	**Jack Huston**
Wells	**Will Brill**
Joy Deitz	**Dominique McElligott**
Joe Patuto	**Brahm Vaccarella**
Skip	**Gregory Perri**
Pat	**James Gandolfini**
Grace Dietz	**Bella Heathcote**

Molly Price (Antoinette), Meg Guzulescu (Evelyn), Christopher McDonald (Jack Dietz), Brad Garrett (Jerry Ragovoy), Isiah Whitlock Jr. (Landers), Gerard Canonico (Schindewulf), F. Michael Haynie (The Bloat), Ken Forman (Vincent Lento), Chris Bannow (Dave Smith), Lisa Lampanelli (Aunt Josie), Louis Mustillo (Johnny Vitelloni), Marylou Mellace (Aunt Louise), John Tormey (Uncle Paul), Robert Funaro (Uncle Murf), Samantha Ryan Maisano (Aunt Jean), Anthony Giaimo (Uncle Beppy), Meredith Forlenza (Cousin Carol), Adam LaFaci (Cousin Paul), Katherine Bralower (Card Table Girl), Rebecca Luker (Marti Dietz), Justine Lupe (Candace), Shannon Esper (Mo Falcone), Marissa Ghavami (Meredith), Natalie Marchelletta (Karen), Lucie Pohl (Severine), Alfie Stewart (Keith), Dominic Sherwood (Mick), Julia Garner (Girl in Car), Randall Newsome (Mr. Gaunt), Susan Knight (Mrs. Gaunt), Audrey Lynn Weston (Lisa), Lauren Culpepper (Patty), Ryan Munzert (Jim DeSouza), Mike Steinmetz (Dennis), Jay Weinberg (Jazz Drummer), Teddy Coluca (Dominic), Charlie Plummer (Grace's Little Brother), Graham Davie (Mike), Julia Barrett-Mitchell (Crying Girl), John Mainieri (Angry Dad), Taylor Young (Hollywood Hippy), Megan Hubbell (Girl Has to Pee), Susie Duekcer, Samantha Hahn, Devon Werden (Singing Girls), Margaret Dorn, Kyle Gordon, Ula Hedwig, Kevin Osborne (Jingle Singers), Bobby Bandiera (Jingle Guitarist), Levi Wilson (Charlie Watts), Allen Wilson-Myers (Orlando), Kevin Dorian (Biker), Jordan Dean (Bob Cisco), William Connell (Wells' Brother), Madeline Rhodes (Doug's First Fan), Brandon Thane Wilson (Guy at Wells' House), Jeff Norris (Garage Operator), Scarlett Thiele (Diane), Stevie Lee Steel (Melissa)

During the 1960s, a Jersey teen becomes so passionate about rock music that he believes his band can be something more than just a lark and possibly make it in the big time, much to the chagrin of his practical father.

James Gandolfini, Molly Price, Meg Guzulescu

THIS IS 40

(UNIVERSAL) Producers, Judd Apatow, Clayton Townsend, Barry Mendel; Co-Producers, Paula Pell, Lisa Yadavaia; Director/Screenplay, Judd Apatow; based on his characters; Photography, Phedon Papamichael; Designer, Jefferson Sage; Costumes, Leesa Evans; Music, Jon Brion; Music Supervisor, Jonathan Karp; Editor, Brent White; Casting, Allison Jones; an Apatow production; Dolby; Panavision; Deluxe color; Rated R; 134 minutes; Release date: December 21, 2012

CAST

Pete	**Paul Rudd**
Debbie	**Leslie Mann**
Oliver	**John Lithgow**
Desi	**Megan Fox**
Sadie	**Maude Apatow**
Charlotte	**Iris Apatow**
Ronnie	**Chris O'Dowd**
Jason	**Jason Segel**
Catherine	**Melissa McCarthy**
Himself	**Graham Parker**
Larry	**Albert Brooks**

Annie Mumolo (Barb), Charlyne Yi (Jodi), Robert Smigel (Barry), Hugh Fink (Boutique Customer), Tom Freund (Graham Parker Solo Band), D.A. Sandoval (Older Pregnant Parent), Megan Grano (School Playdate Parent), Mackenzie Aladjem (School Playdate Child), Tom Yi (Charlotte's Teacher), Molly Shad (Grandma Molly), Michael Ian Black (Accountant), Lena Dunham (Cat), David Wild (Jewish Journal Reporter), Barb Hernandez (Mammogram Technician), Tom Everett (Pete's Doctor), Tim Bagley (Dr. Pellegrino), Damon Gupton (Colonoscopy Technician), Dan Bakkedahl (Dentist), Rebekka Johnson, Eric Vittina Phillips (Gyno Nurses), Jack Metcalf, Travis Metcalf, Bradley Metcalf (Triplets), Lisa Darr (Claire), Johnny Pemberton, Derek Basco (Room Service Waiters), Sam Dissanayake (Eastern Doctor), Tatum O'Neal (Voice of Realtor), Ava Sambora (Wendy), Nyla Durdin (Sadie's Set-Painting Friend), Ryan Lee (Joseph), Wyatt Russell (Flirty Hockey Player), Phil Burke (Hockey Player), R. Matt Carle, Ian Laperrière, James F. Van Riemsdyk, Scott Wesley Hartnell, Billie Joe Armstrong, Ryan Adams (Themselves), Steve Goulding, Andrew Bodnar, Martin Belmont, Bob Andrews, Brinsley Schwarz (The Rumor Band), Joanne Baron (Vice Principal Laviati), Spencer Daniels, Charlotte Townsend (Obnoxious Teenagers in SUV), Phil Hendrie (Man in Range Rover), Nicol Paone (ER Nurse), Christopher Stills, Ian McLagan, Marshall Vore, Cindy Cashdollar, Gus Seyffert (Ryan Adams Band), Bill Hader (Man at Store)

Pete and Debbie struggle with family and financial problems as they both face turning 40. Paul Rudd, Leslie Mann, Maude Apatow, Iris Apatow, and Jason Segel play the same characters they played in the 2007 Universal film *Knocked Up*.

Iris Apatow, Maude Apatow, Paul Rudd, Leslie Mann

Leslie Mann, Megan Fox © Universal Picture

John Lithgow, Albert Brooks

Chris O'Dowd, Paul Rudd, Lena Dunham

CIRQUE DU SOLEIL:WORLDS AWAY

(PARAMOUNT) Producers, Maritn Bolduc, Andrew Adamson, Aron Warner; 3D Executive Producer, Vincent Pace; Executive Producers, James Cameron, Jacques Méthé, Cary Granat, Ed Jones; Director/Screenplay, Andrew Adamson; Photography, Brett Turnbull; Music, Benoit Jutras; Editors, Sim Evan-Jones, Dirk Westervelt; a James Cameron presentation of a Cirque du Soleil production in association with Reel FX/Strange Weather and Cameron/Page Group; Dolby; Color; 3D; Rated PG; 91 minutes; Release date: December 21, 2012

CAST
Mia	**Erica Linz**
Tha Aerialist	**Igor Zaripov**
Ringmaster	**Lutz Halbhubner**
Sad Clown	**John Clarke**
Boss	**Dallas Barnett**

Tanya Drewery, Sarah Houbolt, Ascia Maybury, Damien Gordon, Zach Brickland, Iren Goed, Roufan Gan, Pei Pei Lane, Shaowei Xin, Stephen Cooper, Mengkai Shi, James Fletcher, Wenbo Zheng, Mariska du Plessis, Dan Hales, Graham Candy, Mike Baker, Matt Gillanders, Alan Thompson, Benedickt Negro (Circus Marvelous Cast Members)

An unexpected accident for one of the troupe's top aerialists leads a visitor into a parallel universe where she is shown some of the most spectacular acts of the world famous Cirque du Soleil.

Erica Linz, Benedikt Negro

Erica Linz, Igor Zaripov © Paramount Pictures

Damien Echols

Jessie Misskelley Jr. © Sony Classics

WEST OF MEMPHIS

(SONY CLASSICS) Producers, Peter Jackson, Fran Walsh, Amy Berg, Damien Echols, Lorri Davis; Executive Producer, Ken Kamins; Co-Producer, Matthew Dravitzki; Associate Producers, Katelyn Howes, Alejandra Riguero; Director, Amy Berg; Screenplay, Amy Berg, Billy McMillin; Photography, Maryse Alberti, Ronan Killeen; Music, Nick Cave, Warren Ellis; Editor, Billy McMillin; a Peter Jackson and Fran Walsh presentation of a Wingnut Films production in association with Disarming Films; Dolby; Color; Rated R; 147 minutes; Release date: December 25, 2012. Documentary on how three men were wrongly convicted of the murder of three 8-year-old boys in West Memphis, AK in 1993.

WITH
Pam Hicks, Jerry Driver, Mark Byers, Steve Jones, Bryan Ridge, Jessie Misskelley Jr., Gary Gitchell, John Fogelman, Vicki Hutcheson, Sharon French, David Burnett, Damien Echols, Amanda Hobbs, Terry Hobbs, Lorri Davis, Eddie Vedder, Mara Leveritt, Dan Stidham, Jessie Misskelley Sr., Laura Nirider, Steve Drizin, Joyce Cureton, Gail Grinnell, Frank Peretti, Dr. Vincent DiMaio, Michael Baden, Don Horgan, Rachel Geiser, Erin Moriarty, Barry Scheck, Natalie Maines-Pasdar, David Jacoby, Jaime Ballard, Mildred French, Judy Sadler, Marie Hicks, Cindy Hobbs, Sheila Hicks-Muse, Stephen Braga, Cari Peck, Patrick Benca, Scott Ellington, Holly Ballard, Jason Baldwin

Billy Crystal, Bette Midler

Billy Crystal, Kyle Harrison Breitkopf, Joshua Rush

Billy Crystal, Kyle Harrison Breitkopf, Marisa Tomei, Tom Everett Scott

PARENTAL GUIDANCE

(20TH CENTURY FOX) Producers, Billy Crystal, Peter Chernin, Dylan Clark; Executive Producer, Kevin Halloran; Director, Andy Fickman; Screenplay Lisa Addario, Joe Syracuse; Photography, Dean Semler; Designer, David J. Bomba; Costumes, Genevieve Tyrrell; Music, Marc Shaiman; Music Supervisor, Julia Michels; Editor, Kent Beyda; Casting, Marcia Ross; a Walden Media presentation of a Chernin Entertainment/Face Productions, Inc. production; Dolby; Super 35 Widescreen; Color; Rated PG; 104 minutes; Release date: December 25, 2012

CAST

Artie Decker	**Billy Crystal**
Diane Decker	**Bette Midler**
Alice Simmons	**Marisa Tomei**
Phil Simmons	**Tom Everett Scott**
Harper Simmons	**Bailee Madison**
Turner Simmons	**Joshua Rush**
Barker Simmons	**Kyle Harrison Breitkopf**
Cassandra	**Jennifer Crystal Foley**
Dr. Schveer	**Rhoda Griffis**
Mr. Cheng	**Gedde Watanabe**

Tony Hawk, Steve Levy (Themselves), Cade Jones (Ivan Halloran), Mavrick Moreno (Cody), Madison Lintz (Ashley), Corey James Wright (Drayton Glass), Justin Kennedy (Brad Zolick), Fyodor Cherniavsky (Orchestra Conductor), Brad James (Officer Chernin), Christine Lakin (Helen), Ron Clinton Smith (Umpire Clark), Hunter Weeks (Dino), Joe Knezevich (Kent), Jody Thompson (Aaron), Brooke Jaye Tyalor (Lois), Maia Moss-Fife (Samantha), Jan Harrelson (Babaloo), Dwayne Boyd (Lowell), Tiffany Morgan (Amanda), Kathleen Hogan (Betsy), Gina Herron (Carol), Patricia French (Rose), Nate Panning (Coach Bostick), Joanna Daniel (Lauren), Kendra Goehring (Doris Halloran), Matthew Warzel (Josh), Peter Zimmerman (Nate), Erin O'Connor (Clara), Audray McCroskey (Gwen), Marla Malcolm (Emma), Troy Michael Simeon (Parker), Daniel Fridkin (Chet Halloran), Jade Nicolette (Lulu), Karan Kendrick (Lisa), Bart Hansard (Joey), Ralph Branca (Legendary Judge),

Having just been fired from his long-time position as a sports announcer, Artie Decker and his wife Diane are asked by their daughter to babysit their grandchildren, with whom they try to use a more personal means of child-rearing than their offspring has done.

Joshua Rush, Bailee Madison, Kyle Harrison Breitkopf, Billy Crystal, Bette Midler © 20th Century Fox

Christoph Waltz, Don Stroud

Jamie Foxx, Leonardo DiCaprio

Don Johnson

DJANGO UNCHAINED

(COLUMBIA/WEINSTEIN CO.) Producers, Stacey Sher, Reginald Hudlin, Pilar Savone; Executive Producers, Bob Weinstein, Harvey Weinstein, Michael Shamberg, Shannon McIntosh, James W. Skotchdopole; Director/Screenplay, Quentin Tarantino; Photography, Robert Richardson; Desginer, J. Michael Riva; Costumes, Sharen Davis; Music Supervisor, Mary Ramos; Editor, Fred Raskin; Special Effects Supervisor, John McLeod; Special Makeup Effects Supervisor, Gregory Nicotero; Casting, Victoria Thomas; a Weinstein Co./Columbia Pictures presentation of a Band Apart production; Dolby; Panavision; Deluxe color; Rated R; 165 minutes; Release date: December 25, 2012

CAST

Django	**Jamie Foxx**
Dr. King Schultz	**Christoph Waltz**
Calvin Candie	**Leonardo DiCaprio**
Broomhilda von Schaft	**Kerry Washington**
Stephen	**Samuel L. Jackson**
Billy Crash	**Walton Goggins**
Leonide Moguy	**Dennis Christopher**
Ace Speck	**James Remar**
Mr. Stonesipher	**David Steen**
Cora	**Dana Gourrier**
Sheba	**Nichole Galicia**
Lara Lee Candie-Fitzwilly	**Laura Cayouette**
D'Artagnan	**Ato Essandoh**
Rodney	**Sammi Rotibi**
Big Fred's Opponent	**Clay Donahue Fontenot**
Big Fred	**Escalante Lundy**
Betina	**Miriam F. Glover**
Big Daddy	**Don Johnson**
Old Man Curtis Carrucan	**Bruce Dern**
Amerigo Vessepi	**Franco Nero**
Dicky Speck	**James Russo**
U.S. Marshal Gill Tatum	**Tom Wopat**
Sheriff Bill Sharp	**Don Stroud**
Son of a Gunfighter	**Russ Tamblyn**
Daughter of a Son of a Gunfighter	**Amber Tamblyn**
Big John Brittle	**M.C. Gainey**
Lil Raj Brittle	**Cooper Huckabee**
Ellis Brittle	**Doc Duhame**
Bag Head #2	**Jonah Hill**
Sheriff Gus (Snowy Snow)	**Lee Horsley**

Zoë Bell, Michael Bowen, Robert Carradine, Jake Garber, Ted Neeley, James Parks, Tom Savini (The Trackers), Michael Parks, John Jarratt, Quention Tarantino (The LeQuint Dickey Mining Co. Employees), Amari Cheatom (Roy), Keith Jefferson (Pudgy Ralph), Marcus Henderson, Lil Chuuuch (Slaves on Chain Gang), Kinetic (Franklin), Louise Stratten (Daughtrey Saloon Girl), Kim Robillard (Saloon Keeper Pete), Shana Stein (Daughtrey Bitty), Shannon Hazlett (Daughtery Saloon Girl), Jack Lucarelli (Daughtrey Rifleman), Victoria Thomas (Daughtrey Woman), Sharon Pierre-Louis (Little Jody), Christopher Berry (Willard), Kim Collins (Randy), Dane Rhodes (Tennessee Redfish), J.D. Evermore (O.B.), Rex Linn (Tennessee Harry), Michael Bacall (Smitty Bacall), Ned Bellamy (Wilson), David A. Coennen (Mr. Wigglesworth), Daniele Watts (Coco), Omar Dorsey (Chicken Charlie), Evan Parke, Nicholas P. Dashnaw (Bagheads), Craig Stark (Tommy Gilles), Brian Lee Brown (Hoot Peters), Ritchie Montgomery (Overseer Johnny Jerome), Jarrod Bunch (Banjo), Edrick Browne (Joshua), Jamal Duff (Tatum), Todd Allen (Dollar Bill), Lewis Smith (Jinglebells Cody), Jakel Marshall (House Servant), Carl Singleton (Carl, House Servant)

A bounty hunter agrees to help a runaway slave reunite with his wife who has been sold to a powerful plantation owner.

2012 Academy Award Winner for Best Supporting Actor (Christoph Waltz) and Best Original Screenplay.

This film received additional Oscar nominations for picture, cinematography, and sound editing.

Leonardo DiCaprio

Christoph Waltz, Jamie Foxx

Samuel L. Jackson, Kerry Washington

Christoph Waltz, Jamie Foxx © Weinstein Company

Jamie Foxx, Kerry Washington, Christoph Waltz

Walton Goggins

Jamie Foxx, Franco Nero

PROMISED LAND

(FOCUS) Producers, Matt Damon, John Krasinski, Chris Moore; Executive Producers, Gus Van Sant, Ron Schmidt, Jeff Skoll, Jonathan King; Director, Gus Van Sant; Screenplay, John Krasinski, Matt Damon; Story, Dave Eggers; Photography, Linus Sandgren; Designer, Daniel B. Clancy; Costumes, Juliet Polcsa; Music, Danny Elfman; Music Supervisor, Brian Reitzell; Editor, Billy Rich; Casting, Francine Maisler; a Sunday Night, Pearl Street, Media Farm production, presented in association with Participant Media and Image Nation Abu Dhabi; Dolby; Hawk Scope; Color; Rated R; 106 minutes; Release date: December 28, 2012

John Krasinsky, Frances McDormand

CAST

Steve Butler	**Matt Damon**
Dustin Noble	**John Krasinski**
Sue Thomason	**Frances McDormand**
Alice	**Rosemarie DeWitt**
Jeff Dennon	**Scoot McNairy**
Rob	**Titus Welliver**
Frank Yates	**Hal Holbrook**
David Churchill	**Terry Kinney**
Drew Scott	**Tim Guinee**
Paul Geary	**Lucas Black**

Benjamin Sheeler (Attendant), Carla Bianco (Waitress), Joe Coyle (Michael Downey), Dorothy Silver (Arlene), Lexi Cowan (Drew's Girl), Sara Lindsey (Claire Allen), Frank Conforti (Coach), Garrett Ashbaugh (Basketball Player), Jericho Morgan (Jericho), Max Schuler (Carson Allen), August G. Siciliano (5th Grader), Ken Strunk (Gerry Richards), Karen Baum (Lynn), Gerri Bumbaugh (Jesse the Bartender), Johnny Cicco (Donny), Erin Baldwin (Buddy's Waitress), Kristin Slaysman (Gwen), Andrew Kuebel (6-Year-Old Boy), Matthew Ferrante (Drummer), Justin Cook, Bruce Craven (Guitars), Steven Craven (Bass), Gene Williams (Keyboard), Dan Anders (Large Man), Sandy Medred (Paul's Girlfriend), Carrington E. Vaughn (Colin), Cain Alexander (Danny Thomason), Joy de la Paz (Motel Receptionist), Lennon Wynn (Lemonade Girl at Gym), Payton Godfrey (Lemonade Girl at Fair)

Hal Holbrook

A pair of corporate salesmen arrives in an economically depressed Pennsylvania town with the offer of buying properties for natural gas drilling rights, only to receive opposition from an activist addressing the environmental repercussions of such an act.

Rosemarie DeWitt, Matt Damon

Scoot McNairy © Focus Features

DOMESTIC FILMS B

2012 Releases / January 1–December 31

IT'S ABOUT YOU (MFI Media Group) Producers, Randy Hoffman, Maria Markus; Directors/ Editors/Photography, Kurt Markus, Ian Markus; Screenplay/ Narrator, Kurt Markus; Music, John Mellencamp; a Little b Pictures production; Color; Not rated; 85 minutes; Release date: January 4, 2012. Documentary on singer John Mellencamp's 2009 summer tour; **WITH:** John Mellencamp, T Bone Burnett, Andy York, Miriam Sturm, Dane Clark, Mike Wanchic, Jon E. Gee, Troye Kinnett, David Roe, Jay Bellerose, Marc Ribot.

John Mellencamp in *It's About You* © MFI Media Group

BENEATH THE DARKNESS (Image Entertainment) Producer, Ronnie Clemmer; Executive Producers, Bruce Wilkinson, Scott Mednick; Director, Martin Guigui; Screenplay, Bruce Wilkinson; Photography, Massimo Zeri; Designer, Christopher Stull; Music, Geoff Zanelli; Editor, Eric Potter; Visual Effects, Subterranean VFX; Casting, Donald Paul Pemrick, Dean E. Fronk; a Raincreek Productions in association with Sunset Pictures production; Dolby; Color; Rated R; 97 minutes; Release date: January 6, 2012. **CAST:** Dennis Quaid (Ely), Aimee Teegarden (Abby), Tony Oller (Travis), Stephen Lunsford (Brian), Devon Werkheiser (Danny), Brett Cullen (Sgt. Nickerson), Dahlia Waingort (Ms. Moore), Wilbur Penn (Officer Wainright), Amber Bartlett (Rosemary), Sydney Barrosse (Carolyn), Conrad Gonzales (Officer Alvarez), David Christopher (Sovic), Gabriel Folse (Russell), Melody Chase (Elaine), Cameron Banfield (Collin), Cheryl Chin (Nurse Josie), Richard Dillard (Doctor), Timothy Fall (Jack), Connor James (Young Travis), Steve Larkin (Rabbi), Paige Creswell, Annie Eileen (Classmates), Helen Ingham (Danny's Mom), John Blenn (I.V. Guy), Davi Jay (Ruben), Sam (Max), Troy Streuer (Assistant Mechanic), Chris Winter (Brian's Father)

Devon Werkheiser, Dennis Quaid in *Beneath the Darkness* © Image Entertainment

CODEPENDENT LESBIAN SPACE ALIEN SEEKS SAME (Space Aliens Presentation) Producers, Madeleine Olnek, Laura Terruso; Director/Screenplay, Madeleine Olnek; Photography, Nat Bouman; Designers, Rebecca Conroy, Bryan Heyboer; Costumes, Linda Gui, Julie Langer; Music, Clay Drinko; Editor, Curtis Grout; Special Effects Supervisor, Eugene Lehnert; a Space Aliens presentation; Black and white/color; HD; Not rated; 76 minutes; Release date: January 6, 2012. **CAST:** Lisa Haas (Jane), Susan Ziegler (Zoinx), Jackie Monahan (Zylar), Cynthia Kaplan (Barr), Dennis Davis (Senior Agent), Alex Karpovsky (Rookie Agent), Rae C. Wright (Jane's Therapist), Clay Drinko (Alien News Anchor), Julian Brand (James)

Lisa Haas, Susan Ziegler in *Codependent Lesbian Space Alien Seeks Same* © Space Aliens Presentation

LOOSIES (IFC Films) Producers, Chad A. Verdi, Peter Facinelli, Noah Kraft, Glenn Ciano; Executive Producers, Michelle Verdi, Robert Tarini, Gino Pereira, Robert DeFranco, Michael Corso, Anthony Gudas, John Santilli; Director, Michael Corrente; Screenplay, Peter Facinelli; Photography, Sam Oliver Fleischner; Designer, Robert Rotundo, Jr.; Costumes, Caroline Errington; Music, Chad Fischer; Music Supervisor, Michelle Verdi; Editor, Daniel Boneville; Casting, Adrienne Stern; a Chad A. Verdi presentation of a Verdi production, a Facinelli Films production; Color; Rated PG-13; 88 minutes; Release date: January 11, 2011. **CAST:** Peter Facinelli (Bobby), Jaimie Alexander (Lucy), Michael Madsen (Lt. Nick Sullivan), Vincent Gallo (Jax), William Forsythe (Capt. Tom Edwards), Mary Anne Leone (Rita), Christy Romano (Carmen), Joe Pantoliano (Carl), Eric Phillips (Donny), Tom DeNucci (Det. Jeffrey), Tom Paolino (Det. Verdi), Ara Boghigian, Anthony Paolucci (Officers), Glenn Ciano (Gomer), Johnny Cicco (Stoner Adam), Stella Schnabel (Girl with Fish), Travis Atwood (Mickey), Tyler Atwood (Nicky), Peter Berkrot (Waiter), Anne Mulhall (Nurse), Sera Verdi (Girl in Train Station), Chad A. Verdi (Father in Train Station), Jeannine Light (Subway Patron), Benny Salerno (Man on Subway), David Goggin (Policeman), Rebecca Forsythe (Pretty Girl in Bar), Billy Vigeant, Barry Blair (Goons), Rob DeFrano, Robert Tarini, Michael Tang, Chad A. Verdi (Bar Guys), Ray Brooks (Bartender), Daniel Boneville (Man on Phone)

Peter Facinelli, Jaimie Alexander in *Loosies* © IFC Films

MAN ON A MISSION: RICHARD GARRIOTT'S ROAD TO THE STARS
(First Run Features) Producer, Karen Yates; Executive Producer, Brady Dial; Director, Mike Woolf; Photography, Andrew Yates; Music, Brian Satterwhite, John Constant; Editor, Catie Cacci; a Beef and Pie production; Color; HD; Not rated; 83 minutes; Release date: January 13, 2012. Documentary on computer game mogul-turned-private space traveler Richard Garriott; **WITH:** Richard Garriott, Owen Garriott, Sergey Brin, Stephen Colbert, Anousheh Ansari, Greg Olsen, Mike Finke, Greg Chamitoff, Mike Barratt, Yuri Lonchakov, Sergey Volkov, Oleg Kononenko

Harry Belafonte in *Sing Your Song* © S2BN Films

Richard Garriott in *Man on a Mission* © First Run Features

DON'T GO IN THE WOODS (Tribeca Film) Producers, Erika Hampson, Ken Christmas; Director, Vincent D'Onofrio; Executive Producers/Screenplay, Joe Vinciguerra, Sam Bisbee; Photography, Michael J. Latino; Designer, Janet Kim; Costumes, Pashelle L. Clayton; Music, Sam Bisbee, Bo Boddie; Editor, Jennifer Lee; a 5 Minutes Production; Color; Not rated; 83 minutes; Release date: January 13, 2012. **CAST:** Bob Boddie (Carson), Eric Bogosian (Executive), Gwynn Galitzer (Felicity), Jorgen Jorgensen (Carlo), Tim Lajcik (Creature), Soomin Lee (Johnny), Kate O'Malley (Callie), Matt Sbeglia (Nick), Casey Smith (Anton), Nick Thorp (Robbie), Ali Tobia (Melinda), Cassandra Walker (Ashley)

SING YOUR SONG (S2BN Films) Producers, Michael Cohl, Gina Belafonte, Jim Brown, William Eigen, Julius R. Nasso; Co-Producer, Sage Scully; Director/Screenplay/Editor, Susanne Rostock; Music, Hahn Rowe; Editors, Susanne Rostock, Jason L. Pollard; a Michael Cohl presentation of a Belafonte Enterprises and S2BN Entertainment Production in association with Julius R. Nasso Productions; Not rated; 104 minutes; Release date: January 13, 2012. Documentary on singer-actor-activist Harry Belafonte; **WITH:** Harry Belafonte, Sidney Poitier, Marge Champion, Fran Scott Attaway, Julian Bond, George Schlatter, Adrienne Belafonte-Biesmeyer, Diahann Carroll, Mike Merrick, Julie Belafonte, Gloria Lynne, Bob DeCormier, Cora Weiss, Nelson Mandela, Taylor Branch, David Belafonte, Shari Belafonte, Gina Belafonte, John Lewis, Willie Blue, Tony Bennett, Clarence Jones, Petula Clark, Whoopi Goldberg, Tom Smothers, Dick Smothers, Buffy Sainte Marie, Dennis Banks, Russell Means, Quincy Jones, Ken Kragan, Dr. Lloyd Grieg, Bishop Desmond Tutu, Bo Taylor, Nane Alejandrez, Marian Wright Edelman, Ruby Dee, Andrew Young, Ade, Abd Al Malik (This film premiered on HBO on Oct. 17, 2011).

FAKE IT SO REAL (4th Row Films) Producers, Douglas Tirola, Susan Bedusa, Robert Greene; Director, Robert Greene; Photography, Sean Price Williams, Robert Greene; Music, Nikki Shapiro; Editors, Robert Greene, Deanna Davis; a 4th Row Films/Prewar Cinema Prods. production; Color; DV; Not rated; 94 minutes; Release date: January 13, 2012. Documentary on a group of pro wrestlers in Lincolnton, North Carolina; **WITH:** Chris Baldwin, Alex Boyles, Gabriel Croft, David Hayes, Tyler Hayes, Howard Hill, Chris Isenberg, J-Prep, Van Jordan, Richie Owenby, Pitt, Zane Riley, Jeff Roberts, Brandon Weese

Gabriel Croft in *Fake it So Real* © 4th Row Films

THE DIVIDE (Anchor Bay) Producers, Ross M. Dinerstein, Darryn Welch, Juliette Hagopian, Nathaniel Rollo; Executive Producers, Tony Rollo, Cathy Rollo, Chris Ouwinga, Bobby Schwartz, Michael Horn, Jamie Carmichael, Kevin Iwashina, Manoj Jain, Ross Bryan; Director, Xavier Gens; Screenplay, Karl Mueller, Eron Sheean; Photography, Laurent Barés; Designer, Tony Noble; Costumes, Mary Hyde Kerr; Music, Jean-Pierre Taieb; Editor, Carlo Rizzo; Casting, Lindsey Hayes Kroeger; a Preferred Content/Instinctive Film/Julijette Inc. production in association with BR Group and Ink Connection; American-Canadian; Dolby; Color; HD; Not rated; 110 minutes; Release date: January 13, 2012. **CAST:** Lauren German (Eva), Michael Biehn (Mickey), Milo Ventimiglia (Josh), Courtney B. Vance (Delvin), Ashton Holmes (Adrien), Rosanna Arquette (Marilyn), Iván González (Sam), Michael Eklund (Bobby), Abbey Thickson (Wendi), Jennifer Blanc (Liz)

Courtney B. Vance, Michael Biehn, Iván Gonzalez, Lauren German, Ashton Holmes, Milo Ventimiglia, Michael Eklund in *The Divide* © Anchor Bay

THE CITY DARK (Argot Pictures) Producer/Director/Screenplay, Ian Cheney; Photography, Ian Cheney, Taylor Gentry; Designer, Tyler Morogren; Music, The Fishermen Three, Ben Fries; Editors, Ian Cheney, Frederick Shanahan; Animation, Sharon Shattuck; a Rooftop Films & Edgeworx Studios presentation of a Wicked Delicate Films production; Stereo; Color; HD; Not rated; 84 minutes; Release date; January 18, 2012. Documentary on light pollution and the disappearing night sky; **WITH:** Neil deGrasse Tyson, Don Pettit, Ann Druyan, Jack Newton, Chris Impey, Jeffrey Kuhn, Roger Ekirch, Jane Brox, Bill Sharpe, Susan Elbin, Dr. Steven Lockley, Dr. Richard Stevens, Dr. George Brainard, Dr. David Blask, Jon Shane, Herve Descottes

The City Dark © Argot Pictures

THE PRUITT-IGOE MYTH (First Run Features) Producers, Chad Freidrichs, Jaime Freidrichs, Paul Fehler, Brian Woodman; Director, Chad Freidrichs; Screenplay, Chad Freidrichs, Jaime Freidrichs; Music, Benjamin Balcom; Narrator, Jason Henry; a Unicorn Stencil production; Color; Not rated; 83 minutes; Release date: January 20, 2012. Documentary on the failure of the St. Louis Pruitt-Igoe housing development; **WITH:** Sylvester Brown, Robert Fishman, Joseph Heathcott, Brian King, Joyce Ladner, Ruby Russell, Valerie Sills, Jacquelyn Williams.

The Pruitt-Igoe Myth © First Run Features

ULTRASUEDE: IN SEARCH OF HALSTON (Tribeca Film) Producers, Whitney Sudler-Smith, Anne Goursaud, Adam Bardach, Tim Maloney, Nicholas Simon; Executive Producers, Shawn Simon, Mark Urman; Director, Whitney Sudler-Smith; Screenplay, Whitney Sudler-Smith, Anne Goursaud; Photography, Scott Miller; Music, Christopher Franke, Edgar Rothermich; Editor, John Paul Horstmann; a Vainglorious Pictures production; Dolby; Color; HD; Not rated; 85 minutes; Release date: January 20, 2012. Documentary on fashion designer Roy Halston and his iconic place in 1970's pop culture; **WITH:** Patricia Altschul, Phillip Bloch, Thom Browne, Stephen Burrows, Pat Cleveland, Bob Colacello, Richard DuPont, Robert DuPont, Amy Fine-Collins, Anthony Haden-Guest, Cathy Horyn, Anjelica Huston, Billy Joel, Randy Jones, Naeem Khan, Christopher Makos, Boaz Masur, Patrick McMullen, Liza Minnelli, Georgette Mosbacher, Glenn O'Brien, Adam Rapoport, Andy Rapoport, Nile Rodgers, Chado Ralph Rucci, Whitney Smith, André Leon Talley, Diane von Fürstenberg, Paul Wilmot

16-LOVE (E1 Entertainment) Producers, Ilyssa Goodman, Adam Lipsius; Executive Producers, Linda Appel Lipsius, Noor Ahmed, Ben Reder, Lindsey Shaw, Alan Caso, Leigh Dunlap; Director, Adam Lipsius; Screenplay, Leigh Dunlap; Photography, Alan Caso; Designers, Eric Conger, Maynard Mendoza; Music, Russ Howard III; Editor, Tina Pacheco; Casting, Linda Phillips-Palo; an Uptown 6 presentation; Color; HD; Rated PG; 88 minutes; Release date: January 20, 2012. **CAST:** Lindsey Shaw (Ally Mash), Chandler Massey (Farrell Gambles), Keith Coulouris (Dave Mash), Lindsey Black (Rebecca Fisher), Alexandra Paul (Margo Mash), Susie Abromeit (Katina Upranova), Mark Elias (Nate), Steven Christopher Parker (Stuart), Josh Blaylock (Red Bull), Sasha Formoso (Lindsey Benfield), Kelly Gould (Ellen), Josh Cooke (Jim), Fabienne Guerin (Debbie), Vivica Schwartz (Vivica), Scott Butler (British Chair Umpire, AJC Finals), Aurelien Drumilion Serand (Aurelein Drumillon), Nick Falls (La Jolla Photographer), Asmar Fontenot (Paul, Ally's Personal Trainer), Layla Zbinden (Milla Christman), Kyron Griffith (Milon Christman), Julia Kelleher (Ashley), Lindsay Kirk (Hayley), Elle Labadie (Young Ally), Sarah Lilly (Amy), Lainey Lipson (Lily), Michael M. McGuire (Pizza Man), Lauryn Moses (Bailey), Brendan Nyhan (Derek Hydon), Michelle Page (Kylie), David Tillman (Chair Umpire, La Jolla), Billy St. John (Farrell's Coach), Jordan Engle (Head Shoe Rep), Mark-Paul Barro (Head Photographer), Ilyssa Goodman (Reporter), Robert W. LeBuhn (Chair Umpire, AJC Doubles Finals), Ned Hill, Steven H. Lipsius (Chair Umpires, La Costa), Jacqueline Hites (Eleanor Henderson), Brendan Nyhan (Derek Hydon), Katelynn Bickle (Irina), Eric Conger (Angry Basketball Player), Dorothy Lipsius, Eli Lipsius (Kids at Pool)

Chandler Massey, Lindsey Shaw in *16-Love* © E1 Entertainment

SCALENE (Along the Tracks) Producers, Carlos Jimenez Flores, Zack Parker; Executive Producer, Mike Khamis; Director/Editor, Zack Parker; Screenplay, Brandon Owens, Zack Parker; Photography, Jim Timperman; Designer, Cameron Bourquein; Music, The Newton Brothers; Casting, Rosemary Welden; an Along the Tracks presentation in association with Kachi Films; Color; Widescreen;

HD; Not rated; 96 minutes; Release date: January 20, 2012. **CAST:** Margo Martindale (Janice Trimble), Hanna Hall (Paige Alexander), Adam Scarimbolo (Jakob Trimble), Jim Dougherty (Charles), LaDonna Pettijohn (Mrs. Alexander), Raymond Kester (Mr. Alexander), Sean Blogett (Public Defender), Angela Steele (City Prosecutor), Frank T. Ziede (Dr. Khamis), Mark A. Nash (Daniel Trimble), Eric Monroe (Butch), Micah Shane Ballinger (Jimmy), Benjamin Riley (Jason), Samantha Eileen DeTurk (Waitress), Alli Miller, Stephanie Lochbihler, Nubia Tamayo Perez (Paige's Friends), Stefania Marcone (Hostess), Megan Magdalene (Girl in Classroom)

Margo Martindale, Adam Scarimbolo in *Scalene* © Along the Tracks

WATCHING TV WITH THE RED CHINESE (Roam Films) Producers, Shimon Dotan, Netaya Anbar; Executive Producers, Ari Weinberger, Dan Anbar, Zev London; Director, Shimon Dotan; Screenplay, Netaya Anbar, Shimon Dotan; Based on the 1992 novel by Luke Whisnant; Photography, Michael Rossetti; Designer, Tania Bijlani; Costumes, Carisa Bush; Music, Nat Osborn; Editor, Netaya Anbar; an Emmkens presentation of a Blue Water Films production; Color/black and white; HD; Not rated; 105 minutes; Release date: January 20, 2012. **CAST:** Ryan O'Nan (Dexter Mitchell), Leonardo Nam (Chen), Gillian Jacobs (Suzanne), James Chen (Tzu), Keong Sim (Wa), Michael Esper (Billy), Peter Scanavino (Czapinczyk), Ron C. Jones (Little), Constance Wu (Kim Hu), Idara Victor (Antigone), Adeel Ahmed (Big Tree Guy), Kenneth Anderson (Junkie), Elijah Cook (Cortez), Daniel Fainman (Paramedic), Alan Feirer (Mark, Radio Reporter), Tom Galantich (Mortician), Mike Holt, Josh Presin (Police Officers), Max Jenkins (Boy in Gladiator Costume), Rebecca Keren (Hooker), Lil Rhee, Charles D. Roden (Doctors), Lyn Saga (Ballerina), Sandro Scenga (Roger, Radio Anchor), Derrick Simmons (Mugger), Aubrey Sinn (Teri), Dale Soules (Bag Lady), Hisham Tawfiq (James)

AN INCONSISTENT TRUTH (Rocky Mountain Pictures) Producer/Screenplay, Phil Valentine; Executive Producers, David Harper, Joseph Edwards, Michael Constanza; Co-Producer, Ann Cates; Director, Shayne Edwards; Photography, Alex Hall, Rich Hawkinson, James King, Ed Lamberg, Phil Loiacono, Art Shirley, Brock Slagle; Music, Michael Thomas Benoit; Editors, Shayne Edwards, Phil Valentine; an Epicstar Pictures presentation of an Extragood production; Rated PG; 89 minutes; Release date: January 27, 2012. Documentary on alternate theories about global warming; **WITH:** Newt Gingrich, Sen. James Inhofe, Dr. John Christy, Dr. Fred Singer, Dr. Roy Spencer, Greg Walden, Sen. Jim DeMint, Dr. Ken Green, Steven Milloy, Drew Johnson.

5 TIME CHAMPION (Bear Media) Producers, Ezra Venetos, Berndt Mader; Director/ Screenplay, Berndt Mader; Photography, Jimmy Lee Phelan; Designer, Javier Bonafont; Costumes, Stephanie A. Steele; Music, Graham Reynolds; Editors, Brent Joseph, Don Howard; a Shark Films/Bear Media production; Color; Not rated; 92 minutes; Release date: January 27, 2012. **CAST:** Ryan Akin (Julius), Betty Buckley (Fran), Dana Wheeler-Nicholson (Danielle), Jon Gries (Melvin

Glee), Justin Arnold (Levi), Noell Coet (Shirley), Robert Longstreet (Harold), Don Pirl (Alwyn), Juli Erickson (Betty), Jill Blackwood (Ms. Klein), Shakei Brown (Duane), Jessie Tilton, Ashley Donigan (Checkout Girls), Susan Mansur (Mrs. Sylvester), Jarrett Randall (Bernard), Cameron Rostami (Rigoberto), Gabi Walker (Teena), Meygan Washington (Claire)

SPLINTERS (SnagFilms) Producers, Perrin Chiles, Adam Pesce; Executive Producers, Paul Morgan, Catherine Davila, Daniel Davila, Alan Siegel, Danielle Robinson; Director/ Photography, Adam Pesce; Music, Jesse Voccia; Editor, Kim Roberts; an In Effect Films production in association with Divisadero Pictures & Little House Prods. presentation; Color; HD; Not rated; 94 minutes; Release date: February 3, 2012. Documentary on the popularity of surfing in the Papua New Guinea village of Vanimo; **WITH:** Andy Abel, Ezekiel Afara, Angelus Lipahi, Steve Tekwie, Lesley Umpa, Susan Umpa.

Splinters © SnagFilms

BAD FEVER (Factory 25) Producer, Dustin Guy Defa; Executive Producers, Melinda McIlwain, Rick Hubbard, Judi Stauffer, Richard Nelson, Toni Nelson; Director/Screenplay, Dustin Guy Defa; Additional Material, Kentucker Audley, Eléonore Hendricks; Photography, Mike Gioulakis; Art Directors/Costumes, Moey Nelson, Allison Baar; Editors, Dustin Guy Defa, David Lowery; Color; HD; Not rated; 77 minutes; Release date: February 3, 2012. **CAST:** Kentucker Audley (Eddie), Eléonore Hendricks (Irene), Annette Wright (Mama), Allison Baar (Yoko), Dustin Guy Defa (Larry), Rebecca McIntosh (Waitress), Duane Stephens (Burt), Rakesh Bhatia (Motel Clerk), Kelly McCraig, Donald Ashvie, Robert Forsland (Tree Workers), Ryan Schlegel, Ashley Anderson (Comedians)

Kentucker Audley in *Bad Fever* © Factory 25

WINDFALL (SnagFilms) Producers, Laura Israel, Autumn Tarleton; Executive Producer, Don Faller; Director, Laura Israel; Photography, Brian Jackson; Music, Wade Schuman, Hazmat Modine; Editors, Laura Israel, Stacey Foster, Alex Bingham; a Cat Hollow Films production; Color; HD; Not rated; 83 minutes; Release date: February 3, 2012. Documentary on the negative effects of wind turbines; **WITH:** Scott Alexander, Frank Bachler, Ron Bailey, Sue Bailey, Rick Beyer, Tara Collins, Eve Kelley, Rosemary Nichols, T. Boone Pickens, Rachel Polens, Marge Rockefeller, Bob Rosen, Marc Schneider.

Windfall © SnagFilms

DYSFUNCTIONAL FRIENDS (Datari Turner Prods.) Producers, Greg Carter, Datari Turner; Executive Producers, Robert Hunt, Patrick Thomas Jr., Neil Harrington, Scott Lang, Ira Antelis, Gordon Bijelonic; Director/ Screenplay, Corey Grant; Photography, Richard J. Vialet; Designer, Rhonda Marie Wagner; Costumes, Ca-Trece Mas'Sey; Music, Ira Antelis, Jason Grey; Editors, Ralph Jean-Pierre, Datari Turner; Casting, Phaedra Harris; Color; Not rated; 111 minutes; Release date: February 3, 2012. **CAST:** Stacey Dash (Lisa), Reagan Gomez-Preston (Ebony), Wesley Jonathan (Brett), Datari Turner (Aaron), Jason Weaver (Gary), Persia White (Trenyce), Tatyana Ali (Alex), Terrell Owens (Jackson), Stacy Keibler (Storm), Hosea Chanchez (Jamal), Christian Keyes (Stylz), Antwon Tanner (Nick), Dennis L.A. White (Minister), Essence Atkins (Alice), Tracy Z. Francis (Madison), Meagan Good (Ms. Stevens), Melissa Grimmond (Trixi), Junie Hoang (Star), Erica Hubbard (Catrece), Sue Lyn (Kelly), Meghan Markle (Terry), Suelyn Medeiros (Kelly), Brittanya O'Campo (Lexus), Laila Odom (Taylor), Samantha Presley (Aliana), J.B. Ricks (Newscaster), Keith Robinson (Dennis), Vanessa Simmons (Hanna), Richard Van Slyke (Ad Company Executive), Adebola Afolabi, Rufaro Walls-Lumbly (Church Ladies)

Stacey Dash in *Dysfunctional Friends* © Datari Turner Prods.

BONSAI PEOPLE: THE VISION OF MUHAMMAD YUNUS (Hummingbird Pictures) Producer/Director/Photography, Holly Mosher; Screenplay, Lisa Gold; Music, Bappi Rahman, Khayem Ahmed; Editor, Natasha Uppal; American Public Television, FilmBuff, VPD; Not rated; 79 minutes; Release date: February 3, 2012. Documentary on the humanitarian work of Muhammad Yunus; **WITH:** Muhammad Yunus, Anarkuli Hossain, Amir Hossain, Aroti & Surinder, Ayesha, Melancho Uddin, Md. Helal Uddin, Shahnaj Hoque, Samsul Hoque, Surjobano, Sumon, Kolopona, Firuza, Amena, Azila, Kodbanu, Suma Rani.

Ayesha in *Bonsai People* © Hummingbird Pictures

THE SKINNY (TSBB) Producer/Director/Screenplay/Music/Editor/Casting, Patrik-Ian Polk; Photography, Eun-ah Lee; Designer, Lisa Green; Costumes, Joe Exclusive; a Tall Skinny Black Boy Prods. presentation in association with Logo Features; Color; HD; Not rated; 100 minutes; Release date: February 10, 2012. **CAST:** Jussie Smollett (Magnus), Anthony Burrell (Kyle), Blake Young-Fountain (Sebastian), Shanika Warren-Markland (Langston), Jeffrey Bowyer-Chapman (Joey), Jennia Fredrique (Samantha), Wilson Cruz (Doctor), B. Scott (Candy), Darryl Stephens (Nurse), Joshua Cruz (Evan), Michael Franklin (Michael), Austin Patrick McBride (Kyle's White Boy), Dustin Ross (Ryan), Robb Sherman (Junot)

Shanika Warren-Markland, Jeffrey Bowyer-Chapman, Jussie Smollett, Blake Young, Anthony Burrell in *The Skinny* © TSBB

KUNG FU JOE (Indican) Producers, Glen Berry, Michael Kutcher; Executive Producers, Wilson Large, Glenn Biernacki; Director/Screenplay/Editor, Glen Berry; Designer, Alex Cassun; Music, Darius Holbert; a Kung Fu Joe Movie production; Color; Not rated; 89 minutes; Release date: February 10, 2012. **CAST:** Zak VanWinkle (Kung Fu Joe), Jeremy Parrish (The Detective), Wilson Large (W), Victoria Maurette (Femme Fatale)

Zak VanWinkle in *Kung Fu Joe* © Indican

THE DISH & THE SPOON (Submarine Entertainment) Producers, Alison Bagnall, Amy Seimetz, Peter Gilbert; Director/Story, Alison Bagnall; Screenplay, Alison Bagnall, Andrew Lewis; Photography, Mark Schwartzbard; Designers, Jade Healy, Chris Trujillo; Costumes, Lisa Hennessy; Editors, Darrin Navarro, Brett Jutkiewicz; a Lake Effect Media Group presentation of a Humble Pictures production in association with 40 Day Prods.; Color; HD; Rated R; 92 minutes; Release date: February 10, 2012. **CAST**: Greta Gerwig (Rose), Olly Alexander (Boy), Eleonore Hendricks (Emma Hicks), Adam Rothenberg (Husband), Amy Seimetz (Emma's Friend)

Greta Gerwig, Olly Alexander in *The Dish & the Spoon* © Submarine Entertainment

RE: GENERATION (D&E Entertainment) Producers, Jules Daly, Tom Dunlap; Executive Producers, Steve Bender, Nick Davidge, Dominic Sandifer; Director, Amir Bar-Lev; Photography, Nelson Hume; Editors, Dan Swietlik, Darrin Navarro; a Hyundai Veloster presentation of an RSA Films production; Color; Not rated; 75 minutes; Release date: February 16, 2012. Documentary in which DJs remix and re-imagine five traditional styles of music; **WITH:** DJ Premier, Mark Ronson, Skrillex, The Crystal Method, Pretty Lights, Nas, Erykah Badu, Martha Reeves, LeAnn Rimes, Mos Def, Dr. Ralph Stanley, The Berklee Symphony Orchestra, Zigaboo Modeliste, The Funk Brothers, Bruce Adolphe, Dennis Coffey, The Dap-Kings, John Desmore, Robby Krieger, Ray Manzarek, Trombone Shorty, Stephen Webber

Re: Generation © D&E Entertainment

JESS + MOSS (Strand) Producers, Clay Jeter, Brian Harstine, Will Basanta, Isaac Hagy; Executive Producers, Jason Michael Berman, Debra Jeter, Harley Tat, Bill Fletcher, John Rowley, David Gelb, Kevin Iwashina; Director/Photography, Clay Jeter; Screenplay, Clay Jeter, Will Basanta, Isaac Hagy, Debra Jeter; Story, Debra Jeter, Nikki Jeter Wilbanks; Designer, Gregory Grover; Editor, Isaac Hagy; a Blood River Pictures presentation in association with Love Stream, agnés b. Productions and Liquid Crystal Productions; Stereo; Color; Super 16; Not rated; 83 minutes; Release date: February 17, 2012. **CAST:** Sarah Hagan (Jess), Austin Vickers (Moss), Haley Strode (Jess' Mother), Donald Fleming (Jess' Father), Haley Parker (Haley), Cliff Coleman (Moss' Grandfather), Marie Coleman (Moss' Grandmother)

Sara Hagan, Austin Vickers in *Jess + Moss* © Strand Releasing

ON THE ICE (Silverwood Films) Producers, Cara Marcous, Lynette Howell, Marco Londoner, Zhana Londoner; Executive Producers, Doug Dey, Susanne Adamski, Nick Quested, Cary Fukunaga, Rick Rosenthal, Nick Morton, Greg Smith; Director/Screenplay, Andrew Okpeaha MacLean; Photography, Lol Crawley; Designer, Chad Keith; Costumes, Courtney McClain; Music, iZLER; Editor, Nat Sanders; Casting, Cara Marcous, Andrew Okpeaha MacLean; a Treehead Films production, presented in association with Whitewater Films & Goldcrest Films; Color; Rated R; 96 minutes; Release date: February 17, 2012. **CAST:** Josiah Patkotak (Qalli), Frank Qutuq Irelan (Aivaaq), Teddy Kyle Smith (Egasak), Adamina Kerr (Michelle), Sierra Jade Sampson (Uvlu), John Miller (James), Rosabelle Kunnanna Rexford (Aaka), Vernon Kanayurak (Roscoe), Billyjens Hopson (Jens), Jay Rapoza (Max), Allison Warden (Sigvaun), Denae Brower (Darlene), Tara Sweeney (Dora), Tasha Taaqpak Panigeo (Charlene), Jerica Aamodt (Ellie), Gage Saxton (DJ), Richard Enlow IV (Trace), Johnnie Kunaq Brower (Nathaniel), Olemaun Rexford (Olemaun), Jack Packer (Helicopter Pilot), Thomas Ahtuangaruak Jr. (Jimmy), Robert Allen Brouilette (Trooper Tagak), Katie Roseberry (Teen Girl)

THE FORGIVENESS OF BLOOD (Sundance Selects) Producer, Paul Mezey; Executive Producers, Janine Gold, Eric Abraham, Domenico Procacci, Hunter Gray, Tyler Brodie; Director, Joshua Marston; Screenplay, Joshua Marston, Andamion Murataj; Photography, Rob Hardy; Designer, Tommaso Ortino; Costumes, Emir Turkeshi; Music, Jacobo Lieberman, Leonardo Heiblum; Editor, Malcolm Jamieson; Casting, Adamion Murataj; a Fandango Portobello presentation in association with Artists Public Domain and Cinereach and Lissus Media of a Journeyman Pictures production; American-Albanian-Danish-Italian; Dolby; HD; Technicolor; Not rated; 109 minutes; Release date: February 24, 2012. **CAST:** Tristan Halilaj (Nik), Sindi Laçej (Rudina), Refet Abazi (Mark), Ilire Vinca Çelaj (Drita), Çun Lajçi (Ded), Zana Hasaj (Bardha), Erjon Mani (Tom), Luan Jaha (Zef), Veton Osmani (Sokol), Selman Lokaj (Kreshnik), Kol Zefi (Shpend), Esmeralda Gjonlulaj (Bora), Elsajed Tallali (Dren), Ibrahim Ymeri (School Director), Servete Haxhija (Mara), Arlind Lleshi (Loran), Alfred Lisi (Fatmir), Edmond Pepkolaj (Police Captain), Geg Zefi (Afrim), Pjeter Noshi (Besim), Gjon Lula (Cen), Isuf Duraj (Gjergi), Sabri Haxhija (Lekë), Ruzhdi Pirnaq (Genc), Xhevdet Shima (Mr. Skendaj), Gjin Basha (Hasan Pema), Arben Buhaj (Burim), Injac Marku, Haxhi Brati, Eduard Beqiri (Cigarette Vendors), Fatmir Shabaj (Horse Buyer)

Tristan Halilaj, Erjon Mani in *The Forgiveness of Blood* © Sundance Selects

AROUND JUNE (Indican) Producers, Ralph King, James Savoca, Jeremiah Birnbaum; Executive Producers, Greg Corbin, Alyssa Weisberg, Eric Cleage; Director/Screenplay, James Savoca; Photography, Peter Hawkins; Designer, Stacey Ransom; Music, Didier Lean Rachou; Animation, Charlie Canfield; Casting, Alyssa Weisberg; a Fog City Pictures presentation in association with Caviar Films; Color; Not rated; 93 minutes; Release date: February 24, 2012. **CAST:** Samaire Armstrong (June), Brad William Henke (Henry), Jon Gries (Murry), Oscar Guerrero (Juan Diego), David Fine (Crane), Spencer Park (Kid), Maggie Grant (Mrs. Baedeker), Celik Kayalar (Mr. Herbert), Rocky LaRochelle (Mr. Bandini), Renee Sweet (Punk Kid)

GONE (Summit) Producers, Tom Rosenberg, Gary Lucchesi, Sidney Kimmel, Dan Abrams, Chris Salvaterra; Executive Producers, Andrew Lamal, Eric Reid, Ted Gidlow, Bruce Toll, Jim Tauber, Matt Berenson; Director, Heitor Dhalia; Screenplay, Allison Burnett; Photography, Michael Grady; Designer, Charisse Cardenas; Costumes, Lindsay Ann McKay; Music, David Buckley; Editor, John Axelrad; Casting, Deborah Aquila, Tricia Wood; a Lakeshore Entertainment, Sidney Kimmel Entertainment production; Dolby; Color; Rated PG-13; 94 minutes; Release date: February 24, 2012. **CAST:** Amanda Seyfried (Jill), Daniel Sunjata (Powers), Jennifer Carpenter (Sharon Ames), Sebastian Stan (Billy), Wes Bentley (Peter Hood), Nick Searcy (Mr. Miller), Socratis Otto (Jim), Emily Wickersham (Molly), Joel David Moore (Nick Massey), Katherine Moennig (Erica Lonsdale), Michael Paré (Lt. Ray Bozeman), Sam Upton (Officer McKay), Ted Rooney (Henry Massey), Erin Carufel (Officer Ash), Amy Lawhorn (Tanya Muslin), Susan Hess Logeais (Dr. Mira Anders), Jeanine Jackson (Mrs. Cermak), Blaine Palmer (Conrad Reynolds), Victor Morris (Officer Dubois), Jeff Cole (Customer #1), Tracy Pacana, Madison Wray (School Girls), Hunter Parrish (Try), Casey O'Neill (Jill's Opponent), Aaron

Thomas (Busboy), Jordan Fry (Jock), Meredith Adelaide (Jock's Girlfriend), Alles Mist (Jock's Friend), Noel Taylor (Skate Rat), Danny Belrose (Custodian), Danny Wynands (Officer Johnson), Wade Allen (Officer Cummins), Jade Marx-Berti (Officer Ruffolo), Grant Reschke (Older Boy), Bruce Lawson (Det. Lawson), Robert Blanche (Officer Johnson), Sean Goodearl (Dojo Classmate), Tim Harrold (Police Officer), Tom Hestmark (Dock Worker), Zachary Olson (College Student)

Amanda Seyfried in *Gone* © Summit Entertainment

FATHER'S DAY (Troma) Producers, Lloyd Kaufman, Michael Herz; Executive Producers, Matt Manjourides, Adam Brooks; Director/Photography/Screenplay, Astron-6; Music, Jeremy Gillespie; Editor, Adam Brooks; Special Effects, Steven Kostanski, Adam Brooks, Jeremy Gillespie; a Lloyd Kaufman and Michael Herz presentation of a Troma Team Production; American-Canadian; Color; Not rated; 99 minutes; Release date: February 24, 2012. **CAST:** Adam Brooks (Ahab), Matt Kennedy (Father John Sullivan), Conor Sweeney (Twink), Amy Groening (Chelsea), Brent Neale (Det. Stegel), Garrett Hnatiuk (Walnut), Meredith Sweeney (Sleazy Mary), Mackenzie Murdock (Chris Fuchman), Kevin Anderson (Father O'Flynn), Zsuzsi (The Chainsaw Ripper/Angel), Lloyd Kaufman (God/Devil), Billy Sadoo (Twink's Dad), Falcon Van Der Baek (Heaven Guide), Kyle Young (Mark), Murray Davidson (Artie), Ted Kennedy (Ahab's Dad), Wilmar Chopyk (Angry Priest), William O'Donnell (Hallway Gimp), Gary Johnston (Narrator), Rob McLaughlin (Marty), Mike Schmidt (Lowlife DJ), Jeremy Gillespie (Disfigured Bill Cummings/Bounty Man), Jason McDonald (Bill Cummings), Kaiden Dupuis (Young Ahab), Dylan Gyles (Teenage Ahab), Jynx (Stripper/Angel), Andrea Felldin (Bartender/Angel), James Mitchell (Lowlife Perv), Cynthia Wolfe-Nolin (Space Princess), McKinley Morton (Count Zadar), Sommer Spendlow (Scary Lady in Hell), Steven Kostanski (Masked Satanist), Screamin' Mimi (Young Chelsea), Stephanie Kennedy, Linda Hyslop (Nuns)

Adam Brooks in *Father's Day* © Troma

TIM AND ERIC'S BILLION DOLLAR MOVIE (Magnet) Producers, Adam McKay, Will Ferrell, Chris Henchy, Ben Cosgrove, Todd Wagner, Tim Heidecker, Eric Wareheim, Dave Kneebone, Jon Mugar; Executive Producer, Mark Cuban; Directors/Screenplay, Tim Heidecker, Eric Wareheim; Photography, Rachel Morrison; Designer, Rosie Sanders; Costumes, Diana Contreras-Gonzalez; Music, Davin Wood; Editors, Daniel Haworth, Doug Lussenhop; Casting, Clark Reinking, James Levine/Typecasting Inc.; a 2929 Productions presentation in association with Funny or Die Productions and Absolutely Productions; Dolby; Color; Rated R; 93 minutes; Release date: March 2, 2012. **CAST:** Tim Heidecker (Tim), Eric Wareheim (Eric), William Atherton (Earle Swinter), Jeff Goldblum (Chef Goldblum), Robert Loggia (Tommy Schlaaang), Ray Wise (Dr. Doon Struts), Bill A. Jones (Serious Announcer), Bob Odenkirk (Schlaaang Announcer), Frank Slaten (Super Seat Customer), Bob Ross, Tennessee Winston Luke, Robert Axelrod, James Quall, David Liebe Hart (Themselves), Ronnie Rodriguez (Diamond Jim/Johnny Depp), Nancy Stelle (Woman on Paris Street), Jean-Michel Richaud (Paris Policeman), Marilyn Porayko (Woman being Ticketed), Erica Durance (Paris Waitress), Michael Gross (Narrator), Jon Baggio (Jason), Kristopher Logan, Andy Spencer, Christopher Guckenberger (Studio Executives), John Downey III (Cornell), Mary Bly (Mrs. Heidecker), Lillian Adams (Mrs. Wareheim), Jay Mawhinney (Bartender), Loki (Tattoo Artist), Harry Elmayan (Delivery Man), Ted Neubauer (Man on Street), Dena Roe (Woman on Street), Twink Caplan (Katie), Kimberly Ables Jindra (Woman giving Birth), Kirk Diedrich (Roy), Doug Foster (Customer), Matt O'Toole (Reggie), Noah Spencer (Jeffrey), Rae Sunshine Lee (Shrim Dancer), Palmer Scott (Large Man), Mobin Khan (El Hat Proprietor), Cole Carl Mangham, Zachariah James-Jadon Evans, Frunzik Ayvazyan Jr., Joshua Briscoe (Shrim Kids), Todd Wagner (Hobo), Howie Slater (Steven Spielberg), Will Ferrell (Damien Weebs), Will Forte (Allen Bishopman), Zach Galifianakis (Jim Joe Kelly), John C. Reilly (Taquito)

Tim Heidecker, Eric Wareheim in *Tim and Eric's Billion Dollar Movie* © Magnet Releasing

RANCHERO (Indican) Producer/Screenplay, Brian Johnson; Director, Richard Kaponas; Photography, Michael Bratkowski; Art Director, Kathryn DiLego; Music, Don DiLego; Editor, Don Burton; Lamppost Productions in association with Stage 6 Productions; Color; Not rated; 98 minutes; Release date: March 2, 2012. **CAST:** Roger Gutierrez (Jesse Torres), Brian Eric Johnson (Tom McCoy), Christina Woods (Lil' Bit), Danny Trejo (Capone), Ruth Livier (Carmen), Jade Gordon (Claudia Ross), Rodger Hoopman (Mr. McCoy), Blake Kushi (Apartment Manager), Baldwin Sykes (Homeless Man), Brandon Brown (YoungThug), Nate Williams, Jeff Hampton (Drug Dealers), Dave Silva (Hopscotch Girl), Nicole Wordes (Receptionist), Ramon Ayala (Mr. Torres), Elias Chairez III, Ricardo Villalpando, Martin Carrillo (Ranch Workers), Ricardo VIIlalpando Jr. (Young Jesse), Hunter Hansen (Young Tom), Anthony Montes (Sign Acrobat), Jesse Freeman (Skateboarder), Robert Botteri (Biker), Gary Eddington (Dope Man), Elisa Dyann (Girl in Breakroom), Poli (Barber), Maleri Mitchell (Girl in Bar), Scott Lurie (Art Gallery Patron)

ART IS ... THE PERMANENT REVOLUTION (First Run Features) Producer/Director/Editor, Manfred Kirchheimer; Photography, Zachary Alspaugh, Peter Rinaldi, Taiki Sugioka; Narrator, Deborah Schneer; a Streetwise Films production; Color/black and white; Not rated; 82 minutes; Release date: March 2, 2012. Documentary on the outrage captured by artists throughout history; **WITH:** Sigmund Abeles, Ann Chernow, Paul Marcus, James Reed

Sigmund Abeles in *Art Is ... The Permanent Revolution* © First Run Features

LAST DAYS HERE (Sundance Selects) Producer, Sheena M. Joyce; Directors/Photography, Don Argott, Demian Fenton; Music, Stars of the Lid, Rachel Grimes, Pentagram; Color; Not rated; 90 minutes; Release date: March 2, 2012. Documentary on cult metal performer Bobby Liebling's efforts to resurrect his career; **WITH:** Bobby Liebling, Sean "Pellet" Pelletier, Diane Liebling, Joe Liebling, Hallie Miller, Geof O'Keefe, Greg Mayne, J.B. Beverly, Murray Krugman, Ian Christie, Jimmy Bower, Phil Anselmo, Joe Hasselvander, Victor Griffin, Russ Strahan, Callae Goltz, Gary Isom, Kayt Vigil; **CAST:** Jeremy Blessing (Young Bobby Liebling), Bob Sweeney (Young Greg Mayne), Chad Pfeiffer (Young Vincent McAllister), Sean-Paul Fenton (Young Geof O'Keefe), Derrick Hans (Crabby Roommate), Demian Fenton (Gene Simmons), Domenic Malandro (Paul Stanley)

Bobby Liebling in *Last Days Here* © Sundance Selects

HEIST: WHO STOLE THE AMERICAN DREAM? (Connecting the Dots Production) Producers/Directors, Donald Goldmacher, Frances Causey; Executive Producers, Earl Katz, Sally Holst; Screenplay, Frances Causey, Hollis Rich; Photography, Rogelio Garcia; Music, David Raiklen; Editors, Maureen Gosling, Rogelio Garcia; Narrator, Thom Hartmann; Color; HD; Not rated; 85 minutes; Release date: March 2, 2012. Documentary charting the events that led to the current economic crisis; **WITH:** Gar Aplerovitz, Jovanka Beckles, Kim Berry,

Deepak Bhargava, Alan Blinder, David Brock, Robert Crandall, Donna Edwards, Jeff Faux, Leo Gerard, David Green, Jakada Imani, David John, David Clay Johnston, Van Jones, Robert Kuttner, Kimber Lanning, Michael Lind, Lou Mattis, Lawrence E. Mitchell, Nomi Prins, Bernie Sanders, Elizabeth Warren, Drew Westen

Heist: Who Stole the American Dream © Connecting the Dots

BETTER THAN SOMETHING: JAY REATARD (Children of Productions) Producer, Alex Hammond; Directors/ Photography/Editors, Ian Markiewicz, Alex Hammond; Music, Jay Reatard; Color; HD; Not rated; 89 minutes; Release date: March 2, 2012. Documentary on garage-punk musician Jay Reatard; **WITH:** Jimmy Lee Lindsey Jr., King Louie Blankston, Scott Bomar, Chad Booth, Alix Brown, Alicia Trout, Eric Friedl, Jeffrey Novak, Ryan Rousseau, Shawn Foree, Stephen Pope.

Jay Reatard in *Better Than Something* © Children of Productions

PATRIOCRACY (Cinema Libre Studios) Producers, Cindy Malone, Brian Malone; Executive Producer, Stephen Nemeth; Director/Screenplay/Photography/Music/Editor, Brian Malone; Political Cartoons, Ed Stein; Graphic Animations, James King; a Fast Forward Films production; Color; Not rated; 90 minutes; Release date: March 2, 2012. Documentary on the polarization of America, because of differing politics; **WITH:** Bob Schieffer, Alan Simpson, Pat Buchanan, Ken Rudin, Eleanor Clift, Kent Conrad, Mark Warner, Mike Crapo, Mark Udall, Ben Cardin, Mickey Edwards, Bob Inglis, Rob Andrews, Jason Altmire, Sheila Jackson, William Cassidy, Bart Stupak, Jared Polis, Todd Young, Kent Collins, Arnie Thomas, Stephen Wayne, William Galston, Gene Policinski

THE WOODS (Cinemad) Executive Producers, Max Nova, Emily Wiedemann, Mike King; Producers, Jett Steiger, Max Knies, Matthew Lessner; Director/Screenplay, Matthew Lessner; Additonal Dialogue, Toby David, Justin Phillips; Contributing Writer, Adam Mortemore; Photography, Wyatt Garfield; Designer, Erin Staub; Costumes, Jessica Matz; Music, Lydia Ainsworth; a Monte Lomax, Greencard Pictures and Team G in association with Kickstarter.com production;

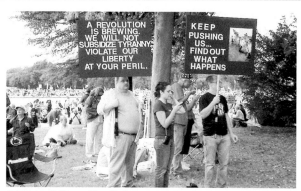

Patriocracy © Cinema Libre Studios

The Woods © Cinemad

Color; Not rated; 90 minutes; Release date: March 2, 2012. **CAST:** Toby David (Daniel), Justin Phillips (Dean), Nicola Persky (Maggie), Brian Woods (Tanner), Anne-Sophie (Nadia), Lauren Hamersmith (Genevieve), Adam Mortemore (Lucas), Chris Edley (Bryce), Amanda Furches (Annakate), Salvador Gonzalez (Luis-Fernando), Carlos Vasquez (Sergio)

THE BALLAD OF GENESIS AND LADY JAYE (Adopt Films) Producers, Steve Holmgren, Marie Losier, Martin Marquet; Director/Photography/Editor, Marie Losier; Music, Bryin Dall; Color; Not rated; 65 minutes; Release date: March 8, 2012. Documentary on performance artist Genesis Breyer P-Orridge; **WITH:** Genesis Breyer P-Orridge, Lady Jaye Breyer P-Orridge, Big Boy Breyer P-Orridge, Bryin Dall, Edley O'Dowd, Tony Conrad, Gibby Haynes, Clyde Magid, Caresse P-Orridge Balpazari, Genesse P-Orridge, Lili Chopra, Peaches, David Max, Alice Genesse, Markus Persson

APART (Gravitas Ventures) Producer, Ryan Rettig; Director/Screenplay/Editor, Aaron Rottinghaus; Photography, J.P. Lipa; Designer, James Fowler; Costumes, Ashlyn Angel; Music, Philip James Gilberti; a SystemX Media presentation; Color; Not rated; 86 minutes; Release date: March 9, 2012. **CAST:** Olesya Rulin (Emily Gates), Josh Danziger (Noah Greene), Bruce McGill (Dr. Thomas Abner), Joey Lauren Adams (Dr. Jane Sheppard), Michael Bowen (Teddy Berg), Sue Rock (Julie Gates), David Born (Joseph Greene), Jason Davis (Oliver Greene), Shiree Nelson (Kelly Corrigan), Brandon Todd (#55), Chris Binum (David Littleton), Harry Buonocore (Young Noah), Scott De La Cruz (Friend of #55), Charlie Guileen (Russ the Bartender), Davi Jay (Doctor), Britney Loerwald (Young Emily), Amy L. Mitchell (Detective), Alex Worley (Ghost Kid)

Oleysa Rulin in *Apart* © Gravitas Ventures

SHAKESPEARE HIGH (Cinema Guild) Producers, Brad Koepenick, Lori Miller, Ronnie Planalp, Alex Rotaru; Executive Producers, Kevin Spacey, Dana Brunetti, Dean Devlin, Eugen Rotaru; Director, Alex Rotaru; Photography/Co-Producer, Brian O'Connell; Music, Nathaniel Blume; Editor, Drew Kilcoin; a Trigger Street Productions presentation of an Ifavor Entertainment, Inc. production; Color; Not rated; 81 minutes; Release date: March 9, 2012. Documentary on Southern California teens who study Shakespeare in order to compete in the Drama Teachers Association festival; **WITH:** Luis Cardenas, Richard Dreyfuss, Sue Freitag, Marisa Gold, Val Kilmer, Julian G. Simmons, Kevin Spacey, Mare Winningham.

Shakespeare High © Cinema Guild

PLAYBACK (Magnet) Producers, John M. Bennett, Lawrence Robbins, Randall Emmett, George Furla; Executive Producers, Marc J. Leder, Chris Heldman, John Dalton; Director/Screenplay, Michael A. Nickles; Photography, Mark Petersen; Designer, Merje Veski; Costumes, Lizzie Cook; Music, Woody Pak; Editor, Ellen Goldwasser; Visual Effects Supervisor, Erick Schiele; Casting, Jennifer Levy, Emily Schweber; a Fontenay Films Ltd., Bennett Robbins Productions in association with Emmett/Furla Films presentation; Color; Rated R; 98 minutes; Release date: March 9, 2012. **CAST:** Johnny Pacar (Julian Miller), Toby Hemingway (Quinn), Ambyr Childers (Riley), Jennifer Missoni (DeeDee Baker), Jonathan Keltz (Nate), Alessandra Torresani (Brianna Baker), Christian Slater (Frank Lyons), Luke Bonczyk (Harlan Diehl), Matt Braaten (Detective), Dorien Davies (Ms. Milton), Bernard McConnell (Cop), Mark Metcalf (Chris Safford), Daryl "Chill" Mitchell (Wylie), Lisa Jane Todd (Anne Miller), Jana Veldheer (Susie Diehl), Brian Erickson (Keg Stand Assistant), Kenny Stevenson (Co-Worker), Stephanie Webb (Newscaster)

Christian Slater in *Playback* © Magnet Releasing

SEEKING JUSTICE (Anchor Bay) formerly *The Hungry Rabbit Jumps*; Producers, Tobey Maguire, Ram Bergman, James D. Stern; Executive Producers, Jenno Topping, Christopher Petzel, Julie Goldstein, Douglas E. Hansen; Director, Roger Donaldson; Screenplay, Robert Tannen; Story, Robert Tannen, Todd Hickey; Photography, David Tattersall; Designer, Dennis Washington; Costumes, Caroline Eselin-Schaefer; Music, J. Peter Robinson; Editor, Jay Cassidy; Casting, Mary Vernieu, Venus Kanani; an Endgame Entertainment Company presentation in association with The Aura Film Partnership and Fierce Entertainment, a Material Pictures production, a Ram Bergman production; Dolby; Color; HD; Rated R; 105 minutes; Release date: March 16, 2012. **CAST:** Nicolas Cage (Will Gerard), Guy Pearce (Simon), January Jones (Laura Gerard), Jennifer Carpenter (Trudy), Harold Perrineau (Jimmy), Xander Berkeley (Lt. Durgan), Irone Singleton (Scar), Wayne Pere (Cancer), Marcus Lyle Brown (Det. Green), Dikran Tulaine (Sideburns), Joe Chrest (Det. Rudeski), Demetrius Bridges (Edwin), Brett Gentile (Bourdette), Renwick D. Scott II (Kid #1), Joe Gelini (Charlie), Alex Van (Hodge), Sharon Landry (Doctor), Asif Taj (Oncology Dept. Doctor), Bernard "Bunche" Johnson (Oncology Dept. Guard),), Donna Duplantier (Gina), John McDonnell (Liquor Store Clerk), JD Evermore (Man in Elevator), Mike Pniewski (Gibbs), Cullen Moss (Jones), Brett Rice (Long), Anthony Michael Frederick, Raymond Hebert (Cops), Rey Hernandez (Shooting Instructor), Thomas 'Tah' Hyde (Hotel Valet), Maureen Brennan (Newspaper Woman), Douglas M. Griffin (Resident), Rachel Dupard (Student), Dane Rhodes (AAA Mechanic), Kenneth Brown Jr. (Det. Richards), Kathleen Wilhoite (Mother), Matthew Posey, J. Omar Castro (Rabbits), Juan Pardo (Max), Joseph Ratliff (Elephant Trainer), Danny O'Flaherty (Singer at Wake), Joseph Boudreaux (Singer in Party Scene), Seth Harden (Boy), Casey Bundick (Security Guard), Jean Montes (Conductor), Terence Rosemore (Bartender), Veronica Musgrove, Michael Hill (Reporters)

Guy Pearce, Nicolas Cage in *Seeking Justice* © Anchor Bay

THE UNDERSTUDY (Indican) Producers/Directors/Screenplay, David Conolly, Hannah Davis; Photography, Joe Folley; Designer, Deana Sidney; Cosumes, Andrea Seidel; Music, Carl Davis; Editor, Kate Eales; Casting, Heidi Miami Marshall; a Mansion Pictures, Safehouse Pictures, Untold Pictures production; Dolby; Color; Not rated; 104 minutes; American release date: March 16, 2012. **CAST:** Marin Ireland (Rebecca), Paul Sparks (Bobby), Aasif Mandvi (Sarfras), Kelli Giddish (Simone), Richard Kind (Ian), Tom Wopat (Det. Jones), Gloria Reuben (The Great Greta), Reiko Aylesworth (Kinsky), Amy Redford (Helen), Scott Cohen (Jonny), Neko Parham (Det. Smith), David Melville (Oscar), Emanuele Ancorini (Jesus), Kerry Bishé (April), Jean Boht (Mrs. Davidovitz), Matt Brown (Poseidon), David Conolly (Hollywood Producer), Carl Davis (Mr. Davidovitz), Hannah Davis (Casting Assistant), Marcia DeBonis (Alison), Carole Healey (Pru), Fredrick Helm (Janitor), Charlie Hewson (Douglas), Dee Hoty (Diane Kinsman), Sakina Jaffrey (Nurse), Timothy Karcher (Chris), Jennifer Loryn (Aphrodite), Adam Ludwig (Hermes), Melanie Angelina Maras (Simone's Agent), Adrian Martinez (Guard), Justin Maruri (Cronos), Emily Cass McDonnell (Jackie), Peter McRobbie (Edward), Daya Mendez (Gaia), Billy Merritt (Dennis), Torri Newman (Persephone), Johnny Sanchez (Bill), Brooklyn Scalzo (Medusa), James P. Stephens (Atlas), Myra Lucretia Taylor (Lara), Sarah Yahr Tucker (Athena), Judy Unger (Georgia), J.T. Waite (Thaddeus Battersby), Max Woertendyke (Delivery Boy), Nicky Arezu Akmal (Autograph Hunter #1), Ashley Adler (Waitress), Stephen Anoroso, Pun Bandhu, Mike Silverman (Producers)

Marin Ireland in *The Understudy* © Indican

NATURAL SELECTION (Cinema Guild) Producers, Brion Hambel, Paul Jensen; Executive Producers, Charlie Mason, Justin Moore-Lewy; Director/Screenplay, Robbie Pickering; Photography, Steven Capitano Calitri; Designer, Michael Bricker; Costumes, Colin Wilkes, Jennifer Beck; Music, iZler, Curt Schneider; Music Supervisor, Justin Gage; Editor, Michelle Tesoro; Casting, Sunday Boling, Meg Morman; a Best Medicine Productions presentation; Color; HD; Rated R; 89 minutes; Release date: March 16, 2012. **CAST:** Rachael Harris (Linda), Matt O'Leary (Raymond), John Diehl (Abe), Gayland Williams (Sheila), Jon Gries (Peter), Stephanie King (Shaunice), Berna Roberts (Porno Nun), Drake Dempsey (Porno Priest), Michael Hyland (Handsome Doctor), Gregory Grosh (Sperm Clinic Doctor), Rob Huebel (Martin), Sam Eidson, Salvador Cabral (Homeless Guys), Lauren Nailen (Wigwam Clerk), Roger Hewitt (Old Motel Clerk), Hallie Martin (White Trash Fox), Rick Appleton (Bartender), Melinda DeKay (Stern Nurse), Mark Winslett (Bus Employee), Soleya Rea (Teen Raymond), Connie Hughes (Old Waitress), Kamlesh Patel (Indian Motel Clerk), Loomis Warren (Country Doctor), Joe Miller, Skeeter Sewart (Police Officers), Adrian Rocha (Busboy), Grant James (Family Doctor), Linda White (Distracted Parishioner)

Matt O'Leary in *Natural Selection* © Cinema Guild

THE FP (Drafthouse Films) Producers, Christian Agypt, Brandon Barerra; Executive Producers, Ron Trost, Hal Tryon, Steven Schneider, Jason Blum; Director/Screenplay, Trost Bros.; Story, Jason Trost; Photography, Brandon Trost; Designer, Tyler B. Robinson; Costumes, Sarah Trost; Music, George Holocroft; Editor, Abe Levy; a Secret Identity Productions presentation; Technicolor; Widescreen; HD; Rated R; 82 minutes; Release date: March 16, 2012. **CAST:** Jason Trost (JTRO), Lee Valmassy (L Dubba E), Art Hsu (KCDC), Nick Principe (BLT), Dov Tiefenbach (Triple Decka 1K), James DeBello (Beat Box Busta Bill), Caker Folley (Stacy), Brandon Barrera (BTRO), Bryan Goddard (Sugga Nigga), Rachel Robinson (Lacy), Michael Sandow (Jody), Sean Whalen (Stacy's Dad), Dash Mihok (Cody), James Remar (Narrator), Clifton Collins Jr. (CC Jam), Blayne Weaver (Gas Station Attendant)

Brandon Barrera, Lee Valmassy in *The FP* © Drafthouse Films

AN ENCOUNTER WITH SIMONE WEIL (Line Street Prods.) Producers, Julia Haslett, Fabrizia Galvagno, Enrico Rossini Cullen; Executive Producers, David Menschel, Adam Haslett; Director/Screenplay/Editor/Narrator, Julia Haslett; Photography, Thomas Torres Cordova; Music, Daniel Thomas Davis; American-Italian-Swedish; Color/black and white; HD; Not rated; 85 minutes; Release date: March 23, 2012. Documentary on French philosopher-activist Simone Weil; **WITH:** Anna Brown, Sylvère Lotringer, Sylvie Weil, Florence de Lussy, Raymonde Weil, Father Jobert, Jeanne Duchamp, Soraya Broukhim, Timothy Haslett.

Simone Weil in *An Encounter with Simone Weil* © Line Street Prods.

THE TROUBLE WITH BLISS (Variance) formerly *East Fifth Bliss*; Producers, John Ramos, Michael Knowles, John Will; Executive Producers, Alex Balandin, Jon Finkel, Chuck Goodgal, Nita Goodgal, Bruce Rogoff, Victoria Rogoff, Dong-Chen Tsai, David E. Price, Brady Richter, Eric Strong; Director/ Editor, Michael Knowles; Screenplay, Douglas Light, Michael Knowles; Based on the 2007 novel *East Fifth Bliss* by Douglas Light; Photography, Ben Wolf; Designer, Lucio Seixas; Costumes, Amy C. Bradshaw; Music, Daniel Alcheh; a 7A Productions in association with Torn Sky Entertainment, Topiary Productions & Off Hollywood Pictures presentation; Color; Rated PG-13; 97 minutes; Release date: March 23, 2012. **CAST:** Michael C. Hall (Morris Bliss), Chris Messina (NJ), Brie Larson (Stephanie Jouseski), Brad William Henke (Steven "Jetski" Jouseski), Sarah Shahi (Hattie Skunk/Hattie Rockworth), Peter Fonda (Seymour Bliss), Lucy Liu (Andrea), Scott Johnsen (George), Glenn Kubota (Mr. Charlies), Mary Goggin (Mrs. Cruxo), Melanie Torres (The Cindi), Joshua Alscher (Torc), Liz Holtan (May), Kate Simses (Nancy), Gameela Wright (Nadine), Dana Raja (Girl on Rollerblades), Carl Villaroman (Cab Driver), Christian Campbell (Walter Knotts), Rhea Perlman (Maria)

Michael C. Hall in *The Trouble with Bliss* © Variance Films

BRAKE (IFC Films) Producers, Gabe Torres, James Walker, Nathan West; Executive Producers, Stephen Dorff, Ryan Ross, Walter Zuck; Director, Gabe Torres; Screenplay, Timothy Mannion; Photography, James Mathers; Designer, John R. Mott; Costumes, Marcy Froehlich; Music, Brian Tyler; Editor, Sam Restivo; a Walking West production in association with La Costa productions; Color; Not rated; 91 minutes; Release date: March 23, 2012. **CAST:** Stephen Dorff (Jeremy Reins), Chyler Leigh (Molly Reins), JR Bourne (Henry Shaw), Tom Berenger (Ben Reynolds), Bobby Tomberlin (Trucker), Kali Rocha (911 Operator), King Orba (Good Samaritan), Pruitt Taylor Vince (Voice of Driver/Boss Terrorist), Sammy Sheik (Voice of Marco), Kent Shocknek (News Anchor Jack Stern), Jayleen Moore (Training Agent Ahmadyar), Stephen J. Bridgewater (Training Agent McClane), Matthew Pollino (Training Agent Dipego), Jason Rafael (Paramedic)

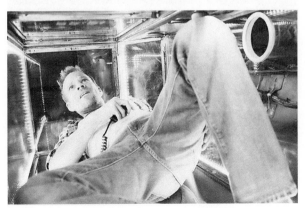

LOSING CONTROL (House Lights Media) Producers, Robert A. Johnson, Matthew Medlin, Alyssa Weisberg, Valerie Weiss; Executive Producer, Jeffrey M. Loeb; Director/Screenplay, Valerie Weiss; Photography, Jamie Urman; Designer, Yoana Wijaya; Costumes, Linde Aseltine; Music, John Swihart; Music Supervisor, Sharon Edelson; Editor, Robin Katz; Casting, Alyssa Weisberg; a PhD Prods. presentation; Color; HD; Rated R; 91 minutes; Release date: March 23, 2012. **CAST:** Miranda Kent (Samantha), Reid Scott (Ben), Kathleen Robertson (Leslie), Theo Alexander (Maurizio), Bitsie Tulloch (Trudy), John Billingsley (Prof. Straub), Lin Shaye (Dolores), Steve Howey (Terry), Ben Weber (Dr. Rudy Mann), Samuel Ball (Tantric Sam), Barry Gordon (Frank), Neil Hopkins (Scott Foote), Jamison Yang (Dr. Chen Wa Chow), Alanna Ubach (Alora), Elise Jackson (Vivienne), Robert A. Johnson (Coty), Alexandre Chen (Chinese Scientist), True Bella Pinci (Little Samantha), Sumalee Montano (Breanna Lee), Heiko Obermöller (Yerdl), Chyna (Bar), Sally Elphick (Tracy Reynolds), Russia Hardy (Amelie), Sonal Shah (Danger), Jade Tailor (Gypsy LaRue), Robbie Tucker (Robbie), Allan Wasserman (Frank), Jeff Witzke (Mark), Tim Camarillo (Harvard Professor), Lauryn Nicole Hamilton, Antoinette Mia Pettis (Body Paint Waitresses), Ben Mark (Dorky Nerd), Steve Rosen (Ticket Agent), Andrew Sarno (Handsome Doctor), Tom Ohmer, Joe Stapleton (FBI Agents), Katie Wallack (Mental Patient)

Lin Shaye, Miranda Kent, Kathleen Robertson in *Losing Control* © House Lights Media

MUSICAL CHAIRS (Paladin) Producers, Janet Carrus, Joey Dedio, Marty Madden, Brian Herskowitz; Executive Producers, Jamin O'Brien, Susan Seidelman; Director, Susan Seidelman; Screenplay, Marty Madden; Photography, Stephen Kazmierski; Designer, Susan Block; Costumes, Kitty Boots; Music, Mario Grigorov; Music Supervisor, Beth Amy Rosenblatt; Editor, Keiko Deguchi; Choreographer, Aubree Marchione; Casting, Sig DeMiguel, Stephen Vincent; a JMC Independent Productions and Active Fox Productions in association with Paladin presentation; Dolby; Color; Rated PG-13; 102 minutes; Release date: March 23, 2012. **CAST:** Leah Pipes (Mia), E.J. Bonilla (Armando), Priscilla Lopez (Isabel), Jaime Tirelli (Bernardo), Laverne Cox (Chantelle), Nelson Landrieu (Wilfredo), Angelica Zambrana (Rosa), Morgan Spector (Kenny), Auti Angel (Nicky), Jerome Preston Bates (Jimmy), Joey Dedio (Chico), Dominic Colon (Julio), Philip Willingham (Daniel), Matthew Clark (Matthew Bowden), Miriam Cruz (Yaira), Mara Davi (Stephanie), John DePalma (Announcer), Tibor Feldman (Mr. Grinker), Capathia Jenkins (Erma), Teresa Kelsey (Therapist), Lisby Larson (Kaye), Graciela Lecube (Yajaira), Heland Lee (Gregory), Aubree Marchione (Tanya Marchione), Steve Routman (Mr. Benson), Marilyn Sokol (Mrs. Greenbaum), Tom Tammi (Henry), Marilyn Torres (Elba), Teresa Yenque (Yadira), Mareo Ryan (Strong Orderly), Hedda Lettuce (Drag Queen)

Stephen Dorff in *Brake* © IFC Films

Leah Pipes, E.J. Bonilla in *Musical Chairs* © Paladin

ALL IN: THE POKER MOVIE (4th Row Films) Producers, Susan Bedusa, Robert Greene, Douglas Tirola; Executive Producer, Amy Brennan; Director, Douglas Tirola; Photography, Nick Higgins, Eric Metgar, Charles Poekel, others; Music, Peitor Angell, Preservation Hall Jazz Band; Editor, Robert Greene; Color/black and white; Not rated; 100 minutes; Release date: March 23, 2012. Documentary on America's fascination with poker; **WITH:** Matt Damon, Annie Duke, Ira Glass, Doris Kearns Goodwin, Frank Deford, Chris Moneymaker, Mike Sexton, Kenny Rogers, James McManus, Thomas "Amarillo Slim" Preston, Daniel Negreanu, Bert Sugar, Peter Alson, Nolan Dalla, Barry Greenstein, Joe Hachem, Phil Laak, Brian Koppleman, Howard Lederer, Chris Ferguson, Scotty Nguyen, Erik Seidel, Isabelle Mercier, Johnny Marinacci, Henry Orenstein, Vanessa Rousso, Richard Anthony, Denny Crum, John Dahl, Alfonse D'Amato, Mori Eskandani, Steve Lipscomb, Mike Scelza, Jennifer Tilly, Vince Van Patten, Karen Abbott, Peter Alson, Nick Brancato, Humberto Brenes, Avery Cardoza, Mark Caro, T.J. Cloutier, Eric Drache, Antonio Esfandiari, Chris "Jesus" Ferguson, Benj Gershman, Jamie Gold, Phil Hellmuth Jr., Ben Jaffe, Lacey Jones, George Joseph, Roger Kimball, John Leland, Jason Lockwood, Shane McCullough, Tom McEvoy, Jon Miller, Marty Morgan, Eric Morris, Jeffrey Pollack, Greg Raymer, Marc Roberge, David Schwartz, Howard Schwartz, Sam Simon, David Singer, Vincent Van Patten, Des Wilson

All In: The Poker Movie © 4th Row Films

THE ISLAND PRESIDENT (Goldwyn) Producers, Richard Berge, Bonni Cohen; Executive Producer, Jon Else; Director/Photography, Jon Shenk; Music, Radiohead, Stars of the Lid; Editor, Pedro Kos; an Afterimage Public Media ITVS and Actual Films in association with Impact Partners presentation; Color; HD; Rated PG; 101 minutes; Release date: March 28, 2012. Documentary on Mohamed Nasheed's aborted term as President of the Maldives; **WITH:** Mohamed Nasheed,

Ahmed Naseem, Mohamed Aslam, Aminath Shauna, Mohamed Zuhair, Laila Ali, Ahmed Moosa, Paul Roberts, Maumoon Abdul Gayoom, Dr. Mohamed Waheed, Mark Lynas, Mohamed Ziyad, Dr. Ahmed Shaheed, Abdul Ghafoor Mohamed, Ibrahim Hussain Zaki, Iruthisham Ada, Gary Streeter, Tillman Thomas, Shyam Saran

Mohamed Nasheed in *The Island President* © Goldwyn Films

SCENES OF A CRIME (New Box Prods.) Producers/Directors, Blue Hadaegh, Grover Babcock; Photography, David Elkins, Brian Mulchy; Editor, Robert DeMaio; Color; HD; Not rated; 86 minutes; Release date: March 30, 2012. Documentary on the interrogation of an unemployed father accused of killing his 4-month-old son; **WITH:** Adrian Thomas, Adam Mason, Ronald Fountain

MONUMENTAL: IN SEARCH OF AMERICA'S NATIONAL TREASURE (Monumental Media) Producers, Duane Barnhart, Kirk Cameron, Angela Alvarez; Executive Producers, John Bona, Bill Hough, Mark Gambee; Director, Duane Barnhart; Screenplay, Kevin Miller; Photography, John Rhode; Editor, Tim Rygh; a Kirk Cameron presentation in association with Camfam Studios, a Pyro Pictures production; Color; Rated PG; 90 minutes; Release date: March 30, 2012. Documentary on actor Kirk Cameron's trek across America to meet the nation's people; **WITH:** Kirk Cameron.

Kirk Cameron in *Monumental* © Monumental Media

DARK TIDE (Wrekin Hill) Producers, Jeanette Buerling, Matthew E. Chausse; Executive Producers, Adi Shankar, Spencer Silna, Maggie Monteith, Martin Shore, Christopher Tuffin, Sukee Chew, John Michaels; Supervising Producer, Chris Curling; Director, John Stockwell; Screenplay, Amy Sorlie, Ronnie Christensen; Story, Amy Sorlie; Photography, Jean-Francois Hensgens; Music, Mark "Dog" Sayfritz; Music Supervisor, Maggie Rodford; Editor, Andrew MacRitchie; Casting, Gail Stevens, Colin Jones; a Magnet Media Productions and Mirabelle Pictures presentation, in association with the Infinite Ammo Motion Picture Company and IM Global, presented in association with Row I Productions; Dolby; Deluxe Color; Super 35 Widescreen; Rated PG-13; 114 minutes; Release date: March 30, 2012. **CAST:** Halle Berry (Kate Mathieson), Olivier Martinez (Jeff), Ralph Brown (Brady), Mark Elderkin (Tommy), Luke Tyler (Nate), Thoko Ntshinga (Zukie), Sizwe Msutu (Walter)

Halle Berry, Olivier Martinez in *Dark Tide* © Wrekin Hill Entertainment

THE MANZANAR FISHING CLUB (Barbed Wire) Producers, Cory Shiozaki, Richard Imamura, Lester Chung, John Gengl; Executive Producer, Alan Sutton; Director, Cory Shiozaki; Screenplay, Richard Imamura; Photography/Editor, Lester Chung; Music, Bill Ungerman, James Achor; Narrators, Scott Sutton, Bonnie Perkinson, Philip Friedman; a Barbed Wire to Barbed Hooks LLC production; Color; Not rated; 74 minutes; Release date: March 30, 2012. Documentary on how several of the Japanese-Americans interred at the Manzanar Relocation Center during World War II kept up their interest in fishing.

The Manzanar Fishing Club © Barbed Wire

GOD SAVE MY SHOES (Caid Productions Inc.) Producer, Thierry Daher; Director/Screenplay, Julie Bensara; Photography, Beatrice Mizrahi, Pierrot Colonna; Music, Elliott Carlson; Editors, Catherine Peix, Jacques Terrien; a Caid Productions & Thierry Daher presentation; Color; Not rated; 60 minutes; Release date: March 30, 2012. Documentary on women's enthusiasm over shoes; **WITH:** Kelly Rowland, Fergie, Dita Von Teese, Christian Louboutin, Manolo Blahnik, Pierre Hardy, Bruno Frisoni, Walter Steiger, Monica von Neumann, Beth Shak, Elizabeth Semmelhack, Filipa Fino, Meghan Cleary, Nikki Schiro, Marshal Cohen

I KISSED A VAMPIRE (Monterey Media) Producer, Laurie Nolan; Executive Producer, Mike Slade; Director/Editor, Chris Sean Nolan; Screenplay, Chris Sean Nolan, Laurie Nolan; Photography, Christopher Gosch; Designer, Elvis Restaino; Costumes, Shannin Carr; Music, Frankie Blue; Casting, Sunday Boling, Meg Morman; an Alter Ego Industries presentation; Color; Rated PG; 91 minutes; Release date: March 30, 2012. **CAST:** Lucas Grabeel (Dylan Knight), Andrew Seeley (Trey Sylvanie), Adrian Slade (Sara Lane), Chris Coppola (Dr. Dan Helsing), Mekia Cox (Nikki No), Amy Paffrath (Luna Dark), Emily Morris (Desiree Damned), Lori Lively (Dr. Lori Light), Sally Slade (Bitty Kilgore), Katie Seeley (Lydia Bloodworthy), Autumn Grabeel (Penny Plasma), Mike Slade (Dr. Payne), Tahlena Chikami (Exchange Student), Molly Nolan, Julie Wolf, Candice Love, Brooke Webber (Customers/Dancers)

Adrian Slade, Lucas Grabeel in *I Kissed a Vampire* © Monterey Media

THE BEAT HOTEL (First Run Features) Producer, Documentary Arts; Director, Alan Govenar; Photography, Didier Dorant, Bob Tullier; Music, Daniel M. Cavanagh, Daniel Cicourel Hanley; Dramatic Reinactments Director/Editor, Alan Hatchett; Animations, Alan Hatchett, Blas Garcia; American-French-British; Stereo; Color; Not rated; 82 minutes; Release date: March 30, 2012. Documentary on how the American beat poets took residence in a Parisian hotel between the years 1957 and 1963; **WITH:** Patrick Amie, Harold Chapman, Peter Golding, Oliver Harris, Jean-Jacques Lebel, Cyclops Lester, Barry Miles, Lars Movin, Claude Odillard, Jürgen Ploog, Elliot Rudie, Regina Weinreich, George Whitman, Sylvia Whitman, Eddie Woods; and Dramatic Reinactments, **CAST:** Kit Hussey (William Burroughs), Andrew Kasten (Harold Chapman), Matt Mitchell (Gregory Corso), Nick Irion (Ian Sommerville), Jason Kendall (Cyclops)

WE THE PARTY (XLrator Media) Producers, Mario Van Peebles, Michael Cohen, Dwjuan F. Fox, Tal Vidgeson; Director/Screeenplay, Mario Van Peebles; Photography, AJ Rickert-Epstein; Designer, Sofia Jimenez; Costumes, Michael McLean; Music, Tree Adams; Editor, George Artope; Casting, Anissa Williams; an Arc Entertainment and MVP Filmz presentation; Dolby; Color/black and white; HD; Rated R; 104 minutes; Release date: April 6, 2012. **CAST:** Mandela Van Peebles (Hendrix), Simone Battle (Cheyenne), Moises Arias (Quicktime), Makaylo

Peter Golding, Robin Page, Madame Rachou in *The Beat Hotel*
© First Run Features

They Call it Myanmar © Autlook Filmsales

Van Peebles (Obama), Patrick Cage II (Chowder), Ryan Vigil (Que), Y.G. (C.C.), Mario Van Peebles (Sutton), Salli Richardson-Whitfield (Principal Reynolds), Michael Jai White (Officer Davis), Tommy "Tiny" Lister (No Shame), China Walker (Shauniqua), Maya Van Peebles (Michelle), B.K. Cannon (Jackie), Quincy Brown (Reggie), Harrison Knight (Calvin), Carlito Olivero (Paco), Soledad St. Hilaire (Mrs. Chavez), Morgana Van Peebles (Megan), Dominic Thomas (H-One), Benjamin "Ben J" Earl (Stunner), Sherri Walker (Artie), Brian Mganga (Barack), Elizabeth Small (Sharon), Chloé Domange (Monique), Darius Love (D-Money), Orlando Brown (Hype DJ), Corde Broadus (Chowder's DJ), Adam Paul (Finklestein), Maurice G. Smith (Johnson), Katarina Garcia (Kailey), Christopher Michael, Gerald Walker (Security Guards), Maxie Santillan Jr. (Mystic), Darlynn L. Moore (Homeless Woman), Marley Van Peebles, Jaimeson Johnson (Mrs. Chavez's Grandson), Michael Reddick, Antonio James Cinotto, Gregg Wayans (Basketball Players), Neil Rodney (Muslim Brother), Tori Irons, Troi Irons (Guitar Twins), Leah Marie Clark (Blonde Girl DJ), Mike Garcia (Edward), Donna Morgan (Executive), MoWii, Pee W33, Bounc3 (Rej3ctz), Jeremy Hawkins (DJ), Snoop Dogg, Melvin Van Peebles (Big D)

ATM (IFC Midnight) Producers, Peter Safran, Paul Brooks; Executive Producers, Joe MacCarthy, Leon Clarance, Scott Niemeyer, Dan Clifton; Director, David Brooks; Screenplay, Chris Sparling; Story, Chris Sparling, Ron Tippe; Photography, Bengt Jan Jönsson; Designer, Craig Sandells; Costumes, Patti Henderson; Music, David Buckley; Editor, David Brooks; Casting, Eyde Belasco; a Gold Circle Films and Safran Company production; Dolby; FotoKem Color; Rated R; 90 minutes; Release date: April 6, 2012. **CAST:** Brian Geraghty (David Hargrove), Josh Peck (Corey Thompson), Alice Eve (Emily Brandt), Mike O'Brien (The Man), Aaron Hughes (Patrolman), Omar Khan (Christian), Will Woytowich (Sargent), Glen Thompson (Harold), Robert Huculak (Robert), Ernesto Griffith (Security Guard), Bryan Clark (Jerry), Daniel De Jaeger (Luke)

Josh Peck, Alice Eve, Brian Geraghty in *ATM* © IFC Midnight

Mario Van Peebles in *We the Party* © XLrator Media

THEY CALL IT MYANMAR: LIFTING THE CURTAIN (Autlook Filmsales) Producers, Deborah C. Hoard, Robert H. Lieberman; Director/Photography, Robert H. Lieberman; Story/Editor, David Kossack; a PhotoSynthesis production; Dolby; Color; Not rated; 84 minutes; Release date: September 21, 2012. Documentary on Burma, the second-most isolated country on the planet;

YOUR BROTHER. REMEMBER? (Independent) Conceived/Director/Editor, Zachary Oberzan; Color; Not rated; 63 minutes; Release date: April 6, 2012. Experimental film in which the Oberzan brothers reenact home movies they made together 20 years earlier; **WITH:** Zachary Oberzan, Gator Oberzan.

PLAYER HATING: A LOVE STORY (Area 23a) Producer/Director, Maggie Hadleigh-West; Photography, Kristen Eccker, Steve McCauley, Emmanual Bastien; Music, Jasun Wardlaw; Editor, Laurie MacMillan; a Film Fatale production; Color; Not rated; 97 minutes; Release date: April 6, 2012. Documentary on hip hop artist Jasun "Half-aMill" Wardlaw.

Zachary Oberzan in *Your Brother, Remember?* © Oberzan

LAST WILL AND EMBEZZLEMENT (Starjack Entertainment) Producers, Pamela S.K. Glasner, Deborah Louise Robinson; Director/Editor, Deborah Louise Robinson; Screenplay, Deborah Louise Robinson, Pamela Glasner; Photography, Jose Luis Rios, Carl Bartels, Marc Saltarelli, Damen Shaqiri; Narrator, Artie Pasquale; Color; Not rated; 82 minutes; Release date: April 13, 2012. Documentary on the financial exploitation of senior citizens; **WITH:** Clifford Berman, Kathy Black, Barbara Bostic, Linda Cramer, Ray Crucet, Pamela Glasner, Richard E. Goble, Natalie Gundrum, Kathleen J. Houseweart, Kim R. Hubbard, Sandy Jolley, Elaine Kaufman, Julie Keegan, Delores Krantz, Connie McManus, Ernie Rinard, Lisa Henderson Rinard, Ralph Robinson, Mickey Rooney, Irene Silver Stender, Ira Wiesner.

Mickey Rooney in *Last Will and Embezzlement* © Starjack Entertainment

DEADLINE (Freestyle) Producers, Molly M. Mayeux, Curt Hahn; Executive Producers, Hunter Atkins, Ron Routson, Curt Hahn; Director, Curt Hahn; Screenplay, Mark Ethridge, based on his 2006 novel *Grievances*; Photography, Paul Marschall; Designer, William J. Blanchard, Jr.; Costumes, Stephen K. Randolph; Music, Dave Perkins; Editor, Robert Gordon; Casting, Aisha Coley, Holly Allen; a Transcendent production; Dolby; Color; Rated PG-13; 95 minutes; Release date: April 13, 2012. **CAST:** Eric Roberts (Ronnie Bullock), Steve Talley (Matt Harper), J.D. Souther (Lucas Harper), Anna Felix (Delana Calhoun), David Dwyer (Everett Hall), Jessejames Locorriere (Earl Thornton), Lauren Jenkins (Trey Hall), Jeremy Childs (Walker Burns), Ian Quinn (Defense Attorney), Jackie Welch (Mary Pell Sampson), Jenny Littleton (Patty Paysinger), Tommy Creswell (Judge Buchanan), Clay Brocker (Possum), Maisha Dyson (Vanessa Brown), Joe

T. Blankenship (Olen Perringer Jr.), Holly Allen (Lab Techician), Denice Hicks (Dr. Deborah Wright), D'Army Bailey (Judge Williams), Darryl Van Leer (Rev. Young), Jenny Helms, Jean Reinke (News Room Reporters), Romonte Hamer (Wallace Sampson), Amelia Hahn (Emma Jean Thornton), Tucker Perry (Young Vanessa Brown), Gemma Holmes (Possum's Wife), David Ditmore (Warren Baxter), Hunter Atkins (Ray), Jonathan Wolf (Courtroom Observer), Travis Warf (Pick-up Passenger), Larry Woods (Max McCallum), Jacqueline Steele (Mail Clerk), Yuri Cunza (Bailiff), Kennedi Hall (Ella Churchwell)

Steve Talley, Eric Roberts in *Deadline* © Freestyle Releasing

THE WOMAN WHO WASN'T THERE (ID Films) Prducer, Amy Rapp; Executive Producers, Meredith Vieira, Ross Kaufman; Director, Angelo J. Guglielmo Jr.; Photography, Andrew Bowley; Music, The Rumor Mill; Editors, Christina Burchard, William Haugse; a Meredith Vieira Prods./4235 production in association with Red Light Films; Color; Not rated; 65 minutes; Release date: April 13, 2012. Documentary on a woman who fabricated her survival of the 9/11 terrorist attacks on the World Trade Center; **WITH:** Tania Head, Gerry Bogacz, Brendan Chellis, Elia Zedeno, Alison Crowther, Marian Fontana, Linda Gormley, Amanda Ripley, Alice Greenwald, Marta Forn, Jeff Glor, Lori Mogol, Janice Cilento, Richard Zimbler.

Tania Head in *The Woman Who Wasn't There* © ID Films

HIT SO HARD (Variance) Producers, Todd Hughes, Christina Soletti; Director/Editor, P. David Ebersole; Screenplay. P. David Ebersole, Todd Hughes; Photography, Larra Anderson, Mark Putnam, John Tanzer; Music, Roddy Bottom; The Ebersole Hughes Company and Tight Ship Productions presentation; Color; HD; Not rated; 103 minutes; Release date: April 13, 2012. Documentary on Hole drummer Patty Schemel; **WITH:** Patty Schemel, Melissa Auf der Maur, Eric Erlandson, Courtney Love Cobain, Roddy Bottom, Alice de Buhr, Izzy, Larry Schemel, Terry Schemel, Gina Schock, Debbi Peterson, Kate Schellenbach, Nina Gordon, Joe Mama-Nitzberg, Phranc, Sarah Vowell, Dallas Taylor

Kate Shellenbach, Patty Schemel, Gina Shock in *Hit So Hard* © Variance Films

HERE (Strand) Producers, Braden King, Lars Knudsen, Jay Van Joy; Executive Producer, Julia King; Director, Braden King; Screenplay, Braden King, Dani Valent; Photography, Lol Crowley; Designer, Richard Wright; Costumes, Amanda Ford; Music, Michael Krassner and Boxhead Ensemble; Editors, David Barker, Andrew Hafitz, Paul Zucker; Casting Eyde Belasco (America), Shant Petrossian (Armenia); a K5 International presentation of a Truckstop Media/Parts and Labor production; Dolby; Color; Not rated; 126 minutes; Release date: April 13, 2012. **CAST:** Ben Foster (Will Shepard), Lubna Azabal (Gadarine Najarian), Peter Coyote (Storyteller), Datekiv Kharibyan (Ashtarak Hotel Woman), Nareg Duryan (Drunk Man), Karapet Aleksanyan (Taxi Driver), Narek Nersisyan (Krikor Nazarian), Karine Voskanyan, Ashot Yerighyan (Socialites), Garik Chepchyan (Russian Businessman), Toma Petrosyan (Russian Businessman's Date), Ara Dkhtrikyan (Trade Minister), Alla Sahakyan (Party Hostess), Gauane Manoukyan (Market Woman), Tatevik Manoukyan (Market Girl), Yuri Kostanyan (Gadarine's Father), Sophik Sarkisyan (Gadarine's Mother), Arsen Manouyan, Ashot Khatchatryan (Electric Planet Workers), Gagik Torchyan (Meghri Hitchhiker), Khachik Khachikyan (Soffiya's Father), Christina Hovaguimyan (Soffiya Gargosian), Hovak Galoyan (Jirair Gargosian), Karen Makhsudyan (Soffiy and Jirati's Son), Anna Korstelova (Soffiya and Jirair's Daughter), Vahag Stepanyan, Aren Yengibaryan (Shepherd Boys), Garik Davityan (Karabakh Driver), Hayk Gasparyan (Gandzasar Tour Guide)

Lubna Azabal, Ben Foster in *Here* © Strand Releasing

L!FE HAPPENS (PMK*BNC Films) Producer, Justin L. Levine; Co-Producers, David J. Phillips, Corbin Timbrook, Kat Coiro, Krysten Ritter; Director, Kat Coiro; Screenplay, Kat Coiro, Krysten Ritter; Photography, Doug Chamberlain; Designer, Kathrin Eder; Costumes, Ilaria Urbinati; Music, Mateo Messina; Music Supervisor, Robin Urdang; Editors, Adam Catino, Eli Nilsen; Casting, Leslie Woo; a Dot Dot Dot Productions presentation of a Stardust Pictures production; American-Canadian; Color; Techniscope; Rated R; 100 minutes; Release date: April 13, 2012. **CAST:** Krysten Ritter (Kim), Kate Bosworth (Deena), Rachel Bilson (Laura), Geoff Stults (Nicolas), Justin Kirk (Henri), Fallon Goodson (Jayde), Andrea Savage (Patti), Kristen Johnston (Francesca), Rhys Coiro (Marc), Seymour Cassel (Poppop), Louis Silvers (Barry Robert Phillips), Jason Biggs (Sergei), Connor Ross, Zachary Ross (Baby Max), Colin Egglesfield (Ivan #1), Ivan Shaw (Ivan #2), Jenny Mollen (Rita the Receptionist), Abby Brammell (Shiva the Yoga Teacher), Marguerite Moreau (Pauline), Lauren Conrad (Herself), Katie Morgan (Dr. Katie), Nic Novicki (Nurse Nic), Merrin Dungey (Hester), Tesla Allgood (Baby J.J.J.), Laura Silverman (Ms. Crenshaw), Devan Leos (Billy), Brody Nicholas Lee, Cody Benjamin Lee (Alternative Teens), Bruce Robert Cole (Bob the Broker), Shelby Janes (Diner Waitress), Carissa Blades (Allison), Darrel Davenport (Hot Jogger), Alexandra Essoe (Girl in Waiting Room), Edith Jefferson (Elderly Woman), Allie McCulloch (Pregnant Woman), Jevin Rae Udcoff (J.J.J. at 1 Year), Milana Vayntrub (Tanya Takeme), Jem Walrath (Max at 1 Year)

Krysten Ritter, Rachel Bilson, Kate Bosworth in *L!fe Happens* © PMK*BNC

COMIC-CON EPISODE IV: A FAN'S HOPE (Wrekin Hill Entertainment) Producers, Morgan Spurlock, Thomas Tull, Jeremy Chilnick, Matthew Galkin; Executive Producers, Gill Champion, Harry Knowles, Stan Lee, Jack Selby, Benjamin Statler, Joss Whedon; Director, Morgan Spurlock; Screenplay, Jeremy Chilnick, Morgan Spurlock; Photography, Daniel Marracino; Music, Jingle Punks; Editors, Tim K. Smith, Tova Goodman; a Neca Films presentation of a Thomas Tull/Warrior Poets and Pow! Entertainment production; Dolby; Color; Rated PG-13; 88 minutes; Release date: April 13, 2012. Documentary on some of the intense fans who attended the 2010 Comic-Con convention; **WITH:** Holly Conrad, Chuck Rozanski, James Darling, Se Young Kang, Skip Harvey, Erc Henson, Seth Rogen, Seth Green, Kevin Smith, Stan Lee, Eli Roth, Paul Scheer, Paul Dini, John Schnepp, Jessica Merizan, Mish'al Samman, Scott Mantz, Maxim Stoyalov, Tayler Hudson, Stephenie Werner, Edgar Gallego, Tank Rigormortis, Michael Bender, Andrew Page

HOW TO GROW A BAND (Intl. Film Circuit) Producers, Michael Bohlmann, Mark Meatto; Director/Photography, Mark Meatto; Editors, Mark Meatto, Purcell Carson; a Shaftway Productions presentation; American-British; Color; Not rated; 88 minutes; Release date: April 13, 2012. Documentary on how Chris Thile dealt with his marital breakup by writing music to be performed by a bluegrass quintet; **WITH:** Chris Thile, Gabe Witcher, Noam Pikelny, Chris Eldridge, Greg Garrison, Paul Kowert, Yo-Yo Ma, John Paul Jones, Edgar Meyer, Jerry Douglas, Sara Watkins

Comic-Con Episode IV: A Fan's Hope © Wrekin Hill Entertainment

Chris Thile in *How to Grow a Band* © Intl. Film Circuit

DETENTION (Goldwyn) Producers, Richard Weager, Maryann Tanedo; Executive Producers, Bob Abramoff, David Kang, Josh Hutcherson, Clayton Reaser, Vernon Reaser; Director, Joseph Kahn; Screenplay, Joseph Kahn, Mark Palmero; Photography, Christopher Probst; Designer, Marcelle Gravel; Costumes, Kim Bowen; Music, Brian and Melissa; Editor, David Blackburn; Casting, Judy Cook; Dolby; Hawk Scope Widescreen; Color; Rated R; 93 minutes; Release date: April 13, 2012. **CAST:** Josh Hutcherson (Clapton Davis), Spencer Locke (Ione), Dane Cook (Principal Verge), Shanley Caswell (Riley Jones), Lindsey Marie Morgan (Alexis Spencer), Walter Perez (Elliot Fink), Jesse Heiman (Nerd), Aaron Perilo (Mike), Will Wallace (Doug Jones), Richard Brake (Mr. Nolan), Parker Bagley (Billy Nolan), Carrie Wiita (Cinderhella), Arthur Darbinyan (Dr. Murdock), Jessica Lee (Cheerleader), Kate Kelton (Madison), Ryan Heinke (Dork), James Black (Mr. Cooper), Erica Shaffer (Sloan), Michael Esparza (Pedro), Jan Anderson (Ms. Macintire), Tiffany Boone (Mimi), Tammy Minoff (Wendy), Aaron David Johnson (Sander Sanderson), Alison Woods (Taylor Fisher), Marque Richardson II (Toby T.), Melanie Abramoff (Lollapalooza Girl), Nicolo Dorian (Sophomore Chump), Joseph Keane (Metro), Travis Fleetwood (Gord), Jonathan Park (Toshiba), Julie Dolan (Taylor's Mom), Kristine Caluya (Bikini Waxer), Ilana Cohn (Officer Marge McNally), Aaron Albert (Young Verge), Erich Lane (Young Doug Jones), Matthew Philips (Greg, Delinquent), Jay Brian Winnick (Principal Woodruff), Yves Bright (Mr. Kendall), Patrick Babbitt (Uber Nerd), Eliot Bitting (Young Billy Nolan), Justin Charles Smith (Red), Harry Anthony Shelley (Officer Randy Randazzo), Logan Stalarow (Taylor's Little Brother), Josh Breeding (Hipster Thief), Marco Garcia (Janitor), Mickey Jury (Punk), Percy Daggs (Jock Kid), JR Osborne (Truman), Jonathan "Dumbfoundead" Park (Toshiba), Sophia Zach (Round Teen Girl), Lucas Alifano (Random Jock), Amanda Leatherman (Monica Lafontaine), Brian Guest (Clapton's Shaman), Jean Elie, Bryan East (Wrestlers), Jeff Olen (Mr. Kendall's Boyfriend), Yimmy Yim (Angry Dudette), Tyler Sean Palmer (Burnout Kid), Aaron

Albert (Young Principal Verge), John Reha (Nerd 1992), Pierangelo Buonamici (Reject), Aaron Perilo (Mike), Matthew Albrecht (Greg), Ron Jeremy (Beauty Beast), Alexandros S. Potter (Indian Clerk)

Josh Hutcherson in *Detention* © Goldwyn Films

UNRAVELED (Showtime Networks) Producers, Marc H. Simon, Matthew Brian Makar, Steven Cantor, Miranda Bailey; Executive Producer, Tony Tamberelli; Director, Marc H. Simon; Photography, Bob Richman; Music, Chris Hajian; Editors, Alyse Ardell Spiegel, Christina Burchard; a Stick Figure Production in association with Ambush Entertainment, Argyle Productions and Elementary Films; Stereo; Color; HD; Not rated; 84 minutes; Release date: April 13, 2012. Documentary on a massive fraud scheme orchestrated by Manhattan attorney Marc Dreier; **WITH:** Gerald L. Shargel, Ross M. Kramer, Spencer Dreier, Marc S. Dreier, Bob Hart, Rich DeFilippo, Phil Scala, Robert Gilmore, Joel Sickler

Marc S. Dreier in *Unraveled* © Showtime Networks

WOMAN THOU ART LOOSED: ON THE 7ᵀᴴ DAY (Codeblack Entertainment) Producers, Jeff Clanagan, Nina Henderson Moore; Executive Producers, T.D. Jakes, Jonathan Babineaux, Jordan Babineaux, Michael Turner; Director, Neema Barnette; Screenplay, Cory Tynan; Story, TD Jakes; Photography, Keith Smith; Designer, Cecil Gentry; Costumes, Shauna Leone; Music, Mark Kilian; Editor, David Beatty; Casting, Twinkie Byrd; Presented in association with T.D. Jakes Productions; Color; Rated PG-13; 101 minutes; Release date: April 13, 2012. **CAST:** Blair Underwood (David Ames), Sharon Leal (Kari Ames), Nicole Beharie (Beth Hutchins), Clyde Jones (Lamont), Pam Grier (Det. Barrick), Jaqueline Fleming (Tia), T.D. Jakes (Himself), Nicoye Banks (Wil Bennett), Reed R. McCants

(Les), Zoe Carter (Mikayla Ames), Samantha Beaulieu (Pam), Ameer Baraka (Joye), Nick Blady (Detective), Bruce Gerard Brown Jr. (Reporter), Jamie Alyson Caudle (White Trash Girl), Kiara Edwards (Lynette's Daughter), Matty Ferraro (Ed Lainer), Tim Francis (Wayne), Ken Massey (Police Officer), Sabrina Mayfield (Lynette), Denis O'Mahoney (Foot Cop), Terrence Parks (CSI Frank), Thanh Phan (Ed's Girlfriend), Garin Sparks (Swamp Team Kid-looker), Patrick Weathers (Remy), Douglas Wilcox II (Police Officer), Tommye Myrick (Anne), Lance Guidry (Polgraph Examiner), Nick Blady (Detective), Jamie Alyson Caudele (Pimp Girl), Gralen Banks (Hustler in Car), Darnell "Dyce" Jackson (Hustler at Pimp House), Travis Williams (Drug Dealer in Bar).

Justin Welborn, Marshall Allman in *Blue like Jazz* © Roadside Attractions

Jaqueline Fleming, Samantha Beaulieu, Sharon Leal in *Woman Thou Art Loosed* © Codeblack Entertainment

BLUE LIKE JAZZ (Roadside Attractions) Producers, Clarke Gallivan, Steve Taylor; Executive Producers, Coke Sams, Chip Murray, Marshall Allman, Scott Lewis, Dan Raines, Erick Goss; Director, Steve Taylor; Screenplay, Donald Miller, Ben Pearson, Steve Taylor; Photography, Ben Pearson; Designer, Cyndi Williams; Music, Danny Seim; Editor, Matthew Sterling; Visual Effects & Animation, Jonathan Richter; Casting, Corbin Bronson, Elizabeth Barnes; a Ruckus Film Production; Dolby; Color; Rated PG-13; 108 minutes; Release date: April 13, 2012. **CAST:** Claire Holt (Penny), Tania Raymonde (Lauryn), Jason Marsden (Kenny), Marshall Allman (Don Miller), Eric Lange (The Hobo), Justin Welborn (The Pope), Natalia Dyer (Grace), Matt Godfrey (Yuri), Susan Isaacs (Crazed Fan), Donald Miller (Trendy Writer), Becky Fly (Professor), Jenson Goins (Quinn), Jeffery Buckner Ford (James Larkin), Chuck David Willis, Zephyr Benson (Robots), Jenny Littleton (Don's Mom), Barak Hardley (Town Crier), Jeff Obafemi Carr (Dean Bowers), Travis Nicholson (Bookstore Clerk), David Alford (Priest), Henry Reegus Flenory (Guard), William McKinney (Jordan), Scott Kerr (Houston Pastor), Joshua Childs (Bookstore Manager), Valerie Parker (Aqua-Babe), Terra Strong (Lauryn's Friend), Rhyan Schwartz (Bicyclist), Traber Burns (Phillipe Nouvel), Bobby Daniels (Convenience Store Clerk), Erin McGarry (Debate Moderator), Ciana Griggs (Sophie), Tiffany Montgomery (Astro Girl), Marin Miller (Reed Receptionist), John Birkel (Brody), Robert Fitzgerald (Black Jesus), Joseph Lopez (Levi), Andrew T. Vandergriff (Neptune), Austin Johnson (Drunk Freshman), Alexander Tan (Boy with Balloon).

TOUCHBACK (Anchor Bay) Producers, Brian Presley, Kevin Matusow, Carissa Buffel; Executive Producers, George Furla, Randall Emmett, Alexandria Kupstein, Patricia Eberle, Richard Rionda Del Castro, Shannon Gardner, Derek Belmer, Michael Corso, Antony Gudas, Paul Ross, Tony Stacy; Director/Screenplay, Don Handfield; Photography, David Morrison; Designer, Roshelle Berliner; Costumes, Jane Johnston; Music, William Ross; Music Supervisor, Tricia Holloway; Casting, Kerry Barden, Paul Schnee; a Freedom Films production in association with Palo Verde, Hannibal Classics and Sakonnet Capital Partners; Dolby; Color; Rated

Kurt Russell, Brian Presley in *Touchback* © Anchor Bay

PG-13; 118 minutes; Release date: April 13, 2012. **CAST:** Brian Presley (Scott Murphy), Kurt Russell (Coach Hand), Melanie Lynskey (Macy), Marc Blucas (Hall), Christine Lahti (Thelma), Sarah Wright (Jenny), Sianoa Smit-McPhee (Sasha), Drew Powell (Dwight Pearson), Kevin Covais (Todd White), Steve Turner (Gig Bird), James Duval (Rodriguez), Barry Sanders (Cuyahoga Coach), Austin Ross (Moss), Jacquelyn Evola (Krista Murphy), Ella Anderson (Jamie Murphy), Bryan Price (Norman), Harrison Flechsig (Norman's Friend), David Lowing (NFL Commissioner), Richard "Rocky" Rector (Red Robinson).

BAD ASS (Samuel Goldwyn Films) Producer, Ash R. Shah; Executive Producer, Ben Feingold; Director/Screenplay, Craig Moss; Photography, John Barr; Designer, Russell M. Jaeger; Costumes, Ariyela Wald-Cohain; Music, Todd Haberman; Editor, Jim Flynn; Casting, Mary Jo Salter, Shannon Makhanian; a Silver Nitrate presentation; Dolby; Color; Rated R; 90 minutes; Release date: April 13, 2012. **CAST:** Danny Trejo (Frank Vega), Charles S. Dutton (Panther), Joyful Drake (Amber Lamps), Shalim Ortiz (Frank Vega, 17-25 years), Ron Perlman (Mayor Williams), Patrick Fabian (Officer Malark), John Duffy (Martin), Winter Ave Zoli (Tatiana), Danny Woodburn (Sluggy Korn-nuts), Donzaleigh Abernathy (Mother), David A. Arnold (James Worthy), Erik Betts (Terence), Jennifer Blanc (Frances), Tonita Castro (Juanita Vega), Andy Davoli (Renaldo), Patricia De Leon (Marissa), Jack Freshkin (Priest), Craig Johnson (Sebastian), Heidi Kramer (Rebecca Parker), Frank Maharajh (Det. Shah), Craig Moss (Generous Bus Driver), Makenzie Moss (Nikki Kendall), Olivia Moss (Emily Kendall), Jillian Murray (Lindsay Kendall), Harrison Page (Klondike Washington), Richard Riehle

(Father Miller), Tommy Rosales (Bartender), Sam Rubin (Interviewer), Craig Sheffer (Attorney), Chris Spencer (Martin Sr.), C.C. Taylor (Militant Guy), Tyler Tuione (Churchill), Duane Whitaker (Rex, Pawnshop Owner), John Dixon, Kevin Patrick Burke (Skinheads), Ezra Buzzington (Store Clerk), Christine Clayburg (News Anchor), Eddie J. Fernandez (Tattoo Guy), Anthony Martins, Marco Morales, Chad Guerrero (Gangbangers), Jessica Lee (Woman in Purple), Davenia McFadden (Rita), Larry Richardson (Calvin), Mackenzie King (Girl on Bus), Austin Scott (Austin Linkler), Brian Schlesinger (Aldo the Office Boy), Christine Clayburg (News Anchor), Joe Holiday (Baller), Norma Michals (Elderly Woman), Sebastian Valdes (Guy in Jeep)

Danny Trejo in *Bad Ass* © Goldwyn Films

LIFE, LOVE, SOUL (Noel Calloway Films) Producers, Noel Calloway, Dedra N. Tate, Devon O'Reagan; Executive Producers, Allen West, Benny Pough; Director/Screenplay, Noel Calloway; Photography, Jon Fine; Designer, Victor Medina-San Andrés, Raven Robinson; Editor, Keith Salmon; an Allen West Enterprises presentation of a Kingdom Come production; Color; Rated PG; 100 minutes; Release date: April 13, 2012. **CAST:** Chad Coleman (Earl Grant), Jamie Hector (Mr. Roundtree), Robbie Tate-Brickle (Roosevelt Jackson), Tamara Fay (Jennifer Grant), Tami Roman (Renee Jackson), Egypt Sherrod (Carrie), Valerie Simpson (Dr. Tunney), Terri J. Vaughn (Tiffany), Allen West (Mark Tate), Mia Michelle (Kyna Tate)

Nellie McKay, Philippe Quint in *Downtown Express* © Intl. Film Circuit

DOWNTOWN EXPRESS (International Film Circuit) Producers, David Grubin, Michael Hausman; Executive Producer, Tyrone Brown; Director, David Grubin; Screenplay, Kathleen Cahill; Photography, Edward Marritz; Designer/Costumes, Hilary Rosenfeld; Music, Michael Bacon, Nellie McKay; Editor, Jeffrey Wolf; Casting, Pat Golden; a Downtown Express LLC Film; Color; Not rated; 90 minutes; Release date: April 20, 2012. **CAST:** Philippe Quint (Sasha), Nellie

McKay (Ramona), Michael Cumpsty (Vadim), Carolyn McCormick (Marie), Ashley Springer (Arkady), Declan Bennett (Carter), Jade Synstelien (Rabbit), Chris Eddleton (Anthony), Igor Fonberg (Ivan), Marcia Jean Kurtz (Woman on the Subway Platform), David Brown (Master of Ceremonies), Elizabeth Abate, Jerry Barnard, John Carlton, Elaine Chambers, Rolyne Joseph, Andrew Roole (Underground Judges), Norris Bennett, Gloria Gassaway, Ohenio H. Prince, Ali Rahmad, William Salter (The Ebony Hillbillies)

MURDER CAPITAL OF THE WORLD (J&M Prods.) Producer/Director, Charlie Minn; Photography, Donnie Laffoday; Music, Kyle Hildenbrand; Editors, Yota Matsuo, Aaron Thomas; Stereo; Color; Not rated; 83 minutes; Release date: April 20, 2012. Documentary on the drug wars in Ciudad Juárez, Mexico; **WITH:** Daniel Borunda, Charles Bowden, Howard Campbell, Paul Cicala, Darren Hunt, Molly Molloy, Hector Murguia, Justus Opot, Tony Payan, Diana Washington-Valdez

FIGHTVILLE (MPI Media Group) Executive Producers, Michael W. Gray, Dan Cogan, Rachel Schnipper; Directors/Editors, Michael Tucker, Petra Epperlein; Photography, Michael Tucker; Music, Alex Kliment; a Pepper & Bones Film; Color; Not rated; 85 minutes; Release date: April 20, 2012. Documentary on young athletes in Louisiana hoping to become professional mixed martial arts fighters; **WITH:** "Bad" Chad Broussard, Jere Folley Chaisson, "Crazy" Tim Credeur, Dick Gauthier, Gil "The Thrill" Guillory, Lori Guillory, Corey Judice, Derrick Krantz, Ronny Lis, Dustin "The Diamond" Poirier, Paul Solieau, Albert Stainback.

Albert Stainback in *Fightville* © MPI Media Group

SNOW ON THA BLUFF (Screen Media) Producer, Chris Knittel; Executive Producer, Michael K. Williams; Director, Damon Russell; Screenplay, Damon Russell, Curtis Snow; Photography, Pancho Perez, Damon Russell; Music, Lil' Curt, King Kun, Young Blo & Boston, Lucci Dollaz; Editor, Takashi Doscher; a Freedome Productions & Screen Media Ventures presentation; Color; Rated R; 79 minutes; Release date: April 20, 2012. Documentation of the rampant crime in their Atlanta neighborhood as recorded by Curtis Snow and Damon Russell; **WITH:** Curtis Snow, Damon Russell, Curtis Lockett, Tamala Davis, Adrienne Lockett, Young Blo, Baby Curtis, HP "The Ghost," Pancho Perez, Amber Russell, Cat Erickson, D-Lo Snow, Brandon Snow, Brian McCray

JESUS HENRY CHRIST (Entertainment One) Producers, Philip Rose, Lisa Gillian, Sukee Chew; Executive Producers, Julia Roberts, Deepak Nayer; Director/Screenplay, Dennis Lee; Photography, Danny Moder; Designer, Robert Pearson; Costumes, Debra Hanson; Music, David Torn, Simon Taufique; Music Supervisor, Koo Abuali; Casting, Tina Gerussi, Stephanie Corsalini; a Red Om Films and Reliance Big Entertainment presentation of a JHC production in association with

IM Global; Dolby; Color; Rated PG-13; 92 minutes; Release date: April 20, 2012. **CAST:** Michael Sheen (Dr. Slavkin O'Hara), Toni Collette (Patricia Herman), Jason Spevack (Henry James Herman), Samantha Weinstein (Audrey O'Hara), Frank Moore (Stan Herman), Sarah Orenstein (Mother Herman), Aaron Abrams (Malcolm's Dad/Nurse Stewart), Melyssa Ade (Kindergarten Teacher), Dewshane Williams (Malcolm), Paul Braunstein (Dr. Gunther Flowers), Hannah Brigden (Young Patricia), Luca Castricone (Boy on Bus), Maria Syrgiannis (Mother on Bus), Mark Caven (President Sullivan), Daniel Matmor, Roger Clown (Proctors), Devan Cohen (Young Henry), Keith Dinicol (Father Benet), Kevin Hare (Delivery Room Doctor), Kate Hewlett (Alice O'Hara), Jack Newman, Jack Jessop, Gino Marrocco, Sam Moses (Stan's Cohorts), Jamie Johnston (Young Billy Herman), Cameron Kennedy (Jimmy Herman), Mark MacDonald (Tim Herman), Mickey MacDonald (Tom Herman), Austin Macdonald (Brian the Bully), Rosalba Martinni (Nurse Bruna), Adrienne Merrell (Audrey Stravinowsky), Chris Ratz (Bookstore Salesman), Nora Sheehan (Sister Hathaway), R.H. Thomson (Billy Herman), Peggi Tibenny (Protest Mother), Lucca Tibenny-Agate (Protest Little Girl), Mishu Vellani (Miss Abda), Torri Webster (Girl in Cafeteria), Drew Davis (Young Henry's Classmate), Oprah Winfrey (Oprah)

Snow on tha Bluff © Screen Media

Toni Collette, Michael Sheen, Jason Spevack in *Jesus Henry Christ*
© Entertainment One

GOING DOWN IN LA-LA LAND (Embrem Entertainment) Producer/Director/Screenplay, Casper Andreas; Based on the 2006 novel by Andy Zeffer; Executive Producers, Linda Larson, Gary Russell, Coder Simon Jorna, George M. Taninatz, Mich Lyon; Photography, Timothy Naylor; Designer, Shannon Lee Fitzgerald; Costumes, Sarah Jeanne Mgeni; Music, Michael Barry; Editor, Alexander

Hammer; Casting, Jeremy Gordon; a LA-LA Land Films production; Color; Not rated; 104 minutes; Release date: April 20, 2012. **CAST:** Matthew Ludwinksi (Adam Zeller), Allison Lane (Candy), Michael Medico (John Vastelli), Casper Andreas (Nick), John Schile (Ron), Jesse Archer (Matthew), Bruce Vilanch (Missy Manhandler), Judy Tenuta (Zinnea), Alec Mapa (Himself), Michelle Akeley (Stacy), Kim Allen (Ms. Campbell), Brent Bailey (Dean), Daniel Berilla (Perry), C. Stephen Browder (Marvin), Mark Cirillo (Alec Mapa's Fan), Scott DeFalco (Frank), Daniel Hayes (Lucas), Perez Hilton (Ricky), Angelina Hong (Kim), William Jackson (Older Actor), William Thomas Jones (Robert), Claes Lilja (Scott), Paul Martingetti (Career Waiter), Tom Nobles (Wayne), Erik Passoja (Mr. Katz), Brian Putnam (Paparazzi), Leah Rachel (Sophie), Kurt Scholler (Slave), Todd Sherry (Collin), Sherry Weston (Older Actress), Cesar Arambula, Sean Hemeon (Oscar Party Guests), Anadel Baughn (Beverly Hills Lawyer), Jeremy Bilding (Dark-Haired Model), Spencer Falls (Baby-Faced Model), Gregg Jacobson (Sun-Burned Model), Damian Corboy (Production Assistant), Linda Larson (Casting Director), Taaffe O'Connell (Job Interviewer), Ashley Slaton (Starlet), Billy Snow (Gym Sales Guy), Geoff Stirling (The Football Coach), Annie Wood (Sitcom Wife), Robert Donoway (Paul)

Matthew Ludwinski, Bruce Vilanch in *Going Down in LA-LA Land*
© Embrem Entertainment

BOOKER'S PLACE: A MISSISSIPPI STORY (Tribeca Film) Producer, David Zellerford; Executive Producers, Lynn Roer, Steve C. Beer; Director, Raymond De Felitta; Photography, Joe Victorine; Music, David Cieri; Editor, George Cross; a Hangover Lounge presentation in association with Eyepatch Productions; Black and white; HD; Not rated; 91 minutes; Release date: April 25, 2012. Documentary on how Mississippian Booker Wright caused an uproar when he appeared in a 1966 documentary expressing his feelings about working for whites; **WITH:** Frank De Felitta, Yvette Johnson, Vera Douglas, Katherine Jones, Raymond De Felitta, David Jordan, Leroy Jones, Wililam Winter, Hodding Carter III, John T. Edge, Marie Tribit, Benton Johnson, Margurite Butler, Walter Williams, Grey Evans, Charlot Ray, Allen Wood Jr., Jess Pinkston, Alix Sanders, Silas McGhee, Willie Bailey, Johnnie E. Walls, Calvin E. Collins, Erlene Smith

Leroy Jones, Yvette Johnson in *Booker's Place* © Tribeca Film

INVENTING OUR LIFE: THE KIBBUTZ EXPERIMENT (First Run Features) Producer/ Director/Screenplay, Toby Perl Freilich; Photography, Itamar Hadar; Music, Beit Habubot; Editor, Juliet Weber; Narrator, Tracy Thorne; American-Israeli; Color; Not rated; 80 minutes; Release date: April 25, 2012. Documentary on Israel's modern kibbutz movement.

Inventing Our Life © First Run Features

THE HIGHEST PASS (Cinema Libre) Producers, Adam Schomer, Jon Fitzgerald; Executive Producers, Bobby Chang, David Makharadze; Director, Jon Fitzgerald; Screenplay, Adam Schomer; Photography, Dean Mitchell; Music, Michael R. Mollura; Editor, Dan Perrett; a BackNine Studios production in association with i2i Productions; Stereo; Color; Not rated; 90 minutes; Release date: April 27, 2012. Documentary follows a motorcycle trip through the highest passes of the Indian Himalayas; **WITH:** Eric Braff, Ariane D Bonvoisin, Brooks Hale, Paul Greene, Anand Mehrotra, Mike Owen, Richard Parkerson, Adam Schomer

The Highest Pass © Cinema Libre

THE BROKEN TOWER (Focus World) Producers, Vince Jolivette, Miles Levy, Caroline Aragon; Director/Screenplay/Editor, James Franco; Based on the 2000 book *The Broken Tower: The Life of Hart Crane* by Paul Mariani; Photography, Christina Voros; Designer, Kristen Adams; Costumes, Malgosia Turzanska; Music, Neil Benezra; a RabbitBandini production; Black and white; Not rated; 99 minutes; Release date: April 27, 2012. **CAST:** James Franco (Hart Crane), Michael Shannon (Emile), Dave Franco (Young Hart), Richard Abate (Father Crane), Betsy Franco (Betsy Crane), Paul Mariani (Alfred Stielgitz), Shandor Garrison (Gorham Munson), Stacey Miller (Peggy Cowley), Dylan Goodwin (Young Truck Driver),

John Morrow (Young Sailor), Ivo Juhani (French Man in Library), Vince Jolivette, Fallon Goodsen (Americans in Paris), Caroline Aragon (French Café Owner), Sebastian Celis (Deckhand), Will Rawls (Factory Worker), Kazy Tauginas (Boxer)

James Franco in *The Broken Tower* © Focus World

96 MINUTES (ARC Entertainment) Producers, Lee Clay, Justin Moore-Lewy, Charlie Mason, Paul Gilreath; Executive Producers, Mark Moran, Dan Abrams, Don Mandrik, Jessie Rusu, David Ball, Danny Roth; Director/Screenplay, Aimee Lagos; Photography, Michael Fimognari; Designer, Denise Hudson; Costumes, Luellyn Harper; Music, Kurt Farquhar; Editor, Aram Nigoghossian; Casting, Chemin Sylvia Bernard; an XLrator Media, Content Media Corporation, Perfect Weekend and Katonah Pictures presentation of a First Point Entertainment production; Dolby; Color; Rated R; 93 minutes; Release date: April 27, 2012. **CAST:** Brittany Snow (Carley), Evan Ross (Dre), Christian Serrators (Lena), J. Michael Trautmann (Kevin), David Oyelowo (Duane), Elena Varela (ER Doctor), Sharon Morris (Rhonda), Sylvia Jefferies (Kevin's Mom), Hosea Chanchez (Officer Grooms), Jessie Rusu (Jill), Anna Enger (Rachel), Justin Martin (Raymond), Markice Moore (Keith), Adam Trahan (Michael), Jamila Thompson (Kisha), Charles Van Eman (Carley's Professor), Jon Chaffin (J.J.), Sope Aluko (Prison Worker), Charles Black (Clerk), Orlando Vargas Diaz (Patron), Dale Neal (Tye), Tyrone Rivers (Rodger), Sonja Perryman (Dre's Teacher), Jason Park (Max), Michael Scialabba (Cop at Hospital), Alisa Sherrod (Gina), J. Matthew Davis (Rodney), Birdie Rose Gilreath (Girl in Hospital)

Brittany Snow in *96 Minutes* © ARC Entertainment

MAMITAS (Screen Media) Producers, Adam Renehan, Andrew Daniel Wells; Executive Producer, Andrew Daniel Wells; Director/Screenplay, Nicholas Ozeki; Photography, Andrew M. Davis; Designer, Julie Ziah; Costumes, Gina Correll Aglietti; Music, Joseph Trapanese; Editor, Melissa Brown; Casting, Arlie Day; a Right Brain Films presentation in association with Sofias Pictures; Dolby; Color; Rated R; 109 minutes; Release date: April 27, 2012. **CAST:** E.J.Bonilla (Jordin Juarez), Veronica Diaz-Carranza (Felipa Talia), Pedro Armendáriz Jr. (Ramon "Tat" Donicio), Jesse Garcia (Hector Juarez), Joaquim de Almeida (Prof. Alexander Viera), Jennifer Esposito (Miss Ruiz), Josue Aguirre (Santos), Jorge Borrelli (Dr. Allison), Kimberly Burke (Kika), Max Decker (Dominic), Carl Donelson (Big Sexy), Michael Esparza (Christian), Jennifer Esposito (Miss Ruiz), Alex Fernandez (Alvaro Juarez), Adriana Fricke (Magdalena Juarez), Monica Garcia (Emcee), Mónica Guzmán (Kika's Mother), Stephanie Lugo (Tiffy), Claudia Mercado (Consuela), Jaylen Moore (Frnaco), Melissa Paulo (Esperanza), Lidia Pires (Nurse), Buron Quiros (Manager), Glenn Taranto (Jimmy), Kevin Scott Thompson (College Recruiter), Heather Tom (Casandra), Dana Vaughns (Aldo), Julia Vera (Miss Palenica), Jose Yenque (Julio), Maynor Alvardo (Jordin's Friend), Elena Campbell-Martinez (Teacher), Gina Lopez (Esperanza's Friend), Rosemary Lopez (Water Fountain Girl), Matt Medrano (P.E. Teacher), Sarah Sweet (Receptionist)

E.J. Bonilla, Veronica Diaz-Carranza in *Mamitas* © Screen Media

CARL (AfterLight Pictures) Producers, Jamie Vosseller, Butch Seibert, Greg Daniel; Director/Screenplay, Greg Daniel; Photography/Editor, Ken Ballner; Art Directors, Leigh Ann Reagan-Barnes, Sally Rowe; Costumes, Bridgette Lacher Mont; Music, Christian Wood; Visual Effects, Butch Seibert; an OOTC Films presentation of an Out of the Cage Production; Stereo; Color; Not rated; 90 minutes; Release date: April 27, 2012. **CAST:** Robert Pralgo (Mike Ingram), Cheri Christian (Lisa Ingram), Matt Cornwell (Carl), Peg Thon (Mamma), Candace Mabry (Young Lady), Lynne Ashe (Miss Woodland), Daniel Burnley (Mountain Man), Philip Covin (Store Employee), Chad Fishburne (Lewis), Andrea Haynes (Young Mamma), Bill Pacer (Preacher Man), Bethany Anne Lind (Judy), Michelle Kabashinski (Carol), Anslie Hogan (Young Judy), Hays Hogan (Young Carl), Keelie Hogan (Missy), Chris Moore (Hot Dog Vendor), Megan Oepen (Voice of 911 Operator)

JOFFREY: MAVERICKS OF AMERICAN DANCE (Hybrid Cinema) Producers, Una Jackman, Erica Mann Ramis; Executive Producers, Jay Alix, Harold Ramis; Director/Screenplay, Bob Hercules; Photography, Michael Swanson, Keith Walker; Music, Mark Bandy; Editor, Melissa Sterne; Narrator, Mandy Patinkin; a Lakeview Films in association with Ocean Films presentation; Stereo; Color/Black and white; HD; Not rated; 82 minutes; Release date: April 27, 2012. Documentary on the groundbreaking Joffrey dance company; **WITH:** Kevin McKenzie, Helgi Tomasson, Lar Lubovitch, Gary Chryst, Trinette Singleton, Anna Kisselgoff, Adam Sklute, Dermot Burke, Paul Sutherland, Francoise Martinet, Jonathan Watts, Dianne Consoer, Charthel Arthur, Maia Wilkins, Fabrice Calmels, Sasha Anawalt, Hedy Weiss, April Daly, Mark Goldweber, Meg Gurin-Paul, Suzanne Lopez, Davis Robertson, Willy Shives

Max Zomosa in *Joffrey: Mavericks of American Dance* © Hybrid Cinema

RESTLESS CITY (AFFRM) Producers, Katie Mustard, Matt Parker; Executive Producers, David Raymond, Tony Okungbowa, Andrew Dosunmu, Munu El Fituri; Director, Andrew Dosunmu; Screenplay, Eugene Gussenhoven; Photography, Bradford Young; Designer, Chad Keith; Costumes, Mobolaji Dawodu; Editor, Oriana Soddu; Casting, Lois Drabkin; Clam Productions; Color; Rated R; 80 minutes; Release date: April 27, 2012. **CAST:** Sy Allassane (Djbirl), Nicole Grey (Trini), Tony Okungbowa (Bekay), Danai Gurira (Sisi), Hervé Diese (Lido), Mohamed Dione (Pesher), Ger Duany (Rocky), Khadra Dumar (Kadra), Beverly Hugo (Linda), Osas Ighodaro (Adinike), Zoey Martinson (Minnie), Dee Dee Moss (Bekay's Girl, Honeycomb), Saoko Okano (Kai), Femi Olagoke (Thug One), Babs Olusanmokun (Cravate), Ese Daniel Ovueraye (Midi), Maduka Steady (Ten Step), Aspen Steib (Letta), Lenore Thomas (Candy), Stephen Tyrone Williams (Kareem), Sophia Woodhouse (Annis)

Nicole Grey, Sy Allassane in *Restless City* © AFFRM

A LITTLE BIT OF HEAVEN (Millennium) Producers, John Davis, Adam Schroeder, Mark Gill, Robert Katz; Executive Producers, Neil Sacker, Michael Goguen, Michael J. Witherill, Skot Bright; Director, Nicole Kassell; Screenplay, Gren Wells; Photography, Russell Carpenter; Designer, Stuart Wurtzel; Costumes, Ann Roth; Music, Heitor Pereira; Editor, Stuart A. Rotter; Casting, Jeanne McCarthy, Nicole Abellera; The Film Department presentation of a Davis Entertainment production; Dolby; HD Widescreen; Color; Rated PG-13; 106 minutes; Release date: May 4, 2012. **CAST:** Kate Hudson (Marley Corbett), Gael García Bernal (Julian Goldstein), Rosemarie DeWitt (Renee Blair), Lucy Punch (Sarah Walker), Romany Malco (Peter Cooper), Treat Williams (Jack Corbett), Whoopi Goldberg (God), Kathy Bates (Beverly Corbett), Peter Dinklage (Vinnie), Alan Dale (Dr.

Sanders), Steven Weber (Rob Randolf), Jaqueline Fleming (Salesperson), Jason Davis (Thomas Blair), James Hébert (Matt), Donna Duplantier (Examining Room Nurse), Charlotte Bass, Bailey Bass (Cammie Blair), Brett Rice (Ad Agency Client), Maureen A. Brennan (Waiting Area Nurse), Ivan J. Neville (Band Leader), Joe Greblo, Malcolm Jones (Hang Gliding Instructors)

Gael García Bernal, Kate Hudson in *A Little Bit of Heaven*© Millennium Films

LAST CALL AT THE OASIS (ATO) Producers, Jessica Yu, Elise Pearlstein; Executive Producers, Jeff Skoll, Diane Weyermann, Carol Baum, David Helpern; Director/ Screenplay, Jessica Yu; Suggested by the 2011 book *The Ripple Effect: The Fate of Fresh Water in the Twenty-First Century* by Alex Prud'Homme; Photography, John Else; Music, Jeff Beal; Music Supervisor, Margaret Yen; Editor, Kim Roberts; a Participant Media presentation; Color; Rated PG-13; 105 minutes; Release date: May 4, 2012. Documentary on the world's water crisis; **WITH:** Erin Brockovich-Ellis, Jay Famiglietti, Peter H. Gleick, Robert Glennon, Tyrone Hayes

Erin Brockovich-Ellis in *Last Call at the Oasis* © ATO

FOLLOW ME: THE YONI NETANYAHU STORY (Intl. Film Circuit) Producers, Ari Daniel Pinchot, Jonathan Gruber, Mark Manson, Stuart Avi Savitsky; Executive Producer, Mark Manson; Directors, Jonathan Gruber, Ari Daniel Pinchot; Screenplay, Jonathan Gruber; a Crystal City Entertainment film; Color; Not rated; 87 minutes; Release date: May 4, 2012. Documentary on Yoni Netanyahu who led the raid to free the hostages at Entebbe in 1976; **WITH:** Ben Zion Netanyahu, Benjamin Netanyahu, Daphne Netanyahu, Iddo Netanyahu, Dani Litani, Elisha Barmeir, Matan Vilnai, Simon Peres, Ehud Barak, Yanush Ben Gal, Chani Maayan,

Tirza "Tutti" Goodman, Gideon Remez, Amos Goren, Yiftach Reicher Atir, Shlomi Reisman, Avi Weiss Livine, Gloria Zorea, Shai Avital, Bruria Shaked-Okon, Dani Vesely, Nava Barak, Omer Bar Lev, Hezi Kallner, Efraim Laor, Oscar Wasyng, Avi Armoni, Yehuda Atai, Benzy Barlevy, Amos Ben Avraham, Yosi Ben Chanan, Muki Betser, Dani Dagan, Allan Entis, Elliot Entis, Eli Katz, Ron Levi, Ric Levitt, Avishai Margalit, Luzi Margolin, Yechiam mart, Yossi Afuta, Don Morris, Amir Ofer, Alik Ron, Alon Shemi

Yoni Netanyahu in *Follow Me* © Intl. Film Circuit

MOTHER'S DAY (Anchor Bay) Producers, Richard Saperstein, Brett Ratner, Brian Witten, Jay Stern; Executive Producers, Stuart Berton, Stephen Kessler, Lloyd Kaufman, Charles Kaufman, Kyle Bornais, Andrew Golov, Jessie Rusu, Jonathan Zucker, Curtis Leopardo; Director, Darren Lynn Bousman; Screen Story and Screenplay, Scott Milam; Based on the 1980 screenplay by Charles Kaufman and Warren Leight; Photography, Joseph White; Designer, Anthony Ianni; Costumes, Leslie Kavanagh; Music, Bobby Johnston; Music Supervisor, Jonathan McHugh; Editor, Hunter M. Via; Casting, Lindsey Hayes Kroeger; a LightTower Entertainment in association with Widget Films presentation of a Rat Entertainment/Genre Company production; Dolby; Techniscope; Deluxe color; Rated R; 112 minutes; Release date: May 4, 2012. **CAST:** Rebecca De Mornay (Natalie "Mother" Koffin), Jaime King (Beth Sohapi), Patrick Flueger (Izaak Koffin), Warren Kole (Addley Koffin), Deborah Ann Woll (Lydia Koffin), Briana Evigan (Annette Langston), Matt O'Leary (Jonathan Koffin), Jessie Rusu (Melissa McGuire), Shawn Ashmore (George Barnum), Frank Grillo (Daniel Sohapi), Lisa Marcos (Julie Ross), Lyriq Bent (Treshawn Jackson), Tony Nappo (Dave Lowe), Kandyse McClure (Gina Jackson), Jason Wishnowski (Charlie Kaufman), J. LaRose (Terry), Jennifer Hupe (Young Nurse), Alexa Vega (Jenna Luther), A.J. Cook (Vicky Rice), Mike O'Brien (Officer Skay), Heather Schill (Operating Room Nurse), Chris Sigurdson (Officer #1), Will Woytowich (Paramedic #1), Curtis Moore (Desk Reporter), John Sauder (Weatherman), Omar Khan (Surgeon), Stan Lesk (Sanitation Worker #1), Andrew Bryniarski (Quincy, Sanitation Worker), Lloyd Kaufman, Charles Kaufman (Mortgage Brokers)

Jaime King, Rebecca De Mornay in *Mother's Day* © Anchor Bay

YOU HURT MY FEELINGS (Filmscience) Producers, Anish Savjani, Jonathan Silberberg; Executive Producer, Rajen Savjani; Director/Screenplay/Editor, Steve Collins; Photography, Jeremy Saulnier; Designer/Costumes, Carolyn Merriman; a Filmscience production; Color; HD; Not rated; 85 minutes; Release date: May 4, 2012. **CAST:** John Merriman (John), Courtney Davis (Courtney), Macon Blair (Macon)

John Merriman, Macon Blair, Courtney Davis in *You Hurt My Feelings* © Filmscience

THE PERFECT FAMILY (Variance) Producers, Jennifer Dubin, Cora Olson; Executive Producers, Connie Cummings, Kathleen Turner; Director, Anne Renton; Screenplay, Claire V. Riley, Paula Goldberg; Story, Claire V. Riley; Photography, Andre Lascaris; Designer, Megan Hutchison; Costumes, Oneita Parker; Music, Andrew Kaiser; Music Supervisor, Janine Scalise; Editor, Christopher Kroll; Casting, Ronnie Yeskel; a Certainty Films presentation of a Present Pictures production; Dolby; Color; Rated PG-13; 84 minutes; Release date: May 4, 2012. **CAST:** Kathleen Turner (Eileen Cleary), Emily Deschanel (Shannon Cleary), Jason Ritter (Frank Cleary, Jr.), Michael McGrady (Frank Cleary), Elizabeth Peña (Christina Rayes), Richard Chamberlain (Monsignor Murphy), Sharon Lawrence (Agnes Dunn), Kristen Dalton (Theresa Henessy), Laura Cerón (Carmelita), Scott Michael Campbell (Father Joe), Angelique Cabral (Angela Rayes), June Squibb (Mrs. Punch), Mandy June Turpin (Susan O'Connor), Michael Andrew Stock (Frank Jr.'s Son), Gregory Zaragoza (Louis Reyes), Hansford Rowe (Bishop Donnelly), Rebecca Wackler (Sister Joan), Bess Meisler (Greta Russert), Joe Holt (Nurse)

Kathleen Turner, Richard Chamberlain in *The Perfect Family* © Variance Films

FIRST POSITION (Sundance Selects) Producer/Director, Bess Kargman; Executive Producer, Rose Caiola; Photography, Nick Higgins; Music, Chris Hajian; Editors, Kate Amenda, Bess Kargman; a Bess Kargman production; Dolby; Color; Not rated; 94 minutes; Release date: May 4, 2012. Documentary on the Youth America Grand Prix ballet competition; **WITH:** Miko Fogarty, Jules Fogarty, Joan Sebastian Zamora, Aran Bell, Michaela DePrince

Joan Sebastian Zamora in *First Position* © Sundance Selects

LOL (Lionsgate) Producers, Michael Shamberg, Stacey Sher, Tish Cyrus; Executive Producers, Nathan Kahane, Jérôme Seydoux, Romain Le Grand, Lisa Azuelos; Director, Lisa Azuelos; Screenplay, Lisa Azuelos, Kamir Aïnouz; Based on the 2008 film *LOL (Laughing Out Loud)* written by Lisa Azuelos and Delgado Nans; Photography, Kieran McGuigan; Designer, Happy Massee; Costumes, Hope Hanafin; Music, Rob Simonsen; Music Supervisor, Mary Ramos; Editor, Myron Kerstein; Casting, David H. Rapaport; a Mandate Pictures presentation of a Double Feature Films production; Dolby; Deluxe Color; Rated PG-13; 97 minutes; Release date: May 4, 2012. **CAST:** Miley Cyrus (Lola), Demi Moore (Anne), Ashley Greene (Ashley), Douglas Booth (Kyle), Adam Sevani (Wen), Thomas Jane (Allen), Jay Hernandez (James), Marlo Thomas (Gran), Nora Dunn (Emily's Mother), Gina Gershon (Kathy), Fisher Stevens (Roman), George Finn (Chad), Lina Esco (Janice), Ashley Hinshaw (Emily), Tanz Watson (Lloyd), Austin Nichols (Mr. Ross), Jean-Luc Bilodeau (Jeremy), Michelle Burke Thomas (Lauren), Brady Tutton (Jackson), Bridget M. Brown (Lily), Madelyn Lasky (Joan of Arc), Delphine Pontvieux (Joan of Arc's Mother) Sam Derence (Ashley's Dad), Rebecca Finnegan (Therapist), Vivian Le Borgne (Lily's Mother), Jimmy Carrane (Bilogy Teacher), Felix Dayan (French Father), Trevor Fahnstrom (Ethan), Alix Freihage (Young Wife), Lynette Gaza (Principal), Loretta Higgins (Kyle's Mother), Vichaan Kue (David), Emma Nolan (Emma), Dennis North (Kyle's Father), Barbara Robertson (French Techer), Russell Steinberg (Coach), Armon York (Uniformed Cop)

Douglas Booth, Miley Cyrus in *LOL* © Lionsgate

THIS BINARY UNIVERSE (Indican) Director/Music, BT (Brian Wayne Transeau); Dolby; Color; Not rated; 107 minutes; Release date: May 4, 2012. Visual and aural celebration of the world.

MEETING EVIL (Magnet) Producers, Brad Krevoy, Mike Callaghan, Justin Bursch; Executive Producers, Reuben Liber, James Townsend, Roman Viaris; Director/Screenplay, Chris Fisher; Based on the 1992 novel by Thomas Berger; Photography, Marvin V. Rush; Designer, Tom Lisowski; Music, Ryan Beveridge; Editor, Miklos Wright; Casting, Brent Caballero; a Brad Krevoy presentation in association with Motion Picture Corporation of America; Color; Rated R; 89 minutes; Release date: May 4, 2012. **CAST:** Luke Wilson (John Felton), Samuel L. Jackson (Richie), Leslie Bibb (Joanie Felton), Peyton List (Tammy Strate), Muse Watson (Frank), Tracie Thoms (Latisha Rogers), Bret Roberts (Peter the Pool Guy), Jason Alan Smith (Trevor), Tina Parker (Rhonda), Danny Epper (Redneck Driver), Ryan Scott Lee (Scooter), Samuel Robbins (John Felton Jr.), Gabrielle Harvey (Sam Felton), Danny Hanemann (Bartender), Allie McConnell (Gas Station Attendant), Jillian Batherson (Charlene), Avi Lake (Little Girl with Dog), James Townsend, Ritchie Montgomery (Suburban Cops), Charles Ferrara (Old Diner Patron), Dustan Costine (State Policeman), Samantha Sitzman (Girl at Gas Station)

Samuel L. Jackson in *Meeting Evil* © Magnet Releasing

THE OBSERVERS (Independent) Director/Editor, Jacqueline Goss; Photography, Jesse Cain; Color; Not rated; 67 minutes; Release date: May 10, 2012. Experimental film looking at the weather observatory atop New Hampshire's Mount Washington; **WITH:** Dani Leventhal, Katya Gorker.

Dani Levanthal in *The Observers* © Jacqueline Goss

A BAG OF HAMMERS (MPI Media Group) Producers, Peter Friedlander, Lucy Barzun Donnelly, Jennifer Barrons; Director, Brian Crano; Screenplay, Brian Crano, Jake Sandvig; Photography, Byron Shah, Quyen Tran; Designer, Bradley Thordarson; Costumes, Michelle Sandvig; Music, Johnny Flynn; Editor, Brian A. Kates; Casting, Brad Gilmore; a Manor Film presentation of a Two Ships and Locomotive production; Color; Not rated; 85 minutes; Release date: May 11, 2012. **CAST:** Jason Ritter (Ben), Jake Sandvig (Alan), Rebecca Hall (Mel), Chandler Canterbury (Kelsey), Carrie Preston (Lynette), Todd Luiso (Marty), Gabriel Macht (Wyatt), Amanda Seyfried (Amanda), Sally Kirkland (Older Jewish Lady), Jordan Green (Scott Owen), Johnny Simmons (Kelsey, age 18), Micah Hauptman (Vince Ortega), Barbara Rossmeisl (Hobo), Josh Cooke (Cop), Devika Parikh, Greg Clark (Interviewers), Ricardo J. Chacon (Jorge), Dale Waddington Horowitz (Neighbor), Elmaire Wendel (The Mark)

Jason Ritter in *A Bag of Hammers* © MPI Media Group

STEVE JOBS: THE LOST INTERVIEW (Truly Indie) Producers, John Gau, Paul Sen, Stephen Segaller; Executive Producers, Robert X. Cringely, Ted Mundorff; Director, Paul Sen; Screenplay/Narrator, Robert X. Cringely; Photography, John Booth, Clayton Moore; Editor, Nic Stacey; a Truly Indie/Nerd TV/Furnace/John Gau Prods. presentation; Color; Video; Not rated; 69 minutes; Release date: May 11, 2012. 1995 interview with Apple creator Steve Jobs

Steve Jobs in *Steve Jobs: The Lost Interview* © Truly Indie

OTTER 501 (Paladin) Producer/Screenplay, Josh Rosen; Executive Producers, Clint Jones, Mark Shelley; Director, Bob Talbot; Photography/Story, Mark Shelley; Music, Mark Adler; a Sea Studios Foundation production; Stereo; Color; Rated G; 85 minutes; Release date: May 11, 2012. Documentary on an otter sea pup and the efforts to save its species; **WITH:** Katie Pofahl.

Otter 501 © Paladin

CHANGING THE GAME (Barnholtz Entertainment) Producer, Alain Silver; Executive Producers, Thomas L. Webster, Karen L. Isaac; Director, Rel Dowdell; Screenplay, Rel Dowdell, Aaron R. Astillero; Photography, Bob Demers; Designer, R. Brian Chacon; Costumes, Lauren Palmer; Music, Charles Gregory Washington; Editor, Nicholas Schwartz; Casting, Cyndi Lane; a Philly First Entertainment and Pentragon Film Ltd. Production; Color; Rated R; Release date: May 11, 2012. **CAST:** Jakobi Alvin (Young Darrell Barnes), Suzzanne Douglas (Mrs. Davis), Thomas Staten (Young Andre "Dre" Newell), Karen Isaac (Ms. Brown), Summer Valentine (Angelina), Irma P. Hall (Grandma Barnes), Dennis LA White (Dre as an Adult), Sean Riggs (Darrell as an Adult), Shannon Dorsey (Nichole), Tony Todd (Curtis the Diabolical, FBI Agent), Kendia R. Jones (Reba Jones), Ernest Butts (Troy), Kirk "Sticky Fingaz" Jones (Craig), Nicoye Banks (Goldie), Brandon Ruckdashel (Marty Levine), Mari White (Jennifer), John Frisby (Vince), Ming Leone (Marty's Masseuse), Tom Dwyer (Dean Houseman), Irv Slifkin (Jennifer's Father), Demetria Bailey (Jennifer's Mothre), Ted Taylor (Segar Thuns), David Winning (Scott Haragon), Jessica Czop (Darrell's Secretary), Kaki Burns (Marty's Companion), J. Center (Charles Ryne), Munir Kreidie (Obul Metha), Raw Leiba (Balu), Ted Leblang (Gordon Eissenhart), Brian Anthony Wilson (McCormick), Ted Ferguson (John Morris), Elizabeth Camacho (Sexy Light Attendant), Howard Rubin (Neighborhood Cop), José Alvarez (Bass and Montgomery Guard), Neelah Shah (Obul's Secretary), Monica Peters (Darrell's London Secretary), Steve Izant (Dr. Alfred), Tiffany "Charlie Baltimore" Lane (News Reporter)

JaKobi Alvin, Suzzanne Douglas in Changing the Game © Barnholtz Entertainment

SMALL, BEAUTIFULLY MOVING PARTS (Sacha Pictures) Producers, Annie J. Lowell, Lisa Robinson, Jennifer Dougherty; Executive Producer, Yael Melamede; Directors/Screenplay, Annie J. Howell, Lisa Robinson; Photography, Charles E. Swanson; Music, Xander Duell; Editor, Jennifer Lee; Color; HD; Not rated; 72 minutes; Release date: May 11, 2012. **CAST:** Anna Margaret Hollyman (Sarah Sparks), Richard Hoag (Henry), André Holland (Leon), Mary Beth Peil (Marjorie), Sarah Rafferty (Emily), Susan Kelechi Watson (Towie), Timothy McCracken (George), Jan Sandwich (Guru)

Anna Margaret Hollyman in Small, Beautifully Moving Parts © Sacha Pictures

STASH HOUSE (After Dark Films) Producer, Moshe Diamant; Executive Producers, Dolph Lundgren, Gregory Walker, Steven A. Frankel, Bobby Ranghelov, Courtney Solomon; Director, Eduardo Rodriguez; Screenplay, Gary Spinelli; Photography, Matthew Irving; Designer, Michelle Jones; Costumes, Jennifer Kamrath; Music, Luis Ascanio; Editors, Eduardo Rodriguez, Don Adams; a Signature Entertainment, Ingenious, Au-ton-o-mous [films] production; Dolby; Color; Rated R; 99 minutes; Release date: May 11, 2012. **CAST:** Dolph Lundgren (Andy Spector), Briana Evigan (Amy Nash), Sean Faris (David Nash), Jon Huertas (Ray Jaffe), Alyshia Ochse (Trish Garrety), Don Yesso (Benz), Lance E. Nichols (Priest), Lawrence Turner (Max Farrell), David Lee Valle (Bulldog), David Bottoms, James Rawlings, Michael Rogers (Uniformed Police Officers), Sean Boyd (Fed #2), Javier Carrasquillo (Officer Rushing), Caleb Michaelson (Paramedic), Roger J. Timber (Cop), Douglas Wilcox (SWAT Officer)

Briana Evigan, Sean Faris in Stash House © After Dark Films

HICK (Phase 4 Films) Producers, Steven Siebert, Christian Taylor, Charles de Portes, Jon Cornick; Director, Derick Martini; Screenplay, Andrea Portes, based on her 2007 novel; Photography, Frank Godwin; Designer, Roshelle Berliner; Costumes, Erika Munro; Music, Larry Campbell; Editor, Mark Yoshikawa;

Casting, Eyde Belasco; a Stoneriver Lighthouse Entertainment and Taylor Lane production; Dolby; Panavision; Color; Rated R; 99 minutes; Release date: May 11, 2012. **CAST:** Chloë Grace Moretz (Luli McMullen), Eddie Redmayne (Eddie Kreezer), Rory Culkin (Clement), Juliette Lewis (Tammy), Ray McKinnon (Lloyd), Anson Mount (Nick), Blake Lively (Glenda), Alec Baldwin (Beau), Robert Baker (Ray), Robert J. Stephenson (Lux), Shaun Sipos (Blane), Dartanian Sloan (Angel), Beth Malone (Sherri), Gina Stewart (Crystal), David Allen Vescio (Stranger), Jody Thompson (Bartender), Tim Parati (Barfly), Leon Lamar (Clerk), Jon Cornick (Cop #2), Brian Avery Galligan (EMT), Michael Jefferson (Flannel Drunk), Matt Malloy (Bunny Looker), Troy Rudeseal (Bus Driver)

Eddie Redmayne in *Hick* © Phase 4 Films

EL GRINGO (After Dark Films) Producers, Courtney Solomon, Moshe Diamante; Executive Producers, Scott Adkins, Gregory Walker, Steven A. Frankel, Bobby Ranghelov, Allan Zeman, Joel Silver; Director, Eduardo Rodriguez; Screenplay, Jonathan Stokes; Photography, Yaron Levy; Designer, Nate Jones; Costumes, Kim Martinez; Music, Luis Ascanio; Editors, Eduardo Rodriguez, Don Adams; Casting, Manuel Teil; a Signature Entertainment, Ingenious, Au-ton-o-mous [films] production; Dolby; Color; Rated R; 103 minutes; Release date: May 11, 2012. **CAST:** Scott Adkins (The Man), Christian Slater (Lt. West), Yvette Yates (Anna), Petar Bachvarov (Tortuga), Zachary Baharov (Officer Bell), Mihail Elenov (Pablo), Valentin Ganev (Deputy Chief Logan), Erando González (Chief Espinoza), Israel Islas (Culebra), Georgi Karlukovski (El Jefe), Vlado Mihaylov (Chilango), Velislav Pavlov (Officer Dunn), Bashar Rahal (Officer Sullivan), Marii Rosen (Naco), Edward Joe Scargill (Officer Conner), Sofia Sisniega (Flaca), Atanas Srebrev (Officer Rick), Mimoza Bazova (Bus Station Attendant), Krasimir Rankov (Restaurant Owner), Yoana Temelkova (Shop Keeper)

Christian Slater, Scott Adkins in *El Gringo* © After Dark Films

TRANSIT (After Dark Films) Producer, Courtney Solomon; Executive Producers, Joel Silver, Allan Zeman; Executive Producers, Michael Gaeta, Alison Rosenzweig; Director, Antonio Negret; Screenplay, Michael Gilvary; Photography, Yaron Levy; Designer, Nate Jones; Costumes, Kimberly Martinez; Music, Chris Westlake; Editor, William Yeh; Casting, Shannon Makhanian; a Signature Entertainment production; Dolby; Color; Rated R; 88 minutes; Release date: May 11, 2012. **CAST:** Jim Caviezel (Nate), James Frain (Marek), Diora Baird (Arielle), Elisabeth Röhm (Robyn), Ryan Donowho (Evers), Sterling Knight (Shane), Harold Perrineau (Losada), Jake Cherry (Kenny), J.D. Evermore (Sgt. Doucette), Beau Brasso (Crazy Driver), Robbie Jones (Dallas), Griff Furst (Lt. B. Morgan), Rob Boltin (Sgt. Spurlock), Don Yesso (Sgt. Gazzo), Douglas M. Griffin (Lt. Paolo), Monica Acosta (Driver), Ashley Braud (Voice of News Anchor)

Jim Caviezel in *Transit* © After Dark Films

PORTRAIT OF WALLY (Seventh Art) Producers, Andrew Shea, Barbara Morgan, David D'Arcy; Director, Andrew Shea; Screenplay, Andrew Shea, David D'Arcy; Photography, Sam Henriques; Music, Gary Lionelli; Editor, Melissa Shea; Visual Effects, Ptarmak; a P.O.W. Productions film; Color; Not rated; 90 minutes; Release date: May 11, 2012. Documentary on the controversy behind the theft and exhibition of Egon Schiele's painting *Portrait of Wally*, **WITH:** David D'Arcy, Tom L. Freudenheim, Bonnie Goldblatt, Jane Kallir, Elizabeth Leopold, Sharon Cohen Levin, Robert Morgenthau, Michael B. Mukasey, Morley Safer, Ori Z. Soltes

Portrait of Wally © Seventh Art Releasing

THE PHILLY KID (After Dark Films) Producers, Moshe Diamant, Stephanie Caleb, Kerri O'Reilly, Lauren Ito, Jeffrey Silver, Courtney Solomon; Director, Jason Connery; Screenplay, Adam Mervis; Photography, Marco Fargnoli; Designer, Erika Rice; Costumes, Stacy Ellen Rich; Music, Ian Honeyman; Editor, William Yeh; Casting, Sally Lear; a Signature Entertainment, Ingenious, Au-ton-o-mous [films] production; Dolby; Color; Rated R; 90 minutes; Release date: May 11, 2012. **CAST:** Wes Chatham (Dillon), Devon Sawa (Jake), Sarah Butler (Amy), Neal McDonough (LA Jim), Lucky Johnson (Ace), Chris Browning (Marks), Adam Mervis (Ryan Maygold), Bernard Hocke (Lenny), Ava Bogle (Allison Kaufman), Eric Scott Woods (Spencer), Michael Jai White (Arthur Letts), Andrew Sensenig (Larry), Rich Clementi (Sanchez), Gralen Bryant Banks (Landlord), J.D. Evermore (Parole Officer), Douglas M. Griffin (Internal Affairs Officer), Kaitlin Hoychick, Bliss Kelley, Blaire Noonan (Ring Girls), Vinny Lebelo (Titan Referee), Josh Mancuso (College Wrestler), Scott O'Shaughnessy (Justin Lean), Ross Rouillier (Titov, Corner Man), Brittany Soileau (The Blonde), Marco St. John (Doctor), Jason Stanly (Maury Rosen), Kristopher Van Varenberg (Chase), Glen Warner (Bouncer), Nedal Yousef (Dom)

Neal McDonough, Wes Chatham in *The Philly Kid* © After Dark Films

NESTING (PMK*BNC Films) Producers, Laura Boersma, John Chuldenko; Executive Producers, Jim Stanard, Karen Clark, Jay Nichols; Director/Screenplay, John Chuldenko; Occasional Funny Aside by Sean Blythe; Photography, Frederick Schroeder; Designer, Jem Elsner; Costumes, Sarah Ellis; Music, Julian Wass; Editor, Sam Restivo; Casting, Hannah Cooper; a Dangertrain Films production; Color; Rated PG-13; 92 minutes; Release date: May 11, 2012. **CAST:** Todd Grinnell (Neil), Ali Hillis (Sarah), Kevin Linehan (Graham), Erin Chambers (Katie), Erin Gray (Mrs. Deegan), John Gerbin (Greg), Wes Armstrong (Kenny), Alexi Wasser (Rachel), Ian Jensen (Pete), Sorel Carradine (Nikki), Christine Barger (Jill), Devin Barry (Todd), Jake Borelli (Josh), John Chuldenko (Sound Guy), Xandra Clark (Anna), Sujata Day (Sasha), Anthony Gaudioso (Officer Kelly), Stacy Hall (Officer Powell), Bjorn Johnson (Volvo Man), James Austin Kerr (Travis, the Abercrombie Model), Zarah Kulczycki (Noel), Kevin Manwarren (Alvin), Ben Marks (Matt), John Stewart Muller (Hipster Dude), Mike C. Nelson (Andy), Allison Paige (Ashley), Nathaniel A. Pena (Pedro), Michael Manuel Peña (Pedro's Friend), Jeremy Radin (Ross), David Scales (Ian), Erik Stocklin (Ben), Maryann Strossner (Mrs. Borkowski), Jeffrey Stubblefield (Jeff), Liliana Tandon (Brittany), Jamal Thomas (Brian), Sam Upton (Officer Evans), Katie Wallack (Hannah), Bill Watterson (Scoreboard Pete), Gregory Zarian (Shane)

DRAGON EYES (After Dark Films) Executive Producers, Moshe Diamant, Courtney Solomon, Steven A. Frankel, Stephanie Caleb; Director, John Hyams; Screenplay, Tim Tori; Photography, Stephen Schlueter; Designer, Nate Jones; Costumes, Kim Martinez; Music, Michael Krassner; Editors, Jon Greenhalgh, Andrew Drazek; Casting, Shannon Makhanian; a Signature Entertainment production; Dolby; Color; Rated R; 91 minutes; Release date: May 11, 2012.

Todd Grinnell, Ali Hillis in *Nesting* ©PKM*BNC

CAST: Cung Le (Ryan Hong), Jean-Claude Van Damme (Tiano), Johnny Holmes (Big Jake), Peter Weller (Mr. V), Sam Medina (Biggie), Gilbert Melendez (Trey), Adrian Hammond (Buyer), Danny Cosmo (Junkie), Crystal Mantecon (Rosanna), Danny Mora (Grandpa George), Arielle Zimmerman (Young Woman), Luis Da Silva Jr. (Dash), Arturo Palacios (Jonsey), Edrick Browne (Antoine), Jason Mitchell (J-Dog), Travis Johnson (Mikey), Tony Jarreau (Jail Cop), Trevor Prangley (Lord), Scott Sheeley (Yuri), Eddie Rouse (Beech), Andrew Sikking (Tony), Craig Walker (Sgt. Howe), Kristopher Van Varenberg (Sgt. Feldman), Sari Cummings (Honey Darling), Dan Henderson (Office Fizzari), Monica Acosta (Pedestrian), Robert Dutton (Asian Prisoner), Kasey Emas (Cecilia), Larry Goldstein (Motorcycle Bandit), Lloyd Pitts (James), Adam Sibley (Little Homie), Andy Chapman, Austin Naulty, Eduardo Neves, Michael Patrick Rogers, Joe Williams (6th Street Kings), Rich Clementi, Travis McCoy, Luke Hawx, Micah Lopez, James Rawlings, Bill Waters, Greg Sproles, Josh Thompson (Devil Dogs), David Ali (Theo)

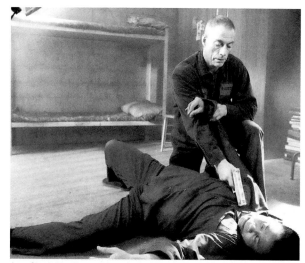

Jean-Claude Van Damme, Cung Le in *Dragon Eyes* © After Dark Films

AMERICAN ANIMAL (Screen Media) Producers, Matt D'Elia, Julian King, Jennifer MacVittie, Patrick Sayre; Executive Producer, Bill D'Elia; Director/Screenplay, Matt D'Elia; Photography, Julian King; Designer, Arthur Martinot; Editors, Matt D'Elia, Julian King; an American Moving Pictures production; Dolby; Color; Rated R; 95 minutes; Release date: May 18, 2012. **CAST:** Matt D'Elia (Jimmy), Brendan Fletcher (James), Mircea Monroe (Blonde Angela), Angela Sarafyan (Not Blonde Angela)

UNDER AFRICAN SKIES (A&E Indie Films) Producers, Joe Berlinger, Jon Kamen, Justin Wilkes; Executive Producers, Molly Thompson, Robert Debitetto, Dave McKillop, Robert Friedman, Frank Scherma, Eddie Simon, Richard Story, Adam Block, Gil Aronow; Director, Joe Berlinger; Photography, Bob Richman; Editor, Joshua L. Pearson; Color; a @Radical Media Production in association with Sony Music Entertainment's Legacy Recordings; American-South African; Color; Not rated; 102 minutes; Release date: May 18, 2012. Documentary on the creation of Paul Simon's classic *Graceland* album; **WITH:** Paul Simon, Maya Angelou, Okeyerama Asante, Harry Belafonte, David Byrne, Tony Cedras, Peter Gabriel, Philip Glass, Whoopi Goldberg, Roy Halee, Quincy Jones, Vusi Khumalo, Bakithi Kumalo, Koloi Lebona, Ladysmith Black Mambazzo, Hugh Masekela, Paul McCartney, Lorne Michaels, Sonti Mndebele, Isaac Mtshali, Jon Pareles, Ray Phiri, Barney Rachabane, Hilton Rosenthal, John Selolwane, Wally Serote, Joseph Shabalala, Dali Tambo, Oprah Winfrey

Miriam Makeba, Paul Simon in *Under African Skies* © A&E Indie Films

D'AGOSTINO (Hollywood Independents) Producers, Jorge Ameer, Zach Voytas, James Vegas; Executive Producers, Jorge Ameer, Fanis Kavalari, Thomas Likourinos, Irini Liourinou; Director/Screenplay/Editor, Jorge Ameer; Photography, Zach Voytas; Music, Brent J. Dickey, Keith Roenke, Chris Tart, Zach Voytas; an A.J. Productions in association with Kavalari and Mama's House production; American-Greek; Color; Not rated; 117 minutes; Release date: May 18, 2012. **CAST:** Jorge Ameer (Niko), Michael Angels (D'Agostino), Angus Malcolm (Larry), Keith Roenke (Allan Dawson), Torie Tyson (Sylvia)

Jorge Ameer in *D'Agostino* © Hollywood Independents

THE DARK SIDE OF LOVE (Hollywood Independents) Producer/Director/ Screenplay/Editor, Jorge Ameer; Photography, Xavier Henselmann; a Casa Granada, The Big Kitchen production, presented in association with A.J. Productions; Dolby; Color; Not rated; 87 minutes; Release date: May 18, 2012. **CAST:** Harsha First (Steven), Carlos Salas (Julian), Raquel Rosser (Chanel), Ramon Estrada (William), Marcelle Lee (Lady Vanessa), Anthea Orlando (Mrs. Winnie), Jason Susag (Michael)

Carlos Salas, Harsha First in *The Dark Side of Love* © Hollywood Independents

THE COLOR WHEEL (Cinema Conservancy) Producer/Director/Editor, Alex Ross Perry; Screenplay, Alex Ross Perry, Carlen Altman; Photography, Sean Price Williams; Designer, Anna Bak-Kvapil; Music, Preston Spurlock; a Dorset Films production; Black and white; HD; Not rated; 83 minutes; Release date: May 18, 2012. **CAST:** Carlen Altman (JR), Bob Byington (Prof. Neil Chadwick), Kate Lyn Sheil (Julia), Anna Bak-Kvapil (Kim Thompson), Ry Russo-Young (Zoe), Craig Butta (Norton the Bully), Alex Ross Perry (Colin), Tom Brown (Antique Tom), Kate Hollowell (Ellie), Anna Margaret Hollyman (Roberta B.), Ethan Smith (Singing Waiter), Jody Smith (Ms. Wagner), Roy Thomas (Motel Clerk), Sarah Virden (Preppie No-Pineapple), C. Mason Wells (Chris "Wheels" Locke), Keith Poulson (Norton's Sidekick)

Alex Ross Perry, Carlen Altman in *The Color Wheel* © Cinema Conservancy

MANSOME (Paladin) Producers, Jeremy Chilnick, Meri Haitkin, Morgan Spurlock; Executive Producers, Will Arnett, Jason Bateman, Drew Buckley, Laura Caraccioli, Ben Silverman; Director, Morgan Spurlock; Screenplay, Morgan Spurlock, Jeremy Chilnick; Photography, Paul Dokuchitz, Matt Goodman, Daniel Marracino; Music, Jingle Punks; Editor, Thomas M. Vogt; Graphics, Nathan Love; a Warrior Poets/Electus/DumbDumb production; Dolby; Color; HD; Rated PG-13; 82 minutes; Release date: May 18, 2012. Documentary on the rising interest in grooming products for men; **WITH:** Morgan Spurlock, Judd Apatow, Will Arnett, Jason Bateman, Adam Carolla, JC Coccoli, Shawn Daivari, Zach Galifianakis, Ricky Manchanda, Chris McLaughlin, Cari Moskow, Isaiah Mustafa, Timothy Nordwind, Jack Passion, Adam Popp, Paul Rudd, John Waters, Doug Willen

Jason Bateman, Will Arnett in *Mansome* © Paladin

LOVELY MOLLY (Image Entertainment) Producers, Robin Cowie, Gregg Hale, Jane Fleming, Mark Ordesky; Executive Producers, J. Andrew Jenkins, Robert Eick; Director/Screenplay, Eduardo Sanchez; Story, Jamie Nash; Photography, John W. Rutland; Designer, Andrew White; Music, Tortoise; Editors, Andrew Vona, Eduardo Sanchez; Special Effect Coordinator, Mark Fenalson; Casting, Pat Moran; a Haxan Films and Amber Entertainment production; Color; HD; Rated R; 100 minutes; Release date: May 18, 2012. **CAST:** Alexandra Holden (Hannah), Johnny Lewis (Tim), Gretchen Lodge (Molly), Ken Arnold (Samuels), Lauren Lakis (Lauren), Tony Ellis (Church Boy), Katie Foster (Stacey), Shane Tunney (Hotel Clerk), Daniel Ross (Victor), Tara Garwood (Saleswoman), Todd Ryan Jones (The Demon), Field Blauvelt (Pastor Bobby), Andrew Vona (Voice of Demon), Mark Redfield (Ronnie's Friend), Brandon Thane Wilson (Spit Cup), Dan Franko (Mall Man), Alexis Savage (Young Molly), Greg Cool (Ben Palmer), Erik Young (Larry, Possessed Civil War Soldier), Kyle David Crosby (Church Band Leader), Kenny Caperton (Mall Walker), Dan Manning (Dr. Dean), Hillary Styer (1940s Mom), Steve Dantzler (Drug Dealer)

Gretchen Lodge in *Lovely Molly* © Image Entertainment

TALES FROM DELL CITY, TEXAS (Philofilm) Producer/Director/Editor, Josh Carter; Color; Not rated; 68 minutes; Release date: May 18, 2012. Documentary on a slowly dying Texas town.

NEVER STAND STILL (First Run Features) Producers/Screenplay, Ron Honsa, Nan Penman; Executive Producer, Ella Baff; Director, Ron Honsa; Photography, Jimmy O'Donnell, Etienne Sauret; Editor, Charles Yurick; Narrator, Bill T. Jones; a

Bobby Jones in *Tales from Dell City, Texas* © Philofilm

Moving Pictures production; Color/Black and white; HD; Not rated; 74 minutes; Release date: May 18, 2012. Documentary on Jacob's Pillow dance troupe; **WITH:** Marge Champion, Merce Cunningham, Suzanne Farrell, Diane Ferlatte, Frederic Franklin, Joanna Haigood, Anna-Marie Holmes, Nikolaj Hübbe, Bill Irwin, Judith Jamison, Jomar Mesquita, Mark Morris, Gideon Obarzanek, Jens Rosén, Shantala Shivalingappa, Paul Taylor, Linda Tillery, Rasta Thomas

Kellye Saunders in *Never Stand Still*
© First Run Features

CROOKED ARROWS (Sports Studio) Producers, J. Todd Harris, Mitchell Peck, Adam Leff; Executive Producers, Jeffrey McCormick, Brandon Routh; Co-Executive Producers, Marc Marcum, Murphy van der Velde, Stephen Brackett; Director, Steve Rash; Screenplay, Todd Baird, Brad Riddell; Photography, Daniel Stoloff; Designer, Carl Sprague; Costumes, Virginia Johnson; Music, Brian Ralston; Music Supervisor, Jeffrey Rabhan; Editors, Danny Saphire, Bart Rachmil; Casting, Rene Haynes; a Peck Entertainment/Branded Pictures Entertainment production in association with the Onondaga Nation and Sports Studio; Dolby; Color; Rated PG-13; 105 minutes; Release date: May 18, 2012. **CAST:** Brandon Routh (Joe Logan), Crystal Allen (Julie Gifford), Chelsea Ricketts (Nadie Logan), Dennis Ambriz (Crooked Arrow), Gil Birmingham (Ben Logan), Tyler Hill (Jimmy), Michael Hudson (Reed), Robert Coffie (Crooked Arrow's Fan), Tom Kemp (Mr. Geyer), Mike Handelman (Chad Bryan), Cindy Lentol (Baccarat Woman), Kelby Akin (Sulgrave Dad), Alex Cook (Titly Sunglasses Guy), Jack van der Velde (Toby Gifford), Aaron Printup (Maug), Cree Cathers (Chewy), Kakaionstha Betty Deer (Grandma Logan), Orris Edwards (Sammy)

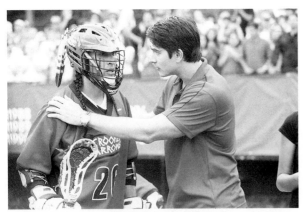

Tyler Hill, Brandon Routh in *Crooked Arrows* © Sports Studio

BILL W. (Page 124 Prods.) Producers/Directors/Screenplay, Kevin Hanlon, Dan Carracino; Photography, Ryo Murakami; Music, Gil Talmi; Editor, Patrick Gambuti Jr.; Dolby; Color/black and white; HD; Not rated; 103 minutes; Release date: May 18, 2012. Documentary on William G. Wilson, the co-founder of Alcoholics Anonymous; **WITH:** Shep S., Tom W., Bill S., Tom I., Sara N., Ruth O., Ernest Kurtz, Bill White, Phil P., Gail L., Merton Minter, Norm E., Candace C., Dr. Abram Hoffer, Mitch K., Mel B., Bob P.; **CAST** (Re-enactments): Blake J. Evans (Bill Wilson), Chris Gates (Dr. Bob), Dennis Lowell (Hank Parkhurst), Julia Schell (Lois Wilson), Tim Intravia (Ebby T.), Leila Babson (Annie Smith), Lenore Pershing (Henrietta Seiberilng), Max Owens (Young Bill), Ron Nagle (Bill's Grandfather), Laura Kauffmann (Martha Deane), Andrew Langton (Bill's Armistice Day Friend), Francis Stallings (Kathleen Parkhurst), Rachel Lynn Jackson (Ruth Hock), Norman Shultz (Father Ed Dowling), Ed Moroney (Tom the Caretaker), Kathleen Emmans (Nell), Catherine Hogan (Waitress), Brendan McMahon, David Caporale, Martin McColgan, Robert Shulman (Men at 182 Clinton St.)

Bill Wilson in *Bill W.* © Page 124 Prods.

OC87: THE OBSESSIVE, COMPULSIVE, MAJOR DEPRESSION, BI-POLAR, ASPERGER'S MOVIE (Fisher Klingenstein Films) Executive Producer, Bud Clayman; Directors, Glenn Holsten, Scott Johnston, Bud Clayman; Screenplay, Scott Johnston, Bud Clayman; Photography, Daniel Traub; Costumes, Andrew Basile; Music, Michael Aharon; Editor, Kathleen Soulliere; a Therapy Prods. Inc. presentation; Color; HD; Not rated; 100 minutes; Release date: May 25, 2012. Documentary on how Bud Clayman dealt with his OCD by making a film about it; **WITH:** Bud Clayman, Lila Clayman, Morton Clayman, Jonathan Grayson, Jeff Bell, Maurice Benard, Wayne Bickerstaff, Carol Caruso, Loren H. Crabtree, Barbara H. Cram, Rachel Davis, Daniel Fisher, Sally F. Gever, JJohn Hart, Susan Heffelfinger, Sally Holmgren, Paul Kiesling, Dustin Knast, Richard Krefertz, Elizabeth McIngvale, Amy Miller, Susan Nelson, Karen Peek, Linda Rauscher, Marie Rennie, Kristen Roberts, Mary Scullion, Robert Serge, Harold Shannon, Carl Steinberg, Glenn Weaver, Jonathan Wolfman

Bud Clayman in *OC87* © Fisher Klingenstein

MIGHTY FINE (Adopt Films) Producers, Ajae Clearway, Kathryn Wallack, Debra Goodstein-Rosenfeld; Executive Producers, Chazz Palminteri, Mark Manuel; Co-Producer, Andie MacDowell; Director/Screenplay, Debra Goodstein-Rosenfeld; Photography, Bobby Bukowski; Designer, Kelly McGehee; Costumes, Kari Perkins; Music, Max Avery Lichtenstein; Editor, Suzy Elminger; Casting, Adrienne Stern; a Mighty Fine Productions presentation; Color; Not rated; 80 minutes; Release date: May 25, 2012. **CAST:** Chazz Palminteri (Joe Fine), Andie MacDowell (Stella Fine), Jodelle Ferland (Natalie Fine), Rainey Qualley (Maddie Fine), Paul Ben-Victor (Bobby), Arthur J. Nascarella (Lenny), Richard Kohnke (Earl), Kent Jude Bernard (Louie), Miles Doleac (Mr. Smith), Ron Flagge (Sam), Ann McKenzie (Poetry Contest Judge), Joseph Miessner (Veterinarian), Geraldine Singer (Gracie), Todd Williams (Boris), John T. Wilson Jr. (Wiseguy), Sally Winters (Narrator)

Andie MacDowell, Rainey Qualley, Jodelle Ferland, Chazz Palminteri in *Mighty Fine* © Adopt Films

COWGIRLS N' ANGELS (Goldwyn) Producers, Ben Feingold; Shawn Griffith, Jim Busfield, Timothy Armstrong; Co-Producers, Carlos D. De Mattos, Marcus M. De Mattos, Steve Kantola; Director, Timothy Armstrong; Screenplay, Timothy Armstrong, Stephan Blinn; Photography, John Barr; Designer, Rebekah Bell; Music, Alan Williams; Editor, Michael Rafferty; Casting, Mary Jo Slater, Shannon Makhanian; a Sense and Sensibility Ventures presentation; Dolby; Color; Rated PG; 91 minutes; Release date: May 25, 2012. **CAST:** Bailee Madison (Ida Clayton), James Cromwell (Terence Parker), Jackson Rathbone (Justin Wood), Alicia Witt (Elaine), Frankie Faison (Augustus), Kathleen Rose Perkins (Rebecca), Dora Madison Burge (Kansas), Leslie-Anne Huff (Madison), Drew Waters (Rollie), Louanne Stephens (Joan), Noell Coet (Nora), Mark Nutter (Walker), Calley Luman (Sierra), Denise Lee (Alice), Haley Ganzel (Rose), Aimee Crowther (Kim), Amber Hayes (Amber Grant), Bill Story, Monty Stueve, Shawn Griffith (Rodeo Announcers), Ashley D. Merritt (Brooke), Lindsay Sawyer (Jeannie), Richie McDonald (Doug Grant), Richard Levi (Security Guard), Madison Freeman (Ricky Rodeo), Dusta Kimzey (Dusta), Bill Poague (Mr. Stucky), Brian Capshaw (Mark Winters), Joyce Galloway (Gracie), Cristela Carrizales (Marta), Kent Jones (Doctor), Daniel Armstrong, Lilly Armstrong, Macy Armstrong, Natalia Lopez, Julia Lopez (Autograph Kids), Grayson Griffith (Fan #1), Karena Richmond (Young Elaine), Justin Lauer (Jim Clayton), Robert Paschall Jr. (Cowboy), Keaton Cunningham (Violin Girl)

Jackson Rathbone, Dora Madison Burge in *Cowgirls n' Angels* © Goldwyn Films

QUALITY CONTROL (Picture Palace Pictures) Producers, Kevin Jerome Everson, Madeleine Molyneaux; Director/Photography/Editor, Kevin Jerome Everson; a Trilobite-Arts-DAC production; Black and white; Not rated; 80 minutes; Release date: May 25, 2012. Documentary on an Alabama dry cleaner's daily operations; **WITH:** Shay Wright, Annette Speight, Eric Brown, Tyhesha Dawkins, Omar Diamond, Sam Ervin Jr., Sandra Gully, Patricia Isaack, Cora Pair, Doshier Thomas, Ann Thrash, Sheila Wells

REDLEGS (Arts Fund/Nappinati Films) Producers, Brett Greene, Brandon Harris, Evan Louison; Executive Producers, Adam Hootnick, Bryan Kane, Schuyler Murdock; Director, Brandon Harris; Screenplay, Brandon Harris, Andrew Katz, Evan Louison, Nathan Ramos; Story, Brandon Harris, Nick D'Agostino; Photography, Miranda Rhyne; Designer, Kelsey Koble; Costumes, Kelsey Wing; Editors, Brandon Harris, Jackeline Tejada; Casting, Charlotte Bence; Color; Not rated; 65 minutes; Release date: May 25, 2012. **CAST:** Evan Louison (Willie), Andrew Katz (Aaron), Nathan Ramos (Marco), Aimee Cucchiaro (Marjorie), T.J. Hamper (Wired Guy), Jill Donenfeld (Blonde Girl), Brandon Harris (Pot Dealer), Jeseca Davis (Ricky's Sister), Tony Davis (Preacher), Ben Ferrell (Ron), Greg Stanforth (Farmer)

HIDE AWAY (MMC Joule Films) formerly *A Year in Mooring*; Producers, Sally Jo Effenson, Chris Eyre, Kevin Reidy; Executive Producer, Jeff Honeck; Director, Chris Eyre; Screenplay, Peter Vanderwall; Photography, Elliot Davis; Designer, Sharon Lomofsky; Costumes, Susanna Puisto; Music, Tony Morales, Edward

Rogers; Editors, Devin Maurer, Jonathan Lucas; Color; Rated PG-13; 88 minutes; Release date: May 25, 2012. **CAST:** Josh Lucas (Young Mariner), Ayelet Zurer (The Waitress), James Cromwell (The Ancient Mariner), Jon Tenney (The Divorced Man), Taylor Nichols (The Boss), Casey LaBow (Lauren), Anne Faba (Helen), Ele Bardha (The Buyer), Austin Bickel (Owen), Bryan Crough (Curmudgeon), Taylor Groothuis (Young Lauren), David Herbst (The Seller)

Josh Lucas in *Hide Away* © MMC Joule Films

WISH ME AWAY (First Run Features) Producers/Directors, Bobbie Birleffi, Beverly Kopf; Executive Producers, Rhonda Eiffe, Richard Bever; Photography, Paul Mailman; Editor, Lisa Palattella; Dolby; Color; HD; Not rated; 96 minutes; Release date: June 1, 2012. Documentary on how Chely Wright's decision to come out as gay had an impact on her life as a country music singer; **WITH:** Chely Wright, Jennifer Archer, Howard Bragman, Tony Brown, Russell Carter, Cherie Combs, Rodney Crowell, Charlene Daniels, Welton Gaddy, Blair Garner, Natalie Morales, Rosie O'Donnell, Meredith Vieira, Chuck D. Walter, Christopher Wright, Stan Wright

Chely Wright in *Wish Me Away* © First Run Features

6 MONTH RULE (Abramorama) Producers, Brandon Barrera, Steak House; Executive Producer, James Ballengee; Director/Screenplay, Blayne Weaver; Photography, Daniel Stoloff; Designer, Michael Fitzgerald; Costumes, Sarah Trost; Music, Andrew Hollander; Editor, Abe Levy; Casting, Lauren Bass; a Secret Identity Productions in association with Steakhaus Productions presentation; Color; HD; Rated R; 99 minutes; Release date: June 1, 2012. **CAST:** Blayne Weaver (Tyler),

Martin Starr (Alan), Natalie Morales (Sophie), Patrick J. Adams (Julian), Vanessa Branch (Wendy), Dave Foley (Charles), John Michael Higgins (Paul), Jaime Pressly (Claire), Brandon Barrera (Kenny), Kristina Klebe (Reese), Nate Rubin (Bookstore Teen), Samantha Shelton (Melissa), Lena Clark (Savannah), Sarah Jane Morris (Beth), Erin Cahill (Missy), Erin Howell (Jordan), Sheeri Rappaport (Kristi), Kendrick Hudson (Deno), Bryan T. Donovan (Lyndsey), Relia Aphrodite (Julia), David Giuntoli (Jared), Derek Wayne Johnson, Rachael Lee Magill (Reality TV), Hal Tryon (Parker Wallace), Christopher Lee Moore (Liquor Exterminator), Alleigh Schulz (Groupie)

Martin Starr, Blayne Weaver in *6 Month Rule* © Abramorama

U.N. ME (Visio Entertainment) Producers/Directors/Screenplay, Matt Groff, Ami Horowitz; Executive Producers, Thor Halvorssen, Bill Siegel; Photography, Bob Richman, Wolfgang Held; Music, Richard Friedman; Editor, Doug Abel; a Visio Entertainment presentation in association with the Moving Picture Institute of a Disruptive Pictures film; Dolby; Color; Rated PG-13; 90 minutes; Release date: June 1, 2012. Documentary on several instances where the invervention of the United Nations has had a negative impact; **WITH:** David Bosco, Ken Cain, Roberta Cohen, Norm Coleman, Simon Deng, Charles Duelfer, Frank Gaffney, Stephen Groves, Jean-Marie Guéhenno, Peggy Hicks, Michael Hussey, Colin Keating, Mark Kirk, Moise Lida Kouassi, Joe Loconte, Linda Melvern, Gary Milhollin, Abou Moussa, Joshua Muravchik, Danielle Pletka, Claudia Rosett, Javier Ruperez, Christopher Shays, Rob Simmons, Henry Sokolski, Michael Soussan, Shashi Tharoor, James Woolsey

BATTLEFIELD AMERICA (Cinedigm) Producers, Christopher B. Stokes, Marques Houston, Jerome Jones, J. Owen, Zeus Zaman, Sharif Armed; Executive Producers, Marsha Powell, London Boys; Director/Screenplay, Christopher B. Stokes; Photography, Miko Dannels; Designer, Tema L. Staig; Costumes, Marlena Campbell; Music, Michael J. Leslie; Editors, Harvey White, Sherril Schlesinger; Choreographers, Kolanie Marks, Free Crawford; Casting, Natasha Ward; a Brian & Barrett Pictures presentation; Deluxe color; Rated PG-13; 106 minutes; Release date: June 1, 2012. **CAST:** Marques Houston (Sean Lewis), Mekia Cox (Sarah Miller), Lynn Whitfield (Ms. Parker), Tristen M. Carter (Eric Smith), Chandler Kinney (Chantel), Tracey Heggins (Kimberly Aimes), Christopher Michael Jones (Hank "The Shockwave" Adams), JoJo Wright (Ernie Garrison), Valarie Pettiford (Ms. Williams), Gary Anthony Sturgis (Eric Smith Sr.), Kida Burns (Thomas "Tommy" Brown), Neiko Keiyan (Jeremiah Williams), Gavin Pecson (Tyrone "Chocolate" Jackson), Adam Cravens (Trey "Mute" Jordan), Zach Belandres (Chu), Russell Ferguson (Prime), Alexus Scelsi (Samantha), Alyssa Chang (Natalie), Michael Toland (Mr. Greenwald), Big Boy (Battlefield America Host), Edward Mandell (Marv), Kyle Brooks (Roger), Camren Bicondova (Prissy), Kristopher Mangonon (Kris), Kaela Elmido (Gi Gi), Alexandria Porter (Caroline), David Michie (Glen Downing), Erika Guillory (Casey), Bruce Katzman (Judge Robinson), Ricky Harris (Tyrone Jackson Sr.), Clifford McGee (The Alley Battle Host), Andre "Zone" McGee (Drug Dealer), Bruno Gioiello (Officer Ward), Tomi Townsend (Naomi Jones), Kolanie Marks, Taki (Audition Judges), Cameron Diskin

(Dr. Stone), Harry Zinn (Mr. Taylor), Christopher Britto (Opening Battle Security), Marques Stokes (Battlefield America Kid Announcer – Jordan), Hannah Star Esser (Battlefield America Kid Announcer – Julia), Dylan K. Shepherd, Miles Brown (Little Rascals Intro Battle Crew), Mikayylan Williams (Don & Roberts Employee), Kyler Lein, Kailani Buhain, Marina Morga, Jennique Derousseau, Aneeka Acode, Paiton Hamilton, Erin Anderson (Show Stoppers)

Battlefield America © Cinedigm

CELLMATES (Viva Pictures) Producers, Jesse Baget, Daniel Bort, Andrea Bottigliero, Karuna Eberl, Andrea Monier, Stefania Moscato; Executive Producers, Sean Gowrie, Héctor Jiménez; Director/Editor, Jesse Baget; Screenplay, Jesse Baget, Stefania Moscato; Photography, Bill Otto; Designer, Elvis Strange; Costumes, Belen Ricoy; Music, Jim Lang; a White Knights Films LLC presentation in association with Producciones a Ciegas; Color; Not rated; 85 minutes; Release date: June 1, 2012. **CAST:** Tom Sizemore (Leroy Lowe), Héctor Jiménez (Emilio), Stacy Keach (Warden Merville), Olga Segura (Madalena), Kevin Farley (Bubba), Bob Rickard (Judge), Rock Williams, Tom Gulager, Kaj Sturdivant (Prison Guards), Leighton R. Shields (Minister), Orock Orock, Scott Forrester, Pedro Alvarado, Darrell Britt, Carlos Soto-Montes (Prisoners)

Héctor Jiménez in *Cellmates* © Viva Pictures

HIGH SCHOOL (Anchor Bay) Producers, Arcadiy Golubovich, Warren Zide, Raymond J. Markovich; Executive Producers, John Stalberg Jr., Stephen Susco, Olga Mirimskaya; Director, John Stalberg, Jr.; Screenplay, Erik Linthorst, John Stalberg Jr., Stephen Susco; Story, John Stalberg Jr., Erik Linthorst; Photography, Mitchell Amundsen; Designer, Seth Reed; Costumes, Marie France; Music, The Newton Brothers; Editor, Gabriel Wrye; a Parallel Media presentation of a Flipzide production in association with Zero Hour Films; Dolby; Super 35 Widescreen; Color; Rated R; 99 minutes; Release date: June 1, 2012. **CAST:** Adrien Brody

(Psycho Ed), Sean Marquette (Travis Breaux), Matt Bush (Henry Burke), Colin Hanks (Brandon Ellis), Adhir Kalyan (Sebastian Saleem), Mykelti Williamson (Paranoid), Michael Chiklis (Dr. Leslie Gordon), Cody Longo (Chad), Yeardley Smith (Computer Skills Teacher), Michael Vartan (Calculus Teacher), Curtis Armstrong (Mr. Thompson), Luis Chávez (Big Dave), Alicia Sixtos (Sharky Ovante), Max Van Ville (Little Dave), Mary Birdsong (Mrs. Gordon), Julia Ling (Charlyne), Camille Mana (Dana), Brett Kelly (Martin Gordon), George Back (Malcolm), Andrew Wilson (Hippie Dude), Erica Vittina Phillips (Tameka), Arcadiy Golubovich (Edwin Hunter), Julia Ling (Charlyne), Alex Biats (Spelling Bee Rival), Wyatt Russell (Drug PSA Stoned Teenager), Joseph Julian Soria (Rubin), Nadine Crocker (Emily Tooms), Kellie Rasmus (Hippie Chick), Kevin Yon (Mr. Cavanaugh), Robert Bailey Jr. (Jeffrey), Rhys Coiro (Vato), Emily Sutton-Smith (Mrs. Breaux), John Beard, Barret Swatek (News Desk Reporters), Terri Lyn Rodriguez (Vivian), Shirley Benyas (Older Donor), Wallace Bridges (African American Donor), Harry Carlson, Randall Godwin, Mike Evans (Donors), Linda Boston (Head Nurse), Heather Regan (Sexy Cheerleader), Rene Santana, Sammy A. Publes (Cooks), Michael Eshaq (Lead Terrorist), David Herbst (School Security Guard), Heather Kleisner (Voice of Henry's Mom), Rachel Quaintance, Peter Tocco (Angry Parents), Billye Thompson (Cop #1), Clarence Smith (Chess Opponent), Ron Ayres (Stunned Lawn Blower), Karl Murphy (Band Teacher), Mike Woods (Announcer), Kerry Birmingham (Reporter), John O'Hurley (Drug PSA Voiceover), John Stalberg Jr. (Voice of Grandpa Frodo)

Matt Bush, Dave Herbst in *High School* © Anchor Bay

HARDFLIP (Digital Filmz Intl.) Producer/Director, Johnny Remo; Executive Producers, Allan Camaisa, Megan Camaisa; Screenplay, Daniel Backman, Johnny Remo; Photography, Rudy Harbon; Designer, Allison Veilleux; Music, Jason Brandt; Editor, Vahe Douglas; a Risen Media presentation of a Skipstone Pictures production; Color; Rated PG-13; 112 minutes; Release date: June 1, 2012. **CAST:** Randy Wayne (Caleb), John Schneider (Jack Sanders), Rosanna Arquette (Bethany Jones), Sean Michael Afable (Joey), Jason Dundas (Ryder), Corey Sorenson (Stupack), Christopher Michael (Ralph), Christian Hosoi (Hosoi), Brian Sumner (Brian), Mathew Ziff (Jeff), Louise Griffiths (Denise), Yves Bright (Dr. Sheldon), Mary Jo Gruber (Jasmine), Ed V. Morgan (Pastor), Luis Tolentino (Roberto), Tennille Williams (Tennille), Lorraine Ziff (Kaia), Raquel Ames (Bank Teller), Daniel Backman (Mailman), Matt Beachman (Arresting Officer), Kinga Rylend (Receptionist)

PIRANHA 3DD (Dimension) Producers, Mark Canton, Marc Toberoff, Joel Soisson; Executive Producers, Bob Weinstein, Harvey Weinstein, Ben Ormand, Matthew Stein, Chako van Leeuwen; Director, John Gulager; Screenplay, Patrick Melton, Marcus Dunstant, Joel Soisson; Based on characters created by Peter Goldfinger, Josh Stolberg; Photography, Alexandre Lehmann; Designer, Ermanno Di Febo-Orsini; Costumes, Carol Cutshall; Music, Elia Cmiral; Editors, Devin C.

Randy Wayne in *Hardflip* © Digital Filmz

Lussier, Martin Bernfeld, Kirk Morri; Special Makeup & Creature Effects Designer, Gary J. Tunnicliffe; Visual Effects Supervisor, Adam Stern; Stunts, John Copeman; Casting, Nancy Nayor; a Dimension Films presentation of a Mark Canton/IPW production in association with Neo Art & Logic; Dolby; Color; 3D; HD; Rated R; 83 minutes; Release date: June 1, 2012. **CAST:** Danielle Panabaker (Maddy), Matt Bush (Barry), Katrina Bowden (Shelby), Jean-Luc Bilodeau (Josh), David Koechner (Chet), Chris Zylka (Kyle), Adrian Martinez (Big Dave), Paul James Jordan (Travis), Meagan Tandy (Ashley), David Hasselhoff (Himself), Christopher Lloyd (Mr. Goodman), Paul Scheer (Andrew), Gary Busey (Clayton), Clu Gulager (Mo), Sierra Fisk (Bethany), Matthew Lintz (Freckled Boy), Sylvia Jefferies (Young Mother), Jenna Hurt (Rochelle), Rozlyn Papa (Dawn), Alisa Harris (Hysteric/Stocky Woman), Stacy Rabon (Fearful Woman), Nate Panning (Waterpark Patron), Kathy Sue Holtorf (Bimbo Lifeguard), Irina Voronina (Kiki), Katie Garner (Lizzie Guard), Ving Rhames (Deputy Fallon)

Piranha 3DD © Dimension Films

RICHARD'S WEDDING (Factory 25) Producers, Jason Klorfein, Devoe Yates; Executive Producers, Andrew Krucoff, Onur Turkel; Director/Screenplay/Editor, Onur Turkel; Photography, Jason Banker, Jorge Torres-Torres; Designers, Devoe Yates, Richard Gambill; Costumes, Christine Bean; Music Supervisor, Devoe Yates; Casting, Onur Turkel, Alex Karpovsky; Color; HD; Not rated; 88 minutes; Release date: June 1, 2012. **CAST:** Onur Turkel (Tuna), Jennifer Prediger (Alex), Darrill Rosen (Russell), Randy Gambill (Louis), Thomas J. Buchmueller (Simon), Josephine Decker (Phoebe), Dustin Guy Defa (Taco), Jamie Dobie (Deedee), Heddy Lahmann (Amy), Lawrence Michael Levine (Richard), Theresa Lu (Lyndsey), Oona Mekas (Kristin), Adam Schartoff (Andrew)

ONE DAY ON EARTH (The One Day on Earth Community) Producer, Brandon Litman; Executive Producers, Tony Goldman, Jessica Goldman Srebnick, Kyle Ruddick, Brandon Litman; Director/Screenplay, Kyle Ruddick; Music, Joseph Minadeo; Editors, Michael Martinez, Mark Morgan; United Nations Foundation; Color; Not rated; 104 minutes; Release date: June 1, 2012. Footage from around the world, all taken on a single day, October 10, 2010; **WITH:** Vincent Miedema

One Day on Earth © One Day on Earth Community

THE OREGONIAN (Constellation) Producers, Christian Palmer, Roger M. Mayer, Christo Dimassis, Wen Marcoux, Ryan K. Adams, Scott Honea, Joey Marcoux; Executive Producers, Steven Schardt, Elana Kruasz; Director/Screenplay, Calvin Lee Reeder; Photography, Ryan K. Adams; Costumes, Brady Hall; Music, Scott Honea, Clavin Lee Reeder; Editor, Buzz Pierce; Color; HD; Not rated; 81 minutes; Release date: June 8, 2012. **CAST:** Lindsay Pulsipher (The Oregonian), Robert Longstreet (Herb), Matt Olsen (Blond Stranger), Lynn Compton (Redheaded Stranger), Roger M. Mayer (Omelette Man), Barlow Jacobs (Bud), Chadwick Brown (Ronnie), Jed Maheu (Murph), Tipper Newton (Julie), Zumi Rosow (Carlotta), Scott Honea (James), Christian Palmer (Handsome Deadman), Christo Dimassis (Bud's Friend), Mandy M. Bailey, Meredith Binder, Sharon Delong, Sherry Penoyer (Strangers), Michael Adams (Dead Child), Rick Jensen (Voice on the Radio)

Lindsay Pulsipher in *The Oregonian* © Constellation

FOR THE LOVE OF MONEY (Archstone) Producers, Jenna Mattison; Executive Producers, Izek Shomof, Ken Topolsky; Director, Ellie Kanner; Screenplay, Jenna Mattison; Story, Michael Micco; Photography, Andrzej Sekula; Designer, Travis Zariwny; Costumes, Ariyela Wald-Cohain; Music Supervisor, Wendy Marino?; Editor, Karl Hirsch; Casting, Mary Jo Slater, Dori Zuckerman; an All Cash Productions presentation in association with Cheshire Smile Productions; Dolby; Widescreen; Color; HD; Rated R; 93 minutes; Release date: June 8, 2012. **CAST:** Yuda Levi (Isaac), Delphine Chanéac (Aline), Joshua Biton (Yoni), Cody Longo (Young Isaac), Jeffrey Tambor (Mr. Solomon), Steven Bauer (Hector), Jonathan Lipnicki (Young Yoni), Michael Benyaer (Jacob), Richard Gunn (Vince), Hal Ozsan (Abe), Meredith Scott Lynn (Mazal), Inbar Lavi (Talia), Leilani Sarelle (Nancy), Robb Skyler (Frishka), Edward Furlong (Tommy), Oded Fehr (Levi), Paul Sorvino (Red Parker), James Caan (Micky), Noel Guglielmi (Ramon), Michael Papajohn (Little Guy), J.C. MacKenzie (Mr. Phillips), Sammy Sheik (Kaleb), Omed Zader (Manuel), Carole Ita White (Rosie), Ronnie Marmo (Carmine), Emilio Roso (Tito), Gary Sievers (Rabbi), Linda Bisesti (Sarah), Luke LaFontaine (Billy), Caroline Jaden Stussi (Bank Teller), Carolina Bonetti (Miriam), Alex Luria (Cain), Alan Gray (Shuk Merchant), Angela Nordeng (Beach Girl), Kaye Marie Talise (Bathing Beauty), Andrew Schlessinger (Josef), Michael Raynor (Martz), Eric Michael Kochmer (Drunk at Party), Johnny Soto (Pepe), Stephen Gabriel (Tyler), Travis Merindino (Banker Robber), Robert Dill (Morris), Maya Farshoukh (Little Sarah), Luis Aldana (Carlos), Jason Talmadge (Cop), Mariano Mendoza (Bouncer), Chuy Garcia (Gardener), Claudio Cultrera (Gangster), Max Daniels (Beat Cop), Kaye Marie Talise (Bathing Beauty), Carlo Corbellini (Bartender)

Oded Fehr in *For the Love of Money* © Archstone Distribution

THE PIGEONEERS (Alessandro Croseri Productions) Producers, Alessandro Croseri, Avon Jong; Executive Producer/Director/Screenplay/Photography, Alessandro Croseri; Color; Not rated; 111 minutes; Release date: June 8, 2012. Documentary on 103-year-old Col. Clifford A. Poutre, who trained homing pigeons for combat mission during WWII; **WITH:** Col. Clifford A. Poutre.

IN BED WITH ULYSSES (Independent) Producers/Directors, Alan Adelson, Kate Taverna; Narration Written and Read by Alan Adelson; Photography, Michael Berz, Scott Sinkler, Marc DeGenaar; Music, Mark De Gli Antoni, Joel Goodman, Dave Soldier, Ilir Bajri; Editor, Kate Taverna; Color; No t rated; 80 minutes; Release date: June 11, 2012. Documentary on James Joyce's classic novel *Ulysses* (including readings of excerpts); **WITH:** Kathleen Chalfant (Molly Bloom), Allyn Burrows (Leopold Bloom and Others), Chris Ceraso (Leopold Bloom and Others), Rufus Collins (Leopold Bloom/Stage Manager/Others), Jerry Matz (Leopold Bloom and Others), Paul McIsaac (Narrator/Leopold Bloom), Robert Zukerman (Leopold Bloom and Others); AND: Michael Barsanti, Sylvia Beach, Christopher Cerf, Michael Groden, Colum McCann, Helen Monaghan, Robert Nicholson, Rafael Siev

MARINA ABRAMOVIC: THE ARTIST IS PRESENT (Music Box Films/ HBO Documentary Films) Executive Producers for HBO, Sheila Nevins, Nancy Abraham; Producers, Jeff Dupre, Maro Chermayeff; Director/Photography, Matthew Akers; Co-Director, Jeff Dupre; Music, Nathan Halpern; Editor, E. Donna Shepherd; a Show of Force production; Color; 105 minutes; Release date: June 13, 2012. Documentary on Serbian performance artist Marina Abramovic and her retrospective at the Museum of Modern Art; **WITH:** Marina Ambramovic, Ulay, Klaus Biesenbach, Davide Balliano, Chrissie Iles, Arthur Danto, David Blaine, James Franco

Marina Abramovic in *The Artist is Present* © HBO

THE TORTURED (IFC Films) Producers, Mark Burg, Oren Koules, Carl Mazzocone; Executive Producers, Curtis Leopardo, Jonathan Zucker, Kari Hollend, Tom Strnad; Director, Robert Lieberman; Screenplay, Marek Posival; Photography, Peter Florian Woeste; Designer, Brian Davie; Costumes, Nancy Bryant; Music, Jeff Rona; Editor, Jim Page; Casting, Michelle Gertz (US), Susan Brouse (Canada); a Twisted Pictures and Lighttower Entertainment presentation; American-Canadian; Color; Not rated; 79 minutes; Release date: June 15, 2012. **CAST:** Erika Christensen (Elise Landry), Jesse Metcalfe (Craig Landry), Fulvio Cecere (Det. Berger), Bill Lippincott (Galligan), Thomas Greenwood (Ben Landry), Bill Moseley (John Kozlowski), Stephen Park (Man in Condo), Samantha Gutstadt (Woman in Condo), Zak Santiago (Younger Cop), Alfonso Quijada (Clerk), John Taylor (Pastor), Viv Leacock (Officer Patterson), Darryl Scheelar (Officer Alvarez), Peter Abrams (Judge Stanley), Paul Herbert (Bailiff), Chelah Horsdal (District Attorney), Donita Dyer (Woman in Courtroom), Carl Mazzocone Sr. (Defense Attorney), John Stewart (Prison Van Driver), Kurt Runte (Prison Van Guard), J. LaRose (Hunter), Bill Dow (Hospital Doctor), Sheilah Shah (Coffee Server), Linda Curial (Woman Behind Cash Register), Lynn Colliar (Anchorwoman), Marke Driesschen (Reporter at Crash Site), Brent Stait (U.S. Marshal), Jessie Rusu (Kate), Albert Patterson McPeake (Newborn Ben), Liam Turchanaksi (10-week-old Ben), Torren Pritchard (10-month-old Ben)

Erika Christensen, Jesse Metcalfe, Bill Lippincott in *The Tortured* © IFC Films

THE GIRL FROM THE NAKED EYE (Archstone Distribution) Producer, Jason Yee; Executive Producer, Henry Mu; Director, David Ren; Screenplay, Larry Madill, Jason Yee, David Ren; Photography, Max Da-Yung Wang; Designer, Suzanne Rattigan; Costumes, Hazel Yuan; Music, Danny Manor; Editors, Greg Babor, Richard Halsey; a Lifted Productions, in association with Mu-Yee Productions presentation; Dolby; Color/Black and white; HD; Widescreen; Rated R; 84 minutes; Release date: June 15, 2012. **CAST:** Jason Yee (Jake), Samantha Streets (Sandy), Ron Yuan (Simon), Dominique Swain (Alissa), Gary Stretch (Frank), Jerry C. Ying (Johnny), Sasha Grey (Lena), Wilson Jermaine Heredia (Bobby), Chris Ufland (Edward Bates), Assaf Cohen (Miles), Brandy M. Grace (Angela), James Lew (Eddie), Peter Scott Antico, Kovar D. McClure, Christopher Tranchina (Detectives), Lateef Crowder (Maximillion), Woon Young Park (Frankie), Art Hsu (Sammy), Gina Jackson (Honey), Angelina Valentine (Cimone), Alan M. Tow (Yao), Jen Sung Outerbridge (Marlon), Somaya S. Reece (Wendy), Michael Patrick Wilson (Nathan), Lee Whittaker (Andy), Sidney S. Liufau (Moses), Elizabeth McDonald (Fiona), Buddy Sosthand (Bouncer), Jennifer Hughes (Linda), Sno E. Blac (Bunny), Michelle C. Lee (Cop), Henry Mu (Club Promoter), Masaaki Endo, Panuvat Anthony Nanakornpanom (Guards), Thomas Braxton Jr. (Card Player), Dan Marshall (John), Sonny Sison, Chad Guerrero (Security Guards)

Jason Yee (right) in *The Girl from the Naked Eye* © Archstone Distribution

IKLAND (Spectacle Films) Producer, Cevin Soling; Directors, Cevin Soling, David Hilbert; Photography, David Pluth; Music, Sacha Lucashenko; Editor, David Hilbert; American-Ugandan; Stereo; Color; HD; Not rated; 88 minutes; Release date: June 15, 2012. Documentary on the quest to study the Ik, a northern Ugandan tribe, described as "the worst people in the world;" **WITH:** Thomas Lomogin, Gregory Lotukufa, Tuliakung Marwath, Anna Nabilo, Martin Longole, Fabiano Kiyonga, Matthew Kiyonga, Hilary Lokwang, Esther Nacham, Eisa Nialetcha, Charilki Moding, Elizabetha Lomeyana, Anna Kokoi, Chelina Natuk, Marco Terho; AND: Loritong Dakai (Scrooge), Paul Lokoi (Bob Cratchit), Monica Kunumer (Tiny Tim), Hilary Ekale (Ancestor), Alice Naroo (Soothsayer)

KUMARÉ (Kino Lorber) Producers, Bryan Carmel, Brendan Colthurst; Executive Producers, Stephen Feder, Cristian Gill, Nadia Muna, Eli Nhaissi; Director, Vikram Gandhi; Photography, Kahlil Hudson, Daniel Leeb; Costumes for Kumaré, Maytinee Redding; Music, Alex Kliment, Hisham Bharoocha, Sanjay Khanna; Editors, Adam Barton, Nathan Russell; aa Disposable production; Dolby; Color; Not rated; 84 minutes; Release date: June 20, 2012. Documentary on how filmmaker Vikram Gandhi transformed himself into a fake guru named Kumaré and managed to cultivate a following; **WITH:** Vikram Gandhi, Purva Bedi, Kristen Calgaro

Ikland © Spectacle Films

Vikram Gandhi in *Kumaré*
© Kino Lorber

ORDINARY MIRACLES: THE PHOTO LEAGUE'S NEW YORK (Daedalus Prods.) Producers/Directors, Daniel Allentuck, Nina Rosenblum; Screenplay, Daniel Allentuck; Photography, Dejan Georgevich, Kennth Ortiz; Editors, Peter Maugeri, Russell Greene, Angelo Corrao; Narrator, Campbell Scott; Stereo; Color/black and white; Not rated; 75 minutes; Release date: June 22, 2012. Documentary on New York's Photo League (1936-51), which promoted "social change through photography;" **WITH:** Miriam Grossman Cohen, Morris Engel, Walter Rosenblum, Joe Schwartz

Ordinary Miracles © Daedalus Prods.

GRASSROOTS (Goldwyn) Producers, Peggy Rajski, Michael Huffington, Matthew R. Brady, Brent Stiefel, Peggy Case; Executive Producers, Jane Charles, Gary Allen Tucci; Director, Stephen Gyllenhaal; Screenplay, Justin Rhodes, Stephen Gyllenhaal; Based upon the 2005 book *Zioncheck for President: A True Story of Idealism and Madness in American Politics* by Phil Campbell; Photography, Sean Porter; Designer, Laurie Hicks; Costumes, Ron Leamon; Music, Nick Urata; Editor, Neil Mandelberg; Casting, Robert Gurland; an MRB Productions film in association with Votiv Films and Lanai Productions; Dolby; Color; HD; Rated R; 100 minutes; Release date: June 22, 2012. **CAST:** Jason Biggs (Phil Campbell), Joel David Moore (Grant Cogswell), Lauren Ambrose (Emily Bowen), Cedric the Entertainer (Richard McIver), Tom Arnold (Tommy), Cobie Smulders (Clair), Todd Stashwick (Nick Ricochet), Emily Bergl (Theresa Glendon), Christopher McDonald (Jim Tripp), D.C. Pierson (Wayne), Michael Nardelli (Willis), Russell Hodgkinson (Pernell Alden), Noah Harpster (Marvin), Basil Harris (News Producer), M.J. Sieber, Todd Licea, Erin Mayovsky, Steve Pool, Talena Bennett, John Misner (Reporters), Frank Buxton (Old Man), Lance Rosen (ACLU Lawyer), Rachel Pate (Suit), Rodney Sherwood (Tate Austin), Tom Ricciardelli (Campaign Supporter), Anthony L. Fuller Jr. (Agent Sikora), Ian Bell (Birkenstocks), Garr Godfrey (2nd Questioner), Amy Frear (Lisa), Brent Stiefel (Volunteer), Dave Berseford (Snow Wolf), Imogen Love, Brennan Murphy (Questioning Democrats), Sarah Harlett (Receptionist), Branden Romans (Genzlinger), Joe Mandragona (Kevin), Nik Doner (Doug), Connie Thompson (Connie), Barbara Deering (Moderator), Claire Vardiel (Augusta D'Amico), Sarah Dunne (ACLU #2), Mt. St. Helens Vietnam Band (Comet House Band), John Ulman (Agent Goecker), Carolyn Crabtree (Older Woman), Sean Nelson (Musician), Lauren Guity (Mary Jane)

Jason Biggs, Joel David Moore in *Grassroots* © Goldwyn Films

THE LAST RIDE (Category One) Producers, Douglas Jackson, Benjamin Gaither; Executive Producers, Tim Jackson, Rodney Stone, Harry Thomason, Benjamin Gaither; Director, Harry Thomason; Screenplay, Howie Klausner, Dub Cornett; Photography, Jim Roberson; Designer, Dwight Jackson; Costumes, Doug Hall; Music, Benjy Gaither; Editor, Leo Papin; Casting, Fran Bascom; a Live Bait Entertainment and Mozark Productions presentation; Dolby; Color; Rated PG-13; 105 minutes; Release date: June 22, 2012. **CAST:** Henry Thomas (Mr. Wells, Hank Williams), Jesse James (Silas), Fred Dalton Thompson (O'Keefe), Kaley Cuoco (Wanda), Stephen Tobolowsky (Ray), Ray McKinnon (Stan), Rick Dial (Dirty Black John), James Hampton (Judge Matheny), Will Koberg (Leroy), Matt Lindahl (Guitar Player), Gary Newton (Usher), Jennifer Pierce (Good Looking Woman)

TOP PRIORITY: THE TERROR WITHIN (Fleur de Lis Film Studios) Producers, Asif Akbar, Julia Davis, BJ Davis, Lindsay Hudson; Director/Screenplay/Photography, Asif Akbar; Music, Cleveland Bledsoe Jr.; Editor, Paul Robinson; Narrator, Ron Peterson; Color; Not rated; 114 minutes; Release date: June 29, 2012. Documentary on how former Customs and Border Protection Officer Julia Davis suffered after exposing the shortcomings in the processing of aliens from terrorist countries admitted into the U.S.; **WITH:** Julia Davis, BJ Davis, Mykola Kot, Galyna Kovalska, Chance E. Gordon

Henry Thomas, Jesse James in *The Last Ride* © Category One

United in Anger © Hubbard/Schulman

NEIL YOUNG JOURNEYS (Sony Classics) Producers, Jonathan Demme, Elliot Rabinowitz; Executive Producers, Marc Benioff, Bernard Shakey; Director, Jonathan Demme; Photography, Declan Quinn; Music, Neil Young; Editor, Glenn Allen; a Shakey Pictures/Clinica Estetico production in association with Salesforce Films; Dolby; Color; Rated PG; 87 minutes; Release date: June 29, 2012. Documentary in which singer Neil Young drives to his hometown of Omemee, Ontario to perform the last two nights of his solo world tour; **WITH:** Neil Young

Neil Young in *Neil Young Journeys* © Sony Classics

UNITED IN ANGER: A HISTORY OF ACT UP (Hubbard/Schulman) Producers, Jim Hubbard; Sarah Schulman; Director, Jim Hubbard; Screenplay, Ali Cotterill, Jim Hubbard; Photography, James Wentzy; a Jim Hubbard/Sarah Schulman presentation; Color; Not rated; 93 minutes; Release date: July 6, 2012. Documentary on how ACT UP was formed to combat the political and medical worlds' indifference towards the AIDS epidemic; **WITH:** Ron Goldberg, Tom Kalin, Ann Northrup, Eric Sawyer, Peter Staley

CRAZY EYES (Strand) Producer, Hagai Shaham; Director, Adam Sherman; Screenplay, Adam Sherman, Rachel Hardisty, David Reeves; Photography, Sharone Meir; Designer, Celine Diano; Costumes, Erica Nicotra; Music, Bobby Johnston; Editor, Sam Bauer; Casting, Sunday Boling, Meg Morman; Dolby; Color; Not rated; 96 minutes; Release date: July 6, 2012. **CAST:** Lukas Haas (Zach), Madeline Zima (Rebecca), Jake Busey (Dan Drake), Tania Raymonde (Autumn), Blake Garrett Rosenthal (Boy), Ray Wise (Zach's Father), Valerie Mahaffey (Zach's Mother), Moran Atias (Ex), Ned Bellamy (Bob), Laura Miro (Ping), Regine Nehy (Latisha), P.D. Mani (Indian Guy), Josh Thorpe (Brad), Harvey Shield (British Man), Natalie Floyd (Blond), Michael Pasternak (Rabbi), Bruce Gray (Lawyer)

Madeline Zima, Lukas Haas in *Crazy Eyes* © Strand Releasing

THE PACT (IFC Midnight) Producer, Ross M. Dinerstein; Executive Producer, Jamie Carmichael; Director/Screenplay, Nicholas McCarthy; Photography, Bridger Nielson; Designer, Walter Barnett; Costumes, Azalia Snail; Music, Ronen Landa; Editor, Adriaan Van Zyl; Visual Effects Supervisor, Padraic Culham; Casting, Lindsey Hayes Kroeger; a Content Media Corporation presentation of a Preferred Content production; Stereo; Color; DV; Not rated; 89 minutes; Release date: July 6, 2012. **CAST:** Caity Lotz (Annie), Casper Van Dien (Bill Creek), Agnes Bruckner (Nichole), Mark Steger (Charles), Haley Hudson (Stevie), Kathleen Rose Perkins (Liz), Sam Ball (Giles), Bo Barrett (Jesse), Dakota Bright (Eva), Jeffrey T. Ferguson (Officer Benson), Tse Ho-kwan (Rudy Fong), Petra Wright (Jennifer Glick), Anjini Taneja Azhar (Hindi Kid), Rachael Kahne (Waitress), Santiago Segura (Dishwasher), Sam Zuckerman (County Clerk)

THE DO-DECA-PENTATHLON (Red Flag Releasing/Fox Searchlight) Producers, Jay Duplass, Mark Duplass, Stephanie Langhoff; Directors/Screenplay, Jay Duplass, Mark Duplass; Photography, Jas Shelton; Music, Julian Wass; Editors, Jay Deuby, Nat Sanders; Color; Rated R; 76 minutes; Release date: July 6, 2012. **CAST:** Steve Zissis (Mark), Mark Kelly (Jeremy), Jennifer Lafleur (Stephanie), Julie Vorus (Alice), Brendan Robinson (Young Mark), Brock Patrick Kaufman (Young Jeremy, age 10), Reid Williams (Hunter), Noël Wells (Stripper), Jordan Stidham (Young Jeremy), Elton LeBlanc, Alex Lipschultz, Brett Patron (Poker Players)

Steve Zissis in *The Do-Deca-Pentathlon* © Red Flag Releasing

PONIES (Creative Chaos Ventures) Producers, Ginny Galloway, Tom Donahue; Executive Producers, Pamela Gwaltney, Lee Ackerley, Carmen Ackerley; Director, Nick Sandow; Screenplay, Michael Batistick, based on his 2004 play; Photography, Dane Lawing; Designer, Elizabeth Jones; Costumes, Natalia Fedner; Music, Jim Farmer; Editor, Tom Donahue; a GreenBox presentation in association with Sibs Productions; Color; Not rated; 72 minutes; Release date: July 13, 2012. **CAST:** John Ventimiglia (Drazen), Kevin Corrigan (Wallace), Babs Olusanmokun (Ken), Tonye Patano (Cashier), Joe Caniano (Guard), Meital Dohan (Aliah), Sean Patrick Folster (The Cop), Peter Iasillo Jr., Sui Keung Wong (OTB Bettors), David Kaplan (Hasidic Gambler), Stephen Lin (Simon), Darlene Violette (Homeless Woman)

DECONSTRUCTING DAD: THE MUSIC, MACHINES AND MYSTERY OF RAYMOND SCOTT (CAVU Pictures) Producer/Director/Photography/Editor, Stan Warnow; Co-Producer, Jeff Winner; Animation Sequence, Scott SanGiacomo; a Waterfall Films production; Color; Not rated; 98 minutes; Release date: July 13, 2012. Documentary on electronic music pioneer Raymond Scott; **WITH:** Wayne Barker, Gert-Jan Blom, Don Byron, Irwin Chusid, Jeremy Cohen, Herb Deutsch, Greg Ford, Will Friedwald, Skip Heller, Carolyn Makover, Mark Mothersbaugh, Mitzi Scott, DJ Spooky, Pearl Warnow Winters, Alexander Warnow, Stan Warnow, Hal Willner, Jeff Winner, John Williams

Raymond Scott in *Deconstructing Dad* © CAVU Pictures

THE OBAMA EFFECT (BRO Distribution) Producers, Harry Smith, Rob Johnson; Executive Producers, Barry Hankerson, Harry Smith, Corey Large; Director, Charles S. Dutton; Screenplay, Charles S. Dutton, Sidra Smith, Celeste Walker, Samuel Z. Jean; Story, Barry Hankerson; Photography, Daniel Pearl; Costumes, Kathryn Langston; Music, Cee Lo Green; Editor, Sean Hubbert; Presented in association with Smith Global Management; Color; Rated PG-13; 85 minutes; Release date: July 13, 2012. **CAST:** Charles S. Dutton (John Thomas), Katt Williams (MLK), Vanessa Bell Calloway (Molly Thomas), Glynn Turman (Slim Sugar), Meagan Good (Tamika Jones), Emilio Rivera (Hector Santiago), Jenny Gago (Dede Santiago), Mark Ashworth (Nigel the Butler), Giselle Bonilla (Maria Santiago), Bill Lee Brown (Tank), Reggie Brown (Barack Obama), John Diehl (Steve Warren), Lonnie Henderson (Sebastian Thomas), Xango Henry (Duane the Guard), Vernetta Jenkins (Michele Obama), Wesley Jonathan (Kalil Thomas), Zab Judah (Jamel Thomas), Cleo King (Rebecca Thomas), Julie Lancaster (Nancy Reilly), William Mitchell (Dr. Mosley), Ashley Noel (Karen Thomas), Shanga Parker (Prison Guard), Shelley Robertson (Lola Jackson), Bryan Ross (Joshua Thomas), Jamie Tisdale (Nicole Reilly), Diego Torres (Luis Santiago), Jeremy Ray Valdez (Hector Santiago Jr.), Eric Wright (Scottie Jackson), Becky Wu (Asian Store Owner), Richie Gibbs (Redneck Friend), Carlos Moreno Jr. (Young Latino Man)

Zab Judah (center) in *The Obama Effect* © BRO Distribution

BALLPLAYER: PELOTERO (Strand) Producer, Isaac Solotaroff; Executive Producers, Andrew J. Muscato, Bobby Valentine, Robert Castrignano, Douglas Lorentz, Robert Musumeci; Directors/Screenplay, Joss Finkel, Jon Paley, Trevor Martin; Photography, Ross Finkel; Editors, Mary Manhardt, Isaac Solotaroff; Narrator, John Leguizamo; a Guagua Productions, Makurhari Media production; American-Dominican Republic; Color; Not rated; 77 minutes; Release date: July 13, 2012. Documentary on two baseball players from the Dominican Republic who hope to play in the big leagues; **WITH**: Miguel Angel Sanó, Juan Carlos Batista, Astín Jacobo Jr., Vasilio "Moreno" Tejeda

Juan Carlos in *Ballplayer: Pelotero* © Strand Releasing

2016: OBAMA'S AMERICA (Rocky Mountain Pictures) Producers, Gerald R. Molen, Ann Balog, Doug Sain; Executive Producers, Dinesh D'Souza, John Sullivan, Christopher Williams; Directors/Screenplay, Diniseh D'Souza, John Sullivan; Based on the books *The Roots of Obama's Rage* (2011) and *Obama's America* (2012) by Dinesh D'Souza; Editors, Victoria Sillano, Simon James, Michael Nicholas; an OAF, LLC presentation of a Gerald R. Molen production; Color; Rated PG; 89 minutes; Release date: July 13, 2012. Documentary attempting to paint a bleak portrait of the country under a second term in office for President Barack Obama; **WITH:** Dr. Paul Vitz, Dr. Alice Dewey, Dr. Paul Kengor, Willy Kauai, George Obama, Philip Ochieng, Joseph Ojiru, Daniel Pipes, David Walker

Barack Obama in *2016: Obama's America* © Rocky Mountain Pictures

DRUNKBOAT (Seven Arts/Lantern Lane) Producers, Steven A. Jones, Daniel J. Walker; Executive Producers, Chase Bailey, Anthony J. Tomaska, Joseph J. Tomaska, Thomas H. Baur, James Andrew Cameron; Director/Screenplay, Bob Meyer; Based on the 1985 play by L. Randall Buescher, Bob Meyer; Photography, Lisa Rinzler; Designer, Richard Hoover; Costumes, Susan Kaufmann; Editor, Mario Battistel; a Magnificent Mile Productions and Leftbank Films presentation; Color; HD; Rated PG; 88 minutes; Release date: July 13, 2012. **CAST:** John Malkovich (Mort), John Goodman (Mr. Fletcher), Dana Delany (Eileen), Brian Deneen (Dave), Jim Ortlieb (Morley), Bryce Pegelow (Morley's Son), Jacob Zachar (Abe), Skipp Sudduth (Earl), Rae Gray (Girl on Bike), Zach Gray (Boy on Bike), Aaron Benjamin Miller (Baseball Boy), Elizabeth Hipwell (Mommy)

John Malkovich in *Drunkboat* © Seven Arts

WAGNER'S DREAM (Metropolitan Opera) Producers, Susan Froemke, Douglas Graves; Director, Susan Froemke; Photography, Don Lenzer; Editor, Bob Eisenhardt; Susan Froemke Productions; Color; Not rated; 115 minutes; Release date: July 19, 2012. Documentary on Robert Lepage's staging of Richard Wagner's *Ring* cycle at the Metropolitan Opera; **WITH:** Carl Fillion, Peter Gelb, Robert Lepage, James Levine, Fabio Luisi, Jay Hunter Morris, Lisette Oropesa, Deborah Voigt

Wagner's Dream © Metropolitan Opera

30 BEATS (Roadside Attractions) Producers, Molly Conners, Carl Ford, Alexis Lloyd; Executive Producers, Susan Batson, Ronald Guttman, Perre Lagrange; Director/Screenplay, Alexis Lloyd; Photography, Lisa Rinzler; Designer, Brian Rzepka; Costumes, Katie Calcaterra; Music, CC Adcock; Editors, Xavier Loutreuil, Roberto Silvi; Casting, Billy Hopkins; a Latitude 49 and Studio 37 presentation in association with Black Nexxus Productions, Worldview Entertainment and Highbrow Entertainment; American-French; Dolby; Color; HD; Rated R; 88 minutes; Release date: July 20, 2012. **CAST:** Condola Rashad (The Virgin - Julie), Justin Kirk (The Anthropologist - Adam), Jennifer Tilly (The Psychic - Erika), Jason Day (The Bike Messenger - Diego), Paz de la Huerta (The Girl with a Scar - Laura), Lee Pace (The Chiropractor - Matt), Vahina Giocante (The Operator - Kim), Thomas Sadoski (The Speechwriter - Julian), Ingeborga Dapkunaite (The Call Girl - Alice), Ben Levin (The Young Man - Sean), Antone Pagan (Harlem Concierge), Aliyaah Hashi (The Other Girl), Ronald Guttman (Sean's Father), Jean Rene Mbeng (Man with Ice Pack), Cheutine Fong, Carla Collado (Girls in Bed), Kimberli Alexis Flores (One Night Stand Girl), Shawn Parsons (The Bartender), Mr. T. Shan (Fruit Stand Vendor), Treena David Chirico (Office Assistant)

Vahina Giocante, Thomas Sadoski in *30 Beats* © Roadside Attractions

RITES OF SPRING (IFC Midnight) Producers, Wes Benton, E. Thompson; Executive Producers, Bobby Benton, John Norris; Director/Screenplay, Padraig Reynolds; Photography, Carl Herse; Designer, Mary Goodson; Costumes, Kerrie Kordowski; Music, Holly Amber Church; Editor, Ed Marx; Casting, Cher Foley; Creature Special Effects Makeup, Toby Sells Creature Makeup, "Puppet" Chris Brown; a Red Planet Entertainment and White Rock Lake Productions in association with Vigilante Entertainment presentation; Color; Not rated; 80 minutes; Release date: July 27, 2012. **CAST:** AJ Bowen (Ben Geringer), Anessa Ramsey (Rachel Adams), Katherine Randolph (Amy), James Bartz (Ryan Hayden), Shanna Forrestall (Gillian Hayden), Sarah Pachelli (Jessica), Hannah Bryan (Alyssa Miller), Marco St. John (The Stranger), Skylar Page Burke (Kelly Hayden), Sonny Marinelli (Paul Nolan), Andrew Breland (Tommy Geringer), Amile Wilson, John Evenden, Jeff Nations (Creatures)

Anessa Ramsey in *Rites of Spring* © IFC Midnight

FALLING OVERNIGHT (Osiris Entertainment) Producers, Jed Rhein, Elizabeth Jackson; Executive Producers, Conrad Jackson, Aaron Golden, Parker Croft, Christian Yeager, Sangeeta Parekh, Lou Fusaro; Director/Photography/Editor, Conrad Jackson; Screenplay, Aaron Golden, Parker Croft, Conrad Jackson; Designer, Sarah Taub; Music Supervisor, Marcela May Wojtczak; a DPO Productions in association with Cerebroscope Films and Dried Lemon Productions presentation; Color; HD; Not rated; 87 minutes; Release date: July 27, 2012. **CAST:** Parker Croft (Elliot Carson), Emilia Zoryan (Chloe Webb), Barak Hardley (Toby), Millie Zinner (Mel), Jake Olson (Kevin), Elizabeth Levin (Samantha), Natalie Antonia (Eva), Lydie Ben-Zakin (French Lady), Christopher Blim (Andrew), Bubba Ganter (Daniel), Jesse Garcia (Miguel), Aaron Golden (Waiter), Corin Grant (Rich Bully), Chad Matheny (Tunnel Concert Musician), Aly Mawji (Cab Driver), Sascha Rasmussen (Doctor), Christian Yeager (Jake), Ari Davis (Kyle), Michael Finn (Tyler), Andreea Florescu (Vanessa), Brian Foyster (Marty), Jon Michael Hill (Troy), Ashli Johnson (Paige), Jeffrey Parker (Rich Bully), Yamil Urena (Ecliserio), Conrad Jackson (Voice of Greggers), Joan McMurtrey (Voice of Mom)

Emilia Zoryan, Parker Croft in *Falling Overnight* © Osiris Entertainment

RUNAWAY SLAVE (Rocky Mountain Pictures) Producer, Beverly Zaslow; Executive Producer, Luke Livingston; Director/Screenplay, Prichett Cotten; Concept, C.L. Bryant; Editors, Matthew Perdie, Pritchett Cotten; a Ground Floor Video presentation of a Riddled with Bullets Film in association with FreedomWorks Foundation and Filmcrest Entertainment; Color; Rated PG; 108 minutes; Release date: July 27, 2012. Documentary on how America's welfare state continues to create a form of "modern slavery" for many black citizens; **WITH:** Glenn Beck, Andrew Breibart, C.L. Bryant, Herman Cain, Alveda King, Star Parker, Jesse Lee Petterson, Thomas Sowell, David Webb, Allen West, Armstrong Williams

HOME RUN SHOWDOWN (Image Entertainment) Producers, Dena Hysell, Joe Gressis; Director, Oz Scott; Screenplay, John Bella, Tim Cavanaugh; Photography, David Stockton; Designer, Bruton Jones; Editor, Joe Gressis; Casting, Richard Pagano, Russell Boast; a Shoreline Entertainment presentation of a Secret Handshake film; Color; Not rated; 94 minutes; Release date: July 27, 2012. **CAST:** Matthew Lillard (Joey), Dean Cain (Rico), Annabeth Gish (Michelle), Wayne Duvall (Simpson), Kyle Kirk (Lori), Barry Bostwick (Big Al), Stephanie Koenig (Aunt Janey Moore), Emma-Lee Hess (Fassi), Brandon Balog (Tanker), Carlos L. Faison (Coach Jeff), Joshua Saba (Dave), Jordan March (Bobby DeLuca), Jesse Harper (Sal), Mike Evans (Admiral), Gary Sheffield (Gonzo), Dmitri Young (Tank Turpino), Anthony Talley (Cub #1), Molly Gundry (Osprey's 2nd Baseman), Cristina V. Sasso (Coach Joules), Conner Wise (Carter Ford), Kaleigh Ryan (Felicia Lee), Mark Ellis, Dave Marcon (Umpires), Vic Faust (Reporter, Channel 7), Darren Daulton (Harrington), Harold Martin (Himself)

Matthew Lillard, Annabeth Gish in *Home Run Showdown* © Image Entertainment

ASSASSIN'S BULLET (ARC Entertainment) formerly *Sofia*; Producer, David E. Ornston; Director, Isaac Florentine; Screenplay, Hans Feuersinger, Nancy L. Babine; Story, Elika Portnoy; Photography, Ross Clarkson; Designer, Valya Mladenova; Costumes, Irina Kocheva; Music, Simon Stevens; Editor, Irit Raz; an XLRator Media and Mutressa Movies presentation; Color; HD; Rated R; 91 minutes; Release date: August 3, 2012. **CAST:** Christian Slater (Robert), Donald Sutherland (Ambassador Ashdown), Elika Portnoy (Vicky), Timothy Spall (Dr. Kahn), Vasil Mihaylov (Host), Mariana Stanisheva (Zoey), Ivaylo Gersakov (Aleks), Ivan Kotsev (Vicky's Dad), Tanya Mitskov (Vicky's Mom), Bashar Rahal (Abdullah Said), Marian Valev (Spasov), Kiril Efremov (Boris), Yordanka Angelova (Gypsy Woman), David Krumov (Pavel), Filip Avramov, Martin Ghiaurov (Muslims), Petyo Petkov (The Turk), Margarita Dilova, Kalina Stancheva (Young Vicki)

THE BABYMAKERS (Millennium) Producers, Jason Blum, Brian Kavanaugh-Jones, Jay Chandrasekhar; Executive Producers, Charles Layton, Stuart Ford, Kevin Heffernan; Director, Jay Chandrasekhar; Screenplay, Peter Gaulke, Gerry Swallow; Photography, Frankie G. DeMarco; Designer, Katie Bryon; Costumes,

Donald Sutherland, Christian Slater in *Assassin's Bullet* © ARC Entertainment

Tricia Gray; Music, Edward Shearmur; Editor, Brad Katz; Casting, Mary Vernieu, Venus Kanani; an IM Global presentation of a Blumhouse Automatik Duck Attack Films production; Dolby; Super 35 Widescreen; Color; Rated R; 98 minutes; Release date: August 3, 2012. **CAST:** Paul Schneider (Tommy Macklin), Olivia Munn (Audrey Macklin), Kevin Heffernan (Wade), Wood Harris (Darrell), Nat Faxon (Zig-Zag), Aisha Tyler (Karen), Collette Wolfe (Allison), Hayes MacArthur (Leslie Jenkins), Jay Chandrasekhar (Ron Jon), Michael Yurchak (Sommellier), Jude Ciccolella (Coach Stubbs), Noureen DeWulf (Bride), Helena Mattsson (Tanya), Desi Lydic (Julie), Will Chandrasekhar (Billy), Bill Fagerbakke (Clark), Jeanne Sakata (Wanda), Constance Zimmer (Mona), M.C. Gainey (Officer Malloy), Miles Fisher (Groom), Tommy Dewey (Todd), Sharon Maughan (Dr. Roberts), Jenica Bergere (Officer Kanani), Rick Overton (Officer Raspler), Jason Piccioni (Officer Pigeon), Ray King (Christopher), Nicole Moore (Jenny), Lindsey Kraft (Greta), Charlie Finn (Sperm Bank Receptionist), Candace Smith (Roxie), Philippe Brenninkmeyer (Dr. Vickery), Sophia Marzocchi (Vanessa), Carrie Clifford (Lynda), Jennifer Ingrum (Birthing Nurse), Alena Savostikova (Farm Girl), Reva Rose (Receptionist), Jeanne Sakata (Wanda), Phillip Daniel (Officer Hawk), BJ Averell (Jesus), Ryan Falkner (Flipoff Man), Tony Sancho (Pedro), James Grace (Bus Driver)

Paul Schneider, Olivia Munn in *The Babymakers* © Millennium Entertainment

SUSHI: THE GLOBAL CATCH (Kino Lorber) Producer/Director, Mark Hall; Executive Producers, Dan Green, Scott Graynor, Alberto Tamura, Robert Barnhart, Lynn Edmundson; Director, Mark Hall; Photography, Jason Faust, Matt Franklin, Kazu Furuya, others; Music, Brian Satterwhite; Editors, Sandra Adair, Catie Cacci; an Alive Mind Cinema presentation of a Sakana Film production; American-Australian-Japanese-Polish; Dolby; Color; Not rated; 75 minutes; Release date: August 3, 2012. Documentary on the downside of sushi; **WITH:** Alistair Douglas, Hagen Stehr, Mamoru Sugiyama, Mike Sutton, Casson Trenor, Tyson Cole

Tyson Cole in *Sushi: The Global Catch* © Kino Lorber

MOSQUITA Y MARI (Wolfe Releasing) Producers, Chad Burris, Charlene Blanc Agabao; Executive Producers, Moctesuma Esparza, Jim McKay, Ky Chaffin, Simone Ling, Jim McKay, Jose Martinez Jr.; Director/Screenplay, Aurora Guerrero; Photography, Magela Crosignani; Designer, Dalila Méndez; Music, Ryan Beveridge; Editor, Augie Robles; Casting, Michael Sanford; a Maya Entertainment, Indion Entertainment Group presentation; Color; Not rated; 85 minutes; Release date: August 3, 2012. **CAST:** Fenessa Pineda (Yolanda), Venecia Troncoso (Mari), Melissa Uscanga (Vicki), Marisela Uscanga (Vero), Laura Patalano (Mrs. Olveros), Joaquin Garrido (Mr. Olveros), Dulce Maria Solis (Mrs. Rodriguez), Armando Cosio (Don Pedro), Omar Leyva (Mr. G), Paul Alayo (Pablo), Sammy Zaragosa (Olivia), Virginia Montero (Photo Shop Owner), Johnny F. Rios (Marlon), Ezquiel Jimenez, Carlos Rios (Boner Survey Boys), Annie McKnight (Security Guard), Georgina Cuautencos (Grandma), Tonita Castro (Dona Herlinda)

Fenessa Pineda, Venecia Troncoso in *Mosquita y Mari* © Wolfe Releasing

CRAIGSLIST JOE (CLJ Films) Producers, Eve Marson Singbiel, Joseph Garner; Executive Producers, Zach Galifianakis, Uday Sehgal; Director, Joseph Garner; Photography, Kevin Flint; Music, David G. Garner; Graphics/Animation, James Anderson; Editor, Drew Kilcoin; Color; HD; Not rated; 90 minutes; Release date: August 3, 2012. Documentary in which filmmaker Joseph Garner attempts to spend a month living off freebies accessed through Craigslist; **WITH:** Joseph Garner, Kristos Andrews, Gina Keatley, 357 Magnumm, Fran McGee, Travis Shivers.

NITRO CIRCUS: THE MOVIE (ARC Entertainment) Producers, Gregg Godfrey, Jeremy Rawle, Travis Pastrana, Dave Hunter; Executive Producers, Bill Gerber, David Brooks, Jared Knight; Directors, Gregg Godfrey, Jeremy Rawle; Photography, Donny Anderson; Costumes, Shelley Godfrey; Music, Damien Starkey, Paul Phillips; Editor, Seth Torok; Special Effects Coordinator, Chuck Johnson; Narrator, Travis Pastrana; a Godfrey Entertainment production in association with Red Bull Media House, Wasserman Media Group and Gerber Pictures; Color; 3D; Rated

Joe Garner (left) in *Craigslist Joe* © CLJ Films

PG-13; 92 minutes; Release date: August 8, 2012. Documentary on extreme stunts; **WITH:** Jim DeChamp, Aaron "Wheelz" Fortheringham, Johnny Knoxville, "Street Bike" Tommy Passemante, Travis Pastrana, "Special" Greg Powell, Jeremy Rawle, Erik Roner, Channing Tatum, Joelen Van Vugt, Parks Bonifay, Dusty Wygle, Aaron "Crum" Sauvage, Cameron McQueen, Rob Dyrdek, Ryan Sheckler, Ken Block, Bill Gerber, David Brooks, Dick Godfrey, Bob Burnquist, Dov Ribnick, Jeff Tremaine

Nitro Circus: The Movie © ARC Entertainment

WE WOMEN WARRIORS (Todos Los Pueblos) a.k.a. *Tejiendo Sabiduría*; Producer/Director, Nicole Karsin; Screenplay, Nicole Karsin, Gabriel Baudet; Photography, Diego Barajas, Daniel Valenica; Music, Daniel Hamuy, Richard Cordoba; Editors, Cristina Malavenda, Gabriel Baudet; American-Colombian; Color; Not rated; 82 minutes; Release date: August 10, 2012. Documentary on three Colombian women who attempt to use nonviolent resistance to defend indigenous rights; **WITH:** Doris Puchana, Ludis Rodriguez, Flor Ilva Trochez

THIS TIME (Village Art Pictures) Producers, Mark Bower, Victor Mignatti; Director/ Photography/Editor, Victor Mignatti; Music, Peitor Angell; an Inspiration 101 production;; Color; HD; Not rated; 111 minutes; Release date: August 10, 2012. Documentary on backup group The Sweet Inspirations, **WITH:** Peitor Angell, Bobby Belfry, Estelle Brown, Portia Griffin, Pat Hodges, Cissy Houston, Myrna Smith, The Sweet Inspirations; Joey Reynolds, Steven Ray Watkins, Thommie Walsh, Alexis Sanders, Tracy Kennedy, John Skaliski, Johanna Pinzler, Peter Mastroangelo, Sylvia Shemwell, Alan Douches, Roger Cohen, Matt Koke, Jerry Heer, Paul Casey, David Budway, Andy Weston, Luca Colombo, Brian Springer, Kristi Rose, Monte Carlo, Alex Barkus, Roland Belmares

The Sweet Inspirations in *This Time* © Village Art Pictures

GOATS (Image Entertainment) Producers, Christopher Neil, Daniela Taplin Lundberg, Shannon Lail, Eric Kopeloff; Executive Producers, Richard Arlook, Daniel Crown, Riva Marker, Peter Touche, Peter Fruchtman, Jai Stefan, Eva Maria Daniels; Director, Christopher Neil; Screenplay, Mark Jude Poirier, based on his 2000 novel; Photography, Wyatt Troll; Designer, Mark A. Duran; Costumes, Kate Deblasio; Music, Jason Schwartzman, Woody Jackson; Editors, Jeremiah O'Driscoll, Kevin Tent; a Red Crown Productions and Sandia Media presentation in association with The Arlook Group; Dolby; Color; Rated R; 94 minutes; Release date: August 10, 2012. **CAST:** David Duchovny (Goat Man), Vera Farmiga (Wendy), Graham Phillips (Ellis), Justin Kirk (Bennet), Keri Russell (Judy), Anthony Anderson (Coach), Dakota Johnson (Minnie), Adelaide Kane (Aubrey), Ty Burrell (Frank), Alan Ruck (Dr. Eldredge), Evan Boymel (Aubrey's Boyfriend), Justin Wheelon (Bully), Olga Segura (Serena), Nicholas Lobue (Barney), Tommee May (Fiona), Shenita Moore (Nurse), Peter Cavnoudias (Sozos), Musashi Alexander (Mr. Lin), Caleb Dane Horst (Bicycle Thief), Ronnie Rubalcaba (Rosenberg), Jacqui Getty (Barney's Mother), Geoff Elsworth (Jonathan the Mailman), Steve Almazan (Jesus), Amanda Crown (Mailroom Clerk), Paul Buchheit (Skycap)

Graham Phillips, David Duchovny in *Goats* © Image Entertainment

THE LION OF JUDAH (JEC Prods.) Producers, Matt Mindell, Joe Kavitski; Director/ Screenplay, Matt Mindell; Photography, Joe Kavitski, Ben Donnellon; Music, Matt Turk; American-Polish; Color; Not rated; 60 minutes; Release date: August 10, 2012. Documentary on Holocaust survivor Leo Zisman; **WITH:** Leo Zisman, Eric Gorenstein, Adriana Celis, Noah Lederman, Agnes Furtak.

SUPERCAPITALIST (Random Art Workshop) Producers, Derek Ting, Joyce Yung, Diana Footitt; Executive Producers, James C. Chie, Sam Kwok, Phillip Yin, John C. Hsu; Director, Simon Yin; Screenplay, Derek Ting; Story, Derek Ting, Young Cho; Photography, Derrick Chung; Designer, Niquan Riley; Costumes, Molly Maguire; Music, Dennis Ting; Editors, Victor Pena; a Random Art Workshop production in association with 408 Films; American-Hong Kong; Color; HD; Not rated; 96 minutes; Release date: August 10, 2012. **CAST:** Derek Ting (Conner Lee), Linus Roache (Mark Patterson), Richard Ng (Donald Chang), Kathy Uyen (Natalie Wang), Darren E. Scott (Quentin Wong), Michael Park (Morris Brown), Kenneth Tsang (Victor Chang), Robin Baker (Anita), Jake Boswell (Michael Baker), Chit-Man Chan (Mr. Chau), Bryan Tang (Kelvin Chau), Roger De Leon (Andy), Thomas Daniel (Chance), Eugene Kang (Richard Chang), Tom Kemnitz Jr. (Gamble), Sofia Regan (Clara), Paul Sheehan (James McIntyre), Vivek Mahbubani (Raj), Eric Ng (Gary), Damon Howe (Jorge), Kathryn Tarwater (Hendricks), Louisa Ward (Secretary), Danny Boushebel, Michael Jacobs (Bankers), Andrew Dasz (Fighter), John Michael Kennedy, Phil Sauers (Wall Street Investors), LoDeon (Dice Man), Jacquees London (Dice Player), Alexandra Moore (Ajay's Girlfriend), Natalie Murray (Reporter), Harry Du Young (Homeless Man)

Linus Roache in *Supercapitalist* © Random Art Workshop

FREELANCERS (Lionsgate) Producers, Randall Emmett, Curtis Jackson, George Furla; Executive Producers, Stepan Martirosyan, Remington Chase, Rick Jackson, Barry Brooker, Stan Wertlieb, Fredrik Malmberg, Daniel Wagner, Michael Blencowe, Martin Richard Blencowe, Jeff Rice, Brandt Andersen, James Gibb, Feng Yang, Iiro Seppänen, Brett Granstaff; Director, Jessy Terrero; Screenplay, L. Philippe Casseus; Photography, Igor Martinovi; Designer, Philip Toolin; Costumes, Mia Maddox; Music, Stanley Clarke; Editor, Kirk Morri; Casting, Barbara Fiorentio; a Grindstone Entertainment Group, Cheetah Vision and Emmett/ Furla Films presentation in association with Paradox Entertainment Inc., Rick Jackson Films and Envision Entertainment; Dolby; Color; Rated R; 96 minutes; Release date: August 10, 2012. **CAST:** Curtis "50 Cent" Jackson (Jonas "Malo" Maldonado), Forest Whitaker (Lt. Det. Dennis LaRue), Robert De Niro (Capt. Joe Sarcone), Matt Gerald (Billy Morrison), Beau Garrett (Joey), Malcolm Goodwin (A.D. Valburn), Robert Wisdom (Terrence Burke), Dana Delany (Lydia Vecchio), Vinnie Jones (Sully), Pedro Armendáriz Jr. (Gabriel Baez), Michael McGrady (Robert Jude), Andre Royo (Daniel Maldonado), Jeff Chase (Angie), Ryan O'Nan (Lucas), Anabelle Acosta (Cyn), Roger Edwards (Ricky), La'Jessie Janoard Smith (Young Malo), Dominique DuVernay (Latin Girl), Cassie Shea Watson (Karlin),

Javier Carrasquillo (Uptown Felix), Raeden Greer (White Girl), Craig Leydecker (Flashback Officer), Danny A. Abeckaser (Louie), Douglas M. Griffin (Harrison), Ambyr Childers (Elaine Morrison), Hilary Cruz (Sexy Girl), Amin Joseph (Shady Guy #2), Shantel Jackson (Tanisha), Phil Laak, Antonio Esfandiari (Undercover Detectives), Jesse Pruett (Mercer Bartender)

Robert De Niro, 50 Cent in *Freelancers* © Lionsgate

IT IS NO DREAM (Moriah Films) Producers, Rabbi Marvin Hier, Richard Trank; Director/Screenplay, Richard Trank, based on original material written by Richard Trank and Rabbi Marvin Hier; Photography, Jeffrey Victor; Music, Lee Holdridge; Editor, Nimrod Erez; Narrator, Sir Ben Kingsley; a Moriah Films production in association with the Friends of Simon Wiesenthal Center for Holocaust Studies; Color/black and white; DV; Not rated; 97 minutes; Release date: August 10, 2012. Documentary on Austro-Hungarian journalist-playwright Theodor Herzl; **VOICES:** Christoph Waltz (Theodor Herzl), Steve Schub (David Ben Gurion), Matthew Asner, Athena Demos, Brian McArdle, Tom Metcalf

Theodor Herzl in *It is No Dream* © Moriah Films

DEATH BY CHINA (Area 23a) Producers, Peter Navarro, Joe Zarinko, Michael Addis, Greg Autry; Executive Producer/Director/Screenplay, Peter Navarro; Based on the 2011 book *Death by China: Confronting the Dragon – A Global Call to Action* by Peter Navarro and Greg Autry; Photography, Kasey Kirby; Music, Christophe Eagleton; Editor, John A. Carr; Animation, Friends of Mine; Narrator, Martin Sheen; a DBC Productions and Area 23a presentation; American-Chinese; Color; HD; Not rated; 79 minutes; Release date: August 17, 2012. Documentary on China's increasing dominance in world trade; **WITH:** Carolyn Bartholomew, Tom Danjczek, Richard McCormack, Peter Morici, Patrick Mulloy, Tim Ryan, Richard L. Trumka, Harry Wu, Chris Smith, Dana Rohrabacher, Jared Bernstein, Gordon Chang, Thea Lee, Kevin MacDonald, Lynn MacDonald, Alan Tonelson

Lana Wachowski, Andy Wachowski in *Side by Side* © Tribeca Film

Death by China © Area 23a

SIDE BY SIDE (Tribeca Film) Producers, Keanu Reeves, Justin Szlasa; Director, Chris Kenneally; Photography, Chris Cassidy; Music, Brendan Ryan, Billy Ryan; Editors, Mike Long, Malcolm Hearn; a Company Films production; Color; Not rated; 98 minutes; Release date: August 17, 2012. Documentary in which several filmmakers discuss the pros and cons of digital filmmaking; **WITH:** Derek Ambrosi, Michael Ballhaus, Andrezej Bartkowiak, Dion Beebe, Jill Bogdanowicz, Danny Boyle, Geoff Boyle, James Cameron, Michael Chapman, Don Ciana, Anne Coates, Lorenzo Di Bonaventura, Lena Dunham, Gary Einhaus, Jonathan Faulkner, David Fincher, Shruti Ganguly, Greta Gerwig, Geoffrey Gilmore, Michael Goi, Terry Haggar, Bob Harvey, Charlie Herzfeld, Jim Jannard, Caroline Kaplan, Glenn Kennel, Jason Kliot, John Knoll, Ellen Kuras, Chris Lebenzon, Barry Levinson, Richard Linklater, George Lucas, David Lynch, John Malkovich, Anthony Dod Mantle, Darnell Martin, Donald McAlpine, Phil Meheux, Reed Morano, Walter Murch, Dennis Muren, Christopher Nolan, Vince Pace, Wally Pfister, Dick Pope, Ari Presler, Keanu Reeves, Robert Rodriguez, Tom Rothman, Ted Schilowitz, Joel Schumacher, Martin Scorsese, Alec Shapiro, Sandi Sissel, Steven Soderbergh, Stefan Sonnenfeld, Tim Stipan, Vittorio Storaro, Edward E. Stratmann, David Stump, David Tattersall, Jost Vacano, Adam Valdez, Lars von Trier, Andy Wachowski, Lana Wachowski, Tim Webber, Craig Wood, Bradford Young, Vilmos Zsigmond.

WHY STOP NOW (IFC) a.k.a. *Predisposed*; Producers, Neda Armian, Ron Nyswaner, Brice Dal Farra, Claude Dal Farra, Lauren Munsch, Paul Prokop; Executive Producers, Wendy Cox, Peter Sterling, Peter Graham, Stephen Hays; Directors/Screenplay, Philip Dorling, Ron Nyswaner; Photography, Ben Kutchins; Designer, Jane Musky; Costumes, Sysan Lyall; Music, Spencer David Hutchings; Editors, Colleen Sharp, Suzy Elmiger; Casting, Kerry Barden, Paul Schnee; a Strategic Motion Ventures presentation of a BCDF Pictures Production in association with Armian Pictures and Blue Days Films; Dolby; Super 35 Widescreen; Color; Not rated; 86 minutes; Release date: August 17, 2012. **CAST:** Jesse Eisenberg (Eli Bloom), Melissa Leo (Penny Bloom), Tracy

Morgan (Sprinkles), Emma Rayne Lyle (Nicole Bloom), Sarah Ramos (Chloe), Isiah Whitlock Jr. (Black), Stephanie March (Trish), Tanya Wright (Lisa), Paul Calderon (Eduardo), Neal Huff (Dave Epstein), Jayce Bartok (Nurse Mike), Harper Dill (Lucy), Marilyn Berry (Charlene), Luna Catarevas (Marina), Susan Barnes (Jennifer Michaels), Kai Chapman (Pat), Stephen Payne (Old Junkie), Nicole Quinn (Receptionist), Ryan McCarthy (British Soldier), Jay Israelson, Sebastion Blanck, Hannah Cohen (Band Members)

Jesse Eisenberg, Isiah Whitlock Jr., Emma Rayne, Tracy Morgan, Melissa Leo in *Why Stop Now* © IFC Films

SPEAK (Tumbleweed Entertainment) Producers/Directors, Paul Galichia, Brian Weidling; Executive Producer, Michael Maloy; Photography, Brian Weidling, Paul Galichia, Matthew Talesfore, others; Music, Philip White; Editors, Brian Weidling, Chris Ross Leong; American-Canadian; Janson Media; Color; Not rated; 89 minutes; Release date: August 17, 2012. Documentary on the art of public speaking; **WITH:** Rich Hopkins, Robert Mackenzie, Dr. Katherine Morrison, Martin Presse, LaShunda Rundles, Charlie Wilson, David Brooks, Mark Brown, Brian Collins, John Daly, Jock Elliott, Henry Flowers, Ann Hastings, Kristi Hopkins, Vikas Jinghram, Richard Kim, Loghandran Krishnasami, Darren LaCroix, Chris Matthews, Susan Milledge, Tammy Miller, Sonya Rundles, Gary Schmidt, Chad Tate, Caite Upton, Colin William, Caroline Wilson

OLD GOATS (ShadowCatcher Entertainment) Producers, Taylor Guterson, Johnathan Boyer; Executive Producers, David Skinner, Tom Gorai; Director/Screenplay/Photography/Editor, Taylor Guterson; Elliot Bay Productions; Color; Not rated; 91 minutes; Release date: August 17, 2012. **CAST:** Britton Crosley (Britt), Bob Burkholder (Bob), David Vander Wal (David), Stephen Stolee (Doug Carlson), Gail Shackel, Benita Staadecker

TRUE WOLF (Shadow Distribution) Producers/Photography, Rob Whitehair, Pam Voth; Executive Producers, Chris Palmer, Bruce Weide; Director/Editor, Rob Whitehair; Screenplay, Rob Whitehair, Bruce Weide; Music, Cody Westheimer; a Tree and Sky Media Arts production; Color; HD; Not rated; 76 minutes; Release date: August 17, 2012. Documentary about a Montana couple who raised a wolf in captivity; **WITH:** Alan Applebury, Jesse Applebury, Ed Bang, Tempe Stahl Conway, Ron Gillette, Graham Neale, Chris Palmer, Nancy Spagnoli, Pat Tucker, Dan Franklin Welch

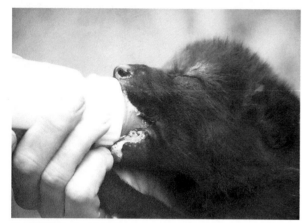

True Wolf © Shadow Distribution

BROTHER, CAN YOU SPARE A DOLLAR (Thomas Hoffman Prods.) Producer/ Director/ Screenplay/Music/Editor, Thom Hoffman; Color; Not rated; 69 minutes; Release date: August 17, 2012. Documentary comparing the Great Depression to today's economic state.

Brother, Can You Spare a Dollar © Thomas Hoffman Prods.

THE APPARITION (Warner Bros.) Producers, Joel Silver, Andrew Rona, Alex Heineman; Executive Producers, Steve Richards, Sue Baden-Powell, Daniel Alter; Director/Screenplay, Todd Lincoln; Photography, Daniel C. Pearl; Designer, Steve Saklad; Costumes, Kimberly Adams; Music, Tomandandy; Editors, Jeff Betancourt, Harold Parker; Visual Effects Coordinators, Christopher Custodio, Jaqgravan Sananikone; Casting, David H. Rapaport; Presented in association with Dark Castle Entertainment; Dolby; Panavision; Color; Rated PG-13; 82 minutes; Release date: August 24, 2012. **CAST:** Ashley Greene (Kelly), Sebastian Stan (Ben), Tom Felton (Patrick), Julianna Guill (Lydia), Luke Pasqualino (Greg), Rick Gomez (Mike), Anna Clark (Maggie), Tim Williams (Office Executive), Marty Martulis (Apparition)

Tom Felton, Ashley Greene, Sebastian Stan in *The Apparition* © Warner Bros.

THUNDERSTRUCK (Warner Premiere) Producer, Mike Karz; Executive Producers, Eric Goodwin, Director, John Whitesell; Screenplay, Eric Champnella, Jeff Farley; Photography, Shawn Maurer; Designer, Meghan C. Rogers; Music, Ali Dee Theodore; Editor, Tony Lombardo; a Karz Entertainment/Goodwin Sports production; Rated PG; 93 minutes; Release date: August 24, 2012. **CAST:** Kevin Durant (Himself), Taylor Gray (Brian), Brandon T. Jackson (Alan), Laramie Doc Shaw (Mitch), James Belushi (Coach Amross), Tristin Mays (Isabel), Robert Belushi (Assistant Coach Dan), Spencer Daniels (Connor), Williams Ragsdale (Joe Newall), Hana Hayes (Ashley Newell), Daniel Amoss, Randall D. Cunningham (W.O.W. Clan Members), Andrea Frankle (Math Teacher), Beau Brasseaux (Drillers Basketball Player), Glen Warner (Photographer), Brie Lybrand (Isabel's Friend), George Wilson (Spider, Janitor), Sean Michael Cunningham (High School Announcer), Lorrie Chilcoat (Security Guard), Nicole Barré (Laurie Newell), Donovan Dunn (Nader), Candace Parker Williams (Herself)

Kevin Durant in *Thunderstruck* © Warner Premiere

A LONELY PLACE FOR DYING (Humble Magi) Producers, Justin Eugene Evans, Brent Daniels, Ross Marquand; Executive Producers, Margery Sinclair, James Cromwell; Director, Justin Eugene Evans; Screenplay, Justin Eugene Evans, Catherine Doughty; Photography, Justin Eugene Evans, Nick Bongianni; Designer, Catherine Doughty; Music, Brent Daniels; Editor, Brad Stoddard; Dolby; Color; Not rated; 94 minutes; Release date: August 24, 2012. **CAST:** Ross Marquand (Nikolai Dzerzhinsky), Michael Scovotti (Robert Harper), Michael Wincott (Anthony Greenglass), James Cromwell (Howard Simons), Luis Robledo (Staff Sgt. Solares), Brad Culver (Capt. Altman), Jason R. Moore (Staff Sgt. Friedkin), Mike Peebler (1st Lt. Hill), Stephen Jules Rubin (Buck Sgt. Konigsberg)

Ross Marquand in *A Lonely Place for Dying* © Humble Magi

Wild Horse, Wild Ride © Screen Media

GENERAL EDUCATION (Well Go USA) Producers, Elliot Feld, Jaz Kalkat, Kevin Liang, Tom Morris; Executive Producers, Kevin Matusow, Gary Abrams, Jag Kalkat, Jessica Liang; Director, Tom Morris; Screenplay, Elliot Feld, Jaz Kalkat, Tom Morris; Photography, Brooks Ludwick; Designer, Kristi Uribes; Costumes, Erica Rice; Music, T.J. Hill, Jesse Pruett; Editor, Tyler MacIntyre; Casting, Danielle Aufiero, Amber Horn; a Pelican House Productions presentation in association with Greenhouse Studios; Color; Not rated; 94 minutes; Release date: August 24, 2012. **CAST:** Chris Sheffield (Levi Collins), Maiara Walsh (Katie), Elaine Hendrix (Ms. Bradford), Bobby Campo (Brian Collins), Tom Maden (Chad), Seth Cassell (Shady Nick), McKaley Miller (Emily Collins), Mercedes Masöhn (Bebe), Janeane Garofalo (Gale Collins), Larry Miller (Rich Collins), Sam Ayers (Samson), Skylan Brooks (Charles), Federico Dordei (Samuel Goldstein), Harvey Guillen (Andy), Stacy Hall (Officer Bob), Susan McCarthy (Principal Lynch), Jesse Pruett (Creepy Donut Buck), Sean Przano (Dan), Todd Quillen (Donald), Kerry Rhodes (Daryl), Sam Tiger (Veggie Oil Vic), Peter S. Williams (Opie), Jimmy Wong (Bo Chang)

Chris Sheffield, Maiara Walsh in *General Education* © Well Go USA

WILD HORSE, WILD RIDE (Screen Media) Producer, Alex Dawson; Directors, Alex Dawson, Greg Gricus; Photography, Greg Gricus; Music, Anthony Lee Rogers, Steve Mullen; Editor, Jude Leak; a Fish Creek Films presentation; Color; HD; Not rated; 106 minutes; Release date: August 24, 2012. Documentary on the annual Extreme Mustang Makeover Challenge; **WITH:** Carlos Chee, Charles Chee, Patti Colbert, Evelyn Gregory, George Gregory, Jesus Jauregui, Melissa Kanzelberger, Kris Kokal, Nik Kokal, Wylene Wilson.

THE REVANANT (Lightning Entertainment) Producers, Kerry Prior, Jacques Thelemaque, Liam Finn; Director/Screenplay, Kerry Prior; Photography, Peter Hawkins; Designer, Thomas Hallbauer; Costumes, Charlotte Kruse; Music, Wendell Hobbs; Editor, Walter Montague Urch; a Wanko Toys production; Color; Rated R; 117 minutes; Release date: August 24, 2012. **CAST:** David Anders (Bart Gregory), Chris Wylde (Joey Luebner), Louise Griffiths (Janet), Jacy King (Mathilda), Philippe Durand (Translator), Mark Elias (Silverlake Jake), Eric Payne (Baily), Wally White (Minister), Theda Reichman, Richard Reichman (Bart's Parents), Stacy Michelle Gold (Nurse Julia), Yvette Freeman (Scientological Nurse), Yvette Freeman (Scientological Nurse), Robert Axelrod (Racially Confused Veteran), Mike Rad (Homophobic Shopping Cart Guy), Zana Zefi (Joey's Neighbor), Emilian Torres (Miguel), Michael J. Gonzalez, Ruben Ferrer, Vinni Ali'l Mesa (Miguel's Friends), Clint Jung (Marty Kim), Cathy Shim (Anita Chung), Twain Taylor (ATM Patron), David Ury (ATM Robber), Beau Clark (The Hood), Tina-Elena Martinez (Victim of Skinheads), David Ross Paterson (Coroner), Amy Correa (Latina Nurse), Ciro Suarez (Blue Collard Leader), Colin Follenweider (LAPD Officer), Braxton Davis Honeycutt (SWAT Captain), Annie Abbott (Tour Guide), Marica Loring (Blonde Woman), Jeff Rector (Military Guy), Codaway King (Chimaera Baby), Bobby King, Marque Ohmes (SWAT Officers), Jerry Pennington, Ron Smith (Cemetery Workers)

David Anders, Chris Wylde in *The Revnant* © Lightning Entertainment

THE VICTIM (Anchor Bay) Producers, Lorna Paul, Jennifer Blanc; Executive Producers, Brock Morse, Morgan Johnson, Ryan Honey; Director/Screenplay, Michael Biehn; Story, Reed Lackey; Photography, Eric Curtis; Music, Jeehun Hwang; Editor, Vance Crofoot; a Blanc/Biehn Production in association with The Mud Show presentation; Color; Rated R; 83 minutes; Release date: August 24, 2012. **CAST:** Michael Biehn (Kyle Limato), Jennifer Blanc (Annie), Ryan Honey (James Harrison), Danielle Harris (Mary), Denny Kirkwood (Jonathan Cooper), Tanya Newbould (Christy Gonzales), Dana Daurey (Waitress), Alyssa Lobit (Lisa Kim), Sam Beneves (Lisa Kim's Boyfriend), Nidah Barber (Spiritual Advisor), Nicole Bilderback, Phoebe Price, Kym Jackson, Amy Honey, Linoria Aghakhani, Juliette Chloe, Brianne Davis, Jamielyn Kane, J.C. Brandy, Caitlin Keats (Missing Girls)

Michael Biehn in *The Victim* © Anchor Bay

SOMEWHERE BETWEEN (Ladylike Films) Producer/Director, Linda Goldstein Knowlton; Executive Producers, Bobby Chang, Jon Fitzgerald, Catherine A. Johnston, Paul E. Li; Photography, Nelson Hume, Christine Burrill; Music, Lili Haydn; Editor, Katie Flint; a Long Shot Factory and Ladylike Films presentation; Color; Not rated; 88 minutes; Release date: August 24, 2012. Documentary on four Chinese adoptees growing up in the United States; **WITH:** Ann Boccuti, Haley Butler, Jenna Cook, Fang "Jenni" Lee.

Fang Lee in *Somewhere Between* © Ladylike Films

THE OOGIELOVES IN THE BIG BALLOON ADVENTURE (Kenn Viselman Presentation) Producers, Kenn Viselman, Gayle Dickie; Executive Producers, Michael A. Chirco, Scot J. Moceri, David R. Schwarcz; Director, Matthew Diamond; Screenplay, Scott Stabile; Photography, Peter Klein; Designer, Bob Kayganich; Costumes, Stacy Lauwers; Music, Joe Alfuso, Rob Rettberg; Editor, Girish Bhargava; Visual Effects Supervisor, James Gilmore; Casting, Valerie McCaffrey, Dayna Polehanki; Dolby; Deluxe color; HD; Rated G; 88 minutes; Release date: August 29, 2012. **VOICE CAST:** Cary Elwes (Bobby Wobbly), Christopher Lloyd (Lero Sombrero), Jaime Pressly (Lola Sombrero), Cloris Leachman (Dotty Rounder), Chazz Palminteri (Marvin Milkshake), Toni Braxton (Rosalie Rosebud), Misty Miller (Goobie), Stephanie Renz (Zoozie), Malerie Grady (Toofie), Maya Stange (Windy Window), Nick Drago (J. Edgar), Steve Blackwood (Sheep), Alecia Jai Fears (Rochelle Rosebud), Kylie O'Brien (Jubilee Rounder), Taras Los (Schluufy the Pillow), Guistina Chirco (Marna), Sonya A. Avakian, Squeakie Starr (Mice), Toby Murray, Dave Doran (Ducklings), Randy Carfagno (Ruffy)

The Oogieloves in The Big Balloon Adventure © Kenn Viselman Presentation

THE DAY (Anchor Bay) Producer, Guy A. Danella; Executive Producers, Michael Finley, Tim James, Antonina Armato, Ross M. Dinerstein, Doug Aarniokoski; Co-Producers, Shawn Ashmore, Dominic Monaghan; Director, Doug Aarniokoski; Screenplay, Luke Passmore; Photography, Boris Mojsovski; Designer, Lisa Soper; Costumes, Candice Beuckx; Music, Rock Mafia; Editor, Andrew Counts; a WWE Studios and Anchor Bay Films presentation of a Guy A. Danella production in association with Follow Through Prodsuctions LLC, Rock Mafia, Preferred Content, Faction M.; Dolby; Color; DV; Rated R; 85 minutes; Release date: August 29, 2012. **CAST:** Shawn Ashmore (Adam), Ashley Bell (Mary), Michael Eklund (Father), Cory Hardrict (Henson), Dominic Monaghan (Rick), Shannyn Sossamon (Shannon), Brianna Barnes (Nikki), Kassidy Verreault (Ava), Brayden Edwards (Timmy), Steffi Hagel (Sally), Robert Baldwin, Frank Beaudoin, Patrick Beriault, Patrick Blais, Alex Brown, Andre Deveaux, Jose Garcia, Tarlee Gerhard, Andre Givogue, Daniel Lavigne, Duncan Milloy, Sean Morel, Alain Moussi, Myra Quinonez, Kelly Rigole, Cameron Tecarton, Migel Woleston (Survivalists), Shimon Moore (Boss)

Cory Hardrict, Dominic Monaghan, Shannyn Sossamon in *The Day* © Anchor Bay

LITTLE BIRDS (Millennium) Producers, Alan Polsky, Gabe Polsky, Jamie Patricof; Executive Producers, Kevin Iwashina, Stefan Nowicki; Director/Screenplay, Elgin James; Photography, Reed Morano; Designer, Todd Fjelsted; Costumes, Trayce Field; Music, Elgin James; Editor, Suzanne Spangler; Casting, Wendy O'Brien; a Burger Collection presentation of a Hunting Lane Films Production in association with Polsky Films and Sundial Pictures; Dolby; Techniscope; Deluxe color; Rated R; 95 minutes; Release date: August 29, 2012. **CAST:** Juno Temple (Lily Hobart), Kay Panabaker (Alison Hoffman), Kyle Gallner (Jesse MacNamara), Chris Coy (David Riley), Carlos Pena (Louis Estes), Neal McDonough (Hogan), JR Bourne (John Gretton), Kate Bosworth (Bonnie Muller), Leslie Mann (Margaret Hobart), David Warshofsky (Joseph Hoffman), Kathleen Gati (Sally Heron), Lauren Whitney Pennington (Shawna Cawley), Bob Larkin (Mr. Kovacs), Mike Erwin (Mark Muller), Erik Ellington (Dealer), Scotty Noyd Jr. (Ray Cawley), Elizabeth James (LA Hipster Girl), Todd Fjelsted (LA Hipster Boy), J.W. Buckley (Skate Shop Owner), Marc Rose (Man), Lydia Blanco (Cashier), Mindy Vela-Henderson (Realtor), Katie Nehra (Realtor's Assistant), Joel McKinnon Miller (Michael White), Chad Gilbert (Guy with Drink), Jake Devine, George Hathaway, Jared Huss (Salton Sea Skateboarders), Arto Saari, Geoff Rowley, David Gonzales, Rune Glifberg, Ewan Bowman (Los Angeles Skateboaders), Gibby Miller, Matthew Boettcher, Chad Glissmeyer (Partygoers)

Kay Panabaker, Juno Temple in *Little Birds* © Millennium Entertainment

THE TALL MAN (Image Entertainment) Producers, Jean-Charles Levy, Kevin DeWalt, Clément Miserez, Scott Kennedy; Executive Producers, Jessica Biel, Thierry Desmichelle, Lionel Uzan, Steven Schneider, Gerard Demaer, Lisa Donahue, Mark Montague, David Cormican, Nicolas Manuel, Olivier Piasentin, Matthieu Warter, Frank White; Director/Screenplay, Pascal Laugier; Photography, Kamal Derkaoui; Designer, Jean Carriere; Costumes, Angus Strathie; Music, Todd Bryanton; Editor, Sebastien Prangere; Visual Effects Supervisor, Mark Savela; Casting, Carmen Kotyk, Bonnie Timmerman; a Minds Eye Entertainment, Radar Films and Forecast Pictures co-production in association with SND, Highwire Pictures and Iron Ocean Films with the participation of M6 and Canal +; American-Canadian-French; Dolby; Color; Rated R; 106 minutes; Release date: August 31, 2012. **CAST:** Jessica Biel (Julia Denning), Jodelle Ferland (Jenny), Stephen McHattie (Lt. Dodd), William B. Davis (Sheriff Chestnut), Samantha Ferris (Tracy), Colleen Wheeler (Mrs. Johnson), Eve Harlow (Christine), Janet Wright (Trish), Ferne Downey (Mrs. Parker Leigh), John Mann (Douglas), Teach Grant (Steven), Garwin Sanford (Robert), Jakob Davies (David), Lucas Myers (Deputy Campbell), Pat Henman (Nurse at Police Infirmary), Katherine Ramdeen (Carol), Alicia Gracy (Young Mother #3), G. Michael Gray (Young Father #2), Georgia Swedish (Mrs. Ashcroft), Jenna Gatschene (Waitress at Diner), Priya Lily Campbell (Tiffany), John Ryan, Kevin DeWalt (Prison Guards), Melissa Gibson (Guard), Melissa Patenaude, Michele Mungall, Jacqueline Eggie, Angela Stott (Inmates), Ricardo Hubbs (Tall Cook), Rene Mousseux (Silhouette), Josh Strait (Anonymous Voice #1), Jodi Sadowsky (David's New Mother)

Jessica Biel in *The Tall Man* © Image Entertainment

UNTIL THEY ARE HOME (Vanilla Fire Prods.) Producer, Tamara Henry; Executive Producer, Tim Shelton; Director, Steven C. Barber; Screenplay/Editor, Paul Freedman; Photography, Matthew Hausle; Music, Clint Black; Narrator, Kesley Grammer; Color; Not rated; 66 minutes; Release date: August 31, 2012. Documentary on the efforts of Joinh POW/MIA Accounting Command to retrieve the bodies of U.S. servicemen killed in the Battle of Tarawa in 1943; **WITH:** Eddie Albert, Norm Hatch, Larry King, John Savage.

Until They are Home © Vanilla Fire Prods.

DOGGIE B (Phase 4) a.k.a. *Doggie Boogie – Get Your Grrr On!*; Producers, Romanus Wolter, Delicia Niami, Delphine Suter; Director/Screenplay, Romanus Wolter; Photography, Maurice Freeman; Designer, Cheryl Parrott; Music, Jacob Yoffee; Editor, Robin Lee; Casting, Ashley George; a Kaboom! Entertainment presentation; American-Canadian; Dolby; Color; HD; Rated PG; 87 minutes; Release date: August 31, 2012. **CAST:** Pijo (Pijo) Jesse Draper (Cassie Barbizon), Scott Cox (Peter Wolfe), Bettina Devin (Gertrude Spinner), Patrick Davis (Roman Spinner), Jane Wiedlin (Dottie), Barbara Tintori (Karen Barbizon), Erica Gerard (Rachelle), Constance Hasapopoulos (Pinkie), Judith Sims (Kia Tuel), Keith Myer (Mortgage Man), Chris Marsol (Candler), Daniel Will-Harris (Dr. Loren), Janlee Marshall (Tabitha), Robin Griffin (Dognositist), Ken Baggott, Linden King (Announcers), Michael Sean Roads (Taxi Driver), Athena Radomski (Rosie), Vince Weigel (James), Bob Vickers, Karim Mayfield, Loretta Carpenter, Dr. Hal (Judges), Ronkat Spearman, Gabby La La, Evelyn Taft (Nationals Judges), Paula O'Rourke McFadden, Caleb Hessing, Peter Suter (Bongo Players), Shelah Barr (Dog Masseuse), Erin Shredder (Hula Hooper), Gregangelo Herrera (Whirling Dirvish Performer), Cesar Sanchez, Andrew Swan (Security Guards), Rick Torres (Elvis), Eva Grady (Elvis' Girlfriend), Beverly Ulbrich, Margaret Hahn (Dognosis Students), Shane Silveira (Jasper), Bella Nickel (Young Cassie), Alyssa Ferrari (Young Karen)

Pijo, Jesse Draper in *Doggie B* © Phase 4 Films

Paul Dano in *For Ellen* © Tribeca Film

HOLLYWOOD TO DOLLYWOOD (Bloodrush Films) Producers, Gary Lane, Larry Lane; Executive Producers, Gary Lane, Larry Lane, Mike Bowen; Co-Producers, Chad Allen, Christopher Racster; Director/Editor, John Lavin; Photography, Jennifer D'Urso; Designer, Mike Bowen; Music, Greg Delson; Color; Not rated; 79 minutes; Release date: August 31, 2012. Documentary on twins Gary and Larry Lane's efforts to get their script to their idol, Dolly Parton, **WITH:** Gary Lane, Larry Lane, Mike Bowen, Chad Allen, Beth Grant, Ann Walker, Manouschka Guerrier, Dustin Lance Black, Leslie Jordan, Dolly Parton

GIRL MODEL (First Run Features) Consulting Producers, Marcy Garriott, Robert Garriott; Directors/Photography/Editors, David Redmon, Ashley Sabin; Music, Matthew Dougherty, Eric Taxier; American-Russian-Japanese-French; Stereo; Color; Not rated; 77 minutes; Release date: September 5, 2012. Documentary on Russian girls who go abroad in search of modeling jobs; **WITH:** Ashley Arbaugh, Rachel Blais, Nadya Vall

Larry Lane, Leslie Jordan, Gary Lane in *Hollywood to Dollywood* © Bloodrush Films

Girl Model © First Run Features

FOR ELLEN (Tribeca) Producers, Jen Gatien, Bradley Rust Gray, So Yong Kim; Executive Producers, Paul Dano, Tricia Quick, Jonathan Vinnik, Michael Clofine, Dave Berlin, Rui Costa Reis; Director/Screenplay, So Yong Kim; Photography, Reed Morano; Designer, Ryan Smith; Music, Jóhann Jóhannsson; Editors, So Yong Kim, Bradley Rust Gray; Casting, Sig De Miguel, Stephen Vincent; a Deerjen and Soandbrad production; Color; Not rated; 93 minutes; Release date: September 5, 2012. **CAST:** Paul Dano (Joby Taylor), Jon Heder (Fred Butler), Jena Malone (Susan), Margarita Levieva (Claire Taylor), Dakota Johnson (Cindy), Julian Gamble (Mr. Hamilton), Shaylena Mandigo (Ellen Taylor), Peter Roberts, William Roberts (Tow-Truck Guys), Ronald Walter Mandigo (Claire Taylor's Fiancé), Mara Pelifian (Mrs. Butler)

SERVING UP RICHARD (Dance On Productions) formerly *The Guest Room*; Producer, Diane Levine; Executive Producer, Susan Priver; Director, Henry Olek; Screenplay, Henry Olek, Jay Longshore; Based on a story by Jay Longshore; Photography, Bruce Alan Greene; Designer, Freddy Naff; Costumes, Drew Bird; Music, Stephen Graziano; Editor, Bob Joyce; Casting, Russell Boast; Color; Not rated; 106 minutes; Release date: September 7, 2012. **CAST:** Ross McCall (Richard Reubens), Susan Priver (Glory Hutchins), Jude Ciccolella (Everett Hutchins), Brian Burke (Stanley), Adam Kulbersh (Dennis), Darby Stanchfield (Karen), Doug Sinclair, Michael Austin (Rescue Workers), Kirkaldy Myers, Eugene Conde (Cab Drivers), Jeanne Heileman (Dog Walker)

GREEN (Factory 25) Producer, Lawrence Michael Levine; Director/Screenplay/Editor, Sophia Takal; Photography, Nandan Rao; Music, Ernesto Carcamo; a Reality Pictures, Little Teeth Pictures production; Stereo; Color; DV; Not rated;

73 minutes; Release date: September 7, 2012. **CAST:** Kate Lyn Sheil (Genevieve), Sophia Takal (Robin), Lawrence Michael Levine (Sebastian), Louis Cancelmi (Dustin), Alex Ross Perry (Phillip Roth Expert), Robert Malone (Bill)

Lawrence Michael Levine, Kate Lyn Sheil, Sophia Takal in *Green* © Factory 25

THE COLD LIGHT OF DAY (Summit) Producers, Trevor Macy, Marc D. Evans; Executive Producers, Steven Zaillian, Scott Wiper, Jesús Martínez Asencio, Kevin Mann, Matthew Perniciaro, Mark Canton; Director, Mabrouk El Mechri; Screenplay, Scott Wiper, John Petro; Photography, Remi Adefarasin; Designer, Benjamín Fernández; Costumes, Bina Daigeler; Music, Lucas Vidal; Editor, Valerio Bonelli; Special Effects Supervisor, Chris Reynolds; Stunts, Lee Sheward, Jordi Casaraes; a Summit Entertainment and Intrepid Pictures presentation in association with Galavis Film of an Intrepid Pictures/Film Rites production, a Fría Luz Del Día A.I.E. production; American-Spanish; Dolby; Super 35 Widescreen; Color; Rated PG-13; 93 minutes; Release date: September 7, 2012. **CAST:** Henry Cavill (Will), Verónica Echegui (Lucia), Bruce Willis (Martin), Sigourney Weaver (Carrack), Joseph Mawle (Gorman), Caroline Goodall (Laurie), Rafi Gavron (Josh), Emma Hamilton (Dara), Michael Budd (Esmael), Roschdy Zem (Zahir), Óscar Jaenada (Maximo), Joe Dixon (Dixon), Jim Piddock (Meckler), Fermí Reixach (Carlos), Lolo Herrero (Reynaldo), Luiggi López (Puerto Serena Fisherman), Alex Amaral (Cesar), Paloma Bloyd (Christiana), Simón Andreu (Pizarro), Morgan Johnson (Habib), Mark Ullod (Vicente), Borja Chantres (Bus Driver), Andrea Ros Buerrero (SP College Girl), Carlos Martínez (Young Cop), José Alias (Garbage Man), Sílvia Sabaté (Mother at Pharmacy), Colm Meaney (Bandler)

Verónica Echegui, Henry Cavill in *The Cold Light of Day* © Summit Entertainment

DETROPIA (Loki Films) Producers, Heidi Ewing, Rachel Grady, Craig Atkinson; Directors, Heidi Ewing, Rachel Grady; Executive Producers, Dan Cogan, David Menschel; Photography, Tony Hardmon, Craig Atkinson; Music, Dial.81; Editor, Enat Sidi; a Loki Films presentation in association with Ford Foundation, Justfilms and ITVS, Impact Partners and Vital Projects; Color; Not rated; 91 minutes; Release date: September 7, 2012. Documentary looks at the decline of Detroit.

Detropia © Loki Films

BEAUTY IS EMBARRASSING (Future You Pictures) Producers, Neil Berkeley, Chris Bradley, Milan Erceg, Morgan Neville; Executive Producers, Aimee Bothwell, Bart McDonough, Eddie Schmidt; Director, Neil Berkeley; Screenplay, Neil Berkeley, Chris Bradley, Kevin Klauber; Photography, Chris Bradley, Neil Berkeley; Editor, Chris Bradley; a Future You Pictures presentation in association with Tremolo Productions; Color; Not rated; 87 minutes; Release date: September 7, 2012. Documentary on designer-painter-puppeteer-sculptor-musician Wayne White; **WITH:** Cliff Benjamin, Tony Crow, Jonathan Dayton, Valerie Faris, Matt Groening, Mark Mothersbaugh, Todd Oldham, David Pagel, Gary Panter, Paul Reubens, Charles Stone, Fred Sullivan, Kurt Wagner, Wayne White, Paul Zaloom.

Wayne White in *Beauty is Embarrassing* © Future You Pictures

DESPERATE ENDEAVORS (LBYL Films) Producer/Director, Salim Khassa; Screenplay, Don L. Wilhelm, Salim Khassa; Based on the 1991 book *Seeking Home: An Immigrant's Realization* by Jayant Patel; Photography, Scott Henderson; Designer, Roger Ambrose; Costumes, Tomoko Khassa; Music, Tony Finno; Editors, Ryan M. Fritzsche, Salim Khassa; a Look Before You Leap Film production; Color; Rated PG-13; 110 minutes; Release date: September 7, 2012. **CAST:** Ismail Bashey (Ram Patel), Gulshan Grover (Dada Baghwan), Michael Madsen (Skeeter), Robert Clohessy (Mark),Samrat Chakrabarti (Adesh), Shikha Jain (Rani), Lavrenti Lopes (Dilip), Geeta Citygirl Chopra (Kali), Terence Exodus (Floyd), Kevin Gebhard (Ed Radford), Reggie Green (Whitey the Butcher), Paul Ben-Victor (Bill Loney), Joseph R. Gannascoli (Neil Bates), Deborah Green (Serene), Jessica Minhas

(Gira), Ismhail Khassa (Street Urchin), Bobby Abido (Sajay G), Caitlin Abrams (Marsha), Kevin Arbouet (Rufus), Ralph Bracco (Carl, Angry Neighbor), Romeo D'Costa (Deepak), Alyssa Daver (Tara), Sarah Ellis (Patty), Aiden Eyrick (Sick Child), Sujata Eyrick (Madhu), Nimo Gandhi (Bagesh), John Gibson (Quincy), Kelvin Hale (Bruno), George Kayaian (Businessman), Kristina Klebe (Lambchop), Sherry Locher (Dora Hunt), Kimberly Magness (Rhonda Flaherty), Roni Mazumdar (Kareem), Brittany Moore (Eleanor), Daniel Moya (Johnny), Vince Parenti (Officer Coolidge), Nona Pipes (Yolanda), Dennis Rees, Michael A. Russo (Police Officers), Timothy Ryan (Lowell), Philip Seidman (Oscar), Tom E. Ford (Colin), Laura Summerhill (Chastity), Shawn Tracy (Lucious), Robert Yougren (Howie)

Shika Jain, Ismail Bashey in *Desperate Endeavors* © LBYL Films

VERSAILLES '73: AMERICAN RUNWAY REVOLUTION (Coffee Bluff Pictures) Executive Producers, Deborah Riley Draper, Michael A. Draper, Caralene Robinson; Director/Screenplay, Deborah Riley Draper; Photography, Jonathan Hall; Editors, Ryan Kerrison, Bill Bowen; Color; Not rated; 91 minutes; Release date: September 7, 2012. Documentary on the importance in fashion of the 1973 Grand Divertissement at Versailles; **WITH:** Marisa Berenson, Billie Blair, Stephen Burrows, Alva Chinn, Dennis Christopher, Anna Cleveland, Pat Cleveland, Laurent Cotta, Norma Jean Darden, Charlene Dash, Tom Fallon, Didier Grumbach, Bethann Hardison, Pierre-Andre Helene, Jean-Luce Hure, Barbara Jackson, Sandy Jordan, Harold Koda, Carla Lemonte, Simone Levitt, China Machado, Karen Bjornson McDonald, Karine McGrath, Grace Mirabella, Nancy North, Carola Polakova, Beatrix Saule, Cameron Silver, Barbara Summers, Mikki Taylor, John Tiffany, Charles Tracy.

Marisa Berenson, Halston, Liza Minnelli in *Versailles '73* © Coffee Bluff Pictures

I'M CAROLYN PARKER (Clinica Estetico) Producers, Lindsay Jaeger, Daniel Wolff, Stephen Apkon; Executive Producer, Rocco Caruso; Music, Zafer Tawil; Editor, Ido Haar; a Clinica Estetico/Jacob Burns Film Center production; Black and white/color; Not rated; 93 minutes; Release date: September 12, 2012. Documentary on the last woman to leave her New Orleans neighborhood when a mandatory evacuation order was issued in anticipation of the arrival of Hurricane Katrina; **WITH:** Carolyn Parker.

MULBERRY CHILD (American Dream Pictures) Producer/Director/Screenplay, Susan Morgan Cooper; based on the 2009 book *Mulberry Child: A Memoir of China* by Jian Ping; Executive Producer, Ellis Goodman; Photography, Quyen Tran; Music, Kyle Eastwood, Matt McGuire; Editor, Sean Valla; Narrator, Jacqueline Bisset; a Morgan Cooper production; Color/Black and white; Not rated; 85 minutes; Release date: September 7, 2012. Documentary-drama based on Jian Ping's memoir of her childhood in Sino, China; **WITH:** Jian Ping, Lisa Xia; **AND:** Jody Choi (Little Jian), Bruce Akoni Yong (Father/Hou Kai), Christine Chiang (Mother/Gu Wenxiu), Yang Juan Xue (Nainai), Vanessa Chiu (Big Jian), Charlotte Kong (Ping), Kayley Kong (Wen), Megan Kong (Schoolmate), Cody Choi (Mean Boy), Lia Tian (Binbin), Lily Sang (Mrs. Zhang), Vincent Lee (Mr. Wang), Tony Li (Old School Director), Phannie Choi (Landlord's Wife), Eric Choi (Guard), Eddie Chiu (Chauffeur), Thomas Fung (Red Guard)

Mulberry Child © American Dream Pictures

BRAWLER (XLrator Films) Producers, Nathan Grubbs, Marc Senter; Executive Producer, Captain Jack Grubbs; Director/Screenplay, Chris Sivertson; Story, Nathan Grubbs, Chris Sivertson; Photography, Zoran Popovic; Designer, Denise Greenwood; Costumes, Shareen Chehade; Music, Tim Rutili; Editors, Abe Levy, Philip Norden; Casting, Jory Weitz, Brent Caballero; a GFY Films presentation; Color; Rated R; 84 minutes; Release date: September 7, 2012. **CAST:** Nathan Grubbs (Charlie Fontaine), Marc Senter (Bobby Fontaine), Bryan Batt (Fat Chucky), Michael Bowen (Rex Baker), Pell James (Kat), Lance E. Nichols (McSweeney), Megan Henning (Chloe), Kenny Bordes (Tony), Sean Paul Braud (Big Guy), J. Omar Castro (Juan), Garrett Hines (Nickels), Ann McKenzie (Margaret), Dane Rhodes (Atwater), Tom Sicola (Wrestling Partner), Lindsay Soileau (Sarah), Brian Stapf (Walter), Lawrence Turner (Richard), Doc Whitney (Anthony), Zac Cino (Meek Frat Kid), Shane Guilbeau (Chapel Manager), Oren Hawxhurst (Fighter)

Nathan Grubbs in *Brawler*
© XLrator Films

Jennifer O'Neill in *Last Ounce of Courage* © Veritas Entertainment

THE RIGHT TO LOVE: AN AMERICAN FAMILY (Jaye Bird Prods.) Producers, Christina Clack, Cassie Jaye, Nena Jaye, Ford Austin, Marc Wasserman; Executive Producer, Jay Pugh; Director, Cassie Jaye; Photography, Cassie Jaye, Nena Jaye; Music, Edwin Wendler; Editor, Cassie Jaye; a Jaye Bird Productions presentation; Color; HD; Not rated; 88 minutes; Release date: September 7, 2012. Documentary on a Northern California family consisting of two fathers and two adopted kids; **WITH:** Justin R. Cannon, Jay Foxworthy, Anne Leffew, Brandon Leffew, Bryan Leffew, Chuck Leffew, Daniel Leffew, Selena Leffew, Denise Miney.

Bryan Leffew, Jay Foxworthy in *The Right to Love* © Jaye Bird Prods.

LAST OUNCE OF COURAGE (Veritas Entertainment) Producer, Kevin McAfee; Executive Producers, Steve Griffin, Richard Headrick, Gina Headrick, Gen Fukunaga, Cindy Fukunaga, Doug Pethoud, Lynn Dean McAfee, Rooney Stone; Directors, Darrel Campbell, Kevin McAfee; Screenplay, Darrel Campbell; Story, Richard Headrick, Gina Headrick, Darrel Campbell; Photography, Jason Cantu; Music, Ronald Owen; Editor, Miles Hanon; Presented in association with Hellfighters Productions, Be-Still Pictures, Outpost Worldwide & Veritas Marketing Group; Color; Rated PG; 101 minutes; Release date: September 11, 2012. **CAST:** Marshall Teague (Bob Revere), Jennifer O'Neill (Dottie Revere), Fred Williamson (Warren Hammerschmidt), Jenna Boyd (Mattie Rogers), Rusty Joiner (Greg Rogers), Hunter Gomez (Christian Revere), Darrel Campbell (Renaldo Boutwell), Nikki Novak (Kari Revere), Sarah McMullen (Reagan), Adelie Campbell (Lindsay), Steve Nave (Walter Putman), Bill O'Reilly (Himself), Benjay Gaither (Ernie), Michelle Davidson (Connie Lee), Katherine McNamara (Caroler), Sharon Marie Wright (Reporter)

FRANCINE (Factory 25) Producers, Joshua Blum, Katie Stern; Executive Producer, Anna Gerb; Directors/Screenplay, Brian M. Cassidy, Melanie Shatzky; Photography, Brian M. Cassidy; Designer/Costumes, Christina Cole; Editors, Brian M. Cassidy, Benjamin Gray, Melanie Shatzky; a Washington Square Films and Pigeon Projects presentation; American-Canadian; Color; Not rated; 74 minutes; Release date: September 12, 2012. **CAST:** Melissa Leo (Francine), Keith Leonard (Ned), Victoria Charkut (Linda), Dave Clark (Pet Store Manager), Dr. Mike Halstead (Veterinarian), Marietta Hanley (Prison Guard), Brendan Burke (Prison Administrator), Robert J. Meredith (Cab Driver), Danica Brodehead (DMV Clerk), Colin Mulholland (Customer with Hamster), Angelo Decelie, Shane Lake, Kevin Rhoades, Matthew Slater, Eric Willows (Snapring, Band), Karen Keefe (Customer with Bird), Joey Hoeber (Older Man), Barbara Forman (Pastor's Wife), Alder Lakish (Pastor), Brenda Roach (Nurse), Deborah Scott (Receptionist)

Melissa Leo in *Francine* © Factory 25

STOLEN (Millennium) Producers, René Besson, Jesse Kennedy, Matthew Joynes; Executive Producers, Joseph McGinty, Mary Viola, Avi Lerner, Danny Dimbort, Trevor Short, Boaz Davidson, John Thompson, Kristina Dubin, Jib Polhemus, Cassian Elwes; Director, Simon West; Screenplay, David Guggenheim; Photography, James Whitaker; Designer, Jaymes Hinkle; Costumes, Christopher Lawrence; Music, Mark Isham; Editor, Glenn Scantlebury; Casting, Amanda Mackey, Cathy Sandrich; a Nu Image production in association with Saturn Films; Dolby; Super 35 Widescreen; Color; Rated R; 96 minutes; Release date: September 14, 2012. **CAST:** Nicolas Cage (Will Montgomery), Danny Huston (Tim Harlend), Malin Akerman (Riley Jeffers), M.C. Gainey (Hoyt), Sami Gayle (Alison Loeb), Mark Valley (Fletcher), Josh Lucas (Vincent), Edrick Browne (Jacobs), Barry Shabaka Henley (Reginald), J.D. Evermore (Rookie), Garrett Hines (Aaron), Kevin

Foster (Motorcycle Cop), Tanc Sade (Pete), Dan Braverman (Lefleur), Jon Eyez (Bertrand), Marcus Lyle Brown (Matthews), Matt Nolan (Tessler), Tyler Forrest (Teenage Cab Driver), Shanna Forrestall (Harlend's Assistant), Brian Kinney, Joe Nin Williams (FBI Agents), Derek Schreck (FBI Guard #1), Tim Bell (Cop #1), Kyle Russell Clements, Mustafa Harris (FBI Surveillance), John McConnell (Drunk Businessman), Dave Davis (Taylor), Bernadette Ralphs (Kiosk Girl), Emily West (Frightened Girl in Car), Randall Nelms (Stakeout Agent), Demetrice Jackson (Mark), Matt McHugh (FBI)

Matt Nolan, Nicolas Cage, Marcus Lyle in *Stolen* © Millennium Entertainment

THE TROUBLE WITH THE TRUTH (Winning Edge Partners/1428 Films) Producers, Daniel Farrands, Thommy Hutson; Executive Producers, James W. Hemphill, Nancy Yudchitz; Director/ Screenplay, Jim Hemphill; Photography, Roberto Correa; Designer, C.J. Strawn; Music, Sean Schafer Hennessy; Editor, Michael Benni Pierce; Casting; Dean E. Fronk, Donald Paul Pemrick; Color; Rated R; 96 minutes; Release date: September 14, 2012. **CAST:** Lea Thompson (Emily), John Shea (Robert), Danielle Harris (Jenny), Keri Lynn Pratt (Heather), Rainy Kerwin (Staci), Ira Heiden (Restaurant Host), Adrienne Rusk (Waitress)

John Shea, Lea Thompson in *The Trouble with the Truth*
© Winning Edge Partners

AFTER (Seabourne Pictures) Producers, Brandon Gregory, Sabyn Mayfield; Executive Producers, Michael Gangwisch, Scott Healy, Chris Schmid; Director/ Screenplay, Ryan Smith; Photography, Blake McClure; Designer, Edward Gurney; Costumes, Anna Redmon; Music, Tyler Smith; Editor, David Kiern; Casting, Sabyn Mayfield; Visual Effects Supervisor, Julian Herrera; Presented in association with Quite Quick Productions; Deluxe color; J-D-C Scope; Rated PG-13; 99 minutes; Release date: September 9, 2012. **CAST:** Steven Strait (Freddy), Karolina Wydra (Ana), Sandra Lafferty (Aunt Lu), Madison Lintz (Young Ana), Ric Reitz, Steve

Coulter (Doctors), Jackson Walker (Phil), Bob Penny (Elderly Man), Chase Presley (Young Freddy), April Billingsley (Caretaker), Sabyn Mayfield (Carnival Attendant), Jennfier Spriggs, Jacqueline Springfield (Nurses), Tyrin Niles Wyche (Chuck), Michael Dinardo (Clay)

Karolina Wydra, Steven Strait in *After* © Seabourne Pictures

THE STAND UP (Cinema 59) Producers, Eli Wolstan, David Wexler; Co-Producer, Shane Tilston; Director/Screenplay, David Wexler; Photography, Bart Grieb; Designer, Keith Garvey; Costumes, Stephanie Yarger; Music, Kevin Drew; Editor, Alex Ricciardi; Casting, Rob Decina; a Cinema 59 Productions presentation; Not rated; 82 minutes; Release date: September 14, 2012. **CAST:** Jonathan Sollis (Zoe), Margarita Levieva (Veronica), Aidan Quinn (Sandy), Jonathan Reed Wexler (Clem), Arija Bareikis (Mrs. Rundgren), Julia Dennis (Miranda), Justine Cotsonas (Rosaline), Quinn Broggy (Ethan), Jennifer Mudge (Mrs. Schumacher), Bryanna Adames (Rachel), Duncan Bindbeutel (MC at Comedy Club), Gianni Echeverria (Sasha), Ashley Gerasimovich (Claire), Ryan Hoffman (Comic), Leonardo Larocca (Dominick), William Liao (Clark), Christopher Martinez (Juan), Jackson Nicoll (Sebastian), Ursula Parker (Yvonne), Janet Passanante (DJ), Jake Schlueter (Trevor), Adam Smith Jr. (Weird Teacher), Joseph Theisen (Luke)

Jonathan Sollis in *The Stand Up* © Cinema 59

IT'S SUCH A BEAUTIFUL DAY (Bitter Films) Producer/Director/Screenplay/ Photography, Don Hertzfeldt; Editor, Brian Hamblin; Dolby; Color; Not rated; 70 minutes; Release date: September 14, 2012. Animated feature consisting of three short films: *Everything Will Be Okay* (2006), *I am So Proud of You* (2008), and *It's Such a Beautiful Day* (2012).

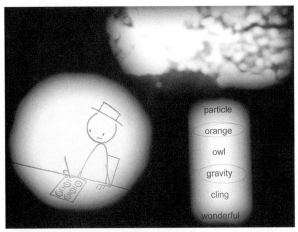

It's Such a Beautiful Day © Bitter Films

LIBERAL ARTS (IFC Films) Producers, Brice Dal Farra, Claude Dal Farra, Lauren Munsch, Jesse Hara, Josh Radnor; Executive Producers, Peter Graham, Stephen Hays, Paul Prokop; Director/Screenplay, Josh Radnor; Photography, Seamus Tierney; Designer, Jade Healy; Costumes, Deborah Newhall; Music, Ben Toth; Music Supervisor, Andy Gowan; Editor, Michael R. Miller; Casting, Suzanne Smith Crowley, Jessica Kelly, Deborah Maxwell Dion; a Strategic Motion Ventures presentation of a BCDF Pictures production in association with Tom Sawyer Entertainment; Color; Not rated; 97 minutes; Release date: September 14, 2012. **CAST:** Josh Radnor (Jesse Fisher), Elizabeth Olsen (Zibby), Richard Jenkins (Prof. Peter Hoberg), Allison Janney (Prof. Judith Fairfield), John Magaro (Dean), Elizabeth Reaser (Ana), Kate Burton (Susan), Robert Desiderio (David), Zac Efron (Nat), Kristen Bush (Leslie), Ali Ahn (Vanessa), Ned Daunis (Eric), Gregg Edelman (Robert), Michael Weston (Miles)

Elizabeth Olsen, Josh Radnor in *Liberal Arts* © IFC Films

KNUCKLEBALL! (FilmBuff) Producers, Ricki Stern, Annie Sundberg, Dan Cogan, Christine Schomer; Executive Producers, Neil Barsky, William T. Conway, Morgan Spurlock; Directors, Ricki Stern, Annie Sundberg; Photography, Charles Miller; Music, Paul Brill; Editor, Pax Wasserman; an Amelia & Theo Films presentation of a Break Thru Films Production, in association with Major League Baseball Productions, How Am I Doing Productions, New Mexico Media Partners; Color; Not rated; 93 minutes; Release date: September 18, 2012. Documentary on two Major League pitchers who continue the tradition of knuckleballing; **WITH:** R.A. Dickey, Tim Wakefield, Charlie Hough, Phil Niekro, Jim Bouton, Wilbur Wood

Knuckleball!!! © FilmBuff

RADIO UNNAMEABLE (Kino Lorber) Producers/Directors, Paul Lovelace, Jessica Wolfson; Executive Producers, P. Ellen Borowitz, MJ Glembotski, Caryl Ratner; Photography, John Pirozzi; Music, Jeffrey Lewis; Editor, Gregory Wright; a Lost Footage Films production, presented in association with Twelve O'Cock Films; Stereo; Color/black and white; HD; Not rated; 87 minutes; Release date: September 19, 2012. Documentary on influential radio personality Bob Fass; **WITH:** Margot Adler, David Amram, Steve Ben Israel, Joe Boyd, David Bromberg, Len Chandler, Simeon Coxe, Judy Collins, Robert Downey Sr., Marshall Efron, Ken Freedman, Bob Fass, Danny Goldberg, Wavy Gravy, Arlo Guthrie, Larry Josephson, Paul Krassner, Kenny Kramer, Julius Lester, Judith Malina, Ed Sanders, Steve Post, Vin Scelsa, Jerry Jeff Walker

Bob Fass in *Radio Unnameable* © Kino Lorber

186 DOLLARS TO FREEDOM (Blairwood Entertainment) a.k.a. *The City of Gardens*; Producers, Monty Fisher, Alicia Rivera Frankl; Executive Producers, Lucho Llosa, Roger Burlage, Kevan Michaels; Director, Camilo Vila; Screenplay, Monty Fisher; Photography, Henry Vargas; Designer, Fernando Gagliuffi; Costumes, Paula Vila; Editors, Richard Halsey, Coleen Halsey; Casting, Pixie Monroe; a Four Fish Films Productions presentation; Color; Not rated; 101 minutes; Release date: September 21, 2012. **CAST:** John Robinson (Wayne), Michael DeLorenzo (Gutierrez), Alex Meraz (Nicaragua), Johnny Lewis (Jorge), Grant Bowler (Jesus Christ), Deborah Kara Unger (Consul Powers), Oscar Carrillo (Luna), David Michie (Colonel Ramos), Anahí de Cárdenas (Maritza), Paul Ramirez (Israel), Coco Gutierrez (Aurelio), Gabriel Ledesma (Cornejo), Luis Alberto Urrutia (Walter), Diego Cáceres (Sergeant), Carlos Cano (Gen. Cardenas), Rafael Horna (Gustavo Mayer), Renzo Schuller (Chino), Roberto Sifuentes (Transsexual Singer)

John Robinson, Alex Meraz in *186 Dollars to Freedom*
© Blairwood Entertainment

Yoram Gross in *Blinky & Me* © Kalejdoskop Film

BACKWARDS (Dada Films/Required Viewing) Producer/Screenplay, Sarah Megan Thomas; Director, Ben Hickernell; Photography, Harlan Bosmajian; Designer, Alex Brook Lynn; Costumes, Sarah Beers; Music, David Torn; Editor, Phillip J. Bartell; Casting, Stephanie Holbrook; a 13th Night Productions, LLC presentation; Color; Rated PG; 89 minutes; Release date: September 21, 2012. **CAST**: Sarah Megan Thomas (Abi Brooks), James Van Der Beek (Geoff), Margaret Colin (Mrs. Brooks), Glenn Morshower (Coach Spriklin), Alexandra Metz (Hannah), Meredith Apfelbaum (Susan), Wynn Everett (Reba), David Alan Basche (Cox), Ellis Walding (Preston), Alysia Reiner (Meghan), Armen Badkerhanian (Bartender), Brea Bee (Giselle), Brian Cheng (Loud Cashier), Nicole Colina (Rude Waitress), Jennette Daley (Kelsey), Liz Holtan (Beth), Marceline Hugot (Mrs. Atkinson), Traci Law (Waitress), Christopher Mann (Man), Alexa Salamé (Vanessa), Michelle Santiago (Party Guest), Chuck Schanamann (Airline Agent), April Yvette Thompson (Airport Worker), Kiandra Wilshire (Coxswain), Reema Zaman (Ticket Agent)

Sarah Megan Thomas, James Van Der Beek in *Backwards* © Dada Films

BLINKY & ME (Kalejdoskop/Smoking Mirror) Producer, Janusz Slalkowski; Director/Screenplay/Editor, Tomasz Magierski; Photography, Andrzej Adamczak, Tomasz Magierski; Music, Guy Gross; Animation, Pawel Pawlicki; a Kalejdoskop Film, Smoking Mirror Productions presentation; American-Polish; Black and white/Color; Not rated; 75 minutes; Release date: September 21, 2012. Documentary on Australian animator Yoram Gross; **WITH:** Yoram Gross.

FRED WON'T MOVE OUT (Footnote Four) Producer, Ged Dickersin; Executive Producer, Joseph Infantolino; Director/Screenplay, Richard Ledes; Photography, Valentina Caniglia; Designer, Brian Rzepka; Costumes, Tere Duncan; Music, Robert Miller; Editor, Pete Street; Casting, Billy Hopkins; a Footone Four production; Color/black and white; HD; Not rated; 74 minutes; Release date: September 21, 2012. **CAST:** Elliott Gould (Fred), Fred Melamed (Bob), Stephanie Roth Haberle (Carole), Judith Roberts (Susan), Mfoniso Udofia (Victoria), Ariana Altman (Lila), Robert Miller (The Music Therapist), Richard Ledes (Bob's Friend)

Elliott Gould in *Fred Won't Move Out* © Footnote Four

DOCTORED (Jeff Hays Films/Working Pictures) formerly *Medical Inc.*; Producers, Bobby Sheehan, Jeff Hays; Director/ Screenplay/Photography, Bobby Sheehan; Music, Lucinda Bell, Paul James Riggio; Editors, Michael Caso, Erin Talgo, Robert Whitney; a Jeff Hays Films & Working Pictures in association with Submarine Deluxe presentation; Color; Not rated; 105 minutes; Release date: September 21, 2012. Documentary in support of chiropractic care.

ELECTORAL DYSFUNCTION (Trio Pictures) Producers/Directors/Screenplay, David Deschamps, Leslie D. Farrell, Bennett Singer; Executive Producer, Don Epstein; Photography, Joseph Friedman; Music, Adi Yeshaya; Editor, Jay Keuper; Animation, David Tristman, K-hwa Park; a Center for Independent Documentary presentation; Color; HD; Not rated; 90 minutes; Release date: September 21, 2012. Documentary on how America's voting system falls short; **WITH:** Mo Rocca.

Mo Rocca in *Electoral Dysfunction* © Trio Pictures

UNCONDITIONAL (Harbinger Media Partners) Producers, Jason Atkins, J. Wesley Legg; Executive Producer, Shannon Atkins; Director/Screenplay, Brent McCorkle; Photography, Michael Regalbuto; Designer, Kay Lee; Music, Mark Petrie, Brent McCorkle; Casting, Sunday Boling, Meg Morman; a Free to Love production, presented in association with Veracity Moving Pictures; Dolby; Color; PG-13; 92 minutes; Release date: September 21, 2012. **CAST:** Lynn Collins (Samantha Crawford), Michael Ealy ("Papa Joe"), Bruce McGill (Det. Miller), Kwesi Boakye (Macon), Diego Klattenhoff (Billy Crawford), Cedric Pendleton (Anthony Jones), Joanne Morgan (Mattie), Danielle Lewis (Denise), Gabriella Phillips (Keisha), Emily Rollins (Young Sam), Amanda Bailey (Medical Examiner), Michael Beasley (Manager), Jacinte Blankenship (Nurse), Steven Brown (Snuffy), Claudia Church (Emergency Room Nurse), Roger D. Eldridge (Detective), Reegus Flenory (Big Mac), John W. Gray (Murphy), William J. Harrison (Jimmy), Manon Guy, Morgan Hennum, Hannah Rollins (Students), Erik Hollander (Gunman), Sidmar Holloman (Inmate), Tarren Mason (Young Joe), Montrel Miller (Grady), Gower Mills (Prison Guard Tower Supervisor), Vernon Mitchell (Drunk Pedestrian), James D. Owens (Det. Turner), Sonny Shroyer (Pauly), Bill Stinchcomb (White Leader)

Michael Ealy in *Unconditional* © Harbinger Media

HEAD GAMES (Variance) Producers, Bruce Sheridan, Steve James; Executive Producers, Steve Devick, Anthony Athanas, Carol Quimby-Bonan, Casey Cowell, Jon Cronin, Andrew E. Filipowski, Frank Murane, Hank Neuberger, Jim O'Donovan; Director, Steve James; Based on the book by Chris Nowinski; Photography, Keith Walker, Dana Kupper; Music, Billy Corgan, Craig Snider; Editor, David E. Simpson; a Head Games the Film LLC in association with Variance Films presentation; Color; Rated PG-13; 91 minutes; Release date: September 21, 2012.

Documentary on the effects of silent concussions suffered by American athletes; **WITH:** Christopher Nowinski, Alan Schwarz, Keith Primeau, Cindy Parlow Cone, Bob Costas, Isaiah Kacyvenski, Bill Daly, Brendan Shanahan, Robert Cantu, Ann McKee, Robert Stern, Hunt Batjer, Gary Dorshimer, Ruben Echemendia, Douglas Smith, Steven Galetta, Laura Balcer, Christina Master, Eric Laudano

Head Games © Variance Films

DREDD (Lionsgate) Producers, Andrew Macdonald, Allon Reich, Alex Garland; Producers for Reliance, Jason Kingsley, Chris Kingsley; Executive Producers, Deepak Nayar, Stuart Ford, Adi Shankar; Co-Producer, Michael S. Murphey; Co-Executive Producer, Michael Elson; Director, Pete Travis; Screenplay, Alex Garland; based on the comicbook created by John Wagner and Carlos Ezquerra; Photography, Anthony Dod Mantle; Designer, Mark Digby; Costumes, Michael O'Connor, Diana Cilliers; Music, Paul Leonard-Morgan; Editor, Mark Eckersley; Special Effects Supervisors, Max Poolman, Richard Conway; Visual Effects Supervisor, Jon Thum; Casting, Denton Douglas, Kate Dowd, Sarah Halley Finn; a Lionsgate and Reliance Entertainment presentation in association with IM Global, a DNA Films production; Dolby; Widescreen; Color; 3D; Rated R; 96 minutes; Release date: September 21, 2012. **CAST:** Karl Urban (Judge Dredd), Olivia Thirlby (Cassandra Anderson), Lena Headey (Madeline Madrigal 'Ma-Ma'), Wood Harris (Kay), Langley Kirkwood (Judge Lex), Junior Singo (Amos), Luke Tyler (Freel), Jason Cope (Zwimer), Domhnall Gleeson (Clan Techie), Warrick Grier (Caleb), Rachel Wood, Patrick Lyster (Control Operators), Andile Mngadi (Passenger), Porteus Xandau Steenkamp (Driver), Emma Breschi (Hostage), Rakie Ayola (Chief Judge), Tamer Burjaq (Ma-Ma Bodyguard), Shoki Mokgapa (Woman with Child), Yohan Chun, Eden Knowles (Girls in Window), Desmond Lai Lan (Homeless Man), Deobia Oparei (Paramedic TJ), Travis Snyders, Chad Phillips (Slo-Mo Junkies), Joe Vaz (Big Joe), Scott Sparrow (Japhet), Martin Kintu (Big Joe Gang Member), Nicole Bailey (Cathy), Daniel Hadebe, Francis Chouler (Judges at Entrance), Edwin Perry (Judge Alvarez), Karl Thaning (Judge Chan), Michele Levin (Judge Kaplan).

Karl Urban, Olivia Thirlby in *Dredd* © Lionsgate

OCCUPY UNMASKED (Magnet) Producers, David N. Bossie, Dan Fleuette; Executive Producers, Andrew Breibart, Laurence Solov, Glenn Bracken Evans, Lawrence Kadish, David N. Bossie; Director/ Screenplay, Stephen K. Bannon; Photography/Editor, Kasey Kirby; Music, David Cebert; a Citizens United Productions presentation of a David N. Bossie production in association with Victory Film Group of a David N. Bossie production; Color; Not rated; 75 minutes; Release date: September 21, 2012. Documentary that attempts to find sinister motives behind the Occupy Wall Street movement; **WITH:** Andrew Breibart, Bryan Carmody, Brandon Darby, Christian Hartsock, David Horowitz, Pam Key, Mandy Nagy, Anita MonCrief, Dan Sandini, Lee Stranahan

Occupy Unmasked © Magnet Releasing

BROOKLYN BROTHERS BEAT THE BEST (Oscilloscope) Producers, Jason Michael Berman, Kwesi Collisson; Executive Producers, Ruth Mutch, Sergio Agüero, Sandra R. Berman, Thomas B. Fore, Mark G. Mathis; Director/Screenplay, Ryan O'Nan; Photography, Gavin Kelly; Designer, Ola Maslik; Costumes, Derek Sullivan; Music, Rob Simonsen, Crayon Rosary; Editor, Annette Davey; a Soaring Flight Productions in association with Tiderock Films Characters Brigade and Taggart Productions presentation; Color; Not rated; 97 minutes; Release date: September 21, 2012. **CAST:** Ryan O'Nan (Alex), Michael Weston (Jim), Arielle Kebbel (Cassidy), Melissa Leo (Sarah), Andrew McCarthy (Brian), Christopher McDonald (Jack), Jason Ritter (Kyle), Wilmer Valderrama (Jason), Jake Miller (Jackson), Charles Chu (Joe), Philip Ettinger (John John), Steven Boyer (Fibber), Charlie Hewson (Tibber), Carolyn Barrett (Mother), Christina Blithe (Biker Chick), Teena Byrd, Tanya Davis(Goth Groupies), Cori Dioquino (Frat Party Girl), Joy Gohring (Jim's Drunk Date), Caleb J. Jackson (Security), Anthony Keating (Goth), Amber Nelson (Smoker), Bobby Rickert (Drummer), Douglas Watson (Grandpa)

Ryan O'Nan, Michael Weston in *Brooklyn Brothers Beat the Best*
© Oscilloscope Laboratories

ABOUT CHERRY (IFC Midnight) Producers, Liz Destro, Jordan Kessler, Rick Dugdale, Elana Krausz, Taylor Phillips; Executive Producer, Bendrix Bailey; Director, Stephen Elliott; Screenplay, Stephen Elliott, Lorelei Lee; Photography, Darren Genet; Designer, Michael Grasley; Music, Jeff Russo; Editor, Michelle Botticelli; an IFC Midnight, Enderby Entertainment, Kink.com and Visualiner presentation; Dolby; Color; Rated R; 102 minutes; Release date: September 21, 2012. **CAST:** Ashley Hinshaw (Angelina), Lili Taylor (Phyllis), Dev Patel (Andrew), Diane Farr (Jillian), Jonny Weston (Bobby), James Franco (Frances), Heather Graham (Margaret), Maya Donato (JoJo), Vincent Palo (Paco), Elana Krausz (Lana), Lorelei Lee (Sophie), K.Lee (Sweet), Michael Torres (PO), Robert Nelson (Officer), Viva Celso (Viva Nova), Cully Fredricksen, Donald Lacy Jr. (Pool Players), Leo Galelan McKeown Hickel, James Cotton (Bartenders), Nkechi (Tanya), Ernest Waddell (Vaughn), Sarah Curtiss (Brande), Ben Simonetti (Miller), Nelson Lee (Jessica), Megan Boone (Jake), Karyn Hunt (Karyn), Jordan Kessler (Paul), Momo Juniper Hurley (Evany), Mike Bessoni (Chuck), Melissa Tan (Chellis), Tom McGraw (Customer #1), Darryl Fong, Dennis Smith (Men), Amy Huckabay (Sheila), Patrick Alparone (Rudy), Dan Weiss (Danny), Tim Weiss (Danny), Tim Lewis (Duke), Peter Alton (Director #3), Windy Chien (Audrey), Ricky Saenz, Mark Silversten (Workers), Peter Kepler (Co-Worker), Tristin Hagen (Girl #1), Andy Miller (Manager), Veronica Valencia (Amber), Sensi Pearl (Vicki), Nina Ljeti (Nina), Sean Thomas (Waiter), Alexa Inkeles (Terra), Isaac Fitzgerald (Mike)

Ashley Hinshaw, James Franco in *About Cherry* © IFC Midnight

MY UNCLE RAFAEL (Slater Brothers Entertainment) Producers, Michael Garrity, Vahik Pirhamzei; Executive Producers, Anahid Avanesian, Randy Simon, Todd Slater; Director/Editor, Marc Fusco; Screenplay, Scott Yagemann, Vahik Pirhamzei; based on characters from the play *Rafael Qeroo Gandzere* by Vahik Pirhamzei; Photography, Keith Holland; Designer, David Storm; Costumes, Kelli Jones; Music, Joey Newman, Chris Westlake; Casting, Dorian Frankel; a World Entertainment Connections and Slater Brothers Entertainment presentation of a Nickel Palace Production in association with Richmond Media Entertainment; Color; HD; Rated PG-13; 103 minutes; Release date: September 21, 2012. **CAST:** John Michael Higgins (Damon), Missi Pyle (Blair), Vahik Pirhamzei (Rafael/ Hamo), Anthony Clark (Jack), Rachel Blanchard (Michele), Carly Chaikin (Kim), Tadeh Amirian (Robo), Anahid Avanesian (Linda), Austin Robert Butler (Cody Beck), Giovanni Cirfiera (Pietro), Amanda Leigh Cobb (Angela), Fred Cross (Sam), Arthur Darbinyan (Vardan), Brooke Dillman (Francine Lamb), Yvonne Farrow (Principal Dorothy Johnson), Lafe Jordan (Mr. Wang's Son), Matt Kelley (Humbled Man), Joe Lo Truglio (Father Jim), Lupe Ontiveros (Mrs. Gonzales), Mila McConaughey (Megan), Malina Moye (Vogel's Secretary), Erica Piccininni (Mariella), Ellington Ratliff (Photographer), Sage Ryan (Beau), Keri Safan (Tina), Oren Skoog (Skoogs), Ursula Taherian (Helen), Samir Younis (Sevak), Jason D. Avalos (Groom's Guest)

Vahik Pirhamzei in *My Uncle Rafael* © Slater Brothers

THE WAITING ROOM (Intl. Film Circuit) Producers, Linda Davis, Peter Nicks, William B. Hirsch; Executive Producers, Scott Verges, Sally Jo Fifer; Director/Photography, Peter Nicks; Music, William Ryan Fritch; Editor, Lawrence Lerew; an ITVS in association with Peer Review Films presentation; Color; HD; Not rated; 83 minutes; Release date: September 26, 2012. Documentary on the struggle to provide healthcare to uninsured Americans; **WITH:** Demia Bruce, Eric Morgan, Davelo Lujuan, Carl Connelly, Barbara Johnson, Cynthia Y. Johnson, Dr. Douglas White, Liz Lynch, Matthew Rehrer, Amandeep Singh, Aaron Harries, Jocelyn Garrick, Ricka White-Soso

Cynthia Y. Johnson in The Waiting Room © Intl. Film Circuit

MY LIFE AS ABRAHAM LINCOLN (Four Reel Films) Producer/Director/Screenplay/Editor, Shari Berman; Photography, Chris Benker; Music, Ken Lampl; a Saberman … Too production; Color; Not rated; 91 minutes; Release date: September 28, 2012. **CAST:** Caroline Luft (Cindy), Gerry Birnbach (Calvin/Psychiatrist), Jennifer Lynn Malloy (Holly), Trevor Nelson (Fiancé/Man #275), Leisha Shorey (Sophie), Wendy Taylor (Michele), Jason Steffan (George), Brandon DeSpain (Larry), Jerry Rago (Paulie), Takumi Mitobe (John), Erzen Krivca (Photographer/Detective/Seth), Colleen Cosgrove (Mother/Receptionist), Stewart Schneck (Albert), Peter Zerneck (Barry), Corinne Callahan (Young Cindy), Kimberly Ann Maguire (Young Holly), Catherine Melillo (Young Michele), Lindsey Wales (Young Sophie), Ryan Cody Connor (Young Barry), Russell Kahn (Young Michael), John Kovaleski (Waiter), Brian Guillaudeu (Friend/Man in Mask)

THE OTHER DREAM TEAM (The Film Arcade) Producers, Jon Weinbach, Marius Markevicius; Director, Marius Markevicius; Screenplay, Marius Markevicius, Jon Weinbach; Photography, Jesse Feldman; Music, Dustin O'Halloran; Editor, Dan Marks; Animation, Jeff Goelz; The Basketball Future Foundation in association with Sorrento Productions and Berliner 76 Entertainment presentation; American-Lithuanian; Color; Not rated; 89 minutes;

Release date: September 28, 2012. Documentary on how the Lithuanian basketball team triumphed at the 1992 Olympics; **WITH:** Valdas Adamkus, Kim Bohuny, Jouzas Butrimas, P.J. Carlesimo, Valdemaras Chomicius, Chad Ford, Fran Fraschilla, Vladas Garastas, Mickey Hart, Žydrunas Ilgauskas, Sergéjus Jovaiša, Arturas Karnišovas, Rimas Kurtinaitis, Jim Lampley, Vytautas Landsbergis, Dan Majerle, Šarunas Marciulionis, Dennis McNally, Chris Mullin, Donnie Nelson, Arturas Povillionas, David Remnick, Mitch Richmond, Arvydas Sabonis, Tommy Sheppard, Charles Smith, Greg Speirs, David Stern, Jonas Valanciunas, Danuté Valancuinas, Alexander Volkov, Bill Walton, Alexander Wolff

The Other Dream Team © The Film Arcade

THE IRAN JOB (Paladin) Producers, Sara Nodjoumi, Till Schauder; Executive Producer, Abigail Disney; Director/Screenplay/Photography, Till Schauder; Music, Kareem Roustom; Editor, David Teague; a Fork Films presentation; Color; Not rated; 90 minutes; Release date: September 28, 2012. Documentary on how pro basketball player Kevin Sheppard signed with an Iranian Super League team; **WITH:** Kevin Sheppard, Leah Sheppard, Laleh, Elaheh, Hilda, Zoran "Z" Milicic, Kami Jamshidvand, Ali Doraghi, Mehdi Shirjang, Gholamreza Khajeh, Asadollah Kabir, Fereidoon Reisi, Mohammad Ahmadi

Kevin Sheppard in *The Iran Job* © Paladin

BEARCITY 2: THE PROPOSAL (TLA Releasing) Producers, Tracy Utley, Jim A, Landé, Henry White; Executive Producers, Henry White, David Stephen Martin, Jim A. Landé; Director/Screenplay/Editor, Doug Langway; Photography, Michael Hauer; Art Director, Alexandra Schaller; Costumes, Lydia Popper; Music, Peter Calandra; Casting, Anne Teutschel; a Sharpleft Studios production; Color; Not rated; 101 minutes; Release date: September 28, 2012. **CAST:** Gerald McCullouch (Roger Beam), Joe Conti (Tyler Hall), Stephen Guarino (Brent), Brian Keane (Fred), Gregory Gunter (Michael), James Martinez (Carlos), Alex Di Dio (Simon) Aaron Tone (Nate), Blake Evan Sherman (Melvin), Susan Mosher (Rachel), Jason Stuart (Scott-O), Richard Riehle (Gabe), Kathy Najimy (Rose), Kevin Smith, Mike Ruiz, Frank DeCaro, Mark Caruso, Dan Choi, Justin Elzie, Tawny Heatherton (Themselves), Peter Finland (Ken), Jeffery Roberson (Varla Jean Merman), Will Bethencourt (Jack), Spyridon Boviatsos (Cristos), Nathan Butera (Dean), Frank Liotti (Reggie), J. Andrew Mullins (Jimmy), Johnny Skandros (Johnny), Matthew Vecera (Gary), Robert Hollenbeck Jr. (Warren), Paul Romero (Pat), T. Doyle Leverett (Big Dan), Jesse Leonard (James), Andrew Criss (Jake), David Stephen Martin (Sam), Patrick Spike (Steve), Jonny Mack (Ted), Ken Kleiber (Coat Check Checker), Steven Stein-Grainger (Cole), Sam Kite (Ray), Jack Bethke (Randy), Mike Benford (Dave), Shawn Patrick Hunt (Ryno), Don Regan (Ron), Joe Scibetta (Chef), Mike Flanagan (Bouncer), Eric Peterson (Denny), Christopher MacDow (Masseuse), Stephen Lambeth (Tim), Steve Zuley (Bruce), Tim Hooper (Jay), Brad Allison (Beach Party Bear)

Gerald McCullouch, Joe Conti in *BearCity 2* © TLA Releasing

HARVEST OF EMPIRE (SnagFilms) Producers, Wendy Thompson-Marquez, Eduardo López; Directors, Peter Getzels, Eduardo López; Based on the 2001 book *Harvest of Empire: A History of Latinos in America* by Juan González; Photography, James M. Felter; Music, Lenny Williams, Chris Biondo; Editor, Catherine Shields; an Onyx Films, EVS Communications, Loquito Productions presentation, in association with Getzels Gordon Productions; Color; Not rated; 90 minutes; Release date: September 28, 2012. Documentary on how the U.S. intervention in Latin America has had a direct effect on immigration.

STARS IN SHORTS (Shorts HD) Producers, Carter Pilcher, Leif Nelson; a Shorts HD production; American-British; Color; Not rated; 113 minutes; Release date: September 28, 2012. **7 Short Films:** *The Procession:* Producers, Tatiana Kelly, Roberta Munroe; Director/Screenplay, Robert Festinger; **CAST:** Lily Tomlin (Mom), Jesse Tyler Ferguson (Jason), Lucy Punch (Julie); *Steve:* Producers, Rupert Friend, Jess Cole, Rachel Kennedy, Anthony Haas; Director/Screenplay, Rupert Friend; **CAST:** Colin Firth (Steve), Keira Knightley (Woman), Tom Mison (Man); *Not Your Time:* Producers, Dawn Bridgewater, James L. Honore, Reggie Joseph, Jay Kamen, Marjorie Mann; Director/Screenplay, Jay Kamen; **CAST:** Jason Alexander (Sid Rosenthal), Valarie Pettiford (Angel of Death), Kathy Najimy (Sid's Mother), Sally Kirkland (Madame Ulaila), Jillian Armenante (Debbie), James Avery (Haig), Jesse Burch (Harold), Sean Patrick Flaherty (Young Sid), Jameson Moss (Teenage Sid), Jack Rapke, Sandahl Bergman, Chris Buck, Amy Pascal, Sidney Ganis, Justin Ross, Joe Roth, Ron Dennis, Amy Heckerling,

Stuart Cornfeld, Neal Israel, Laurence Mark, Demetrios Skodras (Themselves); *Sexting:* Producer, Tim Harms; Director/Screenplay, Neil LaBute; **CAST:** Julia Stiles (Young Woman), Marin Ireland (Wife), Jamie Anderson (Other Woman); *Prodigal:* Producers, Benjamin Grayson, Trenton Waterson; Director, Benjamin Grayson; Screenplay, Benjamin Grayson, Travis Crim; **CAST:** Kenneth Branagh (Mark Snow), Jennifer Morrison (Agent Rachel Mintz), Jade Pettyjohn (Samantha O'Neill), Travis Crim (David O'Neill), Taylor Kinney (Brad Searcy), Winter Ave Zoli (Angela O'Neill), Annie Baria (Server), Spencer Kelly (Valet), Josh Latzer (Manager), Daniel Pittack (Mechanic); *After-School Special:* Producer, Andrew Carlberg; Director, Jacob Chase; Screenplay, Neil LaBute; **CAST:** Sarah Paulson (Woman), Wes Bentley (Man), Sam Cohen (Boy), Moira O'Nan (Man's Daughter); *Friend Request Pending:* Producer, Chris Croucher; Director, Chris Foggin; **CAST:** Judi Dench (Mary), Penny Ryder (Linda), Philip Jackson (Trevor), Tom Hiddleston (Tom), John MacMillan (Jason), Andrew Dee Jones (Club Dancer)

Lily Tomlin, Jesse Tyler Ferguson in *Stars in Shorts* © Shorts HD

AMERICAN AUTUMN: AN OCCUDOC (Occudoc.org) Producer/Director/ Screenplay/ Narrator, Douglas Trainor Jr.; Executive Producer, Peggy Kimble; Photography, Kevin Egan, Asher Platts, Douglas Trainor Jr.; Music, Goldi, Mike Lawrence-Yannicelli; Editors, AJ Russo, Douglas Trainor Jr.; an Artful Dodger production; Color; HD; Not rated; 75 minutes; Release date: September 28, 2012. Documentary on the on-going "Occupy Wall Street" movement; **WITH:** Leah Bolger, Lee Camp, Jackie De Salvo, Margaret Flowers, Katie Goodman, Naomi Klein, Michael Moore, Nathan Schneider, Debora Sweet, Douglas Trainor Jr., Vlad Tiechberg, Cornel West

American Autumn: An Occudoc © Occudoc.org

BRINGING UP BOBBY (Monterey Media) Producers, Sofia Sondervan, Famke Janssen; Executive Producers, Phil Hunt, Compton Ross David, Maryann Johndrow, Chad Burris Steve, Renee Knox, Cole Frates; Director/Screenplay, Famke Janssen; Photography, Guido Van Gennep; Designer, Dina Goldman; Costumes, Hala Bahmet; Music, Tom Holkenborg; Editor, Job Ter Burg; a Bankside

Films presentation of a Dutch Tilt Film and EHS Production in association with Head Gear Films, Metrol Technology, Fu Works and Rinkel Film; American-Dutch-British; Dolby; Color; Rated PG-13; 93 minutes; Release date: September 28, 2012. **CAST:** Milla Jovovich (Olive), Bill Pullman (Kent), Marcia Cross (Mary), Rory Cochrane (Walt), Spencer List (Bobby), Renata Batista (Maid), Justin Hall (Jamie), Ray Prewitt (Chuck Lee Buck), Lauren Analla (Darlene), Dan Corley (Tommy Lee Jones), Dalton Olive (Earl), Eric Starkey (John Lewis III), Brandon E. Jackson (Insurance Agent), Ana Anderson (Det. Winters), Paul Dietz, Robin Brooks (Teachers), Deedra Jordon (Doctor), Molly Reilly (Nurse), Sanford Kelly (Kent's Driver, Gerry), Jane Hall (Carol, Secretary), Braden Fowler (Sam), Harry Falter (Policeman), Milton Killen (Man in Parking Lot), Clayton Ingmire, Max Gonzales (Kids), Don Kruzinga (Car Salesman), Cary Hawkins (Young Salesman), Venice Del Valle (Cleaning Lady), Christopher Townsend (Undercover Cop)

Spencer List, Milla Jovovich in *Bringing Up Bobby* © Monterey Media

PRIMUM NON NOCERE: FIRST - DO NO HARM (Asia Geographic) Producer/Director, James Reynolds; Music Supervisor, Stefano Conticello; Editor, Jason Sievert; Color; Not rated; 108 minutes; Release date: September 28, 2012. Documentary on the numerous health risks associated with blood transfusions; **WITH:** Aryeh Shander, Pierre Tibi, Jonathan H. Waters, Dame Marcela Contreras, Bruce D. Spiess, Jonathan S. Stamler, Alice Maniatis, Konrad Messmer, Colonel John Holcomb, Kathleen Sazama, David Gozzard, Sherri Ozawa, Scott A. Scheinin, Simon Towler, Vitaly Slepoushkin, Nathaniel I. Usoro, Richard Daniel, Ken Kipnis, Danilo Kuizon, Gonzalo Cardemil Herrera, Deb Tabert, Qiang Shu, Shunji Kawamoto, Sundar Sankaran, Manish Samson

THE YAKUZA AND THE MERMAID (Four Reel Films) Producer/Director/ Screenplay/ Photography/Editor, Chris Benker; Music, Brian Lease; Color; Not rated; 101 minutes; Release date: September 28, 2012. **CAST:** Peter Hertsgaard (The Writer), Georgiana Avram (The Mermaid), Takumi Mitobe (The Yakuza), Ikuko Ikari (The Girl), Jennifer Malloy (Peggy), Caroline Luft (Lori), Bob Connelly (Werner), Robert Field (Werner's Lawyer), Gerry Birnbach (Jason), Jerry Rago (Patrick), Erzen Krivca, Brandon deSpain (Janitors/Assassins), Patranila Jefferson (Nightclub Singer), Donna Gentry (Edie), David Etkin, Abdul Stone Jackson, Jason Maran (Sushi Diners), Michael Mazzeo (Sushi Bouncer), Ayako Misawa, Aiko Ishikawa, Kaori Ibuki, Allan Fong (Gang Members), Steve Briante, Cynthia Schwartz (Bartenders)

NOW, FORAGER (Argot Pictures) Producers, Julia Halperin, Kit Bland; Directors, Jason Cortlund, Julia Halperin; Screenplay, Jason Cortland; Photography, Jonathan Nastasi; Music, Chris Brokaw; Editor, Julia Halperin; a Small Drama production; American-Polish; Stereo; Color; HD; Not rated; 93 minutes; Release date: October 3, 2012. **CAST:** Jason Cortlund (Lucien Echevarría), Tiffany Esteb (Regina Echevarría), Gabrielle Maisels (April Garrison), Almex Lee (Mas), Tom Cherwin (Fisherman), Marty Clarke (Babe), Brandon deSpain (Lev), Jason Howard

(Clark Garrison), Roberta Kirshbaum (Loli), Alex Mayzlin (Sergei), Nicholas Mikovich (Francesca Garrison), Sabrina Morand (Hanna), Nick Raio (Little Johnnie), T. Guava Sands (Sammy), Eric Dean Scott (Duncan), Kim Weiler (Marili)

Jason Cortlund in *Now, Forager* © Argot Pictures

GIVE UP TOMORROW (Thoughtful Robot) Producer, Marty Syjuco; Executive Producers, Ramona Diaz, Eric Daniel Metzgar; Director, Michael Collins; Screenplay, Michael Collins, Eric Daniel Metzgar, Marty Syjuco; Photographer, Michael Collins, Joshua Z. Weinstein; Music, Adam Crystal; Editor, Eric Daniel Metzgar; an Independent Television Service production in association with the BBC and the Sundance Documentary Film Program; American-British; Color; HD; Not rated; 95 minutes; Release date: October 1, 2012. Documentary on how Paco Larranaga was wrongly convicted of the rape and murder of a young woman in 1997; **WITH:** Paco Larrañaga, Mimi Larrañaga, Thelma Chiong, Solita Monsod, Manuel Larrañaga, Margo Larrañaga, Leo Lastimosa, Suzzanne Salva, Pablo Labra, Napoleon Estilles, Teresa Galanida

Give up Tomorrow © Thoughtful Robot

JUST 45 MINUTES FROM BROADWAY (Rainbow) Producer, Rosemary Marks; Director/ Screenplay, Henry Jaglom; Photography, Hanania Baer; Art Director, Tobias Mehler; Costumes, Cynthia Obsenares; Editor, Ron Vignone; The Rainbow Film Company; Color; Not rated; 106 minutes; Release date: October 3, 2012. **CAST:** Tanna Frederick (Pandora Isaacs), Judd Nelson (James Archer), Julie Davis (Betsy Isaacs), Jack Heller (George Isaacs), David Proval (Larry Cooper), Diane Salinger (Viviene Cooper Isaacs), Harriet Schock (Sally Brooks), Michael Emil (Uncle Misha), Mary Crosby (Sharon Cooper), Emily Alexander (Linda Lewis), Linda Carson (Aunt Karla), Sabrina Jaglom (Judy Cooper), Simon Orson Jaglom (Willy Lewis), Jack Quaid (Danny), Eliza Roberts (Aunt Kit), Peter Townend (Barry Lewis)

Judd Nelson, Tanna Frederick in *Just 45 Minutes from Broadway*
© Rainbow Film Co.

THE PROSECUTION OF AN AMERICAN PRESIDENT (Lost Soldier Films) Producer, Jim Shaban; Executive Producers, Peter Miller, Nathan Folks, Channsin Berry; Directors, David J. Burke, Dave Hagen; Screenplay, Vincent Bugliosi, based on his 2008 book *The Prosecution of George W. Bush for Murder*; Photography, Francis Kenny; Music, Kenneth Lampl; Editors, David Hagen, Brian Singbiel; a Naftc Studios presentation of a Lost Soldier Films production; Color; Not rated; 101 minutes; Release date: October 5, 2012. Documentary on former prosecutor Vincent Bugliosi's contention that George W. Bush should be prosecuted for the murders of over 4,000 soldiers killed during the Iraq War; **WITH:** Vincent Bugliosi, Elizabeth de la Vega, Alan Dershowitz, Alan Ides.

BUTTER (Radius-TWC) Producers, Michael De Luca, Jennifer Garner, Alissa Phillips; Executive Producers, Bob Weinstein, Harvey Weinstein, Kelly Carmichael, Juliana James, Benjamin Ormand; Director, Jim Field Smith; Screenplay, Jason Micallef; Photography, Jim Denault; Designer, Tony Fanning; Costumes, Susie DeSanto; Music, Mateo Messina; Music Supervisor, Dana Sano; Editors, Dan Schalk, Matt Garner; Casting, Carmen Cuba; a Michael DeLuca/Vandalia Films production; Dolby; Super 35 Widescreen; Color; Rated R; 90 minutes; Release date: October 5, 2012. **CAST:** Jennifer Garner (Laura Pickler), Ty Burrell (Bob Pickler), Olivia Wilde (Brooke Sinkowski), Rob Corddry (Ethan Emmet), Ashley Greene (Kaitlen Pickler), Alicia Silverstone (Julie Emmet), Yara Shahidi (Destiny), Hugh Jackman (Boyd Bolton), Kristen Schaal (Carol-Ann Stevenson), Pruitt Taylor Vince (Ned Eaten), Phyllis Smith (Nancy), Dodie Brown (June Carmichael), Mark Oliver (Martin Caswell), Ted Ferguson (The Minister), Corena Chase (Mrs. Schram), Cindy Creekmore (Danielle Mattingly), Rachel Greene (Miss Daisy), Betsy Lou Holt), Robin McGree (Clerk), Keri Shahidi (Biological Mother), Garrett Schenck (Orval Flanagan), Brett Hill (Hayden), Kelly Tippens (Mrs. Moore), Jennifer Benton (Car Buyer), Rj Hanson (Technician), Judy Leavell (Helen), Andrew Daly (Radio Announcer)

Jennifer Garner in *Butter* © Radius-WTC

DECODING DEEPAK (SnagFilms) Producers, Gotham Chopra, Scott Carlin, Mark Rinehart, Josh Soskin; Executive Producers, Emilio Diez Barroso, Darlene Caamaño Loquet; Director/ Screenplay, Gotham Chopra; Photography, Mark Rinehart; Music, Huma Human; Editor, Julian Robinson; a NALA Films production; Color; Not rated; 74 minutes; Release date: October 5, 2012. Documentary on spiritual self-help guru Deepak Chopra; **WITH:** Deepak Chopra, Gotham Chopra.

Deepak Chopra, Gotham Chopra in *Decoding Deepak* © SnagFilms

HOLD YOUR BREATH (The Asylum) Producer, David Michael Latt; Executive Producer, David Rimawi; Director, Jared Cohn; Screenplay, Geoff Meed; Story, Kenny Zinn; Photography, Stuart Brereton; Designer, Sabine Asanger; Costumes, Nicole Katherine Mamuzich; Music, Chris Ridenhour; Editor, Bobby K. Richardson; a Global Asylum production; Dolby; Color; Rated R; 87 minutes; Release date: October 5, 2012. **CAST:** Katrina Bowden (Jerry), Randy Wayne (Johnny), Erin Marie Hogan (Natasha), Steve Hanks (McBride), Josh Allen (Young McBride), Brad Slaughter (Tony), Seth Cassell (Kyle), Darin Cooper (Warden Wilkes), Jordan Pratt-Thatcher (Heath), Lisa Younger (Samantha), Keith Allen (Van Hausen), Devanny Pinn (Woman with Scar), Natalie Sterling (Scar Woman's Sister), Gerald Webb (Park Ranger), Alex Ball (Burly Guard #2), John Marsch, Michael Sadler (Victim's Family Members), Quillian Hightower, Erik Monrad (Press)

Jordan Pratt-Thatcher, Erin Marie Hogan in *Hold Your Breath* © The Asylum

V/H/S (Magnet) Producers, Gary Binkow, Brad Miska, Roxanne Benjamin; Executive Producers, Tom Owen, Zak Zeman; Anthology Concept, Brad Miska; The Collective in association with Bloody Disgusting; Dolby; Color; Rated R; 115 minutes; Release date: October 5, 2012. *Tape 56:* Producers, Simon Barrett, Kim Sherman; Director/Editor, Adam Wingard; Screenplay, Simon Barrett; **CAST:** Calvin Reeder (Gary), Lane Hughes (Zak), Kentucker Audley (Rox), Adam Wingard (Brad), Frank Stack (Old Man), Sarah Byrne (Abbey), Melissa Boatright

(Tabitha), Simon Barrett (Steve), Andrew Droz Palermo (5th Thug); *Amateur Night:* Producers, Linda Burns, David Bruckner; Director, David Bruckner; Screenplay, David Bruckner, Nicholas Tecosky; **CAST:** Hannah Fierman (Lily), Mike Donlan (Shane), Joe Sykes (Patrick), Drew Sawyer (Clint), Jas Sams (Lisa), Nicholas Tecosky (Bartender), Rob Mosca (Bouncer), Lisa Marie Thomas (Lisa's Friend), Sunita Patel & Family (Motel Office Staff), Elizabeth Davidovich, Kat Slatery (Walking Girls); *Second Honeymoon:* Producers, Peter Phok, Ti West; Director/Screenplay, Ti West; **CAST:** Joe Swanberg (Sam), Sophia Takal (Stephanie), Kate Lyn Sheil (Girl), Graham Reznick (Local DJ); *Tuesday the 17th:* Producers, Glenn McQuaid, Lee Nussbaum; Director/Screenplay, Glenn McQuaid; **CAST:** Norma C. Quinones (Wendy), Drew Moerlein (Joey), Jeannine Yoder (Samantha), Jason Yachanin (Spider), Bryce Burke (The Glitch), Jennifer Sacks (Victim by Wall), Glenn McQuaid (Victim in River); *The Sick Thing That Happened to Emily When She Was Younger:* Producers, Simon Barrett, Joe Swanberg; Director, Joe Swanberg; Screenplay, Simon Barrett; **CAST:** Helen Rogers (Emily), Daniel Kaufman (James), Liz Harvey (The New Girl), Isaiah Hillman, Corrie Lynne Fitzpatrick, Taliyah Hillman (Little Girl Alien); *10/31/98:* Producers/Directors/Screenplay, Radio Silence (Matt Bettinelli-Olpin, Tyler Gillett, Justin Martinez, Chad Villella); **CAST:** Chad Villella (Chad), Matt Bettinelli-Olpin (Matt), Tyler Gillett (Tyler), Paul Natonek (Paul), Nicole Erb (The Girl), John Walcutt (Cult Leader), Bilal Mir, Damion Stephens, Koz McCrae (Cult Dudes), Eric Curtis (Roommate), Nicole Boccumini (Niky), Melinda Fleming (Melinda)

Escape Fire © Roadside Attractions

Fame High © Black Valley Films

Calvin Reeder in V/H/S © Magnet Releasing

ESCAPE FIRE: THE FIGHT TO RESCUE AMERICAN HEALTH CARE (Roadside Attractions) Producers/Directors, Matthew Heineman, Susan Froemke; Executive Producer, Doug Scott; Photography, Wolfgang Held; Music, Chad Kelly, Moby; Editor, Bradley J. Ross; an Aisle C Productions & Our Time Projects production; American-Chinese-German; Color; Rated PG-13; 99 minutes; Release date: October 5, 2012. Documentary on America's faulty health care system; **WITH:** Dr. Don Berwick, Shannon Brownlee, Steve Burd, Gen. David Fridovich, Dr. Wayne Jonas, Roy Litton, Dr. Erin Martin, Dr. Steve Nissen, Dr. Dean Ornish, Yvonne Osborn, Wendell Potter, Dr. Andrew Weil, Sgt. Robert Yates

FAME HIGH (Black Valley Films) Producers, Leilani Makuakane Potter, Scott Hamilton Kennedy; Executive Producers, Rick Rosenthal, Chip Rosenbloom, Leilani Makuakane Potter, Scott Hamilton Kennedy; Director/Photography, Scott Hamilton Kennedy; Music, Doug DeAngelis; Editors, Jillian Moul, Scott Hamilton Kennedy; Presented in association with Whitewater Films; Color; Not rated; 101 minutes; Release date: October 5, 2012. Documentary on one school year at Los Angeles County High School for the Arts.

JANEANE FROM DES MOINES (Wilsilu Pictures) Producers/Screenplay, Grace Lee, Jane Edith Wilson; Executive Producer, Chip Rosenbloom; Director, Grace Lee; Photography, Jerry A. Henry; Music, Ceiri Torjussen; Editor, Aldo Velasco; Presented in association with Open Pictures; Stereo; Color; Not rated; 78 minutes; Release date: October 5, 2012. Documentary on ultra-conservative Iowa housewife and political activist Janeane (Jane Edith) Wilson; **WITH:** Janeane Wilson, Diane Sawyer, David Muir, Mitt Romney, Ralph Reed, Herman Cain, Newt Gingrich, Rick Santorum, Michele Bachmann, Pastor Jeff Mullen, Pastor Tom Allen, Ron Paul, Anita Perry, Rick Perry; **AND:** Michael Oosterom (Fred Wilson), Mary Manofsky (Bible Study Leader), Melanie Merkosky (Lissi), Mark Fite (Janeane's Brother), Cheryl Elizabeth Grant (Tara), Maile Flanagan (Amy), Cindy Drummond, Nosmo King (Friends in Park), Jennifer Courtney (Janeane's Boss), Sam Riegel (Sam), Loretta Fox (Doctor)

TRADE OF INNOCENTS (Monterey Media) Producers, William Bolthouse, Laurie Bolthouse, Jim Schmidt; Executive Producer, Dave Ross; Director/Screenplay, Christopher Bessette; Photography, Philip Hurn; Designer, Mona Nahm; Costumes, Chantika Kongsillawat; Music, Timothy Hosman; Editor, Diane Robb; Casting, Beverly Holloway; Presented in association with Dean River Productions; American-Thai; Color; Rated PG-13; 91 minutes; Release date: October 5, 2012. **CAST:** Dermot Mulroney (Alex Becker), Mira Sorvino (Claire Becker), John Billingsley (Malcolm Eddery), Sahajak Boonthanakit (Police Chief Pakkadey), Trieu Tran (Duke), Guzjung Pitakporntrakul (Lie-U), Tanapol Chuksrida (Brothel Man), Saichia Wongwirot, Kecha Khamphakdee (Brothel Thugs), ithaya Pansringarm (Nath), Jonathan James Isgar (Stan), Teerawat Mulvilai (Kosal), Oak Keerati Sivakuae (Thanh Le), James Tang (Police Translator), Jan Yousagoon (Sophea), Xanny Disjad (Be), Deedee Kumphasee (Chantra), Fah Nilratsirikul (Tuyen), Thawanrat Tantituvanont (Amy), Ashlyn Bellamy (Abigail Becker), Tharinee Thaima (Kim Ly's Mother)

Dermot Mulroney in *Trade of Innocents* © Monterey Media

FAT KID RULES THE WORLD (ARC Entertainment) Producers, Rick Rosenthal, Nick Norton, Matthew Lillard, Jane Charles, Jennifer Mass, Evan Hoyt Wasserstrom, Talan C. Torriero; Director, Matthew Lillard; Screenplay, Michael M.B. Galvin, Peter Speakman; Based upon the 2004 novel by K.L. Going; Photography, Noah M. Rosenthal; Designer, Tania Kupczak; Costumes, Ashley Russell; Music, Mike McCready; Music Supervisor, Sandy Wilson; Editor, Michelle M. Witten; Casting, Jennifer Ricchiazzi; a Whitewater Films production in association with Whippany Park Productions and Buffalo Bulldog Films, Inc.; Color; Rated R; 96 minutes; Release date: October 5, 2012. **CAST:** Jacob Wysocki (Troy), Matt O'Leary (Marcus), Billy Campbell (Mr. Billings), Lili Simmons (Isabel), Dylan Arnold (Dayle), Sean Donavan (Ollie), Jeffrey Doornbos (Mr. Sherman), Vivan Dugré (Victoria), Julian Gavilanes (Matt), Russell Hodgkinson (Marcus's Stepfather), Brian Sutherland (Dino), Tyler Trerise (Manoj), Megan Day, Devon Nichols, Lorin Prangley, Vanessa Prangley (Band Groupies), Jeannine Johnson (Megan's Roommate), Heidi Korndorffer (Hot Chick), Keri Owen (Girl at Counter), Stephanie Sarreal Park (Girl #1)

Matt O'Leary, Jason Wysocki in *Fat Kid Rules the World* © ARC Entertainment

AN AFFAIR OF THE HEART (Films Transit International) Producers, Sylvia Caminer, Melanie Lentz-Janney; Executive Producers, Melanie Lentz-Janney, Dancy Myers; Director, Sylvia Caminer; Photography, Douglas Bachman; Editor, David Dean; a Yellow Rick Road Productions, Dolger Films, Doverwood Communications production; Color; Not rated; 94 minutes; Release date: October 10, 2012. Documentary on musician-songwriter-actor Rick Springfield; **WITH:** Rick Springfield, Jill Antipas, Steve Antipas, Laurie Bennett, Linda Blair, JoAnn Camporeale, Doug Davidson, Rev. Kate Dennis, Sue DeVita, Corey Feldman, Mark Goodman, Dustin Walker, Jacklyn Zeman.

Rick Springfield in *An Affair of the Heart* © Films Transit Intl.

GAYBY (Wolfe) Producers, Amy Hobby, Anne Hubbell; Executive Producers, Zeke Farrow, Laura Hebberton; Director/Screenplay, Jonathan Lisecki; Photography, Clay Liford; Designer, Cat Navarro; Costumes, David Tabbert; Music, Giancarlo Vulcano; Editor, Ann Husaini; a Hubbhobb presentation; Color; HD; Not rated; 89 minutes; Release date: October 12, 2012. **CAST:** Jenn Harris (Jenn), Matthew Wilkas (Matt), Mike Doyle (Scott), Jonathan Lisecki (Nelson), Jack Ferver (Jamie), Anna Margaret Hollyman (Kelly), Louis Cancelmi (Louis), Alycia Delmore (Linda), Dulé Hill (Adam), Charlie Barnett (Daniel), Joanne Tucker (Valerie), Sarita Choudhury (Dr. Ushma), Adam Driver (Neil), Zach Shaffer (Tom), Christian Coulson (Arron), Alex Karpovsky (Peter), Samanthan Buck (Sophia), Victoire Charles (Maude), Corinne Colon (Kate), Bridget Everett (Bridget), Randy Harrison (Waiter), Tommy Heleringer (Adrian), Zoe Leathers (Baby Logan), Lawrence Michael Levine (Nick), Jeff Hiller (*Showgirls* Fan Customer), Satchel Shure (Parker), Maria McConville (Pink Thing Customer), Ryan McGinnis (Logan), Kenny Mellman (Kenny), Sophia Takal (Honey), Emily Watchel (Sconce Customer), Liz Coakley, Joshua Marston, David Tabbert (Hair Salon), Douglas Hiller, Mandy Lawrence, Laura Terruso, Lauren Wolkstein (Yoga Class)

Jack Ferver, Jenn Harris in *Gayby* © Wolfe Releasing

LEAST AMONG SAINTS (Brainstorm Media) Producers, Robert A. Papazian, James G. Hirsch; Director/Screenplay, Martin Papazian; Photography, Guy Skinner; Music, Gary Lionelli; Editor, Robert Florio; Casting, Mary Vernieu, Lindsay Graham; a Papazian Hirsch Entertainment presentation; Color; Rated R; 107 minutes; Release date: October 12, 2012. **CAST:** Martin Papazian (Anthony), Tristan Lake Leabu (Wade), Laura San Giacomo (Jolene), Azura Skye (May),

Audrey Marie Anderson (Jenny), A.J. Cook (Cheryl), Ronnie Gene Blevins (Ronnie), Charles S. Dutton (George), Taylor Kinney (Jessie), Lombardo Boyar (Armando), Doug Purdy (Billy), Kari Nissena (Beth), Nayo Wallace (Balek, Sandy), Braden Plagge (Jeremy), Max Charles (Dylan), M.D. Walton (Security Guard), Natasha Cayman (Iraqi Mother), Kanin Howell (Jessie's Partner), Lynne Alana Delaney (Social Worker), Jeanne Taylor (Diane Cougar), Gabriel Aslan (Boy at Hospital), Ryan Heinke, Jordan Wells (Teens), La-Niece (ER Nurse), Connor Mac (Bully's Friend), Alison Rood (I.C.U. Nurse)

ETHEL (HBO Films) Producers, Rory Kennedy, Jack Youngelson; Executive Producer, Sheila Nevins; Director/Narrator, Rory Kennedy; Screenplay, Mark Bailey; Photography, Buddy Squires; Music, Miriam Cutler; Editor, Azin Samari; a Moxie Firecracker production; Color; Not rated; 97 minutes; Release date: October 12, 2012. Documentary on the life of Ethel Kennedy, widow of former Attorney General and Senator Robert F. Kennedy

Ethel Kennedy, Robert Kennedy in *Ethel* © HBO Films

A WHISPER TO A ROAR (The Moulay Hicham Foundation) Producers, Ben Moses, Amy Martinez; Director/Screenplay, Ben Moses; Executive Producers, Larry Diamond, Lynne Moses; Photography, Harris Done; Music, Christopher Thomas; Editor, Sharon Franklin; Narrator, Alfred Molina; an Appleseed Entertainment production; Color; Not rated; minutes; Release date: October 12, 2012. Documentary on democracy advocate Larry Diamond; **WITH:** Larry Diamond, Prince Moulay Hicham Ben Abdallah.

3, 2, 1 ... FRANKIE GO BOOM (Variance) Producers, Marcel Langenegger, Pavlina Hatoupis, Katayoun A. Marciano; Executive Producers, Elliott Lewitt, Julie Kirkham; Director/Screenplay, Jordan Roberts; Photography, Mattias Troelstrup; Designer, Michael Fitzgerald; Costumes, Ann Foley; Music, Mateo Messina; Editor, Michael Hofacre; Casting, Wendy O'Brien; Produced in association with Ministry of Content; a Defenderfilms and Kirkham-Lewitt Productions presentation; Color; HD; Not rated; 88 minutes; Release date: October 12, 2012. **CAST:** Charlie Hunnam (Frankie), Chris O'Dowd (Bruce), Lizzy Caplan (Lassie), Ron Perlman (Phyllis), Chris Noth (Jack), Whitney Cummings (Claudia), Nora Dunn (Mom, Karen), Sam Anderson (Dad, Chris), Kate Luyben (Dharma), David Marciano (David), Sarah Rush (Natalie), Frank Alvarez (Cholo), Ramon "Ray" Chavez (Grandfather), Leonard Kelly-Young (Arthur), Jordan Black (Kip), Adam Pally (Brandon), James Mitchell Miller (Sydney), Sophia Curan (Blushing Intern), Justin Dray (Guy in Park), Marcel Langenegger (Taxi Driver)

SPLIT: A DEEPER DIVIDE (Feature Presentations Releasing) Producers, Kelly Nyks, Jared Scott, Kelly Nyks, Peter Hutchison, Jeff Beard; Director/Screenplay, Kelly Nyks; Photography, Tarina Reed; Music Supervisor, Malcolm Francis; a PF Pictures production; Color; Not rated; 72 minutes; Release date: October 12,

Ron Perlman in *3,2,1 ... Frankie Go Boom* © Variance Films

2012. Documentary about the partisanship that is paralyzing America's politics, **WITH:** Evan Bayh, Chuck Hagel, Al Franken, Tom Price, John Dingell, Lawrence Lessig, Paul Starr, Norman J. Ornstein, Grover Norquist, Noam Chomsky, Robert G. Kaiser, Nicholas D. Kristof, Ezra Klein, Tucker Carlson, Amy Goodman, Thomas Frank.

SMILEY (Fever Prods/AMC) Producer, Michael Wormser; Executive Producers, Michael Gallagher, Elaine Gallagher, Glasgow Phillips; Director, Michael Gallagher; Screenplay, Glasgow Phillips, Michael Gallagher; Photography, Nicola B. Marsh; Designer, Alec Contestabile; Costumes, Adrienne Young; Music, Dave Porter; Editor, Zach Anderson; Special Effects Make-Up, Steve Costanza, Greg McDougall; Casting, Lisa Essary; a Fever Productions in association with Level 10 Films presentation; Color; HD; Rated R; 90 minutes; Release date: October 12, 2012. **CAST:** Caitlin Gerard (Ashley), Melanie Papalia (Proxy), Shane Dawson (Binder), Andrew James Allen (Zane), Roger Bart (Prof. Clayton), Keith David (Diamond), Toby Turner (Mark), Michael Traynor (Smiley), Liza Weil (Dr. Jenkins), Jana Winternitz (Maria), Nikki Limo (Stacy), Richard Ryan (Kells), Jason Horton (Flasher), Elizabeth Greer (Mom), Patrick O'Sullivan (Cooper), Darrien Skylar (Mary), Bree Essrig (Kim), Spencer John Olson (Weird Guy), Snake (Engineer), Billy St. John (Dad)

Caitlin Gerard, Michael Traynor in *Smiley* © Fever Prods.

HOTEL NOIR (Shangri-La Entertainment) Producers, Steve Bing, Sebastian Gutierrez, Zach Schwartz; Director/Screenplay, Sebastian Gutierrez; Photography, Cale Finot; Desiger, Jeffrey MacIntyre; Costumes, Betsy Heimann; Music, Robin Hannibal, Mathieu Schreyer; Editor, Lisa Bromwell; a Gato Negro Films production; Black and white; Not rated; 97 minutes; Release date: October 12, 2012. **CAST:** Malin Akerman (Swedish Mary), Kevin Connolly (Vance), Rosario Dawson (Sevilla), Danny DeVito (Eugene Portland), Robert Forster (Jim Logan), Carla Gugino (Hanna Click), Mandy Moore (Evangeline Lundy), Rufus Sewell

(Felix), Aaron Behr (Paul), Michael B. Jordan (Leon), Kim Mahair (Bettie Page), Michael Raif (Mysterious Gentleman), Cameron Richardson (Maureen Chapman), Derek Schreck (Mickey), Genny Sermonia (Nightclub Dancer), Jade Wiley (Man at Train Station)

Carla Gugino, Rufus Sewell in *Hotel Noir* © Shangri-La Entertainment

PHOTOGRAPHIC MEMORY (First Run Features) Executive Producers/Screenplay, Marie-Emmanuelle Hartness, Ross McElwee; Director/Photography/Narrator, Ross McElwee; Music, Charles Mingus, DJ Flack, Dane Walker; Editor, Sabrina Zanella-Foresi; a St. Quay Films presentation in co-production with French Connection Films in association with Arte France; American-French; Stereo; Color; HD; Not rated; 87 minutes; Release date: October 12, 2012. Documentary on how filmmaker Ross McElwee traveled back to St. Quay-Portrieux in Brittany to retrace his journey into adulthood; **WITH:** Ross McElwee, Adrian McElwee, Helene Landouar, Maud Corbel-Rouchy.

Ross McElwee, Adrian McElwee in *Photographic Memory* © First Run Features

SHEER (Virgilio Prods.) Producer, Juan Cruz Pochat; Executive Producers, Ruben Mazzoleni, Richard Tarczaly, Juan Cruz Pochat; Director, Ruben Mazzoleni; Screenplay, Ruben Mazzoleni, Juan Cruz Pochat; Photography, Daniele Napolitano; Music, Martin Capella; Editor, Anderson Boyd; a Juan Cruz Pochat production; Black and white; Not rated; 91 minutes; Release date: October 12, 2012. **CAST:** Michael Jefferson (Joe Romanowski), Aaron Barcelo (Nicholas Quinn), Frances E. Koepenick (Martha), Rachel Brookner (Jenny), Juan Cruz

Pochat (Hector Gastaldi), Kazy Tauginas (Super), Alec Beard (Matt), Peter Reznikoff (Karol), Robert Ross (Mr. Carver), Ginger Grace (Helena), Anthony M. Pizzuto (Tony), Charles Kopelson (Bob), Eric Vill Springer (Henry), Sasha Kelly (Samantha), Teniece Divya Johnson (Lydia), Juan Tourn (Hector's Bodyguard), Michael R. Richards (Mr. Whyte), Meliza Fernandez (Bartender)

EXCUSE ME FOR LIVING (Dada Films/Required Viewing) Producer/Director/Screenplay, Ric Klass; Photography, Chase Bowmam; Designer, Kristen Adams; Costumes, David Tabbert; Music, Robert Miller; Editor, Scott Conrad; Casting, Donna McKenna; an EMFL presentation; Color; HD; Not rated; 107 minutes; Release date: October 12, 2012. **CAST:** Tom Pelphrey (Dan), Christopher Lloyd (Lars), Wayne Knight (Albert), Jerry Stiller (Morty), Robert Vaughn (Jacob), Melissa Archer (Laura), Ewa Da Cruz (Charlie), James McCaffrey (Barry), Dick Cavett (Rev. Pilatus), Tonja Walker (Elaine), David A. Gregory (Bruce), Kevin Brown (Officer Franklin), Alysia Joy Powell (Nurse Linda), Shenaz Treasury (Bhadra), Kai Chapman (Ronnie), Tom Creel (Rob), Cal Crenshaw (David), Todd Davis (Thomas), Eric Deskin (Blinder), Chris Dunn (Orderly), Dale Grand (Tracy), Tyler Holinger (Mason), Eliza Huberth (Olga), Bari Hyman (Helen Clausen), David Kenner (Chip), Morty Kessler (Glen), Nikolas Kontomanolis (Achilles), Michael LaMarca (Proselyte), Richard V. Licata (Judge Karmel), David B. Martin (Sam), Jeronimo Medina (Pirot), Emily Morden (Ally), Maureen Mueller (Harriet), Sonja O'Hara (Olga's Friend), William Otterson (Dr. Heine), George Peck (Bertrand the Butler), Christopher Roach (Joe), Nicole Rutigliano (Waitress), Dawn Sobolewski (Daisy), Michael Willis (Harry)

Christopher Lloyd, Jerry Stiller in *Excuse Me for Living* © Dada Films

UNMASKED JUDEOPHOBIA (DocEmet) Producer/Director/Screenplay, Gloria Z. Greenfield; Executive Producers, George Violin, Andrea Levin, Alex Safian; Photography, Richard Chisholm; Music, Sharon Farber; Editor, David Grossbach; American-Israeli-Belgian-British-Canadian-French; Color; HD; Not rated; 88 minutes; Release date: October 19, 2012. Documentary on anti-Jewish ideology; **WITH:** Anne Bayefsky, John R. Bolton, Catherine Chatterley, Phyllis Chesler, Irwin Cotler, Ron Dermer, Alan M. Dershowitz, Daniel Diker, François Fillon, Mark Gardner, Manfred Gerstenfeld, Caroline B. Glick, Jeffrey Herf, Radu Ioanid, Anthony Julius, Matthias Küntzel, Richard Landes, Andrea Levin, Joe Lieberman, Itamar Marcus, Kenneth L. Marcus, Benny Morris, Yisrael Ne'eman, Hillel Neuer, Fiamma Nirenstein, Michael Oren, Emanuele Ottolenghi, Melanie Phillips, Nidra Poller, Pilar Rahola, Alvin H. Rosenfeld, Tammi Rossman-Benjamin, Barry Rubin, Jonathan Sacks, Alex Safian, Shimon Samuels, Natan Sharansky, Robin Shepherd, Charles Asher Small, Gerald Steinberg, Bret Stephens, Shmuel Trigano, Meir Waintrater, Elie Weisel, Ruth R. Wisse, Robert S. Wistrich, R. James Woolsey, Moshe "Bogie" Ya'alon, Ben-Dror Yemini

PARANORMAL ACTIVITY 4 (Paramount) Producers, Jason Blum, Oren Peli; Executive Producers, Akiva Goldsman, Steven Schneider, Christopher Landon; Directors, Henry Joost, Ariel Schulman; Screenplay, Christopher Landon; Story, Chad Feehan; based on the 2009 film *Paranormal Activity* directed and written by Oren Peli; Photography, Doug Emmett; Designer, Jennifer Spence; Costumes, Leah Butler; Editor, Gregory Plotkin; Special Effects Coordinator, Mark Gullesserian; Visual Effect Supervisor, Eddie Pasquarello; Prosthetic Makeup Effects, Almost Human Inc.; Stunts, James Armstrong; Casting, Terri Taylor; a Blumhouse/Solana Films/Room 101 Production; Color; Rated R; 88 minutes; Release date: October 19, 2012. **CAST:** Kathryn Newton (Alex), Matt Shively (Ben), Aiden Lovekamp (Wyatt), Brady Allen (Robbie), Stephen Dunham (Doug), Alexandra Lee (Holly), Katie Featherstone (Katie), Sprague Grayden (Kristi), Brian Boland (Daniel), William Juan Prieto (Hunter), Sara Mornell (Debbie), Alisah Boe (Tara), Brendon Eggertsen (Derek), Georgia Pettus (Sarah), Rightor Doyle (Referee), Constance Espisito (Robbie's Mom's Friend), Ty Dawson, Jonah Pasco (Shadow Boys)

Katie Featherstone in *Paranormal Activity 4* © Paramount Pictures

SEXY BABY (Two To Tangle Productions) Producers, Jill Bauer, Ronna Gradus, Brittany Huckabee; Directors, Jill Bauer, Ronna Gradus; Executive Producers, Abigail E. Disney, Chandra Jessee, Jill Bauer; Photography, Ronna Gradus; Music, Paul Brill; Presented in association with Fork Films; Not rated; 83 minutes; Release date: October 19, 2012. Documentary on the preponderance of sexual images in our culture and specifically its effect on three females; **WITH:** Winnifred Bonjean-Alpart, Jennifer Bonjean, Ken Alpart, Nichole Romagna, Dave Romagna, Laura Castle, Terry Castle, Dr. Bernard Stern.

Sexy Baby © Two to Tangle Prods.

NOBODY WALKS (Magnolia) Producers, Jonathan Schwartz, Andrea Sperling, Alicia Van Couvering; Executive Producers, Audrey Wilf, Zygi Wilf; Director, Ry Russo-Young; Screenplay, Lena Dunham, Ry Russo-Young; Photography, Christopher Blauvelt; Designer, Linda Sena; Costumes, Kim Wilcox; Music, Fall on Your Sword; Music Supervisor, Tiffany Anders; Editor, John Walter; Casting,

Kerry Barden, Paul Schnee; a Super Crispy Entertainment & Jonathan Schwartz/ Andrea Sperling Productions presentation; Dolby; Color; Rated R; 82 minutes; Release date: October 19, 2012. **CAST:** John Krasinski (Peter), Olivia Thirlby (Martine), Rosemarie DeWitt (Julie), India Ennenga (Kolt), Dylan McDermott (Leroy), Justin Kirk (Billy), Rhys Wakefield (David), Emanuele Secci (Marcello), Sam Lerner (Avi), Mason Welch (Dusty), David Call (Man), Jane Levy (Caroline), Anthony Saludares (Actor), Samantha Ressler (Actress), Stacy Barnhisel (Teacher), Emma Dumont (Yma)

John Krasinski, Olivia Thirlby in *Nobody Walks* © Magnolia Films

YOGAWOMAN (Second Nature Films) Producers, Michael S. McIntyre, Kate McIntyre, Saraswati Clere; Directors/Screenplay, Katie McIntyre Clere, Saraswati Clere; Photography, Michael S. McIntyre; Music, Jim Fish; Editors, Melanie Sandford, Wayne Hyett; Narrator, Annette Bening; a Yogakula Productions presentation; Dolby; Color; Not rated; 84 minutes; Release date: October 19, 2012. Documentary on the global phenomenon of women teaching yoga; **WITH:** Katchie Ananda, Caroline Shola Arewa, Beryl Bender Birch, Beth Berila, Gabriela Bozic, Elena Brower, Jnani Chapman, Donna Farhi, Angela Farmer, Sara Gottfried, Gabriella Guibilaro, Dona Holleman, Jenny Sauer Klein, Judith Lasater, Cyndi Lee, Claire Missingham, Indra Mohan, Tina Navarez, Anne O'Brien, Anne Ornish, Kaitlin Quistgaard, Shiva Rea, Constantina Rhodes, Desirée Rumbaugh, Deborah Saliby, Ellen Saltonstall, Cathy Stallworth, Janet Stone, Shirley Telles, Abby Willis, Colleen Saidman Yee

Shiva Rea in *Yogawoman* © Second Nature Films

THAT'S WHAT SHE SAID (Phase 4 Films) Producers, Joshua Astrachan, Lucy Barzun Donnelly, Mona Panchai, Carrie Preston; Executive Producers, Mark Holmes, James Vasquez; Director, Carrie Preston; Screenplay, Kellie Overbey; Photography, William Klayer; Designer, Bobby Berg; Costumes, Meghan Kasperlik; Music, Tim Adams, Mike Viola; Editor, Anita Brandt-Burgoyne; Casting, James Calleri, Paul Davis, Erica Jensen; a Daisy 3 Pictures presentation in association with Locomotive; Color; Rated R; 84 minutes; Release date: October 19, 2012. **CAST:** Anne Heche (Dee Dee), Marcia DeBonis (Bebe), Alia Shawkat (Clementine), Kellie Overbey (Elyse), Kate Rigg (Lu), Miriam Shor (Rhoda), Heather Lindell (Little Miss Nutcracker), Mandy Siegfried (Mary), Marylouise Burke (Phyllis), Charisse Bellante (Spa Receptionist), Kristine Nielsen (Judith), William Jackson Harper (Harry), Nick Gregory (Dick), Tanisha T. Long (Opening Credits Woman), Alexandra Rosario, Dani Spieler (Kickline Dancers), Cassandra Taylor (UWS Coffee Shop College Student), Brandi Nicole Wilson (Menage a Trois Woman), Teresa Hui (Scissor-Happy Chinese Beautician), Sean Patrick Murray (Hipster Kid), John G. Preston (Tom), Otoja Abit (Menage a Trois Man), Vanessa Hardy (East Village Hipster), Migina Tsai, Judy W. Chen (Beauticians), Makenzie Caine, Melissa Ferraro, Briana Yacavone (Secretaries), Maggie Levin (Disinterested Goth Girl), Saoko Okano (Spa Technician), Virginia Bartholomew (UWS Coffee Shop Wife), Dana Pelevine (Hair Salon Secretary), Katherine McDonald, Laura Darrell (Coffee Shop Girls), Scott Price (Rowdy Twenty-Something), Annie Henk (Latina Officer), Maria Scavullo (Perky Barista), Kelley Jackson Garcia (Coffee Shop Snob), Sujata Eyrick (Pharmacist), Eric Rizk (NYPD Officer), Emma Katz (UWS Coffee Shop Mom), Sheila Cockburn (SoHo Shopper), Rashelle Stocker (NYPD Coroner), Griffin DuBois (EMT), Sarah Pencheff (Hipster Chick), Lori Richardson (UWS Coffee Shop Patron)

Marcia DeBonis, Anne Heche in *That's What She Said* © Phase 4 Films

QUESTION ONE (Fly on the Wall Prods.) Producers/Directors, Joe Fox, James Nubile; Screenplay, Joe Fox; Editor, James Nubile; Color; Color; Not rated; 113 minutes; Release date: October 19, 2012. Documentary on the debate over same-sex marriage; **WITH:** Marc Mutty, Linda Seavy, Rev. Bob Emrich, Darlene Huntress, Sarah Dowling,

Question One © Fly on the Wall Prods.

THE FIRST TIME (Goldwyn) Producers, Martin Shafer, Liz Glotzer; Executive Producers, Liah Kim, Carol Fuchs; Director/Screenplay, Jonathan Kasdan; Photography, Rhet Bear; Designer, Keith Cunningham; Costumes, Michelle Posch; Music, Alec Puro; Editor, Hugh Ross; Casting, Amy McIntyre Britt, Anya Colloff; a Destination Films presentation of a Jerimaca Films production; Color; Rated PG-13; 98 minutes; Release date: October 19, 2012. **CAST:** Dylan O'Brien (Dave Hodgman), Brittany Robertson (Aubrey Miller), Craig Roberts (Simon Daldry), Maggie Elizabeth Jones (Stella Hodgman), Lamarcus Tinker (Big Corporation), Christine Taylor (Aubrey's Mom), Joshua Malina (Aubrey's Dad), Victoria Justice (Jane Harmon), James Frecheville (Ronny), Halston Sage (Brianna), Molly C. Quinn (Erika #1), Christine Quynh Nguyen (Erika #2), Matthew Fahey (Brendan Meltzer), Corianna Di Julio (Park Mom), Chandler Chasen (Jilted Girlfriend)

Brittany Robertson, Dylan O'Brien in *The First Time* © Goldwyn Films

ALTER EGOS (Phase 4) Producers, Dan Farah, Milan Chakraborty, Carlos Velazquez, Jordan Galland; Director/Screenplay, Jordan Galland; Photography, Chris LaVasseur; Designer, Lucio Seixas; Costumes, Carisa Kelly; Music, Sean Lennon; Music Supervisor, Jonathan Leahy; Editor, Dan Schecter; Casting, Eve Battaglia; a Gallard/Velazquez/Attic Light Films/Farah Films production in association with Off Hollywood Pictures and Cloud 9 Film Partners; Color; Rated R; 79 minutes; Release date: October 19, 2012. **CAST:** Kris Lemche (Fridge), Brooke Nevin (Claudel), Joey Kern (C-Thru), Danny Masterson (Jimmy), John Ventimiglia (Shrink), Christine Evangelista (Emily), Geneva Carr (Newscaster), Marina Squerciati (Dr. Sara Bella), Carlos Velazquez (Moon Dog), Daniel Sauli (Sunburn), Sean Lennon (Electric Death), Kristina Klebe (Ice Scream), Adam LeFevre (Local Man), Nathan Harlan (Restore-O), Aurelie Claudel (Rich Woman), Tim Barker (Cop), Marie Masters (Waitress), Milan Chakraborty (Hater), Lou Carbonneau (Marvin Chase), Carmen Goodine (Truth Fairy), Mike Landry (Talk Show Host)

Joey Kern, Kris Lemche in *Alter Egos* © Phase 4 Films

WE ARE LEGION: THE STORY OF THE HACKTIVISTS (Ro*co Films Intl/FilmBuff) Producers, Luminant Media; Director/Screenplay, Brian Knappenberger; Photography, Scott Sinkler, Dan Krauss, Lincoln Else; Music, John Dragonetti; Editor, Andy Robertson; a Luminant Media presentation; American-British; Color/Black and white; Not rated; 93 minutes; Release date: October 19, 2012. Documentary on Anonymous, a radical "hacktivist" collective; **WITH:** Anon2World, Anonyops, Aaron Barr, Barrett Brown, Adrian Chen, Gabriella Coleman, Joshua Corman, Josh Covelli, Peter Fein, Mercedes Haefer, Homocarnula, Gregg Housh, Tim Hwang, Jericho, Steven Levy, Brian Mettenbrink, Quinn Norton, Ryan Singel, Richard Thieme, Vendetta, Mike Vitale, Chris Wysopal, Commander X

We are Legion © FilmBuff

HATING BREITBART (Rocky Mountain Pictures) Producers, Maura Flynn, Evan Maloney; Director/Screenplay, Andrew Marcus; Music, Chris Loesch; Editors, Michael Kadela, Andrew Marcus; a Pixel & Verse in association with Speakeasy Video and Filmcrest Entertainment presentation; Color; Rated R; 85 minutes; Release date: October 19, 2012. Documentary on how Andrew Breitbart changed the rules of citizen journalism through new media; **WITH:** Andrew Breitbart, Orson Bean, Dick Armey, Michelle Bachmann, Stephen K. Bannon, Tucker Carlson, Nick Gillespie, Sean Hannity, Steve King, Dana Loesch, Rachel Maddow, Alley Mills, Terry Moran, Larry O'Connor, James O'Keefe, Keith Olbermann, Rick Perry, Kerry Picket, Larry Solov, Matthew Vadum, David Webb

Andrew Breitbart in *Hating Breitbart* © Rocky Mountain Pictures

BIGFOOT: THE LOST COAST TAPES (XLrator Media) Producers, Chevez Frazier, Corey Grant, Chris Beal; Executive Producers, Eddie Booze, Albert Sandoval, Charlene Castarjon, Neil Harrington, Patrick Thomas, Robert Salazar, Matthew Shreder, James Andrew Felts; Director, Corey Grant; Screenplay, Brian Kelsey, Bryan O'Cain; Photography, Richard Vialet; Designer, Chris Davis; Costumes, Tiffany Kay; Music, Eddie Booze; Editor, Ralph Jean-Pierre; Visual Effects, Alexis Nelson, Rick Sandler; Casting, Phaedra Harris; a New Breed Entertainment presentation; Color; Not rated; 85 minutes; Release date: October 19, 2012. **CAST:** Drew Rausch (Sean Reynolds), Rich McDonald (Darryl Coleman), Ashley Wood (Robyn Conway), Noah Weisberg (Kevin Lancaster), Frank Ashmore (Carl Drybeck), Rowdy Kelley (LaRoche), Japheth Gordon (Curtis), Sweetie Sherrié (Latonya), Chrison Thompson (The Shape), Alan Carnes (The Second Shape), Brittani Ebert (News Anchor), Travis McHenry (Reporter), Loren Lester, Donal Thoms-Cappello (Executives)

Ashley Wood in *Bigfoot: The Lost Coast Tapes* © XLrator Media

SASSY PANTS (Phase 4 Films) Producers, Adam Wilkins, Pavlina Hatoupis; Executive Producers, Eyde Belasco, Paul Korver; Director/Screenplay, Coley Sohn; Photography, Denis Maloney; Designer, Rachel Payne; Costumes, Mairi Chisholm; Music, Angela Correa; Music Supervisor, Kasey Truman; Editors, Robin Katz, Kinda Marra; Casting, Eyde Belasco; a Spruce Street Films and Ubranite presentation in association with the Ministry of Content and Cinelicious; Dolby; Color; Not rated; 87 minutes; Release date: October 19, 2012. **CAST:** Anna Gunn (June Pruitt), Ashley Rickards (Bethany Pruitt), Haley Joel Osment (Chip Hardy), Martin Spanjers (Shayne Pruitt), Diedrich Bader (Dale Pinto), Rene Rosado (Hector), Shanna Collins (Brianna), Drew Droege (Michael Paul), Jenny O'Hara (Grandma Pruitt), Aaron Perilo (Cory), Maynor Alvarado (Gangsta Wannabe), Brenan Baird (Dean Kupka), Mathew Botuchis (Brandon), Sabrena No'mani, Angie Dick (Cholas), Anthony Gaudioso (Oversized Senior), Maria Lazam Hanson (Elderly Filipino Woman), Jenna Kanell (Anna), Tara Karsian (Bank Teller), Shanica Knowles (Amber), Tara Jean O'Brien (Jr. College Clerk), Keith Page (Rodney), Carlos Pratts (Hector's Homey), Jennifer Robertson (Misty), Austin Rogers (Counter Boy), Soledad St. Hilaire (Hector's Mom), M.D. Walton (Officer Sneed), Matthew McKelligon (Line Dancer), Candace McKinney (Party Girl)

Haley Joel Osment, Ashley Rickards in *Sassy Pants* © Phase 4 Films

THE ZEN OF BENNETT (Abramorama) Producers, Danny Bennett, Jennifer Lebeau; Executive Producers, Danny Bennett, Ted Sarandos; Director, Unjoo Moon; Photography, Dion Beebe; Editors, Wyatt Smith, Katherine McQuerry; a Benedetto Films presentation; Color; HD; Not rated; 85 minutes; Release date: October 24, 2012. Documentary looks at legendary singer Tony Bennett as he records his *Duets II* album; **WITH:** Tony Bennett, Andrea Bocelli, Michael Bublé, Natalie Cole, Aretha Franklin, Norah Jones, Lady Gaga, John Mayer, Willie Nelson, Carrie Underwood, Amy Winehouse

Tony Bennett in *The Zen of Bennett* © Abramorama

THE REVISIONARIES (Kino Lorber) Producers, Pierson Silver, Orlando Wood, Scott Thurman; Executive Producers, Jim Butterworth, Vijay Dewan; Director, Scott Thurman; Screenplay, Jawad Metni, Scott Thurman; Photography, Zac Sprague, Scott Thurman; Music, Mark Orton; Editor, Jawad Metni; a Silver Ligining Pictures & Magic Hour Entertainment in participation with Naked Edge Films presentation; Color; Not rated; 92 minutes; Release date: October 26, 2012. Documentary on a creationist's efforts to get Texas schools to question evolution; **WITH:** David Anderson, Connie Barlow, Jessica Beckham, Kimberly Bilica, Heidi Boles, Chris Comer, Bob Craig, Michael Dowd, Cynthia Dunbar, Raymond Eve, Laura Ewing, Kevin Fisher, Barbara Forrest, Julie Fry, Steve Fuller, Michael Hudson, Lee Hughes, Stephanie Klenzendorf, Norman Lear, Gail Lowe, Arturo De Lozanne, Don McLeroy, Kathy Miller, Ken Miller, Matthew Ogilvie, Thomas Ratliff, Jonathan Saenz, Steven Schafersman, Gary Scharrer, Eugenie Scott, Gerald Skoog, Srinivasan Srivilliputher, Bill Takington, Ruthanne Thompson, Ide Trotter, Amanda Walker, Ron Wetherington

Ron Wetherington in *The Revisionaries* © Kino Lorber

DISTRICT OF CORRUPTION (Judicial Watch) Producers, Dan Fleuette, Stephen K. Bannon; Executive Producers, Brandon L. Millett, Glenn Bracken Evans, Tom Fitton, Chris Farrell, Paul Orfanedes; Director/Screenplay, Stephen K. Bannon; Photography, Fernando Ortega, Chris Winter; Music, David Cebert; Editors, Kasaey Kirby, Penny Lee; a Victory Film Group production in association with Constant Motion Entertainment; Color; Not rated; 71 minutes; Release date: October 26, 2012. Documentary takes a negative look at liberal Washington politics; **WITH:** Tom Fitton, Chris Farrell, Paul Orfanedes, Peter Schweizer, Katie Pavlich, Mark Tapscott, Louis Gohmert, Anita Moncrief, J. Christian Adams, David Webb, Matthew Boyle, Mike Flynn, Kerry Picket, Matthew Vadum, Vern McKinley, Hans von Spakovsky

FUN SIZE (Paramount) Producers, Stephanie Savage, Josh Schwartz, Bard Dorros, David Kanter; Executive Producers, Michael Beugg, Steve Golin, Paul Green; Director, Josh Schwartz; Screenplay, Max Werner; Photography, Yaron Orbach; Designer, Mark White; Costumes, Eric Daman; Music, Deborah Lurie; Editors, Mike Sale, Wendy Greene Bricmont; Casting, Alyssa Weisberg; a Nickelodeon Movies presentation of an Anonymous Content/Fake Empire production; Dolby; Deluxe Color; Rated PG-13; 86 minutes; Release date: October 26, 2012. **CAST:** Victoria Justice (Wren), Thomas Mann (Roosevelt), Jane Levy (April), Chelsea Handler (Joy), Thomas McDonell (Aaron Riley), Osric Chau (Peng), Thomas Middleditch (Fuzzy), Jackson Nicoll (Albert), Ana Gasteyer (Jackie), Josh Pence (Keevin), Kerri Kenney-Silver (Barb), Johnny Knoxville (Jörgen), Carrie Clifford (Pumpkin Mom), Barry Livingston (Halloween Dad), Ele Bardha (Mariposa Dad), Zamani Munashe (Spider Girl), Bobby Thomas (Old Spider-Man), James Pumphrey (Brueder), Dean Ogle, Manny Liotta, Amiri Zaire (Tweens), Abby Elliott (Lara), Peter Navy Tuiasosopo (Mr. Mahani, Samoan Man), Lori Pelenise Tuisano (Mrs. Mahani, Samoan Woman), Patrick de Ledebur (Mike Puglio), Stefan Gatt (Hulk), Sara Lindsey (Sexy Nurse), Riki Lindhome (Galaxy Scout), Erin Scerbak (Andrea, Drive Thru Girl), Gabrielle McClinton (Galaxy Scout Friend), Jeremy Earl (Officer Savage), Rachel Sterling (Kassi), Holmes Osborne (Mr. Brueder), Annie Fitzpatrick (Mrs. Brueder), Nick Varricchio (Jonathan, Mad Hatter), Maria Perossa (Hailey, Pirate Wench)

Osric Chau, Thomas Mann in *Fun Size* © Paramount Pictures

DINOTASIA (Picturehouse/Discovery) Producer, Erik Nelson; Executive Producers, Dave Harding, Alan Eyres, Brooke Runnette; Directors, David Krentz, Erik Nelson; VFX Supervisor, Douglas Martin; Music, Mark Leggett; Editors, Randall Boyd, Paul Marengo; Narrator, Werner Herzog; a Picturehouse, Discovery Channel and Creative Differences presentation; Color; Not rated; 83 minutes; Release date: October 26, 2012. Documentary on the survival tactics of he dinosaurs.

Dinotasia © Picturehouse

IN THE NIGHT (UnitedRain Prods.) Producer/Director/Screenplay/Music, Götz Neumann; Photography, Jörg Pumpa, Alicia Robbins, Valentin Steiner; Designer, Ray Luckey; Costumes, Wiebke Wardenbach, Stacy Ellen Rich; Editor, Christian Löw; Color; Not rated; 85 minutes; Release date: October 26, 2012. **CAST:** Nicole Dionne (Jane), Sara Brophy (Laura), Eric Dysart (Jerome), Heather Gault (Mary), Michiko Sasaki (Sachiko), Bryana Servedio (Debby), Andrew Start (Paul), Corey Wright (Aaron)

CHASING MAVERICKS (20th Century Fox) Producers, Curtis Hanson, Mark Johnson, Brandon Hooper, Jim Meenaghan; Executive Producers, Gerard Butler, Alan Siegel, Georgia Kacandes, David Weil; Directors, Curtis Hanson, Michael Apted; Screenplay, Kario Salem; Story, Jim Meenaghan, Brandon Hooper; Photography, Bill Pope; Designer, Ida Random; Costumes, Sophie de Rakoff; Music, Chad Fischer; Music Supervisor, Andrea von Foerster; Editor, John Gilbert; Special Effects Coordinator, J.D. Streett; Stunts, Brock Little; Casting, Mary Vernieu, Venus Kanani; a Fox 2000 Pictures and Walden Media presentation of a Gran Via/Deuce Three production; Dolby; FotoKem Color; Rated PG; 115 minutes; Release date: October 26, 2012. **CAST:** Gerard Butler (Frosty Hesson), Jonny Weston (Jay Moriarty), Elisabeth Shue (Kristy Moriarty), Abigail Spencer (Brenda Hesson), Leven Rambin (Kim Moriarty), Greg Long (Magnificent One), Peter Mel (Magnificent Two), Zach Wormhoudt (Magnificent Three), Devin Crittenden (Blond), Taylor Handley (Sonny), Cooper Timberline (Young Jay), Maya Raines (Roquet), Harley Graham (Young Kim), Jenica Bergere (Zeuf), James Anthony Cotton (Frank), Channon Roe (Bob Pearson), Thomas Freil (Bells), L. Peter Callender (Biology Teacher), Andrew Pierno, Coy Coffman (Sonny Crew), Richard Gross (Brenda's Father), Gary Griffis (Young Blond), Brandon Fleschner (Beach Cruiser), Adam Del Rio (Capitola Mall Druggie), Keegan Boos (Young Sonny), Kaila Pearson (Student), Christopher Sweeney (Eli), Elina Wells (Melia), Brandon Hooper (Photographer on Boat), Nate Feix (Little Grommet)

Gerard Butler, Jonny Weston in *Chasing Mavericks* © 20th Century Fox

LONG SHOT: THE KEVIN LAUE STORY (Dutchmen Films) Producers, Franklin Martin, Billy Raftery; Executive Producers, Dain Blair, Julian McMahon, Charles Loventhal; Director/ Screenplay, Franklin Martin; Music, Robin Soper; Music Supervisor, Dain Blair; Editors, Sam Citron, Tyler Lindsay, Jason Summers; Color; Not rated; 93 minutes; Release date: October 26, 2012. Documentary on how Kevin Laue overcame his handicap of a missing left arm to become a high school basketball star; **WITH:** Kevin Laue, Barry Rohrssen

Kevin Laue in *Long Shot* © Dutchmen Films

THE LAST FALL (Image Entertainment) Producers, Scott Hebert, Nikki Love; Executive Producers, Ellis Hobbs, Monique Hobbs, Matthew A. Cherry, Lance Gross; Director/Screenplay, Matthew A. Cherry; Photography, Richard Vialet; Designer, Gustaf Aspegren; Costumes, Neiman Tate, Paige Michelle; Music, Tremaine Williams; Editors, Michael Norville, Matthew A. Cherry; Casting, Michelle D. Adams; a Transparent Filmworks in association with Outerstratosphere Productions; Color; Not rated; 98 minutes; Release date: October 26, 2012. **CAST:** Lance Gross (Kyle Bishop), Nicole Behaire (Faith Davis), Vanessa Bell Calloway (Marie Bishop), Obba Babatundé (Larry Armstrong), Darrin Dewitt Henson (Rell Lee), Harry Lennix (Ron Davis), Keith David (Sydney Bishop), Michael Moss (Marcus Sparks), Sinorice Moss (Drew Irving), Sayeed Shahidi (Von Davis), Yaani King (Chris), Ellis Williams (Mr. Edwards), Trisha Mann (Beverly Davis), Brandon Dmico Anderson (Vincent), Sam Scarber (Coach Green), Rayan Lawrence (The Turk), Brittany Loren (Stacy), Lonn McCraley (Anthony), Michelle Joan Papillon (Agent's Assistant), Taylor Reed (Assistant Coach)

Nicole Behaire, Lance Gross in *The Last Fall* © Image Entertainment

ORCHESTRA OF EXILES (First Run Features) Producer/Director/Screenplay, Josh Aronson; Executive Producers, Michael Marks, Carole Marks, Victor Elmaleh, Sono Elmaleh, Vincent Mai, Anne Mai, Dorit Straus; Photography, Amnon Zalait, Nitay Netzer; Music, Wlad Marhulets; Editor, Nancy Kennedy; Narrator,Tim Elliot; an Aronson Films production; Stereo; Color; Not rated; 85 minutes; Release date: October 26, 2012. Documentary-drama on how Polish violinist Bronislaw Huberman rescued some of the top musicians from the Nazis and formed the Palestine Symphony Orchestra; **WITH:** Itzhak Perlman, Zubin Mehta, Pinchas Zukerman, Leon Botstein, Joshua Bell, Amnon Weinstein; **CAST:** Thomas Kornmann (Adult Huberman), Elin Kolev (14-Year-Old Huberman), Henk Reinicke (8-Year-Old Huberman), Geno Lechner (Ida Ibbeken), Jan Uplegger (Jacob Huberman), Alex Ansky (Arturo Toscanini), Yigal Sachs (William Steinberg), Vladsto Peyitch (Chaim Weizmann), Gil Baxpehler (Horst Salomon), Brett Lorier (Lorand Fenyves), Stefan Hauser (Wilhelm Furtwängler), Harald Magarin (Joseph Goebbels), Wolfgang Ronfeldt (Jacob Surowicz)

Bronislaw Huberman in *Orchestra of Exiles* © First Run Features

DEMOCRACY AT WORK (Sand/Dollar Prods./Melody Makers Prods.) Producers, Susan Metzger, Sergio Crego; Director/Screenplay, Wasko Khouri; Photography, Charles DeRosa; Designer, Kathryn Kenneth; Costumes, Tomika Smalls; Editor, Susan Metzger; Presented in association with Kearns and Mariande and ReKon Prods.; Black and white; Not rated; 90 minutes; Release date: November 2, 2012. **CAST:** Michael Scovotti (Ted Float), Matt Jones (Adrian Bluoff), Toks Olagundoye (Meghan Oliver), Sean Spence (Steven Mime), Meredith Thomas (Jill Kirk), Bruno Oliver (Travis), Ed Refuerzo (Hector), Robin Shelby (Debra Mime), Marty Lodge (Dr. Mike), Debbie Kagy (Tiffany), Sherri Lewandowski (Sheila), Sasha Carrera (Marilyn), Ericka Kreutz (Cindy Doolan), Christian Levatino (The Fixer), Kyle Steven Templin (Tom Stern), Alex Knudsen (The Photographer), Anastasia Savko (Photographer's Assistant), John Kearns Jr. (Mark Thomas), Robert Evans, Toni Perkins (Models)

BURN (General Motors Entertainment Marketing) Producers/Directors, Tom Putnam, Brenna Sanchez; Executive Producers, Denis Leary, Jim Serpico, Steve Tihanyi, Morgan Neville; Photography, Mark Eaton, Nicola B. Marsh, Matt Pappas; Music, BC Smith, Alessandro Cortini; Editors, Kevin Jones, Morgan R. Stiff, Miranda Yousef; an Apostle & TBVE presentation; Color; Not rated; 86 minutes; Release date: November 2, 2012. Documentary on Detroit's firefighters and their often thankless job of trying to save their depressed city; **WITH:** Donald Austin, Brendan Doogie Milewski, Craig Dougherty, Terrell Hardaway, Dennis Hunter, Dave Miller, Chris Palm, Dave Parnell, Jeff Urbas

Burn © General Motors

FESTIVAL OF LIGHTS (Industry Works Pictures) Producers, Graziano Bruni, Shundell Prasad, Ritu Singh Pande; Director/Screenplay, Shundell Prasad; Photography, Valentina Caniglia; Designer, Mark Gebel; Costumes, Francyne Granico; Music, Ronen Landa; Editor, Barry Alexander Brown; a Durga Entertainment presentation of an SP Films International production; Dolby; Deluxe color; Not rated; 120 minutes; Release date: November 2, 2012. **CAST:** Melinda Shankar (Reshma), Jimi Mistry (Vishnu), Aidan Quinn (Adem), Ritu Singh Pande (Meena), Stephen Hadeed Jr. (Ravin), Nandanie Dudhnath (Asha), Isabella A. Santos (Sandy), Kamla Bhagroo (Sheila), Puneet Prasada (Justin), Ramesh Deochand (Shah), Chunilall Narine (Pandit), Mark Epperson (INS Agent), Ashley Rebecca Farley (Sam), Lalit Ahluwalia (Warden), Dion Matthews (Warden's Assistant), Zoe Anastasiou (Guidance Counselor), Jason Downs (Emory), Hoji Fortuna (Mr. Wright), Laila Harrison (Sunita), Dhanpaul Narine (Devin), Nirvani Prasad (12-Year-Old Rehsma), Shundell Prasad (Nurse), Gregg Prosser (Barry), Fawad Siddiqui (Mike Singh), Danny Wiseman (Doctor), Natalia Laspina, Brittney Palazzo (Office Girls), George S. Matsuo (Mover #1), Kimberly Ramirez (Oversized Woman)

Jimi Mistry in *Festival of Lights* © Industry Works Pictures

HIGH GROUND (Red Flag Releasing) Producers, Don Hahn, Michael Brown; Director/ Photography, Michael Brown; Screenplay, Brian Mockenhaupt; Music, Chris Bacon; Editor, Scott McElroy; a Stone Circle Pictures and Serac Adventure Films presentation of a Khumbu Pictures production; Stereo; Color; HD; Not rated; 92 minutes; Release date: November 2, 2012. Documentary on how 11 veterans returning from Iraq and Afghanistan joined an expedition to climb Mount Lobuche in the Himalayas; **WITH:** Steve Baskis, Chad Butrick, Ashley Crandall, Aaron Isaacson, Chad Jukes, Nicolette Maroulis, Cody Miranda, Justin Moore, Matt Nyman, Katherine Ragazzino, Dan Sidles, Lona Parten

High Ground © Red Flag Releasing

AMBER ALERT (Wrekin Hill Entertainment) Producers, Kerry Bellessa, Summer Bellessa, Trevor Engelson; Executive Producers, Joshua Oram, Nick Osborne; Director, Kerry Bellessa; Screenplay, Kerry Bellessa, Joshua Oram; Photography, Kendall Hurley; Designer, Clark Bellessa; Editor, Joshua Oram; Casting, Summer Smith; a Bluefields Entertainment and Underground Films presentation; Color; Rated R; 80 minutes; Release date: November 2, 2012. **CAST:** Summer Bellessa (Samantha Green), Chris Hill (Nathan Riley), Jasen Wade (Michael Muller), Caleb Thompson (Caleb), Brook Thompson (Brooke), Tom Murray (Officer Murray)

JACK AND DIANE (Magnolia) Producers, Jen Gatien, Karin Chien, So Yong Kim, Bradley Rust Gray; Executive Producers, Riaz Tyab, Leonardo Guerra Seragnoli, Gene Reed, Tricia Quick, Rui Costa Reis, Ricardo Costa Reis, Eliad Josephson; Director/Screenplay, Bradley Rust Gray; Photography, Anne Misawa; Designer, Chris Trujillo; Music, múm; Editors, Bradley Rust Gray, So Yong Kim; Creature Design, Gabe Bartalos; Animation, Quay Brothers; Casting, Sig De Miguel, Stephen Vincent; a Deer Jen and Soandbrad production in association with A Space Between and RCR Media Group; Dolby; Color; Rated R; 110 minutes; Release date: November 2, 2012. **CAST:** Juno Temple (Diane/Karen), Riley Keough (Jack), Cara Seymour (Aunt Linda), Kylie Minogue (Tara), Dane DeHaan (Chris), Haviland Morris (Jack's Mom), Michael Chernus (Jaimie), Leo Fitzpatrick (Joby), Lou Taylor Pucci (Tom), Neal Huff (Jerry), Rock Kohli (Cab Driver), Jen Ponton (Stacy), Samantha Anderson Ives (Business Lady), Lena Gora (Kissing Girl), Zohren Weiss (Punk Kid), Hayley Hunt (Punk Kid's Girl), Thysson George Williams (Club Smoker), Blake Daniel (Greg, Curley-Haired Boy), T. Oliver Reid (Transvestite), Jackson Ning (Bus Driver)

Juno Temple, Riley Keogh in *Jack and Diane* © Magnolia Films

GIRL WALK: ALL DAY (Independent) Producer, Youngna Park; Director/ Photography, Jacob Krupnick; a Wild Combination production; Color; Not rated; 75 minutes; Release date: November 2, 2012. A dance through New York City, **WITH:** Anne Marsen (The Girl), Dai Omiya (The Gentleman), John Doyle (The Creep), Amanda Turner (Teacher), Dustin John (Transporter), Beat Club (The Crew), Shari Rosenblatt, Linda Fingerson, Deborah Blau (Flower Girls), Luciano Acuna Jr. (Thief), Alyssa Chloe (Waacker), Stephen Retchless (Pole Dancer)

Stephen Retchless in *Girl Walk: All Day* © Wild Combination

GREGORY CREWDSON: BRIEF ENCOUNTERS (Zeitgeist) Producer/ Director/ Photography, Ben Shapiro; Music, Dana Kaproff, Little Silver; Editors, Tom Patterson, Nancy Kennedy; Produced with the support from IFP in co-production with AVRO Television/The Netherlands and in association with SVT/ Sweden; American-Dutch-Swedish; Stereo; Color; Not rated; 77 minutes; Release date: November 2, 2012. Documentary on photographer Gregory Crewdson; **WITH:** Gregory Crewdson, Russell Banks, Rick Moody, Laurie Simmons, Melissa Harris, Richard Sands

Gregory Crewdson (left) in *Gregory Crewdson: Brief Encounters* © Zeitgeist Films

NATURE CALLS (Magnet) Producer, Lisa Muskat; Executive Producers, David Gordon Green, Michael B. Clark, John Hodges, David Bausch; Director/ Screenplay, Todd Rohal; Photography, Steve Gainer; Designer, Matthew Munn; Costumes, Jacki Roach; Music, Eric D. Johnson, Ryan Miller, Teese Gohl; Editors, Alan Canant, Nat Sanders; Casting, Avy Kaufman; a Troop 41 Productions in association with Muskat Filmed Properties; Dolby; Color; Rated R; 79 minutes; Release date: November 9, 2012. **CAST:** Patton Oswalt (Randy), Johnny Knoxville (Kirk), Rob Riggle (Gentry), Maura Tierney (Janine), Patrice O'Neal (Mr. Caldwell), Darrell Hammond (Ranger Deakins), Eddie Rouse (Little Eddie), Ivan Dimitrov

(Ivan), Kelly Coffield Park (Mrs. Hartnett), Nilaja Sun (Moses Mother), Joshua Ormond (Leonard), Robert Longstreet (Drew Pritchard), Regan Mizrahi (Kent), Jill de Jong (Motorcycle Lady), Adam Dorfman (Leachman), Eric Ruffin (Moses), Joseph Paul Kennedy (Gary), Santana Pruitt (Shane), Francisco Burgos (Tibbits), Lisa Sample (Nun), John Tobias (Stuart), Thiecoura Cissoko (Dwande), Serenity Martorell (Tibbit's Little Sister)

Patrice O'Neal, Rob Riggle in *Nature Calls* © Manget Releasing

COMING UP ROSES (Dada Films) Producers, Adam Folk, Jonathan Mason, Mona Lessnick; Director, Lisa Albright; Screenplay, Christine Lazaridi, Lisa Albright; Photography, Ryan Samul; Designer, Daniel R. Kersting; Costumes, Michael Anzalone; Music, Dominic Matar; Editor, Ray Hubley; Casting, Margery Simkin, Judy Henderson; a Bullet Pictures in association with Dada Films presentation of a Mary Sunshine Films Production; Color; HD; Not rated; 88 minutes; Release date: November 9, 2012. **CAST:** Bernadette Peters (Diane), Rachel Brosnahan (Alice), Peter Friedman (Charles), Reyna de Courcy (Cat), Michael Anzalone (Barry), Jayce Bartok (Jimmy), David Cale (Joe), Amelia Campbell (Mrs. Doyle), Ann Dowd (Lynne), Christopher Durham (Dr. Go-Light), Shannon Esper (Cherie), Sadie Feighan (Young Alice), Adam Henry Garcia (Bobby), Jamie Hurley (Receptionist), Erik Jonsun (Stage Manager), Neal Matarazzo (Officer Kapp), Malachy McCourt (Priest), Daniel Oreskes (Gerry), Andrew Polk (Charles' Boss), Kate Rogal (Prostitute), Michael Willis (Counselor), Mike Catapano (Delinquent #1), Kendahl Ferguson, Andrew Parker Greenwood, Joshua Gunn, Michael Haayen, Rhett Kalman, Billy Keyes, Graham Kurtz (Dancers), Olan Montgomery (Phil Diet Center Patron), Caroline Strong (Woman)

Rachel Brosnahan, Bernadette Peters in *Coming Up Roses* © Dada Films

28 HOTEL ROOMS (Oscilloscope) Producers, Lynette Howell, Louise Runge, Samantha Housman; Executive Producers, Chris Messina, Andrew Meleran, Stefan Nowicki, Joey Carey, Alex Sagalchik; Director/Screenplay, Matt Ross; Photography, Doug Emmett; Costumes, Julia Caston, Jamie Bresnan; Music, Fall On Your Sword; Editor, Joseph Krings; a Silverwood Films presentation of a OneZero Films production in association with Sundial Pictures/Mott Street Pictures; Stereo; Color; Not rated; 82 minutes; Release date: November 9, 2012. **CAST:** Chris Messina (Man), Marin Ireland (Woman), Robert E. Deamer Jr. (Bartender), Brett Collier (Bar Patron)

Chris Messina, Marin Ireland in *28 Hotel Rooms* © Oscilloscope Laboratories

CHRISTMAS IN COMPTON (Barnholtz Entertainment) Producers, Murillo Penchel, Marcia Penchel, Michael Hubbard, Beth Hubbard; Executive Producers, Joe Hubbard III, Reshaun Frear, Ivan Alexander Ramirez; Director, David Raynr; Screenplay, David Raynr, Suzanne Broderick, Robert Fedor; Photography, Sandra Valde; Designer, Shaun Motley; Costumes, Mikel Padilla; Music, James Poyser, Zukhan Bey; Songs, Luke Christopher; Editor, Richard Halsey; Casting, Mathew Gray, Peter Wise; a Bright Idea Entertainment presentation; Color; Digital; Rated PG-13; 93 minutes; Release date: November 9, 2012. **CAST:** Omar Gooding (Derrick Hollander), Keith David (Big Earl), Sheryl Lee Ralph (Abuta), Eric Roberts (Tommy Maxell), Miguel A. Nuñez Jr. (Delicious), Orlando Brown (Tyrone), Alycia Bellamy (Shante), Jayda Brown (Sierra), Christopher Carroll (Butler), Porscha Coleman (Kendra Campbell), Marcos De Silvas (Ernesto Martinez), Kristinia DeBarge (Lola), Fefe Dobson (Kim), Cynthia Graham (Mrs. Hubbard), Edwin Hodge (Pookie), Spencer Hubbard (DJ Killionaire), Budd Jackson (Heckler), Leslie Jones (Tiny), Charles Kim (Steve Ho), Arif S. Kinchen (Squeaky), Roland "Buddy" Lewis (Mr. Hubbard), Karen McClain (Mrs. Jones), Jermanne Perry, Jonathan McHugh (Policemen), "Big" LeRoy Mobley (Heckler), Zion Otano (Leon), Evan Rayner (E-Ray), Darrly Alan Reed (Sly), Emiliano Torres (Tre), Matthew Willig (Charlie), Malin Yhr (Lost White Woman), Heather Rae Young (Paulette)

Omar Gooding in *Christmas in Compton* © Barnholtz Entertainment

THE COMEDY (Tribeca) Producers, Mike S. Ryan, Brent Kunkle; Executive Producers, Chris Swanson, Darius Van Arman, Ben Swanson, Jonathan Cargill, David Gordon Green, Jody Hill, Danny McBride, Alex Plapinger, Matt Reilly; Director, Rick Alverson; Screenplay, Rick Alverson, Robert Donne, Colm O'Leary; Photography, Mark Schwartzbard; Designer, Shawn Annabel; Editors, Michael Taylor, Rick Alverson; Casting, Brandon Powers, Harley Kaplan; a Jagjaguwar presentation of a Greyshack Films/Glass Eye Pix Production in association with Made Bed Productions; Color; Not rated; 90 minutes; Release date: November 9, 2012. **CAST:** Tim Heidecker (Swanson), Eric Wareheim (Van Arman), Kate Lyn Sheil (Waitress), Alexia Rasmussen (Young Woman), Gregg Turkington (Bobby), James Murphy (Ben), Jeff Jensen (Cargill), Liza Kate Walter (Sister in Law), Yianni Kool (Taxi Driver), Mike S. Ryan (Construction Foreman), Robert Wallin, Angelo Velentzas (Construction Workers), Lester Stepien, Nina Polan (Poles), Katie Vitti, Liam O'Connor (Children), Seth Koen (Male Nurse), David Olsen (Old Man in Hospital), Roxanne Ferris (Prostitute), Kender Jones (Swanson's Father), Angus Hepburn (Hampton's Elderly Man), Grace Kiley (Hampton's Elderly Woman), Meyhem Lauren (Bar Patron, Top), Gerard Amyzial (Bartender, Top), Adam Scarimbolo (Restaurant Manager), Ryan Raftery (Antique Shop Patron), Grace Rex (Hospital Nurse), Alice Maziuman (Hospital Woman), Ryan Schreiber (Record Store Clerk), Will Sheff (Will), Kevin Townley (Waiter), Rock Kohli (The Driver), Luke Wasserman (Beach Child), Sarah Trogden (Beach Mother), Richard Swift (Richard), Gregory M. Brown (Doctor), Joe Mele (Head Trauma Man), Russell Boyle (Antique Store Clerk)

Tim Heidecker, Eric Warenheim, James Murphy in *The Comedy* © Tribeca Film

SHADY LADY (Fact Not Fiction Films) Producer/Director/Editor, Tristan Loraine; Executive Producers, Adrian G. Pop, Ian Ryder Smith, John Davison, Ken Fitzpatrick, Andy Jacob; Screenplay, Tristan Loraine, Viv Young; Photography, Nathalie Grace; Designer, Chloë Potter; Music, Moritz Schmittat; Narrator, Michael Dorn; Color; HD; 87 minutes; Release date: November 9, 2012. Documentary-drama on the B-24 Liberator aircraft *Shady Lady* and its mission to bomb the oil refineries in Borneo during WWII; **CAST:** Ross Neuenfeldt (1st Lt. Douglas S. Craig), Gregory Kanter (2nd Lt. Robert L. Jackson), Jim Alexander (Lt. Col. William Miller), Robert H. Wainwright (RAF Group Captain), Shaun Morton (Flt. Lt. Burr), Ben L'Abbe (T/Sgt. Louis D. Joseph), Jonathan W. Colby (2nd Lt. John B. Nash), Jonathan Michael Anderson (2nd Lt. Randall E. Packard), Josh Coleman (Maurice V. Powers), Mike Cali (S/Sgt. William J. Mynock), Marc Ferrante (T/Sgt. Rupert J. Daugherty), Andrew Adler (Flying Officer Len Ruston), Charles Doug Craig (S/Sgt. William F. Klenn), George L. Craig (S/Sgt. Vernon A. Krout), Andrew Harwood Mills (Capt. Bob Horn), James Baxter (Jeep Driver), Christian Knight (Flt. Lt. David Arrowsmith), Clement Maraltadj (Balangarra Elder), Donald Morrison (Lt. Gus Connery), Paris Stangl (USAAF Ground Radio Operator), Alice Craig (Herself), Derek Charles, Kevin Williams (Wunambal Gaambera Traditional Owners)

Ben L'Abbe in *Shady Lady* © Fact Not Fiction Films

BUFFALO GIRLS (Paladin) Producers, Lanette Philips, Jonathon Ker; Executive Producers, Paul Rachman, Michael Raimondi, Noah Hauessner; Director, Todd Kellstein; Music, Scott Hackwith; Editor, Zimo Huang; a 108 Media and Paladin presentation of a Buffalo Girls Movie in association with Union Entertainment; Color; Not rated; 66 minutes; Release date: November 14, 2012. Documentary on two eight-year-old girls who become child boxers to earn money for their families; **WITH:** Stam Sor Con Lek, Pet Chor Chanachai

Pet Chor Chanachai in *Buffalo Girls* © Paladin

16 ACRES (Tanexis Productions) Producer, Mike Marcucci, Matt Kapp; Director/Editor, Richard Hankin; Screenplay, Matt Kapp; Photography, Antonio Rossi; Music, Max Avery Lichtenstein; Editors, Richard Hankin, Joe Murphy; Color; Not rated; 92 minutes; Release date: November 16, 2012. Documentary on the endless disagreement over rebuilding the World Trade Center; **WITH:** Michael Bloomberg, Michael Arad, Roland Betts, David Childs, Daniel Libeskind, Janno Lieber, George Pataki, Larry Silverstein, Rosaleen Tallon, Chris Ward

16 Acres © Tanexis Prods.

FIRST WINTER (Ghost Robot) Producers, Mark De Pace, Zachary Mortensen, Lindsay Burdge, Benjamin Dickinson; Executive Producer, Jon Watts; Director/Screenplay, Benjamin Dickinson; Photography, Adam Newport-Berra; Designer, Katie Hickman; Editors, Benjamin Dickinson, Jen Lame, Andrew Alan; Casting, Lindsay Burge; a Ghost Robot production in association with RSA Films; Color; Not rated; 88 minutes; Release date: November 16, 2012. **CAST:** Lindsay Burdge (Marie), Paul Manza (Paul), Jennifer Kim (Jen), Samantha Jacober (Sam), Matthew Chastain (Matt), Kate Lyn Sheil (Kate), Haruka Hashimoto (Monika), Fonlin Nyeu (Fonlin), Luke Simon (Luke), Jeff Thrope (Jeff), Benjamin Dickinson (Thomas), Jaffe Zinn (Jaffe), Bill Dunn (Radio Announcer), Paul Green (Radio DJ)

Paul Manza in *First Winter* © Ghost Robot

WHO BOMBED JUDI BARI? (Hokey Pokey Prods.) Producer, Darryl Cherney; Executive Producer, Elyse Katz; Director/Editor, Mary Liz Thomson; Music, The Matt Eakle Band; Color; HD; Not rated; 93 minutes; Release date: November 16, 2012. Documentary on the 1990 car bombing that injured environmental activists Judi Bari and Darryl Cherney; **WITH:** Judi Bari, Dennis Cunningham, Darryl Cherney, Frank Doyle

THE NORMALS (K5 Intl.) Producers, Kevin Connors, Chris Ciancimino, Jason Orans; Executive Producer, Kerry Orent; Director, Kevin Connors; Screenplay, Chris Ciancimino; Based on the 2004 novel by David Gilbert; Photography, Andre Lascaris; Designer, Jade Healy; Costumes, Elisabeth Vastola; Music, Fall on Your Sword; Editor, Todd Holmes, Casting, Kerry Barden, Paul Schnee, Allison Estrin; a Woodshed Entertainment Production in association with Gigantic Pictures; Color; Not rated; 100 minutes; Release date: November 16, 2012. **CAST:** Bryan Greenberg (Billy Schine), Jess Weixler (Gretchen), Frederick Weller (Lannigan), Josh Pais (Dr. Honeysack), Reg E. Cathey (Rodney), John Sayles (Dr. Marx), Dan Hedaya (Ragnar), Brooke Bloom (Nurse Longley), Bard Calcaterra (Stew), Kelli Crump (Joy), Matt McCarthy (Ossap), Tim O'Halloran (Dullick), Debargo Sanyal (Sameer), Jon Norman Schneider (Do), Peter Mark Bockman, Ralph Bracco, Gerard Cordero, Bryan Williams (Orderlies), Jordan Carlos (Cafeteria Worker), Sara Chase (Nurse), Dorothi Fox (Old Woman), Chris Haemmerle, Michael Monteiro (Technicians), Philip Hernandez (Corker), Michael Jefferson (Yellow Patient), Robert Montano (Victor Munoz), J. Paul Nicholas (Dr. Vartan), Jennifer Regan (Billy's Neighbor), Gaby Sandoval (Patient)

Bryan Greenberg, Josh Pais in *The Normals* © K5 Intl.

MEA MAXIMA CULPA: SILENCE IN THE HOUSE OF GOD (HBO Documentary Films) Producers, Kristen Vaurio, Alex Gibney, Alexandra Johnes, Jedd Wider, Todd Wider; Executive Producers, Lori Singer, Jessica Kingdon, Sheila Nevins; Director/Screenplay/Narrator, Alex Gibney; Photography, Lisa Rinzler; Music, Ivor Guest, Robert Logan; Editor, Sloane Klevin; a Jigsaw production, in association with Wider Film Projects and Below the Radar films, with the participation of Irish Film Board; American-Irish; Color/Black and white; HD; Not rated; 107 minutes; Release date: November 16, 2012. Documentary on sexual abuse in the Catholic Church, specifically the crimes of Lawrence Murphy who taught at St. John's School for the Deaf in Milwaukee; **WITH:** Jeff Anderson, Jason Berry, Arthur Budzinski, Thomas Doyle, Laurie Goodstein, Terry Kohut, Pat Kuehn, Robert Mickens, Marco Politi, Geoffrey Robertson, Richard Sipe, Gary Smith, Patrick J. Wall, Rembert Weakland; **VOICES:** Chris Cooper, Ethan Hawke, Jamey Sheridan, John Slattery

Mea Maxima Culpa © HBO Documentary

PRICE CHECK (IFC Films) Producer, Dolly Hall; Director/Screenplay, Michael Walker; Photography, Sam Chase; Designer, Nadya Gurevich; Costumes, Astrid Brucker; Music, Dean Wareham, Britta Phillips; Editors, Michael Taylor, Jen Lame; Casting, Kerry Barden, Paul Schnee; a Dolly Hall production; Color; Not rated; 92 minutes; Release date: November 16, 2012. **CAST:** Parker Posey (Susan Felders), Eric Mabius (Pete Cozy), Annie Parisse (Sara Cozy), Josh Pais (Doug Cain), Cheyenne Jackson (Ernie), Edward Herrmann (Jack Bennington), Amy Beth Schumer (Lila), Remy Auberjonois (Todd Kenner), Jayce Bartok (Bobby McCain), Brian Berrebbi (Matt Davis), Samrat Chakrabarti (Eddie), Victor Cruz (Dave Scalzod), Finn Donoghue (Henry Cozy), Christopher Douros (Donald), Stephen Kunken (Cartwright), Nicholas Martorell Jr. (Syd), Jennifer Mudge (Janis), Xosha Roquemore (Donna), Faith Sandberg (Bennington's Assistant), Matt Servitto (Jim Brady), Nate Steinwachs (Patrick), Juan Luis Acevedo (Salesman), Natalie Best (Clara), Joe D'Onofrio (Town Car Driver), Selena Mars (Lady in Silver), Elizabeth Masucci (Waitress), Frank Amoruso, Mike O'Brien, Stephen Park (Board Members), Matt Walker (Tony Gomes), Melinda Hull (Daphne's Mother), Marceline Hugot (Mrs. Raphael), John Fugelsang (Jake), Dean Wareham, Britta Phillips (Themselves), Julia Bray (Cheryl)

Parker Posey, Eric Mabius in *Price Check* © IFC Films

SCROOGE & MARLEY (Sam I Am Films) Producers, David Strzepek, Tracy Baim; Directors, Richard Knight, Jr., Peter Neville; Screenplay, Ellen Stoneking, Richard Knight Jr., Timothy Imse; Based on the 1843 novella *A Christmas Carol* by Charles Dickens; Photography, Andrew Parrotte; Designer, Rob Steffen; Costumes, Jill Dunbar; Music, Lisa McQueen; Editor, Peter Neville; Makeup Designer, Lora Michael; Color; Not rated; 93 minutes; Release date: November 21, 2012. **CAST:** David Pevsner (Ebenezer Scrooge), Tim Kazurinsky (Jacob Marley's Ghost), Rusty Schwimmer (Freda), Bruce Villanch (Fezziwig), Megan Cavanagh (Terry, Ghost of Christmas Present), Ronnie Kroell (Randy, Ghost of Christmas Past), David Moretti (Bob Cratchit), Richard Ganoung (Colin), Becca Kaufman (Becca), Judith Light (Narrator), Drew Anderson (Young Scrooge), Nicholas Bailey (Young Marley), Christopher Allen (Bill), JoJo Baby (Ghost of Christmas Future/Spectres/Delivery Person), P.J. Powers (Wraith), Scott Duff (Drew), Amy Matheny (Mary), Fawzia Mirza (Marshall), Peter Mohawk (Kyle), Michael Joseph Mitchell (Scrooge's Father), Richard Knight, Jr. (Dick), Tommy Beardmore (Brent), Allison Torem (Franny), Liam Jones (Tiny Tim), Dixon Kaufman (Cassie), Delaney Kaufman (Ruby), Elijah Pendleton (Rafael), Keante Pendleton (Simon), Michael Termine (Pawnshop Owner), Olin Eargle, Bradley Thomas (Hustlers, Pawnshop), Tom Chiola, Victor Salvo (Cabaret Customers), Sean Walton, Diana Simonzadeh, Alex Weisman (Guests at Freda and Mary's Party), Ellen Stoneking (GPS Voice), Rafael Torres, Steve McQuown (Bullies), David Cerda, Ed Jones (Drag Queens), Colin Spahr, Scott Goehring (Grindr App Men), Alison Cuddy (Television Broadcaster), Beth Behney (Fezziwig's Secretary)

Bruce Villanch in *Scrooge & Marley* © Sam I Am Films

SEEDS OF RESILIENCY (Iron Zeal Films) Producer/Director, Susan Polis Schutz; Photography, Aron Brown, Larry Warner, others; Editor, Bret Granado; Color; Not rated; 58 minutes; Release date: November 23, 2012. Documentary on people who have bounced back from various hardships, illnesses and life challenges; **WITH:** Jackline Arima, Tracy Bennett, Dr. Edith Eger, Aaron Fotheringham, Rufus Hannah, Walter Lam, Fanny Lebovits, Dr. Sang-Mook Lee, Candace Lightner, Ernest Michel, Chad Miller, Laurie Rapp Miller, Maureen Monroe, Moreen Obura, Jared Polis, Barry Soper, Andrea Spiner, Mike Stevens, Susan Stevens, Gerald Womaniala

GOTTFRIED HELNWEIN AND THE DREAMING CHILD (First Run Features) Producer/ Director, Lisa Kirk Colburn; Photography, Nyika Jansco, Robert Brinkman, John Sharaf; Music, Kirk Wesley Bailey; Editor, Alex Gans; a Red Fire Films production; Color; HD; Stereo; Not rated; 72 minutes; Release date: November 23, 2012. Documentary on artist Gottfried Helnwein and his role as production designer on the 2010 Tel Aviv opera *The Child Dreams*; **WITH:** Gottfried Helnwein, Omri Nitzan, Gil Shohat, David Stern, Gregor Seyffert, Ari Yona Bueno, Byeager Blackwell Seelig, Bambi

Seeds of Resiliency © Iron Zeal Films

Gottfried Helnwein and the Dreaming Child © First Run Features

SAVING AMERICA'S HORSES: A NATION BETRAYED (Area 23a) Producer/ Director/ Screenplay/Narrator, Katia Louise; a Wild For Life Foundation presentation of an IMA Studios/Humanion Films production; Color; Not rated; 91 minutes; Release date: November 26, 2012. Documentary on the fate of horses who outlive their owners' needs; **WITH:** Shelley Abrams, Laura Allen, Joy Aten, Paula Bacon, Shane Barbi, Sia Barbi, Michael Blake, Deniz Bolbol, Linda Breitman, Ila Bromberg, Diamond Jim Brooks, Dan Burton, Julie Caramante, Diana Chontos, Sandi Claypool, Calamity Cate Crismani, Neda DeMayo, Dr. Nicholas Dodman, Craig Downer, Jualine Eldridge, Robert Eldridge, Amy Fitzgerald, Leslie Fleming-Mitchell, Twyla Francois, Dr. Lester Friedlander, Elyse Gardner, Temple Grandin, Linda Gray, Laura Hearn, Tippi Hedren, John Holland, Gwen Holloway, Ryan Hopkins, Nick Illia, Margaret Jackson, Dr. Lisa Jacobson, Valeri James-Patten Julie Ann Johnson, Ginger Kathrens, Dr. Elliot Katz, George Knapp, Michelle Laine, Mary Landrieu, Jennifer Lee, Steve Long, Chief Arvol Looking Horse, Debra Lopez, Katia Louise, Peter Max, Victoria McCullough, Sonja Meadows, Amy Nelson, Raelyn Nelson, Willie Nelson, JoAnne Normile, Patience O'Dowd, Madeleine A. Pickens, Jennifer Lee Pryor, Paul Rainbird, Audrey Reynolds, Monty Roberts, Suzanne Roy, Jeff Ruch, Bob Rumnock, Sir Paul Sorvino, Beverly Strauss, Tom Strauss, Virginia Suarez, Sally Summers, Susan Wagner, Ken Wahl, Ed Whitfield, Dr. Nena Winand, Nick Zito

Saving America's Horses © Area 23a

BEWARE OF MR. BAKER (SnagFilms) Producers, Jay Bulger, Andrew Karsch, Fisher Stevens, Erik H. Gordon; Executive Producers, Julie Goldman, Tony Palmer; Director/Screenplay, Jay Bulger; Photography, Eric Robbins; Music Supervisor, Susan Jacobs; Editor, Abhay Sofsky; an Insurgent Media presentation of a Pugilist at Rest production; Color; Not rated; 92 minutes; Release date: November 28, 2012. Documentary on revered drummer Ginger Baker; **WITH:** Ginger Baker, Bob Adcock, Tony Allen, Carmine Appice, Brian Auger, Ginette Baker, Leda Baker, Jack Bruce, Malcolm Cecil, Eric Clapton, Stewart Copeland, Joni Haasrtup, Mickey Hart, Jon Hiseman, Simon Kirke, Femi Kuti, Denny Laine, Bill Laswell, John Lydon, Nick Mason, Neil Peart, Marky Ramone, Mick Rock, Carlos Santana, Chad Smith, Chip Stern, Lars Ulrich, Bill Ward, Charlie Watts, Max Weinberg, Hank Williams III, Steve Winwood, Bernie Worrell

EX-GIRLFRIENDS (Poe/Films) Producer/Editor, Jennifer Gerber; Executive Producers, Alexander Poe, Jennifer Carpenter; Co-Producer, Joseph Varca; Director/Screenplay, Alexander Poe; Photography, Gregory Kershaw; Designers, Joseph Varca, Minji Kang; an Alexander Poe and Jennifer Gerber production and [Poe/Films] presentation; Color; Not rated; 72 minutes; Release date: November 28, 2012. **CAST:** Jennifer Carpenter (Kate), Kristen Connolly (Laura), Alexander Poe (Graham), Liz Holtan (Samantha), Noah Bean (Tom), Will Janowitz (Matt), Matt McGrath (Professor O'Donnelly), Ian Unterman (Ben), Teddy Bergman (Paul), Tara Giordano (Ingrid), Justine Lupe (Lisa), Michael Zegen (Graham's Friend), Ashley Springer, Jordan Klepper, Jay Dunn

Matt McGrath in *Ex-Girlfriends* © Poe/Films

CERTAINTY (FilmBuff) Producers, Will Battersby, Mike O'Malley, Per Melita; Director, Peter Askin; Screenplay, Mike O'Malley, based on his 2003 play *Searching for Certainty*; Photography, Sean Kirby; Designer, Dara Wishingrad; Costumes, Tere Duncan; Music, David Mansfield; Editor, Karen Wynn Weinberg; Casting, Douglas Aibel, Henry Russell Bergstein; a Reno Productions film in association with Cinergy Pictures; Color; HD; Not rated; 104 minutes; Release date: November 30, 2012. **CAST:** Adelaide Clemens (Deb Catalano), Tom Lipinski

(Dom McGuire), Bobby Moynihan (Roddy), Tammy Blanchard (Melissa), Will Rogers (Kevin), Kristen Connolly (Betsy), Giancarlo Esposito (Father Heery), Valerie Harper (Kathryn), Dominic Colon (Hefty Dude), Jo Armenioux (Christine), Larry Clarke (Mike), Maria Dizzia (Serious Lady), Paloma Guzmán (Jennifer), Frank Harts (Khakis), Thomas Middleditch (Game Guy), Kianné Muschett (Eager Lady), Brendan O'Malley (Chad), Kerry O'Malley (Theresa), Kate Reinders (Mary), Loudon Wainright III (Tom), Johnny M. Wu (Rick), Rob Yang (Fred), John Auer, Mike Finazzo, Stephanie Sherry (Acting Students), John Cariani (Odd Interviewer), Robert Arensen (Physical Therapist Patient), David Dantowitz, Thomas Brucia, Hal Cohen (Barbershoppers)

THE COLLECTION (LD Entertainment) Producers, Julie Richardson, Brett Forbes, Patrick Rizzotti, Mickey Liddell, Jennifer Monroe; Executive Producers, Tom Luse, Pete Shilaimon; Director, Marcus Dunstan; Screenplay, Patrick Melton, Marcus Dunstan, based on their characters; Photography, Sam McCurdy; Designer, Graham "Grace" Walker; Costumes, Eulyn Womble; Music, Charlie Clouser; Editors, Mark Stevens, Kevin Greutert; Visual Effects Supervisor, David Karlak; Makeup Effects Creator, Gary J. Tunnicliffe; Casting, Joseph Middleton, Tineka Becker; a Liddell Entertainment presentation of a Fortress Features production; Dolby; Hawk-Scope; Color; Rated R; 82 minutes; Release date: November 30, 2012. **CAST:** Josh Stewart (Arkin), Emma Fitzpatrick (Elena), Lee Tergesen (Lucello), Christopher McDonald (Mr. Peters), Johanna Braddy (Missy Solomon), Michael Nardelli (Josh), Navi Rawat (Lisa), Andre Royo (Wally), Daniel Sharman (Basil), Randall Archer (The Collector), Brandon Molale (Lin), Shannon Kane (Paz), Erin Way (Abby), William Peltz (Brian), Justin Mortelliti (Zack), Tim Griffin (Dre), Robert Pralgo (Doctor), Mel Fair, Anne Marie Howard (Reporters), Courtney Lauren Cummings (Young Elena), Michael H. Cole (Older Man), Laura Marion (Cheryl), Joshua Burion-Mohn (Sick Person), Heather Mote (Brian's Sexy Blonde), Anne Tyler, Tandra Caldwell (DJs), Ryan Cutrona (Police Spokesperson), John Gulager (Agent Gulager), Seth Camillo (Agent Camillo), Jeff Arbaugh (Fire Captain Adam Lynch), Brett Forbes (Sgt. Hoss Wiggins), Jennifer Hilton Moore (Sgt. Hilton), Patrick Rizzotti (Nurse Rizzo), Brita Parker (Nurse Mary Jane), David Landsness (Nurse Snicklefritz), David Karlak (Deceased Cat Lover)

Erin Way, Randall Arhcer in *The Collection* © LD Entertainment

DRIVERS WANTED (Weinstein Film Production) Producers, Jean Tsien, Joshua Z. Weinstein; Director/ Photography, Joshua Z. Weinstein; Music, Adam Crystal; Editor, Jean Tsien; Color; Not rated; 54 minutes; Release date: November 30, 2012. Documentary on a Queens-based taxi company; **WITH:** Johnnie "Spider" Footman, Eric "New Driver," Stanley "Taxi Manager"

NEW JERUSALEM (Factory 25) Producers, Rick Alverson, Colm O'Leary; Executive Producers, Chris Swanson, Darius Van Arman, Jonathan Cargill, Ben Swanson; Director/Photography/Editor, Rick Alverson; Screenplay, Rick Alverson, Colm O'Leary; Music, Champ Bennett, Robert Donne; The Made Bed Productions; Stereo; Color; Not rated; 92 minutes; Release date: November 30, 2012. **CAST:** Colm O'Leary (Sean Murphy), Will Oldham (Ike Evans), Walter Scott (Walt),

Drivers Wanted © Weinstein Film Prod.

Roxanne Ferris (Store Clerk), Ryan O'Neill, Chris Dovi, Eddie Prendergast, Ricky Goran (Ike's Friends)

Louisa Krause in King Kelly © See Think Films

Taylor, Uma Thurman, Marisa Tomei, Evan Rachel Wood, Lois Banner, George Barris, Patricia Bosworth, Sarah Churchwell, Amy Greene, Molly Haskell, Jay Kanter, Richard Meryman, Thomas Schatz, Donald Spoto

Will Oldham in New Jerusalem © Factory 25

KING KELLY (SeeThink Films) Producers, Tom Davis, Luke Meyer, Ethan Palmer, Tom Davis, Andrew D. Corkin; Executive Producers, Laura Heberton, John David, Susan Shopmaker, David F. Schwartz; Director/Story, Andrew Neel; Screenplay, Mike Roberts; Photography, Ethan Palmer; Designer, Annie Simeone; Costumes, Jesse Huber; Music, Jonn Ollsin, Kim Krans; Editor, Brad Turner; Casting, Susan Shopmaker; from GoDigital; Color; Not rated; 85 minutes; Release date: November 30, 2012. **CAST:** Louisa Krause (Kelly), Libby Woodbridge (Jordan), Roderick Hill (Poo Bare), Will Brill (Ryan), Joseph Reiever (Troy), Jonny Orsini (Matt), Joey Auzenne (Drug Dealer), Aaron Cassara (Tom), Ash Christian (Dean), Beth Dzuricky (Mom), Ramsey Faragallah (Liquor Store Clerk), Anthony Fazio (Blake), Peter Ferguson (Blow-Job Guy), Michael Kaycheck (Commanding Officer), Anthony Lumia (Timmy), Diana Masi (Donna), Andrew Mer (Dad), Patrick Murney (Chad), John F. O'Donnell (Jimbo), Jen Ponton (Angela), Micah Stock (Josh), Orien Longo (Guy on Stairs), Emily Fleischer (Girl at Fire)

LOVE, MARILYN (HBO Documentary Films) Producers, Stanley Buchthal, Liz Garbus, Amy Hobby; Executive Producers, Anne Carey, Olivier Courson, Harold Van Lier; Director/ Screenplay, Liz Garbus; Photography, Maryse Alberti; Designer, Mike Barton; Music, Philip Sheppard; Editor, Azin Samari; a Studiocanal presentation of a Diamond Girl and Sol's Luncheonette production; Color; DCP; Not rated; 107 minutes; Release date: November 30, 2012. Documentary on actress Marilyn Monroe, as told through her personal papers; **VOICES:** F. Murray Abraham, Elizabeth Banks, Adrien Brody, Ellen Burstyn, Glenn Close, Hope Davis, Viola Davis, Jennifer Ehle, Ben Foster, Paul Giamatti, Jack Huston, Stephen Lang, Lindsay Lohan, Janet McTeer, Jeremy Piven, Oliver Platt, David Strathairn, Lili

Marilyn Monroe in Love, Marilyn © HBO Documentary Films

CALIFORNIA SOLO (Strand) Producer, Mynette Louie; Executive Producers, Robert Carlyle, Joan Huang, Nick Morton, Rick Rosenthal; Director/Screenplay, Marshall Lewy; Photography, James Laxton; Designer, Eric James Archer; Costumes, Cynthia Ann Summers; Music, T. Griffin; Music Supervisor, Joe Rudge; Editor, Alex Jablonski; Casting, Heidi Levitt, Michael Sanford; a Zambry Films presentation of a Syncopated Films production in association with A Harp Productions/Cherry Sky Films/Whitewater Films; Color; Not rated; 94 minutes; Release date: November 30, 2012. **CAST:** Robert Carlyle (Lachlan), Alexia Rasmussen (Beau), Kathleen Wilhoite (Catherine), A Martinez (Warren), Michael Des Barres (Wendell), Danny Masterson (Paul), Brad Greenquist (Piper), Robert Cicchini (Domenico), Savannah Lathem (Arianwen), Eli Vargas (Julian), Brian Chenoweth (Bartender), Stephen Jared (Patrolman), Wiley Pickett (Deputy), Anna Khaja (Anna), Ping Wu (Judge), William Russ (Rusty), Hal Landon Jr. (Farmer), Ella Joyce (Carol), Patrick Gallagher (ICE Officer), Dale Nieli (Customer), Nice Nicotera (Nick), Adam Arian (Paul's Friend), Heather Fowler (Flashlight #4)

Alexia Rasmussen, Robert Carlyle in *California Solo* © Strand Releasing

UNIVERSAL SOLDIER: DAY OF RECKONING (Magnet) Producers, Moshe Diamant, Craig Baumgarten; Executive Producers, Mark Damon, Borislav Ranghelov, Courtney Solomon, Steven A. Frankel, Gregory Walker, Allen Shapiro, James Gibb; Director, John Hyams; Screenplay, John Hyams, Doug Magnuson, Jon Greenhalgh; Based on a story by John Hyams, Moshe Diamant, based on characters created by Richard Rothstein, Christopher Leitch, Dean Devlin; Photography, Yaron Levy; Designer, Nate Jones; Costumes, Kim Martinez; Music, Michael Krassner, Wil Hendricks, Robin Vining; Editors, John Hyams, Andrew Drazek; Stunts, Chuck Picerni Jr.; Casting, Brent Caballero; a Foresight Unlimited presentation of a Signature Entertainment/BMP production; Dolby; Color; Rated R; 114 minutes; Release date: November 30, 2012. **CAST:** Jean-Claude Van Damme (Luc Deveraux), Dolph Lundgren (Andrew Scott), Scott Adkins (John), Andrei "The Pit Bull" Arlovski (Magnus), Mariah Bonner (Sarah), Rus Blackwell (Agent Gorman), Tony Jarreau (Bouncer), Craig Walker (Earl), Andrew Sikking (Larry), James DuMont (Dr. Timothy Brady), David Jensen (Dr. Su), Audrey P. Scott (Emma), Dane Rhodes (Ron Castellano), Susan Mansur (Madame), Kristopher Van Varenberg (Miles), Sigal Diamant (Claudia), Juli Erickson (Woman), Michelle Jones (Kathryn), Roy Jones Jr. (Mess Hall Unisol)

Dolph Lundgren in *Universal Soldier: Day of Reckoning* © Magnet Releasing

IN OUR NATURE (Cinedigm/Flatiron) Producers, Anish Savjani, Vincent Savino, Brian Savelson; Executive Producers, Susan Bianchi, Robert Savelson, Rajen Savjani, James Black, Mark Dalton, Kurt Dalton, Todd Kessler, James Marciano, Jeremy Mindich; Director/Screenplay, Brian Savelson; Photography, Jeremy Saulnier; Designer, Russell Barnes; Costumes, Anney Perrine; Music, Jeff Grace; Editors, Kate Abernathy, Annette Davey; a FilmScience production; Color; Not rated; 103 minutes; Release date: December 7, 2012. **CAST:** Zach Gilford (Seth), Jena Malone (Andie), John Slattery (Gil), Gabrielle Union (Vicky), David Ilku (Visiting Father), Lisa Velten Smith (Visiting Mother), Lola Cook (Little Girl), Hudson Price (Little Boy)

Gabrielle Union, John Slattery, Jena Malone, Zach Gilford in *In Our Nature* © Cinedigm

THE SHEIK AND I (Factory 25) Producer/Director, Caveh Zahedi; Photography, Colin Nusbaum, Michael Patten; Music, Sammy Miler, Emilie Levienaise-Farrouch; Editors, Caveh Zahedi, Colin Nusbaum; a Reinventing the Wheel production; Color; Not rated; 104 minutes; Release date: December 7, 2012. Documentary on how filmmaker Caveh Zahedi turned his assignment of "art as a subversive act" into a movie poking fun at the Sheik financing the Middle Eastern Biennial; **WITH:** Caveh Zahedi, Alan Berliner, Amanda Field, Mansour, Colin Nusbaum, Michael Patten, Jack Persekian, Abdul Rahman, Rasha Satti, Zuzu Snyder, Beckett Zahedi,

WAITING FOR LIGHTNING (Samuel Goldwyn Films) Producers, Max Leitman, Darryl Franklin, Jacob Rosenberg, Hana Ripperger-Suhler; Executive Producers, Michael Mailis, Ray Ibe, Jay Pollak, Scott Waugh, Mouse McCoy; Director, Jacob Rosenberg; Screenplay, Bret Anthony Johnston; Photography, Michael Svitak; Music, Nathan Furst; Presented in association with DC Shoes; Color; Rated PG-13; 96 minutes; Release date: December 7, 2012. Documentary on skateboarder Danny Way; **WITH:** Danny Way, Mike Blabc, Ken Bloc, Bod Boyle, Grant Brittain, Bob Burnquist, Tommy Caudill, Paul Chek, Adrian Demain, Steve Douglas, Rob Dyrdek, Ty Evans, Darryl Franklin, Bobby Goodsby, Laird Hamilton, Brian Harper, Tony Hawk, Matt Hensley, Mat Hoffman, Christian Hosoi, Greg Hunt, Ray Ibe, Tony Magnusson, Guy Mariano, Jeremy McGrath, Colin McKay, Rodney Mullen, Jim O'Dea, Mary O'Dea, Travis Pastrana, Paul Rodriguez Jr., Jim Ruonala, John Schultes, Dave Swift, John "JT" Tyson, Damon Way, Gale Webb, Kelly Byrd, Mike Carroll, Rick Howard, Bucky Lasek, Alphonzo Rawls, Todd Richards, Jordan Richter; **AND:** Grant Romagnoli (Danny, age 2), Julian Haggart (Danny, age 3), Dondillon Rohrer (Danny, age 7), Crystal Ackley (Mary O'Dea, age 28), Miles Michaud (Boyfriend)

THE FITZGERALD FAMILY CHRISTMAS (Tribeca Film) Producers, Aaron Lubin, Edward Burns, William Rexer II; Executive Producer, Mike Harrop; Director/Screenplay, Edward Burns; Photography, William Rexer II; Music, PT Walkley; Editor, Janet Gaynor; Casting, Maribeth Fox; a Marlboro Road Gang production; Color; Not rated; 103 minutes; Release date: December 7, 2012. **CAST:** Kerry Bishé (Sharon Fitzgerald), Edward Burns (Gerry Fitzgerald), Heather Burns (Erin Fitzgerald), Marsha Dietlein Bennett (Dottie Fitzgerald), Caitlin Fitzgerald

Danny Way in *Waiting for Lightning* © Goldwyn Films

(Connie Fitzgerald), Anita Gillette (Rosie Fitzgerald), Tom Guiry (Cyril Fitzgerald), Ed Lauter (Jim Fitzgerald), Michael McGlone (Quinn Fitzgerald), Nick Sandow (Corey), Noah Emmerich (FX), Connie Britton (Nora), Joyce Van Patten (Mrs. McGowan), Dara Coleman (JJ), Brian D'Arcy James (Skippy), Malachy McCourt (Father), Daniella Pineda (Abbie), John Solo (Johnny Esposito), Michele Harris (Quinn's Assistant), Kevin Kash (Brian)

Edward Burns, Connie Britton in *The Fitzgerald Family Christmas* © Tribeca Film

HAPPY NEW YEAR (One Light Left) Producers, Michael Cuomo, K. Lorrel Manning, Karl Jacob, Victoria Hay, Tom Stein; Executive Produers, Iain Smith, Whitney Arcaro, Terrence Gray; Director/Screenplay, K. Lorrel Manning, based on his 2007 play; Photography, Soopum Sohn; Music, Paul Brill; Editor, William Miller; Casting, Adrienne Stern; an Iain Smith presentation; Color; Rated R; 105 minutes; Release date: December 7, 2012. **CAST:** Michael Cuomo (Staff Sgt. Cole Lewis), J.D. Williams (Jerome), Monique Gabriela Curnen (Lisa), Jose Yenque (Martinez), David Fonteno (Gunny D), Wilmer Calderon (Santiago), Will Rogers (Danny), Noah Mills (Looch), Tina Sloan (Grace), Alan Dale (Bill), John Leighton (Jesus), Frank Harts (Dex), Seth Barrish (Dr. Keith), Karl Jacob (Brian), Joseph Harrell (Joe Wallace), Terrence Gray (Senator Charles), Larry Mitchell (Brant), Miles Solay (Liam), Anne Girard (Gina), Shelley Bennett (Sheila), Teresa Stephenson (Teresa), Hunter Emery (Johnson), Chris Barber (Barnes), Vandal Truong (Luc), Latrice Martin (Rita), Patricia Alexandro (Anesthesiologist), Patrick Blumer (ICU Nurse), Ankara Martinez (Cocktail Waitress), Cheri Haines (Nurse), Francis Cooper, Dan Kaplan (Orderlies), Selena Johnson (Guard), John J. Palomino (Veteran in Gym), Vega (Bouncer), Joseph Marcello (Stripclub Announcer), Josh Mendelow, Taylor Ruckel, Emilio Savone (Bar Patrons), Thomas Reardon (Antwone Dimley, TV Talkshow Host), Cher Santiago (Tina, Talkshow Guest), Maurice Clemons (Marcus, Talkshow Guest), Sarah Babb (Natalie,

Talkshow Guest), Nathan Mirsky (Looch's Son), Stephanie Wise (Woman in Crack Den), Mike Scotti (Marine Radio Voice), Victoria Hay (British Newscast Voiceover)

Michael Cuomo in *Happy New Year*
© One Light Left

HONOR FLIGHT (Freethink Media) Producers, Clay Broga, Eric Schroeder (Wisconsin); Executive Producers, Kmele Foster, Ted Balaker; Director, Dan Hayes; Photography, Benjamin Gaskell, Dan Hayes; Music, Josh Christiansen, Alex Maas; Editor, Hawk Jensen; Color; Rated PG; 82 minutes; Release date: December 7, 2012. Documentary on how a Midwest community came together to send four World War II veterans to Washington DC to see the memorial constructed for them; **WITH:** Harvey Kurz, Joe Demler, Joe Dean, Renee Riddle, Charlie Sykes, Steve Deutsch, Julian Plaster, Orville Lemke, Ann Rasmusson, Mark Grams, Ryan Jazak, Heidi Schmidt, Lisa Goglio-Zarczynski, Bert Brach, Earl Bruss, Donald Esselman, Theodor Gurzynski, Raymond Hasey, Sterling Hasey, Bill Holmes, Kenneth Holzer, John Kruzycki, Loretta Kurz, George Legath, Edward Mikush, Earl Morse, Scott Olsen, Larry Parmalee, Renee Riddle, Bill Rossman, Stephan Sanfelippo, Paul Schmidt, Eugene Schulz, Joseph Turicik

Julian Plaster in *Honor Flight* © Freethink Media

ONLY THE YOUNG (Oscilloscope) Producer, Derek Waters; Executive Producers, Tim Garrett, Daniel A. Murphy, John Kaulakis; Directors/Editors, Jason Tippet, Elizabeth Mims; Photography, Jason Tippet; Music, Nick Thorburn; a THEsaurus LLC presentation; Not rated; 70 minutes; Release date: December 7, 2012. Documentary on how three teens live their lives in a depressed Southern California town; **WITH:** Garrison Saenz, Kevin Conway, Skye Elmore, Samantha Macdonald, Kristen Cheriegate, Shannon Hudson, Robin Levy

Kevin Conway, Garrison Saenz in *Only the Young* © Oscilloscope Laboratories

BAD KIDS GO TO HELL (Red Sea Media) Producers, Barry Wernick, Brad Keller; Executive Producers, Stuart Wernick, James Hallam, David Genecov, Carmrin Agin, Tommy Warren; Director, Matthew Spradlin; Screenplay, Matthew Spradlin, Barry Wernick; Based on the graphic novel; Photography, David Blood; Designer, Jason Hammond; Costumes, Alyssa Wernick; Music, Brian Flores; Editor, Justin Wilson; a Bad Kids presentation in association with Spiderwood Studios and Charlieuniformtango of a BKGTH Production; Color; Rated R; 91 minutes; Release date: December 7, 2012. **CAST:** Ben Browder (Max), Judd Nelson (Headmaster Nash), Cameron Deane Stewart (Matt Clark), Ali Faulkner (Tricia Wilkes), Roger Edwards (Craig Cook), Marc Donato (Tarek Ahmed), Augie Duke (Veronica Harmon), Amanda Alch (Megan McDurst), Jefrey Schmidt (Dr. Day), Chanel Ryan (Ms. Gleason), Eloise DeJoria (Gov. Wilkes), Barry Wernick (Marquez), Doran Ingram (Rainwater), Brandon Noack (Magnus Stubblefield – Paramedic), Steve Jimenez, Phillip Tolle (Detectives), Íce Mrozek (Mr. Ahmed), Rodney Johnson (Mr. Cook), Collin Cole (Wheelchair Kid), Charles Solomon Jr., Steve Kriger (Cops), Wendhy Tobias (Whoa Teacher), Mike Gassaway (Taser Police Officer), Katrina Hill (Kissing Girl), Monica Zelak (Cafeteria Hot Girl), Jim Cates, Kensley Grant, Carol Mazhuvancheril, Hollee McMurray (Crestview Students)

Bad Kids Go to Hell © Red Sea Media

FLYING LESSONS (New Films Intl.) Producers, Jenny Hinkey, Derek Magyar; Executive Producers, Mark Johnson, Chris Carter, Chip Fullerton, Biride Hawthorne, JPL, Nesim Hason, Ron Gell, Straw Weisman, Jak Kamhi, Aylin Filiba; Director, Derek Magyar; Screenplay, Thomas J. Kuehl; Photography, Joshua Hess; Designer, Khari Walker; Costumes, Peter Max-Mueller, Maya Krispin; Music, Jesse Glick; Editor, Richard Harris; Casting, Steve Brooksbank; a Skinny Lee Productions in association with Granvia Productions and Tenthirteen Productions presentation; Color; Rated R; 103 minutes; Release date: December 7, 2012. **CAST:** Maggie Grace (Sophie Conway), Cary Elwes (Steven Jennings), Hal Holbrook (Harry Pleasant), Jonathan Tucker (Billy), Ian Anthony Dale (Lance),

Rick Gonzalez (Benji), Joanna Cassidy (Totty Kuspert), Christine Lahti (Caroline Conway), Nikki Deloach (Mila), Maggie Castle (Shelly), Michael O'Neill (Chief Dobbs), Alyssa de Boisblanc (Annie), Mickey Meyer (Teen Punk #2), Jillian Greene (Little Girl)

Maggie Grace in *Flying Lessons* © New Films Intl.

TCHOUPITOULAS (Oscilloscope) Producers/Directors/Photography, Bill Ross IV, Turner Ross; Executive Producers, Michael Gottwald, Dan Janvey, Josh Penn; Music Supervisor, Joe Rudge; an Epic Match Media presentation; Color; Not rated; 80 minutes; Release date: December 7, 2012. Documentary follows three young brothers as they journey into late-night New Orleans; **WITH:** William Zanders, Bryan Zanders, Kentrell Zanders

Tchoupitoulas © Oscilloscope Laboratories

LOST ANGELS: SKID ROW IS MY HOME (Cinema Libre Studios) Producer, Agi Orsi; Executive Producers, Gary Foster, Joe Wright, Susan Klos; Director, Thomas Q. Napper; Screenplay, Christine Triano; Photography, Seamus McGarvey, Fortunato Procopio, Christopher Gosch; Music, Walter Werzowa; Editor, Tyler Hubby; Narrator, Catherine Keener; an Agi Orsi Productions in association with Krasnoff Foster presentation; Color; Not rated; 77 minutes; Release date: December 7, 2012. Documentary on eight people who have tried to overcome being homeless in Los Angeles; **WITH:** Kevin Cohen, Manuel Compito, Danny Harris, Linda Harris, Terri Hughes, Lee Anne Leven, Albert Olson, Steve Richardson.

THE LOVING STORY (Icarus/HBO) Producers, Nancy Buirski, Elisabeth Haviland James; Executive Producers, Sheila Nevins, Marshall Sonenshine; Director, Nancy Buirski; Screenplay, Nancy Buirski, Susie Ruth Powell; Photography, Rex Miller, Steve Milligan, Abbot Mills; Music, David Majzlin; Editor, Elisabeth Haviland James; an Augusta Films production; Color/Black and white; Not rated; 77 minutes; Release date: December 10, 2012. Documentary on how the 1958 interracial marriage between Richard Loving and Mildred Jeter erupted in controversy; **WITH:** Edward Ayers, Caitlin Congdon, Kenneth Edwards, Raymond Green, Ruthie Holliday, Garnet Jeter, Lewis Jeter, Peggy Loving, Abbot Mills, Robert Pratt, Hope Ryden

Richard and Mildred Loving in *The Loving Story* © Icarus/HBO

CONSUMING SPIRITS (Chris Sullivan Animation) Producer/Director/Screenplay/Editor, Chris Sullivan; Animation, Chris Sullivan, Corinne Faiella, Shelley Dodson; Color; Not rated; 129 minutes; Release date: December 12, 2012. **VOICE CAST:** Robert Levy (Earl Gray), Nancy Andrews (Gentian Violet), Chris Sullivan (Victor Blue), Judith Rafael (Ida Blue), Mary Lou Zelazny (Mother Beatrice Elastica), Chris Harris (Peabody Shampling)

Consuming Spirits © Chris Sullivan Animation

THE GIRL (BrainStorm Media/Film Collectiv) Producer, Paul Mezey; Executive Producers, Philipp Englehorn, Nick Quested; Director/Screenplay, David Riker; Photography, Martin Boege; Designer, Salvador Parra; Costumes, Mariestela Hernandez; Music, Jacobo Lieberman, Leonardo Heiblum; Editors, Malcolm Jamieson, Stephanie Ahn; a Goldcrest Films and Cinereach Films presentation in association with Lulú Producciones of a Journeyman Pictures productions, in association with Axiom Films, Sin Sentido Films and Bonita Films; Dolby; Color; Not rated; 94 minutes; Release date: December 14, 2012, **CAST:** Abbie Cornish

(Ashley), Will Patton (Tommy), Maritza Santiago Hernandez (Rosa), Austin West (Georgie), Annallee Jefferies (Gloria), Giovanna Zacarías (Enriqueta), Luci Christian (Sally), Geoffrey Rivas (Manager), Isabel Sanchez Lara (Grandmother), Angeles Cruz (Rosa's Mother), Katelyn Merricks, Lauren Galley (Tourists), Raúl Castillo (Border Agent), Harold Torres (Isidro), Javier Zaragoza (Felix), Abel Lopez Marroquin (Pancho), Hanne Jiménez Turcott (Waitress), Heber Garnica (Car Wash Man), Joaquin Maldonado Bolaños (Cheko), Palemon Olmedo (Jesus Antonio), Magdalena Heredia (Migrant Mother), Angel Alonso (Prayer Man), Luis Fernando Peña (Beto), Octavio Manuel Corres Pombo (Paco), Wagive Turcott Fiatt (Caretaker), Isabel Cruz Daza (Edith), Ivonne Cruz Daza (Cecilia), Jose Carlos Rodriguez Gutierrez (Police Official), Liliana Alberto (Ofelia)

Maritza Santiago, Abbie Cornish in *The Girl* © BrainStorm Media

LET FURY HAVE THE HOUR (CAVU Pictures) Producers, Antonio D'Ambrosio, James Reid; Executive Producers, Rob McKay, Brian Devine, Jonathan Gray, Mark Urman, Chaz Zelus; Director/Screenplay, Antonio D'Ambrosio; Based on Antonio D'Ambrosio's essays from his 2012 book *Let Fury Have the Hour*; Photography/Editor, Karim Lopez; Music, Wayne Kramer; a La Lutta NMC presentation of a Bricklayers Union Production in association with Gigantic Pictures; Color; Not rated; 87 minutes; Release date: December 14, 2012. Documentary on the creative counter-culture of the 21st century; **WITH:** Lewis Black, Billy Bragg, Staceyann Chin, Chuck D, Edwidge Danticat, Stephen Duncombe, Eve Ensler, Shepard Fairey, Tommy Guerrero, Suheir Hammad, Sean Hayes, Eugene Hutz, Van Jones, Wayne Kramer, Hari Kunzru, Ian MacKaye, El Meswy, Tom Morello, John Sayles, D.J. Spooky, Elizabeth Streb, Richard D. Wolff

Chuck D in *Let Fury Have the Hour* © CAVU Pictures

ANY DAY NOW (Music Box Films) Producers, Travis Fine, Kristine Hostetter Fine, Chip Hourihan, Liam Finn; Executive Producers, Maxine Makover, Anne O'Shea, Wayne Larue Smith, Dan Skahen; Director, Travis Fine; Screenplay, Travis Fine, George Arthur Bloom; Photography, Rachel Morrison; Designer, Elizabeth Garner; Costumes, Samantha Kuester; Music, Joey Newman; Music Supervisor, PJ Bloom; Song: "Metaphorical Blanket" written and performed by Rufus Wainright; Editor, Tom Cross; Casting, Anya Colloff, Michael Nicolo; a PFM Pictures presentation; Color; Rated R; 97 minutes; Release date: December 14, 2012. **CAST:** Alan Cumming (Rudy Donatello), Garret Dillahunt (Paul Fleiger), Isaac Leyva (Marco Deleon), Frances Fisher (Judge Meyerson), Gregg Henry (Lambert), Chris Mulkey (D.A. Wilson), Don Franklin (Lonnie Washington), Jamie Anne Allman (Marianna Deleon), Kelli Williams (Miss Fleming), Alan Rachins (Judge Resnick), Mindy Sterling (Miss Mills), Doug Spearman (Johnny Boy), Randy Roberts (PJ), Miracle Laurie (Monica), Michael Nouri (Miles Dubrow), Jeffrey Pierce (Officer Plitt), Louis Lombardi (Mr. Blum), Donna W. Scott (Kelly Wilson), Clyde Kusatsu (Dr. Nakahura), Anne O'Shea (Mrs. Lowell), Joe Howard (Dr. Watkins), Kirk Fox (Beaux), Ezra Buzzington (Larry), Kamala Lopez (Agent Martinez), Edward James Gage (Sgt. Johnson), Randy Thompson (Coco)

Lizzy Caplan, Mark Webber in *Save the Date* © IFC Films

Garret Dillahunt, Isaac Leyva, Alan Cumming in *Any Day Now* © Music Box Films

SAVE THE DATE (IFC Films) Producers, Jordan Horowitz, Michael Huffington, Michael Roiff; Executive Producer, Gary Gilbert; Director, Michael Mohan; Screenplay, Jeffrey Brown, Egan Reich, Michael Mohan; Photography, Elisha Christian; Designers, Cindy Chao, Michele Yu; Costumes, Mirren Gordon-Crozier; Music, Hrishikesh Hirway; Editor, Christian Masini; Casting, Kerry Barden, Paul Schnee; a Huffington Productions presentation; Color; Rated R; 98 minutes; Release date: December 14, 2012. **CAST:** Lizzy Caplan (Sarah), Alison Brie (Beth), Martin Starr (Andrew), Mark Webber (Jonathan), Geoffrey Arend (Kevin), Melonie Diaz (Isabelle), Timothy Busfield (Benjie), Gigi Bermingham (Mom), Grant Harvey (Trevor), Devin Barry (Soul Patch), Jacob Womack (Jonathan's Friend), Ray Conchado (Steppenwolf), Lauren Nash (Cute Wolfbird Fan), Kristin Slaysman (Michelle), Meghan McCarthy (Not Sarah), Robin Riker (Aunt Mary), Kristen Riley (Checkout Girl), Elizabeth Ho (Bridal Saleswoman), Jessica Morris (Girl in Bar), Rich Cooper (Rabbi), Carlease Burke (Receptionist), Miss Kitty (Ferdinand), Nasa (Herself), Jay Chaffin, Emily Chaffin (Couple getting Married), Aaron Smith (Doctor)

TRASHED (Blenheim Films) Producers, Candida Brady, Titus Ogilvy; Executive Producers, Jeremy Irons, Candida Brady, Titus Ogilvy, Tom Wesel; Director/Screenplay, Candida Brady; Photography, Sean Bobbitt, Titus Ogilvy, Peter Ditch; Art Director, Garry Waller; Music, Vangelis; Editors, James Coward, Kate Coggins, Jamie Trevill; Presented by Jeremy Irons; Stereo; Color; Not rated; 98 minutes; Release date: December 14, 2012. Documentary in which actor Jeremy Irons presents the devastating truth about the effects of global waste.

Jeremy Irons in *Trashed* © Blenheim Films

YELLING TO THE SKY (MPI) Producers, Victoria Mahoney, Ged Dickersin, Billy Mulligan, Diane Houslin; Director/Screenplay, Victoria Mahoney; Photography, Reed Morano; Designer, Kelly McGehee; Costumes, Nia Hooper; Music, David Wittman; Editor, Bill Henry; Casting, Eyde Belasco; a Mahoney/Mulligan Productions presentation; Dolby; Color; Not rated; 94 minutes; Release date: December 14, 2012. **CAST:** Zoë Kravitz (Sweetness O'Hara), Jason Clarke (Gordon O'Hara), Antonique Smith (Ola Katherine O'Hara), Tim Blake Nelson (Coleman), Gabourey Sidibe (Latonya Williams), Marc John Jefferies (Lil' Man), Maurice Compte (Junior Oriol), Adam Tomei (Cal), Sonequa Martin (Jojo Parker), Zabryna Guevara (Aracely Oriol), Shareeka Epps (Fatima Harris), E.J. Bonilla (Rob Rodriguez), Billy Kay (Dobbs), Peter Anthony Tambakis (Drew), Yolonda Ross (Lorene O'Hara), Gleendilys Inoa (Betty Oriol), Gio Perez (Shorty), Deema Aitken (Sean), Hassan Manning (Bohanen), Dennis Kellum Castro (Two Dog), Sarah Shaefer (Moira), Antoine de Pharoah (Hi'Low)

Zoë Kravitz in *Yelling to the Sky* © MPI Media

JASON BECKER: NOT DEAD YET (Kino Lorber) Producer/Director, Jesse Vile; Executive Producers, Oli Harbottle, Dennis Joyce; Photography, Car Burke; Music, Jason Becker, Michael Lee Firkins; Editor, Gideon Gold; an Opus Pocus Films and Dogwoof presentation; Color; Not rated; 86 minutes; Release date: December 14, 2012. Documentary on how guitarist Jason Becker's career was cut short by ALS. **WITH:** Jason Becker, Ehren Becker, Gary Becker, Pat Becker, Ron Becker, Marty Friedman, Steve Hunter, Dave Lopez, Serrana Pilar, Joe Satriani, Steve Vai

Jason Becker in *Jason Becker: Not Dead Yet* © Kino Lorber

SAVING GRACE B. JONES (New Films Intl.) Executive Producers, John Gioia, Nesim Hason, Straw Weisman, Ron Gell, Jak Kamhi, Aylin Filiba; Director, Connie Stevens; Screenplay, Connie Stevens, Jeffry Elison; Photography, Denis Maloney; Music, Peter Golub; Editor, Clarinda Wong; Color; Rated R; 116 minutes; Release date: December 14, 2012. **CAST:** Michael Biehn (Landy Bretthorst), Tatum O'Neal (Grace Bretthorst), Penelope Ann Miller (Bea Bretthorst), Joel Gretsch (Dan Jones), Tricia Leigh Fisher (Ella Jean Jones), Audrey Wasilewski (Opal Lynn Carter), Gregory James (Phil Carter), Piper Laurie (Marta Shrank), Scott Wilson (Reverend Potter), Rylee Fansler (Carrie Staley), Evie Louise Thompson (Lucy Bretthorst), Nora Hennessy (Mollie Jane Carter), Liberty Smith (Little Opal), Melinda Chilton (Jane Belford), Logan Moore (Sean Ryan), L. Charles Taylor (Davey Lund), Scott Crouse (Miles Braddon), Vincent Monachino (Lem Bryerton), Karen Errington (Lynette Bryerton), Byron Thames (Clint Dexter), Desmond S. Peters (Tom Hendryks), Scott Cordes (Senior Orderly), Craig Joe Harris, Todd

R. Terry (Brooklyn Street Fighters), Mark Sweeney (New York Cop), Donn Markel (Orderly), Marie James, Jessie Williams (Gospel Soloists), David Huddleston (Radio Announcer)

Penelope Ann Miller, Tatum O'Neal in *Saving Grace B. Jones* © New Films Intl.

IN THE HIVE (Entertainment One) Producers, Robert Townsend, Messiah Jacobs, Rey Ramsey; Executive Producer, David Saunier; Director, Robert Townsend; Screenplay, Cheryl L. West; Photography, John L. Demps Jr.; Designer, Shaun Motley; Costumes, Nicole Beckett; Music, Dontae Winslow; Editor, Robert Pergament; Casting, Amber Bickham, Eileen Mack Knight; a V Studio production; Color; Rated R; 110 minutes; Release date: December 14, 2012. **CAST:** Loretta Devine (Mrs. Inez), Vivica A. Fox (Billie), Michael Clarke Duncan (Mr. Hollis), Jonathan "Lil J" McDaniel (Xtra Keyz), Ali Liebert (Parker Whitmore), Roger Guenveur Smith (Paris), Percy Daggs III (Rack Robinson), Yutopia Essex (Shay), Jontille Gerard (Gemini), Gordon Greene (Chase), Josh Harp (Lawyer), Jerome Hawkins (Shoot), Kevin Hendricks (Courvousier Carter), Courtney Schleinkofer (Christa), Richard Kuhlman (Dr. V), Joshua Kushner (Mr. Scott), Ronald William Lawrence (Jake), Sebastian Minor (Deuce), Barry O'Neil (Aden Rosen), Kiev Rhyse (Tony), Tre C. Roberts (Que Patterson), Tracey Dukes (Shoot's Lieutenant), B.J. Clinkscales, Marcus Natividad (Inmates), Michael Coley, Lavon Davis, Paul Sims (Hive Boys), Luise Heath (Board Member), Leeah Jackson (Prison Visitor), Bre Scullark (6 8 Gangmember)

Loretta Devine in *In the Hive* © Entertainment One

AMERICAN EMPIRE (HeartFelt Films) Producers, Jack Tucker, Patrea Patrick, Brian Jamieson, Frank Johnson, Sharlene Sullivan; Director/Photography/Editor, Patrea Patrick; Screenplay, Patrea Patrick, Jack Tucker; Music, Shane Jordan; Color; Not rated; 95 minutes; Release date: December 21, 2012. Documentary on how catering to corporate interests has slowly been destroying America; **WITH:** Tariq Ali, G. Edward Griffin, John Perkins, Vandana Shiva, Maude Barlow, Gerald Celente, Jeffrey Smith, John Robbins, Francis Moore Lappe, David Korten

Tariq Ali in *American Empire* © Heartfelt Films

ALLEGIANCE (XLrator Media) formerly *Recalled*; Producers, Daryl Friemark, Sean Mullin; Executive Producer, John Patrick Boyle; Director/Screenplay, Michael Connors; Photography, Danny Vecchione; Designer, Laurie Hicks; Costumes, Kama K. Royz; Music, Immediate; Editor, Jonathan Schwartz; a Five by Eight, Hardball Entertainment production; Color; HD; Rated R; 92 minutes; Release date: December 28, 2012. **CAST:** Aidan Quinn (Lt. Col. Owens), Seth Gabel (Lt. Danny Sefton), Shad "Bow Wow" Moss (Specialist Chris Reyes), Zachary Booth (Carroll), Pablo Schreiber (Lt. Alec Chambers), Malik Yoba (Staff Sgt. Hart), Reshma Shetty (Leela), Jason Lew (Kraft), Dominic Fumusa (Capt. Angelo), Redaric Williams (Pvt. Adams), Gavin-Keith Umeh (Gonzo), Laith Nakli (1st Sgt. Wells), Corey Antonio Hawkins (Willie), Mike Finazzo, Michael O'Neill (Cooks), Brian Smolensky (MP Sgt. Wilkins), Michael Gucciardo (Sgt. Longo), Rey Lucas (Barracks MP Sgt.), Gregg Prosser (Radio Sergeant), Alexander Martin Jones (Barracks MP Sergeant), Kareem Hamdy (Pvt. 1st Class Ryan), David Leviev (Sgt. Janczych), Ed Sordellini (Sgt. 1st Class Sordellini), Dennis Rees (Sgt. Kim), Gregg Prosser (Radio Sergeant), Christopher L. McAllister (Disheveled Sergeant), Jason Gore, Kristen Bartlett (Stockbrokers), Fady Kerko, Trever Sutherland, Joey Giambattista, Stanislav Shkilnyi, Russell Soder (Soldiers)

Seth Gabel, Shad Moss in *Allegiance* © XLrator Med

ONCE UPON A TIME IN ANATOLIA

(CINEMA GUILD) a.k.a. *Bir zamanlar Anadoul'da*; Producer, Zeynep Özbatur Atakan; Co-Producers, Mirsad Purivatra, Ed Arikan, Ibrahim Sahin, Müge Kolat, Murat Akdilek, Nuri Bilge Ceylan; Director, Nuri Bilge Ceylan; Screenplay, Ercan Kesal, Ebru Ceylan, Nuri Bilge Ceylan; Photography, Gökhan Tiryaki; Art Director, Dilek Yapukuöz Ayaztuna; Editors, Bora Göksingöl, Nuri Bilge Ceylan; Casting, Selim Ünel, Minet Atasoy; a Zeyno Film, Production 2006 Sarajevo, 1000 Volt Post-Production, Turkish Radio TV Corp., Imaj, Fida Film, NBC Film production; Turkish, 2011; Dolby; HD; Color; Not rated; 157 minutes; American release date: January 4, 2012

CAST

Doctor Cemal	**Muhammet Uzuner**
Commissar Naci	**Yilmaz Erdogan**
Prosecutor Nusret	**Taner Birsel**
Driver Arab Ali	**Ahmet Mümtaz Taylan**
Suspect Kenan	**Firat Tanis**
Mukhtar	**Ercan Kesal**

Erol Erarslan (Murder Victim Yasar), Ugur Aslanoglu (Courthouse Driver Tevfik), Murat Kiliç (Police Officer Izzet), Safak Karali (Courthouse Clerk Abidin), Emre Sen (Sergeant Önder), Burhan Yildiz (Suspect Ramazan), Nihan Okutucu (Yasar's Wife Gülnaz), Cansu Demirci (Mukhtar's Daughter Cemile),Kubilay Tunçer (Autopsy Technician Sakir), Aziz İzzet Biçici (Hospital Cook Hamit), Salih Ünal (Restaurant Owner Kazim), Celal Acaralp (Pharmacist Saim), Mehmet Eren Topçak (Hamam Scrubber), Ufuk Karaali (Hospital Attendant Sitki), Fevzi Müftüogu (1st Digger Hayrettin), Turgay Kürkçü (2nd Digger Ethem), Fatih Ereli (Gülnaz's Son Adem), Hüseyin Bekeç, Mehmet Öztürk (Soldiers)

A prosecutor, a doctor and the police search throughout the Anatolian steppes for a murder victim the suspect claims to have buried there earlier.

Taner Birsel

Firat Tanis © Cinema Guild

Rinko Kikuchi, Ken'ichi Matsuyama

Kiko Mizuhara © Red Flag

NORWEGIAN WOOD

(RED FLAG) a.k.a. *Noruwei no mori*; Producer, Shinji Ogawa; Executive Producers, Masao Teshima, Chihiro Kameyama; Director/Screenplay, Tran Anh Hung; Based on the 1987 novel by Haruki Murakami; Photography, Mark Lee Ping Bin; Designers, Yen Khe Luguern, Norifumi Ataka; Costumes, Yen Khe Luguern; Music, Jonny Greenwood; Editor, Mario Battistel; a Soda Pictures, Asmik Ace Entertainment and Fuji Television Network presentation in association with Norwegian Wood Film Partners; Japanese, 2010; Dolby; Color; Not rated; 133 minutes; American release date: January 6, 2012

CAST

Toru Watanabe	**Ken'ichi Matsuyama**
Naoko	**Rinko Kikuchi**
Midori	**Kiko Mizuhara**
Dr. Reiko Ishida	**Reika Kirishima**
Kizuki	**Kengo Kôra**
Hatsumi	**Eriko Hatsune**
Nagasawa	**Tetsuji Tamayama**

Shigesato Itoi (University Professor), Tokio Emoto (Storm Trooper), Haruomi Hosono (Record Shop Manager), Takao Handa (Midori's Father), Yukihiro Takahashi (Gatekeeper), Izumi Hirasawa (Midori's Friend), Yuki Ito, Kentaro Tamura, Makoto Sugisawa, Kohei Yoshino (Student Activists)

Watanabe looks back on his relationships with the free-spirited Midori and the mentally troubled Naoko, the girlfriend of his best friend who had committed suicide.

Isaïe Sultan, Béatrice Dalle

Béatrice Dalle, Isaïe Sultan © Strand Releasing

DOMAIN

(STRAND) a.k.a. *Domaine*; Producer, Charlotte Vincent; Co-Producers, Ebba Sinzinger, Vincent Lucassen; Director/Screenplay, Patric Chiha; Photography, Pascal Poucet; Art Directors, Céline Cayron, Maria Gruber; Costumes, Pierre Canitrot; Music, Milkymee; Editor, Karina Ressler; Casting, Tatiana Vialle; an Aurora Film in co-production with WilDart Film presentation; French-Austrian, 2010; Dolby; Color; Not rated; 110 minutes; American release date: January 13, 2012

CAST

Nadia	**Béatrice Dalle**
Pierre	**Isaïe Sultan**
Samir	**Alain Libolt**
John	**Raphaël Bouvet**
Barbara	**Sylvia Rohrer**

Udo Samel (Sanatorium Director), Tatiana Vialle (Jeanne), Bernd Birkhahn (Schwarzbach), Manuel Marmier (Fabrice), Gisèle Viene (Marie), Gloria Pedemonte (Gloria), Thomas Landbo (Sven)

An impressionable gay teen worships his unconventional aunt, whose life is spiraling out of control due to her dependency on alcohol.

LULA, SON OF BRAZIL

(NEW YORKER) a.k.a. *Lula, o Filho do Brasil*; Producers, Paula Barreto, Romulo Marinho Jr.; Director, Fábio Barreto; Screenplay, Daniel Tendler, Denise Paraná, Fernando Bonassi; Based on the 2009 book *Lula, o Filho do Brasil* (*Lula, the Son of Brazil*) by Denise Parana; Photography, Gustavo Hadba; Art Director, Clóvis Bueno; Costumes, Cristina Camargo; Music, Antônio Pinto, Jaques Morelenbaum; Editor, Letícia Giffoni; an ALC LC Barreto, Filmes do Equador, Intervideo Digital production, co-produced by Globo Filmes; Brazilian, 2010; Dolby; Color/black and white; Not rated; 128 minutes; American release date: January 13, 2012

CAST

Lula	**Rui Ricardo Diaz**
Dona Lindu	**Glória Pires**
Lurdes	**Cléo Pires**
Marisa Letíca	**Juliana Baroni**
Artistedes	**Milhem Cortaz**
Teacher	**Lucélia Santos**
Mr. Cristóvão	**Antônio Pitanga**
Mr. Álvaro	**Celso Frateschi**

Marcos Cesana (Cláudio Feitosa), Sóstenes Vidal (Ziza), Antonio Saboia (Vavá), Clayton Mariano (Lambari), Eduardo Acaibe (Geraldão), Marat Descartes (Arnaldo), Nei Piacentini (Dr. Miguel), Felipe Falanga (Lula at 7 years old), Guilherme Tortolio (Lula at 15 years old), Luccas Papp (Lambari at 15 years old), Vanessa Bizarro (Lurdes at 13 years old), Maicon Gouveia (Jamie), Fernando Alvez Pinto (Journalist), Rayana Carvalho (Dona Mocinha), Jonas Melo (Tosinho), Mariah Teixeira (Marinete), Fernanda Laranjeira (Tiana)

The true story of how Luiz Inácio Lula da Silva rose from poverty to become one of Brazil's most beloved presidents.

Rui Ricardo Diaz

Cléo Pires © New Yorker Films

Diva Novita

Jade Or © Zipporah Films

CRAZY HORSE

(ZIPPORAH) a.k.a. *Dèsir*; Producers, Pierre Olivier Bardet, Frederick Wiseman; Director/Editor, Frederick Wiseman; Photography, John Davey; an Idéale Audience & Zipporah Films production in association with Crazy Horse Productions; French-American, 2011; Color; Not rated; 134 minutes; American release date: January 18, 2012. Documentary on the legendary Paris cabaret Crazy Horse

WITH
Naamah Alva, Daizy Blu, Philippe Decouflé, Philippe Katerine

THE FRONT LINE

(WELL GO USA) a.k.a. *Go-ji-jeon*; Producers, Lee Woo-jung, Kim Hyun-cheol; Executive Producer, You Jung-hoon; Director, Jang Hun; Screenplay, Park Sang-yeon; Photography, Kim Woo-hyung; Designer, Ryu Seong-hie; Costumes, Cho Sang-kyung; Music, Jang Young-gyu, Dalparan; Editors, Kim Sang-beom, Kim Jae-beom; Visual Effects Supervisors, Jeong Seong-jin, Heo Dong-hyeok; a Showbox/Mediaplex presentation of a TPS Co. production in association with A-Po Films; South Korean, 2011; Dolby; Color; HD; Not rated; 133 minutes; American release date: January 20, 2012

CAST

Lt. Kang Eun-pyo	**Shin Hay-kyun**
Lt. Kim Su-hyeok	**Ko Soo**
Capt. Shin Il-yeong	**Lee Je-hoon**
Sgt. Oh Gi-yeong	**Ruy Seung-soo**
Yang Hyo-sam	**Ko Chang-seok**
Nam Sung-sik	**Lee Da-wit**
Cha Tae-kyeong	**Kim Ok-bin**
Heyon Jeong-yoon	**Ryoo Seung-yong**

As the conflict in Korean comes to a close, army intelligence officer Kang Eun-pyo is sent to investigate the possible murder of an officer within the Alligator Unit squad.

Lee Je-hoon

Lee Je-hoon © Well Go USA

MISS BALA

(20TH CENTURY FOX) Producer, Pablo Cruz; Executive Producers, Gael García Bernal, Diego Luna, Geminiano Pineda; Director/Editor, Gerardo Naranjo; Screenplay, Gerardo Naranjo, Mauricio Katz; Photography, Matyas Erdely; Designer, Ivonne Fuentes; Costumes, Anna Terrazas; Music, Emilio Kauderer; Music Supervisor, Lynn Fainchtein; Casting, Isabel Cortázar, Andrea Abbiati, Nicole Daniels, Courtney Bright; a Canana and Fox International Productions presentation of a Canana, Fox International Productions, El Instituto Mexicano de Cinematografía Imcine, El Consejo Nacional, Para la Cultura y Las Artes Conaculta and El Fondo de Inversión y Estímulos al Cine (Fidecine) production; Mexican, 2011; Dolby; Hawk Scope; Deluxe color; Rated R; 113 minutes; American release date: January 20, 2012

CAST

Laura Guerrero	**Stephanie Sigman**
Lino Valdez	**Noé Hernandez**
Jessica	**Irene Azuela**
Kike Cámara	**Jose Yenque**
Jimmy	**James Russo**
General Salomón Duarte	**Miguel Couturier**
Agent Bell	**Gabriel Heads**

Juan Carlos Galván (Arturo Guerrero), Javier Zaragoza (Ramón Guerrero), Lakshmi Picazo (Azucena "Suzu" Ramos), Leonor Vitorica (Luisa Janes), Hugo Márquez (Javi Fernández), Eduardo Mendizábal (Quiño) Sergio Gómez Padilla (Parca), Felipe Morales (Tío), Sergio Miguel Martinez (Cali), Luis Francisco Escobedo (Roca), Armando Gutiérrez Flores (Ventura), Andrea Abbiati Correnti (Choreographer), Victor Roldán (Patrolman) Leticia Huijara Cano (Vendor), Gabriel Chávez (Quizmaster), Victor Manuel Rodríguez (Bodyguard), Octavio Velasco (Robles), Claudio León Burstin Campos (Attorney) Angel Galindo (Alonso Gutiérrez)

A teen vying for the Miss Baja California beauty contest ends up in danger after surviving a massacre at a party attended by American DEA agents.

Stephanie Sigman

Stephanie Sigman © 20th Century Fox

César Desseix, Jérémie Elkaïm, Valérie Donzelli

Valérie Donzelli, Jérémie Elkaïm © Sundance Selects

DECLARATION OF WAR

(SUNDANCE SELECTS) a.k.a. *La guerre est declaree*; Producer, Edouard Weil; Executive Producer, Serge Catoire; Director, Valérie Donzelli; Screenplay, Valérie Donzelli, Jérémie Elkaïm; Photography, Sébastien Buchmann; Set Designer, Gaélle Usandivaras; Costumes, Elisabeth Méhu; Editor, Pauline Gaillard; Casting, Kauren Hottois; Canal + and Ciné+ in association with Cofinova 7, Une Etoiler and ARTE/Cofinova G; French, 2011; Color; Widescreen; Not rated; 100 minutes; American release date: January 27, 2012

CAST

Juliette	**Valérie Donzelli**
Roméo Benaïm	**Jérémie Elkaïm**
Adam, 18 months	**César Desseix**
Adam, 8 years	**Gabriel Elkaïm**

The Families: Brigitte Sy (Claudia), Elina Lowensohn (Alex), Michèle Moretti (Geneviève), Philippe Laudenbach (Philippe), Bastien Bouillon (Nikos); *The Doctors*: Béatrice de Staël (Dr. Prat), Anne Le Ny (Dr. Fitoussi), Frédéric Pierrot (Prof. Sainte-Rose), Elisabeth Dion (Dr. Kalifa)

A young couple faces tremendous stress and uncertainty when they learn that their newborn child is very ill.

THE WOMAN IN BLACK

(CBS FILMS) Producers, Richard Jackson, Simon Oakes, Brian Oliver; Executive Producers, Guy East, Nigel Sinclair, Tobin Armbrust, Marc Schipper, Neil Dunn, Xavier Marchand, Tyler Thompson, Roy Lee; Co-Producers, Paul Ritchie, Ben Holder, Todd Thompson; Director, James Watkins; Screenplay, Jane Goldman; Based on the 1983 novel by Susan Lee; Photography, Tim Maurice-Jones; Designer, Kave Quinn; Costumes, Keith Madden; Music, Marco Beltrami; Editor, Jon Harris; Special Effects Supervisor, Bob Hollow; Visual Effects Supervisor, Håkan Blomdahl; Casting, Karen Lindsay-Stewart; a Cross Creek Pictures presentation in association with Hammer and Alliance Films of a Talisman production in association with Exclusive Media Group and The UK Film Council; British-Canadian-Swedish; Dolby; Panavision; Color; Rated PG-13; 95 minutes; American release date: February 3, 2012

CAST

Arthur Kipps	**Daniel Radcliffe**
Daily	**Ciarán Hinds**
Mrs. Daily	**Janet McTeer**
Jennet	**Liz White**
Joseph Kipps	**Misha Handley**
Mr. Bentley	**Roger Allam**
Fisher	**Shaun Dooley**
Mrs. Fisher	**Mary Stockley**
Mr. Jerome	**Tim McMullan**
Nathanial Drablow	**Ashley Foster**
Stella Kipps	**Sophie Stuckey**

Emma Shorey, Molly Harmon, Ellisa Walker-Reid (Fisher Girls), Jessica Raine (Nanny), Lucy May Barker (Nursemaid), Indira Ainger (Little Girl on Train), Andy Robb (Doctor), Alexia Osborne (Victoria Hardy), Alfie Field (Tom Hardy), William Tobin (Charlie Hardy), Victor McGuire (Gerald Hardy), Cathy Sara (Mrs. Jerome), Daniel Cerqueira (Keckwick), Alisa Khazanova (Mrs. Drablow), David Burke (P.C. Collins), Aoife Doherty (Lucy Jerome), Sidney Johnston (Nicholas Daily)

Arriving at the secluded mansion of its recently deceased owner in order to sort through her legal papers Arthur Kipps encounters the presence of a supernatural force.

Janet McTeer, Daniel Radcliffe

Ciarán Hinds

Daniel Radcliffe

Ellisa Walker-Reid, Emma Shorey, Molly Harmon © CBS Films

Michael Smiley, Neil Maskell

Richard Stocks© IFC Midnight

KILL LIST

IFC MIDNIGHT) Producers, Claire Jones, Andy Starke; Executive Producers, Robin Gutch, Katherine Butler, Hugo Heppell; Co-Producer, Barry Ryan; Associate Producer, Ally Gipps; Director, Ben Wheatley; Screenplay, Ben Wheatley, Amy Jump; Photography, Laurie Rose; Designer, Jim Williams; Music, David Butterworth; Editors, Robin Hill, Ben Wheatley, Amy Jump; a UK Film Council & Film4 presentation in association with Screen Yorkshire of a Warp X/Rook Films Production; British, 2011; Color; Not rated; 95 minutes; American release date: February 3, 2012

CAST
Jay	**Neil Maskell**
Gal	**Michael Smiley**
Shel	**MyAnna Buring**
Fiona	**Emma Fryer**
Sam	**Harry Simpson**
The Client	**Struan Rodger**

Esme Folley, Jamelle Ola (Hotel Receptionists), Ben Crompton (Justin), Gemma Lise Thornton (Kiera), Robin Hill (Stuart), Zoe Thomas (Hotel Waitress), Gareth Tunley (The Priest), Mark Kempner (The Librarian), Damien Thomas (The Doctor), Lora Evans (Thorn Blindfold Woman), Bob Hill (High Priest), Rebecca Holmes (The Bride), James Nickerson (MP), David Bowen (Father of the Bride), Sara Dee (News Reader), Alice Lowe, Steve Oram (Radio Reporters), Richard Stocks (Wicker Face)

A paranoid hitman reluctantly accepts a new assignment to carry out three assassinations which only serve to wreck further havoc on his psyche.

PERFECT SENSE

(IFC FILMS) Producers, Gillian Berrie, Malte Grunert; Executive Producers, Jamie Laurenson, Peter Aalbæk Jensen, Peter Garde, Carole Sheridan, David Mackenzie; Co-Producers, Sisse Graum Jørgensen, Tristan Orpen Lynch; Line Producer, Julia Valentine; Director, David Mackenzie; Screenplay, Kim Fupz Aakeson; Photography, Giles Nuttgens; Designer, Tom Sayer; Costumes, Trisha Biggar; Make-up & Hair Designer, Donald McInnes; Music, Max Richter; Editor, Jake Roberts; Casting, Shaheen Baig; a BBC Films presentation in association with Zentropa Entertainment S5 and Scottish Screen with the participation of the Danish Film Institute and Film I Väst and Bord Scannán na Héireann/The Irish Film Board of a Sigma Films production; British-Scottish-Danish, 2011; Color; HD; Not rated; 92 minutes; American release date: February 3, 2012

CAST
Michael	**Ewan McGregor**
Susan	**Eva Green**
James	**Ewen Bremner**
Jenny	**Connie Nielsen**
Stephen Montgomery	**Stephen Dillane**
Boss	**Denis Lawson**

Liz Strange (Deaf Customer), Richard Mack (Apprentice Chef Richard), James Watson (Crying Bus Driver), Caroline Paterson (Woman at Hospital), Shabana Bakhsh (Nurse), Malcolm Shields (Patient), Alastair Mackenzie (Virologist), Duncan James (Kickboxer), Lauren Tempany (Girl in Bed), Judith Anne Christie, Joni Mackay (Waitresses), Anamaria Marinca (Street Performer), Juliet Cadzow, Tam Dean Burn (Couple at Grave), Ferosa Mackenzie (Jenny's Daughter), Luke Mackenzie (Jenny's Son), Gilly Gilchrist (Doctor), Barbara Rafferty (Woman in Car Park), Siu Hun Li (Thai Scientist), Stephen McCole (Nice Official), Paul Thomas Hickey (Grumpy Official), Katy Engels (Narrator), John Mulkeen, David Monaghan (Chefs de Partie), Karen Hepburn, Sean Early (Pastry Chefs), Oscar Balmaseda Villoslada, Max Barr, Amjad Mobaraak (Waiters), Trish Mullin (School Teacher), Fiona Danskin (Crying Traffic Warden), Lewis Roberts (Boy in Sweet Shop), Ian Sexon (Crying Man in Stadium), John Conroy (Wizard), George Robertson (Crying Fishmonger), Allan Brown (Food Critic), Perry Costello (Shopkeeper with Gun), Frank McCabe, Brad Askew (Emergency Response), Euan Williamson (Homeguard), Paul Lambie (Man getting Tattoo), Des Hamilton (Jenny's Husband)

A mysterious epidemic begins sweeping the world in which those afflicted lose their sense of smell and taste.

Eva Green, Ewan McGregor © IFC Films

Erika Bók © Cinema Guild

János Derzsi

THE TURIN HORSE

(CINEMA GUILD) a.k.a. *A torinói ló*; Producers, Gábor Téni, Marie-Pierre Macia, Juliette Lepoutre, Ruth Waldburger, Martin Hagemann; Executive Producers, Elizabeth G. Redleaf, Christine K. Walker; Director, Béla Tarr; Co-Director/Editor, Ágnes Hranitzky; Screenplay, Béla Tarr, László Krasznahorkai; Photography, Fred Kelemen; Sets, Sandor Kallay; Music, Mihály Vig; a T.T. Filmmûhely, MPM Film, Vega Film, Zero Fiction Film presentation in association with Werc Werk Works; Hungarian-French-Swiss-German, 2011; Dolby; Black and white; Not rated; 146 minutes; American release date: February 10, 2012

CAST

Ohlsdorfer	**János Derzsi**
Ohlsdorfer's Daughter	**Erika Bók**
Bernhard	**Mihály Kormos**
Horse	**Ricsi**
Narrator	**Mihály Ráday**

Cart driver Ohlsdorfer and his daughter's already bleak lives take a turn for the worse when their horse suddenly refuses to do his regular duties.

CHICO & RITA

(GKIDS/LUNA FILMS) Producers, Santi Errando, Cristina Huete, Martin Pope, Michael Rose; Executive Producers, Steve Christian, Marc Samuelson; Co-Producer, Andrew Fingret; Associate Producer, Antonio Resines; Directors, Fernando Trueba, Javier Mariscal, Tono Errando; Screenplay, Fernando Trueba, Ignacio Martinez de Pisón; Head of Production, Albert García Vila; Animation Direction, Manolo Galiana; Character Creative Direction, Bojan Pantelic; Music, Bebo Valdés; Editor, Arnau Quiles; a Fernando Trueba PC, Estudio Mariscal, Magic Light Pictures, CinemNX, Isle of Man Film presentation in association with Televisión Española SA, Hanway Films, Televisió de Catalunya SA, with the participation of MesFilms, Televisió de Cataluna SA, with participation of the Ministerio de Cultura – ICAA, ICIC Instituto Catalán de las Industrias Culturales with the support of ICO Instituto de Crédito Oficial, ICF Instituto Catalán de Finanzas; Spanish-British, 2010; Dolby; Not rated; 94 minutes; American release date: February 10, 2012

VOICES

Rita	**Limara Meneses**
Chico	**Eman Xor Oña**
Ramón	**Mario Guerra**

SINGING VOICES

Chico	**Bebo Valdés**
Rita	**Idania Valdés**
Estrella	**Estrella Morente**
Nat King Cole	**Freddy Cole**
Ben Webster	**Jimmy Heath**

Pedrito Martínez (Miguelito Valdés), Michael Phillip Mossman (Dizzie Gillespie), Amadito Valdés (Tito Puente), Germán Velazco (Charlie Parker), Yaroldi Abreu (Chano Pozo), Chico (Celia)

In 1948 Cuba, a young piano player and a singer united by love, find their relationship tested as the pair of them hope to make it in the world of music.

This film received an Oscar nomination for animated feature (2011).

Rita, Chico © GKids

THE SECRET WORLD OF ARRIETTY

(WALT DISNEY STUDIOS) a.k.a. *Kari-gurashi no Arietti*; Producer, Toshio Suzuki; Executive Producers (English Language Version), Frank Marshall, Kathleen Kennedy; Director, Hiromasa Yonebayashi; English Language Version Director, Gary Rydstrom; Screenplay, Hayao Miyazaki, Keiko Niwa; Based on the 1952 novel *The Borrowers* by Mary Norton; English Language Screenplay, Karey Kirkpatrick; Photography, Atsushi Okui; Supervising Animators, Megumi Kagawa, Akihiko Yamashita; Art Directors, Yôji Takeshige, Noboru Yoshida; Music, Cécile Corbel; Editor, Rie Matsubara; a Studio Ghibli, Dentsu, Walt Disney Company, Toho Company production; Japanese, 2010; Dolby; Color; Rated G; 94 minutes; American release date: February 17, 2012

VOICE CAST

Arrietty Clock	**Bridgit Mendler**
Homily Clock	**Amy Poehler**
Pod Clock	**Will Arnett**
Shawn	**David Henrie**
Haru	**Carol Burnett**
Spiller	**Moises Arias**

Gracie Poletti (Aunt Jessica), Dale Sison (Harachi), Frank Marshall, Karey Kirkpatrick, Peter Jason, Steve Alpert (Additional Voices)

The tiny Clock family lives under the floorboards of a cottage, where they are obliged to secretly scrounge for supplies from the full-size residents. The British version of this film featured such voices as Saoirse Ronan, Olivia Colman, Mark Strong, and Phyllida Law. Earlier live-action version of *The Borrowers* was released in 1998 and starred John Goodman.

Pod, Arrietty

Arrietty, Shawn © Walt Disney Studios

Matthias Schoenaerts © Drafthouse Films

BULLHEAD

(DRAFTHOUSE FILMS) a.k.a. *Rundskop*; Producer, Bart van Langendonck; Co-Producers, Peter Bouckaert, Patrick Quinet, Jan Van der Zanden; Director/Screenplay, Michaël R. Roskam; Photography, Nicolas Karakatsanis; Art Director, Walter Brugmans; Music, Raf Keunen; Editor, Alain Dessauvage; Casting, Bernard Falaise; a Savage Film and Eyeworks presentation; Belgian-Dutch, 2011; Dolby; Techniscope; Color; Rated R; 128 minutes; American release date: February 17, 2012

CAST

Jacky Vanmarsenille	**Matthias Schoenaerts**
Diederik Maes	**Jeroen Perceval**
Lucia Schepers	**Jeanne Dandoy**
Eva Forrestier	**Barbara Sarafian**
Marc de Kuyper	**Sam Louwyck**
Anthony De Greef	**Tibo Vandenborre**
Sam Raymond	**Frank Lamers**

Robin Valvekens (Young Jacky), Baudoin Wolwertz (Young Diederik), David Murgia (Young Bruno Schepers), Erico Salamone (Christian Filippini), Philippe Grand'Henry (David Filippini), Kris Cuppens (Jean Vanmarsenille), Sofie Sente (Irene Vanmarsenille), Kristof Renson (Stieve Vanmarsenille), Hein van der Heijden (Renaat Maes), Stefaan Degand (Leon), Mike Reus (Charles Richter), Ludmila Klejnak (Daphne), Bill Barberis, Anneleen Aerts (Surveillance Agents), Jean-Marie LeSuisse (Eddy Vanmarsenille), Jeanne Remy (Young Lucia), Juda Goslinga (Bruno Schepers), Gael Maleux (Vincent), Baloji (Patrick), Renaud Rutten (Louis Schepers), Jurgen Rogier (Daems), Steven Sheeren (BOB Inspector), Marie-Rose Roland (Mother Schepers), Jolente De Keersmaeker, Circé Lethem (Detectives), Stee Aernouts (Specialist), Uwamungu Cornelis (Assistant Specialist), Steph Baeyens (Commissioner), Armand Naessens (Young Stieve), Oliver Boni (Dealer), Jos Geens (Agriculturist), Erna Vandendriessche (Thérèse) Urbain Ilsbroex (Doctor), Abdel Bellabiad, Anabel Lopez (Agents), Isolde Rossilion (Babbie), Cindy Gijsels (Hostess), Mirco Gijsens, Pieter-Jan Coenen, Timothy Vanelderen, Florian Vigilante, Eric Remi (Bruno's Friends), Bert Van Nieuwenhuyse (Bus Driver)

A cattle farmer, addicted to steroids, is approached by an unscrupulous veterinarian to do business with mob-connected meat traders.

This film received an Oscar nomination for foreign language film (2011).

THE FAIRY

(KINO LORBER) a.k.a. *La fée*; Producers, Marin Karmitz, Charles Gillibert, Dominique Abel, Fiona Gordon; Executive Producer, Marina Festré; Directors/Screenplay, Dominique Abel, Fiona Gordon, Bruno Romy; Photography, Claire Chidéric; Sets, Nicolas Girault; Costumes, Claire Dubien; Editor, Sandrine Deegen; a MK2, Courage Mon Amour production in coproduction with France 3 Cinema; French, 2011; Dolby; Color; Not rated; 94 minutes; American release date: February 24, 2012

CAST

Dom	**Dominique Abel**
The Fairy	**Fiona Gordon**
John English	**Philippe Martz**
The Bartender	**Bruno Romy**
The Flying Man	**Didier Armbruster**
The Singer	**Anaïs Lemarchand**
Jimmy	**Lenny Martz**

Vladimir Zongo, Destiné M'Bikulu Mayemba, Wilson Goma (Illegal Immigrants), Emilie Horcholle (Shoe Saleswoman), Sandrine Morin (Nurse), Christophe Philippe (Bart), Alexandre Xenakis (Dave), Ophélie Anfry, Olivier Parenty (Police), Thérèse Fichert (Hotel Owner), Christelle Thibon (Cleaning Lady), Dominique Gallay (Worker), Sarah Bensoussan (The Woman in Red), Abdou Sagna, Marc-Antoine Vaugeois (Security Guards), Hervé Goubert (The Butcher), Fouad Bentalha (The Apprentice Butcher), Chantal Romy (The Doctor), Cyril Colmant (The Fisherman), Pascal Banizet (Guard)

A mysterious woman appears before a night shift porter, claiming to be a fairy and offering to grant him three wishes.

Jafar Panami

Fiona Gordon, Dominique Abel

Jafar Panami © Palisades Tartan

Fiona Gordon, Dominique Abel © Kino Lorber

THIS IS NOT A FILM

(PALISADES TARTAN) a.k.a. *In film nist*; Producer/Editor, Jafar Panahi; Directors, Mojtaba Mirtahmasb, Jafar Panahi; a Jafar Panahi Film production; Iranian-Persian, 2011; Color; Not rated; 75 minutes; American release date: February 29, 2012. Documentary (partially shot on an iPhone) in which director Jafar Panahi documents his house arrest in his Tehran apartment.

WITH
Jafar Panani

Matthew Howard, Marcus Howard, Anthony Groves

Lucas Pittaway, Daniel Henshall © IFC Midnight

THE SNOWTOWN MURDERS

(IFC MIDNIGHT) a.k.a. *Snowtown*; Producers, Anna McLeish, Sarah Shaw; Executive Producers, Robin Gutch, Mark Herbert; Director, Justin Kurzel; Screenplay, Shaun Grant; Story, Shaun Grant, Justin Kurzel; Inspired by the books *Killing for Pleasure* (2006) by Debi Marshall and *The Snowtown Murders* (2005) by Andrew McGarry; Photography, Adam Arkapaw; Designer, Fiona Crombie; Costumes, Alice Babidge, Fiona Crombie; Music, Jed Kurzel; Editor, Veronika Jenet; Casting, Allison Meadows, Mullinars Consultants; a Screen Australia and Warp Films Australia presentation in association with Film Victoria, South Australian Film Corporation, Adelaide Film Festival, Omnilab Media and Fulcrum Media Finance; Australian, 2011; Dolby; Color; Not rated; 120 minutes; American release date: March 2, 2012

CAST

Jamie Vlassakis	**Lucas Pittaway**
John Bunting	**Daniel Henshall**
Elizabeth Harvey	**Louise Harris**
Gavin	**Bob Adriaens**
Jeffrey	**Frank Cwertniak**
Nicholas	**Matthew Howard**

Marcus Howard (Alex), Anthony Groves (Troy), Richard Green (Barry), Aaron Viergever (Robert), Denis Davey (Guitar Player), Allan Chapple (Prayer Reader), Beau Gosling (David), Brendan Rock (Marcus), Bryan Sellars (Minister), David Walker (Mark Haydon), Aasta Brown (Verna), Nigel Howard (Man at Dinner), Joanne Argent, Astrid Adriaens (Women at Dinner), Keiran Schwerdt (Thomas), Craig Coyne (Ray), Kathryn Wissell (Suzanne), Krystle Flaherty (Vikki), Hannah Shelley (Vikki's Baby), Andrew Mayers (Fred), Dr. Gabor Kiss (Doctor), Carol Smith (Doctor's Receptionist), Jenny Hallam (Social Worker), Robert Deeble (Gary)

The true story of how John Bunting enlisted a crew of vigilantes to help him exact revenge on those he considered deviants, resulting in a devastating murder spree.

BOY

(PALADIN) Producers, Ainsley Gardiner, Cliff Curtis, Emanuel Michael; Co-Producer, Merata Mita; Director/Screenplay, Taika Waititi; Photography, Adam Clark; Designer, Shayne Radford; Costumes, Amanda Neale; Music, The Phoenix Foundation; Editor, Chris Plummer; Visual Effects Supervisor, Brett Johnansen; Hair & Makeup, Dannelle Satherley; Casting, Tina Cleary; a Whenua Films, Unison Films and the New Zealand Film Production Fund Trust in association with the New Zealand Film Commission, New Zealand On Air and Te Mangai Paho presentation; New Zealand, 2010; Dolby; Color; Not rated; 88 minutes; American release date: March 2, 2012

CAST

Boy	**James Rolleston**
Rocky	**Te Aho Aho Eketone-Whitu**
Alamein	**Taika Waititi**
Dynasty	**Moerangi Tihore**
Kelly	**Cherilee Martin**
Chardonnay	**RickyLee Waipuka-Russell**

Haze Reweti (Dallas), Maakariini Butler (Murray), Rajvinder Eria (Tane), Manihera Rangiuaia (Kingi), Darcy Ray Flavell-Hudson (Holden), Rachel House (Aunty Gracey), Waihoroi Shortland (Weirdo), Cohen Holloway (Chuppa), Pana Hema Taylor (Juju), Tuhoro Ranihera Christie (Mr. Nepia), Craig Hall (Mr. Langston), Mavis Paenga (Nan), Ngapaki Emery (Mum), Ngaru-toa Puru (Che), Hoanihuhi Takotohiwi (Hucks), Tainui Callaghan (Kiko), Manaia Callaghan (Miria), Montana Te Kani-Williams (Falcon Crest), Rangiteaorere Raki (Young Darcy), Wairangi Herewini (Kingi's Friend), Waimihi Hotere (Teacher), Heke-turoa 'Panache' Ropitini, Ei Kura Albert, Ruataarehu Waititi (Chardonnay's Friends), Te Urikore Waititi-Lake (Noodle)

An eleven-year-old Maori boy growing up in 1980s Waihau Bay, New Zealand, hopes to connect with his absent dad when the man returns to find some money he had buried years before.

Te Aho Aho Eketone-Whitu, James Rolleston © Paladin

Te Aho Aho Eketone-Whitu, James Rolleston, Taika Waititi

Liam Cunningham, Carice van Houten

Liam Cunningham, Carice van Houten © Tribeca Film

BLACK BUTTERFLIES

(TRIBECA) Producers, Frans van Gestel, Richard Claus, Michael Auret, Arry Voorsmit; Executive Producer, Arnold Heslenfeld; Director, Paula van der Oest; Screenplay, Greg Latter; Photography, Giulio Biccari; Designer, Darryl Hammer; Costumes, Rae Donnelly; Music, Philip Miller; Editor, Sander Vos; Casting, Christa Schamberger, Ana Feyder, Jeremy Zimmermann; a Bavaria Film International presentation, with IDTV Film and Cool Beans presentation of a Comet Film and Spier Films in association with Riba Film International; German-Dutch-South African, 2011; Dolby; Widescreen; Color; Not rated; 100 minutes; American release date: March 2, 2012

CAST

Ingrid Jonker	**Carice van Houten**
Jack Cope	**Liam Cunningham**
Uys Krige	**Graham Clarke**
Eugene Maritz	**Nicholas Pauling**
Anna Jonker	**Candice D'Arcy**
Abraham Jonker	**Ruger Hauer**

Ceridwen Morris (Marjorie), Grant Swanby (Jan Rabie), Waldemar Schultz (Ettiene le Roux), Tarryn Page (Irma), Louis Pretorius (Mike Loots), Damon Berry (Pieter Venter), Marthinus van den Berg (Marius Schoon), Florence Masebe (Maria), Jennifer Steyn (Lucille – Lulu), Thamsanqua Mbongo (Nkosi), Sabrina Oschmann (Young Ingrid), Fallin Robertson (Young Anna), Diane Wilson (Ouma), Euodia Sampson (Muslim Woman), Albert Maritz (Bus Conductor), Shannyn Fourie (Eugene's Wife), Chris Majiedt (Fisherman)

The true story of fiercely indepenendent poet Ingrid Jonker's need to establish a bond with her callous, unfeeling father, and how circumstances drove her to be institutionalized.

SOUND OF NOISE

(MAGNOLIA) Producers, Jim Birmant, Guy Pechard, Christophe Audeguis, Olivier Guerpillon; Directors/Screenplay, Ola Simonsson, Johannes Stjärne Nilsson; Story, Ola Simonsson, Johannes Stjärne Nilsson, Jim Birmant; Photography, Charlotta Tengroth; Designer, Cecilia Sterner; Costumes, Gabriella Dinnetz; Music, Fred Avril; Six Drummers Music, Magnus Börjeson & Six Drummers; Editor, Stefan Sundlöf; Casting, Sara Törnkvist; a Magnolia Pictures and Bliss presentation in association with Wild Bunch of a Bliss, Wild Bunch, DFM Fiktion, Kostr-Film, Nordisk Film, Film I Skåne, Film I Vast, Europasound production; Swedish-French-Danish, 2010; Dolby; Super 35 Widescreen; Color; Rated R; 102 minutes; American release date: March 9, 2012

CAST

Amadeus Warnebring	**Bengt Nilsson**
Sanna	**Sanna Persson Halapi**
Magnus	**Magnus Börjeson**
Johannes	**Johannes Björk**
Myran	**Fredrik Myhr**

Marcus Haraldson Boij (Marcus), Anders Vestergård (Anders), Sven Ahlstrom (Oscar Warnebring), Ralph Carlsson (Hagman), Paula McManus (Colette), Peter Schildt (Police Commissioner), Pelle Öhlund (Sanchez), Dag Malmberg (Örjan Levander), Björn Granath (Hospital Director), Anders Jansson (Bosse, Landlord), Axel Bergendal (Amadeus as a Child), Nina Brundahl Warnolf (Mother, Young), Martin Bergendal (Father, Young), Bilo Frenander (Grandfather), Tage Persson (Oscar as a Child), Benjamin Peetre (Policeman with Radio), Lasse Svensson (Motorcycle Police), Mildred Malmros (Old Lady at Police Station), Ulf Homtröm, Dan Holmström, Mats Berg, Pether Book (Dance Band), Per Kockum (Saw Man), Eugen Lichorad (Keyboard Player, SawBand), Ola Simonsson (Man in Music Shop), Irene Lindh (Warenbring's Mother), Iwar Wiklander (Tony, the Mother's New Husband), Ann-Christin Schwartz (Oscar's Wife), Robin Keller (Jean-Pierre), Julia Isaksoon (Lucia the Piano Player), Hans Hansson (Roadworker in Sauna), Elina Du Rietz (Nurse), Alf Christensson (Janitor at Hospital), Zerny Thor (Old Man at Poster), Jaqueline Sjeklöca (Screaming Woman in Bank), Anders Andersson (Screaming Man in Bank), Bengt Ekelund (Man with Queue Ticket in Bank), Fredrik Hammar (Policeman in Bank), Sten Elfström (Professor Backman), David Wiberg (Backman's Secretary), Magnus Bauer (Tattooed Man), Karin Homberg (Minister at Opera), Frederik Nilsson (Mayor at Opera), Tommy Johed (Policeman at Roadblock), Bertil Pålsson (Body Paint Artist), Narinder Singh (Taxi Driver), May Attebring, Ally Backlund (Ladies under Cables), Anders Loosme (Man in Telephone Booth), Patrik A.Edgren (Man holding Dog), Turkes Güclü (Hot Dog Stand Owner), Julian James (Man at Hot Dog Stand), Louise Larsson (Woman at Hot Dog Stand), Krister Jönsson (Man at Resort Restaurant), Jorge Carruillo (Waiter at Resort Restaurant), Juan Carlos Mondoza Fuentes (Spanish Dishwasher)

A tone-deaf police officer who hails from a family of distinguished musicians attempts to track down a quintet of guerilla percussions that is causing an uproar with its random public performances.

Anders Vestergård, Johannes Björk, Sanna Persson Halapi, Fredrik Myhr, Magnus Börjeson, Marcus Haraldson Boij © Magnolia Films

Amr Waked, Ewan McGregor

Ewan McGregor © CBS Films

Kristin Scott Thomas, Amr Waked

Emily Blunt, Ewan McGregor

SALMON FISHING IN THE YEMEN

(CBS FILMS) Producer, Paul Webster; Co-Producer, Nicky Kentish Barnes; Executive Producers, Jamie Laurenson, Paula Jalfon, Zygi Kamasa, Guy Avshalom, Stephen Garrett; Co-Executive Producers, Samuel Hadida, Victor Hadida; Director, Lasse Hallström; Screenplay, Simon Beaufoy; Based on the 2006 novel by Paul Torday; Photography, Terry Stacey; Designer, Michael Carlin; Costumes, Julian Day; Music, Dario Marianelli; Editor, Lisa Gunning; Casting, Fiona Weir; a CBS Films presentation in association with BBC Films, Lionsgate UK and The UK Film Council of a Kudos Pictures production in association with Davis Films productions; British; Dolby; Panavision; Technicolor; HD; Rated PG-13; 107 minutes; American release date: March 9, 2012

CAST

Dr. Alfred Jones	**Ewan McGregor**
Harriet	**Emily Blunt**
Sheikh Muhammed	**Amr Waked**
Patricia Maxwell	**Kristin Scott Thomas**
Capt. Robert Mayers	**Tom Mison**
Mary Jones	**Rachael Stirling**
Peter Maxwell	**Tom Beard**
Ashley	**Catherine Steadman**
Betty Burnside	**Jill Baker**
Bernard Sugden	**Conleth Hill**
Edward Maxwell	**Alex Taylor-McDowall**
Abby Maxwell	**Matilda White**
Joshua Maxwell	**Otto Farrant**
Malcolm	**Hamish Gray**

Clive Wood (Tom Price-Williams), Nayef Rashed (Rebel Leader), Peter Wight (Tory Grandee, Angus Butler), Waleed Akhtar (Essad), Steven Blake (Cabinet Member), Hugh Simon (Brian Fleet), James Cutting, Colin Kilkelly (Journalists)

Hoping to improve Euro-Mideast relations, a Yemeni sheik comes up with the outlandish idea of introducing British sport fishing to his country.

FOOTNOTE

(SONY CLASSICS) a.k.a. *Hearat Shulayim*; Producers, David Mandil, Moshe Edery, Leon Edery; Executive Producer, Michal Graidy; Line Producer, Tamir Kfir; Director/Screenplay, Joseph Cedar; Photography, Yaron Scharf; Designer, Arad Sawat; Costumes, Laura Sheim; Music, Amit Poznansky; Editor, Einat Glaser Zarhin; Casting, Hila Yuval; a Westend Films, United King Films and Movie Plus production, with the support of Israel Film Fund, Jerusalem Film and Television Fund, Avi Chan Foundation; Israeli, 2011; Dolby; Super 35 Widescreen; Color; Rated PG; 105 minutes; American release date: March 9, 2012

CAST

Eliezer Shkolnik	**Shlomo Bar Aba**
Uriel Shkolnik	**Lior Ashkenazi**
Yehudit Shkolnik	**Alisa Rosen**
Dikla Shkolnik	**Alma Zak**
Josh Shkolnik	**Daniel Markovich**
Yehuda Grossman	**Micah Lewesohn**
Noa, Newspaper Reporter	**Yuval Scharf**
Yair Fingerhut	**Nevo Kimichi**
The Costume Designer Lady	**Edna Blilious**
Sara Foddor	**Idit Teperson**
Dvir Oded	**Albert Iluz**
Herman	**Shmulik Shilo**

Neli Tagar, Itay Polishuk (Security Guards), Tsipi Gal (Mystery Woman), Michael Koresh (Yona Solomon), Daria Robichek (Devora), Nina Traub (Yonat), Natalia Faust (Nurse), Jacky Levi (Talk Show Host), Dali Shachnaey (Young Uriel), Jonnie Shualy (Soundman), Dan Caner (Narrator), Dana Glozman (Silit), Gad Kaynar (Committee Member), Hanna Hacohen (Israel Prize Producer), Edna Blilious (Costume Designer)

When Talmudic scholar Eliezer Shkolnik is told he is about to be awarded the Israel Prize for his work, further tension erupts between himself and his ambitious son, who has also dedicated his life to similar studies.

This movie received an Oscar nomination for foreign language film (2011).

Alma Zak, Lior Ashkenazi

Alisa Rosen, Shlomo Bar Aba

Tsipi Gal, Shlomo Bar Aba

Shlomo Bar Aba © Sony Classics

Inge Rademeyer, Cohen Holloway

Toa Waaka © Screen Media

GOOD FOR NOTHING

(SCREEN MEDIA) Producers, Mike Wallis, Inge Rademeyer; Executive Producers, Jamie Selkirk, Brett Gamble; Director/Screenplay, Mike Wallis; Photography, Mathew Knight; Designer, Zoe Wilson; Costumes, Marianna Rademeyer; Music, John Psathas; Editor, Greg Daniels; Visual Effects Supervisors, Paul Story, Steve Cronin; a Mi Films presentation in association with Chopper Productions; New Zealand, 2011; Dolby; Color; Rated R; 92 minutes; American release date: March 9, 2012

CAST
The Man	**Cohen Holloway**
Isabella Montgomery	**Inge Rademeyer**
The Sheriff	**Jon Pheloung**
Will	**Richard Thompson**
The Doc	**Toby Leach**

Toa Waaka (Native American Medicine Man), Charles Lum (Chinese Medicine Man), Tao Jrang (Chinese Interpreter), Mark Norrie (Mexican), Barnie Duncan (Mexican Tracker), Tony Wyeth (The Texan), Sean McChesney (Drifter), Steve Cronin (Slim), Pana Hema Taylor (Young Native American), Norman Chieng (Chinese Rockstacker), Alex Chan (Chinese Digger), Terry MacTavish (Chaperone), Robin Gamble (Henry), Nigel Harbrow (Fernando), Mike Wallis (Harry), Allen Hemberger (Undertaker)

In this spoof of spaghetti westerns, an English lady arrives in the Old West and is promptly kidnapped by a gunslinger who intends to have his way with her only to discover he is suffering from impotency.

DELICACY

(COHEN MEDIA GROUP) a.k.a. *La délicatesse*; Producers, Xavier Rigault, Marc-Antoine Robert; Directors, David Foenkinos, Stéphane Foenkinos; Screenplay, David Foenkinos, based on his 2009 novel *La délicatesse*; Photography, Rémy Chevrin; Set Designer, Maamar Ech-Cheikh; Costumes, Emmanuelle Youchnovski; Music/Songs, Emilie Simon; Editor, Virginie Bruant; a 2.4.7. Films Production co-production with Studiocanal France 2 Cinéma with the participation of Canal + Ciné+ and France Télévisions; French; Dolby; Super 35 Widescreen; Color; Rated PG-13; 109 minutes; American release date: March 14, 2012

CAST
Nathalie Kerr	**Audrey Tautou**
Markus Lundl	**François Damiens**
Charles	**Bruno Todeschini**
Chloé, Nathalie's Secretary	**Mélanie Bernier**
Sophie	**Joséphine de Meaux**
François	**Pio Marmaï**
Madeleine	**Monique Chaumette**

Marc Citty (Pierre), Alexandre Pavloff (Benoît), Vittoria Scognamiglio (François' Mother), Olivier Cruveiller (François' Father), Ariane Ascaride (Nathalie's Mother), Christophe Malavoy (Nathalie's Father), Audrey Fleurot (Ingrid), Bénédicte Ernoult (Theatre Usher), Nicolas Guimbard (Parking Attendant), Asa Verdin Kallman (Markus' Mother), Dan Dan Lau (Waitress at Chinese Restaurant), Pom Klementieff (Waitress at Charles' Restaurant), Nadège Perrier (The Doctor), Benoît Pétré (Coffee House Waiter), Stellan Sundlof (Markus' Father), Lara Suyeux (Cocktail Waitress), Sébastien Thiery (Aggressive Man), Michaël Bensoussan, Renan Carteaux, Charley Fouquet, Gwendoline Gourvenec (Pierre's Friends), Violette Renard (Sophie's Daughter)

Three years after the unexpected death of her husband, Nathalie becomes romantically interested in a somewhat slovenly Swedish co-worker.

Audrey Tautou

François Damiens © Cohen Media Group

Thomas Doret, Cécile de France

Thomas Doret

Thomas Doret, Cécile de France © Sundance Selects

THE KID WITH A BIKE

(SUNDANCE SELECTS) a.k.a. *Le gamin au vélo*; Producers, Jean-Pierre Dardenne, Luc Dardenne, Denis Freyd; Executive Producer, Delphine Tomson; Co-Producer, Andrea Occhipinti; Directors/Screenplay, Jean-Pierre Dardenne, Luc Dardenne; Photography, Alain Marcoen; Costumes, Maïra Ramedhan-Levi; Editor, Marie-Hélène Dozo; a Les Films du Fleuve, Archipel 35, Lucky Red, France 2 Cinéma, RTBF (Belgian Television), Belgacom production; Belgian-French-Italian, 2011; Dolby; Color; Rated PG-13; 87 minutes; American release date: March 16, 2012

CAST

Samantha	**Cécile de France**
Cyril Catoul	**Thomas Doret**
Guy Catoul	**Jérémie Renier**
Bookseller	**Fabrizio Rongione**
Wes	**Egon Di Mateo**
Bar Patron	**Olivier Gourmet**
Teachers	**Baptiste Sornin, Samuel De Rijk, Carl Jadot, Sandra Raco**
Man at the Bus Station	**Claudy Delfosse**
Val Polet, Neighbor	**Jean-Michel Balthazar**
Concierge	**Frédéric Dussenne**
Medical Assistant	**Myriem Akheddiou**

Hicham Slaoui (Director), Romain Clavareau (Logan), Charles Monnoyer (Brian), Jasser Jaafari (Nabil), Mireille Bailly (Baker), Mourad Maimuni (Garage Owner), Neda Luga (Salon Client), Laurent Caron (Gilles), Selma Alaoui (Nadine), Youssef Tiberkanine (Mourad), Michèle Romus (Wes' Grandmother), Bilal Covino (Garage Apprentice), Valentin Jacob (Martin), Lara Persain (Mediator), Jérémie Segard (Market Vendor). Sabrina Mastratisi (Cashier)

An 11-year-old boy abandoned by his father is befriended by a hairdresser who is determined to help see him through this difficult time.

Jérémie Renier, Thomas Doret

THE DEEP BLUE SEA

(MUSIC BOX) Producers, Sean O'Connor, Kate Ogborn; Executive Producers, Katherine Butler, Lisa Marie Russo, Peter Hampden, Norman Merry; Line Producer, Eliza Mellor; Director/Screenplay, Terence Davies; Based on the 1952 play by Terence Rattigan; Photography, Florian Hoffmeister; Designer, James Merifield; Costumes, Ruth Myers; Music (Concerto for Violin and Orchestra, Op. 14), Samuel Barber; Editor, David Charap; Hair and Make-Up Designer, Lizzie Yianni Georgiou; Casting, Jane Arnell; a UK Film Council and Film4 in association with Protagonist Pictures, Lip Sync Productions and Artifical Eye presentation of a Camberwell/Fly Film Production; British, 2011; Dolby; Super 35 Widescreen; Deluxe color; Rated R; 98 minutes; American release date: March 23, 2012

Tom Hiddleston, Rachel Weisz

CAST
Hester Collyer	Rachel Weisz
Freddie Page	Tom Hiddleston
Sir William Collyer	Simon Russell Beale
Mrs. Elton	Ann Mitchell
Philip Welch	Jolyon Coy
Mr. Miller	Karl Johnson
Jackie Jackson	Harry Hadden-Paton
Liz Jackson	Sarah Kants
Hester's Father	Oliver Ford Davies
Collyer's Mother	Barbara Jefford
Ede and Ravenscroft's Assistant	Mark Tandy
Singing Man in Tube	Stuart McLoughlin
Mr. Elton	Nicholas Amer

Hester Collyer's privileged married life is shattered by her affair with a former RAF pilot with whom she shares little interest beyond the physical. Previous film version of Rattigan's play was released by 20th Century Fox in 1955 and starred Vivien Leigh and Kenneth More.

Rachel Weisz

Tom Hiddleston, Rachel Weisz

Simon Russell Beale, Rachel Weisz © Music Box Films

THE RAID: REDEMPTION

(SONY CLASSICS) a.k.a. *Serbuan maut*; Producer, Ario Sagantoro; Executive Producers, Rangga Maya Barack-Evans, Irwan D. Mussry, Nate Bolotin, Todd Brown; Director/Screenplay/Action Director, Gareth Evans; Photography, Matt Flannery; Art Director, Moti D. Setyanto; Music, Mike Shinoda, Joseph Trapanese; Action Choreographers, Iko Uwais, Yayan Ruhian, Gareth Huw Evans; Released in association with Stage 6 Films, PT.Merantau Films in association with XYZ Films and Celluloid Nightmares; Indonesian, 2011; Dolby; Color; Rated R; 100 minutes; Release date: March 23, 2012

CAST
Rama	**Iko Uwais**
Mad Dog	**Yayan Ruhian**
Jaka	**Joe Taslim**
Andi	**Doni Alamsyah**
Tama	**Ray Sahetapy**
Wahyu	**Pierre Gruno**
Bowo	**Tegar Satrya**
Gofar	**Iang Darmawan**
Dagu	**Eka "Piranha" Rahmadia**
Budi	**Verdi Solaiman**

R. Iman Aji (Eko), Ananda George (Ari), Yusuf Opilus (Alee), Yandi "Piranha" Sutisna (Prisoner), Hengky Solaiman (Rama's Father), Fikha Efendi (Rama's Wife), Umi Kulsum (Gofar's Wife), Alfridus Godfred, Rully Santoso, Melkias Ronald Torobi, Johanes Tuname, Sofyan Alop (Machete Gang), Mus Danang Danar Dono, Sunarto (Special Force Drivers), Hanggi Maisyra (Hanggi, Special Force #10), Zaenal Arifin (Zaenal, Special Force #1), Abraham Joshua B. Sitompul, Aji Setianto, Fachrudin Midun, Ardiansyah Putra, Engelius Rumbindi, Bastian Riffanie, Aliusman (Special Forces), Ubay Dillah (Naga, Mad Dog's Man #1), Taufik Arrahman, Acip Sumardi (Mad Dog's Men), Muhammad Yazid, Saifan Nur (Andi's Men), Fiqih Hardana Yuanza, Dafa Sikumbang (Spotter Boys)

A raid on an apartment block run by a sadistic crime lord turns into a bloodbath when the special-forces team assigned to the task is trapped inside with the deadly inhabitants instructed to wipe them out.

Joe Taslim, Yayan Ruhian

Doni Alamsyah, Yayan Ruhian © Sony Classics

Iko Uwais

Helene Bergsholm

Matias Myren, Helene Bergsholm © Sony Classics

TURN ME ON, DAMMIT!

(NEW YORKER) a.k.a. *Få meg på, for faen*; Producers, Brede Hovland, Sigve Endresen; Dierctor/Screenplay, Jannicke Systad Jacobsen; Based on the 2005 novel *Få meg på, for faen* by Olaug Nilssen; Co-Producer, Frida Ohrvik; Photography, Marianne Bakke; Art Director, Sunniva Rostad; Costumes, Sabina Cavenius; Music, Ginge Anvik; Editor, Zaklina Stojcevska; Casting, Ellen Michelsen; a Motlys presentation; Norwegian, 2011; Dolby; Color; Not rated; 76 minutes; American release date: March 30, 2012

CAST
Alma	**Helene Bergsholm**
Sara	**Malin Bjørhovde**
Alma's Mother	**Henriette Steenstrup**
Ingrid	**Beate Støfring**
Artur	**Matias Myren**
Kjartan	**Lars Nordtveit Listau**
Sebjørn	**Jon Bleiklie Devik**

Julia Bache-Wiig (Maria), Julia Elise Schacht (Elisabeth), Arthur Berning (Terje), Hilde-Gunn Ommedal (Magda), Ole Johan Skjelbred (Turnip Factory Boss), Finn Tokvam (Math Teacher), Per Kjertstad (Stig, Sex Hotline), Olaug Nilssen (Voice of Sebjørn's Wife), Yngve Hustad Reite (Careful Guy at Supermarket), Ronny Brede Aase (Truck Driver), Platon (Bingo, Alma's Dog)

Feeling trapped by her small town existence, 15-year-old Alma hopes to act on the sexual fantasies that are consuming her.

INTRUDERS

(MILLENNIUM) Producers, Enrique López-Lavigne, Belén Atienza, Mercedes Gamero; Executive Producers, Jesús de la Vega, Ricardo García Arrojo; Director, Juan Carlos Fresnadillo; Screenplay, Nicolás Casariego, James Marques; Photography, Enrique Chediak; Designer, Alain Bainée; Costumes, Tatiana Hernandez; Music, Roque Baños; Editor, Nacho Ruiz Capillas; Special Effects Makeup, DDT; Visual Effects Supervisor, David Heras; Casting, Shaheen Baig, Esther Cocero; a Universal Pictures International presentation of Apaches Entertainment and Antena 3 Films production in association with Canal Plus; Spanish-British, 2011; Dolby; Deluxe color; Rated R; 99 minutes; American release date: March 30, 2012

CAST
John Farrow	**Clive Owen**
Susanna	**Carice van Houten**
Father Antonio	**Daniel Brühl**
Mia	**Ella Purnell**
Dr. Rachel	**Kerry Fox**
Luisa	**Pilar López de Ayala**
Juan	**Izán Corchero**

Lolita Chakrabarti (Dr. Roy), Mark Wingett (Dave), Imogen Gray (Lilly), Ella Hunt (Ella Foster), Héctor Alterio (Old Priest), Adrian Rawlins (Police Inspector), Michael Nardone (Frank), Mary Woodvine (Teacher), Ralph Ineson (Alamar Installer), Adam Leese, Raymond Waring (Policemen), Natalia Rodriguez (Babysitter), Natasha Dosanjh (Aisha)

A young boy in Spain keeps receiving nightly visits from a mysterious, black-hooded figure, an occurrence repeated across the miles in London where a little girl is visited by a similar spectre.

Clive Owen, Ella Purnell

Clive Owen © Millennium Entertainment

Willem Dafoe, Sam Neill

Willem Dafoe © Magnolia Films

THE HUNTER

(MAGNOLIA) Producer, Vincent Sheehan; Executive Producers, Liz Watts, Anita Sheehan, Paul Wiegard; Director, Daniel Nettheim; Screenplay, Alice Addison; Original Adaptation, Wain Fimeri, Daniel Nettheim; Based on the 1999 novel by Julia Leigh; Photography, Robert Humphreys; Designer, Steven Jones-Evans; Costumes, Emily Seresin; Music, Matteo Zingales, Michael Lira, Andrew Lancaster; Music Supervisor, Andrew Kotatko; Casting, Jane Norris; a Screen Australia presentation with Screen NSW, Screen Tasmania, Fulcrum Media Finance, Madman Entertainment and Entertainment One of a Porchlight Films production; Australian, 2011; Dolby; Super 35 Widescreen; Color; Rated R; 101 minutes; American release date: April 6, 2012

CAST

Martin	**Willem Dafoe**
Lucy	**Frances O'Connor**
Jack	**Sam Neill**
Sass	**Morgana Davies**
Bike	**Finn Woodlock**
Milddeman	**Jacek Koman**

Callan Mulvey (Rival Hunter), John Brumpton (Publican), Dan Wyllie (Pool Player), Sullivan Stapleton (Doug), Jamie Timony (Free), Dan Spielman (Simon), Maia Thomas (Shakti), Marc Watson-Paul (Jarrah)

A mercenary is hired by an anonymous company to trek into the Tasmanian wilderness to hunt for a tiger believed to be extinct.

THE ASSAULT

(SCREEN MEDIA) a.k.a. *L'assaut*; Producers, Julien Leclercq, Julien Madon; Line Producer, Marc Olla; Director, Julien Leclercq; Screenplay, Simon Moutairou, Julien Leclercq; Based on the 2007 book by Roland Môntins and Gilles Cauture; Photography, Thierry Pouget; Designer, Jean-Philippe Moreaux; Costumes, Muriel Legrand; Music, Jean-Jacques Hertz, Francois Roy; Editors, Michael Dumontier, Christine Lucas Navarro, Frédéric Thoraval; Visual Effects, Buf Compagnie; Casting, Pierre-Jacques Benichou; a Julien Leclerg and Julien Madon presentation of a co-production of Labyrinthe Films and Mars Films with the participation of Canal+ and Cinecinema; French, 2011; Dolby; HD; Color; Rated R; 91 minutes; American release date: April 6, 2012

CAST

Thierry	**Vincent Elbaz**
Commandant Denis Favier	**Grégori Derangère**
Carole	**Mélanie Bernier**
Yahia	**Aymen Saïdi**
Mustapha	**Chems Dahmani**
Makhlouf	**Mohid Abid**

Djanis Bouzyani (Salim), Marie Guillard (Claire), Naturel Le Ruyet (Emma), Philippe Bas (Didier Sniper GIGN), Philippe Cura, Grégoire Taulère (GIGNs), Charlie Costillas, Ludovic Meacci (Young GIGN Recruits), Laurent Paillot (GIGN Administrator), Antoine Basler (Solignac), Louis Arene (Solignac Assistant), Hugo Becker (Leroy), Hugues Martel (d'Orsay Director), Hervé Dubourjal (Beauvau Director), François Lescurat (Aeronautics Expert), Thierry Pietra (DST Agent), Abdelhafid Metalsi (Ali Touchent), Jean-Philippe Puymartin (Captain), David Sevier (Copilot), Marc Robert (Mechanic), Samira Lachhab (Leila), Samira Sedira (Leila's Mother), Lounès Tazairt (Leila's Father), Nicolas Melocco (Yannick Beugnet), Farid Badaoui (Algerian Policeman), Abdelkrim Bahloul (Melki), Bing Yin (Vietnamese Hostage), Zorah Benali (Yahia's Mother), Kader Kada (Negotiator Ninja), Fatima Adoum (Djia, 1st Class Passenger), Jane Resmond (Airline Hostess), Thierry Jennaud (Stewart), Lassâad Salaani (Algerian Maintenance Man), Bruno Seznec (Marignane Airport Director)

The true story of how a group of Islamic terrorists hijacked a plane in Algiers and headed for Paris, with the intention of flying the aircraft into the Eiffel Tower.

Vincent Elbaz © Screen Media

Nanni Moretti

Michel Piccoli

Michel Piccoli

Nanni Moretti © Sundance Selects

WE HAVE A POPE

(SUNDANCE SELECTS) a.k.a. *Habemus Papam*; Producers, Nanni Moretti, Domenico Procacci; Director, Nanni Moretti; Story and Screenplay, Nanni Moretti, Francesco Piccolo, Federica Pontremoli; Photography, Alessandro Pesci; Designer, Paola Bizzarri; Costumes, Lina Nerli Taviani; Music, Franco Piersanti; Editor, Esmeralda Calabria; a Sundance Selects, Nanni Moretti and Domenico Procacci presentation of a Sacher Film, Fandango (Rome), Le Pacte, France 3 Cinema (Paris) co-production in collaboration with RAI Cinema; Italian-French, 2011; Dolby; Color; Not rated; 104 minutes; American release date: April 6, 2012

CAST
The Pope	**Michel Piccoli**
Male Psychotherapist	**Nanni Moretti**
Female Pyschotherapist	**Margherita Buy**
Spokesperson	**Jerzy Stuhr**
Cardinal Gregori	**Renato Scarpa**
Cardinal Bollati	**Franco Graziosi**
Cardinal Pescardona	**Camillo Milli**
Cardinal Cevasco	**Robert Nobile**
Cardinal Brummer	**Ulrich von Dobschütz**
Master of Ceremonies	**Mario Santella**

Gianluca Gobbi (Swiss Guard), Camilla Ridolfi, Leonardo Della Bianca (Children), Dario Cantarelli, Manuela Mandracchia, Rossana Mortara, Teco Celio, Roberto De Francesco, Chiara Causa (Theater Company), Tony Laudadio (Chief of Police), Enrico Ianniello (Journalist), Cecilia Dazzi (A Mother), Lucia Mascino (Shop Assistant), Maurizio Mannoni (TV Journalist), Giovanni Ludeno (Hall Porter), Giulia Giordano (Girl at Bar), Francesco Brandi (Bartender), Leonardo Maddalena (Boy at the Bus), Salvatore Miscio (Priest), Salvatore Della'Aquila (Doctor), Diapason (Musical Band), Peter Boom, Erik Merino, Kevin Murray, Harold Bradley, Jelle Bruinsma, Alfredo Cairo, Mauro Casanica, Don Somasiry Jayamanne (Cardinals)

A Cardinal who never expected to be elected Pope, is thrown into such a panic at the news of his appointment that the help of a psychiatrist is sought.

LOCKOUT

(FILMDISTRICT/OPEN ROAD) Producers, Marc Libert, Leila Smith; Line Producer, Andjelija Vlaisavljevic; Directors, Saint & Mather (Stephen Saint Leger, James Mather); Screenplay, Stephen Saint Leger, James Mather, Luc Besson; Photography, James Mather; Designer, Romek Delimata; Costumes, Olivier Beriot; Music, Alexandre Azaria; Digital Visual Effects, Windmill Lane Visual Effects, Dublin; Editors, Camillle Delamarre, Eamonn Power; Special Effects Coordinator, Muhamed M'Barek-Toske; Special Effects Supervisor, Mike Crowley; Stunts, Slavisa Ivanovic; a Luc Besson and FilmDistrict presentation of a Europacorp production with the participation of Canal+and Cine+; French-American; Dolby; Widescreen; Color; Rated PG-13; 95 minutes; American release date: April 13, 2012

Joseph Gilgun (front)

CAST

Marion Snow	**Guy Pearce**
Emilie Warnock	**Maggie Grace**
Alex	**Vincent Regan**
Hydell	**Joseph Gilgun**
Harry Shaw	**Lennie James**
Scott Langral	**Peter Stormare**
Hock	**Jacky Ido**
John James Mace	**Tim Plester**
Barnes	**Mark Tankersley**
Kathryn	**Anne-Solenne Hatte**

Peter Hudson (President Warnock), Nick Hardin (Hostage Negotiator), Dan Savier (Duke), Damijan Oklopdzic (Slick), Bojan Peric, Evan Timothy Moses (LOPD Technicians), Greg De Cuir (Radio Technician), Thomas Kelly, Daryl Fidelak (White House Doctors), Miodrag Stevanovic (Frank Armstrong), Charles Robertson (Safe Room Technician), Michael Sopko (Rupert), Yan Dron, Vanja Lazin (Hitmen), Marko Janjic, Stefan Buzurovic (LOPD Pilots), Peter Chaffey (MS1 Control Room Doctor), Bojana Bregovic (Secretary), Milorad Kapor (Scar), Jason Ryan (Corridor Inmate with Knife), Jovan B. Todorovic (New Technician), Milana Milunovic (Street Girl), Patrick Cauderlier (Shuttle Pilot)

An unjustly convicted prisoner is offered his freedom if he can rescue the president's daughter from a space prison that has been taken over by the inmates.

Guy Pearce

Maggie Grace, Guy Pearce

Maggie Grace © FilmDistrict

Fellag

Emilien Nëron, Sophie Nélisse

MONSIEUR LAZHAR

(MUSIC BOX FILMS) Producers, Luc Déry, Kim McCraw; Line Producer, Claude Paiement; Director/ Screenplay, Philippe Falardeau; Based on the 2002 play *Bashir Lazhar* by Evelyne de la Chenelière; Photography, Ronald Plante; Designer, Emmanuel Fréchette; Costumes, Francesca Chamberland; Music, Martin Léon; Editor, Stéphane Lafleur; Casting, Nathalie Boutrie, Emanuelle Beaugrand-Champagne, Constance Demontoy; a micro_scope production; Canadian, 2011; Dolby; Super 35 Widescreen; HD; Color; Rated PG-13; 94 minutes; American release date: April 13, 2012

CAST

Bachir Lazhar	**Fellag**
Alice	**Sophie Nélisse**
Simon	**Émilien Néron**
Mrs. Vaillancourt	**Danielle Proulx**
Claire	**Brigitte Poupart**
Janitor	**Louis Champagne**
Gaston	**Jules Philip**
Mrs. Dumas	**Francine Ruel**
Audrée	**Sophie Sanscartier**
Abdelmalek	**Seddik Benslimane**
Marie-Frédérique	**Marie-Eve Beauregard**
Boris	**Louis-David Leblanc**
Victor	**Vincent Millard**

André Robitaille (Commissioner), Daniel Gadouas (Me. Gilbert Danis), Stéphane Demers (Marie-Frédérique's Father), Evelyne de la Chenelière (Alice's Mother), Marie Charlebois (Prosecutor), Nico Lagarde (Psychologist)

Taking a job as a substitute teacher after his predecessor has committed suicide, an Algerian immigrant tries to bridge the cultural gap between himself and his French Canadian students.

This film received a 2011 Oscar nomination as foreign language film.

Danielle Proulx, Fellag

Fellag and class © Music Box Films

Lola Créton, Sebastian Urzendowsky

Sebastian Urzendowsky, Lola Créton © Sundance Selects

GOODBYE FIRST LOVE

(SUNDANCE SELECTS) a.k.a. *Un amour de jeunesse*; Producers, Philippe Martin, David Thion; Co-Producers, Roman Paul, Gerhard Meixner; Director/Screenplay, Mia Hansen-Løve; Photography, Stéphane Fontaine; Designer, Mathieu Menut, Charlotte de Cadeville; Costumes, Bethsabée Dreyfus; Editor, Marion Monnier; Casting, Elsa Pharaon, Antoinette Boulat; a Les Films Pelléas and Razor Film presentation; French-German, 2011; Dolby; Color; Not rated; 110 minutes; American release date: April 20, 2012

CAST
Camille	**Lola Créton**
Sullivan	**Sebastian Urzendowsky**
Lorenz	**Magne-Håvard Brekke**
Camille's Mother	**Valérie Bonneton**
Her Father	**Serge Renko**
Sullivan's Mother	**Özay Fecht**

Max Ricat (Sullivan's Brother), Louis Dunbar (A Friend), Philippe Paimblanc, Patrice Movermann (Antiquarians), Arnaud Azoulay (Camille's Brother), Amélie Robin, Justine Dhouilly (Lycée Friends), Charlotte Faivre (Leader), François Buot (History Professor), Elisabeth Guill (English Teacher), Marie-Hélène Peyrat (French Professor), Guy-Patrick Sainderichin (Architecture Professor), Jean-Paul Dubois (Demolition Boss), Grégoire Strecker (Nightclubber), Eric Fraticelli (Yard Boss), Frédéric Liévain (The Doctor)

Fifteen-year-old Camille experiences her first serious love affair with an older boy who then devastates her by deciding to leave her behind and travel through South America.

CHIMPANZEE

(DISNEYNATURE) Producers, Alastair Fothergill, Mark Linfield, Alix Tidmarsh; Executive Producer, Don Hahn; Directors, Alastair Fothergill, Mark Linfield; Photography, Martyn Colbeck, Bill Wallauer; Music, Nicholas Hooper; Editor, Andy Netley; Narrator, Tim Allen; Great Ape Productions; Tanzanian-American; Dolby; Color; Rated G; 78 minutes; American release date: April 20, 2012. Documentary following a baby chimpanzee's efforts to survive after he is orphaned during an attack by a rival group of chimps.

Oscar

Oscar, Freddy

Oscar © Disneynature

Nikolaj Coster-Waldau, Synnøve Macody Lund

Nikolaj Coster-Waldau

Aksel Hennie

Aksel Hennie © Magnolia Film

HEADHUNTERS

(MAGNOLIA) a.k.a. *Hodejegerne*; Producers, Asle Vatn, Marianne Gray; Executive Producers, Anni Faurbye Fernandez, Ole Søndberg, Mikael Wallén, Christian Fredrik Martin; Co-Producers, Lone Korslund, Hans-Wolfgang Jurgan; Director, Morten Tyldum; Screenplay, Ulf Ryberg, Lars Gudmestad; based on the 2008 novel by Jo Nesbø; Photography, John Andreas Andersen; Designer, Nina Bjerch-Andresen; Costumes, Karen Fabritius Gram; Music, Trond Bjerknæs, Jeppe Kaas; Editor, Vidar Flataukan; Casting, Jannecke Bervell; a Yellow Bird, Frilandfilm presentation of a co-production with Nordisk Film & Degeto Film; Norwegian, 2011; Dolby; Super 35 Widescreen; Color; Rated R; 100 minutes; American release date: April 27, 2012

CAST

Roger Brown	**Aksel Hennie**
Clas Greve	**Nikolaj Coster-Waldau**
Diana Brown	**Synnøve Macody Lund**
Ove Kjikerud	**Eivind Sander**
Lotte	**Julie Ølgaard**
Jeremias Lander	**Kyrre Haugen Sydness**
Brede Sperre	**Reidar Sørensen**
Stig	**Nils Jørgen Kaalstad**
Brugd	**Joachim Rafaelsen**
Sunded	**Mats Mogeland**

Gunnar Skramstad Johnsen, Lars Skramstad Johnsen (Monsen), Signe Tynning (Morning Show Hostess), Nils Gunnar Lie (Morning Show Host), Baard Owe (Sindre Aa), Sondre Abel (Okonomisjef), Morten Hennie (Chairman), Kyrre Mosleth (Vekter Nils), Martin Furulund (Vekter Per), Mattis Herman Nyquist (Ferdinand), Togrim Mellum Stene (Atle Nerum), Camilla Augusta Hallan (Sykepleier), Anjum Salwan (Drosjesjafer)

When his gallery owner wife introduces him to a former mercenary who owns a highly valuable painting, Roger Brown makes it his goal to steal it.

THE PIRATES! BAND OF MISFITS

(COLUMBIA) Producers, Peter Lord, David Sproxton, Julie Lockhart; Executive Producer, Carla Shelley; Director, Peter Lord; Screenplay, Gideon Defoe, based on his 2004 book *The Pirates! In an Adventure with Scientists*; Co-Director, Jeff Newitt; Photography, Frank Passingham; Designer, Norman Garwood; Supervising Art Director, Matt Perry; Visual Effects Supervisor, Andrew Morley; Music, Theodore Shapiro; CG Animation Supervisor, Lesley Headrick; CG Character Animator, Boris Hiestand; a Sony Pictures Animation presentation of an Aardman production; British-American; Dolby; Digital Widescreen; Color; 3D; Rated PG; 88 minutes; American release date: April 27, 2012

Queen Victoria, Pirate Captain, Polly

VOICE CAST

The Pirate Captain	**Hugh Grant**
The Pirate with a Scarf (Number 2)	**Martin Freeman**
Queen Victoria	**Imelda Staunton**
Charles Darwin	**David Tennant**
Black Bellamy	**Jeremy Piven**
Cutlass Liz	**Salma Hayek**
Peg Leg Hastings	**Lenny Henry**
The Pirate King	**Brian Blessed**
The Albino Pirate	**Anton Yelchin**
The Pirate with Gout	**Brendan Gleeson**
The Surprisingly Curvaceous Pirate	**Ashley Jensen**
The Pirate Who Likes Sunsets and Kittens	**Al Roker**
Admiral Collingwood	**Mike Cooper**
Scarlett Morgan	**David Schneider**

Tom Doggart, Sophie Jerrold, Sophie Laughton, Peter Lord, Kayvan Novak, David Schaal (Additional Voices)

Pirate with Gout, Surprisingly Curvaceous Pirate, Albino Pirate, Pirate Who Likes Sunsets and Kittens, Pirate with a Hook for a Hand, Pirate with Accordion

A band of misfit buccanneers seize their chance to win Pirate of Year after a chance encounter with Charles Darwin makes them aware of the scientific value of their beloved mascot, Polly.

This film received an Oscar nomination for animated feature.

Pirate Captain, Polly, Pirate with a Scarf

Pirate Captain

Pirate with a Scarf, Pirate Captain

Cutlass Liz

Charles Darwin, Pirate Captain

Mister Bobo

Pirate with a Scarf, Pirate with Gout, Pirate Captain, Albino Pirate

Charles Darwin, Pirate Captain, Polly, Pirate with a Scarf, Pirate with Gout, Albino Pirate © Columbia Pictures

Maggie Smith

Judi Dench

Tena Desae, Dev Patel

Celia Imrie, Diana Hardcastle, Ronald Pickup

Penelope Wilton © Fox Searchlight

Judi Dench, Tom Wilkinson, Bill Nighy

Tom Wilkinson

Judi Dench, Celia Imrie

THE BEST EXOTIC MARIGOLD HOTEL

(FOX SEARCHLIGHT) Producers, Graham Broadbent, Pete Czernin; Executive Producers, Jeff Skoll, Ricky Strauss, Jonathan King; Co-Producers, Caroline Hewitt, Sarah Harvey; Director, John Madden; Screenplay, Ol Parker; Based on the 2004 novel *These Foolish Things* by Deborah Moggach; Photography, Ben Davis; Designer, Alan MacDonald; Costumes, Louise Stjernsward; Music, Thomas Newman; Editor, Chris Gill; a Blueprint Pictures production, presented in association with Patricipant Media and Imagenation Abu Dhabi; British; Dolby; Color; Rated PG-13; 124 minutes; American release date: May 4, 2012

CAST

Evelyn Greenslade	**Judi Dench**
Douglas Ainslie	**Bill Nighy**
Jean Ainslie	**Penelope Wilton**
Sonny Kapoor	**Dev Patel**
Madge Hardcastle	**Celia Imrie**
Norman Cousins	**Ronald Pickup**
Graham Dashwood	**Tom Wilkinson**
Muriel Donnelly	**Maggie Smith**
Sunaina	**Tena Desae**
Graham's Colleague	**Patrick Pearson**
Judge	**Hugh Dickson**
Estate Agent	**James Rawlings**
Dr. Ghurjarapartidar	**Paul Bhattacharjee**
Staff Nurse	**Liza Tarbuck**
Judith	**Lucy Robinson**
Madge's Son-in-Law	**Simon Wilson**
Madge's Daughter	**Sara Stewart**
Madge's Grandchildren	**Ramona Marquez, Raoul Marquez**
Taxi Driver	**Glen Davies**
Evelyn's Son	**Jay Villiers**
Evelyn's Lawyer	**Paul Bentall**
Hairdresser	**Loo Brealey**
Graham's Cleaner	**Catherine Terris**
Douglas' Golf Partner	**Richard Cubison**
Paramedic	**Josh Cohen**
Airport Security Guard	**Josh Cole**
Muriel's Physiotherapist	**Bhuvnesh Shetty**
Young Wasim	**Honey Chhaya**
Public Records Official	**Shubraojyoti Barat**
Rickshaw Driver for Graham	**N. Kumar**
Boy Playing Cricket	**Hem Acharya**
Rickshaw Driver for Evelyn	**Kailash Vijay**
Jay	**Sid Makkar**

Seema Azmi (Anokhi), Vishnu Sharma (Mr. Maruthi), Lillete Dubey (Mrs. Kapoor), Denzil Smith (Viceroy Club Secretary), Jagdish Sharma (Maharajah), Sandeep Lele (Viceroy Club Barman), Diana Hardcastle (Carol), Neeraj Kadela (Market Salesman), S.N. Purohit (Tap Shop Owner), Shiv Palawat (Tea Room Waiter), Mahesh Udeshi (Doctor at Clinic), Neena Kulkarni (Gaurika), Rajendra Gupta (Manoj), Gagan Mishra (Restaurant Owner), A.R. Rama (Jean, Rickshaw Driver)

A group of British retirees decide to take up residence in a "newly restored" hotel in India, hoping for a cheaper and more exotic locale in which to spend their autumn years.

Dev Patel

DEATH OF A SUPERHERO

(TRIBECA) Producers, Astrid Kahmke, Philipp Kreuzer, Michael Garland; Executive Producers, Matthias Esche, Jan S. Kaiser, Anthony McCarten, Paul Donovan; Co-Producers, Mark Porsche, Michael Coldewey, Christian Sommer; Associate Producers, Alish McElmeel, Lukas Batthyány, Tilo Seiffert; Line Producers, Gilbert Möhler, Paul Myler; Director, Ian Fitzgibbon; Screenplay, Anthony McCarten, based on his 2007 novel; Photography, Tom Fährmann; Designer, Mark Geraghty; Costumes, Kathy Strachan; Music, Marius Ruhland; Editor, Tony Cranstoun; VFX/Animation Supervisor, Alessandro Cioffi; Make-up, Louise Myler; Casting, Ros Hubbard, Louise Kiely, Siegfried Wagner; a Bavaria Pictures and Grand Pictures in co-production with Picture Circle and Cinemendo/Trixter in association with Cinepostproduction; German-Irish; Dolby; Color; Not rated; 97 minutes; American release date: May 4, 2012

CAST
Dr. Adrian King	**Andy Serkis**
Donald Clarke	**Thomas Brodie-Sangster**
Shelly	**Aisling Loftus**
James Clarke	**Michael McElhatton**
Renata Clarke	**Sharon Horgan**
Tanya	**Jessica Schwarz**
Jeff Clarke	**Ronan Raferty**

Ned Dennehy, Matthias Beier (The Glove), Emma Eliza Regan (Morna Pinkerton), Olga Wehrly, Amelia Growley, Nina Gnädig, Amy Huberman (Nursey Worsey), Jane Brennan (Dr. Rebecca Johnston), Mella Caron (Wendy), Aisling Bodkin (Joanna), Ben Harding (Michael), Dónal Haughey (Guy at Laptop), Killian Coyle (Hugo), Enda Oates (English Teacher), Alan Bradley (Patient #2), Julie Sharkey (Nurse), Lilli Forgách, Ian Fitzgibbon (Shrinks), Sean Duggan (Teacher), Rebecca Thompson (Sharon), Peter Sexton (Billy), Simon Mulcahy (Teenage Guy), Holly Gregg (Maja), Billy Gibson (Rugby Jock), Mary Murray, Rachel Dunne (Prostitutes)

Dying of cancer, a bitter teenager wants only to have some physical intimacy with a girl before he faces the inevitable.

Aisling Loftus, Thomas Brodie-Sangster

Thomas Brodie-Sangster © Tribeca Film

Ohshiro Maeda

Joe Odagiri, Koki Maeda, Nene Ohtsuka, Ohshiro Maeda © Mangolia Films

I WISH

(MAGNOLIA) Producers, Kentaro Koike, Hijiri Taguchi; Director/Screenplay/Editor, Hirokazu Kore-Eda; Photography, Yutaka Yamazaki; Set Designer, Ayako Matsuo; Costumes, Miwako Kobayashi; Music, Quruli; a Shirogumi Inc. production; Color; Not rated; 128 minutes; American release date: May 11, 2012

CAST
Koichi	**Koki Maeda**
Ryunosuke	**Ohshiro Maeda**
Tasuku	**Ryoga Hayashi**
Makoto	**Seinosuke Nagayoshi**
Megumi	**Kyara Uchida**
Kanna	**Kanna Hashimoto**
Rento	**Rento Isobe**

Nene Ohtsuka (Nozomi, Mother), Joe Odagiri (Kenji, Father), Yui Natsukawa (Kyoko, Megumi's Mother), Masami Nagasawa (Ms. Mimura, Teacher), Hiroshi Abe (Mr. Sakagami, Teacher), Yoshio Harada (Wataru, Grandfather's Friend), Kirin Kiki (Hideko, Grandmother), Isao Hashizume (Shukichi, Grandfather)

A twelve-year-old boy, living with his divorced mother and grandparents in Kagoshi, tries to reunite with his brother who has been living with his father in the Northern region of Japan.

Oxana Chihane, Olga Yerofyeyeva, Anneta Bousaleh

Nadine Labaki, Julien Farhat © Sony Classics

WHERE DO WE GO NOW?

(SONY CLASSICS) a.k.a. *Et maintent on va où?*; Producers, Anne-Dominique Toussaint; Executive Producers (Lebanon), Ginger Beirut Productions; Co-Producers, Romain Le Grand, Hesham Abdel Khalek, Tarak Ben Ammar; Director, Nadine Labaki; Screenplay, Nadine Labaki, Jihad Hojeily, Rodney Al Haddad, with the participation of Thomas Bidegain; Photography, Christophe Offenstein; Set Designer, Cynthia Zahar; Costumes, Caroline Labaki; Music, Khaled Mouzanar; Editor, Véronique Lange; a Les Films des Tournelles, Pathé, Les Films de Beyrouth, United Artistic Group, Chaocorp, France 2 Cinéma, Prima TV co-production with the participation of Canal+, Cinéncinéma, France Télévisions in association with The Doha Film Institute; French-Lebanese-Italian-Egyptian, 2011; Dolby; Color; Rated PG-13; 100 minutes; American release date: May 11, 2012

CAST
Takla	**Claude Baz Moussawbaa**
Afaf	**Layla Hakim**
Amale	**Nadine Labaki**
Yvonne	**Yvonne Maalouf**
Saydeh	**Antoinette Noufaily**
Rabih	**Julien Farhat**

Ali Haidar (Roukoz), Kevin Abboud (Nassim), Petra Saghbini (Rita), Mostafa Al Sakka (Hammoudi), Sasseen Kawzally (Issam), Caroline Labaki (Aida), Anjo Rihane (Fatmeh), Mohammad Akil (Abou Ahmad), Khalil Bou Khalil (Maire), Samir Awad (Pretre), Ziad Abou Absi (Cheikh), Adel Karam (Bus Driver), Oxana Chihane (Katia), Anneta Bousaleh (Svetlana), Olga Yerofyeyeva (Anna), Yulia Maroun (Tatiana), Oksana Beloglazova (Olga), Fouad Yammine (Boutros), Sami Khorjieh (Abou Ali), Gisèle Smeden (Gisele), Georges Khoury (Youssef), Mounzer Baalbaki (Sassine)

Tired of losing so many of their men in battle, the women in a remote Lebanese village come up with several ruses to keep further wars from erupting.

ELENA

(ZEITGEIST) Producers, Alexander Rodnyansky, Sergey Melkumov; Director, Andrey Zvyagintsev; Screenplay, Oleg Negin, Andrey Zvyagintsev; Photography, Mikhail Krichman; Designers, Vasiliy Gritskov, Valeriy Zhukov; Costumes, Anna Bartuli, Nastia Vishnevskaya, Tatyana Chernyakova; Editor, Anna Mass; Casting, Elina Ternyeva; a Non-Stop Prod. production with the support of Fonds du Cinema; Russian, 2011; Dolby; Color; Widescreen; Not rated; 109 minutes; American release date: May 16, 2012

CAST
Elan	**Nadezhda Markina**
Vladimir	**Andrey Smirnov**
Katerina	**Elena Lyadova**
Sergey	**Alexey Rozin**
Tatyana	**Evgenia Konushkina**
Sasha	**Igor Ogurtsov**
Lawyer	**Vasiliy Michkiv**
Vitek	**Alexey Maslodudov**

A former nurse who has married into wealth must take desperate steps when she realizes that her potential inheritance might be in jeopardy.

Nadezhda Markina, Andrey Smirnov

Nadezhda Markina © Zeitgeist Films

Rupert Everett

Felicity Jones, Jonathan Pryce, Hugh Dancy

Sheridan Smith, Hugh Dancy

HYSTERIA

(SONY CLASSICS) Producers, Sarah Curtis, Judy Cairo, Tracey Becker; Executive Producers, Michael A. Simpson, Eric Brenner, Ken Atchity, Sandra Segal, Leo Joseph, Natalie Joseph, Mark Kress, Hakan Kousetta, Claudia Blümhuber, Florian Dargel, Peter Fudakowski, Stephen Dyer; Co-Producers, Anouk Nora, Jimmy de Brabant, Bob Bellion; Line Producer, Paul Sarony; Director, Tanya Wexler; Screenplay, Stephen Dyer, Jonah Lisa Dyer; Photography, Sean Bobbitt; Designer, Sophie Becher; Costumes, Nic Ede; Music, Gast Waltzing, Christian Henson; Editor, Jon Gregory; Casting, Gaby Kester; an Informant Media & Forthcoming Films production in association with Beachfront Films & Chimera Films in co-production with By Alternative Pictures, Delux Productions, Arte France Cinema and TataFilm in association with Silver Reel, Lankin Partners and The UK Film & TV Production Company PLC; British-French-German-Luxembourg; Dolby; Super 35 Widescreen; Deluxe Color; Rated R; 100 minutes; American release date: May 18, 2012

CAST

Dr. Mortimer Granville	**Hugh Dancy**
Charlotte Dalrymple	**Maggie Gyllenhaal**
Dr. Robert Dalrymple	**Jonathan Pryce**
Emily Dalrymple	**Felicity Jones**
Edmund St. John-Smythe	**Ruper Everett**
Fannie	**Ashley Jensen**
Molly	**Sheridan Smith**
Lady St. John-Smythe	**Gemma Jones**
Lord St. John-Smythe	**Malcolm Rennie**
Mrs. Castellari	**Kim Criswell**
Mrs. Parsons	**Georgie Glen**
Mrs. Pearce	**Elisabet Johannesdottir**

Linda Woodhall (Nurse Smalley), Kim Selby (Lady Wheaton), John Overstall (Mr. Huddleston), Ann Comfort (Mrs. Huddleston), Jonathan Rhodes (PC Fugate), Leila Schaus (Tess), Jules Werner (Jack the Coal Man), Maggie McCarthy (Mrs. Copeland), Michael Webber (Bailiff), Perry Blanks (Prison Guard), Tobias Menzies (Mr. Souters), David Ryall (Judge), Anna Chancellor (Mrs. Bellamy), David Schaal (Tough Guy), Nicholas Woodeson (Dr. Richardson), Ellie Jacob (Nurse), Jack Kelly (Footman #1), Joan Linder (Dispensary Old Woman Patient), Dominic Borrelli (Worker at Edwards), Jimmy de Brabant (Major Dowd), Kate Linder (Lady Cherwell), Corinna Marlowe (Lady Perrigott), Thomas Dennis (Newsboy), Sylvia Strange (Queen Victoria)

In Victorian London, Dr. Mortimer Granville builds himself quite a reputation for his method of helping relieve ladies of their "hysteria," as a chain of events lead to him helping to invent the vibrator.

Rupert Everett, Hugh Dancy, Maggie Gyllenhaal © Sony Classics

QUILL: THE LIFE OF A GUIDE DOG

(MUSIC BOX FILMS) Producers, Nozomu Enoki, Ichiro Yamamoto, Takeo Hisamatsu; Executive Producer, Junichi Sakomoto; Director, Yoichi Sai; Screenplay, Shoichi Maruyama, Yoshihiro Nakamura; Based on the novel *Modoken Quill no Issho* by Ryohei Akimoto and Keigo Ishiguro; Photography, Junichi Fujisawa; Designer, Riki Imamura; Music, Kuricorder Quartet; Editor, Isao Kawase; Dog Trainer, Tadaomi Miya; a Shochiku/TV Tokyo Corporation/Eisei Gekijo/Nippon Shuppan Hanbai production; Japanese; 2004; Dolby; Color; Not rated; 100 minutes; American release date: May 18, 2012

CAST

Mitsuru Watanabe	**Kaoru Kobayashi**
Satoru Tawada	**Kippei Shiina**
Isamu Nii	**Teruyuki Kagawa**
Yoshiko Watanabe	**Keiko Toda**
Mitsuko Nii	**Shinobu Terajima**
Masumi Kubo	**Tomoka Kurotani**
Reno Mito	**Yûko Natori**

Yukika Sakuratani (Mitsuko Watanabe), Yawara Matsuda (Etsuo Watanabe), Tarô Ishida (Hiroshi Totsuka), Kenji Mitzuhashi (Yichi Sakai), Chie Sakagami (Yoko Kamata), Mantarô Koichi (Kawamoto), Kuidaore Uchuutei (Yoshinaga), Kiyomi Tanikawa (Kyoko Yaguchi), Kouzou Satou (Ishibashi), Mariko Miyamoto (Housewife), Kohei Terai (Kenji Mito), Misuru Ochiai (Toru Tsukamoto), Katsuya Nomaura (Tomonori Kataoka), Yukio Hide (Kaneko), Tomohiro Nakagawa (Takano), Kiyohide Yamazaki (Hirata), Reiko Nieda (Sakurai), Akihiko Yamada (Veterinarian), Laffy (Quill), Chibichibi Qoo (Baby Quill), Beat (Quill at 3 months), Chibi Qoo (Quill at 7 months), Eri (Older Quill)

A Labrador Retriever's routine life is changed drastically when he is selected to become a seeing-eye dog.

Chibichibi Qoo © Music Box Films

Kaoru Kobayashi, Laffy

Arnaud Henriet, Jérémie Elkaïm, Nicolas Duvauchelle, Joeystarr

Maïwenn © Sundance Selects

POLISSE

(SUNDANCE SELECTS) Producer, Alain Attal; Director, Maïwenn; Screenplay, Maïwenn, Emmanuelle Bercot; Photography, Pierre Aïm; Designer, Nicolas de Boiscuille; Costumes, Marité Coutard; Music, Stephen Warbeck; Editors, Laure Gardette, Yann Dedet; Casting, Nicolas Ronchi; a Les Productions du Trésor, Arte France Cinéma, Mars Films, Chaocorp, Shortcom production, with the participation of Canal +, CinéCinéma, Arte, in association with Manon, Wild Bunch; French, 2011; Dolby; Color; DV; Not rated; 127 minutes; American release date: May 18, 2012

CAST

Nadine	**Karin Viard**
Fred	**Joeystarr**
Iris	**Marina Foïs**
Mathieu	**Nicolas Duvauchelle**
Melissa	**Maïwenn**
Chrys	**Karole Rocher**
Sue Ellen	**Emmanuelle Bercot**
Balloo	**Frédéric Pierrot**
Bamako	**Arnaud Henriet**
Nora	**Naidra Ayadi**
Gabriel	**Jérémie Elkaïm**

Riccardo Scamarcio (Francesco), Sandrine Kiberlain (Mrs. de la Faublaise), Wladimir Yordanoff (Beauchard), Louis do de Lencquesaing (Mr. de la Faublaise), Carole Franck (Céline), Laurent Bateau (Hervé), Anne Suarez (Alice), Anthony Delon (Alex), Audrey Lamy (Disgraced Mother), Riton Liebman (Franck), Sophie Cattani (Drug-Addicted Mother), Martial di Fonzo Bo (P.E. Teacher), Lou Doillon (Sister Melissa)

A photojournalist is assigned by the Interior Ministry to document the day-to-day events of a group of law inforcement offiers working for the Child Protection Unit in northern Paris.

THE INTOUCHABLES

(WEINSTEIN CO.) Producers, Nicolas Duval Adassovsky, Yann Zenou, Laurent Zeitoun; Line Producer, Laurent Sivot; Directors/Screenplay, Eric Toledano, Olivier Nakache; Photography, Mathieu Vadepied; Set Designer, François Emmanuelli; Costumes, Isabelle Pannetier; Music, Ludovico Einaudi; Editor, Dorian Rigal-Ansous; Casting, GIgi Akoka; a Quad Gaumont, TF1 Films Production, Ten Films, Chaocorp coproduction, with the participation of Canal+ and CinéCinéma in association with Apidev 2 and Cinemage 4 Developpement; French; Dolby; Super 35 Widescreen; Color; Rated R; 102 minutes; American release date: May 25, 2012

Omar Sy

CAST
Philippe	**François Cluzet**
Driss	**Omar Sy**
Yvonne	**Anne Le Ny**
Magalie	**Audrey Fleurot**
Marcelle	**Clotilde Mollet**
Elisa	**Alba Gaïa Bellugi**
Adama	**Cyril Mendy**
Albert	**Christian Ameri**
Antoine	**Grégoire Oestermann**

Joséphine de Meaux (DRH Society of Shopping), Salimata Kamate (Fatou), Absa Diatou Toure (Mina), Dominique Daguier, François Caron (Philippe's Friends), Thomas Solivéres (Bastien), Dorothée Brière Méritte (Eléonore), Marie-Laure Descoureaux (Chantal, the Housemaid), Emilie Caen (Gallery Owner), Sylvain Lazard, Jean-François Cayrey (New Assistant Helpers), Ian Fenelon, Renaud Barse, François Bureloup (Candidates), Nicky Marbot, Benjamin Baroche (Policemen), Jérôme Pauwels, Antoine Laurent (Badly Parked Neighbors), Fabrice Mantegna (Opera Singer), Hedi Bouchenafa (Garage Owner), Caroline Bourg (Frédérique), Michel Winogradoff (Waiter of Deux Magots), Kévin Wamo (Driss's Friend), Elliot Latil (Lycéen), Alain Anthony, Dominique Henry (Paraglider Fliers)

Omar Sy, François Cluzet © Weinstein Co.

A wealthy paraplegic hires streetwise hoodlum Driss to be his nurse, forming an unexpected bond with him because of his unorthodox methods of helping out.

Omar Sy, François Cluzet

Anne Le Ny, François Cluzet, Omar Sy

Emad Burnat

Emad's Mother © Kino Lorber

Adeeb Abu-Rahma

5 BROKEN CAMERAS

(KINO LORBER) Producers, Christine Camdessus, Serge Gordey, Emada Burnat, Guy Davidi; Directors, Emad Burnat, Guy Davidi; Photography, Emad Burnat; Music, Le Trio Joubran; Editors, Véronique Lagoarde-Ségot, Guy Davidi; an Algeria Prods., Burnat Films Palenstein, Guy DVD Films co-production; French-Israeli-Palestinian, 2011; Color; HD; Not rated; 90 minutes; American release date: May 30, 2012. Documentary on the village of Bil'in's resistance to the building of Israeli settlements.

WITH

Emad Burnat, Soraya Burnat, Mohammed Burnat, Yasin Burnat, Taky-Adin Burnat, Gibreel Burnat, Bassem Abu-Rahma, Adeeb Abu-Rahma, Ashraf Abu-Rahma, Bassem Abu-Rahma, Intisar Burnat, Eyad Burnat, Riyad Burnat, Khaled Burnat, Jafar Burnat, Yisrael Puterman

This film received an Oscar nomination for documentary feature.

FOR GREATER GLORY: THE TRUE STORY OF CRISTIADA

(ARC ENTERTAINMENT) Producer, Pablo José Barroso; Director, Dean Wright; Screenplay, Michael Love; Photography, Eduardo Martínez Solares; Designer, Salvador Parra; Costumes, Mariestela Fernandez; Music, James Horner; Editors, Richard Francis-Bruce, Mike Oden Jackson; Casting, Dianne Crittenden, Karen Rea, Manuel Teil; a New Land Films production, presented in association with Dos Corazones Films; Mexican-American; Dolby; Super 35 Widescreen; Deluxe Color; Rated R; 144 minutes; Release date: June 1, 2012

CAST

Enrique Gorostieta	**Andy Garcia**
Father Christopher	**Peter O'Toole**
Tulita Gorostieta	**Eva Longoria**
Ambassador Dwight Morrow	**Bruce Greenwood**
Victoriano "El Catorce" Ramirez	**Oscar Isaac**
President Calvin Coolidge	**Bruce McGill**
Adriana	**Catalina Sandino Moreno**
President Plutarco Elias Calles	**Rubén Blades**

Nestor Carbonell (Mayor Picazo), Santiago Cabrera (Father Vega), Eduardo Verástegui (Anacleto Gonzalez Flores), Patricia Garza (Fernanda Gonzales Flores), Alan Ramírez (Gustavo Gonzales Flores), Estefania Alejandra (Yolanda Gonzales Flores), Raúl Adalid (Father Robles), Erando González (La Guada), Adrián Alonso (Lalo), Ignacio Guadalupe (Bishop Pascual Diaz), Mauricio Kuri (José Luis Sánchez del Rio), Karyme Lozano (Doña María del Río de Sánchez), Louis Rosales (Federal Soldier), Alma Martinez (Mrs. Vargas), Roger Cudney (Secretary of State Kellog), Joaquín Garrido (Minister Amaro), Omar Ayala (Hermano Sanchez), Andrés Montiel (Florentino Vargas), Israel Islas (Gorostieta's Lieutenant), Horacio Garcia Rojas (Flaco), Jorge Luis Moreno (Pablo), Jose Carlos Montes (Gen. Pedroza), Guillermo Larrea (Sgt. Humberto), María Fernanda Urdapilleta (Sandra Gorostieta), Martha Cecilia Flores (Luz Maria Gorostieta), Simón Guevara (Policeman #1), Paulo Galindo (Secret Service Leader), Rodrigo Corea (Messenger), Jorge Uzua (Capt. Quintana), Jake Koenig (Ambassador Sheffield)

The true story of the three year war (1926-29) waged by the people of Mexico against the atheistic government.

Eduardo Verástegui © ARC Entertainment

Dino

Zoe, Dino

Nico © GKids

Nico

A CAT IN PARIS

(GKIDS FILMS) a.k.a. *Une vie de chat*; Producers, Jacques-Rémy Girerd, Annemie Degryse, Arnaud Demuynck; Directors/Dialogue, Alain Gagnol, Jean-Loup Felicioli; Screenplay, Alain Gagnol; Graphic Design, Jean-Loup Felicioli; Music, Serge Besset; Editor, Hervé Guichard; Compositing and Special Effects, Izu Troin; a coproduction of Folimage, Lunanime – Lumière, Digit Anima, France 3 Cinéma, Rhône-Alpes Cinéma, RTBF; French-Dutch-Swiss-Belgian, 2010; Color; Not rated; 70 minutes; American release date: June 1, 2012

VOICE CAST

Jeanne	**Marcia Gay Harden**
Claudine	**Anjelica Huston**
Lucas	**Matthew Modine**
Victor Costa	**JB Blanc**
Nico	**Steve Blum**
Mister Frog	**Gregory Cupoli**
Old Lady	**Barbara Goodson**
Mister Hulot	**Phillipe Hartman**
Mister Baby/Zookeeper	**Mike Pollock**
Mister Potato/Frank	**Marc Thompson**
Zoe	**Lauren Weintraub**

A Parisienne cat lives a double life, as the pet of a mute girl, and as the accomplice to a cat burglar.
This film received a 2011 Oscar nomination for animated feature.

Robert Pattinson © Magnolia Films

BEL AMI

(MAGNOLIA) Producer, Uberto Pasolini; Executive Producer, Simon Fuller; Co-Producer, Laurie Borg; Directors, Declan Donnellan, Nick Ormerod; Screenplay, Rachel Bennette; Based on the novel by Guy de Maupassant; Photography, Stefano Falivene; Designer, Attila F. Kovacs; Costumes, Odile Dicks-Mireaux; Music, Lakshman Joseph de Saram, Rachel Portman; Editors, Masahiro Hirakubo, Gavin Buckley; Casting, Susie Figgis; a Red Wave Productions in association with XIX Film, Protagonist Pictures and RAI Cinema; British-Italian; Dolby; Super 35 Widescreen; Color; Rated R; 102 minutes; American release date: June 8, 2012

CAST

Georges Duroy	**Robert Pattinson**
Madeleine Forestier	**Uma Thurman**
Virginie Rousset	**Kristin Scott Thomas**
Clotilde de Marelle	**Christina Ricci**
Monsieur Rousset	**Colm Meaney**
Charles Forestier	**Philip Glenister**
Suzanne Rousset	**Holliday Grainger**
Rachel the Prostitute	**Natalia Tena**
François Laroche	**James Lance**
Comte de Vaudrec	**Anthony Higgins**
Louis	**Thomas Arnold**
Solicitor	**Timothy Walker**
Paul the Butler	**Pip Torrens**
Police Commissioner	**Christopher Fulford**

Amy Marston (Nanny), Frank Dunne (Bishop), George Potts (Chief Cashier), Eloise Webb (Laurine de Marelle), Iain Stuart Robertson (Innkeeper), Balázs Czukor (Priest), Rebecca Barrett, Tom Muggeridge, Matthew Cheney, Chloe Trend (Dancers)

In 1890's Paris, Georges Duroy trades on his wits and powers of seduction to pull himself up from poverty and enter high society.

Robert Pattinson, Uma Thurman

Christina Ricci, Robert Pattinson

Robert Pattinson, Kristin Scott Thomas

THE WOMAN IN THE FIFTH

(ATO) a.ka. *La femme du Vérne*; Producers, Caroline Benjo, Carole Scotta; Executive Producer, Tessa Ross; Co-Producers, Piotr Reisch, Soledad Gatti-Pascual; Director/Screenplay, Pawel Pawlikowski; Based on the novel by Douglas Kennedy; Photography, Ryszard Lenczewski; Designer, Benoît Barouh; Costumes, Julian Day, Shaida Day; Music, Max de Wardener; Music Supervisor, François Dru; Editor, David Charap; Visual Effects Supervisor, Cedric Fayolle; Casting, Stéphane Batut, Alexandre Nazarian; a co-production of Haut et Court, Film4, SPI International Poland, The Bureau in association with U.K. Film Council, with the participation of Canal & Orange Cinéma Séries, Haut et Court Distribution, Artificial Eye; French-Polish-British, 2011; Dolby; Super 35 Widescreen; Color; Rated R; 84 minutes; American release date: June 15, 2012

CAST

Tom Ricks	**Ethan Hawke**
Margit	**Kristin Scott Thomas**
Ania	**Joanna Kulig**
Sezer	**Samir Guesmi**
Nathalie	**Delphine Chuillot**
Chloé	**Julie Papillon**
Laurent	**Geoffrey Carey**
Omar	**Mamadou Minte**
Moussa	**Mohamed Aroussi**
Dumont	**Jean-Louis Cassarino**
Lorraine L'herbert	**Judith Burnett**

Marcela Iacub (Isabella), Wilfred Benaïche (Lt. Coutard), Pierre Marcoux (The Lawyer), Rosine Favey (The Translator), Grégory Gadebois (Brigade Lieutenant), Anne Benoît (Schoolteacher), Donel Jacks'Man (Customs Officer), Laurent Lévy (Margit's Neighbor), Doug Rand, Tercelin Kirtley (American Writers), Nicolas Beaucaire (Passerby)

Returning to Paris, in hopes of make amends with his estranged wife and daughter, troubled writer Tom Ricks instead finds his life unraveling as he becomes involved with a mysterious woman and accepts a shady job as a night watchman.

Kristin Scott Thomas, Ethan Hawke

Ethan Hawke

Joanna Kulig, Ethan Hawke

Kristin Scott Thomas © ATO

Mathieu Demy, Geraldine Chaplin © MPA Media

AMERICANO

(MPI) Producers, Mathieu Demy, Angeline Massoni; Director/Screenplay, Mathieu Demy; Photography, George Lechaptois; Designer, Arnaud Roth; Costumes, Rosalie Varda; Music, Georges Delerue, Grégoire Hetzel; Editor, Jean-Baptiste Morin; Casting, Alexandre Nazarian; a Les Films de l'Autre production in coproduction with Ciné-Tamaris/Arte France Cinema, with the participation of Canal+, Arte France and Ciné; French, 2011; Color; Super 16; Widescreen; Not rated; 90 minutes; American release date: June 15, 2012

CAST
Martin	**Mathieu Demy**
Lola	**Salma Hayek**
Linda	**Geraldine Chaplin**
Claire	**Chiara Mastroianni**
Luis	**Carlos Bardem**
The Father	**Jean-Pierre Mocky**
Pedro	**Pablo Garcia**
The German	**André Wilms**

Timothy Davis (Customs Officer), Cokey Falkow (Mailman), Kevin Beaty (Doug O'Toole, Property Lawyer), Nick Roberts (The Man in the Machine), Linda Flores Wade (Mexican Woman), Angelina Abeyta (The Lady of the caravan), Samantha Nicole Martinez (Young Translator), Lisa Blok-Linson (Lisa), Mark Mahoney (Mark), Jeanne de France (Cleaning Woman), Romanö (Dead End Bartender), Linda Lee Hopkins (Woman of the Consulate), Eduardo Sainz, Alonso Venegas Flores, Emiliano Suarez (American Waiters), Andrew Shemin, James Gerard (Stripclub Clients)

While settling his mother's estate in Los Angeles, Martin uncovers a photo of her with a Mexican girl, prompting him to journey south of the border to see if he contact the mysterious woman in question.

STELLA DAYS

(TRIBECA) Producers, Maggie Pope, Lesley McKimm, Thaddeus O'Sullivan, Jackie Larkin; Co-Producers, Stein B. Kvae, Finn Gjerdrum; Director, Thaddeus O'Sullivan; Screenplay, Antoine O'Flatharta; Inspired by the memoir *Stella Days: The Life and Times of a Rural Irish Cinema* by Michael Doorley; Photography, John Christian Roselund; Designer, Anna Rackard; Costumes, Judith Williams; Music, Nicholas Hooper; Editor, Dermot Diskin; Casting, Amy Rowan; a Newgrange Pictures Production in association with Paradox, RTÉ, Broadcasting Authority of Ireland, Norwegian Film Institute, Storyline Studios, ZDF/ARTE with the participation of Bord Scannán na Héireann/The Irish Film Board; Irish; Color; Not rated; 90 minutes; American release date: June 22, 2012

CAST
Father Daniel Barry	**Martin Sheen**
Brendan McSweeney	**Stephen Rea**
Tim Lynch	**Trystan Gravelle**
Molly	**Marcella Plunkett**
Bishop Hegerty	**Tom Hickey**
Elaine	**Amy Huberman**

Joey O'Sullivan (Joey Phelan), Derbhle Crotty (Julia McSweeney), Garrett Lombard (Jimmy), Ruth McCabe (Miss Courtney), David Herlihy (Emmet Quinn), Donal O'Kelly (Des), Gary Lydon (Larry), Brendan Conroy (Billy), Barbara Adair (Peggy), Margaret O'Sullivan (Nonie), Hugh O'Conor (Willie), Danny Scully (Frankie), Sean Doyle (Jumper), Gail Fitzpatrick (Sally), Arthur Riordan (Architect), Louis Lovett (Bishop's Secretary), Stephen Gillic (Young Daniel), Philip Judge (Father), Andrea Irvine (Mother), Bernadette McKenna (Woman in Confessional), Gene Rooney, Sheila Cox (Legion of Mary Women), Neil Watkins (Mr. Devoy), Michael John Galvin (Priest), Noel Gaskin (Father Keenan), Nathaniel O'Leary (Jeremiah), Alan Curan (Verger), Sheila Ahearne (Small Girl), Midland Melody Makers (Traditional Band), Bohernanave Church Choir (Choir)

In a small Irish village in 1956, Father Barry is told he must build a new church, but instead defies the local politicians by raising money for a community cinema.

Martin Sheen © Tribeca Film

TO ROME WITH LOVE

(SONY CLASSICS) formerly *The Bop Decameron* and *Nero Fiddled*; Producers, Letty Aronson, Stephen Tenenbaum, Giampaolo Letta, Faruk Alatan; Co-Producers, Helen Robin, David Nichols; Co-Executive Producer, Jack Rollins; Director/Screenplay, Woody Allen; Photography, Darius Khondji; Designer, Anne Seibel; Costumes, Sonia Grande; Editor, Alisa Lepselter; a Medusa Film & Gravier Production, a Perdido Production; Italian-American, Dolby; Color; Rated R; 112 minutes; American release date: June 22, 2012

CAST

Jerry	**Woody Allen**
John	**Alec Baldwin**
Leopoldo	**Roberto Begnini**
Anna	**Penélope Cruz**
Phyllis	**Judy Davis**
Jack	**Jesse Eisenberg**
Sally	**Greta Gerwig**
Monica	**Ellen Page**
Luca Salta	**Antonio Albanese**
Giancarlo	**Fabio Armiliato**
Milly	**Alessandra Mastronardi**
Pia Fusari	**Ornella Muti**
Michelangelo	**Flavio Parenti**
Hayley	**Alison Pill**
Hotel Robber	**Riccardo Scamarcio**
Antonio	**Alessandro Tiberi**
Traffic Policeman	**Pierluigi Marchionne**
Carol	**Carol Alt**
Tim	**David Pasquesi**
Ellen	**Lynn Swanson**
Sofia	**Monica Nappo**
Rocco	**Corrado Fortuna**
Claudia	**Margherita Vicario**
Rosa	**Rosa Di Brigida**

Maurizio Argentieri (Voice of Pilot), Giovanni Esposito (Hotel Clerk), Gabriele Rainone (Gabriele), Camilla Pacifico (Camilla), Massimo Ferroni, Alessandro Procoli, Paolo De Vita (Leopoldo's Co-Workers), Cecilia Capriotti (Serafina), Duccio Camerini, Lina Sastri (Friends at Cinema), Alberto Mangiante (TV Voice), Ruggero Cara, Maria Rosaria Omaggio, Giacomo Fadda (Pedestrians with Directions), Roberto Della Casa (Uncle Paolo), Ariella Reggio (Aunt Rita), Gustavo Frigerio (Uncle Sal), Simona Caparrini (Aunt Giovanna), Sergio Solli (Leopoldo's Chauffeur), Cristina Palazzoni (TG3 Anchorwoman), Massimo De Lorenzo (Film Director), Giuseppe Pambieri (Leopoldo's Boss), Alessio Zucchini, Alessandro Tallarida (Reporters at Leopoldo's Office), Luca Calvani, Marcel Álvarez, Mariella Milani, Roberta Ronconi (Reporters at Movie Premiere), Marta Zoffoli (Marisa Raguso), Lino Guanciale (Leonardo), Fabio Bonini (Max), Brunella Matteucci (Reporter in Leopoldo's Bathroom), Edoardo Leo (Reporter at Barbershop), Claudia Smith (Fashion Show Model), Antonio Rampino (Maitre d'), Anna Teresa Rossini, Gaetano Amato (Restaurant Couple), Marina Rocco (Tanya), Sergio Bini Bustric (Mr. Massucci), Augusto Fornari, Mariano Rigillo, Gianmarco Tognazzi (Anna's Client), Illaria Serrato (Girl outside Barbershop), Vinicio Marchioni (Aldo Romano), Donatella Finocchiaro, Nusia Gorgone (Reporters on Street), Antonino Bruschetta, Carlo Luca De Ruggieri (Hotel Detectives), Giuliano Gemma (Hotel Manager), Margherita Di Rauso (Luca's Wife), Federica Corti (Girl with Autograph), Rita Cammarano (Nedda/Colombina), Matteo Bonetti (Tonio, lo scemo/Taddeo), Antonio Taschini (Silvio), Vinicio Cecere (Peppe/Arlecchino), Francesco De Vito (Man in Window)

Four stories unfold concurrently in Rome: an opera director discovers a talented amateur singer who can only perform in the shower; a successful architect offers advice on love to a young student torn between two women; a newlywed couple accidentally separates, with the wife ending up spending time with a movie star and the husband obliged to pass off a prostitute as his date; an average man unexpectedly finds himself treated like a celebrity for no apparent reason.

Judy Davis, Woody Allen, Alison Pill, Flavio Parenti

Alec Baldwin, Jesse Eisenberg

Ellen Page, Jesse Eisenberg

Alessandro Tiberi, Alessandra Mastronardi

Alessandro Tiberi, Penélope Cruz

Jesse Eisenberg, Greta Gerwig

Alessandro Tiberi, Roberto Della Casa, Penélope Cruz

Alec Baldwin, Ellen Page, Jesse Eisenberg © Sony Classics

Roberto Benigni

Monica Bellucci, Louis Garrel

Monica Bellucci, Jérôme Robart © Sundance Selects

A BURNING HOT SUMMER

(SUNDANCE SELECTS) a.k.a. *Un été brûlant*; Producers, Eduard Weil, Conchita Airoldi, Giorgio Magliulo, Pierre-Alain Meier; Director, Philippe Garrel; Screenplay, Philippe Garrel, Marc Cholondenko, Caroline Deruas; Photography, Willy Kurant; Designer, Manu de Chauvigny; Costumes, Justine Pearce; Music, John Cale; Editor, Yann Dedet; a Rectangle Productions (France), Wild Bunch (France), Faro Film (Italy), and Prince Film (Switzerland) presentation; French-Italian-Swiss, 2011; Dolby; Panavision; Color; Not rated; 95 minutes; American release date: June 29, 2012

CAST
Angèle	**Monica Bellucci**
Frédéric	**Louis Garrel**
Élisabeth	**Céline Sallette**
Paul	**Jérôme Robart**
Roland	**Vladislav Galard**
Achille	**Vincent Macaigne**
Grandfather	**Maurice Garrel**

Benjamin Abitan, Julien Bouanich, Romain Cannone, Jean-Charles Clichet, Rodolphe Congé, Cyrille Hertel, Frédéric Noaille, Alexandre Pallu, Eric Seigne (Soldiers), Jean-Luc Guillotin (Sergeant)

Having just fallen in love, two aspiring actors are invited to spend some time in Rome with a painter, where they witness his stormy relationship with his Italian wife.

UNFORGIVABLE

(STRAND) a.k.a. *Impardonnables*; Producer, Saïd Ben Saïd; Executive Producer, Bruno Bernard; Director, André Téchiné; Screenplay, André Téchiné, Mehdi Ben Attia; Based upon the work of Philippe Djian; Photography, Julien Hirsch; Designer, Michèle Abbé; Costumes, Khadija Zeggaï; Music, Max Richter; Editor, Hervé de Luze; an SBS Films production with CRG International Films, TF1 Droits Audiovisuels, France 3 Cinéma, Soudaine Compagnie; French-Italian; Dolby; Color; Not rated; 112 minutes; American release date: June 29, 2012

CAST
Francis	**André Dussolier**
Judith	**Carole Bouquet**
Alice	**Mélanie Thierry**
Anna Maria	**Adriana Asti**
Jérémie	**Mauro Conte**
Roger	**Alexis Loret**
Vicky	**Zoé Duthion**

Sandra Toffolatti (La Comtese), Andrea Pergolesi (Alvise), Stefano Scandaletti (Dragnet Fisherman), Niccolò Palesa, Massimo Piovesan (Friends of the Dragnet Fisherman), Dominique Muller (Mathilde), Fabio Alessandrini (The Winegrower), Gloria Naletto (The Nurse), Vera Arrivabene (Young Bride), Nicolo Rossi (Young Bridegroom), Sandra Mangini (Market Gardener), Don Mario Sgorlon (Priest), Marko Kosuta (Designer)

When a successful crime writer's new marriage begins to hinder his writing, he hires an ex-con to have his wife followed in order to satisfy his increasing obsession with her daily whereabouts.

André Dussolier, Carole Bouquet

André Dussolier, Adriana Asti © Strand Releasing

Seth Rogen, Michelle Williams

Michelle Williams © Magnolia Films

Luke Kirby, Michelle Williams

Michelle Williams, Sarah Silverman

TAKE THIS WALTZ

(MAGNOLIA) Producers, Susan Cavan, Sarah Polley; Director/Screenplay, Sarah Polley; Photography, Luc Montpellier; Designer, Matthew Davies; Costumes, Lea Carlson; Music, Jonathan Goldsmith; Music Supervisor, Jody Colero; Editor, Christopher Donaldson; Casting, John Buchan, Jason Knight; a Joe's Daughter & Mongrel Media presentation in association with TF1 Droits Audiovisuels; produced with the participation of Telefilm Canada, The Ontario Media Development Corporation, Astral's Harold Greenberg Fund; produced in association with the Movie Network, Movie Central, A Corus Entertainment, Super Écran.; Canada; Dolby; Technicolor; Rated R; 116 minutes; American release date: June 29, 2012

CAST

Margot	**Michelle Williams**
Lou	**Seth Rogen**
Daniel	**Luke Kirby**
Geraldine	**Sarah Silverman**
Karen	**Jennifer Podemski**
Harriet	**Diane D'Aquila**
Tony	**Vanessa Coelho**
James	**Graham Abbey**
Aqualift Instructor	**Damien Atkins**
Aaron	**Aaron Abrams**
Dyan	**Dyan Bell**
Albert	**Albert Howell**

Danielle Miller (Danielle), Matt Baram (Matt), Avi Phillips (Avi), Diane Flacks (Diane), Cheryl MacInnis (Flight Attendant), Ciarán MacGillivray (Soldier), Roy MacNiel (Period Priest), Sandy MacLean (Town Crier), John Dunsworth (Tourist), Barnieta Runnings, Mary Pitt, Rosalind S. Feldman (Shower Ladies), Mike Follert (Man on the Porch), Jean-Michel Le Gal (Police Officer), Samantha Farrow (Threesome Lady), Dustin Peters (Threesome Dude)

After a quick sexual encounter while traveling, Margot is dismayed to discover that the man she is growing increasingly attracted to lives right near her and her husband.

EASY MONEY

(WEINSTEIN CO.) a.k.a. *Snabba Cash*; Producer, Fredrik Wikström; Executive Producer, Michael Hjorth; Director, Daniel Espinosa; Screenplay, Maria Karlsson, in cooperation with Daniel Espinosa, Fredrik Wikström, Hassan Loo Sattarvandi; Based on the 2006 novel *Snabba cash* (*Easy Money*) by Jens Lapidus; Photography, Aril Wretblad; Designer, Roger Rosenberg; Costumes, Denise Östholm; Music, Jon Ekstrand; Editor, Theis Schmidt; a Fredrik Wikström and Tre Vänner Produktion AB production; Swedish, 2010; Dolby; Widescreen; Color; Rated R; 124 minutes; American release date: July 11, 2012

CAST

John "JW" Westlund	**Joel Kinnaman**
Jorge	**Matias Padin Varela**
Mrado	**Dragomir Mrsic**
Sophie	**Lisa Henni**
Abdulkarim	**Mahmut Suvakci**
Fahdi	**Jones Danko**

Lea Stojanov (Lovisa), Dejan Cukic (Radovan), Miodrag Stojanovic (Nenad), Joel Spira (Nippe), Christian Hillborg (Jet Set Carl), Annika Ryberg Whitembury (Paola), Fares Fares (Mahmoud), Hamdisa Causevic (Ratko), Sasa Petrovic (Stefanovic), Alexander Silfverskiöld (Putte), Alexander Stocks (Fredrik), Camilo Alanis (Carlos), Jürgen Uter (German Boss), Godehard Giese (Man in White Coat), Maxim Kovalevski (Serbian Man in Hamburg), Dag Malmberg (Sophie's Dad), Tone Helly-Hansen (Sophie's Mum), Andrea Edwards (Lovisa's Mother), Monica Albornoz (Jorge's Mum), Jan Waldecranz (Sten Malmér), Luis Cifuentes (Gun Dealer), Hugo Ruiz (Sergio), David Marténg (Patrik), Peter Andersson, Joakim Radvanovic, Anders Nyström (Bouncers), Ulla Svedin (Social Secretary), Vuksan Rovcanin (Gym Receptionist), Christopher Wagelin (Andreas), Dzakovic Prvoslav Gane (Dejan), Edin Bajric (Goran), Zoran Milosevic (Slavko), Anders Palm (University Professor)

JW's life as a drug runner gets him entangled with a fugitive on the run from the Serbian mafia and the enforcer who is after him.

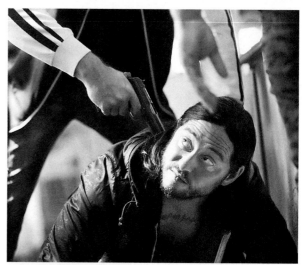

Matias Padin Varela

Matias Padin Varela, Joel Kinnaman, Dragomir Mrsic © Weinstein Co.

Joel Kinnaman

Dragomir Mrsic

THE IMPOSTER

(INDOMINA) Producer, Dimitri Doganis; Line Producer, Vanessa Tovell; Co-Producer, Poppy Dixon; Executive Producers, John Battsek, Simon Chinn, Molly Thompson, Robert DeBitetto, Robert Sharenow, Katherine Butler, Tabitha Jackson; Director, Bart Layton; Photography, Erik Wilson, Lynda Hall; Music, Anne Nikitin; Editor, Andrew Hulme; an A&E Indie Films, Film 4 and Channel 4 presentation of a Raw production in association with Red Box Films and Passion Pictures; British; Dolby; Color; Not rated; 95 minutes; American release date: July 13, 2012. Documentary on serial con artist Frédéric Bourdin;

WITH
Frédéric Bourdin, Carey Gibson, Beverly Dollarhide, Charlie Parker, Nancy Fisher, Bryan Gibson, Codey Gibson, Bruce Perry, Phillip French, Allie Hosteiler, Kevin Hendricks; REINACTMENTS: Adam O'Brian (Frédéric Bourdin), Anna Ruben (Carey Gibson), Cathy Dresbach (Nancy Fisher), Alan Teichman (Charlie Parker), Ivan Villanueva (Social Worker), Maria Jesus Hoyos (Judge), Anton Marti, Amparo Fontanet (Police Officers), Ken Appledorn (U.S. Embassy Official)

Frédéric Bourdin © Indomina

TRISHNA

(IFC FILMS) Producers, Melissa Parmenter, Michael Winterbottom; Executive Producers, Andrew Eaton, Phil Hunt, Compton Ross, Shail Shah; Co-Producers, Anna Croneman, Jessica Ask, Anthony Wilcox; India Co-Producers, Anurag Kashyap, Guneet Monga, Sunil Bohra; Line Producer, Alice Dawson; Director/Screenplay, Michael Winterbottom; Suggested by the 1891 novel *Tess of the d'Urbervilles* by Thomas Hardy; Photography, Marcel Zyskind; Designer, David Bryan; Costumes, Niharika Khan; Music, Shigeru Umebayashi; Original Songs, Amit Trivedi; Editor, Mags Arnold; a Head Gear Films and UK Film Council presentation in association with Metrol Technology and VTR Media Investment of a Revolution Films Production in co-production with Bob Film Sweden and Film i Väst with support from Swedish Film Institute in association with Anurag Kashyap Films; British-Swedish-Indian, 2011; Dolby; Color; Rated R; 115 minutes; American release date: July 13, 2012

CAST

Trishna	**Freida Pinto**
Jay	**Riz Ahmed**
Jay's Father	**Roshan Seth**
Trishna's Mother	**Meeta Vashisht**
Vijay	**Harish Khanna**
Sandeep	**Neet Mohan**
Avit	**Aakash Dahiya**

Leela Madhauram (Devshri), Pratiksha Singh (Pratiksha), Sam Hastings (Sam), Marc Richardson (Marc), Anurag Kashyap (Anurag), Kalki Koechlin (Kalki), Meenakshi Singh (Rita), Chanchal Sharma (Chanchal), Shweta Tripathi (Shweta), Manisha Kakran (Manisha), Shahin Mapker (Shahin), Magan Singh (Head Waiter, Samode Bagh), Ganesh Acharya (Choreographer), Huma Qureshi, Vicky Raushal (Lead Dancers), Pushpendra Singh (Imran), Preeti Kochar (Estate Agent), Bhanu Sharma (Jain Temple Guide), Kavita Seth (Recording Artist), S.N. Purohit, Dr. Agarwal (Doctors), Ashik Khan (Hotel Workers), Suman Sharma (Trishna's Aunt), Lal Singh Rathore (Trishna's Uncle)

Freida Pinto © IFC Films

While working at a resort to make ends meet, Trishna is romanced by the hotel's manager, their affair causing tension between their opposing classes.

Diane Kruger © Cohen Media

Diane Kruger

FAREWELL, MY QUEEN

(COHEN MEDIA GROUP) a.k.a. *Les adieux à la reine*; Producers, Jean-Pierre Guerin, Kristina Larsen, Pedro Uriol; Executive Producer, Christophe Valette; Director, Benoît Jacquot; Screenplay, Gilles Taurand, Benoît Jacquot; Based on the 2002 novel *Les adieux à la reine* (*Farewell, My Queen*) by Chantal Thomas; Photography, Romain Winding; Designer, Katia Wyszkop; Costumes, Christian Gasc, Valérie Ranchoux; Music, Bruno Coulais; Editors, Luc Barnier, Nelly Ollivault; Casting, Antoinette Boulat; a GMT Productions, Les Films du Lendemain, Morena Films presentation; French-Spanish; Dolby; Color; Rated R; 100 minutes; American release date: July 13, 2012

CAST

Agathe-Sidonie Laborde	**Léa Seydoux**
Marie Antoinette	**Diane Kruger**
Duchess Gabrielle de Polignac	**Virginie Ledoyen**
King Louis XVI	**Xavier Beauvois**
Mme. Campan	**Noémie Lvovsky**
Jacob-Nicolas Moreau	**Michel Robin**
Honorine Aubert	**Julie-Marie Parmentier**
Louison	**Lolita Chammah**
Paolo	**Vladimir Consigny**
Monsieur de la Tour du Pin	**Jacques Boudet**
Mme. de Rochereuil	**Dominique Reymond**
Rose Bertin	**Anne Benoît**

Marthe Caufman (Alice), Hervé Pierre Sociétaire (Abbot Hérissé), (Abbot Cornu de la Ballivière), Jacques Nolot (Monsieur de Jolivet), Jacques Herlin (Marquis de Vaucouleurs), Martine Chevalier (Madame de la Tour du Pin), Jean-Chrétien Sibertin-Blanc (Duke de Polignac), Jean-Marc Stehlé (Maréchal de Broglie), Serge Renko (Marquis de la Chesnaye), Gilles David (Vicar Moullet), Pierre Rochefort (Valet Antonin), Rodolphe Congé (Officer of the National Guard), Grégory Gadebois (Count of Provence), Francis Leplay (Count d'Artois), Yves Penay (Monsieur de Barentin), Sonia Joubert (Augustine), Tibo (Gustav), Pierre Berriau, Pascal Vannson (Bailliffs), Maurice Delaistier (Secretary), Emmanuelle Bougerol (Kitchen Girl), Véronique Norey (Madame Tournon), Jean-Pierre Guérin (Monsieur Janvier)

One the eve of the French Revolution, Marie Antoinette strikes up a very intimate relationship with one of the ladies of her court who feels it is to her advantage to be in the queen's good graces.

Virginie Ledoyen, Diane Kruger

Léa Seydoux, Julie-Marie Parmentier

IRON SKY

(ENTERTAINMENT ONE) Producers, Tero Kaukomaa, Samuli Torssonen, Oliver Damian, Cathy Overett, Mark Overett; Executive Producers, San Fu Maltha, Michael Cowan, Sean O'Kelly, Jason Piette; Director, TImo Vuorensola; Screenplay, Michael Kalesniko, Timo Vuorensola; Based on a story by Johanna Sinisalo and an original concept by Jarmo Puskala; Photography, Mike Orasmaa; Designer, Ulrika von Vegesack; Costumes, Jake Collier; Music, Laibach; Editor, Suresh Ayyar; Visual Effects Supervisor, Samuli Torssonen; a Stealth Media Group presentation of a Blind Spot Pictures, 27 Films Production, New Holland Pictures production; Finnish-German-Australia; Dolby; Color; HD; Rated R; 93 minutes; American release date: July 25, 2012

CAST
Renate Richter	**Julia Dietze**
James Washington	**Christopher Kirby**
Klaus Adler	**Götz Otto**
Wolfgang Kortzfleisch	**Udo Kier**
Vivian Wagner	**Peta Sergeant**
President of the United States	**Stephanie Paul**

Tito Prückner (Doktor Richter), Michael Cullen (Secretary of Defense), Kym Jackson (Officer McLennan), Ben Siemer (Sanders), Tom Bossbach (Dieter), Milo Kaukomaa (Siegfried), Vivian Schneider (Brunhilde), Fang You (Chinese Representative), Irshad Panjatan (Indian Representative), Claus Wilke (Russian Representative), Samir Fuchs (Middle East Representative), Monika Gossman (Designer), Jessica Veurman-Betts (Hippie Girl), Mark Mineart (Detective), George Koutros (Neo Nazi #1), Dieter Gring, Harald Koch (Pilots), James Quinn (Reporter), Yuki Iwamoto (Japanese Representative), Jeffrey Coulas (English Representative), Nik Dong Sik (North Korean Representative), Ramin Yazdani (Pakistanti Representative), Tero Kaukomaa (Finnish Representative), Martin Grelis, Andrew Buchanan (GWB Officers), Eugene Schlusser (Nazi General), Jim Knobeloch (Nazi Weapons Officer), Lisa Zoe Bräutigam (Hannelore), Oskar Mahler (Old Man), Kristina Walter (Old Woman), Brett Molloy (Uwe the Pilot)

Seven decades after the end of World War II, a group of Nazi scientists who have been occupying a military base on the dark side of the moon prepare to launch the ultimate warship, the Götterdämmerung.

Udo Kier © Entertainment One

Frank Hvam, Marcuz Jess Petersen

Mia Lynhe, Frank Hvam © Drafthouse

KLOWN

(DRAFTHOUSE) a.k.a. *Klovn the Movie*; Producer, Louise Vesth; Director, Mikkel Nørgaard; Screenplay, Casper Christensen, Frank Hvam; Based on the 2005 television series *Klovn*; Photography, Jacob Banke Olesen; Designer, Rasmus Thjellesen; Costumes, Louise Hauberg; Music, Kristian Eidnes Andersen; Editors, Martin Schade, Morten Egholm; Stunts, Anders Woldike; Casting, Jette Termann, Anders Nygaard; a Zentropa Entertainments/JA-hatten presentation in association with Med TV2 and the Danish Film Institute; Danish, 2011; Color; Rated R; 90 minutes; American release date: July 27, 2012

CAST
Frank	**Frank Hvam**
Casper	**Casper Christensen**
Bo	**Marcuz Jess Petersen**
Mia	**Mia Lynhe**
Iben	**Iben Hjejle**

Lars Hjortshøj (Hjortshøj), Tina Bilsbo (Tina), Mads Lisby (Mads), Anne Møen (Katrine), Niels Weyde (Ole), Elsebeth Steentoft (Pykker), Roger Kormind (Fætter Andreas), Michael Carøe (Carøe), Dya Josefine Hauch (Susan), Marie Mondrup (Ronja), Claus Damgaard (Skolelærer), Bent Fabricius-Bjerre (Bent Fabric), Jørgen Leth (Jørgen), Michael Meyerheim (Michael), Ole Michelsen (Ole), Mads Brügger (Mads), Mikael Bertelsen (Mikael), Ib Michael (Ib), Niels Helveg Petersen (Niels), Ole Sørensen (Bamsefar), Kenneth Carmohn (Jan), Sebastian Christensen (Frederik)

Worried that his pregnant girlfriend thinks he has no rapport with kids, Frank arranges to take her 12-year-old son on a camping trip.

Anthony Hopkins

Djemel Barek, Jamel Debbouze © Magnolia Films

Jud Law, Rachel Weisz

360

(MAGNOLIA) Producers, Andrew Eaton, David Linde, Emanuel Michael, Danny Krausz, Chris Hanley; Executive Producers, Christine Langan, Klaus Lintschinger, Peter Morgan, Fernando Meirelles, Paul Brett, Tim Smith, Graham Bradstreet, Michael Winterbottom, Steven Gagnon, Nikhil Sharma, Chris Contogouris, Jordan Gertner; Director, Fernando Meirelles; Screenplay, Peter Morgan; Photography, Adriano Goldman; Designer, John Paul Kelly; Costumes, Monika Buttinger; Editor, Daniel Rezende; Casting, Leo Davis; a BBC Films, The UK Film Council, ORF, Unison Films, Gravity Pictures and Hero Entertainment presentation in association with Prescience, EOS Pictures, Wild Bunch, Film Location Austria, Austrian Film Institute and Vienna Film Fund, of a Revolution/Dor Film/Fidélité Films production in coproduction with O2 Filmes and Muse Productions; British-Austrian-French-Brazilian, Dolby; Super 35 Widescreen; Deluxe color; Rated R; 111 minutes; American release date: August 3, 2012

CAST
Older Man (John)	**Anthony Hopkins**
Tyler	**Ben Foster**
Michael Daly	**Jude Law**
Fran	**Marianne Jean-Baptiste**
Rose	**Rachel Weisz**
Salesman	**Moritz Bleibtreu**
Valentina	**Dinara Drukarova**
Algerian Man	**Jamel Debbouze**
The Boss	**Mark Ivanir**
Anna	**Gabriela Marcinkova**
Rocco	**Johannes Krisch**

Juliano Cazarré (Rui), Lucia Siposová (Mirka), Maria Flor (Laura), Vladimir Vdovichenkov (Sergei), Danica Jurcová (Alina), Peter Morgan (Salesman #2), Riann Steele (Waitress), François-Xavier Demaison (Taxi Driver), Patty Hannock (Psychiatrist), Djemel Barek (Imam), Chipo Chung (Editor), Sydney Wade (Ellie), Byrd Wilkins (Social Worker), Martin McDougall (Policeman, Airport), Gerard Monaco (Airport Security Desk Official), Youssef Kerkour (Policeman, Phoenix Morgue), Sean Power (AA Secretary), Christoph Zadra (Hotel Security), Tereza Srbova (European Girl), Giorgio Spiegelfeld (Photographer), Lisa Palfrey (Psychologist)

A businessman's decision of whether or not to be unfaithful to his wife sets off a series of events that impacts a wide array of people from various social backgrounds and different countries.

Ben Foster

2 DAYS IN NEW YORK

(MAGNOLIA) Producers, Christophe Mazodier, Scott Franklin, Julie Delpy, Ulf Israel, Hubert Toint, Jean-Jacques Neira; Executive Producers, Helge Sasse, Matthias Triebel; Associate Producers, Dominique Boutonnat, Arnaud Bertrand, Hubert Caillard, Gérard Frydman, Jean-Claude Fleury, David Claikens, Alex Verbaere; Director, Julie Delpy; Screenplay, Julie Delpy, Alexia Landeau; Story, Julie Delpy, Alexia Landeau, Alex Nahon; Based on original characters by Julie Delpy; Photography, Lubomir Bakchev; Designer, Judy Rhee; Costumes, Rebecca Hofherr; Editor, Isabelle Devinck; Casting, Suzanne Smith Crowley, Jessica Kelly; a Christophe Mazodier presentation of a Polaris production in coproduction with Tempête Sous un Crâne, Senator Film, Saga Film, Alvy Productions, In Production, TDY Film Produktion, BNP Paribas Film Fund in association with Protozoa Pictures; French-German-Belgian; Dolby; Color; Rated R; 96 minutes; American release date: August 10, 2012

Julie Delpy, Talen Riley, Chris Rock, Alex Nahon (back to camera), Malinda Williams, Albert Delpy

CAST

Mingus	**Chris Rock**
Marion	**Julie Delpy**
Jeannot	**Albert Delpy**
Rose	**Alexia Landeau**
Manu	**Alex Nahon**
Bella	**Kate Burton**
Ron	**Dylan Baker**
The Oak Fairy	**Daniel Brühl**
Willow	**Talen Riley**
Lulu	**Owen Shipman**
Himself	**Vincent Gallo**

Malinda Williams (Elizabeth), Carmen Lopez (Julia), Emily Wagner (Susan), Arthur French (Lee Robinson), Petronia Paley (Carol Robinson), Alex Manette (John Kelly), Marcus Ho (Johnny), Gregory Korostishevsky (Boris), Mai Loan Tran (Ahn), Pun Bandhu (Joe), Johnny Tran (Van), Darlene Violette (Customs Lady), Seth Barrish (Mingus' Boss), Bhavesh Patel (Justin), Brady Smith (Security Guard Bob), Simon Jutras (French Passenger), Tatina de Marinis, Angela Rago (Italian Ladies), Kendra Mylnechuk (Someone), Luigi Scorcia (Italian Man), Christy Nacinovich (Yoga Teacher), Upendran Panicker (Taxi Driver), David Coburn (TV Journalist)

Chris Rock, Julie Delpy © Magnolia Films

Cultures clash and tensions arise as Mingus and Marion pay host to her larger than life French dad, her oversexed sister and her sister's wastrel boyfriend in their Manhattan apartment.

Albert Delpy, Chris Rock

Chris Rock, Talen Riley, Owen Shipman, Julie Delpy

COSMOPOLIS

(ENTERTAINMENT ONE) Producers, Paulo Branco, Martin Katz; Executive Producers, Gregoire Melin, Edouard Carmignac, Renee Tab, Pierre-Ange Le Pogam; Line Producer, Joseph Boccia; Director/Screenplay, David Cronenberg; Based on the 2003 novel by Don DeLillo; Photography, Peter Suschitzky; Designer, Arv Greywal; Costumes, Denise Cronenberg; Music, Howard Shore; Editor, Ronald Sanders; Special Effects Coordinator, Warren Appleby; Casting, Deirdre Bowen; a Paulo Branco and Martin Katz presentation of an Alfama Films, Prospero Pictures production in co-production with Kinologic Films (DC), France 2 Cinéma, produced with the participation of Telefilm Canada, in association with Talandracas Pictures, with the participation of France Télévisions, Canal+, RAI Cinema, RTP Ontario, Media Development Corporation, Astral Media, The Harold Greenberg Fund, Jouror Productions, Leopardo Filmes; Canadian-French-Italian; Dolby; Deluxe color; Rated R; 109 minutes; American release date: August 17, 2012

Robert Pattinson

CAST

Eric Packer	**Robert Pattinson**
Didi Fancher	**Juliette Binoche**
Elise Shifrin	**Sarah Gadon**
André Petrescu	**Mathieu Amalric**
Shiner	**Jay Baruchel**
Torval	**Kevin Durand**
Brutha Fez	**K'Naan**
Jane Melman	**Emily Hampshire**
Vija Kinski	**Samantha Morton**
Benno Levin	**Paul Giamatti**

Philip Nozuka (Michael Chin), Abdul Ayoola (Ibrahim Hamadou), Bob Bainborough (Dr. Ingram), Milton Barnes (Videographer), Gouchy Boy (Kosmo Thomas), Maria Juan Garcias (Nina Brooks), Anna Hardwick (Jenn the Photographer), Zeljko Kecojevic (Danko), Patricia McKenzie (Kendra Hays), John Batkis, Saad Siddiqui (Photographers), George Touliatos (Anthony Adubato), Jadyn Wong (Cathy Lee), Ryan Kelly, Nadeem Umar-Khitab (Rat Men), Alberto Gomez (Counterman), David Schaap (Arthur Rapp), Warren Chow (Arthur's Attacker), Inessa Frantowski (Woman holding Rat), Jonathan Seinen (Man on Fire)

Robert Pattinson, Sarah Gadon

Stuck in traffic on his way across town to get a haircut, Wall Street billionaire Eric Packer continues to conduct business from his stretch limousine, as he begins to unravel from the stress and pressure of his out-of-control way of life.

Paul Giamatti

Kevin Durand, Mathieu Amalric © Entertainment One

Neta Porat, Tuval Shafir

Neta Porat (center) © Menemsha Films

THE MATCHMAKER

(MENEMSHA) a.k.a. *Once I Was*; Producers, Moshe Ederi, Leon Edery, David Silber, Avraham Pirchi, David Silber, Chilik Michaeli, Avi Nesher, Tami Leon, Natan Caspi; Co-Producers, Shlomo Mograbi, Rami Damri, Eviatar Dotan; Director/Screenplay, Avi Nesher; Inspired by the 2008 novel *When Heroes Fly* by Amir Gutfreund; Photography, Michele Abramowitz; Art Director, Miguel Markin; Costumes, Rona Doron; Music, Philippe Sarde; Editor, Isaac Sehayek; a 6Sales presentation of a United King Films, Metro Communications, United Channel Movies, Artomas Communications production in association with Keshey, Hot, Praxis and the participation of the Yeshoua Rabinovich Tel Aviv Foundation for the Arts and Cinema Project; Israeli, 2010; Dolby; Color; Not rated; 111 minutes; American release date: August 17, 2012

CAST
Yankele Bride	**Adir Miller**
Clara Epstein	**Maya Dagan**
Arik Burstein	**Tuval Shafir**
Meir the Librarian	**Dror Keren**
Yozi Burstein	**Dov Navon**
Nili Burstein	**Yarden Bar-Kochva**

Neta Porat (Tamara), Bat-El Papura (Sylvia), Kobi Faraj (Moshe Abadi), Yael Leventhal (Tikva Abadi), Tom Gal (Beni Abadi), Eyal Shechter (Adult Arik), Ya'ackov Bodo (Adv. Segalson), Eli Jaspan (Uncle Nadgi), Shira Alfandari (The Rabbi's Wife)

An unexpected inheritance causes Arik Burstein to look back on his adolescence in 1968 Haifa where he worked as an assistant to a matchmaker.

BELOVED

(SUNDANCE SELECTS) a.k.a. *Les Bien-Aimés*; Director, Christophe Honoré; Photography, Rémy Chevrin; Designer, Samuel Deshors; Costumes, Pascaline Chavanne; Music, Alex Beaupain; Editor, Chantal Hymans; a Why Not Productions, France 2 Cinéma, Sixteen Films, Negativ co-production with the participation of Canal+, France Télévisions, Orange Cinéma Séries; French, 2011; Super 35 WidescreenColor; Not rated; 135 minutes; American release date: August 17, 2012

CAST
Madeleine	**Catherine Deneuve**
Véra Passer	**Chiara Mastroianni**
Young Madeleine	**Ludivine Sagnier**
Clément	**Louis Garrel**
Jaromil Passer	**Milos Forman**
Henderson	**Paul Schneider**

Michel Delpech (François Gouriot), Rasha Bukovic (Young Jarmoil), Ben Sellem (Omar), Clara Couste (Adolescent Véra), Guillaume Denaiffle (François Gouriot 1), Dustin Segura Suarez (Mathieu), Zuzana Krónerová (Madame Passer), Václav Neuzil (Father Jaromil Prague), Pavel Liska (Karel), Zuzana Onufrankova (Mladka), Francine Beaur (Patroness of Madeleine), Anaïs Chetoui, Amélie Flottat, Julia Marty (Shoestore Salespeople), Jean-Charles Clichet (Madeleine's First Customer), Bonnie Duvauchelle (Infant Véra), Côme Rérat (Pruning Hook), Fabrice Uhel (Young Doctor), Kate Moran (Clément's Fiancée), Robert Liska, Frantisek Krizek (Russian Soldiers), Vaclav Nic (Young Man), Goldy Notay (Nandita)

A musical drama following a mother and daughter's misadventures in love over the course of three decades.

Milos Forman, Catherine Deneuve, Chiara Mastroianni

Rasha Bukovic, Ludivine Sagnier
© Sundance Selects

Maria de Medeiros, Mathieu Amalric

Serge Avédikian, Golshifteh Farahani © Sony Classics

CHICKEN WITH PLUMS

(SONY CLASSICS) a.k.a. *Poulet aux prunes*; Producer, Hengameh Panahi; Line Producer, François-Xavier Decraene; Co-Producers, Christoph Fisser, Charlie Woebcken, Torsten Poeck, Henning Molfenter, Adrian Politowski, Gilles Waterkeyn; Directors/Screenplay, Marjane Satrapi, Vincent Paronnaud; Based on the 2004 graphic novel *Poulet aux prunes* by Marjane Satrapi; Photography, Christophe Beaucarne; Designer, Udo Kramer; Costumes, Madeline Fontaine; Music, Oliver Bernet; Editor, Stéphane Roche; a Hengameh Panahi presentation; French-German-Belgian, 2011; Dolby; Color; Hawk Scope; Rated PG-13; 93 minutes; American release date: August 17, 2012

CAST
Nasser-Ali	**Mathieu Amalric**
Azraël	**Edouard Baer**
Faringuisse	**Maria de Medeiros**
Irâne	**Golshifteh Farahani**
Abdi	**Eric Caravaca**
Adutl Lili	**Chiara Mastroianni**

Mathis Bour (Cyrus), Enna Balland (Lili), Jamel Debbouze (The Beggar and Houshang), Isabella Rossellini (Parvine), Didier Flamand (The Music Teacher), Serge Avédikian (Irâne's Father), Rona Hartner (Soudabeh), Fred Saurel (Mirza), Christian Friedel (Cyrus, 22 years old), Julia Goldstern (Nancy), Julia Camps Y Salat (Young Faringuisse), Jaouen Gouevic (Irâne's Grandson), Timothé Riquet (Young Nasser Ali), Angus Boulaire (Young Abdi), François Legrand (Schoolmaster), Laura Baade (Cyrus's Daughter), Dustin Graf, Nomi Kaisar (Cyrus's Sons), Jean-Michel Dagory (Socrates), Christian Sengewald (Socrates' Student), Adolfo Assor (Rasht Bazaar Man), Ilse Strambowski (Old Woman Bus Driver), Tim Williams (American Doctor), Dietmar Rüttiger (Card Player), Louis-Marie Audubert, Bruno Paviot, Philippe Béglia (Anonymous Cemetery Patrons), Luc Gentil (Family Doctor)

Depressed by the loss of his beloved violin, a musician takes to his bed to await death and experiences a series of surreal memories and revelations about his past and future.

TEDDY BEAR

(FILM MOVEMENT) Producer, Morten Kjems Juhl; Executive Producers, Birgitte Skov, Karoline Leth, Michael Fleischer, Morten Revsgaard Frederiksen,; Director, Mads Matthiesen; Screenplay, Mads Matthiesen, Martin Pieter Zandvliet; Photography, Laust Trier Mørk; Designer, Thomas Bremer; Music, Sune Martin; Editor, Adam Nielsen; an SF Film Production & Bedfilm presentation, co-produced by Bedfilm, Tonemestrene APS & Minerva Film A/S in collaboration with TV2 Danmark; Danish; Dolby; Color; Not rated; 93 minutes; American release date: August 22, 2012

CAST
Dennis	**Kim Kold**
Ingrid	**Elsebeth Steentoft**
Toi	**Lamaiporn Sangmanee Hougaard**
Scott	**David Winters**
Phatnay	**Sukunya Mongkol**
Jeff	**John Winters**

Allan Mogensen (Bent), Sukiyana Suwan (Aoi), Barbara Zatler (Sasha), Songporn na Bangchang (Nuu), Paweena Im-Erb (Nok), Prap Poramabhuti (Prap), Patrick Johnson (Lars), Per Otto Rasmussen (Udlejer), Kristanai Promsiriruk (Miss Mayflower)

A shy bodybuilder, living at home with his overbearing mother journeys to Thailand with the dream of finding a girl to settle down with.

Kim Kold, Elsebeth Steentoft

Kim Kold © Film Movement

HERMANO

(MUSIC BOX FILMS) a.k.a. *Brother*; Producers, Enrique Aular, Marcel Rasquin; Executive Producers, Enrique Aular, Liz Mago Bosch, Enrique Aular; Co-Producers, Juan A. Diaz, Jose V. Scheuren; Director, Marcel Rasquin; Screenplay, Rohan Jones, Marcel Rasquin; Photography, Enrique Aular; Art Director, Maya Oloe; Music, Rigel Mitxelena; Editors, Carolina Aular, Juan C. Melian; Casting, Beto Benites; an Enrique Aular presentation of a production of A&B and Tres Palos Pictures; Venezuelan, 2010; Color; Not rated; 97 minutes; American release date: August 24, 2012

CAST

Daniel	**Fernando Moreno**
Julio	**Eliú Armas**
Max	**Alí Rondón**
Graciela	**Marcela Girón**
Roberto	**Gonzalo Cubero**
Morocho	**Beto Benites**
Eliecer	**Gabriel Rojas**

Two boys raised as brothers in the La Ceniza slums struggle to become professional soccer players.

Fernando Moreno, Eliú Armas

Eliú Armas, Fernando Moreno © Music Box Films

Irma Brown, W.J. Solha, Gustavo Jahn © Cinema Guild

Maeve Jenkins and kids

NEIGHBORING SOUNDS

(CINEMA GUILD) a.k.a. *O som ao redor*; Producer, Emilie Lesclaux; Director/Screenplay, Kleber Mendonça Filho; Photography, Pedro Sotero, Fabricio Tadeu; Art Director, Juliano Dornelles; Costumes, Ingrid Mata; Editors, Kleber Mendonça Filho, João Maria; Casting, Daniel Aragão; a Cinemascópo production; Portuguese; Dolby; Techniscope; FotoKem Color; Not rated; 131 minutes; American release date: August 24, 2012

CAST

Clodoalo	**Irandhir Santos**
João	**Gustavo Jahn**
Bia	**Meve Jinkings**
Francisco	**W.J. Solha**
Sofia	**Irma Brown**
Anco	**Lula Terra**

Yuri Holanda (Dinho), Clébia Souza (Luciene), Albert Tenório (Ronaldo), Nivaldo Nascimento (Fernando), Felipe Bandeira (Nelson), Clara Pinheiro De Oliveira (Fernanda), Sebastião Formiga (Claudio), Mauricéia Conceição (Mariá)

The residents of the coastal town of Recife, Brazil, react with resentment and fear when a private security firm is hired to protect them from the petty criminal acts that have been disrupting the neighborhood.

LITTLE WHITE LIES

(MPI) a.k.a. *Les petits mouchoirs*; Producer, Alain Attal; Executive Producer, Hugo Selignac; Director/Screenplay, Guillaume Canet; Photography, Christophe Offenstein; Designer, Philippe Chiffre; Costumes, Carine Sarfati; Editor, Hervé de Luze; a Caneo Films, Les Prods. du Tresor, EuropaCorp, M6 Films production, in association with Cofinova 6, Compagnie Cinematographique Europeenne, Panache Prods., with the participation of Canal Plus, CineCinema, M6, W9; French, 2010; Dolby; Super 35 Widescreen; Color; Not rated ; 154 minutes; American release date: August 24, 2012

Gilles Lellouch, Laurent Lafitte

CAST

Max Cantara	**François Cluzet**
Marie	**Marion Cotillard**
Vincent Ribaud	**Benoît Magimel**
Éric	**Gilles Lellouch**
Ludo	**Jean Dujardin**
Antoine	**Laurent Lafitte**
Véronique Cantara	**Valérie Bonneton**
Isabelle Ribaud	**Pascale Arbillot**
Jean-Louis	**Joël Dupuch**
Juliette	**Anne Marivin**
Léa	**Louise Monot**
Nassim	**Hocine Mérabet**
Raphaël	**Matthieu Chedid**

Maxim Nucci (Franck), Néo Broca (Elliot), Marc Mairé (Arthur), Jeanne Dupuch (Jeanne), Mado Mérabet (Brigitte), Nikita Lespinasse (Virginie, The Extra), Sara Martins (Marie's Little Friend), Edouard Montoute (Ludo's Mate), Niseema Theillaud (Sabine, Ludo's Mother), Patrice Renson (Juliette's Future Husband), Jean-Claude Lagniez (Training Ship Monitor), Jean-Claude Cotillard (Hotel Architect), Pierre-Benoist Varoclier (Waiter), Benoît Petitjean (Hotel Waiter), François Bredon (Nightcluber), Jean-Louis Fourrier (Funeral Priest), Claude Lellouche, Jean-Claude Farnaud (Football Fans)

Joël Dupuch, François Cluzet, Jean Dujardin, Marion Cotillard, Pascale Arbillot

Problems and unspoken truths arise during the annual vacation taken by a group of friends, who have decided to go through with their holiday, despite their close friend lying near death after a road accident.

Maxim Nucci © MPI Media

Pascale Arbillot, Benoît Magimel

Charlotte Rampling, Geoffrey Rush, Judy Davis © Sycamore Entertainment

THE EYE OF THE STORM

(SYCAMORE ENTERTAINMENT) Producers, Antony Waddington, Gregory Read, Fred Schepisi; Executive Producers, Jonathan Shteinman, Edward Simpson, Bob Marcs, James Vernon; Director, Fred Schepisi; Screenplay, Judy Morris; Based on the 1973 novel by Patrick White; Photography, Ian Baker; Designer, Melinda Doring; Music, Paul Grabowsky; Editor, Kate Williams; Casting, Nikki Barrett; an Antony Waddington presentation, in association with RMB Productions, a Paper Bark Films production; Australian, 2011; Dolby; Super 35 Widescreen; Color; HD; Not rated; 119 minutes; American release date: September 7, 2012

CAST
Sir Basil Hunter	**Geoffrey Rush**
Elizabeth Hunter	**Charlotte Rampling**
Dorothy de Lascabanes	**Judy Davis**
Athol Shreve	**Colin Friels**
Lal	**Robyn Nevin**
Arnold Wyburd	**John Gaden**
Lotte	**Helen Morse**
Flora Manhood	**Alexandra Schepisi**

Maria Theodorakis (Mary DeSantis), Dustin Clare (Col), Jamie Timony (Onslow Porter), Bob Marcs (Queens Club Porter), Jane Menelaus (Maggie), Bille Brown (Dudley), Heather Mitchell (June), Simon Stone (Peter), Nikki Shiels (Janie), Louise Siversen (Carol), May Lloyd (Lurline Skinner), Martin Lynes (Edward), Liz Alexander (Cherry Cheeseman), Barry Langrishe (Doug Cheeseman), Benita Colings (Lady at Lunch), Justin Smith (Club Desk Clerk), David Harris (Onslow Desk Clerk), Peter Houghton (Rory Macrory), Trudy Hellier (Anne Macrory), Monique Heath (Mags Macrory), Charlie Dean, William Fisher, Lachlan Thompson (Macrory Boys), Riley Smith, Darcy Smith (Macrory Baby), Tim Robertson (Dr. Treweek), Laurent Denis Boulanger (French Waiter)

With their mother on her death bed, siblings Basil and Dorothy return to their Australian home to pay their last respects and find out what their financial prospects are from their potential inheritance.

RESIDENT EVIL: RETRIBUTION

(SCREEN GEMS) Producers, Jeremy Bolt, Paul W.S. Anderson, Robert Kulzer, Don Carmody, Samuel Hadida; Executive Producer, Martin Moszkowicz; Director/Screenplay, Paul W.S. Anderson; Photography, Glen MacPherson; Designer, Kevin Phipps; Costumes, Wendy Partridge; Music, tomandandy; Editor, Niven Howie; Digital Effects, Mr. X Inc; Visual Effects Supervisor, Dennis Berardi; Casting, Deirdre Bowen; a Constantin Film International GmbH/Davis Films/Impact Pictures (RE5) Inc production; German-Canadian; Dolby; HD Widescreen; Color; 3D; Rated R; 96 minutes; American release date: September 14, 2012

CAST
Alice	**Milla Jovovich**
Jill Valentine	**Sienna Guillory**
Rain	**Michelle Rodriguez**
Becky	**Aryana Engineer**
Ada Wong	**Li Bingbing**
Luther West	**Boris Kodjoe**

Johann Urb (Leon S. Kennedy), Robin Kasyanov (Sergei), Kevin Durand (Barry Burton), Ofilio Portillo (Tony), Oded Fehr (Todd/Carlos),Colin Salmon (James "One" Shade), Shawn Roberts (Albert Wesker), Toshio Oki (Japanese Policeman), Takato Yamashita (Japanese Businessman), Mika Nakashima (J Pop Girl), Megan Charpentier (The Red Queen), Ave Merson-O'Brian (Voice of the Red Queen), Ray Olubowale, Kevin Shand (The Axe Men)

In the dystopian future, Alice joins forces with a resistance group to fight the Umbrella Corporation and the flesh eating dead. Fifth entry in the Screen Gems series starring Milla Jovovich, following *Resident Evil* (2002), *Resident Evil: Apocalypse* (2004), *Resident Evil: Extinction* (2007), and *Resident Evil: Afterlife* (2010).

Boris Kodjoe, Aryana Engineer, Milla Jovovich, Johann Urb

Milla Jovovich © Screen Gems

Jürgen Rißmann, Thomas Wodianka

Reiner Schöne ©Music Box Films

SNOWMAN'S LAND

(MUSIC BOX) Producer, Boris Michalski; Line Producer, Darko Lovrinic; Director/ Screenplay, Thomasz Thomson; Photography, Ralf Mendle; Designer, Thorsten Sabel; Costumes, Monika Gebauer; Music, Luke Lalonde; Editors, Tomasz Thomson, Stefanie Gross, Georg Steinert; a Noirfilm Filmproduktion in association with ZWR, Debut and Arte; German, 2010; Dolby; Widescreen; Color; Not rated; 98 minutes; American release date: September 14, 2012

CAST
Walter	**Jürgen Rißmann**
Mickey	**Thomas Wodianka**
Berger	**Reiner Schöne**
Sibylle	**Eva-Katrin Hermann**
Kazik	**Waléra Kanischtscheff**

Luc Feit (François), Detlef Bothe (Harry), Andreas Windhuis (Arms Dealer), Anton Weber (Kalle)

As punishment for bungling a job, two urban hitmen are sent to the mountains to protect a crime boss's house and proceed to get themselves into further trouble.

WUTHERING HEIGHTS

(OSCILLOSCOPE) Producers, Robert Bernstein, Douglas Rae, Kevin Loader; Executive Producers, Tessa Ross, Mark Woolley, Tim Haslam, Hugo Heppell, Adam Kulick; Line Producer, Rosa Romero; Directors/Screenplay, Andrea Arnold, Olivia Hetreed; Based on the 1847 novel by Emily Brontë; Photography, Robbie Ryan; Designer, Helen Scott; Costumes, Steven Noble; Editor, Nicolas Chaudeurge; Hair & Make-Up Designer, Emma Scott; Casting, Gail Stevens, Des Hamilton, Lucy Pardee; British; a Film4 and the UK Film Council presentation in association with Goldcrest Film Production LLP and Screen Yorkshire and Hanway Films and Ecosse Films production; British, 2011; Dolby; Color; Not rated; 129 minutes; American release date: October 5, 2012

CAST
Cathy Earnshaw	**Kaya Scodelario**
Heathcliff	**James Howson**
Young Heathcliff	**Solomon Glave**
Young Cathy	**Shannon Beer**
Joseph	**Steve Evets**
Mr. Linton	**Oliver Milburn**

Paul Hilton (Mr. Earnshaw), Simone Jackson (Ellen Dean), Lee Shaw (Hindley Earnshaw), Adam Lock (Pastor), Amy Wren (Frances Earnshaw), Eve Coverley (Young Isabella Linton), Jonathan Powell (Young Edgar Linton), Emma Ropner (Mrs. Linton), Richard Guy (Gamekeeper Robert), Michael Hughes (Hareton), James Northcote (Edgar Linton), Nichola Burley (Isabella Linton), Paul Murphy (Lawyer)

Heathcliff, a poor boy brought to work for a Yorkshire farmer, develops a passionate relationship with his employer's daughter, Cathy. Previous film adaptations include (Goldwyn/UA; Laurence Olivier and Merle Oberon, 1939), and (AIP; Timothy Dalton, Anna Calder-Marshall, 1971).

Solomon Glave, Shannon Beer

Kaya Scodelario © Oscilloscope Laboratories

SISTER

(ADOPT FILMS) a.k.a. *L'enfant d'en haut*; Producers, Denis Freyd, Ruth Waldburger; Line Producer, André Bouvard; Director, Ursula Meier; Screenplay, Antoine Jaccoud, Ursula Meier, with the collaboration of Gilles Taurand; Dialogue, Antoine Jaccoud; Photography, Agnès Godard; Designer, Ivan Niclass; Costumes, Anna Van Brée; Music, John Parish; Casting, Aurélie Guichard; an Archipel 35 and Vega Film presentation, in co-production with RTS Radio Télévision Suisse, Band à Part Films; French; Not rated; 97 minutes; American release date: October 5, 2012

CAST

Louise	**Léa Seydoux**
Simon	**Kacey Mottet Klein**
Mike	**Martin Compston**
Kristin Jansen, the English Lady	**Gillian Anderson**
The Chef	**Jean-François Stévenin**
Bruno	**Yann Trégouët**

Gabin Lefebvre (Marcus), Dilon Ademi (Dilon), Magne-Håvard Brekke (The Violent Skier), Simon Guélat (Golfer), Mike Winter (Dynastar Skier), Yannick Ruiz, Vincent Fontannaz, Alain Borek, Fred Mudry, Ange Ruzé, Enrique Estevez, Frédéric Macé, Luc Tissot (Vacationers), Calvin Oberson (Blue Hands Brother), Eugenia Ferreira (Maria, Cleaning Woman), Antonio Troilo (Minibus Driver), Lisa Harder, Lucien Saint-Denis (English Lady's Children), Luca May (Infant)

A young boy helps to support his sister by stealing from the wealthy guests at a Swiss ski resort.

Kacey Mottet Klein, Léa Seydoux

Kacey Mottet Klein, Léa Seydoux © Adopt Films

Maggie Grace © 20ᵗʰ Century Fox   Liam Neeson

TAKEN 2

(20ᵀᴴ CENTURY FOX) Producer, Luc Besson; Director, Olivier Megaton; Screenplay, Luc Besson, Robert Mark Kamen; Photography, Romain Lacourbas; Designer, Sébastien Inizan; Costumes, Olivier Bériot; Music, Nathaniel Méchaly; Editors, Camille Delamarre, Vincent Tabaillon; Stunts, Alain Figlarz, Mark Vanselow; Casting, John Papsidera; a EuropaCorp, M6 Films, Grive Productions co-production with the participation of Canal+, M6 and Cine +; French; Dolby; Super 35 Widescreen; Color; Rated PG-13; 92 minutes; American release date: October 5, 2012

CAST

Bryan Mills	**Liam Neeson**
Kim	**Maggie Grace**
Lenore	**Famke Janssen**
Sam	**Leland Orser**
Casey	**Jon Gries**

D.B. Sweeney (Bernie), Luke Grimes (Jamie), Rade Sherbedgia (Murad Krasniqi), Kevork Malikyan (Inspector Durmaz), Alain Figlarz (Suko), Frank Alvarez (Car Wash Attendant), Murat Tuncelli (Custom Officer, Albania), Ali Yildirim (Imam), Ergun Kuyucu (Mirko), Cengiz Bozkurt, Atilla Pekoz (Border Guards), Hakan Karahan (Reception Clerk), Saruhan Sari (Waiter), Naci Adigüzel (Cheikh), Aclan Buyukturkoglu (Cheikh's Aide), Mehmet Polat (Hotel Driver), Yilmaz Kovan, Erdogan Yavuz, Luran Ahmeti (Hotel Thugs), Cengiz Daner (Hotel Duty Officer), Melis Erman (Maid Lockers), Erkan Üçüncü (Barber), Ugur Ugural (Man in Street), Alex Dawe (Johnson), Olivier Rabourdin (Jean-Claude), Michaël Vander-Meiren (Jean-Claude's Driver), Rochelle Gregorie (Jean-Claude's Concierge), Luenell (Driving Instructor), Emre Melemez (Hammam Attendant), Ilkay Akdagli (Albanian Intelligence Officer), Mylène Pilutik (Waitress), Nathan Rippy (News Reader), Serdar Okten, Mesut Makul, Mustafa Akin (Custom Officers), Murat Karatas, Cuneyt Yanar (Policemen, Car), Baris Adem, Hasan Karagulle (Policemen, Antiques), Gazenfer Kokoz, Remzi Sezgin (Cops), Ahmet Orhan Ozcam (Taxi Driver Kim), Melike Acar (Pool Attendant), Yasemin Yeltekin (Pool Waiter), Baris Aydin (Pool Man, Newspaper), Kenneth James Dakan (Marine), Adil Sak, Bekir Aslantas, Ercan Kurt, Cetin Arik (Coffin Pullers), Tamer Avkapan (Hammam Cop), Erasian Saglam, Mohammed Mouh (Antiques Shop), Julian Vinay (DJ, Disco), Gaelle Oilleau (Hotel Maid)

While in Istanbul, former CIA agent Bryan Mills becomes the target of the families of the human traffickers he helped thwart previously. Sequel to the 2009 film *Taken* (20ᵗʰ).

SOMEDAY THIS PAIN WILL BE USEFUL TO YOU

(FIIMBUFF) Producers, Elda Ferri, Milena Canonero, Ron Stein; Director, Roberto Faenza; Screenplay, Roberto Faenza, Dahlia Heyman; Based on the 2007 novel by Peter Cameron; Photography, Maurizio Calvesi; Designer, Tommaso Ortino; Costumes, Donna Zakowska; Music Supervisor, Andrea Guerra; Editor, Massimo Fiocchi; a Four of a Kind Productions and Jean Vigo Italia presentation in collaboration with RAI Cinema and the 7th Floor in association with BNL-Gruppo BNP Paribas; Italian-American; Dolby; Color; Not rated; 95 minutes; Release date: October 5, 2012

CAST

James Sveck	**Toby Regbo**
Marjorie Dunfour	**Marcia Gay Harden**
Paul Sveck	**Peter Gallagher**
Life Coach	**Lucy Liu**
Barry Rogers	**Stephen Lang**
Gillian Sveck	**Deborah Ann Woll**
Nanette	**Ellen Burstyn**

Aubrey Plaza (Real Estate Agent), Jonny Weston (Thom), Siobhan Fallon (Mrs. Beemer), Dree Hemingway (Rhonda), Christopher Mann (Guard), Peter Y. Kim (Funeral Waiter), Dieter Riesle (Visitor), Rekha Luther (Olivia), Rainer Judd (German Art Buyer), Gilbert Owuor (John Webster), John Mancini (General), Brooke Schlosser (Sue Kenney), Carmen Lamar (Lawyer), Kyle Coffman (Dakin), Greg McGadden (Robert), Jade Gzi (Restaurant Hostess)

The summer before he starts college, a lonely teen attends therapy sessions in order to figure out his past and what might possibly lie ahead for him.

Toby Regbo, Ellen Burstyn

Toby Regbo, Stephen Lang © FilmBuff

Helen Sjöholm, Jonatan S. Wächter © The Film Arcade

Bill Skarsgård, Katharina Schüttler

SIMON & THE OAKS

(THE FILM ARCADE) a.k.a. *Simon och ekarna*; Producers, Christer Nilson, Per Holst, Steffen Reurter, Patrick Knippel, Marc-Daniel Dichant, Leander Carell, John M. Jacobsen, Sveinung Golimo; Director, Lisa Ohlin; Screenplay, Marnie Bolk; Based on the 1985 novel *Simon och ekarna* (*Simon and the Oaks*) by Marianne Fredriksson; Photography, Dan Laustsen; Designers, Anders Engelbrecht, Lena Selander, Folke Strömbäck; Costumes, Katja Watkins; Music, Annette Focks; Editors, Kasper Leick, Michal Leszczylowski, Anders Nylander; Casting, Annette Mandoki, Simon Gunnarsson; a Gota Film, Asta Film, Schmidtz, Katze Filmkollektiv, Filmkameratene in co-production with Film i Vast, SVT, Film FYN, DR, Flink Film, Avro Television; Swedish-Danish-German-Norwegian, 2011; Dolby; Color; Widescreen; Not rated; 122 minutes; American release date: October 12, 2012

CAST

Simon Larsson	**Bill Skarsgård**
Karin Larsson	**Helen Sjöholm**
Ruben Lentov	**Jan Josef Liefers**
Erik Larsson	**Stefan Gödicke**
Isak Lentov	**Karl Linnertorp**
Young Simon	**Jonatan S. Wächter**
Young Isak	**Karl Martin Eriksson**

Erica Löfgren (Klara), Katharina Schüttler (Iza), Josefin Neldén (Mona), Lena Nylén (Olga Lentov), Cecilia Nilsson(Inga), Jan-Erik Emretsson (Neighbor Klas), Pär Brundin (Neighbor Åke), Frederik Nilsson (Teacher), Hermann Beyer (Ernst Habermann), Sven-Åke Gustavsson (Professor), Jan Holmqvist (Doctor), Iwar Wiklander (Headmaster), Peter Borenstein (Rabbi), Dellie Kamjo (Malin – 5-Years), Johanna Malmsten (Malin, 2 years), Tage Wirenhed (Malin, Baby)

In 1939 Sweden, a sensitive teen befriends a Jewish schoolmate whose family has fled Germany because of the Nazis.

Ilona Bacheleier, Jean Texier © Weinstein Co.

WAR OF THE BUTTONS

(WEINSTEIN CO.) a.k.a. *La nouvelle guerre des boutons*; Producer, Thomas Langmann; Director, Christophe Barratier; Screenplay, Stephane Keller, Christophe Barratier, Thomas Langmann, Philippe Lopes Curval; Based on the 1912 novel *La guerre des boutons* by Louis Pergaud; Photography, Jean Poisson; Designer, François Emmanuelli; Costumes, Jean-Daniel Vuillermoz; Music, Philippe Rombi; Editors, Yves Deschamps, Anne-Sophie Bion; a La Petite Reine production, in association with TF1 Films Production, Studio 37, Mars Films, Canal Plus; French, 2011; Dolby; Color; HD; Rated PG-13; 99 minutes; American release date: October 12, 2012

CAST
Lebrac	**Jean Texier**
Little Gibus	**Clément Godefroy**
Big Gibus	**Théophile Baquet**
Bacaillé	**Louis Dussol**
Simone	**Laetitia Casta**
The Teacher	**Guillaume Canet**

Harold Werner (La Crique), Nathan Parent (Camus), Ilona Bachelier (Violette), Thomas Goldberg (L'Aztec), Kad Merad (Lebrac's Father), Gérard Jugnot (L'Aztec's Father), Marie Bunel (Lebrac's Mother), François Morel (Bacaillé's Father), Grégory Gatignoll (Brochard), Anthony Decadi (Chazal), Eric Naggar (Museum Caretaker), Thierry Nenez (Card Player), Thierry Liagre (Proprietor), Anne Gaydier (L'Aztec's Mother), Vincent Bowen (The Prisoner), Philippe Jeancoux, Sébastien Saint-Martin (Resistance Fighters), Nicolas Clauzel, Olivier Papot (Militiamen), Jean-Michel Coulon (Man Stopped), Elise Le Stume (Woman Stopped)

During World War II, two boy gangs allow their rivalry to escalate into a miniature "war."

THE BIG PICTURE

(MPI MEDIA GROUP) a.k.a. *L'homme qui voulait vivre sa vie*; Producer, Pierre-Ange Le Pogam; Director, Eric Lartigau; Screenplay, Eric Lartigau, Laurent de Bartillat, in collaboration with Emmanuelle Bercot, Bernard Jeanean; Based on the 1997 novel by Douglas Kennedy; Photography, Laurent Dailland; Designer, Olivier Radot; Costumes, Anne Schotte; Music, Evgueni Galperine, Sacha Galperine; Editor, Juliette Welfling; a EuropaCorp, TF1 Films, CiBy 2000 production, in association with Canal Plus and CinéCinéma; French, 2010; Dolby; Super 35 Widescreen; Color; Not rated; 114 minutes; American release date: October 12, 2012

CAST
Paul Exben	**Romain Duris**
Sarah Exben	**Marina Foïs**
Bartholomé	**Niels Arestrup**
Ivana	**Branka Katic**
Anne	**Catherine Deneuve**
Grégoire Kremer	**Eric Ruf**

Enzo Caçote (Hugo Exben), Luka Antic (Baptiste), Rachel Berger (Fiona Exben), Esteban Carvajal Alegria (Valéry Grey), Florence Muller (Clarisse), Jean-Paul Bathany (Jean-Claude), Carole Weiss (Annie), Phlippe Dusseau (Emmanuel), Olivier Rogers (Pierre), Pauline Guimard (Morgane), Valérie Even (Estelle), Eric Thomas (Father of the Family), Pierre-Ange Le Pogam (Erwan), Thibaut de Lussy (Alan), Jules Lachaz, Romain Rouet, Achille Gayrad (Baptiste Doubles), Jadranka Mamic (Judy), Zinaida Dedakin (Linda), Zlata Numanagic (Estate Agent), Stevan Radusinovic (Photo Seller), Vanja Lazin (Gallery Owner), Filip Kalezic (Vilko), Alija Ademovic (Old Gymnast), Ljubica Barac (Grocer), John Rogers (Robin), Kristina Stevovic (Gallery Assistant), Aleksandar Markovic (Albanian Immigrant), Branka Otasevic, Jelena Simic (Waiters), Rajka Gacevic (Newspaper Vendor), Bojana Knezevic (Receptionist), Slobodan Marunovic (Freighter Captain), Petar Buric (Harbor Sailor), Dejan Ivanic, Sejfo Seferovic, Dragan Oluic (Sailors), Zelimir Soso (Freighter Cook) Bogoljub Mitic-Djosa (Lothar), Zef Dedivanovic (Monténégro Homeowner), Simo Trebjesanin, Aleksandar Gavranic (Police), Mihailo Radojicic (Italian Newspaper Boss), Slavko Kalezic (Italian Journalist), Douglas Kennedy (Guy in the Crowd)

After murdering the man he suspects is his wife's lover, Paul Exben decides to erase all traces of the crime and fake his own death.

Marina Foïs, Romain Duris © MPI Media

Woody Harrelson

Woody Harrelson, Christopher Walken

Colin Farrell, Christopher Walken, Sam Rockwell © CBS Films

SEVEN PSYCHOPATHS

(CBS FILMS) Producers, Graham Broadbent, Pete Czernin, Martin McDonagh; Co-Producers, Betsy Danbury, Sarah Harvey; Director/Screenplay, Martin McDonagh; Photography, Ben Davis; Designer, David Wasco; Costumes, Karen Patch; Music, Carter Burwell; Editor, Lisa Gunning; Casting, Sarah Halley Finn; a Film4 and BFI presentation of a Blueprint Pictures production; British-American; Dolby; Super 35 Widescreen; Deluxe color; Rated R; 110 minutes; Release date: October 12, 2012

CAST

Marty	**Colin Farrell**
Billy	**Sam Rockwell**
Hans	**Christopher Walken**
Kaya	**Abbie Cornish**
Charlie	**Woody Harrelson**
Zachariah	**Tom Waits**
Myra	**Linda Bright Clay**
Dennis	**Kevin Corrigan**
Killer	**James Hébert**
Paulo	**Zeljko Ivanek**
Man in Hat	**Harry Dean Stanton**
Larry	**Michael Pitt**
Tommy	**Michael Stuhlbarg**
Sharice	**Gabourey Sidibe**

Helen Mattsson (Blonde Lady), Christopher Gehrman (Cellmate), Christian Barillas (Catholic Priest), Joseph Lyle Taylor (Al), Long Nguyen (Vietnamese Priest), Christine Marzano (The Hooker), Frank Alvarez (Hispanic Guy), Brendan Sexton III (Young Zachariah), Amanda Warren (Maggie), John Bishop (The Butcher), Richard Wharton (The Hippy), Olga Kurylenko (Angela), Johnny Bolton (Barman), Ronnie Blevins (First Cop), Tai Chan Ngo (Fellow Monk), Bonny the ShihTzu (Bonny)

A struggling screenwriter unwittingly gets dragged into the L.A. criminal underworld when his friend kidnaps the dog of a psychotic gangster who will stop at nothing to get the animal back.

Colin Farrell, Sam Rockwell

HOLY MOTORS

(INDOMINA) Producers, Martine Marignac, Maurice Tinchant; Director/ Screenplay, Leos Carax; Photography, Caroline Champetier, Yves Cape; Designer, Florian Sanson; Costumes, Anaïs Romand; Music, Neil Hannon; Editor, Nelly Quettier; Make-up and Hairdressing Creator, Bernard Floch; a co-production of Pierre Grise Productions (France), Theo Films (France), Arte France Cinema (France), Pandora Film (Germany), WDR/Arte (Germany) with the participation of the Centre National du Cinema et de L'image, Animee, Arte France, Canal+, WDR/Arte; French-German; Color; Not rated; 115 minutes; American release date: October 17, 2012

CAST

Monsieur Oscar/Banker/Bum/ Motion-Capture/M. Merde/Father/ Accordion Player/Killer/Victim/ Dying Man/Man in Home	**Denis Lavant**
Céline	**Édith Scob**
Eva Grace/Jean	**Kylie Minogue**
Kay M	**Eva Mendes**
The Man with the Birthmark	**Michel Piccoli**
Léa/Elise	**Elise Lhomeau**
Angèle	**Jeanne Disson**
Sleeper/Limousine Voice	**Leos Carax**
Little Girl	**Nastya Golubeva Carax**
Mo-Cap Acrobat	**Reda Oumouzoune**
The Cyber Woman	**Zlata**
Photographer	**Geoffrey Carey**
Assistant Photographer	**Annabelle Dexter-Jones**

In a 24-hour odyssey through Paris while being chauffeured by limousine, Monsieur Oscar transforms into several different characters.

Kylie Minogue © Indomina

Eva Mendes, Denis Lavant

Édith Scob

Denis Lavant

ALL TOGETHER

(KINO LORBER) a.k.a. *Et si on vivait tous ensemble?*; Producers, Christophe Bruncher, Peter Rommel, Philippe Gompel, Aurélia Grossmann; Co-Producer, Frédérique Dumas; Director/Screenplay, Stéphane Robelin; Photography, Dominique Colin; Designer, David Bersanetti; Costumes, Jürgen Doering; Music, Jean-Philippe Verdin; Editor, Patrick Wilfert; a Les Films de la Butte/Rommelfilm/ Manny Films/Studio 37/Home Run Pictures production; French; Dolby; Color; HD; Not rated; 96 minutes; American release date: October 19, 2012

CAST

Jean Colin	**Guy Bedos**
Dirk	**Daniel Brühl**
Annie Colin	**Geraldine Chaplin**
Jeanne	**Jane Fonda**
Claude Blanchard	**Claude Rich**
Albert	**Pierre Richard**
Bernard	**Bernard Malaka**
Maria	**Camino Texeira**
Sabine	**Gwendoline Hamon**
Soraya	**Shemss Audat**
Funeral Salesman	**Gustave Kervern**
Doctor Lacombe	**Laurent Klug**

Lionel Nakache (Policeman), Stéphanie Pasterkamp (Alleyway Bar Waitress), Philippe Chaine (Bouyer, Firefighter), Caroline Clerc (Madame Rolland), Gaëlle Billaut Danno (Nursing Home Employee), Lili Robelin (Lola), Tom Robelin (Milan), Alexandre Robelin (Hugo), Marie Bruncher (Little Girl in Armbands)

With the tribulations of aging taking its toll on each of them, five friends decide to move in together.

Guy Bedos, Pierre Richard, Claude Rich, Jane Fonda, Geraldine Chaplin

Guy Bedos, Pierre Richard, Jane Fonda, Claude Rich, Geraldine Chaplin

Geraldine Chaplin, Claude Rich, Jane Fonda

Daniel Brühl, Jane Fonda © Kino Lorber

Isabelle Huppert, Benoît Poelvoorde © Strand Releasing

MY WORST NIGHTMARE

(STRAND) a.k.a. *Mon pire cauchemar*; Producers, Philippe Carcassonne, Bruno Pesery, Francis Boespflug, Jérôme Seydoux; Co-Producers, Diana Elbaum, Sébastien Delloye, Patrick Quinet; Director, Anne Fontaine; Screenplay, Nicolas Mercier, Anne Fontaine; Photography, Jean-Marc Fabre; Art Director, Olivier Radot; Costumes, Catherine Leterrier; Music, Bruno Coulais; Editors, Luc Barnier, Nelly Ollivault; Casting, Pascale Béraud; a Ciné@, Maison de Cinéma, F.B. Productions, Pathé, M6Films, Entre Chien et Loup, Artemis Productions, RTBF (Télévision Belge) Belgacom production; French, 2011; Dolby; Color; Not rated; 103 minutes; American release date: October 19, 2012

CAST
Agathe Novic	**Isabelle Huppert**
Patrick Demeuleu	**Benoît Poelvoorde**
François Dambreville	**André Dussollier**
Julie	**Virginie Efira**
Tony	**Corentin Devroey**

Donatien Suner (Adrien), Aurélien Recoing (Thierry), Éric Berger (Sébastien), Philippe Magnan (The Principal), Bruno Podalydès (Marc-Henri), Samir Guesmi (Social Services Inspector), Françoise Miquelis (Psychologist), Jean-Luc Couchard (Milou Demeuleu), Émilie Gavois Kahn (Sylvie), Serge Onteniente (Set Designer), Hiroshi Sugimoto (Sugimoto), Yumi Fujimori (Translator), Valérie Moreau (Evelyne), Antoine Blanquefort (Deputy Mayor), Arielle D'Ydewalle, Émeline Scatliffe, Jessica Lefèvre (Dancers at Carwash), Régis Romele (Painter at Foundation), Léa Gabriele, Laurence Colussi, Marie Boissard (Students' Mothers), Gilles Carballo (Student's Father), Rose Cool (Customer in Bar)

Because their sons are best of friends, an uptight art dealer and an unemployed single dad end up in an unlikely relationship when the latter is hired to remodel her apartment.

THE OTHER SON

(COHEN MEDIA) a.k.a. *Le fils de l'autre*; Producers, Virginie Lacombe, Raphael Berdugo; Executive Producer, Itai Tamir; Director, Lorraine Lévy; Screenplay, Nathalie Saugeon, Lorraine Lévy, Noam Fitoussi; Photography, Emmanuel Soyer; Art Director, Miguel Markin; Costumes, Rona Doron, Valérie Adda; Music, Dhafer Youssef; Editor, Sylvie Gadmer; Casting, Michael Laguens, Esther Kling, Rozeen Bisharat; a Rapsodie Production and Cité Films production, co-produced by France 3 Cinéma, Madeleine Films, Solo Films; French; Dolby; Color; Rated PG-13; 105 minutes; American release date: October 26, 2012

CAST
Orinth Silberg	**Emmanuelle Devos**
Alon Silberg	**Pascal Elbé**
Joseph Silberg	**Jules Sitruk**
Yacine Al Bezaaz	**Mehdi Dehbi**
Leila Al Bezaaz	**Areen Omari**
Saïd Al Bezaaz	**Khalifa Natour**

Mahmood Shalabi (Bilal Al Bezaaz), Diana Zriek (Amina), Marie Wisselmann (Keren), Bruno Podalydès (David), Ezra Dagan (The Rabbi), Tamar Shem Or (Yona), Tomer Ofner (Ilan), Noa Manor (Ethel), Shira Naor (Lisa), Jill Ben David (Hospital Director), Yuval Rozman (Military Doctor), Lana Attinger (Officer), Loai Noufi (Jamil), Majd Bitar (Tarik), Nir Avrashi (Ministry Officiate), Shir Friebach (Sergeant), Beni Eldar, Ori Lachmi, Natan Yadlin (Check-Point Soldiers), Samantha Amouyal (Freezing Client), Oum Abed (Madame Hafiz), Michel Taroni, Keppa, Zaki Mevorach (Beach Hooligans)

Two boys, one Israeli, one Palestinian, are accidentally switched at birth and thereby raised on the opposing sides of the Israeli-Palestinian struggle.

Pascale Elbé, Emmanuelle Devos © Cohen Media

Jules Sitruk, Mehdi Dehbi

Jim Sturgess, Hugo Weaving

Jim Broadbent, Ben Whishaw

David Gyasi, Jim Sturgess

CLOUD ATLAS

(WARNER BROS.) Producers, Grant Hill, Stefan Arndt, Lana Wachowski, Tom Tykwer, Andy Wachowski; Executive Producers, Philip Lee, Uwe Schott, Wilson Qiu; Co-Producers, Peter Lam, Tony Ted, Alexander Van Oulmen; Associate Producer, Gigi Oeri; Directors, Lana Wachowski and Andy Wachowski (1849, 2144 and 2321 Sequences), Tom Tykwer (1936, 1973 and 2012 Sequences); Screenplay, Lana Wachowski, Tom Tykwer, Andy Wachowski; Based on the 2004 novel by David Mitchell; Photography, John Toll, Frank Griebe; Designers, Uli Hanisch, Hugh Bateup; Costumes, Kym Barrett, Pierre-Yves Gayraud; Hair & Makeup & Prosthetics Designers, Jeremy Woodhead, Daniel Parker; Music, Tom Tykwer, Johnny Klimek, Reinhold Heil; Editor, Alexander Berner; Senior Visual Effects Supervisor, Dan Glass; Visual Effects Supervisor, Stephane Ceretti; Casting, Lora Kennedy, Lucinda Syson; a Cloud Atlas Production/X-Filme Creative Pool and Anarchos production in association with A Company and ARD Degeto; German-American-Hong Kong-Singapore; Dolby; Arri Color; Super 35 Widescreen; Rated R; 172 minutes; American release date: October 26, 2012

CAST

Dr. Henry Goose/Hotel Manager/ Isaac Sachs/Dermot Hoggins/ Cavendish Look-a-Like Actor/ Zachry	**Tom Hanks**
Native Woman/Jocasta Ayrs/ Luisa Rey/Indian Party Guest/ Ovid/Meronym	**Halle Berry**
Captain Molyneaux/Vyvyan Arys/ Timothy Cavendish/Korean Musician/Prescient 2	**Jim Broadbent**
Haskell Moore/Tadeusz Kesselring/ Bill Smoke/Nurse Noakes/ Boardman Mephi/Old Georgie	**Hugo Weaving**
Adam Ewing/Poor Hotel Guest/ Megan's Dad/Highlander/Hae-Joo Chang/Adam/Zachry Brother-in-Law	**Jim Sturgess**
Tilda/Megan's Mom/Mexican Woman/Sonmi-451/Sonmi-351/Sonmi Prostitute	**Doona Bae**
Cabin Boy/Robert Frobisher/ Store Clerk/Georgette/ Tribesman	**Ben Whishaw**
Kupaka/Joe Napier/An-kor Apis/ Prescient	**Keith David**
Young Rufus Sixsmith/Old Rufus Sixsmith/Nurse James/Archivist	**James D'Arcy**
Talbot/Hotel Manager/Yoona-939/ Rose	**Xun Zhou**
Autua/Lester Rey/Duophsyte	**David Gyasi**
Madame Horrox/Older Ursula/ Yusouf Suleiman/Abbess	**Susan Sarandon**
Rev. Giles Horrox/Hotel Heavy/ Lloyd Hooks/Denholme Cavendish/Seer Rhee/Kona Chief	**Hugh Grant**
Old Salty Dog/Mr. Meeks/ Prescient 1	**Robert Fyfe**
Mr. Boerhaave/Guard/Leary the Healer	**Martin Wuttke**
Young Cavendish	**Robin Morrissey**
Javier Gomez/Jonas/Zachry's Older Nephew	**Brody Lee**

Ian van Temperley (Enforcer), Amanda Walker (Veronica), Ralph Riach (Ernie), Andrew Havill (Mr. Hotchkiss), Tanja de Wendt (Mrs. Hotchkiss), Raevan Lee Hanan (Little Girl with Orison at Papa Song's/ Catkin/Zachry Relative 1), Götz Otto (Groundsman Withers), Niall Greig Fulton (Haskell Moore's Dinner Guest 2/Mozza Hoggins), Louis Dempsey (Haskell Moore's Dinner Guest 3/Jarvis Hoggins), Martin Docherty (Haskell Moore's Dinner Guest 4/Eddie Hoggins), Alistair Petrie (Haskell Moore's Dinner Guest 1/Musician/Felix Finch/Lascivious Businessman), Zhu Zhu (Megan Sixsmith/12th Star Clone), Sylvestra Le Touzel (Haskell Moore's Dinner Guest 5/Nurse Judd/Aide in Slaughtership), Jojo Schöning (Papa Song Punk), Laura Vietzen (Young Ursula), Thomas Kügel (Ursula's Father), Marie Rönnebeck (Ursula's Daughter), Ruby Kastner (Young Girl), Emma Werz (Ursula's Granddaughter), Mya-Leica Naylor (Miro), Korbyn Hanan (Adam Grandson), Katy Karrenbauer (Axwoman), Dulcie Smart (Ursula's Mother/Herbalist), Anna Holmes (Scientist/Executive), Shaun Lawton (Secretary), Moritz Berg (Porter), Gigi Lee, Genevien Lee, Cody Lee (Zachry Relatives), Heike Hanold-Lynch (Nurse Judd Look-a-Like), Victor Esteban Sole (Mr. Roderick), Kristoffer Fuss (Lead Enforcer), Marco Albrecht (Scan Enforcer), Gary McCormack (Crane Operator), David Mitchell (Union Spy), Heiko Lehmann (Enforcer)

Six interconnecting storylines unfold throughout different periods in time, past and future, spanning 500 years: 1849, the South Pacific: an idealistic lawyer bonds on board ship with a slave who has stowed away; 1936, Scotland: a down-on-his-luck composer takes a job apprenticing for a renowned composer, aspiring to write his symphonic masterpiece; 1973, San Francisco: a journalist uncovers corporate corruption involving a nuclear power plant; 2012, England: a small-time publisher is placed, against his will, in a prison-like senior citizen home; 2144, Neo Seoul: a genetically engineered fabricant is rescued by a revolutionary who hopes to overthrow the oppressive totalitarian government; After the Fall, 2321 and 2346 Hawaii: a peaceful tribe tries to avoid attack from a warring one.

Tom Hanks, Halle Berry

Halle Berry, Keith David

Hugo Weaving

Hugh Grant

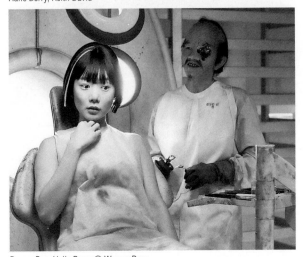
Doona Bae, Halle Berry © Warner Bros.

SLEEP TIGHT

(MPI) a.k.a. *Mientras duermes*; Producer, Julio Fernandez; Executive Producers, Julio Fernandez, Carlos Fernandez, Alberto Marini; Director, Jaume Balagueró; Screenplay, Alberto Marini, based on his novel; Photography, Pablo Rosso; Designer, Javier Alvarino; Costumes, Marian Coromina; a Filmax Entertainment presentation of a Castelao Pictures production with the participation of TVE, Canal Plus, TV; Spanish, 2011; Dolby; Super 35 Widescreen; Color; 105 minutes; American release date: October 26, 2012

CAST

César	**Luis Tosar**
Clara	**Marta Etura**
Marcos	**Alberto San Juan**
Úrsula	**Iris Almeida Molina**
Verónica	**Petra Martinez**

Carlos Lasarte (Neighbor in 4B), Amparo Fernández, Roger Morilla (Clean People), Pep Tosar (Úrsula's Father), Margarita Roset (César's Mother), Ruben Ametllé, Xavier Calvet (Office Workers), Manuel Dueso (Commissioner), Tony Corvillio, Ricard Saudrni, Xavier Pujolràs (Police), Oriol Genis (Administrator), Iker López (Úrsula's Brother), Lola Vidal (Clara's Mother), Patricia Arredondo (Housemaid), Gemma Niergea, Carles Pérez (Radio Voices)

A Barcelona concierge incapable of feeling happy makes it his mission to destroy a relentlessly cheerful tenant.

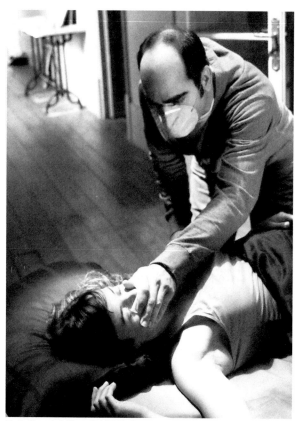

Marta Etura, Luis Tosar © MPI Media

Jelle Florizoone, Mathias Vergels

Jelle Florizoone, Mathias Vergels © Strand Releasing

NORTH SEA TEXAS

(STRAND) a.k.a. *Noordzee, Texas*; Producer, Yves Verbraeken; Director, Bavo Defurne; Screenplay, Bavo Defurne, Yves Verbraeken; Based on the 2005 book *Nooit gaat dit over* by André Sollie; Photography, Anton Mertens; Designer, Kurt Rigolle; Costumes, Nathalie Lermytte; Music, Adriano Cominotto; Editor, Els Voorspoels; an Indeed Films, VRT/één, Mollywood production; Belgian, 2011; Dolby; Color; HD; Not rated; 94 minutes; American release date: November 2, 2012

CAST

Pim	**Jelle Florizoone**
Yvette	**Eva van der Gucht**
Sabrina	**Nina Marie Korekaas**
Gino	**Mathias Vergels**
Marcella	**Katelijne Damen**
Etienne	**Luk Wyns**

Thomas Coumans (Zoltan), Daniel Sikora (Maurice), Victor Ben Van den Heuvel (Young Pim), Patricia Goemaere (Simone), Nathan Naenen (Young Gino), Noor Ben Taouet (Young Sabrina), Ella-June Henrard (Francoise), Mickey (Mirza)

A teenager infatuated with the handsome boy next store, seizes his chance to move in with the lad and his family when his mother hooks up with another man.

Sean Penn, Frances McDormand

Eve Hewson, Sean Penn

Grant Goodman, Sean Penn

THIS MUST BE THE PLACE

(WEINSTEIN CO.) Producers, Nicola Giuliano, Andrea Occhipinti, Francesca Cima, Medusa Film; Co-Producers, Michèle Pétin, Laurent Pétin, Ed Guiney, Andrew Lowe; Director/Story, Paolo Sorrentino; Screenplay, Paolo Sorrentino, Umberto Contarello; Photography, Luca Bigazzi; Designer, Stefania Cella; Costumes, Karen Patch; Music, David Byrne; Lyrics, Will Oldham; Editor, Cristiano Travaglioli; Casting, Laura Rosenthal, Maureen Hughes; Hair, Kim Santantonio; Make-Up, Luisa Abel; an Indigo Film, Lucky Red, Medusa Film production; Italian-French-Irish, 2011; Dolby; Super 35 Widescreen; Technicolor; Rated R; 111 minutes; American release date: November 2, 2012

CAST

Cheyenne	**Sean Penn**
Jane	**Frances McDormand**
Mordecai Midler	**Judd Hirsch**
Mary	**Eve Hewson**
Rachel	**Kerry Condon**
Robert Plath	**Harry Dean Stanton**
Dorothy Shore	**Joyce Van Patten**
Himself	**David Byrne**
Mary's Mother	**Olwen Fouéré**
Ernie Ray	**Shea Whigham**
Richard	**Liron Levo**
Jeffery	**Simon Delaney**
Aloise Lange	**Heinz Lieven**

Grant Goodman (Tommy), Sam Keeley (Desmond), Seth Adkins (Jimmy), Peter Carey (Saks Clerk), Bern Cohen (Rabbi Cohen), Kris Graverson (Saks Shopper), Madge Levinson (Jackie), Gordon Michaels (Tattoo Mike), Ricky Neeble (Pool Man), Johnny Ward (Steven), Fritz Weaver (Voice of Cheyenne's Father), Inga R. Wilson (Ernie Ray's Wife), Antonio Monda (Man on Bench), Jer O'Leary (Bereaved Father in Cemetery), Ross MacMahon (Coffee Waiter), Bronwyn Reed (Escalator Brunette), Robert Herrick (Airport Businessman), Davis Gloff (Gun Shop Owner), Ron Coden (Gun Shop Patron)

A former rock star, living in Dublin, travels to the States for the funeral of his father and decides to follow through on the old man's obsession to track down the Nazi who had humiliated him during the Holocaust.

David Byrne © Weinstein Co.

Mads Mikkelsen, Alicia Vikander

Alicia Vikander

Mikkel Boe Følsgaard, Mads Mikkelsen

A ROYAL AFFAIR

(MAGNOLIA) a.k.a. *En kongelig affære*; Producers, Louise Vesth, Sisse Graum Jørgensen, Meta Louise Foldager; Executive Producers, Lars von Trier, Peter Aalbæk, Peter Garde; Director, Nikolaj Arcel; Screenplay, Rasmus Heisterberg, Nikolaj Arcel; Based on the 2001 novel *Prinsesse af blodet* by Bodil Steensen-Leth; Photography, Rasmus Videbaek; Designer, Niels Sejer; Costumes, Manon Rasmussen; Music, Gabriel Yared, Cyrille Aufort; Editors, Mikkel E. G. Nielsen, Kasper Leick; a Zentropa Entertainments presentation; Danish-Swedish-Czech; Dolby; Cinemascope; Color; Rated R; 138 minutes; American release date: November 9, 2012

CAST

Johann Friedrich Struensee	**Mads Mikkelsen**
Queen Caroline Mathilda	**Alicia Vikander**
King Christian VII	**Mikkel Boe Følsgaard**
Juliane Marie	**Trine Dyrholm**
Ove Høegh-Guldberg	**David Denick**
Schack Carl Rantzau	**Thomas W. Gabrielsson**
Enevold Brandt	**Cyron Bjørn Melville**
J.H.E. Bernstoff	**Bent Mejding**
Augusta, Princess of Wales	**Harriet Walter**

Laura Bro (Louise von Plessen), Jakob Ulrik Lohmann (Julianne's Officer), Søren Malling (Hartmann), Søren Spanning (Munter), Frederik Christian Johansen (Arveprinsen), John Martinus (Reventlow), Rosalinde Mynster (Marie), Nikol Kouklová (Stovlet-Catherine), Egob Nielsen (Mounti), Michaela Horká (Bordelmutter), Alzbeta Jenická (Bondekone), Anna Stiborová (Sophie Livernet), William Jøhnk Juel Nielsen (Frederik VI, at 15), Julia Wentzel Olsen (Louise Augusta, at 12), Frank Rubæk, Klaus Tange, Petr Janis (Ministers), Karin Rørbeck, Josefine Højbjerg Bitsch (Juliane's Ladies-in-Waiting), Zinnini Elkington (Rantzau's Maid), Morten Holst (Lord Chamberlain), Karel Polisenský (Old Doctor), Eva Sitta (English Lady-in-Waiting), Ivan G'Vera (German Doctor), Kristian Fjord (The Fidget), Daniel Bambas (Hamlet), Tereza Terberova (Caroline's Housemaid), Jan Krafka, Peter Varga (Nightwatchers), Ivan Vodochodský (Noble Gentleman), Lukas Kral (Officer), Nora Rajnochova (Prostitute), Jakub Albrecht (Doctor – Smallpox)

As the Danish King Christian VII becomes increasingly irrational, the idealistic royal physician seizes his chance to influence the court.

This film received an Oscar nomination for foreign language film.

Alicia Vikander, Mads Mikkelsen © Magnolia Films

IN ANOTHER COUNTRY

(KINO LORBER) a.k.a. *Da-reun na-ra-e-seo*; Producer, Kim Kyounghee; Director/Screenplay, Hong Sang-soo; Photography, Park Hong-yeol, Jee Yune-jeong; Music, Jeong Yong-jin; Editor, Hahm Sung-won; a Jeonwonsa Film with the participation of Les Films du Camelia; South Korean; Dolby; Widescreen; Color; Not rated; 88 minutes; American release date: November 9, 2012

CAST

Anne	**Isabelle Huppert**
Lifeguard	**Yu Junsang**
Womu	**Jung Yumi**
Park Sook	**Youn Yuhjang**
Jongsoo	**Kwon Hyehyo**
Kumhee	**Moon Sori**

As a film student's script unfolds, three different French women named Anne have varying adventures as they check into the Blue Hotel in a Korean seaside town.

Yu Junsang, Isabelle Huppert

Isabelle Huppert © Kino Lorber

Joshua Close, Selma Blair

Selma Blair, Joshua Close © IFC Midnight

IN THEIR SKIN

(IFC MIDNIGHT) formerly *Replicas*; Producers, Justin Tyler Close, Jeremy Power Regimbal; Executive Producers, Tina Pehme, Kim C. Roberts; Director, Jeremy Power Regimbal; Screenplay, Josh Close; Photography, Norm Li; Designer, Tink; Costumes, Kathi Moore; Music, Keith Power; Editor, Austin Andrews; Casting, Heidi Levitt, Lisa Essary; a Studio Movement Entertainment, Sepia Films, Telefilm Canada production; Canadian; Color; Not rated; 96 minutes; American release date: November 9, 2012

CAST

Mary	**Selma Blair**
Mark	**Joshua Close**
Bobby	**James D'Arcy**
Jane	**Rachel Miner**
Brendon	**Quinn Lord**
Jared	**Alex Ferris**

Leanne Adachi (Medic), Matt Bellefleur (Toby), Agam Darshi (Nurse), Debbe Hirata (Therapist), Terence Kelly (Station Attendant)

Trying to recover from the tragic death of their daughter, an upscale couple and their young son rent a house in woods where they are terrorized by intruders claiming to be their neighbors.

SKYFALL

(COLUMBIA/MGM) Producers, Michael G. Wilson, Barbara Broccoli; Executive Producer, Callum McDougall; Co-Producers, Andrew Noakes, David Pope; Director, Sam Mendes; Screenplay, Neal Purvis, Robert Wade, John Logan; Photography, Roger Deakins; Designer, Dennis Gassner; Costumes, Jany Temime; Music, Thomas Newman; Title song by Adele and Paul Epworth/performed by Adele; Editor, Stuart Baird; Special Effects Supervisor, Chris Corbould; Visual Effects Supervisor, Steve Begg; Stunts, Gary Powell; Casting, Debbie Williams; an Albert R. Broccoli's Eon Productions presentation; British-American; Dolby; Widescreen; Color; Rated PG-13; 143 minutes; American release date: November 9, 2012

CAST

James Bond (007)	**Daniel Craig**
M	**Judi Dench**
Silva	**Javier Bardem**
Gareth Mallory	**Ralph Fiennes**
Eve	**Naomie Harris**
Severine	**Bérénice Lim Marlohe**
Q	**Ben Whishaw**
Kincade	**Albert Finney**
Tanner	**Rory Kinnear**
Patrice	**Ola Rapace**
Clair Dowar MP	**Helen McCrory**
Doctor Hall	**Nicholas Woodeson**
Ronson	**Bill Buckhurst**
Vanessa (M's Assistant)	**Elize du Toit**
MI6 Technician	**Ian Bonar**
M's Driver	**Gordon Milne**
Vauxhall Bridge Police Guards	**Peter Basham, Ben Loyd-Holmes**
Bond's Lover	**Tonia Sotiropoulou**
CNN News Anchor	**Wolf Blitzer**
MI6 Assessors	**David Gillies, James Li, Ken Hazeldine**
Shanghai Barman	**Orion Lee**
Shanghai Art Collector	**Dave Wong**
Severine's Bodyguards	**Tank Dong, Roger Yuan, Liang Yang**
Floating Dragon Cashier	**Yennis Cheung**
Floating Dragon Floor Manager	**Chooye Bay**
Floating Dragon Assistant Floor Manager	**Sid Man**
Floating Dragon Barmaid	**Angela Tran**
Boat Captain	**Milorad Kapor**
BBC News Anchor	**Huw Edwards**
Silva's Isolation Guard	**John Hodgkinson**
M's Inquiry Assistant	**Dominique Jones**

Adebayo Bolaji, Elia Lo Tauro, Amir Boutrous, Kan Bonfils, Nicholas Goh (Boat Crew), Kurt Egyiawan, Oliver Johnstone, Harry Kershaw (Q's Assistants), Burt Caesar, Paul Venables, Crispin Letts, Kammy Darweish, Beatrice Curnew (Inquiry Members), Ross Waiton, Jim Conway (Whitehall Police Guards), Jens Hultén, Michael Pink (Silva's Henchmen), Jo Cameron Brown (Wife at Tube Station), Anthony O'Donnell (Husband at Tube Station), Hannah Stokely (Tube Driver), Wayne Gordon, Enoch Frost, Tom Wu, Jake Fairbrother, Chris Schieuref, Daniel Adegboyega, Selva Rasalingam (Silva's Mercenaries), Jos Skottowe (Helicopter Gunner)

James Bond is called back to duty to track down a cyberterrorist bent on eliminating undercover agents who have been placed within terrorist organizations. The 23rd official Bond entry, released during the 50th anniversary year of the first installment's (*Dr. No*) London opening in the fall of 1962.

2012 Academy Award Winner for Best Original Song ("Skyfall") and Best Sound Editing (tied with *Zero Dark Thirty*).

This film received an additional Oscar nomination for sound mixing.

Naomie Harris

Ola Rapace

Daniel Craig, Bérénice Lim Marlohe

Ralph Fiennes

Daniel Craig, Javier Bardem

Ben Whishaw, Daniel Craig

Daniel Craig

Judi Dench

Daniel Craig © Columbia Pictures

Alicia Vikander, Domhnall Gleeson

Jude Law, Keira Knightley

Aaron Taylor-Johnson, Alicia Vikander

ANNA KARENINA

(FOCUS) Producers, Tim Bevan, Eric Fellner, Paul Webster; Executive Producer, Liza Chasin; Co-Producer, Alexandra Ferguson; Director, Joe Wright; Screenplay, Tom Stoppard; Based on the 1877 novel by Leo Tolstoy; Photography, Seamus McGarvey; Designer, Sarah Greenwood; Costumes, Jacqueline Durran; Hair and Makeup Designer, Ivana Primorac; Music, Dario Marianelli; Choreographer, Sidi Larbi Cherkaoui; Editor, Melanie Ann Oliver; Casting, Jina Jay; a Working Title production; British; Dolby; Panavision; Deluxe color; Rated R; 129 minutes; American release date: November 16, 2012

CAST

Anna Karenina	**Keira Knightley**
Karenin	**Jude Law**
Vronsky	**Aaron Taylor-Johnson**
Dolly	**Kelly Macdonald**
Oblonsky	**Matthew Macfadyen**
Levin	**Domhnall Gleeson**
Princess Betsy Tverskoy	**Ruth Wilson**
Kitty	**Alicia Vikander**
Countess Vronsky	**Olivia Williams**
Countess Lydia Ivanovna	**Emily Watson**
Prince Shcherbatsky	**Pip Torrens**
Princess Shcherbatsky	**Susanne Lothar**
Opera House Wife	**Shirley Henderson**
Matvey	**Eric MacLennan**
Grisha Oblonsky	**Theo Morrissey**
Lili Oblonsky	**Cecily Morrissey**
Masha Oblonsky	**Freya Galpin**
Tanya Oblonsky	**Octavia Morrissey**
Vasya Oblonsky	**Beatrice Morrissey**
Mlle. Rolland	**Marine Battier**
Annushka	**Guro Nagelhus Schia**
Aruhan	**Aruhan Galieva**
Korney	**Carl Grose**
Mikhail Slyudin	**Bryan Hands**
Serhoza	**Oskar McNamara**
Vasily Lukich	**Luke Newberry**

Michael Shaeffer (Doorkeeper), Steven Beard (Elderly Waiter), Alexandra Roach (Countess Nordston), Henry Lloyd-Hughes (Burisov), David Wilmot (Nikolai), Tannishtha Chatterjee (Masha), Joseph Macnab (Guards Officer), Nick Holder (Stationmaster), Claire Greenway (Austrian Princess), Mike Shepherd (Wheel Tapper), Arthur Nightingale (Oblonsky's Servant), Buffy Davis (Agafia), Gala Wesson (Kitchen Maid). Eros Vlahos (Boris), Kyle Soller (Korunsky), Sam Cox (Kapitonich), Max Bennett (Petritsky), Holliday Grainger (Baroness), Jude Monk McGowan (Tuskevitch), Antony Byrne (Colonel Demin), Michelle Dockery (Princess Myagkaya), Emerald Fennell (Princess Merkalova), Sarine Sofair (Anna's Friend), Thomas Howes (Yashvin), Raphaël Personnaz (Alexander Vronsky), Bill Skarsgård (Makhotin), Cara Delevingne (Princess Sorokina), Bodil Blain (Princess Sorokina Senior), Hera Hilmar (Varya), Kenneth Collard (Prince Tverskoy), Steve Evets (Theodore), Conor McCarry (Young Peasant), Giles King (Stremov), Martin Wimbush (Anna's Doctor), James Northcote (Princess Betsy's Footman), Duncan Wisbey (Shopkeeper), Jamie Beamish (Opera House Husband), Simon Muller (Opera House Manager), Nikolai Lester (Piano Prodigy), Tillie-Bett Grant (Baby Anya), Navala "Niku" Chaudhari, Amber Doyle, Damien Fournier, Laura Neyskens, Daniel Proietto, Vebjorn Sundy, Jennifer White, Paul Zivkovich (Ball Dancers & French Theatre Dancers)

Anna Karenina risks her status as the wife of a high-ranking government official when she falls in love with a dashing cavalry officer, Count Vronsky.
Previous versions of the novel include *Love* (MGM, 1927; Greta Garbo and John Gilbert); *Anna Karenina* (MGM, 1935; Greta Garbo and Fredric March); *Anna*

Karenina (20th, 1948; Vivien Leigh and Kieron Moore); and *Leo Tolstoy's Anna Karenina* (WB, 1997; Sophie Marceau and Sean Bean).

2012 Academy Award Winner for Best Costume Design.

This film received additional Oscar nominations for cinematography, production design, and original score.

Aaron Taylor-Johnson

Olivia Williams, Keira Knightley

Aaron Taylor-Johnson, Keira Knightley

Matthew Macfadyen

Keira Knightley

Jude Law © Focus Features

RUST AND BONE

(SONY CLASSICS) a.k.a. *De rouille et d'os*; Executive Producer, Martine Cassinelli; Director, Jacques Audiard; Screenplay, Thomas Biedgain, Jacques Audiard; Based on the short stories "Rust and Bone" and "Rocket Ride" featured in the 2006 collection *Rust and Bone* by Craig Davidson; Photography, Stéphane Fontaine; Designer, Michel Barthélémy; Costumes, Virginie Montel; Music, Alexandre Desplat; Editor, Juliette Welfling; Casting, Richard Rousseau; a Why Not Productions, Page 114, France 2 Cinéma, Les Films du Fleueve, RTBF (Belgian Television), Lumière and Lunanime co-production; French-Belgian; Dolby; HD Wudescreen; Color; Rated R; 120 minutes; American release date: November 23, 2012

Matthias Schoenaerts, Marion Cotillard

CAST

Stéphanie	**Marion Cotillard**
Alain van Versch	**Matthias Schoenaerts**
Sam van Versch	**Armand Verdure**
Louise	**Céline Sallette**
Anna	**Corinne Masiero**
Martial	**Bouli Lanners**
Richard	**Jean-Michel Correia**
Foued	**Mourad Frarema**
Simon	**Yannick Choirat**

Fred Menut (Owner of ELP Security), Duncan Versteegh, Katia Chaperon, Catherine Fa, Andés Lopez Jabois (Orca Trainers), Océane Cartia (Babysitter), Françoise Michaud (Stéphanie's Mother), Irina Coito (Aerobics Teacher), David Billaud (Dog Handler), Fabien L'Allain (Prothesist), Fabien Baïardi (Fisherman), Laetitia Malbranque (Woman in Supermarket), Soulayne Rajraji (Union Representative of Supermarket), Pascal Rozand (Concessionaire), Hedi Touihri (Security Chief at Supermarket), Nathalie Millar (Anna's Colleague), Anne-Marie Tomat (Nurse at Hospital near Lake)

Marion Cotillard

A struggling single father gets a job as a bouncer at a nightclub where he meets Stéphanie, a whale trainer whose job unexpectedly leads to a tragic accident that changes both their lives.

Armand Verdure, Matthias Schoenaerts © Sony Classics

Marion Cotillard, Matthias Schoenaerts

THE GATEKEEPERS

(SONY CLASSICS) Producers, Dror Moreh, Estelle Fialon, Philippa Kowarsky; Co-Producer, Anna van der Wee; Director, Dror Moreh; Photography, Avner Shahaf; Desigenr, Doron Koren; Editor, Oron Adar; a production of Dror Moreh Productions, Les Films du Poisson, Cinephil, in co-production with Mac Guff, Wild Heart Productions, Arte France, IBA, NDR, RTBF, Radio Canada; Israeli-French-German-Belgian; Dolby; Color; Rated PG-13; 96 minutes; American release date: November 26, 2012. Documentary in which six former heads of the Shin Bet, Israel's secret intelligence agency, talk about their organization's tactics

WITH
Ami Ayalon, Avi Dichter, Yuval Diskin, Carmi Gillon, Yaakov Peri, Avraham Shalom

This film received an Oscar nomination for documentary feature.

Ami Ayalon

Avraham Shalom

Avi Dichter © Sony Classics

Pauline Collins, Maggie Smith

Billy Connolly, Tom Courtenay

QUARTET

(WEINSTEIN CO.) Producers, Finola Dwyer, Stewart MacKinnon; Executive Producers, Jamie Laurenson, Dario Suter, Christoph Daniel, Marc Schmidheiny, Dickon Stainer, Thorsten Schumacher, Xavier Marchand, Dustin Hoffman; Director, Dustin Hoffman; Screenplay, Ronald Harwood, based on his 1999 play; Photography, John De Borman; Designer, Andrew McAlpine; Costumes, Odile Dicks-Mireaux; Music, Dario Marianelli; Music Supervisor, Kle Savidge; Editor, Barney Pilling; Associate Producer, Mark Shivas; Line Producer, Nick O'Hagan; Casting, Lucy Bevan; a BBC Films and DCM Productions presentation of a Headline Pictures and Finola Dwyer Productions production in association with Decca and HanWay Films; British; Dolby; Super 35 Widescreen; Color; Rated PG-13; 97 minutes; American release date: December 7, 2012.

CAST

Jean Horton	**Maggie Smith**
Reggie Paget	**Tom Courtenay**
Wilf Bond	**Billy Connolly**
Cissy Robson	**Pauline Collins**
Cedric Livingston	**Michael Gambon**
Dr. Lucy Cogan	**Sheridan Smith**
Bobby Swanson	**Andrews Sachs**

Dame Gwyneth Jones (Anne Langley), Trevor Peacock (George), David Ryall (Harry), Michael Byrne (Frank White), Ronnie Fox (Nobby), Patricia Loveland (Letitia Davis), Eline Powell (Angelique), Luke Newberry (Simon), Shola Adewusi (Sheryl), Jumayn Hunter (Joey), Aleksandra Duczmal (Marta), Denis Khoroshko (Tadek), Sarah Crowden (Felicity Liddle), Colin Bradbury (Olly Fisher), Patricia Varley (Octavia), Ronnie Hughes (Tony Rose), Jack Honeyborne (Dave Trubeck), John Rawnsley (Nigel), Nuala Willis (Norma McIntyre), Melodie Waddingham (Marion Reed), Cynthia Morey (Lottie Yates), John Heley (Leo Cassell), Graeme Scott (Fred), John Georgiadis (Bill), Ita Herbert (Regina), Ania Duczmal (Eva), Cyril Davey ("Flat Piano" Resident), Esme Penry-Davey (Young Pianist), Virginia Bradbury (Daisy), Isla Mathieson, Iona Mathieson (Young Violinists), Claudia Mellor (Lady Gaga Girl), Penelope Zagoul (Cleaner), Helen Bradbury (Daisy's Mother), Jennifer Spillane (Waltzing Neurologist), Catherine Wilson, David Christian, Rashid Karapiet, Arther 'Arturo' Nightingale, Vass Anderson, Desmond Longfield, Michael Pearn, Peta Bartlett, Jill Pert, Marina Banfield, Barbara Head, Martin Kennon, Valerie Barnes, Morrison Thomas (Residents)

At a home for retired musicians, a trio of classical singers are joined by their former partner who had split with the group years ago when her ego dictated she embark on a solo career.

Michael Gambon © Weinstein Co.

Billy Connolly, Maggie Smith, Tom Courtenay, Pauline Collins

HELENO

(SCREEN MEDIA) Producers, José Henrique Fonseca, Rodrigo Teixeira, Eduardo Pop, Rodrigo Santoro; Executive Producers, Beto Bruno, Elaine Ferreira; Director, José Henrique Fonseca; Screenplay, José Henrique Fonseca, Felipe Bragança, Fernando Castets; Photography, Walter Carvalho; Designer, Marlise Storchi; Costumes, Rita Murtinho; Music, Berna Ceppas; Editor, Sérgio Mekler; Brazilian, 2011; Dolby; Super 35 Widescreen; Black and white; Rated R; 116 minutes; American release date: December 7, 2012

CAST
Heleno de Freitas	**Rodrigo Santoro**
Edite	**Priscila Assum**
Carlito Rocha	**Othon Bastos**
Diamantina	**Angie Cepeda**
Silvia	**Aline Moraes**
Alberto	**Erom Cordeiro**

Orã Figueiredo (Bezerra), Jean Pirre Noher (Dr. Souza Lima), Duda Ribeiro (Cesar)

The true story of charismatic Brazilian soccer star Heleno de Freitas, whose wild and self-destructive lifestyle caught up with him at the age of 39.

Rodrigo Santoro

Rodrigo Santoro © Screen Media

Stephen Fry © First Run Features

WAGNER & ME

(FIRST RUN FEATURES) Executive Producers, Lucy Ward, Adam Barker (BBC), John Marshall (Screen East); Producer/Director, Patrick McGrady; Photography, Jeremy Irving; Editor, Amanda Young; a Wavelength Production in association with the BBC; British, 2010 (Originally presented on TV in the UK); Stereo; Color; HD; Not rated; 89 minutes; American release date: December 7, 2012. Documentary in which actor Stephen Fry examines the music of Richard Wagner and his darker associations with anti-Semitism.

WITH
Stephen Fry

Laura Linney, Bill Murray

Olivia Williams, Bill Murray, Olivia Colman, Samuel West

Olivia Williams, Samuel West, Elizabeth Wilson, Olivia Colman, Bill Murray

HYDE PARK ON HUDSON

(FOCUS) Producers, Kevin Loader, Roger Michell, David Aukin; Executive Producer, Tessa Ross; Director, Roger Michell; Screenplay, Richard Nelson; Photography, Lol Crawley; Designer, Simon Bowles; Costumes, Dinah Collin; Music, Jeremy Sams; Editor, Nicolas Gaster; Casting, Gail Stevens, Ellen Lewis; a Film4 presentation of a Free Range film/Daybreak Pictures production; British; Dolby; HD Widescreen; Deluxe color; Rated R; 94 minutes; American release date: December 7, 2012

CAST

Frankin Roosevelt	**Bill Murray**
Margaret "Daisy" Suckley	**Laura Linney**
King George VI (Bertie)	**Samuel West**
Elizabeth	**Olivia Colman**
Missy	**Elizabeth Marvel**
Eleanor	**Olivia Williams**
Mrs. Roosevelt	**Elizabeth Wilson**
Tommy	**Martin McDougall**
Cameron	**Andrew Havill**
Daisy's Aunt	**Eleanor Bron**
Mrs. Astor	**Nancy Baldwin**

Tim Beckmann, Guy Paul, Eben Young (President's Aides), Samantha Dakin (Mary the Maid), Buffy Davis (Cook), Morgan Deare (Plumber), Tim Ahern, Tommy Campbell, Jeff Mash, Kevin Millington (Hungry Drivers), Nell Mooney (Superstitious Maid), Robert G. Slade (Waiter), Jonathan Brewer (Ish-ti-opi), Kumiko Konishi (Princess Te Ata), Blake Ritson (Butler), Parker Sawyers (Thomas), James McNeill (Photographer), The British Imperial Military Band, The Amersham Band (Brass Bands)

President Franklin Roosevelt invites his mistress Daisy Suckley to join him at Hyde Park where he is paying host to the King of England, making an historic US visit.

Olivia Williams, Laura Linney, Bill Murray © Focus Features

BARBARA

(ADOPT FILMS) Producers, Florian Koerner von Gustorf, Michael Weber; Director/Screenplay, Christian Petzold; Photography, Hans Fromm; Designer, K.D. Gruber; Costumes, Anette Guther; Music, Stefan Will; Editor, Bettina Böhler; Casting, Simone Bär; The Match Factory presentation of a Schramm Film Koerner & Weber production in coproduction with ZDF and ARTE; German; Color; Rated PG-13; 105 minutes; American release date: December 21, 2012

CAST

Barbara Wolff	**Nina Hoss**
André	**Ronald Zehrfeld**
Klaus Schütz	**Rainer Bock**
Assistant to Doctor Schulze	**Christina Hecke**
Ward Nurse Schlösser	**Claudia Geisler**
Jörg	**Mark Waschke**
Angelo	**Deniz Petzold**
Stella	**Jasna Fritzi Bauer**
Gerhard	**Peter Benedict**
Caretaker Bungert	**Rosa Enskat**

Peter Weiss, Carolin Haupt (Medical Students), Pee-Uwe Teska (Waiter in Resort Café), Elisabeth Lehmann (Young Waitress), Thomas Neumann (Pensioner at the Car), Thomas Bading (Piano Tuner), Susanne Bormann (Steffi), Jannik Schümann (Mario), Alicia von Rittberg (Angie), Selin Barbara Petzold (Maria), Anette Daugardt, Jean Parschel (Colleagues of Schütz), Christoph Krix (André's Neighbor), Kirsten Block (Friedl Schütz), Irene Rindje (Friedl's Sister)

As punishment for applying for an exit visa from East Germany, Dr. Barbara Wolff is transferred from her prestigious position at a Berlin hospital to a small pediatric facility in the country.

Nina Hoss

Nina Hoss, Ronald Zehrfeld

Ronald Zehrfeld

Nina Hoss

Nina Hoss, Mark Waschke © Adopt Films

THE IMPOSSIBLE

(SUMMIT) Producers, Belén Atienza, Álvaro Augustin, Enrique López-Lavigne, Ghislain Barrois; Executive Producers, Sandra Hermida, Javier Ugarte; Delegate Producer, Jaime Ortiz de Artiñano; Director, J.A. Bayona; Screenplay, Sergio G. Sánchez; Story, María Belón; Photography, Óscar Faura; Designer, Eugenio Caballero; Music, Fernando Velázquez; Editors, Elena Ruíz, Bernat Vilaplana; Casting, Shaheen Baig; Special Effects, EFE-X-Efectos Especiales (Madrid); Miniature Models & Effects, Magicon GmBH (Munich); Wave Design, Edinburgh Designs Limited; a Mediaset España presentation of an Apaches Entertainment and Telecino Cinema production in association with La Trini Canal+, ICAA, IVAC and Generalitat Valenciana; Spanish; Dolby; Super 35 Widescreen; Deluxe color; Rated PG-13; 114 minutes; American release date: December 21, 2012

Naomi Watts, Tom Holland © Summit Entertainment

CAST

Maria	**Naomi Watts**
Henry	**Ewan McGregor**
Lucas	**Tom Holland**
Thomas	**Samuel Joslin**
Simon	**Oaklee Pendergast**
Simone	**Marta Etura**
Karl	**Sönke Möhring**
Old Woman	**Geraldine Chaplin**
Caregiver	**Ploy Jindachote**
Red Cross Nurse	**Jomjaoi Sae-Limh**
Daniel	**Johan Sundberg**
Daniel's Father	**Jan Roland Sundberg**
Old Thai Man	**La-Orng Thongruang**
Young Thai Man	**Tor Klathaley**
Mr. Benstrom	**Douglas Johansson**
Morten Benstrom	**Emilio Riccardi**

Vorarat Jutakeo (Doctor in Stockroom), Karun Konsaman (Young Nurse in Stockroom), Nicola Harrison (Woman in charge of Simon and Thomas), John Albasiny (Oliver Tudpole), Gitte Witt (Norwegian Patient), Bruce Blain, Cecilia Arnold (American Tourists), Peter Tuinstra (American Tourist on Orchid Roof), Esther Davis (Volunteer in Children's Tent), Dominic Power (Tourist Near the Orchid), Sarinrat Thomas (Operating Nurse), Oak Keerati, Namfon Pakdee (Orchid Employees), Wipawee Charoenpura (Woman in Children's Minibus), Laura Power (Young Nurse in Airplane), Kowit Wattanakul (Henry's Pick-Up Driver), Zoe Popham, Danai Thiengdham, Ronnie Eide (Tourists in Henry's Pick-Up), Bonnie Jo Hutchinson, Jean-Loup Pilblad, Franky Gun (Tourists at Bus Station), Giovani Agresti (Tourist looking for Francesca), Georgina Baert, David Bruce, Natalie Lorence, Sverre Golten, Clare Louise Plunkett (People looking for Relatives), Raphaël Dewaerseghers (Naked Man), Pisamai Pakdeevjit, Aratchporn Satead, Jakapong Srichaem (Thai Family in Stockroom), Simon Blyberg (Ferdinand), Christopher Byrd (Dieter), Georgina Winters, Dina Kiseleva, Tan Daniel Demir (Patients in Takua Pa Hospital), Krittanai Yongtrakull (Emergency Nurse), Takashi Hasegawa (Japanese Tourist), Kristen Mandel (Redheaded Woman), Sam Holland, Harry Holland (Kids in Tent), Mara Garcia Garcia (Kid in Car)

Samuel Joslin, Ewan McGregor, Oaklee Pendergast

While vacationing in Thailand at Christmastime of 2004, a young couple and their three sons are separated when an unprecedented Tsunami strikes their resort.

This film received an Oscar nomination for actress (Watts).

Samuel Joslin, Oaklee Pendergast, Tom Holland, Ewan McGregor, Naomi Watts

Sam Reilly, Kristen Stewart, Garrett Hedlund

Sam Reilly, Garrett Hedlund

Sam Reilly, Alice Braga © IFC Films

ON THE ROAD

(IFC FILMS) Producers, Nathanael Karmitz, Charles Gillbert, Rebecca Yeldham, Roman Coppola; Executive Producers, Francis Ford Coppola, John Williams, Jerry Leder, Tessa Ross, Arpad Busson; Associate Producers, Peter Cavaney, Marin Karmitz; Director, Walter Salles; Screenplay, José Rivera; Based on the 1957 novel by Jack Kerouac; Photography, Eric Gautier; Designer, Carlos Conti; Costumes, Danny Glicker; Music, Gustavo Santaolalla, featuring Charlie Haden, Brian Blade; Music Supervisor, Lynn Fainchtein; Editor, Francois Gediger; Casting, David Rubin, Richard Hicks,; a Sundance Selects, MK2 and American Zoetrope presentation of a Jerry Leder Company production in association with Vanguard Films in association with Film4 in co-production with France 2 Cinéma with the participation of France Télévisions, Canal+ and Cine +, MK2 in coproduction with Videofilmes; French-Brazilian; Dolby; Super 35 Widescreen; Color; Rated R; 124 minutes; American release date: December 21, 2012

CAST

Dean Moriarty/Neal Cassady	**Garrett Hedlund**
Sal Paradise/Jack Kerouac	**Sam Riley**
Marylou/LuAnne Henderson	**Kristen Stewart**
Jane/Joan Vollmer	**Amy Adams**
Carlo Marx/Allen Ginsberg	**Tom Sturridge**
Ed Dunkle/Al Hinkle	**Danny Morgan**
Terry/Bea Franco	**Alice Braga**
Ma Paradise	**Marie-Ginette Guay**
Galatéa Dunkle/Helen Hinkle	**Elisabeth Moss**
Camille/Carolyn Cassady	**Kristen Dunst**
Old Bull Lee/William S. Burroughs	**Viggo Mortensen**
Tall Thin Salesman	**Steve Buscemi**
Walter	**Terrence Howard**
Oazacan Girl	**Ximena Adriana**
Vicki	**Sarah Allen**
Newlyweds	**Clara Altimas, Dan Beirne**
Chevy Owner	**Leif Anderson**

Ricardo Andres (Terry's Father), Tetchena Bellange (Walter's Wife), Glen Bowser (Denver Police), Doug Boyd (Grocery Store Owner), Kim Bubbs (Laura), Jason Cavalier (Disgruntled Driver), Joe Chrest (Virginia Cop), Patrick Costello (Chad King), Michael Daigle (Papa Leo Paradise), Eric Davis (Paul), Larry Day (Policeman, New Jersey), Janyève Denoncourt (Joanie, 17 months), Sean J. Dillingham (Cotton Foreman), Paul Dillon (Montana Slim), Joel Figueroa (Victor), Frank Fontaine (Paul's Father), Isa Garcia (Johnny), Kyle Gatehouse (Migrant Worker), Barbara Glover (Okie Woman), David Gow (Parking Lot Boss), Imogen Haworth (Nin Paradise), Matthew Hayes Deano (Ray), Robert Higden (Sam Pharmacy), Arthur Holden (Maitre D'), Tiio Horn (Rita Bettancourt), Omoze Idehenre (Black Woman), Asao Ikegami (Japanese Co-Worker), Giselle Itié (Tonia), Daniel Kash (Henry Glass), Joey Klein (Tom Saybrook), Greg Kramer (Mississippi Gene), Neil Kroetsch (Denver Barber), Jake La Botz (Okie Hitchhiker), Jordane Lavoie (Amy, 1 month), Roc Lafortune (Hotel Clerk), Adam LeBlanc (Remi Boncoeur), Terry Leonard (Pecos Truck Driver), Alison Louder (Dorie), Bronwen Martel (Paul's Mother), Rocky Marquette (Alfred), Lilia Mendoza (Venezuelan Girl), Murphy Ian Moberly (Ray Lee), Luc Morrissette (Old Tramp), George Morris (Old Bartender), Coati Mundi (Slim Gaillard), Jacob Ortiz (Johnny), Felix Pennell (Blond Kid), Chris Ratz (Migrant Truck Driver), Niko Romberg (Migrant Worker), Andaluz Russell (Dona Gregoria), Barry Del Sherman (Dynamite Truck Driver), Mark Trafford (Broadway Sam), Daniela Wong, Gina Vargas (Whorehouse Girls), Madison Wolfe (Dodie Lee, 8), Moira Wylie (Paul's Old Aunt), Giovanna Zacarias (Red Head), Martin Auguste, Wray Downes, Martin Heslop, Moise Yawo Matey (Walter's Jazz Band), Archie Alleyne, Jude Charles, Ronald Johnston (Slim's Band)

A young writer sets out on a cross-country trip with the free-spirited Dean Moriarty and his girlfriend Marylou, the trio hoping to escape the conformity of American life.

Hugh Jackman, Anne Hathaway

Hugh Jackman

Isabelle Allen, Hugh Jackman

LES MISÉRABLES

(UNIVERSAL) Producers, Tim Bevan, Eric Fellner, Debra Hayward, Cameron Mackintosh; Executive Producers, Liza Chasin, Angela Morrison, Nicholas Allott, F. Richard Pappas; Director, Tom Hooper; Screenplay, William Nicholson, Alain Boublil, Claude-Michel Schönberg, Herbert Kretzmer; Based on the 1980 stage musical by Alain Boublil and Claude-Michel Schönberg, from the 1862 novel by Victor Hugo; Photography, Danny Cohen; Designer, Eve Stewart; Costumes, Paco Delgado; Music, Claude-Michel Schönberg; English Lyrics, Herbert Kretzmer; Editors, Melanie Ann Oliver, Chris Dickens; Orichestrations, Anne Dudley, Stephen Metcalfe; Music Director, Stephen Brooker; Visual Effects Supervisor, Richard Bain; Hair & Makeup Designer, Lisa Westcott; Choreographer, Liam Steel; Casting, Nina Gold; a Working Title Films/Cameron Mackintosh production, presented in association with Relativity Media; British; Dolby; Technicolor; Rated PG-13; 157 minutes; American release date: December 25, 2012

CAST

Jean Valjean	**Hugh Jackman**
Javert	**Russell Crowe**
Fantine	**Anne Hathaway**
Cosette	**Amanda Seyfried**
Thénardier	**Sacha Baron Cohen**
Madame Thénardier	**Helena Bonham Carter**
Marius	**Eddie Redmayne**
Enjolras	**Aaron Tveit**
Éponine	**Samantha Barks**
Gavroche	**Daniel Huttlestone**
Bishop	**Colm Wilkinson**
Young Cosette	**Isabelle Allen**
Fauchelevent	**Stephen Tate**
Bamatabois	**Bertie Carvel**
Gillenormand	**Patrick Godfrey**
Courfeyrac	**Fra Fee**
Foreman	**Michael Jibson**
Pimp	**Daniel Evans**

Cavin Cornwall, Josef Altin, David Hawley, Adam Jones, John Barr (Convicts), Tony Rohr (Overseer), Richard Dixon (Mairie Officer), Andy Beckwith (Inkeeper), Stephen Bent (Jailer), Georgie Glen (Madame Baptistine), Heather Chasen (Madame Magloire), Paul Thornley, Paul Howell (Constables), Kate Fleetwood, Hannah Waddingham, Clare Foster, Kirsty Hoiles, Jenna Boyd, Alice Fearn, Alison Tennant, Marilyn Cutts, Cathy Breeze (Factory Women), John Albasiny (Factory Onlooker), Tim Downie (Brevet), Andrew Havill (Cochepaille), Dick Ward (Bamatabois' Valet), Nicola Sloane (Hair Crone), David Stoller, Ross McCormack, Jaygann Ayeh (Sailors), Adrian Scarborough (Toothman), Frances Ruffelle, Lynne Wilmot, Charlotte Spencer (Whores), Julia Worsley (Head Whore), Keith Dunphy (Client), Ashley Artus (Pawn Broker), John Surman (Organ-Grinder), David Cann (Magistrate), James Simmons (Champmathieu), Polly Kemp (Nursing Sister), Ian Pirie (Babet), Adam Pearce (Brujon), Julian Bleach (Claquesous), Marc Pickering (Montparnasse), Natalya Wallace (Young Éponine), Phil Snowden, Hadrian Delacey (Customers), Lottie Steer (Baby), Sam Parks (Tall Customer), Mark Donovan (Portly Customer), Lewis Kirk, Leighton Rafferty (Handsome Soldiers), Peter Mair, Jack Chissick (Father Christmases), Dianne Pilkington, Robyn North (Inn Whores), Norma Atallah (Mother Whore), Mark Roper, Paul Leonard (Citizens), Miles Roughley, Cameron Strefford, Alfie Davis, Joseph West (Gavroche's Urchins), Joel Phillimore, Jacqueline Dankworth, Amelia Jefford, Chris Barnes (Beggars), Richard Cordery (Duc De Raguse), Killian Donnelly (Combeferre), Gabriel Vick (Feuilly), George Blagden (Grantaire), Hugh Skinner (Joly), Stuart Neal (Lesgles), Alistair Brammer (Prouvaire), Iwan Lewis (Bahorel), Katy Secombe (Madame Huchloup), Hadley Fraser (Army Officer), Linzi Hateley, Gemma Wardle, Gina Beck, Katie Hall, Lisa Hull, Andrea Deck, Jessica Duncan, Kerry Ingram (Turning Women), John Warnaby (Majordomo), Mike Sarne (Father Mabeuf), Freya Parks (Café Barmaid), Ellie Beaven (Mother)

Following a 19-year prison sentence, Jean Valjean's efforts to lead a better life are constantly tested by the determined Inspector Javert, who hounds him throughout his life for breaking parole, as France is torn apart by revolution.

2012 Academy Award Winner for Best Supporting Actress (Anne Hathaway), Best Makeup and Hairstyling, and Best Sound Mixing.

This film received additional Oscar nominations for picture, actor (Jackman), costume design,   and original song ("Suddenly").

Helena Bonham Carter, Isabelle Allen, Sacha Baron Cohen

Samantha Barks

Aaron Tveit

Eddie Redmayne, Amanda Seyfried

Russell Crowe

Anne Hathaway © Universal Studios

TABU

(ADOPT FILMS) Producers, Luís Urbano, Sandro Aguilar; Executive Producer, Luís Urbano; Co-Producers, Janine Jackowski, Jonas Dornbach, Maren Ade, Fabiono Gullane, Caio Gullane, Thomas Ordonneau; Director, Miguel Gomes; Screenplay, Miguel Gomes, Mariana Ricardo; Photography, Rui Poças; Designer, Bruno Duarte; Costumes, Silva Grabowski; Editors, Telmo Churro, Miguel Gomes; an O Som e a Fúria presentation in co-production with Komplizen Film, Gullane, Shellac Sud and ZDF/Arte; Portuguese; Black and white; Not rated; 118 minutes; American release date: December 26, 2012

Ana Moreira

CAST
Pilar	**Teresa Madruga**
Old Aurora	**Laura Soveral**
Young Aurora	**Ana Moreira**
Old Ventura	**Henrique Espirito Santo**
Young Ventura	**Carloto Cotta**
Santa	**Isabel Cardoso**
Aurora's Husband	**Ivo Müller**
Mário	**Manuel Mesquita**

Pilar becomes concerned over the increasingly eratic behavior of her elderly neighbor, who, it turns out, was a Portuguse heiress once involved in an elicit affair with a dashing adventurer.

Ana Moreira, Carloto Cotta

Laura Soveral

Isabel Cardoso © Adopt Films

FOREIGN FILMS B

2012 Releases / January 1–December 31

THE HUNTER (Olive Films) a.k.a. *Shekarchi*; Producer, Thanassis Karathanos, Mohammad Reza Takhtkeshian; Director/Screenplay, Rafi Pitts; Photography, Mohammad Davudi; Designer, Malak Khazai; Editor, Hassan Hassandoost; a Twenty Twenty Vision in co-production with Aftab Negaran Film Productions presentation; Iranian-German, 2012; Dolby; Color; Not rated; 92 minutes; American release date: January 4, 2012. **CAST:** Rafi Pitts (Ali Alavi), Mitra Hajjar (Sara P. Alavi, Ali's Wife), Ali Nicksaulat (Policeman, Commander), Hassan Ghalenoi (Policeman, Soldier), Manoochehr Rahimi (Inspector), Ismaïl Amani (Young Man in Warehouse), Nasser Madahi (Basiri, Old Night Guard), Ali Mazinani (Reza, Young Night Guard), Ossta Shah-Tir (Ali's Father), Malak Khazai (Ali's Mother), Saba Yaghoobi (Saba Alavi, Ali's Daughter), Gholamreza Rajabzadeh (Nazem, Police Officer), Mahmoud Babai, Javad Nazari, Arash Faraghinejad, Abbas Hassanzadeh (Policemen), Hossein Nickbakht (Hotel Receptionist), Shoja'edin Ghanaei (Doctor), Said Hajmohammadi, Amir Ayoubi, Mansour Dowlatmand, Ebrahim Safarpour (Police Officers), Sara Kamrani (Orphanage Nurse), Fatemeh Alijani (Orphanage Receptionist)

Rafi Pitts in *The Hunter* © Olive Films

POM POKO (Gkids) a.k.a. *Heisei tanuki gassen ponpoko*; Producers, Ned Lott, Toshio Suzuki, Yasuyoshi Tokuma; Director/Screenplay, Isao Takahata; Based on the story *Futago no hoshi* by Kenji Miyazawa; Photography, Atsushi Okui; Art Director, Kazuo Oga; Animation Director, Shinji Otsuka; Character Design, Shinji Otsuka; Casting, Ned Lott; Japanese, 1994; Dolby; Technicolor; Rated PG; 119 minutes; American release date: January 6, 2012. **VOICE CAST:** Jillian Bowen (Kiyo), Clancy Brown (Gonta), David Oliver Cohen (Ponkichi), Olivia d'Abo (Koru), John Di Maggio (Ryûtarô), Marc Donato (Sasuke), Brian George (Hage Kincho), Jess Harnell (Gyobu), Wally Kurth (Tamasaburô), Maurice LaMarche (Narrator), Tress MacNeille (Oroku), Mark Moseley (Reporter), Brian Posehn (Hayashi), Kevin Michael Richardson (Bunta, Wonderland President), J.K. Simmons (Seizaemon), Andre Stojka (Osho), Russi Taylor (Otama), Jonathan Taylor Thomas (Shoukichi), Reeve Carney, Ike Eisenmann (Additional Voices)

Pom Poko © Gkids

ROBINSON IN RUINS (BFI) Producer/Director/Screenplay/Phiotography/Editor, Patrick Keiller; Executive Producer, Keith Griffiths; a Patrick Keiller at the Royal College of Art production in association with Illuminations Films; British, 2010; Dolby; Color; HD; Not rated; 100 minutes; American release date: January 13, 2012. Experimental film on land reform in England; **WITH:** Vanessa Redgrave (Narrator).

VETTAI (UTV) Producers, N. Subash Chandrabose, Ronnie Screwvala; Director, N. Linguswamy; Screenplay, N. Linguswamy, Brinda Sarathy; Photography, Nirav Shah; Music, Yuvan Shankar Raja; Editor, Anthony Gonsalves; a Thirupathi Brothers production; Indian; Color; Not rated; 150 minutes; American release date: January 13, 2012. **CAST:** Madhavan (Thirumurthi), Arya (Gurumurthi), Sameera Reddy (Vasanthi), Amala Paul (Jayanthi), Nasser (Police), Ashutosh Rana (Annachi), Sreejith Ravi (Suruli), Muthukumar (Mari), Thambi Ramayya (Constable), Shanmugha Rajan (Inspector Kulasekhara Pandian), Rajeev Ravindranathan (Goutham)

ALBATROSS (IFC Films) Producer, Adrian Sturges; Executive Producers, Steve Christian, Marc Samuelson; Director, Niall McCormick; Screenplay, Tamzin Rafn; Photography, Jan Jonaeus; Designer, Paul Cripps; Costumes, Charlotte Holdich; Music, Jack C. Arnold; Editor, Mark Eckersley; Casting, Shaheen Baig; a CinemaNX and Isle of Man Film presentation; British, 2011; Dolby; Widescreen; Color; HD; Not rated; 88 minutes; American release date: January 13, 2012. **CAST:** Sebastian Koch (Jonathan), Julia Ormond (Joa), Felicity Jones (Beth), Peter Vaughan (Grandpa), Jessica Brown Findlay (Emelia), Harry Treadaway (Jake), Thomas Brodie-Sangster (Mark), Josef Altin (Dare), Justin Edwards (Policeman), David Cahn (Grumpy Man), Sheila Monaghan (Edna), Katie Overd (Posy), Billy Seymour (Spotty Youth), Alexis Zegerman (Manageress), Marie-France Alvarez (Customer), Chandra Ruegg (Waitress), Hazel Douglas (Granny), Kenneth Collard (Angry Man), Laura Power (Brainbox Girl), Mark Ryder (Rich), Arthur Nightingale (Porter), Angus Barnett (Guest)

Jessica Brown Findlay, Felicity Jones in *Albatross* © IFC Films

FULLMETAL ALCHEMIST: THE SACRED STAR OF MILOS (Shochiku) a.k.a. *Hagane no renkinjutsushi: Mirosu no seinaru hoshi*; Producers, Masahiko Minami, Hiro Marayuma, Ryo Oyama, Noboyuki Kurashige, Fumi Teraishi, Arimasa Okada, Shin Furukawa; Director, Kazuya Murata; Screenplay, Yuichi Shinbo; Based on characters created by Hiromu Arakawa in the manga *Hagane no renkinjutsushi* (2001-10); Photography, Yoshiyuki Takei; Art Directors, Kazuo Ogura, Tomoaki Okada; Music, Taro Iwashirô; Editor, Kumiko Sakamoto; Character Designer/Chief Animation Director, Ken'ichi Konishi; a Bones production; Japanese, 2011; Dolby; Color; HD; Not rated; 110 minutes; American release date: January 20, 2012. **VOICE CAST:** Rie Kugimiya (Alphonse Elric), Romi Park (Edward Elric), Toshiyuki Morikawa (Melvin Voyager), Fumiko Orikasa (Riza Hawkeye), Kenji Utsumi (Alex Louis Armstrong), Maaya Sakamoto (Julia Crichton), Megumi Takamoto (Winry Rockbell), Shinichirô Miki (Cmdr. Col. Roy Mustang)

Fullmetal Alchemist © Shochiku

THE VIRAL FACTOR (Emperor Motion Pictures) a.k.a. *Jik zin*; Producer, Candy Leung; Director, Dante Lam; Screenplay, Dante Lam, Jack Ng; Story, Dante Lam, Candy Leung; Photography, Kenny Tse; Music, Peter Kam; Editor, Azrael Chung; Hong Kong; Dolby; Super 35 Widescreen; Color; Not rated; 120 minutes; American release date: January 20, 2012. **CAST:** Jay Chou (Jon Man), Nicholas Tse (Man Yeung), Lin Peng (Rachel), Bai Bing (Ice), Andy On (Sean), Carl Ng (Ross), Liu Kai-chi (Man Tin, Jon and Wan's Father), Elaine Jin (Fung Ling, Jon and Wan's Mother), Issam M. Husseini (Doctor), Philip Keung (Russell)

Jay Chou in *The Viral Factor* © Emperor Motion Pictures

AFTER FALL, WINTER (FilmBuff) Producers, Eric Shaeffer, Ed Flaherty, Zach Miller; Director/Screenplay, Eric Schaeffer; Photography, Zoran Veljkovic; Music, Matthew Puckett; Editor, Frank Reynolds; a D3 Pictures and Five Minutes Before the Miracle production; French-American; Color; HD; 130 minutes; Release date: January 27, 2012. **CAST:** Eric Schaeffer (Michael), Lizzie Brocheré (Sophie), Sydney McCann (Chloe), Rebecca Jameson (Nurse), Jimmy King (Thug), Manuel Bonnet (Robert), Anna Gaylor (Cecille), Sylvie Loeillet (Natalie), Christian Mulot (Charles), Akéla Sari (Gypsy), Niseema Theillaud (Sophie's Mother), Deborah Twiss (Caroline), Matthias Van Khache (Antoine)

HOW MUCH DOES YOUR BUILDING WEIGH, MR. FOSTER? (First Run Features) Producer, Elena Ochoa; Executive Producer, Antonio Sanz; Directors, Norberto Lopez Amado, Carlos Carcas; Screenplay/Narrator, Deyan Sudjic; Photography, Valentin Alvarez; Music, Joan Valent; Editor, Paco Cozar; an Art Commissioners production in association with Aiete Ariane Films; British-Spanish, 2010; Dolby; Color; Not rated; 78 minutes; American release date:

January 27, 2012. Documentary on one of the world's premiere architects, Norman Foster; **WITH:** Norman Foster.

Norman Foster in *How Much Does You Building Weigh, Mr Foster?* © First Run Features

ALL'S WELL, ENDS WELL 2012 (China Lion) a.k.a. *Baat seng bou hei*; Producers, Amy Chin, Wong Bak-ming; Director, Chan Hing-ka; Screenplay, Chan Hing-ka, Janet Chun; Photography, Man Po Cheung; Editor, Cheung Ka-fai; a Pegasus Motion Pictures, Icon Pictures production; Chinese; Dolby; Color; Not rated; 115 minutes; American release date; January 27, 2012. **CAST:** Donnie Yen (Carl Tam), Sandra Ng (Chelsia), Chapman To (Hugo), Yan Ni (Cecilia), Louis Koo (Holland Kin), Julie Sun (Kelly Chen), Ronald Cheng (Shalala)

All's Well Ends Well © China Lion

THE WICKER TREE (Anchor Bay) Producers, Peter Snell, Peter Watson-Wood; Executive Producer, Alastair Gourlay; Director/Screenplay, Robin Hardy, based on his 2006 novel *Cowboys for Christ*; Photography, Jan Pester; Designer, Laurel Wear; Costumes, David Blight; Music, John Scott; Additional Music/Songs, Keith Easdale; Editor, Sean Barton; Casting, Kate Plantin; a British Lion presentation; British; Dolby; Color; Rated R; 96 minutes; American release date: January 27, 2012. **CAST:** Graham McTavish (Sir Lachlan Morrison), Jacqueline Leonard (Lady Delia Morrison), Henry Garrett (Steve Thomson), Honeysuckle Weeks (Lolly), Clive Russell (Beame), Christopher Lee (Old Man), Brittania Nicol (Beth Boothby), David Plimmer (Jack), Keira McMillan (Morag), James Mapes (Rev. Moriarty), Ailidh Mackay (Anthea), Kirstin Murray (Celebrity Interviewer), Keith Warwick (Donald Dee), Prue Clarke (Mary Hellier), Lesley Mackie (Daisy), Terry Wale (Murdoch), Iain Stuart Robertson (Peter McNeil), Scott Hoatson (Carl), Christopher Leveaux (Christopher), Will Thompson (Simon), Mark Williams (Paul), Astrid Azurdia (Patricia Gow), Alessandro Conetta (Orlando), Christopher Fosh, Graham Wadsworth (Trailer Trash Video Dancers), St. Clair Leveaux (Marion), Alistair Maxwell (Angus), John Paul McGilvray (Danny), Bill Murdoch (Rev. McLeod), Ben Sullivan (Young Lachlan)

Brittania Nicol in *The Wicker Tree* © Anchor Bay

EK MAIN AUR EKK TU (UTV) Producers, Hiroo Yash Johar, Karan Johar, Ronnie Screwvala; Director, Shakun Batra; Screenplay, Ayesha Devitre, Shakun Batra; Photography, David Macdonald; Designer, Shashaank Tere; Costumes, Manish Malhotra; Music, Amit Trivedi; Lyrics, Amitabh Bhattacharya; Editor, Asif Ali Shaikh; a Dharma Productions presentation; Indian; Color; Not rated; 110 minutes; American release date: February 10, 2012. **CAST:** Imran Khan (Rahul Kapoor), Kareena Kapoor (Riana Braganza), Boman Irani (Mr. Kapoor), Ratna Pathak Shah (Mrs. Kapoor), Ram Kapoor (Mr. Bulani), Rajesh Khattar (Mr. Shah), Manasi Scott (Riana's Sister), Soniya Mehra (Anusha), Zenobia Shroff (Nicole Braganza), Avantika Malik Khan (Auntyji), Dana Lewis (Mrs. Bulani), Kevin Flaherty (Christmas Tree Father), Noah Rotroff (Christmas Tree Son), Mukul Chadda (Riana's Brother in Law)

Imran Khan, Kareena Kapoor in *Ek Main aur Ekk Tu* © UTV

DEATH OF THE VIRGIN (Indican) Producers/Screenplay, Joseph Tito, Silvio Oddi; Director, Joseph Tito; Photography, Michele De Angelis; Music, Luigi Maiello; Editor, Alessandro Giordani; Special Effects Makeup, Domiziano Cristopharo; Jeo Productions; Italian-Canadian, 2009; Dolby; Color; Not rated; 103 minutes; American release date: February 10, 2012. **CAST:** Natasha Allen (May), Daniel Baldock (Father John), Maria Grazia Cucinotta (Claudia), Richard Eckles (Jason), Ingrid Evans (Ruth), Jennifer Healy (Lisa), Silvio Oddi (Inspector), Grace Pieniazek (Laura), Joseph Tito (Mark), Maurizio Vacca (Giuseppe), Linda Valades (Sandra), Marc Aurellio (Alessandro), Kate Sandison (Emma), Jaguse

Vrankova (Julia), Gianluca Rovagna (Jim), Beatrice Ceste (Gianetta), Carla Manera (Iris), Natale Tulipani (Monsignor Tucci), Cici Orsi (Nun), Clelia Riva (Sonya), Enzo Mazzullo, Donato Tito (Police Officers), Paolo Data Blin (David), Elisabeth Yorke (Head Nurse), Laura Della Valle (Nurse), Cecilia Salomone (Young May), Cinzia Tibaldi, Silvia Faedda, Danela Febino (Crazy Women), Roberta Marchetti (Virgin Mary), Stefania Foglia, Elisa Garetto, Concetta Bevilaqua (Witches)

THE FORGOTTEN SPACE (Doc.Eye Film) Producers, Frank Van Reemst, Joost Verheij; Directors/Screenplay, Allan Sekula, Noël Burch; Co-Producers, Vincent Lucassen, Ebba Sinzinger; Photography, Attila Boa, Wolfgang Thaler; Music, Riccardo Tesi, Louis Andriessen; Editor, Menno Boerema; Narrator, Allan Sekula; a co-production with WilDart Film; Dutch-Austrian, 2010; Color; Digibeta; DV; HD; Not rated; 116 minutes; American release date: February 15, 2012. Documentary on changes in maritime trade.

The Forgotten Space © Doc.Eye Film

MICHAEL (Strand) Producers, Nikolaus Geyrhalter, Markus Glaser, Michael Kitzberger, Wolfgang Widerhofer; Executive Producer, Michael Kitzberger; Director/Screenplay, Markus Schleinzer; Photography, Gerald Kerkletz; Set Designers, Katrin Huber, Gerhard Dohr; Costumes, Hanya Barakat; Editor, Wolfgang Widerhofer; Casting, Carmen Loley, Martina Poel; a Les Films du Losange and NGF presentation; Austrian, 2011; Dolby; Color; Not rated; 96 minutes; American release date: February 15, 2012. **CAST:** Michael Fuith (Michael), David Rauchenberger (Wolfgang), Christine Kain (Mother), Ursula Strauss (Sister), Xaver Winkler, Thomas Pfalzmann (Nephews), Viktor Tremmel (Brother-in-Law), Gisela Salcher (Christa), Simon Jaritz (Bernd), Florian Eisner (Markus), Isolde Wagner, Susanne Rachler, Katrin Thurm, Martin Schwehla (Office Colleagues), David Oberkogler (Ehrnsberger), Olivier Beaurepaire (Man in Park), Samy Goldberger (Boy in park), Martina Poel (Compassionate Mother), Mika Sakurai (Daughter), Paul Karall (Hospital Roommate), Helga Karall (The Girl), Gertraud Ball (The Daughter), Sarah Forstner (The Granddaughter), Alicia Limpahan (Nurse), Selma Hönigschnabl (Doctor), Ullah Sefat (News Agent), Gerhard Lutz (Taxi Driver), Hanus Polak Jr. (Christmas Tree Salesclerk), Barbara Willensdorfer (Martina), Jim Holderied (Martina's Son), Philipp Stöger, Niki Guya, Emrah Dzemailoski (Kartbahn Boys), Samuel Jung (Philipp), Simon Jaritz (Bernd), Markus Schleinzer (Vigorous Father), Firas Azman (Young Employee), Margot Vuga (Tyrol Waitress), Dr. Heidi Kastner (Herself)

PUTIN'S KISS (Kino Lorber) Producer, Helle Faber; Director, Lise Birk Pedersen; Photography, Lars Skree; Music, Tobias Hylander; Editors, Janus Billeskov Jansen, Steen Johannessen; Produced by Monday Production in association with Made in Copenhagen in co-production with DR2/Mette Hoffmann Meyer & ITVS Intl./Sally Jo Fifer; Danish-Russian, 2011; Color; Not rated; 85 minutes; American release date: February 17, 2012. Documentary follows teen Masha Drokova as she joins Nashi, a Kremlin-endorsed youth organization; **WITH:** Masha Drokova

Michael Fuith in *Michael* © Strand Releasing

Vladimir V. Putin, Masha Drokova in *Putin's Kiss* © Kino Lorber

LOVE (China Lion) a.k.a. *Ai*; Producers, Wang Zhongjun, Doze Niu Chen-zer; Director, Doze Niu Chen-zer; Screenplay Tseng Li-ting, Wang Qinan, Doze Niu Chen-zer; Photography, Lee Ping-bin; Designer, Huang Mei-ching; Costumes, Fang Chi-lun; Music, Chen Chien-chi; Editor, Tseng Li-ting; a Huyai Brothers Media Corp., Honto Prod. Co. presentation; Chinese-Tai; Color; Widescreen; Not rated; 127 minutes; American release date: February 17, 2012. **CAST:** Shu Qi (Zoe Fang), Vicky Zhao (Jin Xiaoye), Ethan Ruan (Kuan), Mark Jau (Mark), Peng Yu-yan (Kai), Doze Niu Chen-zer (Uncle Lu), Amber Kuo (Ni), Chen Yi-han (Li Yija), Wang Jingchun (Policeman)

Ethan Ruan, Shu Qi in *Love* © China Lion

CIRKUS COLUMBIA (Strand) Producers, Amra Bakšic Camo, Cedomir Kolar, Mirsad Purivatra, Marc Bachet; Director, Danis Tanoviv; Screenplay, Danis Tanovic, Ivica Đikic; Based on the 2003 novel by Ivica Đikic; Photography, Walther Van den Ende; Designer, Dušan Milavec, Sanda Popovac; Costumes, Jasna Hadžiahmetovic Bekric; Editor, Petar Markovic; The Match Factory presentation of an 2006, A.S.A.P. Films, Autonomous, Studio Maj, Razor Film, Man's Film Productions, Art & Popcorn production; Bosnian-Herzegovinian, 2010; Dolby; Color; Not rated; 113 minutes; American release date: February 17, 2012. **CAST:** Miki Manojlovic (Divko Buntic), Mira Furlan (Lucija), Boris Ler (Martin), Jelena Stupljanin (Azra), Milan Štrljic (Ivanda, Mayor), Mario Knezovic (Pivac, Martin's Friend), Svetislav Goncic (Savo, Army Captain), Almir Mehic (Bill, Guy Who Finds Cats for Divko), Mirza Tanovic(Antisa, Café Owner), Miralem Zupcevic(Leon Dilber, Former Mayor), Mirsad Tuka (Dragan), Ermin Bravo (Gudelj), Slaven Knezovic (Miro), Izudin Barhovic (Major Kostelic), Sead Bejtovic (Staklar), Jasna Omela Bery (Marija Ivanda), Vesna Masic (Jelena Dilber), Miroslav Barnjak (Majstor), Ines Fancovic (Starica), Adnan Besirovic (Zeljko)

Boris Ler, Jelena Stupljanin in *Cirkus Columbia* © Strand Releasing

HOW TO START A REVOLUTION (Seventh Art) Producer, Ruaridh Arrow, Richard Shaw; Executive Producer, James Otis; Director, Ruaridh Arrow; Photography, Philip Bloom; Editor, Mike Crozier; The Big Indy production; British-Egyptian-Serbian-American, 2011; Color; Not rated; 85 minutes; American release date: February 24, 2012. Documentary on Gene Sharp and his writings on nonviolent revolution; **WITH**: Gene Sharp, Robert Helvey, Jamila Raqib.

Gene Sharp in *How to Start a Revolution* © Seventh Art

JODI BREAKERS (Prasar Visions) Producer, Rajesh Rajilal; Director/Screenplay, Ashwini Chaudhary; Music, Salim Sulaiman; Lyrics, Irshad Kamil; Art Director, Aparna Raina; Editor, Biren Mohanty; Indian; Color; Not rated; 130 minutes; American release date: February 24, 2012. **CAST:** R. Madhavan (Sid Khanna), Bipasha Basu (Sonali Agnihotri), Omi Vaidya (Nano), Helen Ji (Madonna), Milind Soman (Mark Parera), Dipannita Sharma (Maggie), Mrinalini Sharma (Ira), Tarana Raja Kappor (Dr. Isha)

TOMORROW, WHEN THE WAR BEGAN (Freestyle) Producers, Michael Boughen, Andrew Mason; Executive Producers, Peter D. Graves, Christopher Mapp, Matthew Street, David Whealy; Director/Screenplay, Stuart Beattie; Based on the 1993 novel by John Marsden; Photography, Ben Nott; Music, Johnny Klimek, Reinhold Heil; Editor, Marcus D'Arcy; an Omnilab Media, Screen Australia presentation, in association with Paramount, of an Ambience Entertainment production; Australian, 2010; Dolby; Super 35 Widescreen; Color; Rated R; 103 minutes; American release date: February 24, 2012. **CAST:** Caitlin Stasey (Ellie Linton), Rachel Hurd-Wood (Corrie Mackenzie), Lincoln Lewis (Kevin Holmes), Deniz Akdeniz (Home Yannos), Phoebe Tonkin (Fiona Maxwell), Chris Pang (Lee Takkam), Ashleigh Cummings (Robyn Mathers), Andy Ryan (Chris Lang), Colin Friels (Dr. Clements), Don Halbert (Mr. Linton), Olivia Pigeot (Mrs. Linton), Stephen Bourke (Police Officer), Kelly Butler (Mrs. Maxwell), Julia Yon (Mrs. Takkam), Dane Carson (Mr. Mathers), Matthew Dale (Mr. Coles), Gary Quay (Senior Soldier), Michael Camilleri (Tanker Driver)

Where are You Taking Me? © Icarus

Lincoln Lewis, Deniz Akdeniz, Caitlin Stasey, Ashleigh Cummings in *Tomorrow, When the War Began* © Freestyle Releasing

WHERE ARE YOU TAKING ME? (Icarus) Producer/Director/Photography, Kimi Takesue; Co-Producer, Richard Beenen; Editors, Kim Takesue, John Walter; Kimikat Productions, in association with Lane Street Pictures; Ugandan-American; Color; HD; Not rated; 72 minutes; Release date: March 2, 2012. Documentary on the public and private places in Uganda.

THE SALT OF LIFE (Zeitgeist) a.k.a. *Gianni e le donne*; Producer, Angelo Barbagallo; Executive Producer, Gaetano Daniele; Director, Gianni Di Gregorio; Screenplay, Gianni Di Gregorio, Valerio Attanasio; Based on a story by Gianni Di Gregorio; Photography, Gogò Bianchi; Designer, Susanna Cascella; Costumes, Silvia Polidori; Music, Ratchev and Carratello; Editor, Marco Spoletini; Casting, Fabiola Banzi, Francesca Borromeo; a BiBi Film – Isaria Production, in collaboration with Rai Cinema; Italian, 2011; Color; Not rated; 90 minutes; American release date: March 2, 2012. **CAST:** Gianni Di Gregorio (Gianni), Valeria de Franciscis Bendoni (Mother), Alfonso Santagata (Alfonso), Elisabetta Piccolomini (Gianni's Wife), Valeria Cavalli (Valeria), Alyn Prandi (Alyn), Kristina Cepraga (Cristina), Michelangelo Ciminale (Michelangelo), Teresa Di Gregorio (Teresa), Lilia Silvi (Lilia), Gabriella Sborgi (Gabriella), Laura Squizzato, Silvia Squizzato (Twins)

Gianni Di Gregorio, Valeria de Franciscis Bendoni, Kristina Cepraga, Lilia Silvi in *The Salt of Life* © Zeitgeist Films

LET THE BULLETS FLY (Variance/Well Go USA) a.k.a. *Rang zidan fei*; Producers, Barbie Tung, Zhao Haicheng, Ma Ke, Albert Lee, Yin Homber; Executive Producers, Albert Yeung, Han Sanping, Ma Ke; Director, Jiang Wen; Screenplay, Zhu Sujin, Shu Ping, Jiang Wen, Guo Junli, Wei Xiao, Li Bukong; Adapted from *Ye Tan Shi Ji* by Ma Shitu; Photography, Zhao Fei; Music, Joe Hisaishi; an Emperor Motion Picture (Intl.) Ltd., Beijing Buyilehu Film and Culture Ltd., China Film Group Corp. presentation; Chinese-Hong Kong, 2010; Dolby; Color; Widescreen; Not rated; 132 minutes; American release date: March 2, 2012. **CAST:** Chow Yun-Fat (Master Huang Fox/The Double), Jiang Wen ("Pocky" Zhang Muzhi/The Governor), Ge You (Counselor Tang), Carina Lau (The Mistress), Shao Bing (Number Two), Liao Fan (Number Three), John Do (Number Four), Li Jing (Number Five), Zhang Mo (Number Six), Wei Xiao (Number Seven), Zhou Yun (Flora), Chen Kun (Hu Wan), Yao Lu (Hu Qian), Jiang Wu (Wu Zhichong), Hun Jun (The Fake Pocky Zhang), Bai Bing (Katama Hafumiko), Hu Ming (Sun Shouyi), Feng Xiaogang (The Dead Counselor), Maio Pu (Tang's Jilted Wife)

Jiang Wen in *Let the Bullets Fly* © Variance Films

LONDON PARIS NEW YORK (Fox STAR Studios) Producers, Shrishti Behl, Goldie Behl; Director/Screenplay, Anu Menon; Dialogue, Anu Menon, Ritu Bhatia; Photography, Sameer Arya; Costumes, Shreya Anand, Mandeep Patheja; Music, Zafar Ali; Editor, Sally Salgaonkar; a Rose Movies production; Indian; Color; Rated PG-13; 100 minutes; American release date: March 2, 2012. **CAST:** Ali Zafar (Nikhil Chopra), Aditi Rao Hydari (Lalitha Krishnan), Eric Geynes (Dominic), Judith Musil (Cherie), Samantha Spurgin (Helen)

Adit Rao Hydari, Ali Zafar in *London Paris New York* © Fox STAR Studios

PAAN SINGH TOMAR (UTV) Producer, Ronnie Screwvala; Director, Tigmanshu Dhulia; Photography, Aseem Mishra; Costumes, Namratha Jani; Music, Abhishek Ray; Indian; Color; Not rated; 135 minutes; American release date: March 2, 2012. **CAST:** Irrfan Khan (Paan Singh Tomar), Rajendra Gupta (Major H.S. Randhawa), Imran Hasnee (Matadeen Singh Tomar), Jahangir Khan (Bhawar Singh), Vipin Sharma (Major Masand), Nawazuddin Siddiqui (Gopi Jadav), Brijendra Kala (Journalist)

THE DECOY BRIDE (IFC Films) Producers, Robert Benstein, Douglas Rae, Paul Ritchie; Executive Producers, Steve Christian, Marc Samuelson, Mark Woolley, Carole Sheridan; Director, Sheree Folkson; Screenplay, Sally Phillips, Neil Jaworski; Story, Sally Phillips; Photography, Nanu Segal; Designer, Alison Dominitz; Costumes, Louise Allen; Music, Julian Nott; Editor, Dan Farrrell; Casting, Des Hamilton; a CinemanX and Isle of Man Film in association with Creative Scotland and Harway Films presentation of an Ecosse Films production; British-Scottish, 2011; Dolby; Color; Not rated; 89 minutes; American release date: March 9, 2012. **CAST:** Kelly Macdonald (Katie NicAoidh), David Tennant (James Arber), Alice Eve (Lara Tyler), Hamish Clark (Angus), James Fleet (William), Dylan Moran (Charley), Sally Phillips (Emma), Michael Urie (Steve Korbitz), Federico Castelluccio (Marco Ballani), Danny Bage (Hotel Doorman), Hannah Bourne (Chloe), Maureen Beattie (Iseabail NicAoidh), Muriel Barker (Mrs. Grainie), Jeannie Fisher (Aileen), Sally Howitt (Muireen), Rony Bridges (Roan), Matthew Chalmers (Callum), Victoria Grove (Anais Anais), Alisha Bailey (Suzelle), Patrick Regis (Hollywood Minister), Tina Gray (Elderly Woman), Gil Kolirin (Security Guard), Ben Addis, William Owen, Calum MacNab (Journalists), Ross Armstrong, Samuel Roukin (Paparazzi), Robert Fyfe (Ancient Crofter), Maryann Turner (Ancient Crofter's Wife), Tony Roper (Reverened McDonough), Alex Childs (TV Host), Achara Kirk (Tourist)

David Tennant, Kelly Macdonald, Michael Urie in *The Decoy Bride* © IFC Films

ATTENBERG (Strand) Producers, Maria Hatzakou, Yorgos Lanthimos, Iraklis Mavroidis, Athina Rachel Tsangari, Angelos Venetis; Executive Producer, Christos V. Konstantakopoulos; Director/Screenplay, Athina Rachel Tsangari; Photography, Thimios Bakatakis; Designer, Dafni Kalogianni; Costumes, Thanos Papastergiou, Vassilia Rozana; Editors, Sandrine Cheyrol, Matt Johnson; Casting, Alex Kelly, Christine Akzotis; a Haos Film presentation in co-production with the Greek Film Center, Faliro House Productions, Boo Productions, Stefi Productions; Greek, 2010; Dolby; Color; Not rated; 95 minutes; American release date: March 9, 2012. **CAST:** Ariane Labed (Marina), Vangelis Mourikis (Spryos), Evangelia Randou (Bella), Yorgos Lanthimos (The Engineer)

Ariane Labed, Evangelia Randou in *Attenberg* © Strand Releasing

DISSOLUTION (Transfax) a.k.a. *Hitparkut*; Producers, Marek Rozenbaum, Itai Tamir, Michael Huffington; Executive Producer, Rebecca Hartzell; Director/ Screenplay/Editor, Nina Menkes; Based on the 1866 novel *Crime and Punishment* by Dostoevsky; Photography, Itai Marom, Nina Menkes; Designer, November Wanderin; Costumes, Aline Lazarov; Music, Rich Ragsdale; Editors, Nina Menkes; a Transfax Film Productions, Lanai Productions, Menkesfilm, KNR Productions presentation; Israeli; Stereo; Black and white; HD; Not rated; 88 minutes; American release date: March 9, 2012. CAST: Didi Fire (Man), Nadia Tarazi (Yasmeen), Filina Klutchkin (Malka), Slava Bibergal (Friend), Zeynab Muchareb (Landlady), Yohanan Harrison (Cop)

GERHARD RICHTER – PAINTING (Kino Lorber) Producer, Thomas Kufus; Director/ Screenplay, Corinna Belz; Photography, Johann Feindt, Frank Kranstedt, Dieter Stürmer, Andy Schocken; Editor, Stephan Krumbiegel; a Zeo One Film Production in co-production with Terz Film/WDR/MDR in cooperation with ARTE; German; Dolby; Color; HD; Not rated; 97 minutes; American release date: March 14, 2012. Documentary on German artist Gerhard Richter; **WITH:** Gerhard Richter, Norbert Arns, Hubert Becker, Sabine Moritz-Richter, Konstanze Ell, Marian Goodman, Benjamin Buchloh, Kasper König, Ulrich Wilmes, Sandy Nairne, Paul Moorhouse

Gerhard Richter in *Gerhard Richter – Painting* © Kino Lorber

PRAY FOR JAPAN (AMC Theatres) Producer/Director/Photography, Stu Levy; Executive Producers, Toru Kajio, Ray Klein, Stu Levy, Kazunori Noguchi; Music, Shinya Mizoguchi; Editors, Emiko Kagawa, Susumu Kimura, Noriko Miyakawa, Nobuo Mita, Daisuke Kinouchi, Michelle Klein-Hass, Ayaka Minami, Motohiko Mizutani; a Pray for Japan Film production in association with Animation Studio Art Land, Q-Tec, Studio DEEN; Japanese; Color; HD; Not rated; 97 minutes; American release date: March 14, 2012. Documentary about the efforts to assist the earthquake/tsunami survivors of Ishinomaki, Japan; **WITH:** Yoshiaki Shouji, Najeeb Ullah Ayaz, Keisuke Takahashi, Junichi Sato, Tomiko Okazaki, Chieko Seto, Kento Ito, Shu Chiba, Hideo Otsuki, Manabu Endo, Shuki Ito, Hiroshi Kameyama, Masayuki Satou, Hiroyuke Abe, Kuniaki Shimizu, Takashi Nomura, Manabu Endo, Atsushi Yamashita, Anees Ahmad Nadeem, Kenji Watanabe, Yasunori Sugahara, Seiji Yoshimura, Takato Suzuki, Daisuke Makino, Masumi Kaneda, Kazuko Sato, Hiroko Kudou, Hiromitu Itou.

REUNITING THE RUBINS (Monterey Media) Producers, Yoav Factor, Jonathan Weissler; Executive Producer, Ben White; Director/Screenplay, Yoav Factor; Photography, Miles Cook; Designer, Byron Broadbent; Costumes, Alan Flyng; Music, Tim Atack; Editor, Anthony Stadler; Casting, Gaby Kester; a Factor Films presentation in association with Balagan; British, 2011; Dolby; Color; Rated PG; 97 minutes; American release date: March 16, 2012. **CAST:** Timothy Spall (Lenny Rubin), James Callis (Danny Rubin), Rhona Mitra (Andie Rubin), Honor Blackman (Gran Rubin), Hugh O'Conor (Yona Rubin), Asier Newman (Clarity Rubin), Theo Stevenson (Jake Rubin), Blake Harrison (Nick), Louise Brealey (Miri Rubins), Claudia Coulter (Marta), James Vaughn (Michael Brown), Neil Conrich (Rabbi Cohen), Rez Kempton (Dr. Maniram Nehru), Alison Pargeter (Nurse), Rita

Pray for Japan © AMC Theatres

Davies, Jessica James (Old Ladies), Amy Steel (Midwife), Sian Polhill Thomas (Gill Davies, TV Reporter), Sue Kelvin (Etty), Cassandra French (Receptionist), Sophia Dawnay (Young Gran Rubin), Joanna Adams (Mother in Solicitor's Office), Anthony Eldridge (Maternity Doctor), Georgina Mellor (Mrs. Harper), Anna Brook (Louise), Tom Keller (MC at Convention), Lisa Kerr (Protester), Laura Goodman (Betty Rubins), Lewis Coppen (Yahuda Rubins), Linda Klockare (Blow Out Girl), Mark Tintner (Blow Out Man), Alan Doney (Ship Steward), Duncan Thomas (Young Lenny), Alastair Fleming (Chinese Boy), Joseph Samrai (Sandeep), Jake Lancaster (Young Danny), Hugh Mhlongo (Translator), Nick Lacey (The Mad Man), Hugh Jennings (Young Clarity), Cathryn Brichto (Jennifer Brown), Alfie Hawkins (Meyer Rubins), Carmen Pat (Girl in Holocam Commercial), Eddie Carvalho (Young Yona), Zeph Nzama (Witchdoctor), Elouise Derbyshire (Young Andie), Duke Dam (Chinese Businessman), Zeph Nzama (Witchdoctor), Nicola Brazil (Travel Agent), Martin Friend (Rabbi Braun), Paul Arrowsmith (Writer in Monastery), Pravin Sunwar (Korean Boy), Iain Benjamin, Scott Cohen, Anthony Cowan, Joel Smookler (Yeshiva Students)

Timothy Spall in *Reuniting the Rubins* © Monterey Media

FREE MEN (Film Movement) a.k.a. *Les hommes libres*; Producer, Fabienne Vonier; Director, Ismaël Ferroukhi; Screenplay, Ismaël Ferroukhi, Alain-Michel Blanc; Photography, Jérôme Alméras; Designer, Luca Servino; Music, Armand Amar; Editor, Annette Dutertre; Pyramide Productions in co-production with Solaire Production/VMP, France 2 Cinéma; French, 2011; Dolby; Color; Not rated; 99 minutes; American release date: March 16, 2012. **CAST:** Tahar Rahim (Younes Ben Daoud), Michael Lonsdale (Si Kaddour Ben Ghabrit), Mahmoud Shalaby (Salim Halali), Lubna Azabal (Leila), Christopher Buccholz (Major Von

Ratibor), Farid Larbi (Ali), Stéphane Rideau (Francis), Bruno Fleury (Inspector), François Delaive (Gestapo Chief), Jean-Pierre Becker (Moustached Police), Marie Berto (Maryvonne), Zakariya Gouram (Omar), Slimane Dazi (Larbi), Aïcha Sokrane (Larbi's Mother), Djemel Barek (Maryvonne's Husband), Louna Klanit (Sarah Benssoussan), Lunis Sakji (Eli Benssoussan), Fabien Jegoudez (SS Man), Hassan Madiaf (Beggar), Ahmed Bourkab (Imam), Jamal Latif (Fez Man), Ali Hassan (Ben Ghabrit's Secretary), Jean-Pol Brissart (The Minister), Smail Mekki (Head Doctor), Blandine Pelissier (Woman in Charge of Children), Patrick Bouin (Gestapo Police), Karim Leklou (PPA Tribune), Noureddine Souli, Youssef Hajdi (Resistance Fighters), Abderrahim Oueld El Aijar (Abdelwahab), Maher Kamoun (Abderrahaman), Omar Zeghoudi (Hadj), Raouya (Veiled Woman), Thierry Angelvy (French Police)

Tahar Rahim in *Free Men* © Film Movement

COME ON EILEEN (Blinder Films) Producers, Finola Geraghty, Katie Holly, Kieron J. Walsh; Executive Producer, Frank Murray; Director/Screenplay, Finola Geraghty; Photography, Candida Richardson, Derrick Peters; Editor, Frank Reid; a Foal Film Productions and Blinder Films presentation; British-Irish, 2010; Color; Not rated; 90 minutes; American release date: March 23, 2012. **CAST:** Jackie Howe (Eileen), Mercedes Grower (Gypsy), Felix Malcolm Still (Jimmy), Freddie Jones (Dermot), Keith Allen (Martin), Stephen Taylor (Bill), Mel Hudson (Ann), Noel Fielding (Rex), Julia Davis (Dee), Melanie Hudson (Anne), Pat Tookey-Dickson (Jenny), Jacob Read (Rudy), Jane Kemlo (Jane), Matt Cross (Steve), Peter Barrett (Pete), John Milroy (John), Christian Dunne (Magician), Amber Geraghty (Carly), Louis Crump (Jimmy's Friend), Leon Davies (PC Watson)

Jackie Howe in *Come on Eileen* © Blinder Films

WOMB (Olive Films) Producers, Roman Paul, Gerhard Meixner, Andras Muhl; Director/Screenplay, Benedek Fliegauf; Photography, Péter Szatmári; Designer, Erwin Prib; Costumes, Mariano Tufano; Music, Max Richter; Editor, Xavier Box; Casting, Shaheen Baig, Jacqueline Rietz; a Razor Film, inforg studio, A.S.A.P. Films, Boje Buck Produktion, Arte France Cinéma production; German-Hungarian-French, 2010; Dolby; Color; Not rated; 111 minutes; American release date: March 30, 2012. **CAST:** Eva Green (Rebecca), Matt Smith (Thomas), Peter Wright (Ralph, Thomas' Father), István Lénárt (Henry), Hannah Murray (Monica), Ruby O. Fee (Rebecca, 9 years), Tristan Christopher (Thomas, 10 years), Jesse Hoffmann (Thomas, 5 years), Natalia Tena (Rose, One-Night Stand), Ella Smith (Molly), Wunmi Mosaku (Erica), Alexander Goeller (Marc), Adrian J. Wahlen (Eric), Gina Alice Stiebitz (Dima), Lesley Manville (Judith, Thomas' Mother), Amanda Lawrence (Teacher), Jennifer Lim (Mrs. Muju), Tina Engel (Doctor), Lucas Hawkins, Lukas Sweetwood, Fabian Hundertmark (Teenage Boys)

Tristan Christopher, Eva Green in *Womb* © Olive Films

FOUR LOVERS (Oscilloscope) a.k.a. *Happy Few*; Producer, Sébastien K. Lemercier; Director, Antony Cordier; Screenplay, Antony Cordier, Julie Peyr; Photography, Nicolas Gaurin; Designer, Marie Cheminal; Costumes, Isabelle Pannetier; Music, Frédéric Verrières; Editor, Christel Dewynter; a Why Not U.S. Productions, France 2 Cinéma, Canal+, France Télévision, CinéCinéma; French, 2011; Color; Not rated; 103 minutes; American release date: March 30, 2012. **CAST:** Marina Foïs (Rachel), Élodie Bouchez (Teri), Roschdy Zem (Franck), Nicolas Duvauchelle (Vincent), Jean-François Stévenin (Rachel's Father), Alexia Stresi (Diane), Blanche Gardin (Rachel's Sister), Geneviève Mnich (Franck's Sister), Philippe Paimblanc (Franck's Father), Naomi Ferreira (Margot), Ilona Caly (Thelma), Ferdinand Ledoux (Tim), Ya Hui Chan (Diane's Friend)

Four Lovers © Oscilloscope Laboratories

LOVE IN THE BUFF (China Lion) a.k.a. *Chun giu yu chi ming*; Producers, Pang Ho-cheung, Subi Liang; Executive Producer, John Chong; Directors, Pang Ho-cheung, Jody Luk, Luk Yee-sum; Photography, Jason Kwan; Designer, Lim Chung Man; Music, Janet Yung, Ngai Lun Wong; Editor, Wenders Li; a Media Asia Films, Making Film production; Hong Kong-Chinese; Not rated; 111 minutes; American release date: March 30, 2012. **CAST:** Miriam Yeung Chin Wah (Cherie), Shawn Yue (Jimmy), Mini Yang (You-you), Zheng Xu (Sam), Yat Ning Chan (Isabel), Ekin Cheng, Linda Wong (Themselves), Chim Sui-man (Paul), Huang Xiaoming (Ben), Vincent Kok (Tak), Jo Kuk (KK), June Lam (Brenda), Roy Szeto (Eunuch), Kristal Tin (Olivia), Shaw Yin Yin (Cherie's Mother), Wong So-fun (Masseuse)

Miriam Yeung, Shawn Yue in *Love in the Buff* © China Lion

ARTIFICIAL PARADISES (Interior13 Cine) a.k.a. *Paraísos artificiales*; Producer/Director, Yulene Olaizola; Screenplay, Yulene Olaizola, Fernando del Razo; Photography, Lisa Tillinger; Art Director, Nohemi Gonzalez; Editor, Rubén Imaz; Mexican, 2011; Color; Not rated; 83 minutes; American release date: March 30, 2012. **CAST:** Luisa Pardo (Luisa), Salomón Hernández (Salomón)

Luisa Pardo in *Artificial Paradises* © Interior 13 Cine

SURVIVING PROGRESS (First Run Features) Producers, Daniel Louis, Denise Robert, Gerry Flahive; Executive Producers, Mark Achbar, Betsy Carson, Silva Basmajian, Martin Scorsese, Emma Tillinger Koskoff; Director, Mathieu Roy; Co-Director, Harold Crooks; Screenplay, Harold Crooks, Mathieu Roy; Based on the 2004 book *A Short History of Progress* by Ronald Wright; Photography, Mario Janelle; Music, Patrick Watson, Michael Ramsey; Editor, Louis-Martin Paradis; a Big Pictures Media Corporation and NFB production; Canadian, 2011; Dolby; Color; Not rated; 86 minutes; Release date: April 6, 2012. Documentary on progress and the "traps" facing our civilization in regards to technology, economics, consumption, and the environment; **WITH:** Margaret Atwood, Enio Beata, Colin Beavan, Chen Changnian, Chen Ming, Victor Zhikai Gao, Jane Goodall, Stephen Hawking, Michael Hudson, Simon Johnson, Mark Levine, Gary Marcus, Kambale Musavuli, Daniel Povinelli, Marina Silva, Vaclav Smil, David Suzuki, Raquel Taitson-Queiroz, Jim Thomas, J. Craig Venter, Robert Wright, Ronald Wright

Surviving Progress © First Run Features

MIS HUMAN SECRET WEAPON (UTB) Producers, Ikuya Fuchigami, Ann Haneda, Erika Jones, Yasuhiko Kanazawa; Executive Producers, Hisatake Shibuya, Ryuichi Suzuki; Director/ Screenplay, Junichi Suzuki; Photography, Masahi Kobuchi; Music, Kitaro; Editor, Toru Mihara; Narration, Lane Nishikawa; a UTB presentation; Japanese-American; Color; Not rated; 100 minutes; American release date: April 6, 2012. Documentary on Japanese-Americans enlisted during World War II to work against Japan; **WITH:** Victor Abe, Daniel Akaka, Harry Akune, Ken Akune, Barbara Akune, George Ariyoshi, Paul Bannai, Stanley Falk, George Fujimori, Ichiro Fujisaki, Yoshiaki Fujitani, Harry Fukuhara, Jun Fukushima, Stephen Haller, Dick Hamada, Richard Hamasaki, Colleen Hanabusa, Tadayoshi Hara, Richard Hawkins, Fumie Higa, Takejiro Higa, Warren Higa, Frank Higashi, Irene Hirano Inouye, Mazie Hirono, Grant Ichikawa, Daniel Inouye, Carol Jensen, Bruce Kaji, Frances Kaji, Norman Kikuta, Wayne Kiyosaki, Janelle Kuroda, Al Nakazawa, Frank Masuoka, Mike Masuyama, Victor Matsui, James McNaughton, Craig Middleton, Norman Mineta, Raymond Murakami, James Murata, Joseph Muratsuchi, Herbert Murayama, Al Nipkow, Franklin Odo, James Ogawa, Don Oka, Isao Oka, Stephen Payne, Thomas Sakamoto, Hitoshi Sameshima, Terry Shima, Jake Shimabukuro, Tamlyn Tomita, Rosalyn Tonai, Thomas Tsubota, Ted Tsukiyama, Marvin Uratsu, Miyo Uratsu, Elaine Yagawa, Herbert Yanamura, Akemi Yano, Janet Yokoyama, Haruo Chibana, Seiho Hgia, Seiko Higa, Chosho Kiyuna, Toru Kobayashi, Hatsuko Kyan, Johnny Masuda, Mineko Masuda, Seiko Miyagi, Masahide Ohta, Terry Tsubota

MIS Human Secret Weapon © UTB

HOUSEFUL 2 (Eros) Producer Sajid Nadiadwala; Director, Sajid Khan; Screenplay, Sajid Khan, Tushar Hiranandani, Farhad; Photography, Manoj Soni; Designer, Humphrey Jaeger; Music, Sajid-Wajid, Sandeep Shirodkar; Editor, Rameshwar S. Bhagat; a Nadiadwala Grandson Entertainment production; Indian; Color; Not rated; 145 minutes; American release date: April 6, 2012. **CAST:** Akshay Kumar (Sunny, Jolly 1), Asin (Henna), John Abraham (Max, Jolly 2), Jacqueline Fernandes (Bobby), Shreyas Talpade (Jai, Jolly 3), Shazahn Padamsee (Parul), Ritesh Deshmukh (Jwala, Jolly 4), Zarine Khan (JLo), Rishi Kapoor (Chintu Kapoor), Randhir Kapoor (Daboo Kapoor), Boman Irani (Batook Patel), Mithun Chakraborty (JD), Neelu Kohli (Dolly Kapoor), Johnny Lever (Vishwas Patil), Suparna Marwah (Sweety Kapoor), Shivarna Mitra (Pooja), Chunky Pandey (Aakhri Pasta), Ranjeet (Dr. Pujari), Vindu Dara Singh (Soosa)

KEYHOLE (Monterey Media) Producers, Jody Shapiro, Jean Du Toit; Executive Producer, Phyllis Lang; Director, Guy Maddin; Screenplay, George Toles, Guy Maddin; Photography, Ben Kasulke; Designer, Richardo Alms; Costumes, Heather Neale; Music, Jason Staczek; Editor, John Gurdebeke; an Entertainment One presentation of a Buffalo Gal Pictures and Cinema Atelier Tovar production; Canadian; Black and white/color; Rated R; 94 minutes; American release date: April 6, 2012. **CAST:** Jason Patric (Ulysses Pick), Isabella Rossellini (Hyacinth), Udo Kier (Dr. Lemke), Brooke Palsson (Denny), David Wontner (Manners), Louis Negin (Calypso/Camille), Kevin McDonald (Ogilbe), Daniel Enright (Big Ed), Olivia Rameau (Rochelle), Tattiawna Jones (Lota), Johnny Chang (Chang), Darcy Fehr (Ned Pick), Mike Bell (Milo), Claude Dorge (Belview), David Evans (Nate), Garrett Hnatiuk (Gangster), Reegan McCheyne (Bruce), Brent Neale (Denton), Suzanne Pringle, Cynthia Wolfe-Nolin (Gun Molls), Jorge Requena (Frosty), Tyhr Trubiak (Dwayne), Theodors Zegeye-Gebrehiwot (Heatly), Nihad Ademi, Paula Blair, Jeff Funnell (Ghosts)

Udo Kier in *Keyhole* © Monterey Media

FETIH 1453 (NeoClassics) a.k.a. *Conquest 1453*; Producers, Faruk Aksoy, Servet Aksoy, Ayse Germen; Director, Faruk Aksoy; Screenplay, Atilla Engin, Irfan Saruhan, Faurk Aksoy; Photography, Mirsad Herovic, Hasan Gergin; Art Director, Servet Aksoy; Costumes, Canan Göknil; Music, Benjamin Wallfisch; Editor, Erkan Özekan; Visual Effects Supervisor, Serkan Zelzele; an Aksoy Film; Turkish; Dolby; Color; Not rated; 160 minutes; American release date: April 6, 2012. **CAST:** Devrim Evin (Sultan Mehmed II), Ibrahim Çelikkol (Hasan of Ulubat), Dilek Serbest (Dilek), Recep Aktug (Emperor Constantine), Cengiz Coskun (Guistiniani the Knight), Erden Alkan (Halil Pasha of Çandar), Naci Adigüzel (Grand Duke Notaras), Erdogan Audemir (Master Urban), Sahika Koldemir (Lady Gülbahar), Izzet Çivril (Cardinal Isidor), Ali Riza Soydan (Pope), Adnan Kürtçü (Priest Genadius), Sedat Mert (Zaganos Pasha), Raif Hikmet Çam (Aksemeddin), Mustafa Atilla Kunt (Sahabettin Pasha), Özcan Aliser (Saruca Pasha), Yilmaz Babatürk (Ishak Pasha), Murat Sezal (Isa Pasha), Faik Aksoy (Karaca Pasha), Hüseyin Santur (Baltaoglu Süleyman Pasha), Namik Kemal Yigittürk (Mullah Hüsrev),

Öner As (Mullah Gürani), Halis Bayraktaroglu (Kurtçu Dogan), Songül Kaya (Lady Emine), Tuncay Gençkalan (Eyüp the Prophet), Oguz Oktay (Chieftain Osman), Hüseyin Özay (Ali the Blacksmith), Ilker Kurt (Murad II), Edip Türfekçi (Chieftain Orhan)

Fetih 1453 © NeoClassics

POST MORTEM (Kino Lorber) Producer, Juan de Dios Larrain; Director, Pablo Larrain; Screenplay, Pablo Larrain, Mateo Iribarren; Photography, Sergio Armstrong; Art Director, Polin Garbisu; Editor, Andrea Chignoli; a Fabula production; Chilean-Mexican-German, 2011; Dolby; Color; Not rated; 98 minutes; American release date: April 11, 2012. **CAST:** Alfredo Castro (Mario), Antonia Zegers (Nancy), Jaime Vadell (Dr. Castillo), Amparo Noguera (Sandra), Marcelo Alonso (Victor), Marcial Tagle (Captain Montes), Santiago Graffigna (David Puelma), Ernesto Malbran (Arturo Puelma), Aldo Parodi (Pato), Steve Nave (Lt. Davenport)

Alfredo Castro in *Post Mortem* © Kino Lorber

LATE BLOOMERS (Olive Films) Producers, Sylvie Pialat, Bertrand Faivre; Executive Producer, Sidonie Dumas; Director, Julie Gavras; Screenplay, Julie Gavras, Olivier Dazat; Photography, Nathalie Durand; Designer, Eve Stewart; Costumes, Marianne Agertoft; Music, Sodi Marciszewer; Editor, Pierre Haberer; Casting, Kahleen Crawford; a Gaumont presentation of a Les films du Worso/The Bureau/Gaumont production in co-production with Be-Films; French-Belgian-British, 2011; Dolby; Super 35 Widescreen; Color; Not rated; 95 minutes; American release date: April 13, 2012. **CAST:** William Hurt (Adam), Isabella Rossellini (Mary), Doreen Mantle (Nora), Kate Ashfield (Giulia), Aidan McArdle (James), Arta Dobroshi (Maya), Luke Treadaway (Benjamin), Leslie Phillips (Leo), Hugo Speer (Peter), Joanna Lumley (Charlotte), Simon Callow (Richard), Iona Wayne (Carolyn), Ryan Quarterly (Henry), Nicholas Farrell (Francis), Sushil Chudasama (Sushil), Joanna Bobin (Karen), Danny Rahim (Leon), Phoenix James, Michael

Pourrot (Art Buyers), Lin Blakley, Elsie Kelly (Grey Panthers), Freddy Downham (Carlos), Stuart Martin (Nurse), John Warman (Paramedic), Anthony Errington (Architect Intern), Gino Picciano (European Representative)

Isabella Rossellini, William Hurt in *Late Bloomers* © Olive Films

A SIMPLE LIFE (China Lion) a.k.a. *Tao jie*; Producers, Ann Hui, Lee Yan-lam; Executive Producers, Andy Lau, Dai Song, Dong Yu; Director, Ann Hui; Screenplay, Susan Chan, Lee Yan-lam; Photography, Albert Poon; Music, Law Wing-fai; Editors, Manda Wai, Kwong Chi-leung; Focus Films Ltd.; Hong Kong, 2011; Dolby; Color; Not rated; 118 minutes; American release date: April 13, 2012. **CAST:** Andy Lau (Roger Leung), Deanie Yip (Sister Peach/Chung Chun To), Wang Fuli (Roger's Mother), Qin Hailu (Ms. Choi), Paul Chun (Uncle Kin), Jason Chan (Jason), Dennis Chan (Vincent), Pik Kee Hui (Aunt Kam), Hui So-ying (Mui), Sammo Hung Kam-Bo (Director Hung), Tyson Chak (Air Conditioning Fixer), Lawrence Ah Mon (Ah Chun), Eman Lam (Carmen), Lan Law (Madame Lo), Tin Leung (Headmaster), Mak Yun-sau (Hengzi), Hailu Qin (Ms. Choi), Tam Bing-man (Bing), Billy Lau, Sammuel Leung (Mobsters)

Wang Fuli, Andy Lau in *A Simple Life* © China Lion

KIDS OF TODAY (Factory 25) a.k.a. *Des jeunes gens mödernes*; Producer, Agnès B.; Executive Producers, Mairpol, Julien Tang, Simon Trottier; Director, Jérôme de Missolz; Screenplay, Jérôme de Missolz, Jean-François Sanz; Photography, Jérôme de Missolz, Sarah Blum; Editors, Elisabeth Juste, Vanessa Bozza; a Love Streams, Agnes B Prods. presentation of an Arte France Cinema, Love Streams production; French; Color; HD; Not rated; 97 minutes; American release date: April 13, 2012. Documentary on today's youth; **WITH:** Yves Adrien, Lio, Edwige Belmore, Aurélie Benchekri, Antoine Capet, Mathieu Chausseron, Sabine Noble, Joris Larochelle, Anne-Sophie Le Creuer

MY WAY (CJ Entertainment) a.k.a. *Mai Wei*; Producer, Kang Je-gyu, Kim Yong-hwa; Director, Kang Je-gyu; Screenplay, Kang Je-gyu, Kim Byung-in; Photography, Lee Mo-gae; Designer, Cho Geun-hyun; Costumes, Kim Jong-won; Music, Lee Dong-jun; Editor, Park Gok-ji; an SK Planet presentation of a Directors production; South Korean, 2011; Dolby; Color; Rated R; 137 minutes; American release date: April 20, 2012. **CAST:** Jang Dong-gun (Kim Jun-shik), Jô Odagiri (Tatsu Hasegawa), Fan Bingbing (Shirai), Kim In-kwon (Lee Jong-dae), Lee Yeon-hee (Kim Eun-soo), Kim Hee-won (Choon Bok), Kwak Jung-wook (Min-Woo), Tarô Yamamoto (Noda), Oh Tae-kyung (Kwang-choon), Nicole Jung (Press Conference Guide), Manabu Hamada (Mukai), Shingo Tsurumi (Takakura), Kim Shi-hoo (Tsukamoto), Yoon Hee-won (Sohn Kee-chung), Chun Ho-jin (Jun-shik's Father)

Odagagi Jang, Dong Gu in *My Way* © CJ Entertainment

HELPLESS (CJ Entertainment) a.k.a. *Hoa-cha*; Producers, Shin Hye-eun, Oh Ki-min; Director/Screenplay, Byun Young-joo; Based on the 1999 novel *All She Was Worth* by Miyuki Miyabe; Photography, Kim Dong-young; Music, Kim Hong-jib; Editor, Park Gok-ji; South Korean; Dolby; Color; Not rated; 117 minutes; American release date: April 20, 2012. **CAST:** Lee Seon-gyun (Jang Moon-ho), Kim Min-hie (Kang Seon-yeong), Jo Seong-ha (Jong-geun), Kim Byeol (Han-na), Choi Duek-mun (Ha Seong-sik), Cha Soo-yeon (The Real Kang Seon-yeong), Lee Hee-joon (Noh Seung-joo), Kim Min-jae (Lee Dong-woo), Choi Il-hwa (Moon-ho's Father), Kim Tae-in (Park Myeong-sin)

Lee Seo-gyun in *Helpless* © CJ Entertainment

VICKY DONOR (Eros) Producer, John Abraham; Director, Shoojit Sircar; Screenplay, Juhi Chaturvedi; Photography, Kamaljeet Negi; Music, Abhishek-Akshay Bann, Rochak Kohli, Ayushmann Khurrana; a Rising Sun Films production; Indian; Color; Not rated; 125 minutes; American release date: April 20, 2012. **CAST:** Ayushmann Khurrana (Vicky Arora), Yami Gautam (Ashima Roy Arora), Annu Kapoor (Dr. Baldev Chaddha), Dolly Ahluwalia (Mrs. Arora), Kamlesh Gill (Biji), Jayant Das (Mr. Roy), Bupesh Pandya (Chaman), K.V. Rajni (Nurse Lata), Puja Gupta (Shweta), John Abraham (Himself)

Yami Gautam, Ayushmann Khurrana in *Vicky Donor* © Eros

THE MOTH DIARIES (IFC Films) Producers, Karine Martin, David Collins; Executive Producers, Norton Herrick, Zygi Kamasa, Jon Katz, Jean-Francois Doray, Louis Simon Ménard, Mark Slone, Edward R. Pressman, Sandra Cunningham; Director/Screenplay, Mary Harron; Based on the 2002 novel by Rachel Klein; Photography, Declan Quinn; Designer, Sylvain Gingras; Music, Lesley Barber; Editor, Andrew Marcus; Casting, John Buchan, Jason Knight, Rosina Bucci, Kerry Barden, Paul Schnee; an Alliance Films and Edward R. Pressman presentation of a Mediamax-Samson Films co-production in association with Strada Films and Lionsgate UK with the participation of Mediabiz International, Telefilm Canada, Astral's Harold Greenberg Fund and Windmill Lane Pictures Dublin and Bord Scannan Na Heireann/The Irish Film Board; Canadian-Irish; Dolby; Super 35 Widescreen; Color; Rated R; 82 minutes; American release date: April 20, 2012. **CAST:** Lily Cole (Ernessa), Sarah Gadon (Lucy), Sarah Bolger (Rebecca), Judy Parfitt (Mrs. Rood), Scott Speedman (Mr. Davies), Melissa Farman (Dora), Laurence Hamelin (Sofia), Gia Sandhu (Kiki), Valerie Tian (Charley), Leif Anderson (Policeman), Deena Aziz (Psychiatrist), Roxan Bourdelais (Sofia's Boyfriend), Julian Casey (Rebecca's Father), Anne Day-Jones (Rebecca's Mother), Kathleen Fee (Miss Bobbie), Al Goulem (Detective), Steffi Hagel (Young Rebecca)

Gia Sandhu, Valerie Tian, Sarah Gadon, Sarah Bolger in *The Moth Diaries* © IFC Films

JEAN GENTIL (Northwest Film Forum) Producers, Pablo Cruz, Bärbel Mauch, Israel Cárdenas, Laura Amelia Guzmán; Executive Producers, Sylvia Conde, Eduardo Guzmán, Pedro "Peyi" Guzmán, Gabriel Nuncio, Geminiano Pineda, Desiree Reyes; Directors/Screenplay/Photography, Laura Amelia Guzmán, Israel Cárdenas; Designer/Costumes, Patricia Grassals; Editor, Israel Cárdenas; an Aurora Dominicana/Canana Films/Bärbel Mauch Film; Dominican Republic-Mexican-German, 2010; Color; Not rated; 84 minutes; American release date: April 20, 2012. **CAST**: Jean Remy Genty (Jean Remy), Yanmarco King Encarnación (Yanmarco), Paul Henri Presumé (Polo), Nadal Walcott (Surveyor), Lys Ambroise (Ciryl, Night Watchman)

Jean Remy Genty in *Jean Gentil* © Northwest Film Forum

THE DAY HE ARRIVES (Cinema Guild) a.k.a. *Book chon bang hyang*; Producer, Kim Kyounghee; Director/Screenplay, Hong Sangsoo; Photography, Kim Hyungkoo; Music, Jeong Yongjin; Editor, Hahm Sungwon; a Jeonwonsa Film Co. production; South Korean, 2011; Dolby; Color; Not rated; 79 minutes; American release date: April 20, 2012. **CAST:** Yu Junsang (Seongjun), Kim Sangjoong (Youngho), Song Sunmi (Boram), Kim Bokyung (Kyungjin/Yejeon)

Yu Jungsang, Kim Sangjoong in *The Day He Arrives* © Cinema Guild

PAYBACK (Zeitgeist) Producer, Ravida Din; Director/Screenplay, Jennifer Baichwal; Based on the 2008 book *Payback: Debt and the Shadow Side of Wealth* by Margaret Atwood; Photography, Nicholas de Pencier; Music, Martin Tielli, Gabriel Morley; Editor, Nick Hector; a production of the National Film Board of Canada; Canadian; Color; Not rated; 86 minutes; American release date: April 25, 2012. Documentary on the various forms of "debt" — societal, personal, economic, etc. **WITH:** Margaret Atwood, Raj Patel, Louise Arbour, Conrad Black, Karen Armstrong, William Rees, Lucas Benítez, Gerardo Reyes Chávez, Jon Esformes, Casi Callaway, Gjon Biba, Gjergi Lala, Agrim Loci, Gjin Marku, Donika

Prenaga, Gjin Prenaga, Liliana Prenaga, Llesh Prenaga, Lorenco Prenaga, Pashke Prenaga, Ilir Prenga, Petrit Prenga, Zef Sinani, Florence Barran, Paul Mohammed, Francis Dolan, Gregorio Venegas, Eric Schlosser, Rodney Lyons

Payback © Zeitgeist Films

CITIZEN GANGSTER (IFC Films) formerly *Edwin Boyd*; Producer, Allison Black; Executive Producers, Kirk D'Amico, Daniel Iron; Director/Screenplay, Nathan Morlando; Photography, Steve Cosens; Designer, Aidan Leroux; Costumes, Brenda Broer; Music, Max Richter; Music Supervisor, Linda Cohen; Editor, Richard Comeau; Casting, David Rubin, Richard Hicks; a Myriad Pictures and Entertainment One presentation of a Euclid 431 Pictures production; Canadian; Dolby; Techniscope; Color; Not rated; 105 minutes; American release date: April 27, 2012. **CAST:** Scott Speedman (Edwin Boyd), Kelly Reilly (Doreen Boyd), Kevin Durand (Lenny Jackson), Joseph Cross (Val Kozak), William Mapother (Det. Rhys), Brendan Fletcher (Willy "The Clown" Jackson), Charlotte Sullivan (Mary Mitchell), Brian Cox (Glover Boyd), Melanie Scrofano (Ann Roberts), Joris Jarsky (War Vet), Daniel Kash (Al), Christian Martyn (Billy Boyd), Cynthia Galant (Carolyn Boyd), Tara Nicodemo (Bank Teller, Robbery #1), Marty Adams (Bank Manager, Robbery #1), Sandra Forsell (Bank Teller, Robberies 3 & 4), Robert Bockstael (Bank Manager, Robberies 3 & 4), Craig Snoyer (Dutch), Marianne McIsaac (Lorne Greene Receptionist), Steven McCarthy (Don Jail Reporter), Troy Boudreau (Forest Hill Reporter #1), Jim Calarco (Priest), Patrick Stevenson (Tough Cop), Greg Ellwand (Mayor), Rhaelyn Gillespie (Bank Teller, 1966), Mark Fisher (Plainsclothes Detective), Sandro Frenguelli (Bank Customer, Robbery #3)

Charlotte Sullivan, Joseph Cross in *Citizen Gangster* © IFC Films

DOLPHIN BOY (Dragoman Film Distribution) Producers, Dani Menkin, Yonatan Nir, Judith Manassen Ramon; Directors/Screenplay, Dani Menkin, Yonatan Nir; Photography, Yaron Levisohn, Yoav Kleiman, Yonatan Nir, Uri Ackerman; Music, Isaar Shulman; Editors, Talli Halter-Shenkar, Malenie Margalith; a Judith Manassen Ramon, Dan Menkin & Yonatan Nir presentation in association with ARTE & Channel 4; Israeli; Dolby; Color; Not rated; 72 minutes; American release date; April 27, 2012. Documentary on how swimming with dolphins helped young Morad recover from trauma

Morad in *Dolphin Boy* © Dragoman Film Distrib.

ELLES (Kino Lorber) Producer, Marianne Slot; Executive Producer, Olivier Guerbois; Director, Malgoska Szumowska; Screenplay, Tine Byrckel, Malgoska Szumowska; Photography, Michal Englert; Art Director, Pauline Bourdon; Costumes, Katarzyna Lewinska; Editors, François Tourmen, Jacek Drosio; Casting, Aurélie Guichard; a Slot Machine production; French-Polish-German; Color; HD; Not rated; 96 minutes; American release date: April 27, 2012. **CAST:** Juliette Binoche (Anne), Anaïs Demoustier (Charlotte), Joanna Kulig (Alicja), Louis-Do de Lencquesaing (Patrick), Krystyna Janda (Alicja's Mother), Andrzej Chyra (The Sadistic Client), Ali Marhyar (Saïd), Jean-Marie Bincohe (Anne's Father), François Civil (Florent), Pablo Beugnet (Stéphane), Valérie Dréville (Charlotte's Mother), Jean-Louis Coulloch'h (Charlotte's Father), Arthur Monica (Thomas), Scali Delpeyrat (Charles), Laurence Ragon (Colette), Alain Libolt (Colette's Husband), Swann Arlaud (The Young Client), Nicolas Layani (The Guitar Client), Laurence Jumeaucourt (The Beauty Mark Client), José Fumanal (The Crying Client)

Juliette Binoche, Anaïs Demoustier in *Elles* © Kino Lorber

WHORES' GLORY (Kino Lorber) Producers, Erich Lackner, Tommy Pridnig, Peter Wirthensohn, Mirjam Quinte, Pepe Danquart; Director/Screenplay, Michael Glawogger; Photography, Wolfgang Thaler; Music, Pappik & Regener; Editor, Monika Willi; Austrian-German, 2011; Color; Not rated; 119 minutes; American release date: April 27, 2012. Documentary exploring prostitution in Thailand, Bangladesh, and Mexico.

Whores' Glory © Kino Lorber

WARRIORS OF THE RAINBOW: SEEDIQ BALE (Well Go USA) a.k.a. *Sàidékè balái*; Producers, John Woo, Terence Chang, Jimmy Huang; Director/Screenplay/Editor, Wei Te-Sheng; Photography, Chin Ting-chang; Art Director, Yohei Taneda; a Central Motion Picture Corporation, ARS Film Production presentation; Taiwanese, 2011; Color; Not rated; 150 minutes; American release date: April 27, 2012. **CAST:** Masanobu Andô (Genji Kojima), Umin Boya (Temu Walis), Cheng Chi-wei (Wu Jin-dun), Lin Ching-tai (Mona Rudao), Da-Ching (Mona – young), Jun'ichi Haruta (Egawa Hiromichi), Michio Hayashida (Hua-Lien, Police Chief), Akira Hibino (General Oshima), Vivian Hsu (Obing Tadao), Hsu Yi-fan (Ichiro Hanaoka), Yoshitaka Ishizuka (Yasuichiro Fukabori), Sabu Kawahara (Yahiko Kamada), Yûichi Kimura (Satsuka Aisuke), Bowkeh Kowsang (Dakis Nomin), Ma Ju-lung (Owner of the Trade Center), Minoru Matsumoto (Katsumi Yoshimura), Lo Mei-ling (Obing Nawi), Hirsohi Noguchi (Count Kabayama Sukenori), Chie Tanaka (Matsuno Kojima), Tang Shiang-chu (Lee Ching-fang), Soda Voyu (Jiro Hanaoka), Landy Wen (Mahung Mona)

Umin Boya in *Warriors of the Rainbow* © Well Go USA

CHRONICLING A CRISIS (Israel Film Center) a.k.a. *Chronica shel mashber*; Producers, Osnat Shalev, Amos Kollek, Micahel Tapauch, Talia Kleinhendler; Director, Amos Kollek; Music, Alison Gordy, Robert Aaron; Editors, Miki Kohn, Jeffrey Marc Harkavy; a Hamon Productions Ltd., Pie Films production; Israeli, 2011; Color; Not rated; 90 minutes; American release date: May 4, 2012. Documentary on filmmaker Amos Kollek's efforts to overcome depression and reconnect with his craft, following the failure of his 2003 film *Happy End*; **WITH:** Amos Kollek, Sheila Anderson, Daniele Contarin, Yuri Kapralov, Avigayeel Kollek, Noaa Kollek, Teddy Kollek, Robin Remias, Ally Sheedy, Anna Thomson

Amos Kollek, Robin Remias in *Chronicling a Crisis* © Israel Film Center

PATIENCE (AFTER SEBALD) (Cinema Guild) Producers, Sarah Caddy, Gareth Evans, Di Robson; Executive Producer, Keith Griffiths; Director/Photography, Grant Gee; Music, The Caretaker; Narrator, Jonathan Price; an Illuminations Films production; British; Dolby; HD; Color/black and white; Not rated; 89 minutes; American release date: May 9, 2012. Documentary on writer W.G.Sebald; **WITH:** Arthur Lubow, Tacita Dean, Iain Sinclair, Andrew Motion, Adam Phillips, Robert Macfarlane, Barbara Hui, Rick Moody, Chris Petit, William Firebrace, Dan Gretton, Christopher MacLehose, Jeremy Millar, Katie Mitchell, Bill Swainson, Lise Patt, Marina Warner, Christopher Woodward

SLEEPLESS NIGHT (Tribeca Film) a.k.a. *Nuit blanche*; Producers, Marco Cherqui, Lauranne Bourrachot; Director, Frédéric Jardin; Screenplay, Frédéric Jardin, Nicolas Saada; Adaptation and Dialogues, Frédéric Jardin, Olivier Douyère; Photography, Tom Stern; Set Decoration, Hubert Pouille; Costumes, Uli Simon; Music, DJ Yenn, Ionic Benton, Artaban, Nicolas Errera; Editor, Christophe Pinel; Casting, Swan Pham; a co-production of Chic Films, Paul Thiltges Distributions, Saga Film, Ufilm; French-Belgian-Luxembourg; Color; Not rated; 98 minutes; American release date: May 11, 2012. **CAST:** Tomer Sisley (Vincent), Serge Riaboukine (José Marciano), Julien Boisselier (Lacombe), Joey Starr (Feydek), Laurent Stocker (Manuel), Birol Ünel (Yilmaz), Lizzie Brocheré (Vignali), Samy Seghir (Thomas), Dominique Bettenfeld (Alex), Adel Bencherif (Abel), Catalina Denis (Julia), Pom Klementieff (Lucy), Vincent Bersoulet (Turc 3), Cécile Boland (Barmaid), Pascal Lavancy (Conductor), Hervé Sogne (Young Relief Police), Gabriel Boisante (Inspector), Anne-Elisabeth Chuffart (Young Inspector), Dean Constantin (Police Officer), Albert Dray (Witness), Jean-Michel Correia (Bouncer), Jérôme Gaspard (Thirty), Issam Akel, Thomas Ancora (Barmen), Shom Siddiqi (Sri Lankan), Laurent Hérion (Chef), Pascal Guégan (Billiard Player), Kevin Conseil (Server)

Tomer Sisley in *Sleepless Night* © Tribeca Film

THE ROAD (Freestyle) Producers, Jose Mari R. Abacan, Yam Laranas; Executive Producer, Annette Gozon-Abrogar; Director/Photography, Yam Laranas; Screenplay, Aloy Adlawan, Yam Laranas; Designer, Joey Luna; Costumes, Guada Reyes; Music, Johan Söderqvist; Editors, Mae Carzon, Yam Laranas; Special Effects, Teng Mendoza; Stunts, Lito Castro; a GMA Films production; Philippines, 2011; Dolby; Color; HD; Rated R; 110 minutes; American release date: May 11, 2012. **CAST:** TJ Trinidad (Luis), Carmina Villaroel (Carmela), Marvin Agustin (Boy's Father), Rhian Ramos (Ate Lara), Barbie Forteza (Ella), Alden Richards (Teenage Luis), Lexi Fernandez (Janine), Louise delos Reyes (Joy), Derrick Monasterio (Brian), Ynna Asistio (Martha), Renz Valerio (Boy Luis), Jacklyn Jose (Sisters' Mom), John Regala (Chief), Allan Paule (Greg), Lloyd Samartino (Ella's Father), Gerald Madrid (Allan), Ana Abad Santos (Janine's Mother), Dex Quindoza (Mailman), Mai Fajardo (Lara's Ghost), Dave de Mesa (Mayor), Mart de Mesa (Police Captain), Nick de Mesa (Police Officer)

The Road © Freestyle Releasing

DANGEROUS ISHHQ (Reliance Entertainment) Director/Screenplay, Vikram Bhatt; Dialogue, Girish Dhamija; Photography, Pravin Bhatt; Costumes, Nidhi Yasha; Music, Himesh Reshammiya; Lyrics, Sameer, Shabbir Ahmed; Editor, Kuldip K. Mehan; a BVG Films, DAR Motion Pictures and Reliance Entertainment presentation; Indian; Color; Not rated; 130 minutes; American release date: May 11, 2012. **CAST:** Karisma Kapoor (Sanjana Saksena), Rajneesh Duggal (Rohan), Jimmy Shergill (ACP Singh), Divya Dutta (Dr. Neeta), Ruslaan Mumtaz (Rahul Thakral)

Karisma Kapoor in *Dangerous Ishhq* © Reliance Entertainment

YOU ARE HERE (Cross Country) Producers, Daniel Bekerman, Daniel Cockburn; Executive Producers, Matthew Stone, Brenda Goldstein; Director/Screenplay, Daniel Cockburn; Photography, Cabot McNenly; Designer, Nazl Goshtasbpour; Costumes, Olivia Sementsova; Music, Rick Hyslop; Editor, Duff Smith; Casting, Millie Tom; a ZeroFunction and Scythia Films production; Canadian, 2010; Color; HD; Not rated; 79 minutes; American release date: May 11, 2012. **CAST:** Tracy Wright (Archivist), Shannon Beckner (Verna), Richard Clarkin (Hal), Jenni Burke (Sharon), Robert Kennedy (Bob), R.D. Reid (Dr. Eisenberg), Emily Davidson-Niedoba (Alan, Tracksuit), Anand Rajaram (Subject, Dr. Mayhew), Alec Stockwell (Edgar), Shae Norris (Harue), Rosie Elia (Annie), Isaac Durnford (Tariq), Nadia Capone (Dr. Sheona Nerada), Nadia Litz (Marcie), Peter Solala (The Blond Man), Nobu Adilman (Simon), Max Topplin (Page), Vasanth Saranga (Dennis), LinLyn Lue (Stephanie), Stephen R. Hart (Gerald), Djennie Laguerre (Kristin), Angel Adegboruwa, Scott Anderson, Susan M. Bell, Myles Borins, Stormm Bradshaw, Tessa Cameron, Lisa Charleyboy, Penny Charter, David Grimes, Patrick Hagarty, Christina Elizabeth Hall, Curtis Harrison, Edney Hendrickson, Jeff Muhsoldt, Christen Reynolds, Samuel Rudykoff, Farrah Yip (Alans)

Tracy Wright in *You are Here* © Cross Country

FREESTYLE (Phase 4 Films) Producer, Lincia Daniel; Director, Kolton Lee; Screenplay, Michael Maynard; Photography, Steve Gray; Designer, Dan Taylor; Costumes, Miss Molly; Music, Matt Constantine; Editor, Dominic Stevens; Casting, Leila Bertrand; a B19 Media, Film London, Microwave Film production; British, 2010; Color; Rated PG-13; 86 minutes; American release date: May 11, 2012. **CAST:** Lucy Konadu (Ondene Marchant), Arinze Kene (Leon Chambers), Suzann McLean (Hyacinth Marchant), Alfie Allen (Jez), Eleanor Wyld (Abigail), Rhonda M'Hango (Prunella), James Hamilton (Duane Chambers), Colin Salmon

(Carter), Tarryn Algar (Double S), Loving Valentino Olanrewaju (Man Man), Kristin Milward (Ms. Holloway), Riyan Bissessar (Tameka), Danny John-Jules (Collis), Jerry Ezekiel (Turkish), Martin Okasili, Billy Smith (Burly Men), Chris Wilson (Police Community Support), Zakiya Petty (Production Assistant), Majarah Forbes-Selassie, Reuben Shaljean, Ashley "Bashy" Thomas (Freestyle Competition Judges), TJ (Arena DJ), Nabil Abdulrashid, Tyrone Cole, Big Fen, Robin French, Joe Harding, Lois Haruna, Mohammed Muklar, Wolfgang Mwanje, Eddie Nash, Heron Palmer, Andrew Wilding, Junior Williams (Freestylers)

Arinze Kene, Suzann McLean in *Freestyle* © Phase 4 Films

TONIGHT YOU'RE MINE (Roadside Attractions/Stage 6 Films) a.k.a. *You Instead*; Producer, Gillian Berrie; Executive Producers, Robbie Allen, Carole Sheridan, Phil Hunt, Compton Ross, Geoff Ellis, Malte Grunert, David Mackenzie, Jamie Laurenson, Christine Langan; Director, David Mackenzie; Screenplay, Thomas Leveritt; Photography, Giles Nuttgens; Designer, Judi Ritchie; Costumes, Kelly Cooper Barr; Casting, Kahleen Crawford; a BBC Films presentation in association with Head Gear Films/Metrol Technology and Creative Scotland of a Sigma Films production; British, 2011; Dolby; Color; HD; Rated R; 80 minutes; American release date: May 11, 2012. **CAST:** Luke Treadaway (Adam), Natalia Tena (Morello), Mathew Baynton (Tyko), Ruta Gedmintas (Lake), Alastair Mackenzie (Mark), Gavin Mitchell (Bobby), Joseph Mydell (The Prophet), Sophie Wu (Kim), Kari Corbett (Kirsty), Rebecca Benson (Lucie), Clare Kelly (Justine), Cora Bissett (J.J.), Gilly Gilchrist (Bruce the Roadie), Newton Faulkner, Jo Mango, Kassidy, The Proclaimers, Heather Suttie, The View (Themselves), Jonny Phillips (Jay), Laura McMonagle (Tyko's Friend), John Doherty (Taxi Driver), Hannah Jackson (Jenny), Carl Martin (Fire Marshal), Sinead McKinlay (Bobby's Friend), Jerry Millichip (Security Guard), Stephen Sherriff (Guy at Campfire), Stuart Sloan (Lake Autograph Boy), Becky Wallace (Girl at Campfire), Greg Weir (Stagehand)

Luke Treadaway in *Tonight You're Mine* © Roadside Attractions

THE CUP (Myriad Pictures) Producers, Jan Bladier, David Lee, Simon Wincer; Executive Producers, Lance Hool, Kirk D'Amico, Greg Sitch, Joel Pearlman, Peter de Rauch, James M. Vernon; Director, Simon Wincer; Screenplay, Eric O'Keefe, Simon Wincer; Photography, David Burr; Designer, Lisette Thomas; Costumes, Julie Middleton; Music, Bruce Rowland; Casting, Louise Mitchell, Ann Fay; a Screen Australia, Silver Lion Films, Myriad Pictures and Village Roadshow presentation in association with Film Victoria, coproduced by Ingenious Broadcasting of a Simon Wincer/Lance Hool production; Australian, 2011; Dolby; Color; Rated PG; 99 minutes; American release date: May 11, 2012. **CAST:** Brendan Gleeson (Dermot Weld), Stephen Curry (Damien Oliver), Daniel MacPherson (Jason Oliver), Tom Burlinson (Dave Phillips), Jodi Gordon (Trish Oliver), Alice Parkinson (Jenny), Shaun Micalleff (Lee Freedman), Martin Sacks (Neil Pinner), Colleen Hewett (Pat Oliver), Andrew Curry (Ray Oliver), Meredith Penman (Young Pat), Kate Bell (Claire), Nick Simpson-Deeks (Pat Smullen), Lewis Fitz-Gerald (Sir Michael Smurfit), Rodger Corser (Jason McCartney), Harli Ames (Saeed Bin Suroor), Raj Sidhu (Sheik Mohammed), Claire Chitham (Angela Phillips), Bobby Fox (Niall Phillips), Bill Hunter (Bart Cummings), Rhys McConnochie (George Hanlon), Reg Gorman (Vern), Ian Cover (Himself), Jared Daperis (Frankie Dettori), Mick Lo Monaco (Kerrin McEvoy), Andrew Bongiorno (Corey Brown), Tony Rickards (Chief Steward), Marty Fields (Shearer Bookie), Janet Foye (Damien's Grandmother), Freddie Curry (Damien, 3 years old), Samson Magasanik (Jason, 5 years old), Ian Rooney (Jim Sheridan), Lachlan Macdonald (John Oxx), Brenda Addie (Lady Clague), Patricia Judah (Betty), Lawrence Brewer (Irish Journalist), Lawrence Mooney (Belmont Starter), Ben Grant (Perth ER Doctor), Scott Bowie (Perth Paramedic), Teressa Liane, Tory West (Nurses), Scott Parmeter (Ray Oliver's Doctor), Judy Campbell (Pat's Friend), Rob Gaylard (MC Barrier Draw), Alex Borg (TV Producer), Greg Carroll, Terry Brittingham, Matt Rainey (Punters), Rick Page (Media Puzzle Strapper), Reg Roordink, Will Jones (Miners), Noel Davis, Neil Solomano (Shearers), Phil Hayden (British Commentator), Anthony Guilbert (French Commentator), Paul Didham (Flemington Starter), Brian Markovic (Race Caller, Perth)

Brendan Gleeson in *The Cup* © Myriad Pictures

NOBODY ELSE BUT YOU (First Run Features) a.k.a. *Poupoupidou*; Producer, Isabelle Madelaine; Director, Gérald Hustache-Mathieu; Screenplay, Gérald Hustache-Mathieu, in collaboration with Juliette Sales; Photography, Pierre Cottereau; Music, Stéphane Lopez; Editor, Valérie Deseine; a Dharmasala production, in coproduction with France 2 Cinéma and France Télévisions; French, 2011; Dolby; Scope; Color; Not rated; 102 minutes; American release date: May 18, 2012. **CAST:** Jean-Paul Rouve (David Rousseau), Sophie Quinton (Candice Lecoeur/Martine Langevin), Guillaume Gouix (Brigadier Bruno Leloup), Olivier Rabourdin (Commandant Colbert), Clara Ponsot (Receptionist), Arsinée Khanjian (Dr. Juliette Geminy), Eric Ruf (Simon Denner), Lyès Salem (Gus), Joséphine de Meaux (Cathy), Ken Samuels (Jean-François Burdeau), Antoine Chappey (Bernard-Olivier Burdeau), Fred Quiring (Clément Leprince), Nicolas

Robin (Julien Charlemagne), Milo Hustache-Mathieu (Julien at 11), Anne Le Ny (Victoria Principal Voice), Finnegan Oldfield (Richi), Gérard Bôle du Chaumont (Skier), Marjorie Heirich (The Fromagère), Jérôme Rousselet (France 3 Journalist), Thomas Fisseau (Blanchard Son), Jenny Bellay (Madame Humbert), Dominique Foure (Notary), Arnaud Duléry (Intern)

Sophie Quinton in *Nobody Else but You* © First Run Features

THE SAMARITAN (IFC Films) a.k.a. *Fury*; Producers, Andras Hamori, Suzanne Cheriton, David Weaver, Elan Mastai, Tony Wosk; Executive Producers, Mark Musselman, Lacia Kornylo, Mark Horowitz, Samuel L. Jackson, Eli Selden, Geoffrey Brant, James Atherton, Jan Pace; Director, David Weaver; Screenplay, Elan Mastai, David Weaver; Photography, François Dagenais; Designer, Matthew Davies; Costumes, Patrick Antosh; Music, Todor Kobakov; Editor, Geoff Ashenhurst; Casting, Nina Gold, Jenny Lewis, Sara Kay; an H20 Motion Pictures presentation of an Andras Hamori production, in association with Silver Screen, Lumino Pictures, Middle Child Films and Quickfire Films; Canadian, 2011; Deluxe color; Rated R; 90 minutes; American release date: May 18, 2012. **CAST:** Samuel L. Jackson (Foley), Luke Kirby (Ethan), Ruth Negga (Iris), Tom Wilkinson (Xavier), Gil Bellows (Bartender Bill), Aaron Poole (Jake), Tom McCamus (Deacon), Martha Burns (Gretchen), A. C. Peterson (Miro), Rob Archer (Vernon Hicks), Diana Leblanc (Celia), Rufus Crawford (Construction Foreman), Deborah Kara Unger (Helena), Jonas Chernick (Club Manager), Andrew Butcher (Construction Worker), Frank Moore (Walker), Brian Stillar (Mike, Gretchen's Husband), Harrison Smith (Mike, Gretchen's Son), Tyler Bruce (Dean, Gretchen's Son), Chris Gibbs (Concierge, Ethan's Condo), Sergio Buitrago (Bank Manager)

Luke Kirby, Samuel L. Jackson in *The Samaritan* © IFC Films

MAHLER ON THE COUCH (National Center for Jewish Film) a.k.a. *Mahler auf de Couch*; Producers, Eleonore Adlon, Burkhard Ernst, Constantin Seitz; Directors/Screenplay, Percy Adlon, Felix Adlon; Photography, Benedict Neuenfels; Art Directors, Bernt Amadeus Capra, Veronika Merlin; Costumes, Caterina Czepek; Music, Gustav Mahler; Editor, Jochen Künstler; a Pelemele Film & Stage/Cultfilm Produktion presentation in association with ARD Degeto, BR, ORF; Austrian-German, 2010; Color; Not rated; 98 minutes; American release date: May 18, 2012. **CAST:** Johannes Silberschneider (Gustav Mahler), Barbara Romaner (Alma Mahler), Karl Markovics (Sigmund Freud), Friedrich Mücke (Walter Gropius), Eva Mattes (Anna Sofie Schindler-Moll), Lena Stolze (Justine Mahler-Rosé), Nina Berten (Anna von Mildenburg), Karl Fischer (Karl Moll), Mathias Stein (Alexander von Zemlinsky), Max Mayer (Max Burchard), Michael Dangl (Bruno Walter), Michael Rotschopf (Alfred Roller), Manuel Witting (Gustav Klimt), Simon Hatzl (Arnold Rosé), Johanna Orsini-Rosenberg (Berta Zuckerkandl), Daniele Keberle (Franz Hirn), Jolanda Klaus (Maria Anna "Putzi" Mahler), Lotta Klaus (Anna Justine "Gucki" Mahler), Matthias Franz Stein (Alexander von Zelminsky)

Johannes Silberschneider in *Mahler on the Couch* © National Center for Jewish Film

BEYOND THE BLACK RAINBOW (Magnet) Producers, Oliver Linsley, Christya Nordstokke; Director/Screenplay, Panos Cosmatos; Photography, Norm Li; Designer, Bob Bottieri; Costumes, Kathi Moore; Music, Sinoia Caves; Editor, Nicholas Shepard; Special Effects Coordinator, Brant McIllroy; a Chromewood presentation; Canadian; Color; Panavision; Rated R; 110 minutes; American release date: May 18, 2012. **CAST:** Michael Rogers (Barry Nyle), Eva Allan (Elena), Scott Hylands (Mercurio Arboria), Marilyn Norry (Rosmary Nyle), Rondel Reynoldson (Margo), Geoffrey Condor (Mutant), Chris Gauthier (Fat Hesher), Gerry South (Skinny Hesher), Roy Campsall , Ryley Zinger (Sentionauts), Richard Jollymore (Nurse), Christian Sloan (Test Subject), Sara Stockstad (Anna Arboria)

Michael Rogers in *Beyond the Black Rainbow* © Magnet Releasing

INDIE GAME: THE MOVIE (BlinkWorks) Producers/Directors/Editors, Lisanne Pajot, James Swirsky; Co-Executive Producers, Jeff Lindsay, John McCullah, Jourdain Pajot, Ken Schachter, Matthew Swirsky; Photography/Visual Effects, James Swirsky; Music, Jim Guthrie; Presented in association with Flutter Media;Canadian; HD; Color; Not rated; 95 minutes; Release date: May 18, 2012. Documentary on independent game designers; **WITH:** Jonathan Blow, Phil Fish, Edmund McMillen, Tommy Refenes, Renaud Bédard, Brandon Boyer, Anthony Carboni, Ron Carmel, Chris Dahlen, Gus Mastrapa, Danielle McMillen, Jamie Refenes, Kim Refenes, Ken Schachter, Jamin Warren

THE WOMAN IN THE SEPTIC TANK (Ignatius Films) a.k.a. *Ang babae sa septic tank*; Executive Producers, Chris Martinez, Marlon Rivera, Josabeth Alonso, John Victor Tence; Director, Marlon Rivera; Screenplay, Chris Martinez; Photography, Larry Manda; Designer, Reji Regalado; Music, Vincent de Jesus; Editor, Ike Veneracion; a Cinemalaya presentation of a Martinez-Rivera Films, Quantum Films production in association with Straight Shooters Media; Filipino, 2011; Stereo; Color; Not rated; 87 minutes; American release date: May 23, 2012. **CAST:** Eugene Domingo (Mila), JM de Guzman (Bingbong), Kean Cipriano (Rainier), Cai Coretz (Jocelyn), Jonathan Tadioan (Arthur Poongbato), Carlos Dala (Mila's Son), K.C. Marcelo (Mila's Daughter), Cherry Pie Picache, Mercedes Cabral (Themselves), Lani Tapia (Documentary Mila), Sonny Bautista (Security Guard)

Eugene Domingo in *The Woman in the Septic Tank* © Ignatius Films

ARJUN: THE WARRIOR PRINCE (UTV Communications) Producers, Siddhartha Roy Kapur, Ronnie Screwvala; Director, Arnab Chaudhuri; Screenplay, Rajesh Devraj, R.D. Tailang; Photography, Hemant Chaturvedi; Designers, Rachna Rastogi, K.K. Muralidharan; Music, Vishal Dadlani, Dhruv Ghanekar, Shekhar Ravijani; Editor, A. Sreekar Prasad; a Walt Disney Pictures production; Indian; Color; Not rated; 95 minutes; American release date: May 25, 2012. **VOICE CAST:** Yuddvir Bakolia (Arjun), Ila Arun (Kunti), Anjan Srivastav (Lord Shiv), Sachin Khedekar (Lord Krishna), Ashok Banthia (Bheem), Vishnu Sharma (Bheeshma)

OSLO, AUGUST 31ST (Strand) Producers, Hans-Jørgen Osnes, Yngve Sæther; Director, Joachim Trier; Screenplay, Eskil Vogt, Joachim Trier; Based on the 1931 novel *Le feu follet* by Pierre Drieu La Rochelle; Photography, Jackob Ihre; Designer, Jørgen Stangebye Larsen; Costumes, Ellen Dæhli Ystehede; Music, Ola Fløttum, Torgny Amdam; Editor, Olivier Bugge Coutté; Casting, Christian Rubeck, Emil Trier; The Match Factory presentation of a Don't Look Now, Motlys production; Norwegian, 2011; Dolby; Color; Not rated; 95 minutes; American release date: May 25, 2012. **CAST:** Anders Danielsen Lie (Anders), Malin Crépin (Malin), Aksel M. Thanke (Rehab Counselor), Hans Olav Brenner (Thomas), Ingrid Olava (Rebekka, Thomas' Wife), Øystein Røger (David, Editor), Tone Beate Mostraum (Tove), Kjærsti Odden Skjeldal (Mirjam, Woman Hosting Party), Peter Width Kristiansen (Petter, Man at Party), Emil Lund (Calle, Man Hosting Party), Johanne

Arjun: The Warrior Prince © UTV Communications

Kjellevik Ledang (Johanne, Woman Anders Meets), Renate Reinsve (Petter's Date), Andreas Braaten (Karsten, Dealer), Anders Borchgrevink (Øystein, Man at Bar)

FOUND MEMORIES (Film Movement) a.k.a. *Historias que so existem quando lembradas*; Producers, Lucia Murat, Júlia Murat, Christian Boudier, Felicitas Raffo, Juliette LePoutre, Marie-Pierre Macia; Director, Júlia Murat; Screenplay, Júlia Murat, Maria Clara Escobar, Felipe Sholl; Photography, Lucio Bonelli; Designer, Marina Kosovski; Music, Lucas Marcier; Editor, Marina Meliande; a Taiga Filmes, Bonfilm, MPM Film production; Argentine-Brazilian-French, 2011; Color; Cinemascope; Not rated; 98 minutes; American release date: June 1, 2012. **CAST:** Sonia Guedes (Madalena), Lisa E. Fávero (Rita), Luiz Serra (Antonio), Josias Ricardo Merkin (Padre), Antônio Dos Santos (Carlos)

Lisa E. Fáveros in *Found Memories* © Film Movement

EVERY BREATH YOU TAKE (StarCinema) Supervising Producer, Marizel Samson-Martinez; Executive Producers, Charo Santos-Concio, Malou N. Santos; Director, Mae Czarina Cruz; Screenplay, Mel Mendoza-Del Rosario, Zig Marasigan, Anj Pessumal; Story, Mel Mendoza-Del Rosario, Zig Marasigan; Photography, Manuel Teehankee; Designer, Winston Acuyong; Music, Teresa Barrozo; Editor, Marya Ignacio; an ABS-CBN Film Productions production; Filipino; Color; Not rated; 105 minutes; American release date: June 1, 2012. **CAST:** Piolo Pascual (Leo Dimalanta), Angelica Panganiban (Majoy Marasigan), Nova Villa (Lola Pilar), Ryan Eigenmann (Mario), Smokey Manaloto (King), Carlos Agassi (Ace), Joross Gamboa (Jack), Ketchup Eusebio (Chickoy), Janus del Prado (Boy), Ryan Bang (Ji Sun), Cacai Bautista (Mitch), Dominic Ochoa (Leo's Kuya), Lito Legaspi (Leo's Dad), Wendy Valdez (Dianne), Frenchie Dy (Abbie), Regine Angeles (Leila), Freddie Webb (Lolo Pepe), Marnie Lapus (Mrs. Tan), Roden Araneta (Waiter), Art Mendoza (Senior V.P.), Jojit Lorenzo (Police Officer), JM de Guzman (Carwash Boy), Nico de Luna (The One), Jel Pineda (Pregnant Woman), Mark Villanueva (Mario's Right Hand)

ROWDY RATHORE (UTV) Producers, Ronnie Schewvala, Sanjay Leela Bhansali; Director, Prabhu Deva; Screenplay, Shiraz Ahmed; Based on the film *Vikramarkudu* by S.S. Rajamouli; Photography, Santosh Thundiiayil; Designer, Wasiq Khan; Costumes, Neharika Singh; Music, Sajid Ali, Wajid Ali; Editor, Sanjay Sankla; a Sanjay Leela Bhansali Films presentation; Indian; Color; Not rated; 143 minutes; American release date: June 1, 2012. **CAST:** Akshay Kumar (Shiva/IPS Vikram Singh Rathore), Sonakshi Sinha (Neeraja), Nasser (Baapji), Paresh Ganatra (2G), Supreeth Reddy (Antagonist), Jayant Gadekar (Bhima Goon), Gurdeep Kohli (Inspector Razia Khan), Yashpal Sharma (Inspector Vishal Sharma)

Akshay Kumar, Sonakshi Sinha in *Rowdy Rathore* © UTV Communications

HENNING MANKELL'S WALLANDER: THE REVENGE (Music Box Films) Producer, Malte Forssell; Executive Producers, Ole Søndberg, Anni Faurbye Fernandez, Mikael Wallén, Vibeke Windeløv; Director, Charlotte Brändström; Screenplay, Hans Rosenfeldt; Based on story by Henning Mankell; Photography, Alexander Gruszynski; Designer, Anna Asp; Costumes, Kicki Ilander; Music, Fläskkvartetten; Editor, Håkan Karlsson; a Yellow Bird Films production; Swedish; Color; Not rated; 90 minutes; American release date: June 1, 2012. **CAST:** Krister Henriksson (Kurt Wallander), Lena Endre (Katarina Ahlsell), Fredrik Gunnarson (Svartman), Mats Bergman (Nyberg), Sverrir Gudnason, Nina Zanjani, Douglas Johansson, Stina Ekblad, Marianne Mörck (Originally shown on Swedish TV).

PINK RIBBONS, INC. (First Run Features) Producer/Executive Producer, Ravida Din; Director, Léa Pool; Screenplay, Patricia Kearns, Nancy Guerin, Léa Pool; Based on the 2006 book *Pink Ribbons, Inc.: Breast Cancer and the Politics of Philanthropy* by Samantha King; Photography, Daniel Jobin, Sylvaine Dufaux, Nathalie Moliavko-Visotzky; Music, Peter Scheere; Editor, Oana Suteu Khintirian; Animation, Francis Gélinas; a National Film Board of Canada presentation; Canadian; Color; Not rated; 98 minutes; Release date: June 1, 2012. Documentary on the money raised to fight breast cancer; **WITH:** Judy Brady, Barbara A. Brenner, Nancy G. Brinker, James Brophy, Janet Collins, Carol Cone, Dr. Charlene Elliott, Barbara Ehrenreich, Charlotte Haley, Jane Houlihan, Marc Hurlbert, Dr. Marion Kavanaugh-Lynch, Margaret Keith, Samantha King, Evelyn H. Lauder, Ellen Leopold, Dr. Susan Love, Kim McInerney, Dr. Olufunmilayo L. Olopade

SEXUAL CHRONICLES OF A FRENCH FAMILY (IFC Films) a.k.a. *Chroniques sexuelles d'une famille d'aujourd'hui*; Producers, Pascal Arnold, Teddy Vermeulin, Jean-Marc Barr, Jean-Yves Robin, Nicolas Coppermann, Vanessa Fourgeaud, Jean Holtzmann, Julie Bonvicini; Directors, Pascal Arnold, Jean-Marc Barr; Screenplay, Pascal Arnold; Photography, Jean-Marc Barr; Designer, Gaëlle Guitard; Costumes, Mimi Lempicka; Music, Imaro Quartet; Editor, Teddy Vermeulin; Casting, Laurence Wayser; a Toloda, Monkey Pack Films and Super Sonic Productions production with the participation of Canal Plus and Cine Cinema; French; Color; HD; Not rated; 79 minutes; American release date: June 1, 2012. **CAST:** Mathias Melloul (Romain), Valérie Maes (Claire), Stephan

Pink Ribbons, Inc. © First Run Features

Hersoen (Hervé), Leïla Denio (Marie), Nathan Duval (Pierre), Yan Brian (Michel), Adeline Rebeillard (Coralie), Grégory Annoni (Cédric), Laëtitia Favart (Nathalie), Pierre Perrier (Maxime), Oréade Knobloch (Sophie), Stéphane Clerc (Sébastien), Philippe Duquesne (School Director), Astrid Vermuelin (Secretary)

Mathias Melloul, Adeline Rebeillard in *Sexual Chronicles of a French Family* © IFC Films

MUSIC FROM THE BIG HOUSE (Matson Films) Producers, Erin Faith Young, Jennifer St. John; Director, Bruce McDonald; Screenplay, Tony Burgess, Erin Faith Young; Original Concept, Rita Chiarelli; Photography, Steve Cosens; Music, Chris Guglick; Editor, Eamonn O'Connor; a Caché Film & Television presentation; Canadian, 2010; Color; Not rated; 90 minutes; American release date: June 1, 2012. Documentary in which Canada's "Goddess of the Blues," Rita Chiarelli, performs at the Louisiana State Maximum Security Penitentiary; **WITH:** Rita Chiarelli

THE LOVED ONES (Insurge Pictures) Producers, Mark Lazarus, Michael Boughen; Executive Producers, Christopher Mapp, Matthew Street, David Whealy, Bryce Menzies; Director/ Screenplay, Sean Byrne; Photography, Simon Chapman; Designer, Robert Webb; Costumes, Xanthe Heubel; Music, Ollie Olsen; Editor, Andy Canny; Casting, Anousha Zarkesh; a Screen Australia presentation in association with Omnilab Media, an Ambience Entertainment and Mark Lazarus production in association with Film Victoria in association with the Melbourne International Film Festival Premiere Fund; Australian, 2010; Color; Rated R; 84 minutes; American release date: June 1, 2012. **CAST:** Xavier Samuel (Brent), Robin McLeavy (Lola, "Princess"), Victoria Thaine (Holly), Jessica McNamee (Mia), Richard Wilson (Jamie), John Brumpton (Daddy), Andrew S. Gilbert (Paul), Suzi Dougherty (Carla), Victoria Eagger (Judith), Anne Scott-Pendlebury (Bright Eyes), Fred Whitlock (Dan), Leo Taylor (Teacher), Brandon Burns (Takeaway Shop

Rita Chiardelli in *Music from the Big House* © Matson Films

Kai Lennox in *Apartment 143* © Magnet Releasing

Attendant), Stephen Walden (Timmy Valentine), Igor Svin (Rhys Agnew), Eden Porter (Keri Willis), Tom Mahoney (Duncan Fletcher), Gully McGrath (Keir, 8 Years Old), Stevie-Lou Answerth (Princess, 8 Years Old), Liam Duxbury (Duncan, 8 Year Old), Jedda (Dog)

Xavier Samuels in *The Loved Ones* © Insurge Pictures

APARTMENT 143 (Magnet) a.k.a. *Emergo*; Producers, Adrián Guerra, Rodrigo Cortés; Director, Carles Torrens; Screenplay, Rodrigo Cortés; Photography, Óscar Durán; Art Directors, María de la Cámara, Gabriel Paré; Costumes, Fran Cruz; Music, Victor Reyes; Editors, José Tito, Rodrigo Cortés; Casting, Nicole Daniels, Courtney Bright; a Nostromo Pictures production in association with Kinology; Spanish, 2011; Color; Rated R; 80 minutes; Release date: June 1, 2012. **CAST:** Kai Lennox (Alan White), Gia Mantegna (Caitlin White), Michael O'Keefe (Dr. Helzer), Fiona Glascott (Ellen Keagan), Rick Gonzalez (Paul Ortega), Francesc Garrido (Heseltine), Damian Roman (Benny White), Laura Martuscelli (Cynthia), Fermí Reixach (Lamson), Souleymane Diop (Concierge), Alex van Kuyk (Man in the Subway), Óscar Durán (Photographer), Núria Valls (Benny's Teacher), Marcel Barrena, Vincent Damman, Yatma Sall (Paramedics), Mireia Dalmau Quera, Laura Creus Xifra (Teenagers)

PATAGONIA RISING (First Run Features) Producers, Greg Miller, Scott Douglas; Director/ Photography/Editor, Brian Lilla; Music, Axel Herrera; Chilean-American; Color; Not rated; 88 minutes; American release date: June 8, 2012. Documentary on the controversial plan to build five hydroelectric dams in Chile's wilderness; **WITH:** Lalo Romero.

Patagonia Rising © First Run Features

DOUBLE TROUBLE (China Lion) a.k.a. *Bao dao shuang xiong*; Producers, Michelle Yeh, Liu Jing; Director, David Hsun-wei Chang; Screenplay, Zhang Hongyi, Yeh Sho-heng; Photography, Horace Wong; Designer, Cheng Yi-feng; Action Choreographer, Nicky Lee; a Zhujiang Film Group, Serenity Entertainment Co. Ltd., Beijing East Light Film Co., Ltd. Distribution Workshop presentation; Tai-Chinese; Dolby; Color; Not rated; 87 minutes; American release date: June 8, 2012. **CAST:** Jaycee Chan (Jay), Xia Yu (Ocean), Deng Jiajiia (Jane), Lan Chun-Tian (Captain John), Vivian Dawson (Crime Boss Z), Chen Han Dian (Tour Guide Idol), Jessica C (Treasure Thief V), Shoko (Treasure Thief M)

Jaycee Chan in *Double Trouble* © China Lion

WE WON'T GROW OLD TOGETHER (Filmax Intl.) a.k.a. *Nous ne vieillirons pas ensemble*; Producers, Jacques Dorfmann, Maurice Pialat, Jean-Pierre Rassam; Executive Producer/Director/Screenplay, Maurice Pialat, based on his novel; Photography, Luicano Tovoli; Editors, Arlette Langmann, Corinne Lazare; an Empire Films, Lido Films production; French-Italian, 1972; Eastman color; Not rated; 110 minutes; American release date: June 8, 2012. **CAST:** Marlène Jobert (Catherine), Jean Yanne (Jean), Christine Fabréga (Catherine's Mother), Patricia Pierangeli (Annie), Jacques Galland (Catherine's Father), Maurice Risch (Michel), Harry-Max (Jean's Father), Muse Dalbray (Catherine's Grandmother), Macha Méril (Françoise)

Jean Yanne, Marlène Jobert in *We Won't Grow Old Together* © Filmax Intl.

CORPO CELESTE (Film Movement) Producers, Carlo Cresto-Dina, Jacques Bidou, Marianne Dumoulin, Tiziana Soudani; Director/Screenplay, Alice Rohrwacher; Photography, Hélène Louvart; Designer, Luca Servino; Costumes, Loredana Buscemi; Editor, Marco Spoletini; a Tempesta, JBA production, AMKA Film Productions production in association with RAI Cinema; Italian-French, 2011; Dolby; Color; Not rated; 98 minutes; American release date: June 8, 2012. **CAST:** Yle Vianello (Marta), Salvatore Cantalupo (Don Mario), Pasqualina Scuncia (Santa), Anita Caprioli (Rita), Renato Carpentieri (Don Lorenzo), Paola Lavini (Fortunata)

Yle Vianello in *Corpo Celeste* © Film Movement

TAHRIR: LIBERATION SQUARE (Icarus) Producers, Penelope Bortoluzzi, Marco Alessi; Director/Photography, Stefano Savona; Editor, Penelope Bortoluzzi; a coproduction of Picofilms and Dugong; French-Italian, 2011; Color; Not rated; 91 minutes; American release date: June 11, 2012. Documentary on Egypt's efforts to overcome Mubarak's regime.

Tahrir: Liberation Square © Icarus Films

UFO IN HER EYES (Corazón Intl./Match Factory) Producer, Klaus Maeck; Director, Sabotage Sister (Xiaolu Guo); Screenplay, Xiaolu Guo, Pamela Casey; Based on the 2009 novel by Xiaolu Guo; Photography, Michal Tywoniiuk; Art Director, Jun Yao; Music, Mocky; Editor, Nikolai Hartmann; German-Chinese, 2011; Color; Not rated; 110 minutes; American release date: June 13, 2012. **CAST:** Shi Ke (Kwok Yun), Udo Kier (Steve Frost), Mandy Zhang (Chief Chang), Y. Peng Liu (Bicycle Repairman), Z. Lan (Headmaster Lee), Massela Wei (Secretary Zhao), Dou Li (Old Kwok)

UFO in Her Eyes © Corázon Intl.

EL VELADOR (Icarus) a.k.a. *The Night Watchman*; Producer/Director/Photography, Natalia Almada; Editors, Natalia Almada, Julien Devaux; an Altamura production; Mexican, 2011; Color; Not rated; 72 minutes; American release date: June 14, 2012. Documentary on the night watchman who keeps an eye on the extravagant mausoleums of some of Mexico's most notorious drug lords.

EXTRATERRESTRIAL (Focus World) a.k.a. *Extraterrestre*; Producer, Nahikari Ipioa; Director/ Screenplay, Nacho Vigalondo; Photography/Editor, Jon D. Dominiquez; Designer, Idoia Esteban; Music, Jorge Magaz; a Sayaka Producciones/Apaches Entertainment production; Spanish; Dolby; Color; HD; Widescreen; Not rated; 93 minutes; American release date: June 15, 2012. **CAST:** Julián Villagrán (Julio), Michelle Jenner (Julia), Raúl Cimas (Carlos), Carlos Areces (Ángel)

El Velador © Icarus Films

PATANG (Khushi Films) a.k.a. *The Kite*; Producer, Jaideep Punjabi; Director/Editor, Prashant Bhargava; Screenplay, Prashant Bhargava, James Townsend; Photography, Shanker Raman; Designer, Meera Lakhai; Costumes, Sunjata Sharma; Music, Mario Grigorov; Casting, Anjali Punjabi; Indian; Dolby; Color; HD; Not rated; 105 minutes; American release date: June 15, 2012. **CAST:** Seema Biswas (Sudha), Nawazuddin Siddiqui (Chakku), Sugandha Garg (Priya), Mukkund Shukla (Jayesh), Aakash Maheriya (Bobby), Pannaben Soni (Ba)

SOMETHING FROM NOTHING: THE ART OF RAP (Indomina) Producer, Paul Toogood; Executive Producers, Paul Toogood, Jorge Hinojosa, Ice-T, Alison Toogood, Simon D. Pearce, David Kaplan; Director, Ice-T; Co-Director, Andy Baybutt; Photography, Jeremy Hewson, Andy Baybutt, John Halliday; Editor, Kieran Smythe; a Jolygood Films, Westmount Films and Final Level Entertainment production; British; Color; HD; Rated R; 106 minutes; American release date: June 15, 2012. Documentary on hip-hop; **WITH:** Bun B, B-Real, Afrika Bambaataa, Busy Bee, Joe Budden, Grandmaster Caz, Common, Anthony "Treach" Criss, Ice Cube, Chuck D., Royce Da 59, Dana Dane, Mos Def, Snoop Dogg, Dr. Dre, Eminem, Lord Finesse, Doug E. Fresh, Ice-T, Lord Jamar, Cheryl "Salt" James, Big Daddy Kane, Ras Kass, Kool Keith, KRS-One, MC Lyte, Marley Marl, Darryl McDaniels, Melle Mel, Nas, DJ Premier, Q-Tip, Raekwon, Rakim, Redman, Puerto Rico, Joseph Simmons, Immortal Technique, WC, Kanye West, Chino XL, Xzibit.

Ice-T in *Something from Nothing* © Indomina

MEN ON THE BRIDGE (MoMA) a.k.a. *Köprüdekiler*; Producers, Fabian Massah, Asli Özuge; Director/Screenplay, Asli Özge; Photography, Emre Erkmen; Editos, Vessela Martschewski, Aylín Zoi Tínel, Christof Schertenleib; a co-production of Endorphine Productions, Yení Sínemacilik, Kaliber Film, Bayerischer Rundfunk, ZDF/3SAT, Rush Hour Films; German-Turkish-Dutch, 2009; Dolby; Color; Not rated; 87 minutes; American release date: June 20, 2012. **CAST:** Cemile Ilker (Cemile), Umut Ilker (Umut), Fikret Portakal (Fikret), Murat Tokgöz (Murat)

Men on the Bridge © MoMA

GYPSY (MK2) a.k.a. *Cigan*; Producers, Rudolf Biermann, Martin Sulik; Director, Martin Sulik; Screenplay, Maret Lescak, Martin Sulik; Photography, Martin Sec; Designer, Frantisek Liptak; Music, Peter Mojzis; Editor, Jiri Brozek; an In Film, Titanic, RTVS, CT production; Czech-Slovakian, 2011; Color; Not rated; 100 minutes; American release date: June 27, 2012. **CAST:** Janko Mizigar (Adam), Martin Hangurbadzo (Marian), Martinka Kotlarova (Julka), Ivan Mirga (Father), Miroslava Jarabekova (Mother), Miroslav Gulyas (Zigo), Attila Mokos (Priest)

Gypsy © MK2

ABENDLAND (Geyrhalter Film) Director/Photography, Nikolaus Geyrhalter; Screenplay, Wolfgang Widerhofer, Nikolaus Geyrhalter, Maria Arlamovsky; Editor, Wolfgang Widerhofer; Austrian; 2011; Dolby; Color; Not rated; 90 minutes; American release date: June 27, 2012. Documentary on the "imagined community" of Europe as the filmmaker records various people at work and play throughout the continent.

BUSONG (Solito Arts) a.k.a. *Palawan Fate*; Producers, Auraeus Solito, Hai Balbuena, Baby Ruth Villarama, Chuck Gutierrez, Alfred Vargas; Executive Producer, Jong de Castro; Director, Auraeus Solito; Screenplay, Kanakan Balintagos, Henry Burgos; Photography, Louie Quirino; Designer, Hai Balbuena; Music, Diwa De Leon; Editor, Chuck Gutierrez; a Cinemalaya presentation of a Solito Arts production in association with Alternative Vision Cinema and Voyage Studios; Filipino, 2011; Color; Not rated; 95 minutes; American release date: June

Abendland © Geyrhalter Film

29, 2012. **CAST:** Alessandra de Rossi (Punay), Clifford Bañagale (Aris), Dax Alejandro (Lulong), Bonivie Budao (Ninita), Rodrigo Santikan (Angkadang), Chris Haywood (Landowner), Walter Arenio (Tony)

Rodrigo Santikan in *Busong* © Solito Arts

COLLABORATOR (Tribeca Film) Supervising Producer, Julien Favre; Producer, Luca Matrundola; Executive Producers, Ted Hope, Pascal Vaguelsy, Bryan Gliserman, Charlotte Mickie; Director/ Screenplay, Martin Donovan; Photography, Julie Kirkwood; Designer, Peter Cosco; Costumes, Nadia "Sunny" Sorge; Music, Manels Favre; Music Supervisor, Matt Biffa; Editor, Karen Porter; an Entertainment One/DVF Distribution presentation of a DViant Films production in association with This Is That; Canadian-American; Dolby; Color; Not rated; 87 minutes; American release date: July 6, 2012. **CAST:** Martin Donovan (Robert Longfellow), David Morse (Gus Williams), Olivia Williams (Emma Stiles), Melissa Auf der Maur (Alice Longfellow), Julian Richings (Maurice LeFont), Katherine Helmond (Irene Longfellow), Eileen Ryan (Betty), Mark-Cameron Fraser (SWAT Cop), Phillip Palmer, Leslie Sykes (News Anchors), Jim Pirri (Officer Revel), Russell Yuen (Voice of David Piro), David Rasche, Mary B. Ward (Voices of Radio Hosts)

Martin Donovan, David Morse in *Collaborator* © Tribeca Film

LAST RIDE (Music Box Films) Producers, Nicholas Cole, Antonia Barnard; Executive Producer, Ricci Swart; Director, Glendyn Ivin; Screenplay, Mac Gudgeon; Based on the 2004 novel *The Last Ride* by Denise Young; Photography, Greig Fraser; Designer, Jo Ford; Costumes, Jodie Fried; Music, Paul Charlier; Editor, Jack Hutchings; Casting, Fiona Dann; a Screen Australia presentation of a Talk Films production in association with Film Victoria, South Australian Film Corporation and Adelaide Film Festival; Australian, 2009; Dolby; Color; Not rated; 100 minutes; American release date: July 6, 2012. **CAST:** Hugo Weaving (Kev), Tom Russell (Chook), Anita Hegh (Maryanne), John Brumpton (Max), Sonya Suares (Dr. Zareena Khan), Kelton Pell (Ranger Lyall), Loren Horsley (Girl in Pub), Adam Morgan (Man in Roadhouse), Chrissie Page (Storekeeper), Chris Weir, Michael Allen, Beau Hurren (Locals in Pub), Mick Coulthard (Uncle Mick), Lucy Russell (Girl in the Chicken Shop), Jane Liscombe (News Reporter), Mark Taylor (Police Sergeant), Kate Portus (Mother on Bus), Rachel Francis (Girl Feeding Crooks), Lucas Smith (Boy on the Bus), James Cavanaugh (Old Man in the Store), Reg (Mr. Right)

Hugo Weaving, Tom Russell in *Last Ride* © Music Box Films

STARRY STARRY NIGHT (China Lion) Producers, Wang Zhongjuin, Albert Tong, Frank Liu Chuen, Lu Weijan, Wang Zhonglei; Director/Screenplay, Tom Shu-yu Lin; based on the 2009 illustrated book *The Starry Starry Night* by Jimmy Liao; Photography, Jake Pollock; Designer, Tsai Pei-ling; Costumes, Wei Shiang-rong; Music, World's End Girlfriend; a Huayi Brothers Media Corporation, Media China Corporation Ltd., Sky Land Entertainment Ltd. and Trends Media Group presentation of a Big Feet production; Taiwanese-Chinese, 2011; Dolby; Color; Not rated; 120 minutes; American release date: July 6, 2012. **CAST:** Xu Jiao (Xiao Mei), Eric Lin (Lee), Lin Hui-min (Zhou Yu-jie), Harlem Yu (Mei's Father),

Rene Liu (Mei's Mother), Gwei Lun-mei (Older Xiao Mei), Kenneth Tsang (Mei's Grandfather), Janel Tsai (Xiao Jie's Mother)

Eric Lin, Xu Jiao in *Starry Starry Night* © China Lion

CHINA HEAYWEIGHT (Zeitgeist) Producers, Bob Moore, Peter Wintonick, Yi Han, Zhao Qi; Executive Producers, Mila Aung-thwin, Lixin Fan, Daniel Cross; Director/Screenplay, Yung Chang; Photography, Sun Shaoguang; Music, Olivier Alary; Editors, Hannele Halm, Xi Feng; an Eyesteelfilm, Yuanfang Media, CNEX production, supervised by China Film Co-production Company; Chinese-Canadian; Color; Not rated; 89 minutes; American release date: July 6, 2012. Documentary on former boxer Qi Moxiang and his efforts to recruit new athletes from the impoverished farms of the Sichuan province; **WITH:** Qi Moxiang, Zhao Zhong, Miao Yunfei, He Zongli, Ye Xinchun

Qi Moxiang, Ahikiro Matsumoto in *China Heavyweight* © Zeitgeist Films

BOL BACHCHAN (Fox Star Studios) Producers, Ajay Devgn, Shree Ashtavinayak; Director, Rohit Shetty; Screenplay, Yunus Sajawal; Dialogues, Farhad-Sajid; Photography, Dudley; Art Director, Narendra Rahurikar; Music, Himesh Reshammiya; Lyrics, Swanand Kirkire, Farhad-Sajid, Shabbir Ahmed; Background Score, Amar Mohile; Editor, Steven Bernard; a Shree Ashtavinayak, Cine Vision Ltd. and Ajay Devgn Ffilms production; Indian; Color; Rated PG; 150 minutes; American release date: July 6, 2012. **CAST:** Ajay Devgn (Prithviraj Raghuvanshi), Asin (Sania Ali/Apeksha), Abhishek Bachchan (Abbas Ali/Abhishek Bachchan), Prachi Desai (Radhika Raghuvanshi), Krishna Abhishek (Ravi Shastri), Asrani (Shastri), Amitabh Bachchan (Item), Archana Puran Singh (Zohra/Madhumati), Jeetu Verma (Vikrant Raghuvanshi), Neeraj Vora (Maakhan)

Ajay Devgan in *Bol Bachchan* © Fox Star Studios

INVISIBLE (Plan b Prods.) a.k.a. *Lo roim alaich*; Producer, Ronen Ben Tal; Director, Michael Aviad; Screenplay, Michal Aviad, Tal Omer; Photography, Guy Raz; Designer, Adi Sagi-Amar; Costumes, Laura Sheim; a Tag/Traum Filmproduktion in association with ZDF/Arte, Metro Communications; Israeli-German, 2011; Dolby; Color; Not rated; 89 minutes; American release date: July 9, 2012. **CAST:** Ronit Elkabetz (Lily), Evgenya Dodina (Nira), Sivan Levy (Dana), Gil Frank (Amnon), Gal Lev (Yuval)

Evgenya Dodina, Ronit Elkabetz in *Invisible* © Plan b Prods.

RED LIGHTS (Anchor Bay) Producers, Adrián Guerra, Rodrigo Cortés; Executive Producers, Cindy Cowan, Irving Cowan, Lisa Wilson; Director/Screenplay/Editor, Rodrigo Cortés; Photography, Xavi Gimenez; Designer, Antón Laguna; Costumes, Patricia Monné; Music, Víctor Reyes; Visual Effects, Alex Villagrasa; Casting, Ronna Kress; a Parlay Films presentation of a Nostromo Pictures production in association with Cindy Cowan Entertainment, Antena3 Films and Televisió de Catalunya; Spanish-American; Dolby; Widescreen; Color; Rated R; 113 minutes; American release date: July 13, 2012. **CAST:** Cillian Murphy (Tom Buckley), Sigourney Weaver (Margaret Matheson), Robert De Niro (Simon Silver), Toby Jones (Paul Shackleton), Joely Richardson (Monica Hansen), Elizabeth Olsen (Sally Owen), Craig Roberts (Ben), Leonardo Sbaraglia (Leonard Palladino), Adriane Lenox (Rina), Garrick Hagon (Howard McColm), Burn Gorman (Benedict Cohen), Mitchell Mullen (Jim Carroll), Nathan Osgood (Michael Sidgwick), Madeleine Potter (Sarah Sidgwick), Eloise Webb (Susan Sidgwick), Jeany Spark (Traci Northop), Jan Cornet (David Matheson), Robert G. Slade (Interviewer – 70's), Eugenio Mira (Young Simon Silver), Lynn Blades (Dana), Eben Young (Dick), Becci Gemmell (Lucy Marconi), Jee Yun Lee (Fiona Stewart), Emma Reynolds, Peter Brooke, Liliana Cabal, Karen David, Molly Malcolm, Robert Paterson, Jason Lewis, Jeff Mash, Harris Gordon (Reporters), Josette Simon

(Corrine), Carlos Bermúdez Sagrera (Stevie), Anselmo Cuesta (Stevie's Father), Grant Russell (Pilot), Patricia Potter (Doctor), Bola Olubowale (Bodyguard), Anna Dorca (Katia Novkova), Joel Vigo (Richard Vargas), Jajube Mandiela (Girl with Piercings), Jesse Bostick (Guy), Gina Bramhill (Judi Cale), Jean Daigle (Sally's Father), Ann Turnbull (Sally's Mother), Eric Loren (Policeman), Max Hausmann (Dr. Campbell), Mercé Vidal (Dr. Heynes), Miguel Bordoy (Prof. Franklin), Benjamin Nathan-Serio (Student in Magna Room), Paulette Sinclair (Woman in Wheel Chair), Simon Lee Phillips (Standing Spectator), Aidan Shipley (Tom's Soldier Son), Roscoe van Dyke (Biker), Brian Lehane (Psychic Surgery Patient), Markus Parillo (Notebook Man), Kathy Imrie (Indigent Woman), Howard Swinson (Old Man on Bench), Larissa Bouvier (Teenager on Bench), Syd Mostow (Martin Weiner), Ignacio Carreño López, Richard Felix, Joshua Zamrycki (Men in Bathroom), Wendy Boyd (45-Year-old Sally), Anna Ferguson (Older Sally), Xavier Capdet (Beadle), Alicia Caycho (Maria Vargas), Clelia Bain (Dorina Vargas), Óscar Rodriguez (Decoy), Lex Lang, Grant George (Presenters), Bridget Hoffman, Rif Hutton (Radio Voices), Angelina Wahler (Voice of Susan Sidgwick)

Robert De Niro, Joely Richardson, Toby Jones in *Red Lights* © Anchor Bay

IT'S THE EARTH NOT THE MOON (Goncalo Tocha) a.k.a. *na Terra não é na Lua*; Producer/Director/Photography, Gonçalo Tocha; Screenplay, Gonçalo Tocha, Dídio Pestana, Rui Ribeiro, Rui Gulherme Lopes; Music, Didio Pestana; Editors, Rui Ribeiro, Gonçalo Tocha, Catherine Villeret; a Goncalo Tocha, Baraca 13 production; Portugeuse; Color; DV; Not rated; 183 minutes; American release date: July 13, 2012. Documentary/travelogue on the remote mid-Atlantic island of Corvo.

It's the Earth not the Moon © Goncalo Tocha

ALPS (Kino Lorber) a.k.a. *Alpeis*; Producers, Athina Rachel Tsangari, Yorgos Lanthimos; Director, Yorgos Lanthimos; Screenplay, Yorgos Lanthimos, Efthimis Filippou; Photography, Christos Voudouris; Designer, Anna Georgiadou; Costumes, Thanos Papastergiou, Vassilia Rozana; Editor, Yorgos Mavropsaridis; a Haos Film presentation and production; Greece, 2011; Dolby; Widescreen; Color; Not rated; 93 minutes; American release date: July 13, 2012. **CAST:** Aggeliki Papoulia (Nurse), Johnny Verkis (Coach), Ariane Labed (Gymnast), Aris Servetalis (Mont Blanc), Stavros Psillakis, Efthimis Filippou, Maria Kirozi

Aggeliki Papoulia in *Alps* © Kino Lorber

FAMILY PORTRAIT IN BLACK AND WHITE (First Pond Entertainment) Producer, Boris Ivanov; Director/Screenplay/Photography/Editor, Julia Ivanova; Photography, Stanislav Shakhov; Music, Boris Sichon; Editor, Mike Jackson; Interfilm Productions; Ukranian-Canadian, 2011; Color; Not rated; 85 minutes; American release date: July 13, 2012. Documentary on Olga Nenya and her 27 children: 4 biological, 23 adopted or foster; **WITH:** Olga Nenya.

Olga Nenya and her children in *Family Portrait in Black and White* © First Pond Entertainment

COCKTAIL (Eros) Producers, Saif Ali Khan, Dinesh Vijan; Director, Homi Adajania; Screenplay, Imtiaz Ali, Sajid Ali; Photography, Anil Mehta; Music, Pritam Chakraborty; Editor, A. Sreekar Prasad; an Illuminati Films production; Indian; Color; Not rated; 144 minutes; American release date: July 13, 2012. **CAST:** Saif Ali Khan (Gautam Kapoor), Deepika Padukone (Veronica D'Costa), Diana Penty (Meera Sahni), Dimple Kapadia (Kavita Kapoor), Boman Irani (Randhir "Randy" Malhotra), Randeep Hooda (Kunal Ahuja), Nathan Brine (Pedro)

VALLEY OF STRENGTH (Dan Wolman Prods.) a.k.a. *Gei oni*; Director/ Screenplay, Dan Wolman; Based on the 1982 novel *Gei oni* by Shulamit Ladid; Photography, Ran Aviad; Music, Ori Vidslavski; Editor, Shoshi Wolman; Israeli, 2010; Color; Not rated; 102 minutes; American release date: July 13, 2012. **CAST:** Tamar Alkan (Fania), Zion Ashkenazi (Yechiel), Ya'ackov Bodo, Levana Finkelstein, Ezra Dagan.

THE WELL-DIGGER'S DAUGHTER (Kino Lorber) a.k.a. *La file du puisatier*; Producers, Alain Sarde, Jerome Seydoux; Director/Screenplay, Daniel Auteuil; based on the 1940 screenplay by Marcel Pagnol; Photography, Jean-Francois Robin; Designer, Jean-Marc Pacaud; Costumes, Pierre-Yves Gayraud; Music, Alexandre Desplat; Editor, Joelle Hache; Casting, Elodie Demey; an A.S. Films, Zack Films, Pathé, TF1 Films production, in association with Canal Plus, CinéCinéma; French, 2011; Dolby; Color; Not rated; 107 minutes; American release date: July 20, 2012. **CAST:** Daniel Auteuil (Pascal Amoretti, The Well-Digger), Kad Merad (Félipe Rambert), Sabine Azéma (Mme. Mazel), Jean-Pierre Darroussin (M. Mazel), Nicolas Duvauchelle (Jacques Mazel), Astrid Bergès-Frisbey (Patricia Amoretti), Emilie Cazenave (Amanda), Marie-Anne Chazel (Nathalie), Coline Bosso (Isabelle), Chloé Malarde (Marie), Brune Coustellier (Leonore), Ilona Porte (Roberte), Jean-Louis Barcelona (Clerk), Patrick Bosso (Waiter), François-Eric Gendron (Captain)

Nicolas Duvauchelle, Astrid Bergès-Frisbey in *The Well-Digger's Daughter* © Kino Lorber

HARA-KIRI: DEATH OF A SAMURAI (Tribeca) a.k.a. *Ichimei*; Producers, Toshiaki Nakazawa, Jeremy Thomas; Director, Takashi Miike; Screenplay, Kikumi Yamagishi; Based on the story *Ibun rônin-ki* by Yasuhiko Takiguchi; Photography, Nobuyasu Kita; Art Director, Yuji Hayashida; Costumes, Kazuko Kurosawa; Music, Ryûichi Sakamoto; Editor, Kenji Yamashita; Stunts, Keiji Tsujii; Casting, Yuriko Kitada; a Sedic Intl., Dentsu, Shochiku, Kodansha, OLM, Recorded Pictures Company, Yamanashi Nichinichi Shimbun, YBS, Amuse Soft Entertainment, Yahoo! Japan, Asahi Shimbun & Shochiku presentation; Japanese, 2011; Dolby; Color; 3D; 128 minutes; American release date: July 20, 2012. **CAST:** Ebizô Ichikawa (Hanshirô Tsugumo), Eita (Motome Chijiiwa), Hikari Mitsushima (Miho), Naoto Takenaka (Tajiri), Munetaka Aoki (Hikokuro Omadaka), Hirofumi Arai (Hayatonosho Matsuzaki), Kazuki Namioka (Umanosuke Kawabe), Yoshihisa Amano (Sasaki), Takehiro Hira (Lord Li Kamonnokami Naokata), Ippei Takahashi (Naito), Ayumu Saitô (Fujita), Goro Daimon (Landlord), Takashi Sasano (Priest), Baijaku Nakamura (Jinnai Chijiiwa), Kôji Yausho (Kageyu Saito)

PLANET OF SNAIL (Cinema Guild) Producers, Kim Min-chul, Gary Kam; Executive Producer, Cho Dong-sung; Director/Photography, Yi Seung-jun; Music, Min Seongki; Editors, Simon El Habre, Yi Seung-jun; a Creativeast, Dalpaengee presentation of Music, Min Seong-ki; Editors, Simon El-Habre, Yi Seung-jun; a Creativeast, NKH co-production in association with YLE, Finnish Film Foundation;

Ebizio Ichikawa in *Hara-Kiri* © Tribeca Film

South Korean-Japanese-Finnish, 2011; Dolby; Color; HD; Not rated; 87 minutes; American release date: July 25, 2012. Documentary on deaf and blind Young-chan and his relationship with his dedicated wife Soon-ho; **WITH:** Young-chan, Soon-ho

Young-chan, Soon-ho in *Planet of Snail* © Cinema Guild

BIG BOYS GONE BANANAS!* (WG Film) Producer, Margarete Jangård; Director/ Screenplay/Narrator, Fredrik Gertten; Photography, Joseph Aguirre, Frank Pineda, Kiki Allgeier, others; Music, Dan Gisen Malmquist Conny Malmqvist; Editors, Jesper Osmund, Benjamin Binderup; Swedish-Danish-German-American-British, 2011; Stereo; Color; Not rated; 90 minutes; American release date: July 27, 2012. Documentary on how Dole Food Company tried to prevent a pair of Swedish filmmakers from showing a documentary about a lawsuit against their company; **WITH:** Alex Rivera, Alfonso Allende, Arvid Jurjaks, Bart Simpson, Bernt Hermele, Charlotte Lundgren, Dan Koeppel, David Magdael, Dawn Hudson, Jesper Osmund, Juan J. Dominquez, Ken Silverstein, Lars Åström, Lincoln Bandlow, Luciano Astrudillo, Margarete Jangård, Mats Johansson, Michael Carter, Mikael Wiehe

Fredrik Gertten in *Big Boys Gone Bananas!* © WG Film

SACRIFICE (Goldwyn) a.k.a. *Zhao shi gu er*; Producers, Ren Zhonglun, Long Qiuyun, Qin Hong, Chen Hong; Executive Producers, Chen Hong, Qin Hong; Director/Screenplay, Chen Kaige; Based on a screenplay by Gao Xuan, Ren Baoru, Zhao Ningyu, from the play *The Orphan of Zhao*; Photography, Yang Shu; Designer, Liu Qing; Costumes, Chen Tongxun; Music, Ma Shangyou; Editor, Derek Hui; Action Choreographer, Ku Huenchiu; a Huaxia Film Distribtuion, Easter Mordor, Stella Mega Films Co. production; Chinese, 2010; Dolby; Super 35 Widescreen; Color; Rated R; 122 minutes; American release date: July 27, 2012. **CAST:** Ge You (Cheng Ying), Wang Xueqi (Tu'an Gu), Huang Xiaoming (Han Jue), Fan Bingbing (Zhuang Ji), Hai-Qing (Cheng Ying's Wife), Zhang Fengyi (Gongsun Chujiu), Zhao Wenzhuo (Zhao Shuo), Bao Guo'an (Zhao Dun), Wang Han (The Orphan of Zhao, Child), Zhao Wenhao (The Orphan of Zhao, Youth), Peng Bo (Ling Gong), Wang Jinsong (Advisor), Arthur Chen (The Young King), Dong Wenjun (Ling Zhe), Li Dongxue (Timi Ming), Li Geng (Noodle-Eating Man), Liu Yajin (Patient), Zhao Shili (Messenger)

Fan Bingbing in *Sacrifice* © Goldwyn Films

SHUT UP AND PLAY THE HITS (Oscilloscope) Producers, Lucas Ochoa, Thomas Benski, James Murphy; Executive Producers, Christine Vachon, Keith Wood. The Creators Project; Co-Executive Producers, Terry Felgate, Randall Poster; Directors, Dylan Southern, Will Lovelace; Photography, Reed Morano; Music Supervisors, Jane Bridgeman, Candy Rebbeck; Editor, Mark Burnett; a Pulse Films production; British; Color; HD; Not rated; 108 minutes; American release date: July 27, 2012. Documentary captures LCD Soundsystem's farewell engagement at Madison Square Garden in April of 2011; **WITH:** James Murphy, Pat Mahoney, Nancy Whang, Al Doyle, Gavin Russom, Tyler Pope, Matt Thornley, Keith Wood, Chuck Klosterman

James Murphy in *Shut Up and Play the Hits* © Oscilloscope Laboratories

NUIT #1 (Adopt Films) Producer, Nancy Grant; Director/Screenplay, Anne Émond; Photography, Mathieu Laverdière; Designer, Eric Barbeau; Costumes, Yola Van Keeuwenkamp; Music, Martin M. Tetrault; Editor, Mathieu Bouchard-Malo; a Metafilms production; Canadian, 2011; Color; Not rated; 91 minutes; American release date: July 27, 2012. **CAST:** Catherine de Léan (Clara), Dimitri Storoge (Nikolai), Véronique Rebizov, Raphaël Boulanger, Mika Pluviose, Maïsa Bastien (Children)

Dimitri Storoge, Catherine de Léan in *Nuit #1* © Adopt Films

BURNING MAN (IFC Films) Producers, Andy Paterson, Jonathan Teplitzky; Executive Producers, Daria Jovicic, Cedric Jeanson, Sam Tromans; Director/Screenplay, Jonathan Teplitzky; Photography, Garry Phillips; Designer, Steven Jones-Evans; Costumes, Lizzy Gardiner; Music, Lisa Gerrard; Editor, Martin Connor; Casting, Nikki Barrett; a Screen Australia in association with Screen NSW, Filmbox and Latitude Media presentation of an Andy Paterson production; Australian, 2011; Dolby; Widescreen; Color; HD; Not rated; 109 minutes; American release date: July 27, 2012. **CAST:** Matthew Goode (Tom), Bojana Novakovic (Sarah), Essie Davis (Karen), Kerry Fox (Sally), Rachel Griffiths (Miriam), Anthony Hayes (Brian), Jack Heanly (Oscar), Kate Beahan (Lesley), Gia Carides (Carol), Marta Dusseldorp (Lisa), Robyn Malcolm (Kathryn), Matthew Moore (Luke), Simone Kessell (Oscar's Teacher), Jack Campbell (Ian), Kathryn Beck (Marti), Laura Brent (Crying Nurse), Elena Carapetis (Jane), James Cheney (Motel Manager), Rodger Corser (Jack), Katie Fitchett, Lauren Hamilton Neill (Mums), Alan Flower (Fish Man), Genevieve Hegney (Constable Judith Higgs), Aimee Horne (Ms. Woodcock), Martin Lynes (Graham), Lech Mackiewicz (Blind Man), Garry McDonald (Dr. Burgess), Dan Prowse (Peter Gardener), Sue-Ann San (Toni), Justin Smith (Dr. Allen), Alin Sumarwata (Post Op Eye Nurse), Ben Tate (Butcher), Karl Diercke, Kristin McGroder, Mikey Wise (Tom's Paranorma Staff), Elizabeth Black (Oncology Receptionist), Jenna Lind (ER Nurse)

Bojana Novakovic, Matthew Goode in *Burning Man* © IFC Films

FREE RADICALS: A HISTORY OF EXPERIMENTAL FILM (Kino Lorber) Producers, Ron Dyens, Aurélia Prévieu; Director, Pip Chodorov; Screenplay, Lucy Allwood, Pip Chodorov; Photography, Nicolas Rideau, Pip Chodorov, Ville Piippo; Music, Slink Moss; Editor, Nicolas Sarkissian; French; 80 minutes; Release date: August 3, 2012. **WITH:** Stan Brakhage, Robert Breer, Pip Chodorov, Stephan Chodorov, Ken Jacobs, Peter Kubelka, Maurice Lemaître, Jonas Mekas, John Mhiripiri, MM Serra, Michael Snow, Stan Vanderbeek

DREAMS OF A LIFE (Strand) Producers, Cairo Cannon, James Mitchell; Executive Producers, Katherine Butler, Tabitha Jackson, Alan Maher, Paul McGowan, André Singer; Director/ Screenplay, Carol Morley; Photography, Mary Farbrother, Lynda Hall; Designer, Chris Richmond; Costumes, Leonie Prendergast; Music, Barry Adamson; Editor, Chris Wyatt; Visual Effects Supervisor, Jonathan Privett; Casting, Robert Sterne; a Film4 and U.K. Film Council, in association with Shoot for the Moon, with the participation of Bord Scannán na Héireann/ Irish Film Board, of a Cannon and Morley production with Soho Moon Pictures; Irish-British; Color; Not rated; 95 minutes; American release date: August 3, 2012. Documentary-drama on the mystery behind a 38-year-old woman found dead in her London apartment more than two years after she had expired; **WITH:** Zawe Ashton (Joyce Vincent), Neelam Bakshi (Mother), Alix Luka-Cain (Young Joyce), Cornell John (Father), Jay Simpson (Lock Smith), Ki'juan Whitton (Kyle), Lee Colley (Sound Engineer), Daren Elliott Holmes (Bailiff), Frances Cooper (Joyce's Sister), Jonathan Harden (Eddie), Sophie Leonie (Vincent's Sister)

Donald Trump in *You've Been Trumped* © Montrose Pictures

Rhydian Vaughan, Chang Hsiao-chuan, Gwei Lun-mei in *Girlfriend Boyfriend* © China Lion

Zawe Ashton in *Dreams of a Life* © Strand Releasing

YOU'VE BEEN TRUMPED (Montrose Pictures) Producer, Richard Phinney; Director, Anthony Baxter; Screenplay, Richard Phinney, Anthony Baxter; Photography, Anthony Baxter, Susan Munro, David Milne; Music, Jónsi; Editor, William Rice; Animation Production, Fifty Nine Productions; a Bell Rock production; British; Dolby; Color; HD; Not rated; 96 minutes; American release date: August 3, 2012. Documentary on how mogul Donald Trump callously destroyed ecologically unspoiled real estate in Northern Scotland in order to build a pricy golf course and luxury hotel; **WITH:** Michael Forbes, Molly Forbes, Martin Ford, Ian Francis, Sarah Malone, David McCue, David Milne, Susan Munro, Paul O'Connor, Donald Trump

GIRLFRIEND BOYFRIEND (China Lion) a.k.a. *Gf*Bf*; Producer, Weijan Liu; Director/Screenplay, Gillies Yang Ya-che; Photography, Jake Pollock; an Atom Cinema production; Taiwanese; Color; Not rated; 106 minutes; American release date: August 3, 2012. **CAST:** Chang Hsiao-chuan (Liam), Gwei Lun -Mei (Mabel), Rhydian Vaughan (Aaron), Bryan Shu-Hao Chang (Sean)

SOLDIERS OF FORTUNE (Roadside Attractions) Producers, Robert Crombie, Jeff Most, Natalya Smirnova; Executive Producers, Richard Salvatore, Freddy Brady, Paul Hudson, Jeff Rice; Director, Maxim Korostyshevsky; Screenplay, Alexandre Coscas, Joe Kelbley, Robert Crombie; Story, Alexandre Coscas, Joe Kelbley; Photography, Maria Solovieva; Designer, Nikolay Ryabtsev; Costumes, Natalya Sokolova; Music, Joseph Loduca; Editors, Tim Alverson, Danny Saphire, Igor Litoninsky; Casting, Shannon Makhanian; a Highbridge Production presentation in association with Globus Films and Crombie Film and Most/Rice Films; Russian-American; Super 35 Widescreen; Color; Rated R; 94 minutes; Release date: August 3, 2012. **CAST:** Christian Slater (Craig McCenzie), Sean Bean (Dimidov), Ving Rhames (Grimaud), Dominic Monaghan (Sin), Colm Meaney (Mason), Oxana Korostyshevskaya (Cecelia), Charlie Bewley (Charles Vanderbeer), Ryan Donowho (Ernesto), Gennadi Vengerov (Col. Lupo), Freddy Rodriguez (Reed), James Cromwell (Haussman), Sarah Ann Schultz (Magda Lupo), Martina Jagodkina (Helen), Gary Wasniewski (Captain), Romuald Makarenko (Grimaud's Client), Svetlana Tsvichenko (Elize), Shawn Parsons (The Pitchman), Marusja Korostyshevskaya (Reed's Daughter), Ekaterina Suslova (Haussman's Wife), Nikolay Sileverstov (Vanderbeer's Butler), Ali Voenmij (Village Leader), Edem Abdulaev (Boy with Donkey), Asanov Ajder (Man with Goggle Eye), Elena Lubimtceva, Valentina Shapovalenko, Anna Liboletova, Irina Ponomaryova (Blond Girls), Jon Barton (Team Leader), Brett Lynch, Jeff Hamilton (Soldiers), Timothy S. Abell (Special Operations Ranger)

Sean Bean, Dominic Monaghan, James Cromwell, Ving Rhames, Christian Slater in *Soldiers of Fortune* © Roadside Attractions

Aurora Marion in *Almayer's Folly* © Doc & Film Intl.

MEET THE FOKKENS (Kino Lorber) a.k.a. *Ouwehoeren*; Producers, Femke Wolting, Bruno Felix; Directors, Rob Schröder, Gabrielle Provaas; Photography, Wiro Felix, Rob Schröder; Music, Danny Malando; Editor, Sander vos Nce; a Teledoc, CoBO Fund, The Netherlands Film Fund and NPO production; Dutch, 2011; Color; Not rated; 70 minutes; American release date: August 8, 2012. Documentary on a pair of 69-year-old twins, Louise and Martine Fokkens, who continue to ply their trade in Amsterdam's red light district; **WITH:** Louise Fokkens, Martine Fokkens.

THE GREEN WAVE (Dreamer Joint Venture) Producers, Jan Krueger, Oliver Stoltz; Director/ Screenplay, Ali Samadi Ahadi; Based on an idea by Ali Samadi Ahadi, Oliver Stoltz; Music, Ali N. Askin; Photography, Peter Jeschke, Ali Samadi Ahadi; Editors, Barbara Toennieshen, Andreas Menn; Art Director, Ali Soozandeh; a co-production with Wizard UG; German, 2010; Color; HD; Not rated; 80 minutes; American release date: August 10, 2012. Documentary on Iran's uprising following its 2009 elections; **WITH:** Dr. Shirin Ebadi, Prof. Dr. Payam Akhavan, Dr. Mohsen Kadivar, Mehdi Mohseni, Mitra Khalatbari, Babak, Emir Farshad Ebrahimi; **CAST:** Pegah Ferydoni (Azadeh), Navid Akhavan (Kaveh)

Louise Fokkens, Martine Fokkens in *Meet the Fokkens* © Kino Lorber

ALMAYER'S FOLLY (Doc & Film International) a.k.a. *La folie Almayer*; Producers, Patrick Quinet, Chantal Akerman; Executive Producer, Serge Zeitoun; Director/Screenplay, Chantal Akerman; Based on the 1895 novel by Joseph Conrad; Photography, Rémon Fromont; Designers, Patrick Dechesne; Costumes, Catherine Marchand; Editor, Claire Atherton; Casting, Marion Touitou; a Paradise Film, Artémis Productions, Liaison Cinématographique production; French, 2011; Color; Not rated; 127 minutes; American release date: August 10, 2012. **CAST:** Stanislas Merhar (Almayer), Aurora Marion (Nina), Marc Barbé (Captain Lingard), Zac Andrianasolo (Daïn), Sakhna Oum (Zahira), Solida Chan (Chen), Yucheng Sun (Captain Tom), Bungthang Khim (Ali)

The Green Wave © Dreamer Joint Venture

EK THA TIGER (Yash Raj) Producer/Story, Aditya Chopra; Executive Producer, Aashish Singh; Director, Kabir Khan; Screenplay, Kabir Khan, Neelesh Misra; Photography, Aseem Mishira; Costumes, Alvira Khan, Ashley Rebello, others; Music, Sohail Sen, Sajid-Wajid; Lyrics, Kausar Munir, Neelesh Misra, Anvita Dutt; Choreographers, Vaibhavi Merchant, Ahmed Khan; Editor, Rameshwar S. Bhagat; Action Consultant, Conrad E. Palmisano; a Yash Chopra presentation; Indian; Color; Not rated; 132 minutes; American release date: August 15, 2012. **CAST:** Salman Khan (Tiger/Manish/Avinash Singh Rathod), Katrina Kaif (Zoya), Girish Karnad (Shenoy), Ranveer Shorey (Gopi), Roshan Seth (Anwar Jamal Kidwai), Troi Gre (ISI Agent Feroz), Lisa Byrne (Amelie), Bella Boyd (Sexy Shotgun Killer), Olivia Jackson (Tiger's Killer Ex-Girlfriend), Rochelle Okoye (Ring Card Girl)

PAINTED SKIN: THE RESURRECTION (Well Go) Producer, Chen Guo-fu, Wang Zhonglei, Pang Hong, Yang Hongtao, Wang Ruojun; Director, Wuershan; Screenplay, Ran Ping, Ran Jia'nan; Photography, Taylor Wong; Art Director, Hao Yi; Costumes, Liu Qian; Music, Katsunori Ishida; Editor, Xiao Yang; Action

Salman Khan in *Ek Tha Tiger* © Yash Raj

Choreographer, Li Cai; Visual Effects Supervisor, Chang Hongsong; a Ningxia Movie Group Col, Dinglonda (Beijing) Movie 7 Culture Media Co., Huayi Brothers Intl. presentation; Chinese; Dolby; Widescreen; Color; Not rated; 131 minutes; American release date: August 17, 2012. **CAST:** Zhou Xun (The Fox), Zhao Wei (Princess Jing), Chen Kun (Huo Xin), Yang Mini (Que'er, The Bird), Feng Shaofeng (Pang Lang, the Monster Slayer), Chen Kun (The Warrior), Chen Tingjia (Queen of Tianlang), Fei Xiang (The Wizard), Morgan Benoit (Wolf Boy of Tianlang)

Zhou Xun in *Painted Skin: The Resurrection* © Well Go USA

THE AWAKENING (Cohen Media) Producers, David M. Thompson, Sarah Curtis, Julia Stannard; Executive Producers, Jenny Borgars, Will Clarke, Olivier Courson, Norman Merry, Joe Oppenheimer, Carole Sheridan; Director, Nick Murphy; Screenplay, Nick Murphy, Stephen Volk; Photography, Eduard Grau; Designer, Jon Henson; Costumes, Caroline Harris; Music, Daniel Pemberton; Music Supervisor, Alison Wright; Editor, Victoria Boydell; Visual Effects Supervisor, Sean Farrow; Casting, Shaheen Baig; a Studiocanal Features presentation, a BBC Films presentation in association with Creative Scotland and Lipsynch Productions, an Origin Pictures production; British-Scottish, 2011; Dolby; Widescreen; Color; Rated R; 107 minutes; American release date: August 17, 2012. **CAST:** Rebecca Hall (Florence Cathcart), Dominic West (Robert Mallory), Imelda Staunton (Maud Hill), Lucy Cohu (Constance Strickland), John Shrapnel (Rev. Hugh Purslow), Diana Kent (Harriet Cathcart), Richard Durden (Alexander Cathcart), Alfie Field

(Victor Parry), Tilly Vosburgh (Vera Flood), Ian Hanmore (Albert Flood), Cal Macaninch (Freddie Strickland), Isaac Hempstead Wright (Tom Hill), Anastasia Hille (Dorothy Vandermeer), Andrew Havill (George Vandermeer), Shaun Dooley (Malcolm McNair), Joseph Mawle (Edward Judd), Nicholas Amer (Edgar Hirstwit), Steven Cree (Sgt. Paul Evans), Ben Greaves-Neil (Child Impostor), Sidney Johnston (John Franklin), Charlie Callaghan (Chris Hartley), Spike White (Alistair Howell), James Kirkham (William Ramsbottom), Felix Soper (Julian Dowden), Daniel Pirrie (Capt. Mills), Ewan Andrew Walker (Richard McGorian), Adam Thomas Wright (Max Tebbits), Katie Hart (Katie Forbes), Joseph M. Jenkins (Child Ghost), Molly Lewis (Child Florence), Nick Murphy (Teacher)

Rebecca Hall, Dominic West in *The Awakening* © Cohen Media

ALMS FOR A BLIND HORSE (National Film Development Corporation of India) a.k.a. *Anhey gorhey da daan;* Producer, Mani Kaul; Director/Screenplay, Gurvinder Singh; Based on a story by Gurdial Singh; Photography, Satya Rai Nagpaul; Designer, Pankaj Dhimaan; Music, Catherine Lamb; Editor, Ujjwal Chandra; Indian, 2011; Color; Not rated; 112 minutes; American release date: August 22, 2012. **CAST:** Mal Singh (Father), Samuel Sikander John (Melu), Serbjeet Kaur (Dayalo), Dharminder Kaur (Mother), Emmanuel Singh (Bhupi, Melu's Brother-in-Law), Kulwinder Kaur (Ballo, Melu's Wife), Lakha Singh (Lakha), Gurinder Makna (Dulla)

Mal Singh in *Alms for a Blind Horse* © Natl. Film Development Corp. of India

KNIGHT KNIGHT (Hermit Film Prods.) Producer/Director, Christina Bucher; Screenplay, Nicholas Horwood; Photography/Editor, Bastiaan Los; Music, Stuart Wood; British; Color; Not rated; 85 minutes; Release date: August 24, 2012. **CAST:** Tom Eykelhof (Edgar), David Wayman (Gilbert), Nick Von Schlippe (King Vince), Jonathan Hansler (Cedric), Christina Bucher (Katrina), Mingus Johnston

(Capt. Greaves), Claira Watson Parr (Rachael), Henry Jameson (Ralph), Alex Nowak (Eric), Vidal Sancho (Mysterious Knight), Mark Joseph (Tristan, the Stupid Guard), Robert Feldman (Bugler), Ben Shockley (Relic Seller), Isadora Bucher (Pants Seller), James Harrison (Bishop), Thiago Los (Stick Seller), Klisman Murati (Nigel), Maggie Erotokritou (Veg Seller), Alexandre Guedes de Sousa (Lazy Guard), Nicholas Horwood (Cheerful Guard), Jonathan Davies (Simon of Ayelsbury), David Orpheus (Guard with an Arrow in His Head)

Tom Eykelhof, David Wayman in *Knight Knight* © Hermit Film Prods.

THE DAY I SAW YOUR HEART (Film Movement) a.k.a. *Et Soudain tout le monde me manque*; Producers, Aïssa Djabri, Farid Lahouassa; Executive Producers, Farid Chaouche, Denis Penot; Director/Screenplay, Jennifer Devoldère; Co-Writers, Romain Lévy, Cécile Sellam; Photography, Laurent Tangy; Designer, Hervé Gallet; Costumes, Emmanuelle Youchnavski; Music, Nathan Johnson; Music Supervisor, Valérie Lindon; Editor, Stéphanie Pereira; a Vertigo Productions production in association with TF1 Droits Audiovisuels, UGC and TF1 Films production; French, 2011; Dolby; Color; Not rated; 98 minutes; American release date: August 24, 2012. **CAST:** Mélanie Laurent (Justine Dhrey), Michel Blanc (Eli Dhrey), Florence Loiret Caille (Dom Dhrey), Claude Perron (Suzanne Dhrey), Guillaume Gouix (Sami), Sébastien Castro (Bertrand), Géraldine Nakache (Cécilia), Manu Payet (Atom), Karina Beuthe (Kirsten), Jean-Yves Roan (Dr. Katz), Romain Lévy (Alex), Alexandre Steiger (Mathias), Habibur Rahman (Mahhoob), Assane Seck (Malik), Achille Ndari (Jeff), Samir de Luca (Seb), Luce Mouchel (Dr. Carlier), Gisèle Torterolo (Psychoanalyst), Xavier Goulard (Cardiologist), Arnaud Lemort (Golf Store Clerk), Jeanne Ferron (Wee Lady), Valérie Flan, Jean-Christophe Clément (Neighboring Table), Nicolas Chupin, Indiana Rhazal (Starbucks Clerks), Françoise Vallon (Sandrine), Camille Chamoux (Camille), Danièle Cohen (Maternity Nurse), Malik Bentalha, Kev Adams (Stand-Up Comedians), Eric Delva (Obstetrician), Daniel Cohen (Rabbi Youchnovski)

Guillaume Gouix, Mélanie Laurent in *The Day I Saw Your Heart*
© Film Movement

THE AMBASSADOR (Drafthouse Films) Producers, Peter Engel, Carsten Holst; Executive Producers, Peter Aalbaek Jensen, Peter Garde; Director, Mads Brügger; Screenplay, Maja Jul Larsen, Mads Brügger; Photography, Johan Stahl Winthereik; Music, Niklas Schak, Tin Soheili; Editors, Carsten Sosted, Kimmo Taavila, Leif Axel Kjeldsen; a Zentropa Real Aps presentation, in association with New Danish Screen, in co-production with Film i Väst, Zentropa Intl. Sweden AB; Danish-Swedish, 2011; Color; HD; Not rated; 93 minutes; American release date: August 29, 2012. Documentary following Mads Brügger as he passes himself off as a diplomat in order to show how easy it is to smuggle blood diamonds from Central Africa; **WITH:** Mads Brügger, Dalkia Gilbert, Colin Evans, Eva Jakobsen, Varney Sherman

Toga McIntosh, Mads Brügger in *The Ambassador* © Drafthouse Films

FLYING SWORDS OF DRAGON GATE (Indomina) a.k.a. *Long men fei jia*; Producers, Nansun Shi, Yu Dong, Tsui Hark; Director/Screenplay, Tsui Hark; Photography, Choi Sung-fai; Designer, Yee Chung-man; Costumes, Lai Hsuan-wu; Music, Wu Wai-lap; Li Han-chiang, Gu Xin; Action Choreographers, Yuen Bun, Lan Hai Han, Sun Jiankui; a Bon Film Group Co. Ltd., China Film Co., SMG Pictures, Shine Show Interactive Media Co. and Bona Entertainment Co. presentation of a Film Workshop production; Chinese, 2011; Dolby; Widescreen; Color; 3D; Rated R; 122 minutes; American release date: August 31, 2012. **CAST:** Jet Li (Zhou Huai-an), Zhou Xun (Ling Yanqui), Chen Kun (Yu Huatian), Li Yuchun (Guo Shao Tang), Gewi Lun-Mei (Chang Xiaowen), Mavis Fan (Su Huai Yong), Fan Siu-wong (Ma Jin Liang), Sheng Chien (Tan Lu Ji), Sun Jiankui (Liang Cai), Du Yiheng (Ji Xueyong), Wang Shuangbao (Pingan Zhao), Xue Jian (Lei Chongcheng)

Flying Swords of Dragon Gate
© Indomina

BREATHING (Kino Lorber) a.k.a .*Atmen*; Producers, Dieter Pochlatko, Nikolaus Wisiak; Director/ Screenplay, Karl Markovics; Photography, Martin Gschlacht; Costumes, Caterina Czepek; Music, Herbert Tucmandl; Editor, Alarich Lenz; an EPO Filmproduktion, with the collaboration of ORF Film/Television-Agreement; Austrian, 2011; Color; Not rated; 93 minutes; American release date: August 31, 2012. **CAST:** Thomas Schubert (Roman), Karin Lischka (Margit), Gerhard Liebmann (Walter Fakler), Georg Friedrich (Rudolf Kienast), Stefan Matousch (Gerhard Schorn), Georg Veitl (Jürgen Hefor), Klaus Rott (Leopold Wesnik), Luna Mijovic (Mona), Reinhold G. Moritz (Josef Kallinger), Martin Oberhauser (Prison Guard #3), Magdalena Kronschläger (Young Lady), David Oberkogler, Michael Duregger (Policemen), Peter Raffalt (Judge), Stephanie Taussig (Daughter-in-Law), Gabriela Schmoll (Home Help), Elena Dörfler (Roberta), Werner Wultsch (Man in Sweatsuit), Robert Putzinger (Train Vendor)

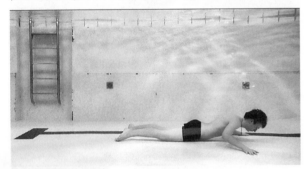

Thomas Schubert in *Breathing* © Kino Lorber

JOKER (UTV) Producers, Farah Khan, Akshay Kumar; Director/Screenplay/Editor, Shirish Kunder; Photography, Sudeep Chatterjee, Anay Goswami; Designers, Samir Chanda, Shashank Tere; Costumes, Rick Roy, Uma Biju; Music, G.V. Prakash Kumar, Gaurav Dagaonkar; Choreographer, Farah Khan; Hari Om Entertainment; Indian; Color; Not rated; 100 minutes; American release date: August 31, 2012. **CAST:** Akshay Kumar (Rajkumar/Agastya), Sonakshi Sinha (Diva), Shreyas Talpade (Babban), Gurpreet Ghuggi (Bobby), Darshan Jariwala (Baba), Asrani (Guruji), Minisha Lamba (Anya), Greg Heffernan (Mr. Smith), Alexx O'Neill (Simon), Pitobash (Kachua), Sonakshi Sinha (Manali), Sanjai Mishra (Rajaji), Vindu Dara Singh (Sundi)

Akshay Kumar in *Joker* © UTV Communications

THE BULLET VANISHES (China Lion) a.k.a. *Xiao shi de zi dan*; Producers, Albert Lee, Zhang Zhao; Director, Law Chi-leung; Screenplay, Law Chi-leung, Yeung Sin-ling; Photography, Chan Chi-ying; Designer, Silver Cheung; Costumes, Stanley Cheung; Music, Teddy Robin Kwan, Tomy Wai; an Unlimited Production Limited; Chinese; Dolby; Color; Not rated; 103 minutes; American release date: August 31, 2012. **CAST:** Nicholas Tse (Guo), Lau Chin-wan (Song Donglu), Yang Mi (Little Lark), Boran Jing (Xiaowu), Liu Kai-chi (Boss Ding), Yumiko Cheng (Li Ja), Wu Gang (Jin), Wang Ziyi (Wang Hai)

The Bullet Vanishes © China Lion

LOVE-CARROT 3 (Fox Intl.) a.k.a. *Lyubov-Morkov 3*; Producers, Renat Davletyarov, Aleksander Kotelevsky, Alexander Oleynikov Director, Sergei Ginzburg; Screenplay, Renat Davletyarov, Yuriy Kortkov, Alexander Oleynikov; Photography, Artur Gimpel; Art Director, Eduard Galkin; Costumes, Aleksandr Osipov; Editors, Aleksandr Albitsky, Dmitry Regan; Russian, 2011; Color; Rated PG-13; 100 minutes; American release date: August 31, 2012. **CAST:** Kristina Orbakayte (Marina Golubeva), Gosha Kutsenko (Andrey Golubev), Denis Paramonov (Gleb Golubev), Alina Bulynko (Sveta Golubeva), Liya Akhedzhakova (Elizaveta Nikolaevna), Vladimir Menshov (Vladimir Andreevich), Aleksey Guskov (Edik), Vyacheslav Manucharov (Misha), Mikhail Kozakov (Dr. Kogan), Andrey Urgant (Oleg Lvovich), Lyudmila Gavrilova (Lyudmila Petrovna), Alla Budnitskaya (Natalia Antonovna), Darya Drozdovskaya (Sonya), Olga Orlova (Lena), Stanislav Govorukhi

TOYS IN THE ATTIC (Hannover House) formerly *In the Attic or Who Has a Birthday Today?*, a.k.a. *Na pude aneb Kdo má dneska*; Producer, Milos Šmídmajer; Director/Screenplay/Set Designer, Jiří Barta; Photography, Zdenik Pospišil, Ivan Vít; Music, Michal Pavlicek; Editor, Lucie Haladová; English Adaptation Written, Produced and Director, by Vivian Schilling; a Eurocine International and Hannover House in association with Bio Illusion Films, Ceska TV, Upp, Krátký Film, Continentaql Film and AT ARMZ presentation; Czech-French, 2009; Dolby; Color; Rated PG; 74 minutes; American release date: September 7, 2012. **VOICE CAST:** Forest Whitaker (Teddy), Joan Cusack (Madam Curie), Cary Elwes (Sir Handsome), Vivian Schilling (Buttercup), Marcelo Tubert (Laurent), Douglas Urbanski (The Head), Emily Hahn (Andrejka), Sandy Holt (Mrs. Nemachkova), Joy Ellison (Rosie), Rico Simonini (Black Cat), Roy Vongtama (School Boy & Monkey)

THE INBETWEENERS MOVIE (Wrekin Hill Entertainment) Producer, Christopher Young; Executive Producers, Iain Morris, Damon Beesley, Shane Allen, Caroline Leroy; Director, Ben Palmer; Screenplay, Iain Morris, Damon Beesley; Photography, Ben Wheeler; Designer, Dick Lunn; Editors, William Webb, Charlie Fawcett; Casting, Nadira Seecoomar; a Film4 presentation of a Young Bwark production; British; Dolby; Color; Rated R: 97 minutes; American release

Buttercup in *Toys in the Attic* © Hannover House

date: September 7, 2012. **CAST:** Simon Bird (Will McKenzie), James Buckley (Jay Cartwright), Blake Harrison (Neil Sutherland), Joe Thomas (Simon Cooper), Emily Head (Carli D'Amato), Lydia Rose Brewley (Jane), Laura Haddock (Alison), Tamla Kari (Lucy), Jessica Knappett (Lisa), Theo Barklem-Biggs (Richard), Theo James (James), Anthony Head (Will's Dad), Victoria Willing (Mrs. Cartwright), Greg Davies (Mr. Gilbert), Henry Lloyd-Hughes (Mark Donovan), Belinda Stewart-Wilson (Polly MacKenzie), Robin Weaver (Pamela Cooper), Martin Trenaman (Alan Cooper), Alex MacQueen (Kevin Sutherland), David Schaal (Jay's Dad), Sophie Colquhoun (Susie), Carolin Stoltz (Woman on Laptop), Etalia Turnball (Jay's Sister), Dominic Frisby (Customer), Lauren O'Rourke (Nicole), Lily Lovett (Rachel), John Seaward (Big John), Cush Jumbo (Check in Woman), Bobby Hirston (Burnley Lad), Tracy Temperton (Holiday Rep), Jimmy Roussounis (Greek Man), Matthew Wilson (Hard Steve), Eloise Joseph (PR Girl), Andrew Spiers (Barman), Cathy Breeze (Neil's Northern Bird), Christopher Miltiadou (Greek Boy), Malcolm Scates (Angry Man), David Mumeni (Hotel Staff Member), Storme Toolis (Wheelchair Girl), Fernando Lopez (Fernando), David Chrysanthou (Nicos), Katarina Gellin (Donna)

Simon Buckley, Blake Harrison, Joe Thomas, Simon Bird in
The Inbetweeners Movie © Wrekin Hill Entertainment

LAS ACACIAS (Outside Pictures) Producers, Veronica Cura, Ariel Rotter, Alex Zito, Pablo Giorgelli, Eduardo Carneros, Javier Ibarrexte, Esteban Ibarrexte; Director, Pablo Giorgelli; Screenplay, Pablo Giorgelli, Salvador Roselli; Photography, Diego Poleri; Art Director, Yamila Fontan; Costumes, Violetta Gauvry, Laura Donari; Editor, Maria Astrauskas; an Airecine, Utópica Cine, Proyecto Experience production in association with Armonika Entertainment, Tarea Fina, Hibou Producciones, Travesia Producciones; Argentine-Spanish; 2011; Color; Widescreen; HD; Not rated; 82 minutes; American release date:

September 7, 2012. **CAST:** Germán de Silva (Rubén), Hebe Duarte (Jacinta), Nayra Calle Mamani (Anahi), Monica Coca (Shop Assistant)

Hebe Duarte in *Las Acacias* © Outside Pictures

[REC)3: GENESIS (Magnet) Producer, Julio Fernández; Executive Producers, Julio Fernández, Carlos Fernández, Alberto Marini; Director, Paca Plaza; Screenplay, Luiso Berdejo, Paco Plaza; Photography, Pablo Rosso; Art Director, Gemma Fauría; Editor, David Gallart; a Canal + and Filmax Entertainment presentation; Spanish; Color; HD; Not rated; 80 minutes; American release date: September 7, 2012. **CAST:** Leticia Dolera (Clara), Diego Martín (Koldo), Ismael Martínez (Rafa), Alex Monner (Cousin Adrián), Claire Baschet (Natalia), Sr. B (Atún), Jana Soler (Tita, Clara's Sister), Emilio Mencheta (Uncle Víctor), Adolf Bataller (Domingo), Dolores Martín (Manoli), Blai Llopis (Quiquín), Mireia Ros (Menchu), José de la Cruz (Grandpa Matías), Xavier Ruano (Cura)

Leticia Dolera, Diego Martin in *[REC]3: Genesis* © Magnet Releasing

BRANDED (Roadside Attractions) Producers, Jamie Bradshaw, Aleksandr Dulerayn; Executive Producers, Aleksandr Lyubimov, Roman Petrenko, Boris Yukhananov; Directors/Screenplay, Jamie Bradshaw, Aleksandr Dulerayn; Photography, Rogier Stoffers; Designer/Costumes, Anastasia Nefedova; Music, Eduard Artemev; Editor, Michael Blackburn; Casting, Stephanie Corsalini; a Barbossa production in association with Mirumir and TNT-Broadcasting Network; Russian-American; Dolby; Color; Rated R; 106 minutes; American release date: September 7, 2012. **CAST:** Ed Stoppard (Misha Galkin), Leelee Sobieski (Abby Gibbons), Jeffrey Tambor (Bob Gibbons), Max von Sydow (Marketing Guru), Ingeborga Dapkunaite (Dupcek), Roman Petrenko, Anastasia Nefedova, Nick Harvey, John Laskowski, Douglas Reno, Gary Brierely (Fast Food Executive), Maria Ignatova (Host), Andrei Kaikov (Pavel), Atanas Srebrev (Jon), Viktoria Popova (Screaming Woman), Jamie Bradshaw (Mr. Johnson), Ulyana Lapteva (Veronika), Alexdander Motasov (Surgeon), Yury Kharikov (Coma Expert), Inna Kolosova (Russian Marketing Guru's Assistant), Aleksandr Dulerayn (Roman

Schwartz), Vladislav Kopp, Pavel Lychkin, Michael Blackburn, Vladimir Rodimov (Guru's Assistants), Dmitry Troitsky (TV Analyst), Teodor Elmazov (Husband in Smolensk), Tsvetomira Daskalova (Wife in Smolensk), Mikhail Lukashev (Prison Guard), Oleg Akulich (Mr. Ivanov), Sergey Koryagin (Police Investigator), Danila Kirsanov (Robert), Evgeniy Kim (Dim Song Top Executive), Artem Martynishin (Man in Beef Tester Ad), Olga Dashkevich (Lady in Beef Tester Ad), Michael Everard (News Analytic), Vladislav Kopp, Emma Stickgold (News Reporters), Lacey Hoff (News Host #1), Egor Popov (Minister of Food and Agriculture), Alexandr Kukolenko, Marianna Storozhenko, Stephen Kukolenko (Diaper Ad), Gleb Aleinikov (Russian President), Alexander Dulerain Jr. (Young Misha)

Ed Stoppard in *Branded* © Roadside Attractions

BAIT (Anchor Bay) Producers, Gary Hamilton, Todd Fellman, Peter Barber; Executive Producers, Russell Mulcahy, Mike Gabrawy, Ian Maycock, Ying Ye, Chris Brown; Director, Kimble Rendall; Screenplay, Russell Mulcahy, John Kim; Photography, Ross Emery; Designer, Nicholas McCallum; Costumes, Phil Eagles; Music, Joe Ng, Alex Oh; Editor, Rodrigo Balart; Visual Effects Supervisor, Marc Varisco; Casting, Matthew Lessall, Ben Parkinson; a Screen Australia and Media Development Authority of Singapore presentation of a Darclight and Blackmagic Design production, in association with Pictures in Paradise, Story Bridge Films, Screen Queensland; Australian-Singapore; Dolby; Color; 3D; Rated R; 92 minutes; American Release date: September 9, 2012. **CAST:** Richard Brancatisano (Rory), Xavier Samuel (Josh), Chris Betts (Lockie), Sharni Vinson (Tina), Simon Edds (Lifeguard), Miranda Deakin (TV Reporter), Julian McMahon (Doyle), Dan Wyllie (Kirby), Alice Parkinson (Naomi), Phoebe Tonkin (Jaimie), Damien Garvey (Colins), Lincoln Lewis (Kyle), Cariba Heine (Heather), Alex Russell (Ryan), Adrian Pang (Jessup), Yuwu Qi (Steven), Martin Sacks (Todd), Rhiannon Dannielle Pettett (Assistant Manager), Skye Fellman (Young Girl), Nicholas McCallum (Oceania Store Owner)

Sharni Vinson, Alice Parkinson in *Bait* © Anchor Bay

MARK LOMBARDI – DEATH DEFYING ACTS OF ART AND CONSPIRACY (Rise and Shine World Sales/MoMA) a.k.a. *Mark Lombardi – Kunst und Konspiration*; Producer, Titus Kreyenberg; Executive Producer, R. Paul Miller; Director/Screenplay, Mareike Wegener; Photography, Sophie Maintigneux; Music, Kevin Haskins; Editors, Eli Cortiñas, Elisabeth Cortinas Hidalgo; a Unafilm production; German-American; Dolby; Color; Not rated; 84 minutes; American release date: September 13, 2012. Documentary on artist Mark Lombardi; **WITH:** Joe Amrhein, James Harithas, Robert Hobbs, Donald Lombardi, Shirley Lombardi, Matthew Lombardi, Lisa Lombardi LaRue, Laura Lombardi Mills, Hilary Ann Maslon, James Siena, Greg Stone, Susan Swenson, Fred Tomaselli, Edward Tufte, Rafael Vargas-Suarez.

Mark Lombardi in *Death Defying Acts of Art and Conspiracy* © Rise and Shine World Sales

BANGKOK REVENGE (China Lion) formerly *Rebirth*; a.k.a. *Yokame no semi*; Producer, Cédric Jimenez; Director/Screenplay, Jean-Marc Minéo; Executive Producer/Music, Christophe Gerber; Photography, Teerawat Rujinatum; Designer, Rapee Chamchean; Editors, Hugo Picazo, Nicolas Sarkissian; Visual Effects Supervisor, Sébastien Drouin; a Le Cercle production in association with G&G; French-Thai, 2011; Color; Not rated; 82 minutes; American release date: September 14, 2012. **CAST:** Jon Foo (Manit), Caroline Ducey (Clara), Michaël Cohen (Simon), Aphiradi Phawaphutanon (Chanticha), Winai Kraibutr (Samat), Kowitch Wathana (Adjan), Lioutsia Goubaidoullina (Jessy), Julaluck Ismalone (Ying), Thiraphong Riawrukwong (Superintendent), Dom Hetrakul (Pichai), Pream Busala-Khamvong (Ananda), Nicky Pimp (Chaiya), Jaturong Kolimart (Wanit), Howard Wang (Gang Leader), Ratthawish Saksirikoon (Manit as a Kid)

Jon Foo in *Bangkok Revenge* © China Lion

STEP UP TO THE PLATE (Cinema Guild) a.k.a. *Entre les Bras*; Producers, Everybody On Deck, Gaëlle Bayssière, Didier Creste; Director/Screenplay, Paul Lacoste; Photography, Yvan Québec; Music, Karol Beffa; Editor, Anthony Brinig; a co-produciton with Le-Lokal, Jaime Mateus-Tique, Jour2Fète; French; Dolby; Color; HD; Not rated; 88 minutes; American release date: September 14, 2012. Documentary shows French chef Michel Bras preparing his son Sébastien to take over his renowned restaurant; **WITH:** Michel Bras, Sébastien Bras

Sébastien Bras, Michel Bras in *Step Up to the Plate* © Cinema Guild

RAAZ 3: THE THIRD DIMENSION (Fox STAR) Producer, Mukesh Bhatt; Director, Vikram Bhatt; Screenplay, Shagufta Rafique; Photography, Pravin Bhatt; from Vishesh Films; Indian; Color; Rated R; 150 minutes; American release date: September 14, 2012. **CAST:** Bipasha Basu (Shanaya), Emraan Hashmi (Aditya), Esha Gupta (Sanjana), Manish Chaudhary (Tara Dutt)

BARFI! (UTV Motion Pictures) Producers, Ronnie Screwvala, Siddharth Roy Kapur; Director/Screenplay, Anurag Basu; Dialogues, Sanjeev Datta; Photography, Ravi Varman; Editor, Akiv Ali; Action Director, Sham Kaushal; Presented in association with Ishana Movies; Indian; Color; Not rated; 151 minutes; American release date: September 14, 2012. **CAST:** Ranbir Kapoor (Murphy, Barfi), Priyanka Chopra (Jhilmil Chatterjee), Ileana D'Cruz (Shruti Gosh/Sengupta), Roopa Ganguly (Shruti's Mother), Arun Bali (Jhilmil's Dad), Haradhan Bannerjee (Daju), Sumona Chakravarti (Shruti's Friend), Akash Kurana (Barfi's Father), Bhola Raja Sapkota (Ranbir's Friend), Jishu Sengupta (Ranjit Sengupta), Saurabh Shukla (Police Sub-Inspector), Nigram Thakur (Constable in Police Station), Uday Tikekar (Shruti's Dad), Ashish Vidyarthi (Mr. Chakraborty)

Ranbir Kapoor (right) in *Barfi!* © UTV

TEARS OF GAZA (Nero Media) a.k.a. *Gazas tårer*; Producer, Terje Kristiansen; Director/Screenplay, Vibeke Løkkeberg; Photography, Yosuf Abu Shreah, Saed al Sabaa; Music, Marcello De Francisci, Lisa Gerrard; Editor, Svein Olav Sandem; a Nero Media production; Norwegian, 2010; Color; Not rated; 82 minutes; American release date: September 19, 2012. Documentary on the 2008-2009 bombings of Gaza by the Israeli military.

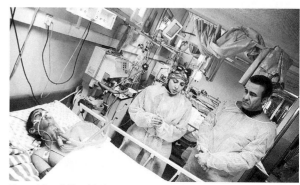

Tears of Gaza © Nero Media

17 GIRLS (Strand) a.k.a. *17 filles*; Producer, Denis Freyd; Directors/Screenplay, Delphine Coulin, Muriel Coulin; Photography, Jean-Louis Vialard; Designer, Benoît Pfauwadel; Costumes, Dorothée Guiraud; Editor, Guy Lecorne; an Archipel 35 production co-produced with ARTE France Cinéma; French; 2011; Dolby; Color; Not rated; 90 minutes; American release date: September 21, 2012. **CAST:** Louise Grinberg (Camille), Juliette Darche (Julia), Roxane Duran (Florence), Esther Garrel (Flavie), Yara Pilartz (Clémentine), Solène Rigot (Mathilde), Noémie Lvovsky (School Nurse), Florence Thomassin (Camille's Mother), Carlo Brandt (Head of the School), Frédéric Noaille (Florian), Arthur Verret (Tom), Philippine Raude Toulliou (Philippine), Sharleen Le Mero Pietruszka (Sharleen), Charlotte Alonso (Charlotte), Julia Ballester (Julia), Manon Denis (Manon), Clémence Thibault (Clémence), Violaine Hayano (Violaine), Eva Kermorvant (Eva), Jeanne Pellan (Jeanne), Pauline Gibert (Pauline), Caroline Darchen (EPS Professor), Pierre Devérines (Physique Professor), Lionel Gonzalez (Math Professor), Antoine Cegarra (French Professor), Benoît Carré (Philosophy Professor), Léo-Antonin Lutinier (Sports Professor), Eric Charon (History Professor), Joëlle Coulin (Feminist Professor), Malou Lucas (A Professor), Samuel Achache (Student), Jocelyne Desverchère (Clémentine's Mother), Luc-Antoine Diquéro (Clémentine's Father), Lucia Sanchez (Aquagym Professor), Antoine Maho (Clémentine's Friend), Puerre Pfauwadel (Stan), Marie-Louise Riou (Pharmacist), Raphaël Poli (Photographer)

17 Girls © Strand Releasing

HELLBOUND? (Area 23a) Producers, David Rempel, Kevin Miller; Executive Producers, David Krysko; Director/Screenplay, Kevin Miller; Photography, Ben Eisner; Music, Marcus Zuhr; Editor, Simon Tondeur; a Kevin Miller XI Productions presentation; Canadian; Color; Not rated; 84 minutes; American release date: September 21, 2012. Documentary questioning whether hell exists and who ends up there; **WITH:** Archbishop Lazar Puhalo, Bob Larson, Brad Jersak, Brian McLaren, Chad Holtz, David Bruce, David Vincent, Frank Schaeffer, Glen Benton, Gregory A. Boyd, Hank Hanegraaff, Jaime Clark-Soles, Jerry Walls, Jonathan & Margie Phelps, Justin Taylor, Kevin DeYoung, Mark Driscoll, Michael Hardin, Mike Bickle, Necrobutcher, Oderus Urungus, Peter Kreeft, Ray Comfort, Robert McKee, Robin Parry, Ron Dart, Sharon Baker, Kevin Miller, Guy Johnson, Richard Duke, Todd Sims, Eddie Oertell, Ole Luger La'fay Walsh, Timothy Preston Woody, William Paul Young

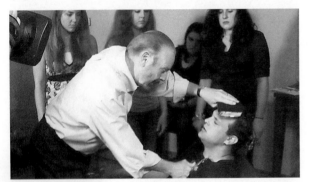

Hellbound? © Are 23a

THREE STARS (First Run Features) Producer/Director, Lutz Hachmeister; Photography, Hajo Schomerus, Dirk Wojcik; Editors, Mechthild Barth, Christian Wagener; Narrator, Deborah Friedman; an HMR, Arte, WDR production; German; Stereo; Color; Not rated; 94 minutes; American release date: September 21, 2012. Documentary focusing on ten Michelin 3-star chefs in some of the world's top restaurants; **WITH:** Jean-Georges Vongerichten, René Redzepi, Juan Mari, Elena Arzak, Yannick Alléno, Olivier Roellinger, Sven Elverfeld, Sergio Herman, Hideki Ishikawa, Nada Santini

Sergio Herman in *Three Stars* © First Run Features

MASQUERADE (CJ Entertainment) a.k.a. *Gwanghae, Wangyidoen namja*; Producers, Jung Ji-hoon, Kim Bo-yeon, Won Dong-yeong, Yim Sang; Director, Choo Chang-min; Screenplay, Choo chang-min, Hwang Jo-yun; Photography, Lee Tae-yoon; Designer, Oh Heung-seok; Costumes, Kwon Yoo-jin; Music, Kim Jun-seong, Mowg; Editor, Nam Na-young; a Realize Pictures production; South Korean; Color; Not rated; 131 minutes; American release date: September 21, 2012. **CAST:** Lee Byung-hun (Ha-seon/King Gwang-hae), Ryoo Seung-yong (Heo Gyun), Han Hyo-ju (Queen), Kim In-kwon (Do), Jang Gwang (Eunuch), Shim Eun-kyung (Sa-wol), Kim Myung-gon (Park Choong-seo)

Lee Byung-hun in *Masquerade* © CJ Entertainment

TALES OF THE NIGHT (Gkids) a.k.a. *Les contes de la nuit*; Producers, Christophe Rossignon, Philip Boëffard; Line Producer Supervisor, Eve Machuel; Director/ Screenplay, Michel Ocelot; Music, Christian Maire; Editor, Patrick Ducruet; Casting, Gigi Akoka; Stereoscopic 3D, Mac Guffligne; a co-production between Nord-Ouest Films, Studio O, Studiocanal with the support of La Region Ile-de-France; French, 2011; Color; 3D; Not rated; 84 minutes; American release date: September 26, 2012. **VOICE CAST:** Julien Béramis (Boy), Christopher Rossignon (Bishop), Marine Griset (Girl), Yves Barsacq (Théo), Michel Elias, Olivier Claverie, Isabelle Guiard, Legrand Bemba Débert, Fatoumata Diawara, Fabrice Daudet Grazaï, Sabine Pakora, Gérard Diby, Umban Gomez de Kset, Firmine Richard, Olivia Brunaux, Serge Feuillard, Michel Ocelot, Louis Rossignon

Tales of the Night © Gkids

SOLOMON KANE (RADiUS-Weinstein Co.) Producers, Samuel Hadida, Paul Berrow; Executive Producers, Victor Hadida, Michael Berrow; Director/Screenplay, Michael J. Bassett; Based on the character created by Robert E. Howard; Photography, Dan Laustsen; Designer, Ricky Eyres; Costumes, John Bloomfield; Music, Klaus Badelt; Editor, Andrew MacRitchie; Hair & Makeup Designer, Paul Pattison; Creatures Designer, Patrick Tatopoulos; Visual Effects Supervisor, Gary Beach; Stunts, Mark Henson; a Davis Films (France)/Wandering Star Pictures (UK)/Czech-Anglo Production (Czech Republic) production; French-British-Czech, 2009; Dolby; Panavision; Deluxe Color; Rated R; 104 minutes; American release date: September 28, 2012. **CAST:** James Purefoy (Solomon Kane), Pete Postlethwaite (William Crowthorn), Rachel Hurd-Wood (Meredith Crowthorn), Alice Krige (Katherine Crowthorn), Mackenzie Crook (Father Michael), Patrick Hurd-Wood (Samuel Crowthorn), Jason Flemyng (Malachi), Max von Sydow (Josiah Kane), Ian Whyte (Devil's Reaper), Lucas Stone (Young Solomon), Mark O'Neal, Robert Orr, Richard Ryan (Kane's Soldiers), Frantisek Deak (Cowering Guard), Christian Michael Dunkley Clark (Lt. Malthus), Thomas McEnchroe (Young Monk), Andrew Whitlaw (Older Monk), Robert Russell (Abbott), James Babson (Skinhead), Marek Vasut (Tattoo), Geoff Bell (Beard), Sam Roukin (Marcus Kane/Overlord), Anthony Wilks (Edward Crowthorn), Isabel Bassett (The Witch), Jeff Smith (Raider Captain), Matt Stirling (Eye Patch), Curtis Matthew (Old Man), Laura Baranik (Prisoner), Andrea Miltnerova (Old Woman Captive), Ryan James, Todd Kramer, Todd Benson, Miek McGuffie (Raiders), Franklin Henson (Landlord), Philip Winchester (Henry Telford), Stewart Moore (Garrick), Madeleine Bassett (Young Sarah), Klara Low (Onlooker), Philip Waley (Drunk), Gordon Truefitt (Stable Master), David Listvan (Gilligan), Jiri Kraus (Smith), Tomás Tobola (Hawkstone), Beryl Nesbitt (Old Crone), Ben Steel (Fletcher), Matthew Blood Smyth (Merton), Rory McCann (McNess), Amy Huck (Prisoner)

James Purefoy in *Solomon Kane* © Weinstein Co.

HEADSHOT (Kino Lorber) Producers, Pawas Sawatchaiyamet, Raymond Phathanavirangoon; Director/Screenplay, Pen-ek Ratanaruang; Based on the 2007 novel *Fon Tok Khuen Fa* by Win Lyovarin; Photography, Chankit Chamnivikaipong; Designer, Wittaya Chaimongkol; Costumes, Visa Kongka; Music, Vichaya Vatanasapt; Editor, Patamanadda Yukol; a Local Color Films Co. production in co-production with Memento Films International in association with Wild Side Films; Thai-French, 2011; Dolby; Color; HD; Not rated; 105 minutes; American release date: September 28, 2012. **CAST:** Nopachai Jayanama (Tul), Sirin Horwang (Rin), Chanokporn Sayoungkul (Joy/Tiwa), Apisit Opasaimlikit (Torpong), Krerkkeiat Punpiputt (Dr. Suang), Theeradanai Suwannahom (Tin)

VULGARIA (China Lion) a.k.a. *Dai juk hei kek*; Producers, Subi Liang, Pang Ho-cheung; Executive Producer, Alex Dong; Director/Story, Pang Ho-cheung; Screenplay, Pang Ho-cheung, Lam Chiu-wing, Luk Yee-sum; Photography, Jason Kwan; Art Director/Costumes, Ho Lok-lam; Music, Alan Wong, Janet Yung; Editor, Wenders Li; Visual Effects Supervisor, Bart Wong; a Sun Entertainment

Chanokorn Sayoungkul in *Headshot* © Kino Lorber

Culture presentation; Hong Kong; Dolby; Color; Not rated; 92 minutes; American release date: September 28, 2012. **CAST:** Chapman To (To Wai-chen), Ronald Cheng (Brother Tyrannosaurus), Dada Chan (Popping Candy), Fiona Sit (Quin), Simon Loui (Lui Wing Shing), Kristal Tin (Tsang), Hiro Kayama, Siu Yam-yam (Themselves), Lawrence Cheng (Professor Cheng), Lam Suet (Tyrannosaurus' Henchman), Nora Miao (Miss Cheung), Vincent Kuk (*Playboy* CEO), Miriam Yeung (Investigator), Mak Ling Ling (Hypnotist)

Vulgaria © China Lion

OMG: OH MY GOD! (Viacom/Grazing Goat Pictures) Producers, Akshay Kumar, Paresh Rawal, Ashvini Yardi; Director, Umesh Shukla; Screenplay, Umesh Shukla, Bhavesh Mandalia; Photography, Sethu Sriram; Costumes, Rahul Agasti; Music, Himesh Reshammiya; Editors, Tusha Shivan, Rajesh Pachal; a Grazing Goat Pictures, Playtime Creations, Viacom 18 Motion Pictures production; Indian; Color; Not rated; 125 minutes; American release date: September 28, 2012. **CAST:** Akshay Kumar (Krishna Vasudev Yadav), Paresh Rawal (Kanji Lalji Mehta), Mithun Chakraborty (Leeladhar Maharaj), Om Puri (Hanif Bhai), Apoorva Arora (Jigna), Honey Chaaya (Jagdeesh Bhai), Yusuf Hussain (Judge), Poonam Jhawer (Gopi Maiyya), Murli Mishra (Laxman Mishra), Govind Namdeo (Siddeshwar Maharaj), Krunal Pandit (Praveen), Jaineeraj Rajpurohit (Dinesh Gandhi), Bhakti Ratnaparkhi (Mangala), Nikhil Ratnaparkhi (Mahadev), Lubna Salim (Sushila), Azaan Rustam Shah (Chintu)

THE DOUBLE STEPS (Tusitala) a.k.a. *Los pasos dobles*; Producers, Luisa Matienzo, Dan Wechsler; Director, Isaki Lacuesta; Screenplay, Isaki Lacuesta, Isa Campo; Photography, Diego Dussuel; Designer, Sebastián Birchler; Music,

Akshay Kumar in *OMG: Oh My God* © Viacom

Gerard Gil; Editor, Domi Parra; Produced in collaboration with Bord Cadre and TVE – Televisión Española; Spanish, 2011; Color; Not rated; 91 minutes; American release date: October 1, 2012. **CAST:** Bokar Dembele (François Augiéras), Alou Cissé (Bandit Boss), Hamadoun Kassogué (Colonel), Miguel Barceló (Painter), Amon Pegnere Dolo (Amon), Amassagou Dolo (Amassagou), Abinum Dolo (Abinum), Soumaila Sabata (Ibrahim), Djenebou Keita (Young Woman), Wani Dolo, Joël Dolo, Emile Dougnon (Bandits), Ilogo Dolo (Adivini), Aguibou Dembele (Official)

AVÉ (MoMA) Producers, Metodius Petrikov, Konstantin Bojanov, Geoffroy Grison, Dimitar Gotchev; Director, Konstantin Bojanov; Screenplay, Konstantin Bojanov, Arnold Barkus; Photography, Nenad Boroevich, Radoslav Gotchev; Designer, Nikolay Karamfilov; Costumes, Marina Yaneva; Music, Tom Paul; Editor, Stela Georgieva; a Kamera, KB Films production; Bulgarian, 2011; Color; Not rated; 86 minutes; American release date: October 3, 2012. **CAST:** Anjela Nedyalkova (Avé), Ovanes Torosian (Kamen), Martin Brambach (Truck Driver), Svetla Yancheva (Viki's Mother), Bruno S. (Viki's Grandfather), Krasimir Dokov (Viktor's Uncle), Katinka Nedyalkova (Viktor's Grandmother), Maria Petrova (Nia), Nikola Dodov (Volvo Driver), Elena Rainova (Viktor's Aunt), Iossif Surchadzhiev (Viktor's Father), Nikolai Urumov (Retired Colonel), Bojka Velka (Avé's Mother), Bojidar Zlatkov (Piri)

Anjela Nedyalkova in *Avé* © KB Films

BEL BORBA AQUI (Abramorama) Producer, Burt Sun; Executive Producer, Debra Winger; Directors/Screenplay, Burt Sun, André Constantini; Photography, André Constantini; Music, André Constantini, Michael Wall, Eliano Braz, Darren Morze, Bob Hart; Editors, Vanessa Reiser Shaw, Daniel Burty, André Constantini; Brazilian; Color; Not rated; 95 minutes; American release date: October 3, 2012. Documentary on Brazilian artist Bel Borba.

Bela Borba Aqui © Abramorama

ENGLISH VINGLISH (Eros) Producers, Sunil Lulla, R. Balki, Rakesh Jhunjhunwala, R. Damani; Director/Screenplay, Gauri Shinde; Photography, Laxman Utekar; Designer, Mustafa Stationawala; Music, Amit Trivedi; Lyrics, Swanand Kirkire; Editor, Hemanti Sarkar; an Eros Intl. & R. Balki presentation; Indian; Color; Not rated; 134 minutes; American release date: October 5, 2012. **CAST:** Sridevi (Shashi Godbole), Adil Hussain (Satish Godbole), Mehdi Nebbou (Laurent), Priya Anand (Radha), Sujata Kumar (Manu), Navika Kotia (Sapna Godbole), Cory Hibbs (David Fischer), Rajeev Ravindranathan (P. Ramamurthy), Maria Romano (Yu Son), Shivash Kotia (Sagar), Ruth Aguilar (Eva), Ross Nathan (Kevin), Damian Thompson (Udumbke), Neelu Sodhi (Meera), Maria Pendolino (Jennifer), Sumeet Vyas (Salman Khan), Nate Steinwachs (Street Clown), Sean LeeRoy Kraemer (New Yorker knocking Papers Down), Rob Murat (Park Drummer), Jared Thompson (Waiter)

Sridevi in *English Vinglish* © Eros

SPECIAL FORCES (Entertainment One) a.k.a. *Forces spéciales*; Producers, Thierry Marro, Benoit Ponsaillé, Stéphane Rybojad; Director, Stéphane Rybojad; Screenplay, Stéphane Rybojad, Michael Cooper, Emmanuel Collomp; Photography, David Jankowski; Designer, Christophe Jutz; Costumes, Céline

El Mazouzi; Music, Xavier Berthelot; Editors, Stéphane Rybojad, Erwan Pecher; an Easy Company presentation and production; French, 2011; Dolby; Super 35 Widescreen; Color; Rated R; 109 minutes; American release date: October 12, 2012. **CAST:** Diane Kruger (Elsa), Djimon Hounsou (Kovax), Benoît Magimel (Tic-Tac), Denis Ménochet (Lucas), Raphaël Personnaz (Elias), Alain Figlarz (Victor), Alain Alivon (Marius), Mehdi Nebbou (Amen), Raz Degan (Ahmed Zaief), Tchéky Karyo (Adrmial Guezennec), Morjana Alaoui (Maina), Didier Flamand (Jacques Beauregard), Jacques Gallo (The Pasha), Bernard Allouf (President of the Republic), Marine Faure (Prime Minister), Eric Soubelet (Boss De La Duse), Jean-Paul Dubois (Minister of Defense), Antoine Blanquefort (Minister of Foreign Affairs), Laurent Claret (Head of State), Jeanne Bournaud (Alex), Isabelle Vitari (Lisa), Anne Caillon (Jeanne), Said Said Kamolidinov (Oakley), Nurullo Abdullayev (Mollah Zukhan), Denis Bracini (Serbian War Criminal), Greg Fromentin (Salemani), Noe Nojoli (Samuel), Juliette Hospitalier (Eva), Ambre Rybojad (Ambre), Armaud Bouchard (Main Dalex), Mathias van Khache (Richard), Jackie Fouquereau (Khabul Ambassador), Eleonore Woodward (Assistant to Beauregard), Elsa Levy, Severin Bavarel, Stephanie Brongniart, Olivier Pierre Richard, Alexandre Brick (Journalists), Eric Kailey, Fabriche Laroche Joubert (Guys at Barbecue)

Diane Kruger in *Special Forces* © Entertainment One

THE THIEVES (Well Go USA) a.k.a. *Dodookdeul*; Producer, Ahn Soo-hyun; Director, Choi Dong-hoon; Screenplay, Choi Dong-hoon, Lee Ki-cheol; Photography, Choi Young-hwan; Designer, Lee Ha-jun; Costumes, Choi Se-yeon; Music, Jang Young-gyu Dalpalan; Editor, Shin Min-kyung; Stunts, Yoo Sang-seob; a Caper Film production; South Korean; Dolby; Widescreen; Color; Not rated; 135 minutes; American release date: October 12, 2012. **CAST:** Kim Yun-seok (Macao Park), Kim Hye-soo (Pepsi), Lee Jung-jae (Popeye), Gianna Jun (Yenicall), Simon Yam (Chen), Kim Hae-sook (Chewingum), Angelica Lee (Julie), Kim Soo-hyun (Zampano), Oh Dal-soo (Andrew)

GRAVE ENCOUNTERS 2 (Tribeca Film) Producer, Shawn Angelski, Martin Fisher; Director, John Poliquin; Screenplay, The Vicious Brothers; Photography, Tony Mirza; Designer, Paul McCulloch; Costumes, Alecia Ebbels; Music, Quynne Alana Paxa; Casting, Laura Brooke Toplass; Darclight, presented in association with Death Awaits Cinema, Pink Buffalo Films and Twin Engine Films Ltd.; Canadian-American; Color; Not rated; 95 minutes; American release date: October 12, 2012. **CAST:** Richard Harmon (Alex Wright), Dylan Playfair (Trevor Thompson), Stephanie Bennett (Tessa Hamill), Howard Lai (Jared Lee), Leanne Lapp (Jennifer Parker), Alex Barima (Michael), Victor Zinc Jr. (Doctor at Party), Peter Chao (Chao), Sean Rogerson (Lance Preston), Garry Garneau (Gary), Justyn Shippelt (The Dentist), Brenda McDonald (Delia Rogerson), Tasha Simms (Caretaker), Javier Caballero (Studio Gate Security Guard), Peter Breeze (Breeze), Ben Wilkinson (Jerry Hartfeld), Gabriel Carter (Studio Security Guard), Sarah Penikett (Jerry's Secretary), The Vicious Brothers (Brothers), Sean Tyson

Kim Yun-seok, Lee Jung-jae, Gianna Jun, Kim Soo-hyun in *The Thieves* © Well Go USA

(Hospital Security Guard), Dalila Cabellero Meranu (Kaitlin), Roy Campsall (The Tall Man), Melissa Valvok, Brenda Anderson (Ghost Nurses), Dale Hall (Ghost Patient), Arthur Corber (Dr. Friedkin), Maddox Valvok (Baby)

Richard Harmon in *Grave Encounters 2* © Tribeca Film

MADRID, 1987 (Breaking Glass Pictures) Producer, Jessica Berman; Director/Screenplay, David Trueba; Photography, Leonor Rodríguez; Designer/Costumes, Laura Renau; Editor, Marta Velasco; a Buenavida Producciones S.L. production; Spanish, 2011; Dolby; Color; Not rated; 105 minutes; American release date: October 12, 2012. **CAST:** José Sacristán (Miguel), María Valverde (Ángela), Ramon Fontserè (Luis), Alberto Ferreiro (Man on Patio), Eduardo Antuña, Francisco Risueño, Miguel Castrejon (Café Commercial Waiters), Gloria Rodríguez, Ricardo Valderde, Teresa Sánchez, Sigfrid Monleón, Isabelle Stoffel, Soledad Osorio, Maria Luisa Osorio (Café Commerical Clients)

Maria Valverde in *Madrid, 1987* © Breaking Glass Pictures

TWO YEARS AT SEA (Soda Pictures/Film London) Director/Screenplay, Ben Rivers; a Flamin Productions presentation, Film London Artists, Moving Image Network in association with the Arts Council England; British; Black and white; Not rated; 88 minutes; Release date: October 12, 2012. Documentary on hermit Jake Williams; **WITH:** Jake Williams.

Jake Williams in *Two Years at Sea* © Soda Pictures

LA VIE AU RANCH (Umedia) a.k.a. *Chicks*; Producer, Emmanuel Chaumet; Director, Sophie Letourneur; Screenplay, Sophie Letourneur, Delphine Agut; Photography, Clare Mathon; Editor, Michel Klochendler; an Ecce Films production; French; Color; Not rated; 92 minutes; American release date: October 19, 2012. **CAST:** Sarah-Jane Sauvegrain (Pam), Eulalie Juster (Lola), Mahault Mollaret (Manon), Elsa Pierret (Chloé), Jade Tong Cuong (Jude), Angèle Ferreux (Olympe), Rafaël Wallon (Ralph), Sacha Naigard (Samson), Vincent Steinebach (Bart), Benjamin Siksou (Benji), Raphaël Haberberg (Louis), Wladimir Schall (Sven), Aurélien Dirler (Christophe), Aurélien Bonnetain (Aurélien), Éric Jolivalt (The Cinéphile), Xavier Bazoge (Xavier), Adrien Lefort (Paxton), Philippe Letourneur (Pam's Brother), Joëlle Robin (Grandmother), Quentin Paliwoda, Antoine Pineau (Boys at Party), Candace Haurie, Maïlys Haurie (Benji Groupies), Laurine Simandre, Adrien Domenec, Thomas Marfisi (Driving School People), Bjorn Frederik Nordin (Fritz), Carmen Letourneur, Lucianna Chardon (Medical Patients), Sylvie Sordelet (Doctor), Malina Deschaux-Beaume (Manon's Niece), Mathilde Charroinx, Antoine Charroinx (Manon's Cousins), Gérard Roche (Farmer), Sara Sperling, Paul Beller (Co-Tenants in Berlin)

La Vie au Ranch © Umedia

STUDENT OF THE YEAR (Dharma Prods.) Producers, Hiroo Yash Johar, Gauri Khan; Director, Karan Johar; Screenplay, Rensil D'Silva; Photography, Ayananka Bose; Cosumes, Manish Malhotra; Music, Vishal & Shekhar; Lyrics, Anvita Dutt; Editor, Deepa Bhatia; a Red Chillies Entertainment presentation; Indian; Color; Not rated; 146 minutes; American release date: October 19, 2012. **CAST:** Varun Dhawan (Rohan Nanda), Alia Bhatt (Shanaya Singhania), Sidharth Malhotra (Abhimanyu Singh), Rishi Kapoor (Dean Yoginder Yashisht), Sana Saeed (Tanya Israni), Sahil Anand (Jeet Khurana), Manasi Rachh (Shruti Pathak), Kayoze Irani (Sudo), Manjot Singh (Dimpy), Ronit Roy (Coach Shah), Ram Kapoor (Ashok Nanda), Gautami Kapoor (Gayatri Nanda), Farida Jalal (Abhimanyu's Grandmother), Akshay Anand (Abhimanyu's Uncle), Manini Mishra (Abhimanyu's Aunt), Prachi Shah (Coach Shah's Wife), Sushma Seth (Yoginder's Mother), Boman Irani, Kajol, Farah Khan, Vaibhavi Merchant (Guest Stars)

Varun Dhawan in *Student of the Year* © Dharma Prods.

BESTIAIRE (Kimstim Films) Producers, Sylvain Corbeil, Denis Côté; Director/ Screenplay, Denis Côté; Photography, Vincent Biron; Editor, Nicolas Roy; a Metafilms/Le Fresnoy, Studio National des Arts Contemporains production; Canadian-French; Dolby; Color; Not rated; 72 minutes; American release date: October 19, 2012. Documentary on mankind's fascination with animals.

Bestiaire © Kim Stim Films

TAI CHI ZERO (Variance/Well Go USA) Producers, Wang Zhongjun, Zhang Dajun, Stephen Fung, Daniel Wu; Director, Stephen Fung; Screenplay, Cheng Hsiao Tse, Zhang Jialui; Story, Chen Kuofu; Photography, Peter Ngor, Lai Yiu Fai, Du Jie; Art Director, Tim Yip; Music, Katsunori Ishida; Editors, Cheng Hsiao Tse, Matthew Hui, Zhang Jialui, Zhang Weili; Action Director, Sammo Hung; a Huayi Brothers Media Corporation presentation; Chinese; Color; Widescreen; Digital; Rated PG-13; 94 minutes; American release date: October 19, 2012. **CAST:** Jayden Yuan (Lu Chan, "The Freak"), Tony Leung Ka Fai (Chen Chang Xing/ Uncle Laborer), Angelababy (Yuniang Chen), Eddie Peng Yu-Yen (Fang Zijing), Feng Shaofeng (Zai Yang Chen), Ying Da (The Governor), Mandy Lieu (Claire Heathrow), Fung Tsui-Fan (Grand Uncle), Bruce Leung Siu-Lung (Dong), Shen Si (Brother Tofu), Feng Hak-On (Lao Zhao), Xiong Naijin (Gang Yun Chen's Wife), Xiong Xin Xin (Uncle Qin), Wu Di (You Zhi Chen), Shu Qi (Lu Chan's Mother), Stephen Fung (Nam), Andrew Lau Wai Keung (Lu Chan's Father), Chen Sicheng (Chen Gang Yun)

Tai Chi Zero © Variance Films

THE FLAT (Sundance Selects) Producers, Arnon Goldfinger, Thomas Kufus; Director/Screenplay, Arnon Goldfinger; Music, Yoni Rechter; Photography, Philippe Bellaiche, Talia "Tulik" Galon; Editor, Tali Helter Shenkar; a Ruth Diskin Films presentation, a co-production of Zero One Film and Arnon Goldfinger with ZDF, SWR, Noga Communications/Channel 8 in cooperation with Arte; Israeli-German; Dolby; Color; Not rated; 97 minutes; American release date: October 19, 2012. Documentary in which filmmaker Arnon Goldfinger chronicles the clues he uncovered cleaning out the flat of his grandparents, immigrants from Nazi Germany; **WITH:** Arnon Goldfinger, Hannah Goldfinger, Harald Milz, Tamar Tuchler, Edda Milz von Mildenstein, Michael Wildt.

Arnon Goldfigner, Edda Milz von Mildenstein in *The Flat* © Sundance Selects

LE GRAND AMOUR (Janus) Producer, Paul Claudon; Director, Pierre Étaix; Screenplay, Pierre Étaix, Jean-Claude Carriere; Photography, Jean Boffety; Designer, Daniel Louradour; Costumes, Daniel Louradour; Music, Claude Stiermans; Editor, Henri Lanoë; a Madeleine Films, C.A.P.A.C., Les Productions de la Guéville production; French; 1969; Color; Not rated; 87 minutes; American release date: October 19, 2012. **CAST:** Pierre Étaix (Pierre), Annie Fratellini (Florence), Nicole Calfan (Agnès), Alain Janey (Jacques), Ketty France (Mme. Girard), Louis Maiss (Mr. Girard), Jacqueline Rouillard (Mme. Louise), Renée Gardès (Gossip), Billy Bourbon (Drunkard), Claude Massot (Café Waiter), Micha Bayard (Bourget's Secretary), Jane Beretta, Odette Duc, Paule Marin, Georgina Pauwels, Judith Pauwels, Denise Péronne (Intriguists), Magali Clément (Irène), Jean-Pierre Elga (M. Bourget), Sandra Fratellini (Young Woman), Mad Letty (Mother Superior), Loriot (Old Man), Marie Marc (Florence's Grandmother), Josette Poirier (Thérèse)

Annie Fratellini, Pierre Etaix in *Le Grand Amour* © Janus Films

SILENT HILL: REVELATION 3D (Open Road) Producers, Samuel Hadida, Don Carmody; Executive Producer, Victor Hadida; Director/Screenplay, Michael J. Bassett; Adapted by Laurent Hadida, based on the game created by Konami; Photography, Maxime Alexandre; Designer, Alicia Keywan; Costumes, Wendy Partridge; Music, Jeff Danna; Editor, Michele Conroy; Visual Effects, Mr. X, Inc.; Creature Designer, Patrick Tatopoulos; Casting, Deirdre Bowen; a Samuel Hadida presentation of a Silent Hill2 DCP/Davis Films production in association with Konami; Canadian-French-American; Dolby; Widescreen; Technicolor; 3D; Rated R; 94 minutes; American release date: October 26, 2012. **CAST:** Adelaide Clemens (Heather/Alessa), Kit Harington (Vincent), Deborah Kara Unger (Dahlia), Martin Donovan (Douglas), Malcolm McDowell (Leonard Wolf), Carrie-Anne Moss (Claudia Wolf), Sean Bean (Harry), Roberto Campanella (Red Pyramid), Radha Mitchell (Rosa Da Silva), Erin Pitt (Sharon/Young Alessa), Peter Outerbridge (Travis Grady), Jefferson Brown (Det. Santini), Milton Barnes (Det. Cable), Heather Marks (Suki), Rachel Sellan (Mannequin Girl), Michel C. Foucault (Businessman), Arlene Duncan (Teacher), Jason Best (The Butcher), Chad Camilleri (Attacker), Sergey Shpakovsky (Fry Cook), Lawrence Dickison (Homeless Man), James Kirchner (Grey Man, Silent Hill Citizen), Jacky Lai (Student Girl), Tig Fong, Dean Copkov (Orderlies), Boyd Banks (Caretaker), Darren Josephs (Uniformed Cop), Peter Schoelier (Vagrant Mumbler)

CHARLIE IS MY DARLING (Brainstorm Media) Producer, Andrew Loog Oldham; Director/ Photography/Editor, Peter Whitehead; Music, Andrew Loog Oldham, Mike Leander; an Andrew Loog Oldham presentation; British; 1966; Black and white; Not rated; 60 minutes; American release date: October 26, 2012. Documentary of the Rolling Stones' 1965 tour of Ireland; **WITH:** Mick Jagger, Keith Richards, Brian Jones, Charlie Watts, Bill Wyman, Andrew Loog Oldham

Adelaide Clemens, Sean Bean in *Silent Hill: Revelation* © Open Road Films

Mick Jagger, Keith Richards in *Charlie is My Darling* © Brainstorm Media

Richard Coyle in *Pusher* © Weinstein Co.

Gabriel Byrne, Don Cheadle, Daniel Day-Lewis, Laurence Fishburne, Jamie Foxx, Jesse Jackson, Spike Lee, Brian McKnight, Prince Charles, Wolfgang Puck, Keanu Reeves, Gavin Rossdale, Ryan Seacrest, Benjamin Silverman, Will Smith, Isaiah Washington, Forest Whitaker, Ray Winstone, Andrew Young

Ozwald Boateng in *A Man's Story* © Wellington Films

PUSHER (RADiUS-TWC) Producers, Rupert Preston, Christopher Simon, Felix Vossen, Huberta von Liel; Executive Producers, Nicolas Winding Refn, Allan Niblo, James Richardson, Nigel Williams, Paul Steadman; Director, Luis Prieto; Screenplay, Matthew Read; Based on the original screenplay *Pusher* by Nicolas Weinding Refn, Jens Dahl; Photography, Simon Dennis; Designer, Sarah Webster; Costumes, Alexandra Mann; Music, Orbital; Editor, Kim Gaster; Casting, Vicky Wildman, Buffy Hall; a Vertigo Films & Embargo Films production in association with Exponential Media; British; Dolby; Color; Rated R; 88 minutes; American release date: October 26, 2012. **CAST:** Richard Coyle (Frank), Bronson Webb (Tony), Agyness Deyn (Flo), Mem Ferda (Hakan), Zlatko Buric (Milo), Paul Kaye (Fitz), Bill Thomas (Jack), Neil Maskell (Marlon), Daisy Lewis (Danaka), Ray Callaghan (Maurice), Badria Timimi (Senior Officer), Adam Foster (Zack), Richard Shanks (Junior Officer), Shend (Meten), Joanna Hole (Frank's Mum), Durassie Kiangangu (Striking Redhead), Tracy Green (Cindy), Amir Jardan (Shop Keeper), Leila Hoffman (Kind Old Lady), Joanne Rayner (Club Kitten), Rob Fry, Pete Meads, Matt Williams (Men in Club), Fredi "Kruga" Nwaka (Bouncer), Eva Dagoo (Pole Dancer), Phillip Gormley (Punter), James Hamilton (Rami), Suki Waterhouse (Mandy)

A MAN'S STORY (Wellington Films) Producers, Rachel Robey, Alastair Clark; Executive Producers, Angus Aynsley, Miel De Bottom Ansley; Director, Varon Bonicos; Music, Chad Hobson; Editor, Tom Hemmings; an Almega Projects presentation of a BBF, a Wellington Films production, produced in association with Molinare; British; Color; Not rated; 98 minutes; American release date: November 2, 2012. Documentary on menswear designer Ozwald Boateng; **WITH:** Ozwald Boateng, Giorgio Armani, Michael Bay, Paul Bettany, Richard Branson,

LUV SHUV TEY CHICKEN KHURANA (UTV Spotboy) Producers, Ronnie Screwvala, Siddharth Roy Kapur, Anurag Kashyap; Director, Sameer Sharma; Screenplay/Story, Sumit Batheja; Photography, Mitesh Mirchandani; Designer, Dhananjay Mondal; Costumes, Bibi Zeeba Miraie; Music, Amit Trivdei; Lyrics, Shellee; Editors, Apurva Motiwale, Ashish Mhatre; an AKFPL production in association with Jar Pictures; Indian; Color; Not rated; 140 minutes; American release date: November 2, 2012. **CAST:** Kunal Kapoor (Omi Khurana), Huma Qureshi (Harman), Rajesh Sharma (Titu Mamaji), Vipin Sharma (Kehar Singh), Dolly Ahluwalia (Buaji), Vinod Nagpal (Daarji), Rahul Bagga (Jeet Khurana), Anjum Batra (Dalidri), Mukesh Chhabra (Lovely), Munish Makhija (Shanty), Herry Tangri (Manty), Rajendra Sethi (Hemraj Khurana), Seema Kaushal (Lata Khurana), Anangsha Biswas (Shama Chatterjee), Nimrat Kaur (Muskaan Khurana)

CITADEL (Cinedigm/Flatiron) Producers, Katie Holly, Brian Coffey; Executive Producers, Gillian Berrie, David Mackenzie, Kieron J. Walsh; Director/Screenplay, Ciaran Foy; Photography, Tim Fleming; Designer, Tom Sayer; Costumes, Anna Robbins; Music, Tomandandy; Editors, Tony Kearns, Jake Roberts; Visual Effects Supervisor, Feidhlimidh Woods; Casting, Shaheen Baig; a Cinedigm and Flatiron Film Company with Blinder Films/Sigma Films presentation in association with Creative Scotland and Bord Scannán na Héireann/Irish Film Board; Irish-Scottish; Dolby; Color; Rated R; 84 minutes; American release date: November 9, 2012. **CAST:** Aneurin Barnard (Tommy), James Cosmo (Priest), Wunmi Mosaku (Marie), Jake Wilson (Danny), Amy Shiels (Joanne), Ian Hanmore (Council Office Clerk), Ingrid Craigie (Dr. Kelly), Chris Hegarty, Matthew Workman, Connor

McGroary, Charlie Graham (Feral Children), Pete Murphy, Scott Mckenzie (Paramedics), Arlowe Saunders (Elsa), Sarah Haworth, James Ramsay (Junkies), Grant Morrison (Taxi Driver), Sandra McFadden, Elizabeth Brady, Agnes Grout (Nurses), Christopher Warbrick (Stout Council Worker), Keith Hutcheson (Bus Driver), Ronnie Johnson (Old Man on Bus)

Aneurin Barnard in *Citadel* © Cinedigm

THE RETURN OF LENCHO (Occularis Films) a.k.a. *El regreso de Lencho*; Producers, Pamela López, Yvie Raij, Mario Rosales; Director/ Screenplay, Mario Rosales; Photography, Raquel Fernández; Art Director, Fernando Gálvez; Costumes, Pablo Estrada; Music, Radio Zumbido; Editor, Gabriel Adderley; Guatamalean, 2010; DuArt color; Not rated; 100 minutes; American release date: November 9, 2012. **CAST:** Mario Lanz (Lencho Aguilar), Tatiana Palomo (Camila Ibarguen), Miriam Arenas (Magali López Cruz), Carlos Chacón (Juan "El Chino" Morales), Emanuel Loarca (Ernesto Pacheco), Manuel Chitay (Marín Pineda), Jorge "El Pumita" Asturias (Carlos Robledo), Douglas Vasquez (Sgt. Rodolfo Rodríguez), Emanuel Loarca (Ernesto "Neco" Pacheco), Roberto Díaz Gomar (Johnny Martinez), Giacomo Buonafina (Alex), Jorge Bac, Marco Mancilla (Police), Marlene Mancilla (Waitress), José Mario Massella (Ramón Aguilar)

CAFÉ DE FLORE (Adopt Films) Producers, Pierre Even, Marie-Claude Poulin; Director/Screenplay/Editor/Co-Producer, Jean-Marc Vallée; Photography, Pierre Cottereau; Designer, Patrice Vermette; Costumes, Ginette Magny, Emmanuelle Youchnowski; Casting, Emmanuelle Beaugrand-Champagne, Nathalie Boutrie, Constance Demontoy; an Item 7, Monkey Pack Films and Crazy Films production; Canadian-French, 2011; Color; Not rated; 120 minutes; American release date: November 9, 2012. **CAST:** Vanessa Paradis (Jacqueline), Kevin Parent (Antoine Godin), Hélène Florent (Carole), Évelyne Brochu (Rose), Marin Gerrier (Laurent), Alice Dubois (Véronique), Evelyne de la Chenelière (Amélie), Michel Dumont (Julien Godin), Linda Smith (Louise Godin), Joanny Corbeil-Picher (Juliette), Rosalie Fortier (Angéline), Michel Laperrière (Psychologist), Caroline Bal (Véronique's Mother), Nicolas Marié (Véronique's Father), Pascal Elso (Paul), Jérôme Kircher (Louis), Claire Vernet (Mrs. Labelle), Manon Balthazar (School Teacher), Émile Vallée (Antoine, 14 years old), Chanel Fontaine (Carole, 14 years old), Emanuele Beaugrand-Champagne (Medium), Misstress Barbara (DJ Piknic Electronik), Luc Raymond (DJ Loft), Yves Perreault (AA Reader), Jean-Marc Vallée (Neighbor), Antoine Duchesneau (Young Cousin)

A LIAR'S AUTOBIOGRAPHY: THE UNTRUE STORY OF MONTY PYTHON'S GRAHAM CHAPMAN (Brainstorm Media/EPIX) Producers, Bill Jones, Ben Timlett; Executive Producers, Mark Sandell, Meyer Shwarzstein, Mark Greenberg, Douglas A. Lee, Aurelio Landolt, Hanspeter Jaberg; Directors/ Screenplay, Bill Jones, Jeff Simpson, Ben Timlett; Based on the 1980 book *A Liar's Autobiography: Volume VI* by Graham Chapman; Animation Producer, Justin Weyers; Music, John Greswell, Christopher Taylor; Editor, Bill Jones; a

Vanessa Paradis, Marin Gerrier in *Café de Flore* © Adopt Films

Ben & Bill Production, presented with Trinity Film; British; Color; 3D; Rated R; 85 minutes; American release date: November 9, 2012. Unconventional documentary about Monty Python member Graham Chapman, as told with various forms of animation; **VOICE CAST:** John Cleese, Carol Cleveland, Terry Gilliam, Terry Jones, Michael Palin; and Philip Bulcock (David Sherlock), Cameron Diaz (Sigmund Freud), Graham Chapman, André Jacquemin (Themselves), Justin McDonald (Young David Sherlock)

Graham Chapman, John Cleese, Michael Palin, Terry Jones in *A Liar's Autobiography* © Brainstorm Media

A SECRET AFFAIR (Viva Films) Executive Producer, Vic Del Rosario, Jr.; Producers, Vicente Del Rosario III, Veronique Del Rosario-Corpus; Director, Nuel Crisostomo Naval; Screenplay, Mel Mendoza-Del Rosario; Photography, Anne Monzon; Designer, Elfren A.P. Vibar Jr.; Music Director, Jesse Lucas; Editor, Marya Ignacio; a G.S.M. Blue, Folded&Hung, Primadonna production; Filipino; Color; Not rated; 110 minutes; American release date: November 9, 2012. **CAST:** Anne Curtis (Rafaela "Rafi" Delgado), Andi Eigenmann (Sam Montinola), Derek Ramsay (Anton), Jaclyn Jose (Ellen), Joel Torre (Jimmy), Jackie Lou Blanco (Cate), Johnny Revilla (Manuel), Jill Yulo (Katie), Say Alonzo (Paula Daza), Tim Yap (Tim), Petra Mahalimuyak (Amie Marielle Ignacio), Jocelyn Oxlade (Marielle Ignacio), Gee-Ann Abraham (Katie), IC Mendoza (Miggy Bernal), Shy Carlos (May Delgado), Paul Jake Castillo (Kevin), Kian Kazemi (Miguel), Nina Girado (Herself)

DANGEROUS LIAISONS (Well Go USA) a.k.a. *Wi-heom-han gyan-gye*; Producer, Chen Weiming; Director, Hur Jin-ho; Screenplay, Yan Geling; Based on the 1782 novel *Les Liaisons dangereuses* by Choderlos de Laclos; Photography, Kim Byung-seo; Music, Jo Seong-woo; Editor, Nam Na-yeong; an Easternlight

Derek Ramsay, Anne Curtis, Andi Eigenmann in *A Secret Affair*
© Viva Films

Films, Zonbo Media production; Chinese-South Korean; Dolby; Color; Not rated; 105 minutes; American release date: November 9, 2012. **CAST:** Zhang Ziyi (Du Fenyu), Jang Dong-gun (Xie Yifan), Cecilia Cheung (Mo Jieyu), Shawn Dou (Dai Wenzhou), Lisa Lu (Madame Du Ruixue), Candy Wang (Beibel), Rong Rong (Mrs. Zhu), Xiao Shuli (Gui Zhen), Zhang Yun (Wen), Ye Xiangming (Wu Shaopu), Wu Fang (Wen, Jieyu's Maid), Chen Guodong (Gen), Zhang Han (Jin Zhihuan)

Jang Dong-gun, Cecilia Cheung in *Dangerous Liaisons* © Well Go USA

THE LAW IN THESE PARTS (Cinema Guild) a.k.a. *Shilton Ha Chok*; Producer, Liran Atzmor; Executive Producers, Laura Poitras, Martin Hagemann; Director/ Screenplay, Ra'anan Alexandrowicz; Photography, Shark De Mayo; Music, Karni Postel; Editor, Neta Dvorkis; Israeli; Color; DCP; Not rated; 100 minutes; American release date: November 14, 2012. Documentary the complicated legal system established after Israel's 1967 occupation of the West Bank and Gaza Strip; **WITH:** Justice Meir Shamgar, Dov Shefi, Abraham Pachter, Alexander Ramti, Jair Rabinovich, Justice Amnon Strashnov, Ilan Katz, Oded Pesensson, Jonathan Livny

BARRYMORE (Image Entertainment) Producer, Garth H. Drabinsky; Director/ Screen Adaptation, Erik Canuel; Based on the 1997 play by William Luce, directed by Gene Saks; Photography, Bernard Couture; Designer, Cameron Porteus; Music, Michel Corriveau; a Steve Kalafer and Peter LeDonne presentation of the Peapack Company/Barrymore Entertainment Film; Canadian; Color; Not rated; 83 minutes; Release date: November 15, 2012. A recorded presentation of Christopher Plummer's award-winning stage role as John Barrymore**; WITH:**

Jonathan Livny in *The Law in These Parts* © Cinema Guild

Christopher Plummer (John Barrymore), John Plumpis (Frank). (Shown with the documentary short *Backstage with Barrymore* featuring Helen Mirren, Julie Andrews, Zoe Caldwell).

Christopher Plummer in *Barrymore* © Image Entertainment

TURNING (Bullitt Film) Producers, Vibeke Vogel, Antony Hegarty; Director/ Photography, Charles Atlas; Music, Antony Hegarty; Editor, Åsa Mossberg; a Turning Film LLC production; Danish-American; Color; Not rated; 78 minutes; Release date: November 16, 2012. Documentary on the performance piece collaboration between experimental filmmaker Charles Atlas and musician Antony Hegarty; **WITH:** Thomas Bartlett, Christian Biegai, Honey Dijon, Antony Hegarty, Will Holshouser, Julia Kent, Parker Kindred, Jeff Langston, Rob Moose, Maxim Moston

GENERATION P (New World) Producers, Victor Ginzburg, Djina Ginzburg; Executive Producers, Andrei Vasiliev, Yuri Krestinski, Leonid Ogorodnikov, Vladimir Yakovlev, Danil Khachaturov, Andrew Paulson; Director, Victor Ginzburg; Screenplay, Victor Ginzburg, Djina Ginzburg; Based on the 1999 novel *Generation (Babylon)* by Victor Pelevin; Photography, Aleksei Rodionov; Designers, Aleksei Tylevich, Daniel Auber, Ant Vasiliev, Ben Stokes; Music, Kaveh Kohen; Michael Nielsen, Alexander Hacke; Editors, Anton Anisimov, Vladimir Markvo, Karolina Machievsky; a Room'Gorky Film Studio/Karo presentation; Russian-American, 2011; Dolby; Widescreen; Color; Not rated; 114 minutes; American release date: November 16, 2012. **CAST:** Vladimir Epifantsev (Babylen Tatarsky), Mikhail Efremov (Leonid Azadovsky), Andrey Fomin (Morkovin), Sergey Shnurov (Gireev), Vladimir Menshov (Farseykin), Oleg Taktarov (Vovchik), Ivan

Okhlobystin (Malyuta), Andrey Panin (Kolya), Leonid Parfyonov (TV Journalist), Renata Litvinova (Alla)

Generation P © New World

HITLER'S CHILDREN (Film Movement) a.k.a. *Meine Familie, die Nazis und Ich*; Producer/Director, Chanoch Ze'evi; Executive Producer, Philippa Kowarsky; Photography, Yoram Millo; Music, Ophir Leibovitch; Editor, Arik Lahav Leibovitz; Narrator, Yael Bedarshi; a Maya Prods./Saxonia Entertainment production in association with MDR, WDR, SWR; Israeli-German; Color/Black and white; HD; Not rated; 80 minutes; American release date: November 16, 2012. Documentary on those who grew up as the children of some of Nazi Germany's leaders; **WITH:** Bettina Göring, Rainier Hoess, Niklas Frank, Monika Goeth, Katrin Himmler, Eldad Beck

Niklas Frank in *Hitler's Children* © Film Movement

LA RAFLE (THE ROUND UP) (Menemsha) Producer, Ilan Goldman; Executive Producer, Christer von Lindequist; Director, Rose Bosch; Photography, David Ungaro; Designer, Olivier Raoux; Costumes, Pierre-Jean Larroque; Music, Christian Henson; Editor, Yann Malcor; Casting, Olivier Carbone, Agathe Hassenforder; a Légende Films, Gaumont, Légende de Siècles, TF1 Films Production, France 3 Cinéma, KS2 Cinéma, Alva Films (France)/EOS Entertainment (Germany)/Eurofilm Bis (Hungary) production; French-German-Hungarian, 2010; Dolby; Panavision; Color; Not rated; 115 minutes; American release date: November 16, 2012. **CAST:** Jean Reno (Dr. David Sheinbaum), Mélanie Laurent (Annette Monod), Gad Elmaleh (Schmuel Weismann), Raphaëlle Agogué (Sura Weismann), Hugo Leverdez (Jo Weismann), Joseph Weismann (Older Jo Weismann), Mathieu Di Concerto, Romain Di Concerto (Nono Zygler), Oliver Cywie (Simon Zygler), Sylvie Testud (Bella Zygler), Anne Brochet (Dina Traube), Denis Ménochet (Corot), Roland Copé (Maréchal Pétain), Jean-Michel Noirey (Pierre Laval), Rebecca Marder (Rachel Weismann), Adèle Exarchopoulos

(Anna Traube), Catherine Allégret ("Tati" Concierge), Thierry Frémont (Capt. Pierret), Jean-Pierre Lorit (Dr. Jousse), Frédéric Moulin (René Bousquet), Isabelle Gélinas (Hélène Timonier), Armelle (Head School Nurse), Caroline Raynaud (Paule Pétiveau), Charlotte Driesen (Charlotte Weismann), Sandra Moreno (Lucienne), Maurice Vaudaux (The Abbot Bernard), Salomé Sebbag (Louise Zygler), Nastasia Juszczak (Renée Traube), Ariane Seguillon, Mathilde Snodgrass (Whores), Nadia Barentin (Grandmother Ida), Catherine Hosmalin (Baker), Marc Rioufol (Jean Leguay), Patrick Courtois (Emile Hennequin)

Mélanie Laurent in *La Rafle* © Menemsha Films

THE MYSTICAL LAWS (Happy Science) a.k.a. *Shinpi no hô*; Producers, Zuisho Motochikawa, Koji Matsumoto; Executive Producer/Original Creator, Ryuho Okawa; Director, Isamu Imakake; Screenplay, *The Mystical Laws* Scenario Project; Art Director, Masaaki Kawaguchi; Music, Yuichi Mizusawa; Visual Effects Supervisor, Yumiko Awaya; an IRH Press Co. Ltd. Production; Japanese; Color; Not rated; 119 minutes; American release date: November 23, 2012. **VOICE CAST:** Ayumi Fujimura, Banjô Ginga, Daisuke Hirakawa, Ken'yû Horiuchi, Miki Itô, Takehito Koyasu, Shinichirô Miki, Rin Mizuhara, Hiroshi Tsuchida, Hiroshi Yanaka, Satsuki Yukino, Ryôka Yuzuki

The Mystical Laws © Happy Science

MAN AT WAR (HBO Films) Producers, Jacek Blawut, Jerzy Dziegielewski, Aleksander Kutela, Anan Skonieczna; Director/Screenplay, Jacek Blawut; Photography, Jerzy Rudzinski, Jacek Blawut, others; Music, Tomasz Stroynowski; Editors, Jacek Blawut, Weronika Blawut; a Produkcja Filmow Jacek Blawut, HBO Central Europe production; Polish; Color; HD; Not rated; 70 minutes; American release date: November 23, 2012. Documentary on the World War II computer game *IL-2 Sturmovik* and its participants; **WITH:** Nicholas Iassogna (Deacon), Christopher C. Johnson (Rooster), Keith Jackson (Clash), Maikel Zaldivar (Mike), Larry Roberts (Persecutor), Anthony Pergolizzi (Magic Merlin), John Spangberg

(Crater), Leszek Niegos (Lesiek), Marcin Nagaj (Marian), Pawel Huta (Lukas), Sebastian Turzaoski (Polrus), Dominik Chmielewski (Pinker), Yury Slabko (Urri), Andrei Kovalev (Addams), Vladimir Paromov (Russian), Oleg Dagurow (Oleg_Da), Roger Glade (Bazi), Frédéric Zamit (Schwarzer Prinz), Heiko Loishen (Lohan), Lars Krämer (Widukind), Steffen Böhm (Bendwick)

Man at War © HBO Films

THE KING (DA Films) a.k.a. *Kralj*; Producer/Director, Dejan Acimovic; Executive Producer, Tatijana Acimovic; Photography, Dario Hacek; Music, Livio Morosin; Editor, Vladimir Gojun; Croatian; Color; Not rated; 75 minutes; American release date: November 23, 2012. Documentary on Paralymic Croatian sportsman Darko Kralj

Darko Kralj in *The King* © DA Films

WALK AWAY RENEE (Sundance Selects) Producers, Pierre-Paul Puljiz, Gérard Lacriox, Gérard Pont, Jonathan Caouette; Director/Story, Jonathan Caouette; Photography, Andres Peyrot, Noam Roubah, Jason Banker, Jorge Torres-Torres, Jonathan Caouette; Editors, Marc Vives, Brian McAllister, Jonathan Caouette; a Love Streams Production; French-Belgian-American, 2011; Color; Not rated; 90 minutes; American release date: November 30, 2012. Documentary in which filmmaker Jonathan Caouette moves his mentally ill mother from Texas to New York; **WITH:** Jonathan Caouette, Renee Leblanc, Adolph Davis, David Paz, Joshua Caouette

SILENT NIGHT (Anchor Bay) Producers, Richard Saperstein, Brian Witten, Phyllis Laing, Shara Kay; Executive Producers, Steve Ruff, Thomas M. Kastelz, Aaron L. Gilbert, John Carbone, John G. Carbone, Mark Sanders, James Gibb, Jayson Rothwell, Edward Mokhtarian, Edmund Mokhtarian, Sean E. DeMott, Adam Goldworm, Vincent Guastini, Kevin Kasha; Director, Steve C. Miller; Screenplay, Jayson Rothwell; Photography, Joseph White; Designer, Kathy McCoy; Costumes, Maureen Petkau; Music, Kevin Riepl; Editor, Seth Flaum; Casting, Eyde Belasco,

Jonathan Caouette, Renee Leblanc in *Walk Away Renee* © Sundance Selects

Jim Heber; a Genre Company/Insidious Pictures production in association with Empire Film & Entertainment Group and Media House Capital, produced with the participation of Manitoba Film & Music; Canadian; Dolby; Color; Rated R; 94 minutes; American release date: November 30, 2012. **CAST:** Malcolm McDowell (Sheriff Cooper), Jaime King (Aubrey Bradimore), Donal Logue (Santa Jim), Ellen Wong (Brenda), Lisa Marie (Mrs. Morwood), Courtney-Jane White (Tiffany), Cortney Palm (Maria), John B. Lowe (Dad), Rick Skene (Ronald Jones Jr./Ronald Jones Sr.), Brendan Fehr (Deputy Jordan), Andrew Cecon (Deputy Giles), Erik Berg (Dennis), Tom Anniko (Mayor Revie), Mike O'Brien (Stein Karsson), Curtis Moore (Rev. Madeley), Adriana O'Neil (Mom), Ali Tataryn (Alan Roach), Cruise Brown (Boy, Ronald Jr.), Clayton T. Stewart (Fake Santa #1), Aaron Hughes (Frank), Kelly Wolfman (Goldie Wallace), John G. Carbone (Joe), Brian Richardson (Mr. McKenzie), Jessica Cameron (Nurse), James Luce (Bartender), Doreen Brownstone (Old Lady in Church), Lane Thiessen Styles (Mindy Lu), Laura Cartlidge (Bratty Girl), Raychell Ruff (Regular Jane), Keenan Lehmann (Timmy), Bryan Clark (Young Deputy Bradimore), Charlyn Olfert, Amanda Borden, Britney Smith, Amy Simoes (Singers)

Jaime King, Malcolm McDowell in *Silent Night* © Anchor Bay

BACK TO 1942 (China Lion) a.k.a. *Yi jiu si er*; Producers, Wang Zhongjun, Han Sanping, Peter Lam, Liu Guangquan, Song Dai, Wang Yiyang, Albert Yeung; Director, Feng Xiaogang; Screenplay, Liu Zhenyun, based on his 1993 novella; Photography, Lü Yue; Costumes, Timmy Yip; Music, Zhao Jiping; Editor, Xiao Jang; a Huayi Brothers Media Corporation presentation; Chinese; Dolby; Color; Not rated; 145 minutes; American release date: November 30, 2012. **CAST:** Zhang Guoli (Master Fan Dianyuan), Adrien Brody (Theodore H. White), Tim Robbins (Father Megan), Xu Fan (Huazhi), Li Xuejian (Li Peiji), Zhang Mo (Shuanzhu), Wang Ziwen (Xingxing), Chen Daoming (Chiang Kai-shek), Zhang Hanyu (Brother

Sim), Fan Wei (Ma), Feng Yuanzheng (Xialu), Duan Yihong (Chen Bulei), Zhang Guoqiang (Dong Yingbin), Yao Jingyi (Lingdang), Peng Jiale (Liubao), Yuan Huifang (Master Fan's Wife), Zhang Shu (Dong Jiayao), Ke Lan (Soong May-ling), Yu Zhen (Jiang Dingwen), Zhang Chenguang (Zhang Lisheng), Peter Noel Duhamel (Joseph Stilwell), James A. Beattle (Clarence E. Gauss), Alec Su (T.V. Soong), Lin Yongjian (County Magistrate Yue)

Adrien Brody in *Back to 1942* © China Lion

I DO BIDOO BIDOO: HETO NAPO SILA! (Studio 5) Producers, Bobby Barreiro, Madonna Tarrayo; Director/Screenplay, Chris Martinez; Photography, Larry Manda; Desiger, Digo Ricio; Music, Vincent de Jesus; Editor, Randy Gabriel; a Unitel Production; Filipino; Color; Not rated; 120 minutes; American release date: November 30, 2012. **CAST:** Eugene Domingo (Rosie Polotan), Gary Valenciano (Nick Fuentebella), Zsa Zsa Padilla (Elaine Fuentebella), Ogie Alcasid (Pol Polotan), Sam Concepcion (Rock Polotan), Tippy Dos Santos (Tracy Fuentebella), Sweet Plantado (Vicky), Neil Coleta (Brent), Frenchie Dy (Lilibeth), Kiray Celis (Jazzy Polotan), Gerald Pesigan (Rap Rap Polotan), Jaime Fabregas (Julio Fuentebella), Ishmael Alshdefat (Austin Fuentebella), John Mark Ibañez (Blake Fuentebella), Nor Domingo (Taxi Driver), Anne Feo (Socialite Lady), Elijah Alejo (Young Tracy), John Lapus (Karaoke Host), Danny Javier (Priest), Jim Paredes, Boboy Garovillo (Godfathers)

PATRICIA (Eagle Eye Prods.) Producer/Director, Juan Carlos Hernandez; Screenplay, Tatiana Smithhart, Juan Carlos Hernandez; Spanish; Color; Not rated; 96 minutes; American release date: November 30, 2012. **CAST:** Eric Del Castillo (Gabriel Hernandez), Tatiana Smithhart (Patricia Hernandez), Claudia Troyo (Veronica Hernandez), Augstín Arana (Mauricio), Alejandro Ruiz (Dr. Caballero)

HECHO EN MÉXICO (Pantelion Films) Producers, Duncan Bridgeman, Lynn Fainchtein; Executive Producer, Bernardo Gomez; Director/Music, Duncan Bridgeman; Photography, Lorenzo Hagerman, Gregory W. Allen; Editors, Gregory W. Allen, Cachi Parisi, Miguel Musálem; Mexican; an El Mall production; Color; Rated R; 98 minutes; American release date: November 30, 2012. Documentary on contemporary Mexican culture; **WITH:** Adanowsky, Héctor Aguilar Camín, Rubén Albarrán, Amandititita, Sergio Arau, Paco Ayala, Venado Azul, Delfines Marching Band, Don Cheto, Juan Cirerol, Oscar D'León, Banda Agua Caliente De Tijuana, Emmanuel del real, Blue Demon, Lila Downs, José Guadalupe Esparza, Laura Esquivel, Alejandro Fernandez, Daniel Giménez Cacho, Ali Guagua, El Humi, Kinky, Natalia Lafourcade, León Larregui, Cuarteto Latinoamericano, Banda Limon, Diego Luna, Angeles Mastretta, Ana Maria Moctezuma, Molotov, Carla Morrison, Elena Poniatowska, Residente, Don Miguel Ruiz, Café Tacuba, Gloria Trevi, Grupo Trotamundos, Los Tucanes de Tijuana, Chavela Vargas, Julieta Venegas, Juan Villoro

Hecho en México © Pantelion Films

TALAASH (Reliance Entertainment) Producers, Ritesh Sidhwani, Aamir Khan, Farhan Akhtar; Director, Reema Kagti; Screenplay, Reema Kagti, Zoya Akhtar; Photography, Mohanan; Designer, Sharmishta Roy; Music, Ram Sampath; Lyrics, Javed Akhtar; Editor, Anand Subaya; Casting, Nandini Skrikent; a Reliance Entertainment presentation in association with Excel Entertainment & Aamir Khan Productions; Indian; Dolby; Color; Not rated; 131 minutes; American release date: November 30, 2012. **CAST:** Aamir Khan (Inspector Surjan Singh Shekhawat), Kareena Kapoor (Rosie/Simran), Rani Mukerji (Roshni Shekhawat), Nawazuddin Siddiqui (Tehmur), Raj Kumar Yadav (Devrath Kulkarni), Om Prakash (Yuvraj), Aditi Vasudev (Mallika), Shernaz Patel (Frenny), Vivan Bhatena (Armaan Kapoor), Sheeba Chaddha (Nirmala), Subrat Dutta (Shashi), Pariva Pranati (Sonia Kapoor), Prashant Prakash (Nikhil)

Aamir Khan in *Talaash* © Reliance Entertainment

WHAT A MAN (Fox Intl.) Producers, Marco Beckmann, Matthias Schweighöfer, Dan Maag, Gabriela Bacher; Director, Matthias Schweighöfer; Screenplay, Doron Wisotzky, Matthias Schweighöfer; Photography, Bernhard Jasper; Designer, Bertram Strauss; Music, Andrej Melita, Peter Horn; Editors, Olivia Retzer, Hans Horn; a Pantaleon Films/Fox International Productions (Germany) production; German; 2011; Dolby; Hawk Scope; Color; Rated R; 94 minutes; American release date: November 30, 2012. **CAST:** Matthias Schweighöfer (Alex), Sibel Kekilli (Nele), Elyas M'Barek (Okke), Mavie Hörbiger (Carolin), Milan Peschel (Volker), Thomas Kretschmann (Jens), Lilay Huser (Okke's Grandma), Vedat Erincin (Okke's Father), Antoine Monot Jr. (Alex' Father), Nora Jokhosha (Laura), Theresa Underberg (Stine), Joel Federico Laczlò Wüstenberg (Alex's Student), Gitta Schweighöfer (Frau Schlupp), Pasquale Aleardi (Etienne), Paul Alhäuser (Frank), Julia Niegel (Henriette), Luise Bähr (Nurse Nina), Friedrich Mücke (Doctor), Thomas Zickler (Doctor's Assistant)

Elyas M'Barek, Sibel Kekilli, Matthias Schweighöfer in *What a Man* © Fox Intl.

MY BROTHERS (Olive Films) Producers, Rebecca O'Flanagan, Robert Walpole; Director, Paul Fraser; Screenplay, Will Collins; Photography, P.J. Dillon; Designer, Mark Geraghty; Costumes, Lara Campbell; Music, Gary Lightbody, Jacknife Lee; Editor, Emer Reynolds; Casting, Oonagh Kearney, Catherine Flanagan; a Bord Scannah na hÉireann/The Irish Film Board and Windmill Lane Pictures presentation of a Rubicon Films production; Irish; Color; Not rated; 88 minutes; American release date: November 30, 2012. **CAST:** Timmy Creed (Noel), Paul Courtney (Paudie), Tj Griffin (Scwally), Don Wycherley (Dad), Kate Ashfield (Kitty), Eamonn Hunt (Tommy), Sarah Greene (Rose), Terry McMahon (Charlie), Aidan O'Hare (Bob), Martin Lucey (Martin), Siobhan Palmer (Emer), Will Collins (Arcade Man), Darragh O'Regan (Young Noel), Jack Archbold (Young Paudie), Andrew Gunkel (School Kid), Eoghan McConville (School Smart Arse), Charlie Crowley, John Crean, David Lane (Hurling Kids), Robert Walpole (Hurling Teacher), Rebecca O'Flanagan (Young Grieving Widow), Veronica Minihane, Emma Field, Laura Fitzgerald (Camogie Girls), Cillian Morrisroe, Sean O'Riordan (Cycle by Kids), Pat Byrne (Man in Car), Kieran Hennessy (Petrol Pump Attendant)

Paul Courtney, Timmy Creel, Tj Griffin in *My Brothers* © Olive Films

ELZA (Autonomous Entertainment) a.k.a. *Le Bonheur d'Elza*; Executive Producer, Eric Basset; Director, Mariette Monpierre; Screenplay, Mariette Monpierre, Mama Keita; Photography, Rémi Mazet; Music, David Fackeure, Max Surla; Editors, Jérome Raim, Virginie Danglades; a coproduction with France Télévisions, Canal+ Overseas; French, 2011; Color; Not rated; 79 minutes; American release date: November 30, 2012. **CAST:** Stana Roumillac (Elza), Vincent Byrd Le Sage (Mr. Désiré), Christophe Cherki (Bernard), Sophie Berger (Mrs. Désiré), Teddy Doloir (Jean-Luc), Eva Constant (Caroline), Jihane Botreau-Roubel (Marie), Auriana Annonay (Christine), Mariette Monpierre (Bernadette), Nancy Fleurival (M. Désiré's Mistress), Michel Reinette (Church Speaker), Yvon Potier (Banker), Chris Mouss (Psychiatric Nurse), Grégory Blaineau (Scooter Salesman), Jack Dugan (Jack), Laurence Joseph (Prostitute), Késiah Geran (Késiah), Sandrine Merguin (M. Désiré's Secretary), Juliana Arconte (Elza's Sister), Laureine Beck (Elza's Girlfriend), Arold Sorbe (Hairdresser in Paris), Kengy Larochelle (Young Man on the Beach), Patrick Chouan (Taxi Driver), Isabelle Kancel, Grégory Jernidier (In front of House), Stan Pasquin (Hotel Employee), Elody Stanislas (Gwo Ka Dancer)

Stana Roumillac in *Elza* © Autonomous Entertainment

YOUNG AND WILD (Sundance Selects) a.k.a. *Joven y alocada*; Producers, Juan De Dios Larraín, Pablo Larraín; Director, Marialy Rivas; Screenplay, Marialy Rivas, Camila Gutiérrez, Pedro Peirano, Sebastián Sepúlveda, María José Viera Gallo; Photography, Sergio Armstrong; Art Director, Polin Garbisu; Editors, Andrea Chignoli, Sebastián Sepúlveda; a Fabula Production; Chilean; Color; Not rated; 96 minutes; American release date: November 30, 2012. **CAST:** Alicia Luz Rodríguez (Daniela Ramírez), Aline Küppenheim (Teresa), María Gracia Omegna (Antonia), Felipe Pinto (Tomás), Alejandro Goic (Raimundo Ramírez), Ingrid Isensee (Isabel), Tomás de Pablo (Cristóbal Ramírez), Pablo Krögh (Josué), Hernán Lacalle (Pastor Simón), Andrea García-Huidobro (Julia Ramírez), Camila Hirane (Barbage), Luis Gnecco (Interviewee), Catalina Saavedra (Converted Woman), Moira Miller (Patricia), Maria Olga Matte (School Headmistress), Jesús Briceño (Young Pastor), Alex Rivera (Rocker Pastor), Franco Bardi, Luka Villalabeitía (Contest Kids), Joris Noordenbos (Pete Montana), Luciana Echeverría, Catalina Silva (Hot Chicks), Javiera Mena (Herself), Catalina Jorquera (Valentina), Macarena Neira (Sofía), Pedro del Carril, Martín Araya (Boys), David Alfonso (Chico Ranura), Claudio Marín (Liberating Pastor), Magdalena Max-Neef (Exorcism Woman), Juan Carlos Cáceres (Dario), Jorge Ramírez (Moses Actor), Hernán Inostroza (Elías), Francesca Díaz (Gip Girl), Marco Antonio González (Doctor), Luis Riveros (Thug), Catalina Benítez (Daniela as a Girl), Valeria Gómez (Julia as a Girl), Marina Ubilla (Betania as a Girl)

Young and Wild © Sundance Selects

PARKED (Olive Films) Producers, Jacqueline Kerrin, Dominic Wright; Line Producer, Annemarie Naughton; Co-Producer, Aleksi Bardy; Director/Screen Story, Darragh Byrne; Screenplay, Ciaran Creagh; Photography, John Conroy; Designer, Owen Power; Costumes, Susan Scott; Music, Niall Byrne; Editor, Guy Montgomery; Casting, Louise Kiely; a Ripple World Pictures presentation in co-production with Helsinki Filmi in association with Sudmen Elokuvasäätiö/Finnish Film Foundation and RTÉ with the participation of Bord Scannán na hÉireann/The Irish Film Board; Irish-Finnish, 2010; Dolby; Color; HD; Not rated; 90 minutes; American release date: November 30, 2012. **CAST:** Colm Meaney (Fred Daly), Colin Morgan (Cathal O'Regan), Milka Ahlroth (Juliana), Stuart Graham (George O'Regan), Michael McElhatton (Frank), David Wilmot (Peter), Tatiana Ouliankina (Aqua Aerobics Instructor), Diarmuid Noyes (Cathal's Brother), Mark Butler (Clippo), Martin Lucey (Appeals Officer), Aoife Maloney (Woman in Garden), Will O'Connell (Welfare Officer), Andy Kellegher (Robbo), Eoin Fleming (Child Pianist), Mary Kelly (Reporter), Conor MacNeill (Youth), Matti Ijäs (Liam)

Colm Meaney in *Parked* © Olive Films

DRAGON (RADiUS-TWC) a.k.a. *Wu xia*; Producers, Jojo Hui Yuet-Chun, Peter Ho-Sun Chan,; Director, Peter Ho-Sun Chan; Screenplay, Aubrey Lam; Photography, Jake Pollock, Lai Yiu-Fai; Designer, Yee Chung Man; Costumes, Dora Ng; Music, Chan Kwong Wing, Peter Kam, Chatchai Pongprapaphan; Editor, Derek Hui; Action Director, Donnie Yen; Visual Effects Producer, Yung Kwok Yin; a We Pictures, Stellar Mega Films, Dingsheng Cultural Industry Investment, Jiangsu Broadcasting Corporation, Yunnan Film Group production; Hong Kong-Chinese, 2011; Dolby; Color; Rated R; 114 minutes; American release date: November 30, 2012. **CAST:** Donnie Yen (Liu Jin-xi), Takeshi Kaneshiro (Xu Baijiu), Tang Wei (Yu), Jimmy Wang Yu (The Master), Kara Hui (13th Madam), Li Xiaoran (Xu Baijiu's Wife), Jiang Wu (Xu Baijiu's Investigator), Zheng Wei (Liu Fangzheng), Li Jiamin (Liu Xiaotian), Ethan Juan (Young Convict), Chun Hyn (Tavern Owner), Wan To-shing (Xu Kun), Yu Kang (Yan Dongsheng)

Donnie Yen in *Dragon* © Weinstein Co.

OTELO BURNING (Autonomous Entertainment) Executive Producer, Kevin Fleischer; Producer/Director, Sara Blecher; Screenplay, James Whyle, Sara Blecher, The Cast; Photography, Lance Gewer; Designer, Juli Vandenberg; Music, Alan Ari Lazar; Editor, Megan Gill; a Cinga Productions Film in association with the National Film and Video Foundation and Sabido Productions; South African; Dolby; Color; HD; Not rated; 96 minutes; American release date: November 30, 2012. **CAST:** Jaffa Mamabolo (Otelo Buthelezi), Thomas Gumede (New Year), Shile Xaba (Mandla Modise), Tshepang Mohlomi (Ntwe Buthelezi), Nolwazi Shange (Dezi), Kenneth Nkosi (Osar Buthelezi), Harriet Manamela (Mother Christmas), Hamilton Dhlamini (Skhumbuzo), Motlasi Mafatshe (Blade), Matthew Oats (Kurt), Dan Robbertse (Potential Sponsor)

Otelo Burning © Autonomous Entertainment

DELHI SAFARI (Applied Art Prods.) Producers, Anupama Patil, Kishor Patil, Mukesh Talreja; Executive Producers, Nishith Takia, Namrata Sharma, Varun Talreja, Fred Dewysocki; Director, Nikhil Advani; Screenplay, Nikhil Advani, Girish Dhamija, Suresh Nair; Music, Loy Mendonsa, Shankar Mahadevan, Ehsaan Noorani; Editor, Aarif Sheikh; Animators, Rahul Bhadri, Umesh Sutar, Rachit Varma; a Fantastic Films Intl. presentation of a Krayon Pictures and People Tree Films production; Indian; Color; 3D; Rated PG; 97 minutes; American release date: December 7, 2012. **VOICE CAST:** Jason Alexander (Male Flamingo/Hyena Cook), Cary Elwes (Sultan/Bee Commander), Brad Garrett (Bagga), Christopher Lloyd (Pigeon, Air India), Jane Lynch (Female Flamingo), Vanessa Williams (Beggum), Tara Strong (Yuvi), Tom Kenny (Alex the Parrot), Brian George (Bat), Troy Baker (Tiger), Fred Tatasciore (Other Hyena), Carlos Alazraqui (Bajrangi), Travis Willingham (Man in Shades), Roger Craig Smith (Bharela/Marela), JB Blanc (Director/Prime Minister), Lex Lang (Another Hyena/News Reporter), G.K. Bowes (News Reporter), Joe Ochman (Man/News Reporter)

Alex, Bajra in *Delhi Safari* © Applied Art Prods.

OFF-WHITE LIES (Film Movement) a.k.a. *Orhim le-rega*; Producers, Yoav Roeh, Aurit Zamir; Director, Maya Kenig; Screenplay, Maya Kenig, Dana Dimant; Photography, Itai Vinograd; Music, Udi Berner; Editor, Or Ben David; a Gum Films production; Israeli, 2011; Dolby; Color; Not rated; 86 minutes; American release date: December 7, 2012. **CAST:** Elya Inbar (Libby), Gur Bentwich (Shaul), Tzahi Grad (Gideon), Arad Yeini (Yuval), Salit Achi-Miriam (Helit), Shimon Mimran, Roni Kuban, Sigal Arad Inbar, Uri Avrahami

Elya Inbar in *Off-White Lies* © Film Movement

CHEERFUL WEATHER FOR THE WEDDING (IFC Films) Producer, Teun Hilte; Director, Donald Rice; Screenplay, Mary Henely Magill, Donald Rice; Based on the 1932 novel by Julia Strachey; Photography, John Lee; Designer, Anna Lavelle; Costumes, Camille Benda; Music, Michael Price; Hair & Make-Up Designer, Magi Vaughan; Editor, Stephen Haren; Casting, Vicky Wildman, Buffy Hall; a Yellow Knife presentation; British; Dolby; Color; Not rated; 93 minutes; American release date: December 7, 2012. **CAST:** Felicity Jones (Dolly Thatcham), Luke Treadaway (Joseph Patten), Elizabeth McGovern (Mrs. Thatcham), Mackenzie Crook (David Dakin), Fenella Woolgar (Nancy Dakin), Zoë Tapper (Evelyn Graham), Julian Wadham (Uncle Bob), Sophie Stanton (Millman), Olly Alexander (Tom), Ellie Kendrick (Kitty Thatcham), Paola Dionisotti (Mrs. Whitstable), James Norton (Owen Bigham), Luke Ward-Wilkinson (Robert), Barbara Flynn (Aunt Bella), John Standing (Horace Spigott), Eva Traynor (Annie), Elizabeth Webster (Betty), Ken Collard (Whitstable), Ben Greaves-Neal (Jimmy Dakin), Jo Hole (Miss Spoon), Camilla Corbett (Alice), Oliver Gilbert (George), Emil Lager (Aunt Bella's Chauffeur), Melanie Gray (Pretty Woman), Edward Saxby (Tony Bigham), Jonathan Saxby (Tiger Bigham), Jim Conway (Photographer), John MacDonald (Piper)

AQUÍ Y ALLÁ (Torch Films) a.k.a. *Here and There*; Producers, Ori Dov Gratch, Tim Hobbs, Pedro Hernández Santos, Diana Wade, Antonio Méndez Esparza; Executive Producers, Alvaro Portanet Hernández, Amadeo Hernández Bueno; Director/Screenplay, Antonio Méndez Esparza; Photography, Barbu Balasoiu; Music, Copa Kings; Editor, Filippo Conz; an Aquí y Allí Films/Torch Films production; Spanish-American-Mexican; DCP; Color; Not rated; 110 minutes; American release date: December 21, 2012. **CAST:** Pedro de los Santos Juárez (Pedro), Teresa Ramírez Aguirre (Teresa), Lorena Guadalupe Pantaleón Vázquez (Lorena), Heidi Laura Solano Espinoza (Heidi), Ángel Joseph de los Santos Leyva (Juan's Nephew), Juan de los Santos Juárez (Juan), Elizabeth Leyva Soriano (Juan's Wife), Cecilia de los Santos Juárez (Mari Luz), María Antonia Juárez Cano (Pedro's Mother), Pascuala Quirina Aguirre Morales (Teresa's Mother), Miguel de los Santos Morales (Miguel), Teodulfa Abelina Cruz Procopio (Teacher), Gloria Verdis Flores (Grieving Mother), Miguel Leyva Velazquez (Café Owner), Jesús Tellez Martínez (Ferryman), Pedro de los Santos Juárez, Juan de los Santos Suárez, Miguel de los Santos Morales, Jorge de los Santos, Ricardo Guevara Victoriano (Copa Kings), Jorge Arias Guzmán (Copa Percussionist), Nicolás Parra Quiroz (Don Nico), Noel Payno Verdiz (Noel), Néstor Tepetate Medina (Leo), Carolina Prado Ángel (Karla), María Cano Díaz (Pedro's Grandma), Susana Aguirre Romano, Tomás Silva Ramírez (Nurses), Gardenia Gaspar Obispo (Doctor), María Marlen Abarca Castro, Miguel Ángel López Sosa (In Pharmacy), Elsa Marisol Cantü Ramírez (Fellow Passenger), Reyna Aguilar Candia (Supermarket Cashier), Lizeidy Susano López, Elia Ramírez Flores (Hospital Receptionists)

Aquí y Allá © Torch Films

Felicity Jones, Luke Treadaway in *Cheerful Weather for the Wedding* © IFC Films

PROMISING NEW ACTORS

2012

Samantha Barks (*Les Misérables*)

Dane DeHaan (*Chronicle, Jack and Diane, Lawless, Lincoln*)

Tom Holland (*The Impossible*)

Emayatzy Corinealdi (*Middle of Nowhere*)

Cody Horn (*End of Watch, Magic Mike*)

Jeremy Jordan (*Joyful Noise*)

Rami Malek (*Battleship, The Master, Breaking Dawn Part II*)

Natalie Martinez (*End of Watch*)

Tyler Ross (*Nate & Margaret, The Wise Kids*)

Analeigh Tipton (*Damsels in Distress*)

Suraj Sharma (*Life of Pi*)

Rebel Wilson (*Bachelorette, Pitch Perfect, What to Expect When You're Expecting*)

ACADEMY AWARDS

Winners and Nominees 2012

BEST PICTURE

ARGO

(WARNER BROS.) Producers, Grant Heslov, Ben Affleck, George Clooney; Executive Producers, David Klawans, Nina Wolarsky, Chris Brigham, Chay Carter, Graham King, Tim Headington; Director, Ben Affleck; Screenplay, Chris Terrio; based on a selection from the 2000 book *The Master of Disguise* by Antonio J. Mendez and the 2007 *Wired* magazine article *The Great Escape* by Joshuah Bearman; Photography, Rodrigo Prieto; Designer, Sharon Seymour; Costumes, Jacqueline West; Music, Alexandre Desplat; Editor, Wililam Goldenberg; Stunts, JJ Perry; Special Effects Supervisor, R. Bruce Steinheimer; Casting, Lora Kennedy; a Smokehouse Pictures production, presented in association with GK Films; Dolby; Deluxe color; Hawk Scope; Rated R; 120 minutes; Release date: October 12, 2012

CAST

Tony Mendez	**Ben Affleck**
Jack O'Donnell	**Bryan Cranston**
Lester Siegel	**Alan Arkin**
John Chambers	**John Goodman**
Ken Taylor	**Victor Garber**
Bob Anders	**Tate Donovan**
Cora Lijek	**Clea DuVall**
Joe Stafford	**Scoot McNairy**
Lee Schatz	**Rory Cochrane**
Mark Lijek	**Christopher Denham**
Kathy Stafford	**Kerry Bishé**
Hamilton Jordan	**Kyle Chandler**
Malinov	**Chris Messina**
Robert Pender	**Zeljko Ivanek**
Bates	**Titus Welliver**
Adam Engell	**Keith Szarabajka**
Cyrus Vance	**Bob Gunton**
Max Klein	**Richard Kind**
OSS Officer Nicholls	**Richard Dillane**

Omid Abtahi (Rez Borhani), Page Leong (Pat Taylor), Philip Baker Hall (C.I.A. Director Stansfield Turner), Farshad Farahat (Azizi Checkpoint #3), Sheila Vand (Sahar), Karina Logue (Elizabeth Ann Swift), Ryan Ahern (Sgt. Sickmann), Bill Tangradi (Alan B. Golacinski), Jamie McShane (William J. Daugherty), Matthew Glave (Col. Charles W. Scott), Roberto Garcia (Sgt. William Gallegos), Christopher Stanley (Thomas L. Ahern Jr.), Jon Woodward Kirby (Fred Kupke), Alborz Basiratmand (Student with Poster), Ruty Rutenberg, Michael Woolston (Marines), Sharareh Sedghi (Lady with Radio), Bobby Zegar (Tear Gas Student), Victor McCay (Malick), Matt Nolan (Peter Genco), J.R. Cacia (Brice), Bill Kalmenson (Hal Saunders), Rob Brownstein (Landon Butler), David Sullivan (Jon Titterton), Jean Carol (Jordan's Secretary), Michael Cassidy (Jordan's Analyst), John Boyd (Lamont), Yuriy Sardarov (Rossi), Nikka Far (Tehran Mary), Aidan Sussman (Ian Mendez), Barry Livingston (David Marmor), Ali Saam (Ali Khalkhali), Araz Vahid Ebrahim Nia (Moradi), Scotty Anthony Leet (The Minotaur), Ashley Wood (Space Lab Nurse), Rob Tepper (Film Director), Ray Porter (First A.D.), Stephen J. Lattanzi (PA), Danielle Barbosa (Lester's Housekeeper), Michael Parks (Jack Kirby), Eric Scott Cooper (Publicist), Adrienne Barbeau (Nina/Serksi the Gallactic Witch), Tom Lenk (*Variety* Reporter), Nelson Franklin (*LA Times* Reporter), Kelly Curran (Princess Aleppa), Mark Rhino Smith (Evil Villain), Scott Elrod (Achilles Crux), Bill Blair (Humanoid Robot), Daston Kalili (Green Jacket), Joseph S. Griffo (Nestor the Android), Andrew Varenhorst (Blue Monster), Amitis Frances Ariano (Persian Dancer), Alison Fiori (Sci Fi Body Suit Girl), Taies Farzan (Middle Class Iranian Woman), Rafi Pitts (Iranian Consulate Official), Allegra Carpenter (British Airways Flight Attendant), Bobby Naderi (Airport Husband), Ray Haratian, Mehrdad Sarlak, Soheil Tasbihchi, Hovik Gharibian (Immigration Officers), Dorianne Pahlvana (Airport Hysterical Wife), Hooshang Tooze (Deputy Minister of Islamic Guidance), Peter-Henry Schroeder (Producer), Ali Farkhonde (Tehran Car Rental Man), Sahm McGlynn (Bearded Fundamentalist in Bazaar), Muhammed Cangören (Bazaar Shopkeeper), Asghar Allah Veirdi Zadeh (Bazaar Angry Man), Leyla Beysülen (Angry Woman), Lindsey Ginter (Hedley Donovan), Tim Quill (Alan Sosa), Larry Sullivan (Engell's Secretary), Danilo Di Julio (Sgt. Gauthier), Fanshen Cox (White House Operator), Tehmina Sunny (Swissair Ticketing Agent), Amir Kamyab (Passport Official), Baris Deli (Carpet Factory Komiteh), Cas Anvar, Bahram Khosraviani, Sam Sheikholeslami, Saba Sarem, Puya Abbassi (Revolutionary Guards), Reza Mir (Komiteh Reza), Jozef Fahey (Lock Up PA), Annie Little (Swissair Gate Agent), Fahim Fazli (Komiteh Subordinate), Brandon Tabassi (Young Komiteh at Airport), Hans Tester (Swissair Pilot), Alex Schemmer (Swissair Co-Pilot), Yan Feldman (Air Traffic Controller), Nancy Stelle (Swissair Flight Attendant), Maz Siam (Iraqi Border Guard), Ken Edling (Assistant Secretary of State), Deborah Deimel Bean (State Department Official), Michael Chieffo (CIA Archives Officer), Taylor Schilling (Christine Mendez)

The true story of how the CIA recruited Hollywood to help invent a fake movie production in order to rescue hostages in Iran.

2012 Academy Award Winner for Best Picture, Best Adapted Screenplay, and Best Film Editing.

This film received additional Oscar nominations for supporting actor (Arkin), original score, sound editing, and sound mixing.

John Goodman, Alan Arkin

John Goodman, Alan Arkin, Ben Affleck

John Goodman, Ben Affleck

Kerry Bishé, Scoot McNairy, Christopher Denham, Tate Donovan,
Rory Cochrane, Clea DuVall

Zeljko Ivanek, Matt Nolan, Titus Welliver, J.R. Cacia, Victor McCay

Ben Affleck

Ben Affleck, Bryan Cranston

Scoot McNairy, Kerry Bishé, Tate Donovan, Christopher Denham, Clea DuVall
© Warner Bros. Pictures

Jean-Louis Trintignant, Emmanuelle Riva

Emmanuelle Riva

Jean-Louis Trintignant, Emmanuelle Riva

BEST FOREIGN LANGUAGE FILM

AMOUR

(SONY CLASSICS) Producers, Margaret Ménégoz, Stefan Arndt, Veit Heiduschka, Michael Katz; Director/Screenplay, Michael Haneke; Photography, Darius Khondji; Designer, Jean-Vincent Puzos; Costumes, Catherine Leterrier; Editors, Monika Willi, Nadine Muse; Casting, Kris Portier de Bellair; a Les Films du Losange, X-Filme Creative Pool, Wega Film presentation co-production of France 3 Cinéma, ARD Degeto, Bayerischer Rundfunk, Westdeutscher Rundfunk in participation with France Télévisions, Canal+ , Cine+, ORF Film/Fernseh-abkommen; French-German-Austrian; Dolby; Color; Rated PG-13; 127 minutes; American release date: December 19, 2012

CAST

Georges	**Jean-Louis Trintignant**
Anne	**Emmanuelle Riva**
Eva	**Isabelle Huppert**
Alexandre	**Alexandre Tharaud**
Geoff	**William Shimell**
Concierge's Husband	**Ramón Agirre**
Concierege	**Rita Blanco**
Nurses	**Carole Franck, Dinara Drukarova**
Police Officers	**Laurent Capelluto, Jean-Michel Monroc**
Neighbor	**Suzanne Schmidt**
Paramedics	**Damien Jouillerot, Walid Afkir**

An elderly, long-married couple finds their bond of devotion tested when the wife's health begins deteriorating from a debilitating illness and the husband struggles to attend to her every need.

This film received additional Oscar nominations for picture, actress (Riva), director, and original screenplay.

Emmanuelle Riva

Isabelle Huppert, Jean-Louis Trintignant

BEST ANIMATED FEATURE

BRAVE

(WALT DISNEY STUDIOS) Producer, Katherine Sarafian; Executive Producers, John Lasseter, Andrew Stanton, Pete Docter; Directors, Mark Andrews, Brenda Chapman; Co-Director, Steve Purcell; Screenplay, Mark Andrews, Steve Purcell, Brenda Chapman, Irene Mecchi; Story, Brenda Chapman; Photography, Robert Anderson; Designer, Steve Pilcher; Art Directors, Matt Nolte (characters), Noah Klocek (sets); Supervising Animators, Alan Barillaro, Steven Clay Hunter; Stereoscopic Supervisor, Bob Whitehill; Music, Patrick Doyle; Editor, Nicholas C. Smith; Casting, Kevin Reher, Natalie Lyon; a Disney presentation of a Pixar Animation Studios production; Dolby; Widescreen; Deluxe color; 3D; Rated PG; 100 minutes; Release date: June 22, 2012

Lord Macintosh, Young Macintosh, Merida, Wee Dingwall, Lord Dingwall, Lord MacGuffin, Young MacGuffin, Queen Elinor, King Fergus

VOICE CAST

Merida	**Kelly Macdonald**
King Fergus	**Billy Connolly**
Queen Elinor	**Emma Thompson**
The Witch	**Julie Walters**
Lord Dingwall	**Robbie Coltrane**
Lord MacGuffin/Young MacGuffin	**Kevin McKidd**
Lord Macintosh	**Craig Ferguson**
Maudie	**Sally Kinghom, Eilidh Fraser**
Young Merida	**Peigi Barker**
Young Macintosh	**Steven Cree**
The Crow	**Steve Purcell**
Wee Dingwall	**Callum O'Neill**
Martin	**Patrick Doyle**
Gordon	**John Ratzenberger**

An independent young princess, who refuses to consent to the limited life her parents have mapped out for her, seeks the help of a witch to change her mother's feelings and accidentally ends up subjecting her to a terrible curse.

Merida © Disney/Pixar

Bear Cubs

Harris, Merida, Hubert, Hamish, King Fergus, Queen Elinor

BEST DOCUMENTARY FEATURE

SEARCHING FOR SUGAR MAN

(SONY CLASSICS) Producers, Simon Chinn, Malik Bendjelloul; Executive Producers, John Battsek, Hjalmar Palmgren, Sheryl Crown, Maggie Montieth; Co-Producers, Malla Grapengiesser (Hysteria Film), George Chignell, Nicole Stott (Passion Pictures) Director/Screenplay/Editor/Interviewer, Malik Bendjelloul; Photography, Camilla Skagerström; Original Songs, (Sixto) Rodriguez; Animation, Filmtechnarna; a Red Box Films & Passion Pictures production in association with Canfield Pictures & The Documentary Company; Swedish-British; Color; Rated PG-13; 85 minutes; Release date: July 27, 2012. Documentary on how '70's singer-songwriter Rodriguez became a cult favorite in South Africa after disappearing into oblivion for years.

WITH

Stephen "Sugar" Segerman, Dennis Coffey, Mike Theodore, Dan DiMaggio, Jerome Ferretti, Steve Rowland, Willem Möller, Craig Bartholomew Strydom, Ilse Assmann, Steve M. Harris, Robbie Mann, Clarence Avant, Eva Rodriguez, Sixto Rodriguez, Regan Rodriguez, Sandra Rodriguez-Kennedy, Rick Emmerson, Rian Malan

Rodriguez

Rodriguez

Rodriguez

Rodriguez © Sony Classics

ACADEMY AWARD WINNER FOR BEST ACTOR: Daniel Day-Lewis in *Lincoln*

ACADEMY AWARD WINNER FOR BEST ACTRESS: Jennifer Lawrence in *Silver Linings Playbook*

ACADEMY AWARD WINNER FOR BEST SUPPORTING ACTOR: Christoph Waltz in *Django Unchained*

ACADEMY AWARD FOR BEST SUPPORTING ACTRESS: Anne Hathaway in *Les Misérables*

ACADEMY AWARD NOMINEES FOR BEST ACTOR

Bradley Cooper in *Silver Linings Playbook*

Hugh Jackman in *Les Misérables*

Joaquin Phoenix in *The Master*

Denzel Washington in *Flight*

ACADEMY AWARD NOMINEES FOR BEST ACTRESS

Jessica Chastain in *Zero Dark Thirty*

Emmanuelle Riva in *Amour*

Quvenzhané Wallis in *Beasts of the Southern Wild*

Naomi Watts in *The Impossible*

ACADEMY AWARD NOMINEES FOR BEST SUPPORTING ACTOR

Alan Arkin, *Argo*

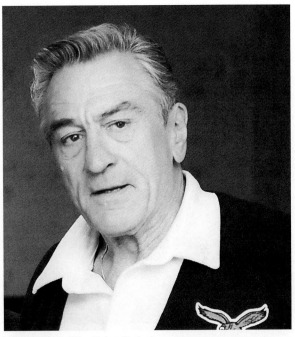

Robert De Niro in *Silver Linings Playbook*

Philip Seymour Hoffman in *The Master*

Tommy Lee Jones in *Lincoln*

ACADEMY AWARD NOMINEES FOR BEST SUPPORTING ACTRESS

Amy Adams, *The Master*

Sally Field, *Lincoln*

Helen Hunt, *The Sessions*

Jacki Weaver, *Silver Linings Playbook*

OTHER AWARDS FOR 2012

ACADEMY AWARDS

Film: *Argo;* Producers: Grant Heslov, Ben Affleck, George Clooney
(nominees: *Amour, Beasts of the Southern Wild, Django Unchained, Les Misérables, Life of Pi, Lincoln, Silver Linings Playbook, Zero Dark Thirty*)
Director: Ang Lee, *Life of Pi*
(nominees: Michael Haneke, *Amour*, David O. Russell, *Silver Linings Playbook*; Steven Spielberg, *Lincoln*; Benh Zeitlin, *Beasts of the Southern Wild*)
Original Screenplay: Quentin Tarantino, *Django Unchained*
(nominees: *Amour; Flight; Moonrise Kingdom; Zero Dark Thirty*)
Adapted Screenplay: Chris Terrio, *Argo*
(nominees: *Beasts of the Southern Wild; Life of Pi; Lincoln; Silver Linings Playbook*)
Cinematography: Claudio Miranda, *Life of Pi*
(nominees: *Anna Karenina; Django Unchained; Lincoln; Skyfall*)
Costume Design: Jacqueline Durran, *Anna Karenina*
(nominees: *Les Misérables; Lincoln; Mirror Mirror; Snow White and the Huntsman*)
Production Design: Rick Carter, Jim Erickson, *Lincoln*
(nominees: *Anna Karenina; The Hobbit; Les Misérables; Life of Pi*)
Original Score: Mychael Danna, *Life of Pi*
(nominees: *Anna Karenina; Argo; Lincoln; Skyfall*)
Original Song: "Skyfall" (Adele, Paul Epworth) from *Skyfall*
(nominees: "Before My Time" from *Chasing Ice;* "Everybody Needs a Best Friend" from *Ted;* "Pi's Lullaby" from *Life of Pi;* "Suddenly" from *Les Misérables*)
Film Editing: William Goldenberg, *Argo*
(nominees: *Life of Pi; Lincoln; Silver Linings Playbook; Zero Dark Thirty*)
Visual Effects: Bill Westenhofer, Guillaume Rocheron, Erik De Boer, Donald Elliott, *Life of Pi*
(nominees: *The Hobbit; Marvel's The Avengers; Prometheus; Snow White and the Huntsman*)
Sound Mixing: Andy Nelson, Mark Paterson, Simon Hayes, *Les Misérables*
(nominees: *Argo; Life of Pi; Lincoln; Skyfall*)
Sound Editing (Tie): Per Hallberg, Karen Baker Landers, *Skyfall* and Paul N.J. Ottosson, *Zero Dark Thirty*
(nominees: *Argo; Django Unchained; Life of Pi*)
Makeup and Hairstyling: Lisa Westcott, Julie Dartnell, *Les Misérables*
(nominees: *Hitchcock; The Hobbit*)
Animated Feature Film: *Brave*, Mark Andrews, Brenda Chapman
(nominees: *Frankenweenie; ParaNorman; The Pirates! Band of Misfits; Wreck-It Ralph*)
Foreign Language Film: *Amour*
(nominees: *Kon-Tiki* – released in the U.S. in 2013; *No* – released in the U.S. in 2013; *A Royal Affair; War Witch* – released in the U.S. in 2013)
Documentary Feature: *Searching for Sugar Man;* Malik Bendjelloul, Simon Chinn
(nominees: *5 Broken Cameras; The Gatekeepers; How to Survive a Plague; The Invisible War*)
Also: George Stevens Jr., Hal Needham, D.A. Pennebaker (Honorary); Jeffrey Katzenberg (Jean Hersholt Humanitarian); *Paperman* (Animated Short); *Curfew* (Live Action Short); *Inocente* (Documentary Short)

NATIONAL BOARD OF REVIEW

Film: *Zero Dark Thirty*
Director: Kathryn Bigelow, *Zero Dark Thirty*
Actor: Bradley Cooper, *Silver Linings Playbook*
Actress: Jessica Chastain, *Zero Dark Thirty*
Supporting Actor: Leonardo DiCaprio, *Django Unchained*
Supporting Actress: Ann Dowd, *Compliance*
Adapted Screenplay: *Silver Linings Playbook*

Daniel Day-Lewis, Joseph Gordon-Levitt in *Lincoln*

Original Screenplay: *Looper*
Animated Feature: *Wreck-It Ralph*
Breakthrough Actor: Tom Holland, *The Impossible*
Breakthrough Actress: Quvenzhané Wallis, *Beasts of the Southern Wild*
Foreign Language Film: *Amour*
Documentary: *Searching for Sugar Man*
Ensemble: *Les Misérables*
Spotlight Award: John Goodman (*Argo, Flight, ParaNorman, Trouble with the Curve*)
NBR Freedom of Expression: *The Central Park Five* and *Promised Land*
William K. Everson Film History Award: 50 Years of James Bond Films
Top Films: *Argo, Beasts of the Southern Wild, Django Unchained, Les Misérables, Lincoln, Looper, The Perks of Being a Wallflower, Promised Land, Silver Linings Playbook*
Top 5 Foreign Language Films: *Barbara, The Intouchables, The Kid with a Bike, No* (2013 US release), *War Witch* (2013 US release)
Top 5 Documentaries: *Ai Weiwi: Never Sorry, Detropia, The Gatekeepers, The Invisible War, Only the Young*
Top 10 Independent Films: *Arbitrage, Bernie, Compliance, End of Watch, Hello I Must be Going, Little Birds, Moonrise Kingdom, On the Road, Quartet, Sleepwalk with Me.*

NATIONAL SOCIETY OF FILM CRITICS

Picture: *Amour*
Director: Michael Haneke, *Amour*
Actor: Daniel Day-Lewis, *Lincoln*
Actress: Emmanuelle Riva, *Amour*
Supporting Actor: Matthew McConaughey, *Magic Mike*
Supporting Actress: Amy Adams, *The Master*
Screenplay: *Lincoln*
Documentary: *The Gatekeepers*
Cinematography: *The Master*
Experimental Film: *This is Not a Film.*

BOSTON SOCIETY OF FILM CRITICS
Film: *Zero Dark Thirty*
Director: Kathryn Bigelow, *Zero Dark Thirty*
Actor: Daniel Day-Lewis, *Lincoln*
Actress: Emmanuelle Riva, *Amour*
Supporting Actor: Ezra Miller, *The Perks of Being a Wallflower*
Supporting Actress: Sally Field, *Lincoln*
Screenplay: *Lincoln*
Ensemble: *Seven Psychopaths*
Animated Film: *Frankenweenie*
Documentary: *How to Survive a Plague*
New Filmmaker: David France, *How to Survive a Plague*
Editing: *Zero Dark Thirty*
Cinematography: *The Master*
Use of Music: *Moonrise Kingdom*

CHICAGO FILM CRITICS ASSOCIATION
Picture: *Zero Dark Thirty*
Director: Kathryn Bigelow, *Zero Dark Thirty*
Actor: Daniel Day-Lewis, *Lincoln*
Actress: Jessica Chastain, *Zero Dark Thirty*
Supporting Actor: Philip Seymour Hoffman, *The Master*
Supporting Actress: Amy Adams, *The Master*
Adapted Screenplay: *Lincoln*
Original Screenplay: *Zero Dark Thirty*
Art Direction: *Moonrise Kingdom*
Cinematography: *The Master*
Film Editing: *Zero Dark Thirty*
Score: *The Master*
Animated Film: *ParaNorman*
Foreign Film: *Amour*
Documentary: *The Invisible War*
Promising Newcomer: Quvenzhané Wallis, *Beasts of the Southern Wild*
Promising Filmmaker: Benh Zeitlin, *Beasts of the Southern Wild*

Eddie Redmayne in *Les Misérables*

NEW YORK FILM CRITICS CIRCLE
Picture: *Zero Dark Thirty*
Director: Kathryn Bigelow, *Zero Dark Thirty*
Actor: Daniel Day-Lewis, *Lincoln*
Actress: Rachel Weisz, *The Deep Blue Sea*
Supporting Actor: Matthew McConaughey, *Magic Mike* and *Bernie*
Supporting Actress: Sally Field, *Lincoln*
Screenplay: *Lincoln*
Foreign Language Film: *Amour*
Animated Feature: *Frankenweenie*
Documentary: *The Central Park Five*
Cinematography: *Zero Dark Thirty*
First Feature: *How to Survive a Plague*

LOS ANGELES FILM CRITICS
Picture: *Amour*
Director: Paul Thomas Anderson, *The Master*
Actress (TIE): Jennifer Lawrence, *Silver Linings Playbook,* and Emmanuelle Riva, *Amour*
Actor: Joaquin Phoenix, *The Master*
Supporting Actor: Dwight Henry, *Beasts of the Southern Wild*
Supporting Actress: Amy Adams, *The Master*
Screenplay: *Argo*
Foreign Film: *Holy Motors*
Documentary: *The Gatekeepers*
Animation: *Frankenweenie*
Film Editing: *Zero Dark Thirty*
Cinematography: *Skyfall*
Score: *Beasts of the Southern Wild*
Production Design: *The Master*
New Generation Award: Benh Zeitlin, *Beasts of the Southern Wild*

SAN FRANCISCO FILM CRITICS
Picture: *The Master*
Director: Kathryn Bigelow, *Zero Dark Thirty*
Actor: Joaquin Phoenix, *The Master*
Actress: Emmanuelle Riva, *Amour*
Supporting Actor: Tommy Lee Jones, *Lincoln*
Supporting Actress: Helen Hunt, *The Sessions*
Adapted Screenplay: *Lincoln*
Original Screenplay: *Zero Dark Thirty*
Cinematography: *Life of Pi*
Film Editing: *Argo*
Production Design: *Moonrise Kingdom*
Animated Feature: *ParaNorman*
Documentary: *The Waiting Room*

WASHINGTON DC AREA FILM CRITICS
Film: *Zero Dark Thirty*
Director: Kathryn Bigelow, *Zero Dark Thirty*
Actor: Daniel Day-Lewis, *Lincoln*
Actress: Jessica Chastain, *Zero Dark Thirty*
Supporting Actor: Philip Seymour Hoffman, *The Master*
Supporting Actress: Anne Hathaway, *Les Misérables*
Adapted Screenplay: *Silver Linings Playbook*
Original Screenplay: *Looper*
Art Direction: *Cloud Atlas*
Cinematography: *Life of Pi*
Score: *The Master*
Animated Feature: *ParaNorman*
Foreign Language Film: *Amour*
Documentary: *Bully*
Acting Ensemble: *Les Misérables*
Youth Performance: *Quvenzhané Wallis, Beasts of the Southern Wild.*

Bruce Willis in *Looper*

GOLDEN GLOBE AWARDS
Picture – Drama: *Argo*
Comedy or Musical: *Les Misérables*
Director: Ben Affleck, *Argo*
Actor – Drama: Daniel Day-Lewis, *Lincoln*
Actress – Drama: Jessica Chastain, *Zero Dark Thirty*
Actor – Comedy or Musical: Hugh Jackman, *Les Misérables*
Actress – Comedy or Musical: Jennifer Lawrence, *Silver Linings Playbook*
Supporting Actor: Christoph Waltz, *Django Unchained*
Supporting Actress: Anne Hathaway, *Les Misérables*
Screenplay: *Django Unchained*
Original Score: *Life of Pi*
Original Song: "Skyfall" from *Skyfall*
Animated Feature: *Brave*
Foreign Language Film: *Amour.*

SCREEN ACTORS GUILD AWARDS
Cast: *Argo*
Male actor in a Leading Role: Daniel Day-Lewis, *Lincoln*
Female Actor in a Leading Role: Jennifer Lawrence, *Silver Linings Playbook*
Male Actor in a Supporting Role: Tommy Lee Jones, *Lincoln*
Female Actor in a Supporting Role: Anne Hathaway, *Les Misérables*
Stunt Ensemble: *Skyfall*

DIRECTORS GUILD AWARDS
Feature Film: Ben Affleck, *Argo*
Documentary: Malik Bendjelloul, *Searching for Sugar Man*
Lifetime Achievement: Milos Forman

PRODUCERS GUILD:
Theatrical Motion Pictures: Ben Affleck, George Clooney, Grant Heslov, *Argo*
Animated Theatrical Motion Pictures: Clark Spencer, *Wreck-It Ralph*
Documentary Theatrical Motion Pictures: Malik Bendjelloul, Simon Chinn, *Searching for Sugar Man.*

WRITERS GUILD AWARDS
Adapted Screenplay: Chris Perrio, *Argo*
Original Screenplay: Mark Boal, *Zero Dark Thirty*
Documentary Screenplay: Malik Bendjelloul, *Searching for Sugar Man.*

BAFTA (British Academy of Film and Television Arts)
Film: *Argo*
Director: Ben Affleck, *Argo*
British Film: *Skyfall*
Leading Actor: Daniel Day-Lewis, *Lincoln*
Leading Actress: Emmanuelle Riva, *Amour*
Supporting Actor: Christoph Waltz, *Django Unchained*
Supporting Actress: Anne Hathaway, *Les Misérables*
Original Screenplay: *Django Unchained*
Adapted Screenplay: *Silver Linings Playbook*
Production Design: *Les Misérables*
Costume Design: *Anna Karenina*
Makeup and Hair: *Les Misérables*
Animated Film: *Brave*
Film Editing: *Argo*
Cinematography: *Life of Pi*
Original Music: *Skyfall*
Sound: *Les Misérables*
Visual Effects: *Life of Pi*
Film Not in the English Language: *Amour*
Documentary: *Searching for Sugar Man*
Outstanding Debut by a British Writer, Director or Producer: Bart Layton, Dimitri Doganis, *The Imposter.*

Matthew McConaughey in *Magic Mike*

AMERICAN FILM INSTITUTE'S TOP 10
Argo; Beasts of the Southern Wild; The Dark Knight Rises; Django Unchained; Les Misérables; Life of Pi; Lincoln; Moonrise Kingdom; Silver Linings Playbook; Zero Dark Thirty.

FILM INDEPENDENT SPIRIT AWARDS
Feature: *Silver Linings Playbook*
First Film: Stephen Chbosky, *The Perks of Being a Wallflower*
Director: David O.Russell, *Silver Linings Playbook*
Male Lead: John Hawkes, *The Sessions*
Female Lead: Jennifer Lawrence, *Silver Linings Playbook*
Supporting Male: Matthew McConaughey, *Magic Mike*
Supporting Female: Helen Hunt, *The Sessions*

Screenplay: *Silver Linings Playbook*
First Screenplay: *Safety Not Guaranteed*
International Film: *Amour*
Cinematography: *Beasts of the Southern Wild*
Documentary: *The Invisible War*
Robert Altman Award: *Starlet*
John Cassavetes Award: *Middle of Nowhere*
Truer Than Fiction Award: *The Waiting Room*
Someone to Watch Award: *Gimme the Loot* (this film received its US commercial run in 2013)
Find Your Audience Award: *Breakfast with Curtis* (no commercial US release in 2012)

TOP BOX OFFICE

Films 2012

TOP 100 BOX OFFICE FILMS of 2012

1. Marvel's The Avengers (BV/Paramount) $623,360,000
2. The Dark Knight Rises (WB) $448,140,000
3. The Hunger Games (Lionsgate) $408,000,000
4. Skyfall (MGM/Columbia) $304,361,000
5. The Hobbit: An Unexpected Journey (WB) $303,004,000
6. Breaking Dawn Part 2 (Summit) $292,312,000
7. The Amazing Spider-Man (Columbia) $262,100,000
8. Brave (Disney) $237,270,000
9. Ted (Universal) $218,670,000
10. Madagascar 3: Europe's Most Wanted (DW/Paramount) $216,400,000
11. Dr. Seuss' The Lorax (Universal) $214,100,000
12. Wreck-It Ralph (Disney) $189,423,000
13. Lincoln (BV) $182,208,000
14. Men in Black III (Columbia) $178,100,000
15. Django Unchained (Weinstein Co.) $162,806,000
16. Ice Age: Continental Drift (20th) $161,140,000
17. Snow White and the Huntsman (Universal) $155,140,000
18. Les Misérables (Universal) $148,810,000
19. Hotel Transylvania (Columbia) $145,330,000
20. Taken 2 (20th) $138,770,000
21. 21 Jump Street (Columbia) $138,450,000
22. Argo (WB) $136,025,000
23. Silver Linings Playbook (Weinstein Co) $132,093,000
24. Prometheus (20th) $126,480,000
25. Safe House (Universal) $126,190,000
26. The Vow (Screen Gems) $125,100,000
27. Life of Pi (20th) $124,977,000
28. Magic Mike (WB) $113,730,000
29. The Bourne Legacy (Universal) $113,210,000
30. Rise of the Guardians (DW/Paramount) $103,413,000
31. Journey 2: The Mysterious Island (WB/New Line) $102,870,000
32. Zero Dark Thirty (Columbia) $95,721,000
33. Flight (Paramount) $93,773,000

Daniel Day-Lewis, Sally Field in *Lincoln*

34. Think Like a Man (Screen Gems) $91,550,000
35. The Campaign (WB) $86,910,000
36. The Expendables 2 (Lionsgate) $84,100,000
37. Wrath of the Titans (WB) $83,680,000
38. Jack Reacher (Paramount) $80,071,000
39. Dark Shadows (WB) $79,730,000
40. Parental Guidance (20th) $76,900,000
41. John Carter (BV) $73,100,000
42. Act of Valor (Relativity Media) $70,100,000
43. This is 40 (Universal) $67,545,000
44. Contraband (Universal) $66,530,000
45. Looper (TriStar) $66,487,000

Scarlett Johansson, Chris Evans, Jeremy Renner in *Marvel's The Avengers*

Samantha Barks, Daniel Huttlestone in *Les Misérables*

Denzel Washington in *Flight*

Russell Brand, Julianne Hough, Diego Boneta, Alec Baldwin in *Rock of Ages*

46. Madea's Witness Protection Program (Lionsgate)	$65,660,000
47. Battleship (Universal)	$65,240,000
48. Pitch Perfect (Universal)	$65,002,000
49. Mirror Mirror (Relativity)	$64,940,000
50. Chronicle (20th)	$64,580,000
51. Hope Springs (Columbia)	$63,540,000
52. Underworld: Awakening (Screen Gems)	$62,330,000
53. The Lucky One (WB)	$60,460,000
54. The Dictator (Paramount)	$59,660,000
55. Total Recall (Columbia)	$58,880,000
56. Titanic (3D reissue) (Paramount)	$57,890,000
57. American Reunion (Universal)	$56,760,000
58. ParaNorman (Focus)	$56,000,000
59. This Means War (20th)	$54,770,000
60. Project X (WB)	$54,740,000
61. The Woman in Black (CBS)	$54,340,000

62. The Devil Inside (Paramount)	$53,270,000
63. Paranormal Activity 4 (Paramount)	$52,890,000
64. The Odd Life of Timothy Green (Disney)	$51,820,000
65. Ghost Rider: Spirit of Vengeance (Columbia)	$51,780,000
66. The Grey (Open Road)	$51,590,000
67. Red Tails (20th)	$49,880,000
68. The Possession (Lionsgate)	$49,130,000
69. Diary of Wimpy Kid: Dog Days (20th)	$49,100,000
70. Sinister (Summit)	$48,100,000
71. Beauty and the Beast (3D reissue) (Disney)	$47,620,000
72. Savages (Universal)	$47,330,000
73. The Best Exotic Marigold Hotel (Fox Searchlight)	$46,413,000
74. Moonrise Kingdom (Focus)	$45,520,000
75. Red Dawn (FilmDistrict)	$44,807,000
76. The Three Stooges (20th)	$44,330,000
77. Here Comes the Boom (Columbia)	$43,600,000
78. Star Wars Episode 1: The Phantom Menace (3D reissue) (20th)	$43,460,000
79. Resident Evil: Retribution (Screen Gems)	$42,350,000
80. The Cabin in the Woods (Lionsgate)	$42,100,000
81. What to Expect When You're Expecting (Lionsgate)	$41,160,000
82. Finding Nemo (3D reissue) (Disney)	$41,100,000
83. End of Watch (Open Road)	$41,004,000
84. Rock of Ages (New Line/WB)	$38,520,000
85. Abraham Lincoln Vampire Hunter (20th)	$37,520,000
86. Lawless (Weinstein Co.)	$37,400,000
87. The Guilt Trip (Paramount)	$37,135,000
88. That's My Boy (Columbia)	$36,940,000
89. Trouble with the Curve (WB)	$35,764,000
90. Step Up Revolution (Summit)	$35,110,000

Sacha Baron Cohen in *The Dictator*

Elsa, Victor, Edgar in *Frankenweenie*

91. Tyler Perry's Good Deeds (Lionsgate) — $35,100,000
92. Frankenweenie (BV) — $34,740,000
93. The Watch (20th) — $34,360,000
94. Monsters, Inc. (3D reissue) (Disney) — $33,824,000
95. 2016: Obama's America (Rocky Mountain) — $33,450,000
96. House at the End of the Street (Relativity Media) — $31,620,000
97. The Pirates! Band of Misfits (Columbia) — $31,100,000
98. Joyful Noise (WB) — $30,940,000
99. Chimpanzee (Disney) — $28,980,000
100. The Five-Year Engagement (Universal) — $28,700,000

Pirate Captain, Polly, Queen Victoria, Charles Darwin in *Pirates Band of Misfits*

OBITUARIES

2012

Ian Abercrombie

Norman Alden

R.G. Armstrong

Luke Askew

Zina Bethune

Turhan Bey

Anita Bjork

Ernest Borgnine

Ray Bradbury

Olympe Bradna

Philip Bruns

Max Bygraves

Frank Cady

Harry Carey, Jr.

Dick Clark

Gary Collins

Hal David

Richard Dawson

Phyllis Diller

Michael Clarke Duncan

IAN ABERCROMBIE, 77, British character actor died in Los Angeles on January 26, 2012 from complications of kidney failure. His film credits include *They Shoot Horses Don't They?*, *Sextette*, *The Ice Pirates*, *The Public Eye*, *Army of Darkness*, *Addams Family Values*, *Grief*, *Mousehunt*, *Wild Wild West*, and *Trust Me*. Survived by his wife and three brothers.

NORMAN ALDEN, 87, Fort Worth-born film and television character actor died in Los Angeles on July 27, 2012 of natural causes. His movies include *Portrait of a Mobster*, *The Nutty Professor* (1963), *Man's Favorite Sport?*, *Andy* (in the title role), *The Wild Angels*, *First to Fight*, *Good Times*, *The Devil's Brigade*, *Tora! Tora! Tora!*, *Kansas City Bomber*, *The Hindenburg*, *I Never Promised You a Rose Garden*, *Semi Tough*, *Victor Victoria*, *Back to the Future*, *They Live*, *Ed Wood*, and *Patch Adams*. Survivors include his longtime partner; his two children; 2 stepsons; a grandson, and a step-granddaughter.

GERRY ANDERSON, 83, British producer-director-writer who created the British sci-fi series *Thunderbirds*, using a technique he dubbed "supermarionation," died in his sleep on December 26, 2012 in Henley-on-Thames, England. He had been diagnosed with mixed dementia two years earlier. In addition to spinning the show into two theatrical features which he wrote and produced, *Thunderbirds are Go* and *Thunderbird 6*, he wrote and produced the live-action feature *Journey to the Far Side of the Sun*. He is survived by his second wife and four children.

R.G. ARMSTRONG (Robert Golden Armstrong, Jr.), 95, Alabama-born character actor died in his sleep at his home in Studio City, CA, on July 27, 2012. His many films include *Garden of Evil*, *The Fugitive Kind*, *Ride the High Country*, *Major Dundee*, *El Dorado*, *The Ballad of Cable Hogue*, *The Great White Hope*, *J.W. Coop*, *Pat Garrett and Billy the Kid*, *Race with the Devil*, *Stay Hungry*, *Heaven Can Wait* (1978), *Raggedy Man*, *Reds* (1981), *Children of the Corn*, *Predator*, and *Dick Tracy*. Survivors include 4 daughters, a son, and 5 grandchildren.

WILLIAM ASHER, 90, New York City-born director-producer-writer responsible for most of AIP's "Beach Party" comedies of the 1960s, and who worked on such popular sitcoms as *I Love Lucy*, *The Patty Duke Show*, and *Bewitched*, died on July 16, 2012 in Palm Desert, CA, of complications from Alzheimer's disease. Although television was principally his field, his theatrical credits as director include *The Shadow on the Window*, *Beach Party*, *Johnny Cool* (also producer), *Beach Blanket Bingo* (also writer), *How to Stuff a Wild Bikini* (also writer), *Fireball 500* (also writer), *Night Warning*, and *Movers & Shakers* (also producer). He is survived by his fourth wife; his two children from his marriage to actress Danni Sue Nolan; his three children from his marriage to actress Elizabeth Montgomery; his son from his marriage to actress Joyce Bullifont; four step-children; nine grandchildren; and eight step-grandchildren.

LUKE ASKEW, 80, Georgia-born character actor died of lung cancer on March 29, 2012 at his home in Lake Oswego, OR. His movies include *Hurry Sundown*, *Cool Hand Luke* (as the prison boss with the reflecting sunglasses), *Will Penny*, *The Green Berets*, *The Devil's Brigade*, *Easy Rider*, *Flareup*, *The Culpepper Cattle Co.*, *The Great Northfield Minnesota Raid*, *Pat Garrett and Billy the Kid*, *Posse*, *Rolling Thunder*, *Wanda Nevada*, *The Beast Within*, *The Newton Boys*, and *The Greatest Game Ever Played*. Survived by his wife; a son; a daughter from a previous marriage; and a grandson.

SIR RICHARD RODNEY BENNETT, 76, British composer-pianist, who earned Oscar nominations for his scores for *Far from the Madding Crowd*, *Nicholas and Alexandra*, and *Murder on the Orient Express*, died at his home in Manhattan on December 24, 2012. His other movie credits include *Indiscreet*, *The Devil's Disciple*, *The Mark*, *The Wrong Arm of the Law*, *Billy Liar*, *The Nanny*, *Billion Dollar Brain*, *Equus*, *The Brink's Job*, *Yanks*, *Enchanted April*, and *Four Weddings and a Funeral*. Survived by his sister.

ZINA BETHUNE, 66, New York City-born dancer-turned-actress was killed on February 12, 2012 after being hit by two different vehicles in Griffith Park, Los Angeles while trying to help a wounded animal. Best known for her role of "Gail Lucas" on the television series *The Doctors and the Nurses*, she also appeared in three theatrical films: *Sunrise at Campobello*, *Who's That Knocking at My Door?*, and *The Boost*. Survived by her husband and her mother, actress Ivy Bethune.

TURHAN BEY (Gilbert Selahettin Schultavey), 90, Austria-born Turkish actor, best remembered for starring in several Technicolor Universal diversions as *Arabian Nights* and *Ali Baba and the Forty Thieves*, died in Vienna on September 30, 2012 after a long struggle with Parkinson's disease. His other credits include *Burma Convoy*, *The Mummy's Tomb*, *White Savage*, *The Mad Ghoul*, *Follow the Boys*, *The Climax*, *Dragon Seed*, *Bowery to Broadway*, *Sudan*, *A Night in Paradise*, *Out of the Blue* (1947), *Adventures of Casanova*, *Song of India*, and *Prisoners of the Casbah*. No immediate survivors.

ANITA BJÖRK, 89, Swedish actress, who came to prominence starring in the 1951 film of *Miss Julie*, died on October 24, 2012. Her other movies include *Night People*, *Secrets of Women*, *Square of Violence*, *Loving Couples* (US: 1964), *Adalen 31*, and *The Best of Intentions*. Survivors include a son and a daughter.

PAUL BOGART, 92, New York City-born film and television director died on April 15, 2012 in Chapel Hill, NC. Although principally a television director, his theatrical film credits include *Marlowe*, *Skin Game*, *Cancel My Reservation*, *Mr. Ricco*, *Oh God! You Devil!*, and *Torch Song Trilogy*. On television he won five Emmy Awards for directing episodes of *The Defenders*, *CBS Playhouse*, and *All in the Family*, and for producing *The Golden Girls*. Survived by his son; his two daughters; his sister; five grandchildren; and four great-grandchildren.

ERNEST BORGNINE (Ermes Effron Borgnino), 95, Connecticut-born actor, who won the Academy Award for his portrayal of a lonely Bronx butcher in search of love in the 1955 Best Picture winner *Marty*, died of kidney failure on July 8, 2012 in Los Angeles. Following his 1951 debut in *China Corsair*, he first made an impact on screen as the brutal stockade sergeant in the classic *From Here to Eternity*. His many other movies include *The Whistle at Eaton Falls*, *The Stranger Wore a Gun*, *Johnny Guitar*, *Demetrius and the Gladiators*, *Vera Cruz*, *Bad Day at Black Rock*, *Violent Saturday*, *Jubal*, *The Catered Affair*, *The Best Things in Life are Free*, *The Vikings*, *The Rabbit Trap*, *Season of Passion* (*The Summer of the 17th Doll*), *Man on a String*, *Pay or Die*, *Barabbas*, *McHale's Navy* (a spin-off from his hit TV series), *The Flight of the Phoenix*, *The Oscar*, *The Dirty Dozen*, *The Legend of Lylah Clare*, *Ice Station Zebra*, *The Wild Bunch*, *The Adventurers*, *Suppose They Gave a War and Nobody Came?*, *Willard* (1971), *Hannie Caulder*, *Bunny O'Hare*, *The Poseidon Adventure*, *Emperor of the North Pole*, *Law and Disorder*, *The Devil's Rain*, *The Greatest* (1977), *Crossed Swords*, *The Black Hole*, *Escape from New York*, *Spike of Bensonhurst*, *Mistress*, *Gattaca*, *September 11*, and *Red*. He is survived by his fifth wife; his four children; six grandchildren; and a sister.

RAY BRADBURY, 91, Illinois-born writer, one of the most revered and popular names in the field of science fiction and fantasy, responsible for such works as *Fahrenheit 451* (filmed in 1966) and *The Martian Chronicles*, died in Los Angeles on June 5, 2012. He was credited with the screenplays for *Moby Dick*, *The Picasso Summer* (as 'Douglas Spaulding'), and *Something Wicked This Way Comes* (from his novel), while such other movies as *It Came from Outer Space* and *The Beast from 20,000 Fathoms* derived from his stories. He is survived by his four daughters and eight grandchildren.

OLYMPE BRADNA, 92, Paris-born actress, who appeared in such Paramount films as *College Holiday* (with Jack Benny) and *Souls at Sea* (opposite Gary Cooper), died on November 5, 2012 at her home in Lodi, CA. Her other U.S. credits include *Three Cheers for Love*, *The Last Train from Madrid*, *Say it in French*, *South of Pago Pago*, and *International Squadron*. She left show business after marrying. Her husband of 70 years predeceased her by 9 months. Survivors include two children; five grandchildren; and several great-grandchildren.

PETER BRECK, 82, Massachusetts-born actor, best known for playing Nick Barkley on the TV series *The Big Valley*, died in Vancouver, British Columbia on Feb. 6, 2012, after a long illness. His films include *I Want to Live!, The Beatniks, Portrait of a Mobster, Lad: A Dog, Hootenanny Hoot, Shock Corridor, The Glory Guys, Benji*, and *Jiminy Glick in Lalawood*. Survivors include his wife.

FAITH BROOK, 90, British actress died on March 11, 2012. The daughter of actor Clive Brook, she made her debut in *Suspicion* in 1941, followed by such movies as *Jungle Book, Finger of Guilt, Chase a Crooked Shadow, The 39 Steps* (1959), *To Sir with Love, ffolkes, The Sea Wolves, Eye of the Needle, The Razor's Edge* (1984), and *Mrs. Dalloway*. Survived by her son.

RICHARD BRUNO, 87, costume designer died from kidney failure in Port Townsend, WA, on Jan. 11, 2012. Among the movies on which he worked were *Wild in the Streets, Two-Lane Blacktop, Steelyard Blues, Heaven Can Wait* (1978), *Ice Castles, Raging Bull, Stripes, The King of Comedy, The Karate Kid* (1984), *The Color of Money, Shoot to Kill, Casualties of War, Goodfellas, Guilty by Suspicion, Under Siege, Eraser*, and *Hoodlum*. Survivors include two daughters, three grandchildren, and one great grandson.

PHILIP BRUNS, 80, Minnesota-born character actor died on Feb. 8, 2012. His movies include *A Thousand Clowns, Jenny, The Out of Towners, Taking Off, The Gang That Couldn't Shoot Straight, Harry and Tonto, The Great Waldo Pepper, Nickelodeon, The Stunt Man, My Favorite Year, Flashdance*, and *The Trigger Effect*. Among his many TV roles was playing the title character's father on *Mary Hartman, Mary Hartman*. Survived by his wife and a sister.

MAX BYGRAVES (Walter William Bygraves), 89, British singer-actor died on August 31, 2012 in Hope Island, Queensland, Australia. He'd been suffering from Alzheimer's disease. In addition to his stage and television appearances, he was seen in a handful of theatrical features; among those that played in the U.S. were *Tom Brown's Schooldays* (1951), *A Cry from the Streets*, and *Bobbikins*. Survivors include his second wife and 6 children.

FRANK CADY, 96, California-born character actor, best remembered for playing the role of "Sam Drucker" on three different series, *Petticoat Junction, Green Acres*, and *The Beverly Hillbillies*, died on June 8, 2012 at his home in Wilsonville, OR. He was also seen in such films as *Flamingo Road, The Asphalt Jungle, Father of the Bride, Ace in the Hole, When Worlds Collide, Rear Window, Trial, The Indian Fighter, The Bad Seed, The Girl Most Likely, 7 Faces of Dr. Lao, The Gnome-Mobile, Zandy's Bride*, and *Hearts of the West*. Survivors include his daughter, his son, three grandchildren, and three great-grandchildren.

HARRY CAREY, JR., 91, California-born actor, who appeared in such westerns for director John Ford as *3 Godfathers* and *She Wore a Yellow Ribbon*, died of natural causes on December 27, 2012 in Santa Barbara, CA. The son of actors Harry and Olive Carey, he made his debut in the 1946 feature *Rolling Home* and was thereafter seen in such movies as *Red River, Wagon Master, Rio Grande, Warpath, Island in the Sky, Beneath the 12-Mile Reef, The Long Gray Line, Mister Roberts, The Searchers, The Great Locomotive Chase, From Hell to Texas, The Great Impostor, Two Rode Together, Shenandoah, The Rare Breed, Alvarez Kelly, The Way West, The Devil's Brigade, The Undefeated, Dirty Dingus Magee, Big Jake, Take a Hard Ride, Nickelodeon, The Long Riders, Gremlins, Mask, The Whales of August, Tombstone*, and *Wyatt Earp*. Survived by his wife, son, two daughters, three grandchildren, and two great-grandchildren.

PETER CARSTEN, 83, German actor died in Lucinja, Slovenia on April 20, 2012. Among his films released in America were *The Devil Strikes at Night, Under Ten Flags, A Study in Terror, The Quiller Memorandum, The Vengeance of Fu Manchu, Dark of the Sun, Hannibal Brooks, Zeppelin, Mr. Superinvisible* (which he also produced), and *Twilight Time*.

CHRISTOPHER CHALLIS, 93, British cinematographer died on May 31, 2012. His credits include *The Tales of Hoffman, The Story of Gilbert and Sullivan, Genevieve, Quentin Durward, Sink the Bismarck!, Damn the Defiant!, The Victors, The Long Ships, A Shot in the Dark, Those Magnificent Men in Their Flying Machines, Arabesque, Two for the Road, Chitty Chitty Bang Bang, The Private Life of Sherlock Holmes, Mary Queen of Scots, The Little Prince, The Deep, The Mirror Crack'd, Evil Under the Sun*, and *Top Secret!* Survived by a son and his daughter.

HAL CHESTER (Harold Ribotsky), 91, Brooklyn-born actor-turned-producer died on March 25, 2012. Billed as Hally Chester he appeared as a teen in such movies as *Juvenile Court, Newsboys' Home, East Side Kids, You're Not So Tough*, and *Boys of the City*. His credits as producer include *Joe Palooka, Champ* (also story; and several follow-up Joe Palooka adventures), *The Highwayman; The Beast from 20,000 Fathoms; Curse of the Demon* (*Night of the Demon*) (also writer), *The Two-Headed Spy, School for Scoundrels* (1960; also writer), *The Double Man*, and *The Secret War of Harry Frigg*. Survived by two sons.

LEONARDO CIMINO, 94, Manhattan-born character actor died of chronic obstructive pulmonary disease at his home in Woodstock, NY, on March 3, 2012. His films include *The Young Savages, Cotton Comes to Harlem, Jeremy, The Man in the Glass Booth, Stardust Memories, Monsignor, Dune, The Monster Squad, Moonstruck, The Freshman* (1990), *Hudson Hawk, Waterworld, Cradle Will Rock*, and *Before the Devil Knows You're Dead*. Survived by his wife.

DICK CLARK, 82, New York-born host of television's *American Bandstand* and *Rockin' New Year's Eve*, died of a heart attack in Santa Monica, CA, on April 18, 2012. He acted in the films *Because They're Young, The Young Doctors, Wild in the Streets, Killers Three* (for which he also wrote the story and produced), and *Spy Kids*, as well as appearing as himself in *Jamboree!* and *The Phynx*. He was producer on such films as *Psych-Out, The Dark*, and *Remo Williams: The Adventure Begins* …On television he received 5 Emmys including three for hosting *The (New) $25,000 Pyramid*. Survived by his third wife, three children from his previous marriages, and two grandchildren.

JOHN CLIVE, 79, London-born actor, whose many roles include providing the voice of John Lennon for the 1968 animated classic *Yellow Submarine*, died on October 14, 2012 in England following a short illness. His other motion pictures include *The Italian Job* (1969), *A Nice Girl like Me, A Clockwork Orange, The Pink Panther Strikes Again*, and *Revenge of the Pink Panther*. Survived by his second wife, two children from his first marriage, and his stepson.

GARY COLLINS, 74, Venice, CA-born actor-emcee died of natural causes on October 13, 2012 in Biloxi, MI. Best known for hosting the syndicated series *Hour Magazine* and serving for a period as the emcee of the Miss America Pageant, he also acted in such motion pictures as *The Pigeon That Took Rome, Angel in My Pocket, Airport, Killer Fish*, and *Beautiful*. He had recently separated from his wife since 1967, actress Mary Ann Mobley.

SAM COPPOLA, 79, Jersey City-born character actor died on February 12, 2012 in Leonia, NJ, of aneurysm complications. His movies include *The Anderson Tapes, Crazy Joe, Saturday Night Fever, Without a Trace, Fatal Attraction, Blue Steel, Jacob's Ladder, Palookaville*, and *Reunion*. He is survived by his two children and three grandchildren.

JEROME COURTLAND (Courtland Jourolman Jr.), 85, Tennessee-born actor-turned-director died of heart disease on March 1, 2012 in Santa Clarita Valley, CA. He acted in such pictures as *Kiss and Tell, The Man from Colorado, Tokyo Joe, Battleground, A Woman of Distinction, The Barefoot Mailman, The Bamboo Prison, Tonka*, and *Black Spurs*. He later directed episodes of such programs as *The Flying Nun, The Love Boat*, and *Knots Landing*. He is survived by his third wife; four sons; three daughters; 16 grandchildren; and one great-grandchild.

Charles Durning

Jake Eberts

Nora Ephron

Chad Everett

James Farentino

William Finley

Al Freeman, Jr.

Jonathan Frid

Ben Gazzara

Don Grady

Andy Griffith

Larry Hagman

Marvin Hamlisch

Levon Helm

Sherman Hemsley

Celeste Holm

Whitney Houston

Davy Jones

Erland Josephson

Alex Karras

HAL DAVID (Harold Lane David), 91, Manhattan born lyricist, who won an Academy Award for the song "Raindrops Keep Fallin' on My Head" from the 1969 film *Butch Cassidy and the Sundance Kid*, died in Los Angeles on September 1, 2012 of complications from a stroke. With his most frequent collaborator Burt Bacharach he was responsible for such pop hits as "Do You Know the Way to San Jose?," "I Say a Little Prayer," "What the World Needs Now is Love," and "Close to You," while they earned additional Oscar nominations for the songs "What's New Pussycat," "Alfie" and "The Look of Love" (from *Casino Royale*). Among the other films for which he contributed lyrics are *The Sad Sack, Country Music Holiday, A House is Not a Home, Send Me No Flowers, Promise Her Anything, After the Fox, On Her Majesty's Secret Service, Lost Horizon* (1973), and *Moonraker*. He is survived by his second wife, two sons, and three grandchildren. His brother, lyricist Mack David, died in 1993.

RICHARD DAWSON (Colin Lionel Emm), 79, British actor-host, best known for acting on the television sitcom *Hogan's Heroes* and hosting the game show *Family Feud* (for which he earned a Daytime Emmy), died in Los Angeles of complications of esophageal cancer on June 2, 2012. His movie credits include *The Longest Day, King Rat, Munster Go Home!, The Devil's Brigade,* and *The Running Man* (1987). Survived by his second wife; their daughter; two sons from his first marriage, to actress Diana Dors; and four grandchildren.

PHYLLIS DILLER (Phyllis Ada Driver), 95, Ohio-born comedian-actress, a former housewife who turned to performing, becoming one of the pioneers in the field of stand-up comedy for women, died in her sleep at her Brentwood, CA, home on August 20, 2012. In addition to her countless nightclub and television appearances, she could be seen in such movies as *Splendor in the Grass, The Fat Spy, Boy Did I Get a Wrong Number!, Mad Monster Party?* (voice), *Eight on the Lam, Did You Hear the One about the Traveling Saleslady?, The Private Navy of Sgt. O'Farrell, The Adding Machine, The Sunshine Boys, Pink Motel, Wisecracks, The Aristocrats,* and *Who Killed the Electric Car?* Survived by her son; two daughters; four grandchildren; and a great-grandchild.

ROBERT DOZIER, 81, screen and television writer died at his home on Martha's Vineyard, MA, on Jan. 6, 2012, following a long illness. Principally a television writer, his five motion picture credits were *The Young Stranger, I Could Go on Singing, The Cardinal, The Big Bounce,* and *When the Legends Die*. Survivors include his wife, actress Diana Muldaur; three sons from his first marriage; his sister; and his stepmother, actress Ann Rutherford (who was married for 38 years to Dozier's father, producer William Dozier).

MICHAEL CLARKE DUNCAN, 54, Chicago-born actor, who earned an Oscar nomination for playing the convict with supernatural powers in the 1999 film *The Green Mile*, died in Los Angeles on September 3, 2012 from complications of a heart attack he'd suffered in July. The former bodyguard's other movie credits include *Bulworth, Armageddon, A Night at the Roxbury, The Whole Nine Yards, Planet of the Apes* (2001), *The Scorpion King, Daredevil, Brother Bear* (voice), *Sin City, The Island* (2005), *Talladega Nights, School for Scoundrels* (2006), *The Last Mimzy, Welcome Home Roscoe Jenkins, Kung Fu Panda* (voice), *The Slammin' Salmon, Redemption Road,* and *Green Lantern* (voice). Survived by his fiancée; his mother; and his sister.

CHARLES DURNING, 89, New York-born character actor, whose vast list of motion picture credits include earning Oscar nominations for his work in *The Best Little Whorehouse in Texas* and the 1983 remake of *To Be or Not to Be*, died of natural causes at his Manhattan home on December 24, 2012. His other titles include *Harvey Middleman – Fireman, I Walk the Line, Dealing, The Sting, The Front Page* (1974), *Dog Day Afternoon, The Hindenburg, Breakheart Pass, Twilight's Last Gleaming, The Choirboys, The Fury, An Enemy of the People, The Muppet Movie, North Dallas Forty, Starting Over, When a Stranger Calls* (1979), *The Final Countdown, True Confessions, Sharky's Machine, Tootsie, Stick, The Man with One Red Shoe, Big Trouble* (1986), *Tough Guys, The Rosary Murders, Cop, Far North, Dick Tracy, The Music of Chance, The Hudsucker Proxy, I.Q., The*

Grass Harp, Home for the Holidays, Spy Hard, Lakeboat, O Brother Where Art Thou?, State and Main, The Golden Boys, and *An Affirmative Act*. Survived by his three children.

JAKE EBERTS, 71, Montreal-born executive producer of the Oscar winners *Driving Miss Daisy* and *Dances with Wolves*, died on September 6, 2012 in Montreal of uveal melanoma, a rare cancer of the eye which had spread to his liver. His other movie credits include *The Name of the Rose, Hope and Glory, The Adventures of Baron Munchausen, Black Robe, A River Runs Through It, Super Mario Bros., James and the Giant Peach, The Legend of Bagger Vance, The Illusionist,* and *The Way Back*. Survivors include his wife and daughter.

BIFF ELLIOTT (Leon Shalek), 89, Massachusetts-born actor, who made his screen debut playing Mickey Spillane's Mike Hammer in the 1953 adaptation of *I, the Jury*, died at his home in Studio City, CA, on August 15, 2012. His other films include *House of Bamboo, Good Morning Miss Dove, Between Heaven and Hell, The True Story of Jesse James, The Enemy Below, Pork Chop Hill, PT 109, The Navy vs. the Night Monsters, Kotch, Save the Tiger, The Front Page* (1974), and *That's Life*. Survivors include his second wife.

NORA EPHRON, 71, New York City-born writer-director, who was responsible for such popular comedies as *Sleepless in Seattle* (Oscar nomination for script) and *Julie & Julia* (which she also produced), died in Manhattan on June 26, 2012 of pneumonia brought on by acute myeloid leukemia. Her other credits as director-writer include *This is My Life, Michael* (also producer), *You've Got Mail* (also prod.), and *Bewitched* (also producer); while she served as a writer on such films as *Silkwood* (Oscar nomination); *Heartburn* (from her *roman a clef* novel based on her marriage to journalist Carl Bernstein); *When Harry Met Sally…* (Oscar nomination); and *My Blue Heaven* (1990). The daughter of the late screenwriters Henry and Phoebe Ephron, she is survived by her third husband, writer Nicholas Pileggi; her two sons from her second marriage; and her three sisters, including Delia Ephron, with whom Nora wrote several screenplays.

CHAD EVERETT (Raymon Lee Cramton), 75, Indiana-born actor, who starred as Dr. Joe Gannon for seven seasons on the CBS TV series *Medical Center*, died at his home in Los Angeles on July 24, 2012, following a long battle with lung cancer. His motion picture credits include *Claudelle Inglish, Rome Adventure, The Chapman Report, Get Yourself a College Girl, Made in Paris, The Singing Nun, Johnny Tiger, First to Fight, The Impossible Years, Fever Pitch,* and *Mulholland Dr.* Survived by his two daughters and six grandchildren. His wife of 45 years, actress Shelby Grant, died in 2011.

JAMES FARENTINO, 73, Brooklyn-born screen and television actor died of complications from a broken hip in Los Angeles on January 24, 2012. Although principally know for his work on the small screen, he was seen in such theatrical motion pictures as *Ensign Pulver, The War Lord, The Pad and How to Use It, Banning, Rosie!; Me, Natalie; Story of a Woman, The Final Countdown, Dead & Buried, Her Alibi,* and *Bulletproof*. Survived by his fourth wife and two sons.

JON FINCH, 71, British actor, who had the leading roles in Roman Polanski's *Macbeth* and Alfred Hitchcock's *Frenzy*, was found dead at his home in Swindon, England, on December 28, 2012. His other movie credits include *The Horror of Frankenstein, Sunday Bloody Sunday, Lady Caroline Lamb, The Last Days of Man on Earth* (*The Final Programme*), *Death on the Nile, Breaking Glass,* and *The Rainbow*. Survivors include his daughter.

WILLIAM FINLEY, 69, New York City-born actor, who played the title role in director Brian DePalma's 1974 cult film *The Phantom of the Paradise*, died on April 14, 2012 in Manhattan from complications following surgery. He also worked with DePalma in *Murder a la Mod, The Wedding Party, Sisters, The Fury,* and *The Black Dahlia*, while his other credits include *Eaten Alive, Wise Blood, Simon, The Funhouse,* and *Silent Rage*. Survived by his wife and his son.

Zalman King

Jack Klugman

Elyse Knox

Sylvia Kristel

George Lindsey

Herbert Lom

Tony Martin

Russell Means

Patricia Medina

Jerry Nelson

Lupe Ontiveros

Cliff Osmond

Morgan Paull

Frank Pierson

Deborah Raffin

Joyce Redman

Tracy Reed

Ann Rutherford

Tony Scott

Dinah Sheridan

JOHN FORREST (John Forsht), 80, Connecticut-born U.K.-based actor died in France on March 28, 2012. Starting in his teens, he appeared in such pictures as *Great Expectations* (1947; as the young Herbert Pocket), *Bonnie Prince Charlie*, *Tom Brown's Schooldays*, *Glory at Sea*, *Nearly a Nasty Accident*, *Very Important Person*, and *The Bawdy Adventures of Tom Jones*.

HARRY FOWLER (Henry James Fowler), 85, London-born actor, who began in films as a teen and continued as a busy character player on screen and television for nearly 50 years, died on Jan. 4, 2012 in London. His credits include *Champagne Charlie*, *Hue and Cry*, *Now Barabbas*, *Mister Drake's Duck*, *13 East Street*, *The Pickwick Papers*, *Idol on Parade*, *Crooks Anonymous*, *The Longest Day*, *Lawrence of Arabia*, *The Nanny*, *Life at the Top*, *Start the Revolution without Me*, *Crossed Swords*, and *Chicago Joe and the Showgirl*. Survived by his second wife.

STEVE FRANKEN, 80, Brooklyn-born character actor whose countless television and movie roles included playing the increasingly drunken waiter in the cult favorite *The Party* died of cancer on August 24, 2012 in Los Angeles. Among his films are *The Americanization of Emily*, *Follow Me Boys!*, *Angel in My Pocket*, *Number One*, *Which Way to the Front?*, *Westworld*, *The Reincarnation of Peter Proud*, *The Missouri Breaks*, *Avalanche*, *The North Avenue Irregulars*, *Hardly Working*, *The Fiendish Plot of Dr. Fu Manchu*, *Can't Buy Me Love*, *Nurse Betty*, and *Angels & Demons*. He is survived by his second wife; their daughter; two daughters from his first marriage; and two grandchildren.

AL FREEMAN, JR., 78, San Antonio-born actor, who had starring roles in the film *Dutchman* (repeating a part he'd played on stage) and the TV movie *My Sweet Charlie* (which also received a theatrical run), died on August 9, 2012 in Washington, DC, where he had taught acting at Howard University. His other motion picture credits include *This Rebel Breed*, *Black like Me*, *The Troublemaker*, *The Detective*, *Finian's Rainbow*, *The Lost Man*, *Castle Keep*, *Malcolm X* (as Elijah Muhammad), *Once Upon a Time … When We Were Colored*, and *Down in the Delta*. On television he won an Emmy for his role as Capt. Ed Hall on the daytime serial *One Life to Live*. No reported survivors.

JONATHAN FRID (John Herbert Frid), 87, Ontario-born actor, best known for playing the vampire Barnabas Collins on the daytime cult serial *Dark Shadows*, died of natural causes in Hamilton, Ontario, Canada on April 14, 2012. He appeared in the theatrical features *House of Dark Shadows* and *Seizure*, and did a cameo in the 2012 *Dark Shadows* revamp, released posthumously. No reported survivors.

ROBERT FUEST, 84, British director of the Vincent Price horror film *The Abominable Dr. Phibes* died in London on March 21, 2012. Although he worked principally on television, his other theatrical features include *Wuthering Heights* (1971), *And Soon the Darkness*, *Dr. Phibes Rises Again* (also writer), and *The Devil's Rain*. He is survived by his wife and their daughter; and three sons from a previous marriage.

BEN GAZZARA (Biagio Anthony Gazzara), 81, New York City-born actor, who starred in such dramas as *Anatomy of a Murder*, *The Young Doctors*, and *Husbands*, died of pancreatic cancer on February 3, 2012. After his breakthrough performance on Broadway in the original production of *Cat on a Hot Tin Roof*, he made his film debut in 1957 in *The Strange One*. His other movies include *The Passionate Thief*, *Convicts 4*, *Conquered City*, *A Rage to Live*, *The Bridge at Remagen*, *The Neptune Factor*, *Capone*, *The Killing of a Chinese Bookie*, *Voyage of the Damned*, *Opening Night*, *Saint Jack*, *Bloodline*, *They All Laughed*, *Inchon*, *Road House* (1989), *Shadow Conspiracy*, *The Spanish Prisoner*, *Buffalo '66*, *The Big Lebowski*, *Happiness*, *Illuminata*, *Summer of Sam*, *The Thomas Crown Affair* (1999), *Dogville*, *Paris je t'aime*, and *Looking for Palladin*. Survived by his third wife and his daughter from his marriage to actress Janice Rule.

NORMAN GRABOWSKI, 79, New Jersey-born actor, best known for playing crew-cutted lugs in Disney movies like *The Monkey's Uncle* and *Blackbeard's Ghost*, died on October 12, 2012 in Cassville, MO after a long illness. Sometimes billed with his nickname of "Woo Woo," he was seen in such other movies as *High School Confidential!*, *The Big Operator*, *The Beat Generation*, *Girls Town*, *College Confidential*, *Sex Kittens Go to College*, *The Misadventures of Merlin Jones*, *Sergeant Dead Head*, *The Gnome-Mobile*, *The Happiest Millionaire*, *Herbie Rides Again*, *The Towering Inferno*, *Hooper*, and *The Cannonball Run*. He was also well known as a custom car builder and designer. Survivors include his sister and several nieces and nephews.

DON GRADY (Don Louis Agrati), 68, San Francisco-born actor, best known for playing Robbie Douglas on the long-running sitcom *My Three Sons*, died at his home in Thousand Oaks, CA, on June 27, 2012 following a long battle with cancer. He was also seen in such theatrical features as *Ma Barker's Killer Brood*, *The Crowded Sky*, and *The Wild McCullochs*. Survived by his second wife; his mother; two children; and a sister.

ANDY GRIFFITH, 86, North Carolina-born actor, who became a household name playing Sheriff Andy Taylor on his 1960s sitcom *The Andy Griffith Show*, died of a heart attack in Manteo, NC, on July 3, 2012. Following his 1957 motion picture debut in *A Face in the Crowd*, he became a star repeating the role he played both on television and Broadway of country bumpkin Will Stockdale in the hit film adaptation of *No Time for Sergeants*. His other theatrical movies are *Onionhead*, *The Second Time Around*, *Angel in My Pocket*, *Hearts of the West*, *Rustlers' Rhapsody*, *Spy Hard*, *Daddy and Them*, *Waitress*, and *Play the Game*. He also starred for nine seasons on the series *Matlock*. Survived by his third wife and his daughter from his first marriage.

ULU GROSBARD, 83, Belgian-born director died in Manhattan on March 19, 2012. His seven credits as a film director are *The Subject Was Roses* (which he had also done on Broadway), *Who is Harry Kellerman and Why is He Saying Those Terrible Things about Me?*, *Straight Time*, *True Confessions*, *Falling in Love*, *Georgia*, and *The Deep End of the Ocean*. His other theater credits include *American Buffalo*, which, like *Roses*, brought him a Tony nomination. Survived by his wife.

TONINO GUERRA, 92, Italian screenwriter, who received Oscar nominations for co-scripting *Casanova '70*, *Blowup*, and *Amarcord*, died at his home in Santarcangelo di Raomgna in Northern Italy on March 21, 2012. Among his other writing credits are *L'avventura*, *La Notte*, *L'Eclisse*, *The Empty Canvas*, *Red Desert*, *Marriage Italian Style*, *The 10th Victim*, *More Than a Miracle*, *A Place for Lovers*, *In Search of Gregory*, *Zabriskie Point*, *Sunflower*, *Sex with a Smile*, *The Night of the Shooting Stars*, *And the Ship Sails On*, *Ginger and Fred*, *Good Morning Babylon*, and *Everybody's Fine* (1990). He is survived by his second wife and a son.

LARRY HAGMAN, 81, Texas-born actor, who became a television icon with his role as the villainous J.R. Ewing on the long-running prime-time serial *Dallas*, died in Dallas on November 23, 2012 of complications from throat cancer. He was reprising the J.R. role on a new update of the series at the time of his death. His motion picture credits include *Ensign Pulver*, *Fail-Safe* (as the U.S. President's interpreter), *The Cavern*, *The Group*, *The Hired Hand*, *Beware! The Blob* (which he also directed), *Harry and Tonto*, *Stardust*, *Mother Jugs & Speed*, *The Big Bus*, *The Eagle Has Landed*, *Superman*, *S.O.B.*, *Nixon*, and *Primary Colors*. He is survived by his wife of 58 years; a son; a daughter; and five granddaughters.

MARVIN HAMLISCH, 68, New York City-born composer, who received 3 Academy Awards in the same year (1974), for *The Way We Were* (for writing the title song and original dramatic score) and *The Sting* (for scoring adaptation), died in Los Angeles on August 6, 2012, following a brief illness. He received additional Oscar nominations for *Kotch* (for the song "Life is What You Make It"), *The Spy Who Loved Me* (for the song "Nobody Does it Better" and the score), *Same Time, Next Year* (for the song "The Last Time I Felt like This"), *Sophie's Choice* (score),

A Chorus Line (for the song "Surprise, Surprise"), Shirley Valentine (for the song "The Girl Who Used to Be Me"), and The Mirror Has Two Faces (for the song "I've Finally Found Someone"). Other film scores include The Swimmer, Take the Money and Run, Bananas, The War Between Men and Women, Save the Tiger, Ice Castles, Starting Over, Chapter Two, Seems Like Old Times, D.A.R.Y.L., 3 Men and a Baby, Little Nikita, and Frankie and Johnny. He received the Tony and the Pulitzer Prize for his work on the classic Broadway musical A Chorus Line. Survived by his wife.

LEVON HELM (Mark Levon Helm), 71, Arkansas-born musician-actor, drummer-singer with The Band, died in New York on April 19, 2012 of complications of cancer. In addition to appearing with the group in the 1978 documentary The Last Waltz, he acted in such films as Coal Miner's Daughter, The Right Stuff, Smooth Talk, End of the Line, Staying Together, The Adventures of Sebastian Cole, The Three Burials of Melquiades Estrada, and Shooter. Survived by his daughter; his wife; and two grandchildren.

SHERMAN HEMSLEY, 74, Philadelphia-born actor who came to prominence playing the character of George Jefferson, first on All in the Family and then on the long-running spinoff series The Jeffersons, died at his home in El Paso, TX, on July 24, 2011 of unspecified causes. Although mainly seen on television, he appeared in such theatrical movies as Love at First Bite, Club Fed, Sprung, Senseless, Jane Austin's Mafia!, and Screwed. No reported survivors.

CELESTE HOLM, 95, New York City-born actress, who won the 1947 Academy Award for Best Supporting Actress for her performance as fashion editor Anne Dettrey in the Best Picture winner Gentleman's Agreement, died at her Manhattan home on July 15, 2012, two days after suffering from a heart attack. First gaining attention as Ado Annie in the original Broadway production of Oklahoma!, she came to Hollywood in 1946 to make her movie debut in Three Little Girls in Blue. Her other motion picture credits include Carnival in Costa Rica, Road House (1948), The Snake Pit, Chicken Every Sunday, Come to the Stable (Oscar nomination), Everybody Does It, A Letter to Three Wives (voice), Champagne for Caesar, All about Eve (Oscar nomination), The Tender Trap, High Society, Bachelor Flat, Tom Sawyer (1973), The Private Files of J. Edgar Hoover, and Three Men and a Baby. She is survived by her fifth husband, two sons, and three grandchildren.

WHITNEY HOUSTON, 48, Newark-born singer-actress was found dead in her Beverly Hills hotel room on February 11, 2012. She had accidentally drowned in the bathtub due to the effects of atherosclerotic heart disease and cocaine use. Her string of number one pop hits include "Saving All My Love," "How Will I Know," and "I Wanna Dance with Somebody." She acted in four movies: The Bodyguard (one of her songs from the film, "I Will Always Love You," became the best-selling single by a female artist in music history), Waiting to Exhale, The Preacher's Wife, and the posthumously-released Sparkle. Survivors include her mother, singer Cissy Houston; and her daughter from her marriage to singer Bobby Brown.

JOHN INGLE, 84, Tulsa-born actor who played Edward Quartermaine on the long-running soap General Hospital over a 19 year period, died of cancer at his home in Altadena, CA, on September 16, 2012. His motion picture credits include True Stories, Heathers, Repossessed, Death Becomes Her, Batman & Robin, Senseless, Hostage (2005), and TiMER. His wife of 57 years had died in February; survivors include their five daughters.

EIKO ISHIOKA, 73, Tokyo-born costume designer, who won an Academy Award for her work on Bram Stoker's Dracula, died in Tokyo of pancreatic cancer on January 21, 2012. Her other credits include The Cell, The Fall, Immortals, and Mirror Mirror (Oscar Nomination), the last released posthumously. She is survived by her husband; her mother; two brothers; and a sister.

STAN JOLLEY, 86, New York City-born art director-production designer who was nominated for an Oscar for his work on Witness died of gastric cancer on June 4, 2012 in Rancho Mirage, CA. His other films include Toby Tyler or Ten

Weeks with a Circus, Mail Order Bride, Young Billy Young, The Phynx, Taps, and The Grass Harp. Jolley also served as one of the designers of Disneyland. He is survived by his 2 daughters and 2 grandchildren.

DAVY JONES, 66, Manchester-born singer-actor, who rose to fame in the 60s as a member of the TV pop group the Monkees, died of a heart attack in Indiantown, FL, on Feb. 29, 2012. He was seen in the theatrical features Head and The Brady Bunch Movie. Survived by his third wife; four daughters; three sisters; and three grandchildren.

KATHRYN JOOSTEN, 72, Florida-born character actress, who won 2 Emmys for playing nosey neighbor Karen McCluskey on the series Desperate Housewives, died of lung cancer at her home in Westlake Village, CA, on June 2, 2012. Her character had died of the same disease on an episode of the show broadcast less than three weeks earlier. Among her movie credits were Grandview U.S.A., The Package, Best Men, Wedding Crashers, The TV Set, Rails & Ties, and Bedtime Stories. Survived by two sons; two grandsons; and a brother.

ERLAND JOSEPHSON, 88, Swedish actor, best known for his many collaborations with Ingmar Bergman, notably Scenes from a Marriage and Face to Face, died in Stockholm on February 25, 2012. He had been suffering from Parkinson's disease. In addition to such other Bergman credits as The Magician, Hour of the Wolf, and After the Rehearsal, he could be seen in Beyond Good and Evil, Montenegro, The Sacrifice, The Unbearable Lightness of Being, Prospero's Books, and Ulysses' Gaze, among other U.S. releases. Survived by his wife and five children.

ALEX KARRAS, 77, Indiana-born football player-turned-actor, who played supporting roles in the classic comedies Blazing Saddles (as the hulking Mongo) and Victor Victoria (as the closeted bodyguard, Squash), died of kidney failure at his home in Los Angeles on October 10, 2012. Following twelve seasons as defensive tackle with the Detroit Lions, he turned to acting after portraying himself in the 1968 film Paper Lion. His other movies include FM, Jacob Two-Two Meets the Hooded Fang, When Time Ran Out ..., Porky's, and Against All Odds. With his wife, Susan Clark, he starred in the popular sitcom Webster. She survives him, along with his three sons and his daughter.

DAVID KELLY, 82, Dublin-born character player, who starred alongside Ian Bannen in the 1998 hit comedy Waking Ned Devine, died on February 12, 2012 in Dublin, after a brief illness. His other movies include The Wrong Box, Young Cassidy, Ulysses (1967), The Italian Job (1969), Quackser Fortune Has a Cousin in the Bronx, Purple Taxi, A Portrait of the Artist as a Young Man, Pirates, Into the West, A Man of No Importance, The Run of the Country, Laws of Attraction, Charlie and the Chocolate Factory, and Stardust. Survived by his wife and his two children.

ZALMAN KING (Zalman Lefkowitz), 70, Trenton-born director-writer-producer-actor died on February 3, 2012 at his Santa Monica home following a 6-year bout with cancer. He acted in such movies as You've Got to Walk it Like You Talk it or You'll Lose That Beat, The Ski Bum, Some Call it Loving, The Passover Plot, Tell Me a Riddle, and Endangered Species (also exec. prod.), while his behind-the-scenes credits include Roadie (1980; exec. prod., story), Nine ½ Weeks (writer, prod.), Two Moon Junction (dir., writer), and Wild Orchid (dir., writer). He is survived by his wife and their two daughters.

JACK KLUGMAN (Jacob Joachim Klugman), 90, Philadelphia-born actor who, after key supporting performances in such movies as 12 Angry Men and Goodbye Columbus, reached his greatest level of fame as the star of TV's The Odd Couple (winning 2 Emmy Awards), died on December 24, 2012 in Northridge, CA. His other motion picture credits include Time Table, Cry Terror!, Days of Wine and Roses, I Could Go on Singing, Act One, Hail Mafia, The Detective (1968), The Split, Who Says I Can't Ride a Rainbow!, Two-Minute Warning, Dear God, and When Do We Eat? He is survived by his second wife, his two sons and two grandchildren.

Robert B. Sherman

Victor Spinetti

Warren Stevens

Mel Stuart

Eric Sykes

Phyllis Thaxter

Susan Tyrrell

Gore Vidal

Simon Ward

Andy Williams

ELYSE KNOX (Elsie Lillian Kornbrath), 94, Hartford-born actress who was active during the 1940s, died at her home in Los Angeles on February 15, 2012. Her credits include *Lillian Russell, Youth Will Be Served, Sheriff of Tombstone, The Mummy's Tomb, Hit the Ice, A Wave, a WAC and a Marine, Moonlight and Cactus, Joe Palooka – Champ* (as Anne Howe, a role she repeated in 5 more films), *Sweetheart of Sigma Chi,* and *There's a Girl in My Heart.* She is survived by three children from her marriage to football player Tom Harmon, including her son, actor Mark Harmon.

SYLVIA KRISTEL, 60, Dutch actress who starred in the 1970s erotic film *Emmanuelle,* died in the Netherlands on October 17, 2012 following a long battle with cancer. Her other theatrical U.S. releases include *The Fifth Musketeer, The Concorde ... Airport '79, The Nude Bomb, Private Lessons, Private School,* and *Red Heat.* She is survived by her partner and her son.

GEORGE LINDSEY, 83, Alabama-born actor, best known for playing the character of "Goober" Pyle on *The Andy Griffith Show, Mayberry RFD,* and *Hee-Haw,* for nearly 30 years, died on May 6, 2012 after an extended illness. He was also seen in such movies as *Ensign Pulver, Snowball Express, Charley and the Angel, Treasure of Matecumbe, Take This Job and Shove It,* and *Cannonball Run II,* as well as doing voices in *The Aristocats, Robin Hood,* and *The Rescuers.* He is survived by his son; his daughter; two grandsons; a cousin; and his companion of many years.

MORT LINDSEY (Morton Lippman), 89, Newark-born musical director-arranger-composer-conductor, best known for his work on *The Judy Garland Show* and *The Merv Griffin Show,* died at his home in Malibu on May 4, 2012, of complications from a broken hip. He provided scores to such films as *40 Pounds of Trouble, I Could Go on Singing* (in which he also appeared on screen), *The*

William Windom

Richard D. Zanuck

Best Man (1964), and *Real Life* (also seen on screen), and was conductor-arranger for *Gay Purr-ee.* He won an Emmy for the 1968 Barbra Streisand special *A Happening in Central Park.* He is survived by his wife, three sons, and three daughters.

HERBERT LOM (Herbert Charles Angelo Kuchacevich ze Schluderpacheru), 95, Prague-born UK-based actor, who created the role of the exasperated Chief Inspector Dreyfuss in the 1964 comedy *A Shot in the Dark* and would reprise it in six more Inspector Clouseau-*Pink Panther* films, died in his sleep at his home in London on September 27, 2012. In addition to appearing in such classic films as *The Ladykillers* and *Spartacus,* his long list of credits include *The Young Mr. Pitt* (as Napoleon), *The Seventh Veil, The Black Rose, Night and the City* (1950), *Mr. Denning Drives North, Twist of Fate, The Love Lottery, War and Peace* (1956; as Napoleon), *Fire Down Below, Action of the Tiger, I Accuse!, The Roots of Heaven, The Big Fisherman, North West Frontier* (*Flame over India*), *Third Man on the Mountain, I Aim at the Stars, Mysterious Island* (as Captain Nemo), *El Cid, The Phantom of the Opera* (1962, title role), *Uncle Tom's Cabin* (as Simon Lagree), *Return from the Ashes, Bang! Bang! You're Dead!, Gambit* (1966), *99 Women, Count Dracula* (as Van Helsing), *Mark of the Devil, Ten Little Indians* (1975 and 1989), *Sam Marlow – Private Eye, Hopscotch, The Dead Zone,* and *The Pope Must Die.* Survivors include his three children and seven grandchildren.

RICHARD LYNCH, 76, Brooklyn-born character actor who specialized in villainous roles, was found dead at his home in Palm Springs, CA, on June 19, 2012. His movies include *Scarecrow, The Seven Ups, The Happy Hooker, The Formula, Twinkle Twinkle ... Killer Kane* (*The Ninth Configuration*), *The Sword and the Sorcerer, Invasion U.S.A., Little Nikita,* and *Bad Dreams.* Survived by his second wife and his brother, actor Barry Lynch.

TONY MARTIN (Alvin Morris), 98, San Francisco-born singer-actor whose career as a crooner spanned some 80 years, died at his home in West Los Angeles on July 27, 2012. He was seen in such films as *Follow the Fleet, Sing Baby Sing* (the first to feature his first wife, Alice Faye), *Pigskin Parade, Banjo on My Knee, You Can't Have Everything, Life Begins in College, Alibi Baba Goes to Town; Sally, Irene and Mary; Music in My Heart; Ziegfeld Girl; The Big Store, Till the Clouds Roll By, Casbah, Two Tickets to Broadway, Here Come the Girls, Easy to Love, Deep in My Heart, Hit the Deck,* and *Meet Me in Las Vegas.* He was married for 60 years to dancer Cy Charisse until her death in 2008. Survived by his stepson and two grandchildren.

JOAQUIN MARTINEZ, 81, Mexican actor whose roles included playing the title character in the 1972 western *Ulzana's Raid,* died at his home in Everdingen, Holland, on Jan. 3, 2012, following a brief battle with cancer. Among his other films are *The Stalking Moon, Joe Kidd, Jeremiah Johnson, Executive Action, Who'll Stop the Rain, Flashpoint, Revenge, House of Cards, The Cowboy Way,* and *Die Another Day.* He is survived by his wife; his son; a daughter; and a stepson.

RUSSELL MEANS, 72, South Dakota-born Indian activist who turned to acting when he played Chingachgook in the 1992 film of *The Last of the Mohicans,* died of esophageal cancer on October 22, 2012 at his ranch in Porcupine, SD. The former leader of the American Indian Movement (AIM), his other movie credits include *Natural Born Killers, Wagons East, Windrunner, Pocahontas* (voice), *Thomas and the Magic Railroad, The Last Shot,* and *Pathfinder.* He is survived by his fifth wife and several children.

PATRICIA MEDINA, 92, British actress, best known for the various swashbuckling adventures she appeared in during the 1950s, died in Los Angeles on April 28, 2012 of natural causes. Her movie credits include *The Foxes of Harrow, The Beginning or the End?, The Three Musketeers* (1948), *The Fighting O'Flynn, Francis, Fortunes of Captain Blood, The Jackpot, Abbott and Costello in the Foreign Legion, Valentino* (1951), *The Lady and the Bandit, The Magic Carpet, Lady in the Iron Mask, Captain Pirate, Siren of Bagdad, Botany Bay, Phantom of the Rue Morgue, Drums of Tahiti, The Black Knight, Mr. Arkadin, Miami Expose, Count Your Blessings, Snow White and the Three Stooges, The Killing of Sister George,* and *Timber Tramp.* Her second husband was actor Joseph Cotten, who died in 1994. No immediate survivors.

CLAUDE MILLER, 70, French filmmaker died on April 4, 2012 in Paris after a long illness. Among his film released in America are *Garde a vue, The Little Thief, The Accompanist, Alias Betty, A Secret,* and *I'm Glad My Mother is Alive.* Survived by his wife and a son.

JOHN MOFFATT, 89, British actor who portrayed Albert Finney's instructor, Mr. Square, in the Oscar-winning 1963 film *Tom Jones,* died on September 10, 2012 in England. While busier on stage, television, and radio, his other films include *The Silent Enemy, Lady Caroline Lamb, Murder on the Orient Express, Galileo,* and *Britannia Hospital.* Survived by a sister.

HANK MOONJEAN, 82, Illinois-born producer, who earned an Oscar nomination for the 1988 film *Dangerous Liaisons,* died on October 7, 2012 at his home in the Hollywood Hills after a battle with pancreatic cancer. Following years as assistant director on such major titles as *Butterfield 8, Cool Hand Luke,* and *The Odd Couple,* he turned to producing with such credits (sometimes as associate) as *The Singing Nun, WUSA, The Great Gatsby* (1974), *The Fortune, The End, Hooper, The Incredible Shrinking Woman, Sharky's Machine,* and *Stealing Home.* Survived by his domestic partner of 51 years and various nieces and nephews.

JERRY NELSON, 79, Tulsa-born puppeteer-actor, who, as one of Jim Henson's Muppet performers, brought life to such characters as Floyd Pepper, Lew Zealand, Robin the Frog, and most famously, *Sesame Street'*s Count, died at his home on Cape Cod, MA, on August 23, 2012. He had been suffering from emphysema for years. He contributed to such films as *The Muppet Movie, The Great Muppet Caper, The Dark Crystal, Sesame Street Presents Follow That Bird, The Muppet Christmas Carol,* and *Muppets from Space.* Survived by his wife.

LUPE ONTIVEROS (Guadalupe Moreno), 69, Texas-born character actress, whose roles included portraying the accused killer of pop star Selena Quintanilla (played by Jennifer Lopez) in the 1997 biopic *Selena,* died on July 26, 2012 in Whittier, CA, after a short battle with liver cancer. Her other films include *The Big Fix, California Suite, Zoot Suit, El Norte, The Goonies, The Rosary Murders, Universal Soldier, Blood In/Blood Out, As Good as it Gets, Chuck & Buck, Real Women Have Curves, This Christmas,* and *Our Family Wedding.* Survived by her husband, three sons, and two granddaughters.

CLIFF OSMOND (Clifford Osman Ebrahim), 75, Jersey City-born character actor, best remembered for his work with filmmaker Billy Wilder, most notably playing the private investigator Purkey in *The Fortune Cookie,* died of pancreatic cancer at his home in Santa Monica, CA, on December 22, 2012. For Wilder he also acted in *Irma la Douce, Kiss Me Stupid,* and *The Front Page,* while his other credits include *How the West Was Won, Wild and Wonderful, The Devil's 8, Oklahoma Crude, Joe Panther, The North Avenue Irregulars,* and *Hangar 18.* He is survived by his wife, his daughter, a son, and a granddaughter.

MORGAN PAULL, 67, character actor died on July 17, 2012 in Ashland, OR, of stomach cancer. His credits include *Patton, Cahill U.S. Marshal, Twilight's Last Gleaming, The Swarm, Norma Rae, Fade to Black, Blade Runner,* and *Out Cold.* Survived by his companion; two daughters; two sisters; a granddaughter and grandson; and his stepmother.

FRANK PIERSON, 87, New York-born writer-director, who won an Academy Award for his screenplay for *Dog Day Afternoon,* died on July 22, 2012 in Los Angeles after a brief illness. He received additional Oscar nominations for his scripts for *Cat Ballou* and *Cool Hand Luke;* wrote such other films as *The Happening* (1967), *The Anderson Tapes,* and *Presumed Innocent;* and served as director and writer on the features *The Looking Glass War, A Star is Born* (1976), and *King of the Gypsies.* From 2001-2005 he served as president of the Academy of Motion Picture Arts and Sciences. Survived by his wife; his son and his daughter; and five grandchildren.

MARTIN POLL, 89, New York City-born producer, who earned an Oscar nomination for *The Lion in Winter,* died in New York on April 14, 2012, of pneumonia and kidney failure. His other credits include *Love is a Ball, Sylvia* (1965), *The Possession of Joel Delaney, The Man Who Loved Cat Dancing, Love and Death, The Sailor Who Fell from Grace with the Sea, Nighthawks, Haunted Summer,* and *My Heroes Have Always Been Cowboys.* Between 1956 and 1961 he ran Gold Medal Studios in the Bronx and served as New York's Commissioner of Motion Picture Arts. Survived by his wife; two sons; a stepson; and three grandchildren.

DORY PREVIN (Dorothy Langdon), 86, New Jersey-born lyricist-singer died of natural causes at her home in Southfield, MA, on February 14, 2012. With her second husband, composer Andre Previn, she received Oscar nominations for the songs "Faraway Part of Town" (from *Pepe*) and "Second Chance" (from *Two for the Seesaw*); and earned her third nod for co-writing "Come Saturday Morning" (from *The Sterile Cuckoo*) with Fred Karlin. Other songs of hers appeared in such films as *Tall Story, Goodbye Charlie, Inside Daisy Clover, The Swinger,* and *Valley of the Dolls.* She is survived by her third husband, actor Joby Baker; three stepchildren; and six step-grandchildren.

DEBORAH RAFFIN, 59, Los Angeles-born actress, who appeared in such 1970s films as *The Dove* and *Once is Not Enough,* died in Los Angeles on Nov. 21, 2012 of leukemia. Her other theatrical releases include *40 Carats, God Told Me To, The Sentinel, Touched by Love, Death Wish 3,* and *Morning Glory* (1993). In addition to her acting career, she created Dove Books-on-Tape. Survived by her brother; her sister; and her daughter.

CARLO RAMBALDI, 86, Italian special effects expert, best known for creating the title character in the sci-fi classic *E.T. The Extra-Terrestrial*, died on August 10, 2012 in Lamezia Terme, Italy after a long-illness. In addition to *E.T.* he also won Academy Awards for his work on *Alien* and the 1976 remake of *King Kong*. He contributed to the effects or served as creature designer/creator on such other films as *Andy Warhol's Frankenstein*, *The Hand*, *Conan the Destroyer*, *Dune*, and *King Kong Lives*. Survived by his two children.

JOYCE REDMAN, 96, Irish actress, who received Oscar nominations for playing Albert Finney's seductive dinner companion in *Tom Jones* and Emilia in *Othello* (1965), died on May 9, 2012 in Kent, England, following a brief illness. She had been suffering from pneumonia. Principally a stage and television performer her handful of other movies include *One of Our Aircraft is Missing* and *Prudence and the Pill*. She is survived by three children and five grandchildren.

TRACY REED (Clare Tracy Compton Pelissier), 69, London-born actress, best remembered for playing George C. Scott's mistress in the classic black comedy *Dr. Strangelove*, died on May 2, 2012 in West Cork, Ireland. Her other films include *A Shot in the Dark*, *You Must Be Joking!*, *Maroc 7*, *Casino Royale*, *Hammerhead*, *Melody*, and *Percy*. She retired from acting in the mid-1970s. Survivors include her daughter from her first marriage, to actor Edward Fox.

JOHN RICH, 86, New York-born director, best known for his television work on such programs as *The Dick Van Dyke Show* and *All in the Family*, both of which won him Emmys, died in Los Angeles on January 29, 2012. He also directed five theatrical features: *Wives and Lovers*, *The New Interns*, *Roustabout*, *Boeing Boeing*, and *Easy Come Easy Go* (1967). Survived by his wife; three children; three stepchildren; and eight grandchildren.

LEE RICH, 93, Cleveland-born producer and co-founder of Lorimar died of lung cancer at his Los Angeles home on May 24, 2012. In addition to winning an Emmy for *The Waltons*, he served as producer or executive producer on such theatrical films as *The Man* (1972), *The Choirboys*, *Who is Killing the Great Chefs of Europe?*, *Hard to Kill*, *Innocent Blood*, and *The Score*. He is survived by his longtime partner, actress Pippa Scott; five children; and seven grandchildren.

MARTIN RICHARDS (Morton Richard Klein), 80, Bronx-born film and stage producer, who won the Academy Award for producing the 2002 Best Picture winner *Chicago*, died in New York on November 26, 2012 of cancer. His other screen credits are *Some of My Best Friends Are*, *The Boys from Brazil*, *The Shining* (as associate producer), and *Fort Apache the Bronx*. On Broadway he earned Tony Awards for *The Norman Conquests*, *Sweeney Todd*, *La Cage aux Folles* (the original production as well as the 2005 revival), *The Will Rogers Follies*, and *The Life*. Survivors include his brother.

J. MICHAEL RIVA, 63, New York City-born production designer, who received an Oscar nomination for his work on the 1985 film *The Color Purple*, died in New Orleans on June 7, 2012 of complications from a stroke. His other credits include *The Hand*, *The Goonies*, *Lethal Weapon*, *Scrooged*, *Tango & Cash*, *A Few Good Men*, *Dave*, *Hard Rain*, *Charlie's Angels*, *The Pursuit of Happyness*, *Iron Man*, and *Django Unchained*. The grandson of cinema legend Marlene Dietrich, he is survived by his wife and four sons.

RICHARD ROBBINS, 71, Massachusetts-born composer, who earned Oscar nominations for the Merchant Ivory productions *Howards End* and *The Remains of the Day*, died of Parkinson's disease at his home in Rhinebeck, NY, on November 7, 2012. His other credits for the Ismail Merchant/James Ivory team include *The Europeans*, *Jane Austen in Manhattan*, *The Bostonians*, *A Room with a View*, *Maurice*, *Slaves of New York*, *Mr. & Mrs. Bridge*, *Jefferson in Paris*, *The Golden Bowl*, *Le Divorce*, and *The White Countess*. He is survived by his longtime partner, composer-artist Michael Schell.

ANN RUTHERFORD (Therese Ann Rutherford), 94, Vancouver-born actress, best remembered for playing Mickey Rooney's girlfriend Polly Benedict in MGM's series of *Andy Hardy* films, died at her home in Beverly Hills on June 11, 2012. Her other films include *Waterfront Lady* (her debut, in 1935), *The Singing Vagabond*, *Of Human Hearts*, *Dramatic School*, *A Christmas Carol* (1938; as the Ghost of Christmas Past); *Gone with the Wind* (as Scarlett O'Hara's sister, Carreen), *Pride and Prejudice*, *Washington Melodrama*, *This Time for Keeps*, *Orchestra Wives*, *Whistling in Dixie*, *Happy Land*, *The Secret Life of Walter Mitty*, *Adventures of Don Juan*, *They Only Kill Their Masters*, and *Won Ton the Dog Who Saved Hollywood*. She is survived by her daughter; her companion; a stepdaughter; and two grandsons.

HARRIS SAVIDES, 55, New York City-born cinematographer died of brain cancer on October 9, 2012 in Manhattan. His credits include *The Game*, *Illuminata*, *The Yards*, *Finding Forrester*, *Elephant*, *Birth*, *Last Days*, *Margot at the Wedding*, *American Gangster*, *Milk*, *Whatever Works*, *Greenberg*, and *Somewhere*. He is survived by his wife and his daughter.

TONY SCOTT, 68, British director, who came to prominence with the 1986 Tom Cruise hit *Top Gun*, jumped to his death on August 19, 2012 from the Vincent Thomas Bridge in San Pedro, CA. His other credits as director include *The Hunger*, *Revenge* (1990), *Days of Thunder*, *The Last Boy Scout*, *True Romance*, *Enemy of the State*, *Spy Game*, and five action films starring Denzel Washington: *Crimson Tide*, *Man on Fire*, *Déjà vu*, *The Taking of Pelham 123* (2009), and *Unstoppable*. He served as producer or executive producer on several of these films as well as titles he did not direct like *In Her Shoes*, *The Assassination of Jesse James*, *Welcome to the Rileys*, *Cyrus*, *The A-Team*, and *The Grey*. Survivors include his third wife; 2 children; and his older brother, director Ridley Scott.

RAVI SHANKAR, 92, sitar master who helped introduce Indian music to the West, died on December 11, 2012 in San Diego. He had been treated for upper-respiratory and heart ailments and had just underwent heart-valve replacement surgery. He appeared as himself in the films *Monterey Pop* and *The Concert for Bangladesh*, and contributed music to such movies as *Pather Panchali*, *The World of Apu*, *Charly*, and *Gandhi*. He is survived by his wife; two daughters, one of whom is singer Norah Jones; three grandchildren, and four great-grandchildren.

DINAH SHERIDAN (Dinah Mec), 92, London-born actress who starred in the classic 1953 British comedy *Genevieve*, died at her home in Northwood, London on November 25, 2012. Among her other movies to be distributed in the U.S. were *Breaking the Sound Barrier*, *The Story of Gilbert and Sullivan*, and *The Railway Children*. Survivors include her children from her first marriage.

ROBERT B. SHERMAN, 86, New York City-born songwriter, who, along with his brother Richard M. Sherman, won 2 Oscars for their most famous score, for *Mary Poppins*, including one for Best Song ("Chim-Chim-Cher-ee"), died in London on March 5, 2012. His other Oscar nominations were for the films *Chitty Chitty Bang Bang* (for the title song); *Bedknobs and Broomsticks* (for scoring adaptation and the song "The Age of Not Believing"); *Tom Sawyer* (for original song score); *The Slipper and the Rose* (for the song "The Slipper and the Rose Waltz–He Danced with Me/She Danced with Me," and for original song score); and *The Magic of Lassie* (for the song "When You're Loved"). Writing principally for Disney, the Sherman's songs were also heard in such films as *The Parent Trap*, *In Search of the Castaways*, *Summer Magic*, *The Sword in the Stone*, *The Monkey's Uncle*, *That Darn Cat*, *The Jungle Book*, *The Happiest Millionaire*, and *The One and Only Genuine Original Family Band*. The Sherman Brothers were the subject of the 2009 documentary *The Boys*. In addition to his brother, he is survived by two sons; two daughters; five grandchildren; and two step-grandchildren.

VICTOR SPINETTI (Vittorio Giorgio Andrea Spinetti), 82, Welsh actor, best known by U.S. audiences for his appearances in the Beatles' films *A Hard Day's Night* (as the TV director) and *Help!* (as a mad scientist), died of cancer on June 18, 2012 in London. His other films include *Sparrows Can't Sing*, *Becket*,

The Taming of the Shrew (1967), *The Biggest Bundle of Them All, Start the Revolution Without Me, Under Milk Wood, The Little Prince, The Return of the Pink Panther, Voyage of the Damned, Under the Cherry Moon,* and *The Krays.* On Broadway he won a Tony Award for *Oh! What a Lovely War.* No reported survivors.

WARREN STEVENS, 92, Pennsylvania-born screen and television actor, died on March 27, 2012 at his home in Sherman Oaks, CA, of respiratory failure complicated by lung disease. He was seen in such motion pictures as *The Frogmen, Phone Call from a Stranger, Deadline U.S.A., The I Don't Care Girl, Gorilla at Large, The Barefoot Contessa, Women's Prison, Forbidden Planet, On the Threshold of Space, Hot Spell, No Name on the Bullet, Madame X* (1966), *An American Dream, Madigan,* and *Stroker Ace.* He is survived by his second wife; their two sons; and a son from his first marriage.

MARTHA STEWART, 89, Kentucky-born actress died of natural causes in Northeast Harbor, ME, on February 25, 2012. Her movies include *Doll Face, I Wonder Who's Kissing Her Now, Daisy Kenyon, In a Lonely Place, Aaron Slick from Punkin Crick,* and *Surf Party.* Survived by two sons from her third marriage.

MEL STUART (Stewart Solomon), 83, New York City-born director-producer, who directed the 1971 cult favorite *Willy Wonka & the Chocolate Factory,* died of cancer in Beverly Hills on August 9, 2012. Principally a documentary maker, his other theatrical movie credits include the documentary *Four Days in November,* for which he received an Oscar nomination; *If It's Tuesday This Must Be Belgium, I Love My Wife,* and *Wattstax.* On television he won an Emmy for the 1963 documentary *The Making of the President 1960.* Survived by his daughter; two sons; and two grandchildren.

BRUCE SURTEES, 74, Los Angeles-born cinematographer, who earned an Oscar nomination for his black and white photography on the 1974 film *Lenny,* died on February 23, 2012. His other credits include *Play Misty for Me, Dirty Harry, High Plains Drifter, Sparkle* (1976), *The Outlaw Josey Wales, The Shootist, Movie Movie, Escape from Alcatraz, Bad Boys* (1983), *Risky Business, Sudden Impact, Tightrope, Beverly Hills Cop, Pale Rider, Men Don't Leave,* and *Corrina Corrina.* He is survived by his wife.

ERIC SYKES, 89, British actor-comedian-writer-director died on July 4, 2012 following a brief illness. On screen he was seen in such films as *Coming-Out Party* (*Very Important Person*), *Invasion Quartet, Heavens Above!, One Way Pendulum, Those Magnificent Men in Their Flying Machines, Rotten to the Core, The Spy with a Cold Nose, The Liquidator, Shalako, Those Daring Young Men in Their Jaunty Jalopies, Theatre of Blood, Splitting Heirs, The Others, Harry Potter and the Goblet of Fire,* and *Son of Rambow.* In the UK he was known for such television series as *Sykes and a …* and *Sykes.* Survived by his wife of 60 years, three daughters and a son.

PHYLLIS THAXTER, 92, Maine-born actress who began her career under contract to MGM, appearing in such popular films as *Thirty Seconds over Tokyo* and *Week-End at the Waldorf,* and ended her movie career playing the adopted Earth mother of Clark Kent in the 1978 blockbuster *Superman,* died in Longwood, FL, on August 14, 2012, following a nine-year bout with Alzheimer's disease. Her other credits include *Bewitched* (1945), *The Sea of Grass, Living in a Big Way, Tenth Avenue Angel, Blood on the Moon, Act of Violence, No Man of Her Own, The Breaking Point, Jim Thorpe – All-American, Come Fill the Cup, She's Working Her Way Through College, Springfield Rifle, Women's Prison,* and *The World of Henry Orient.* Survivors include her daughter, actress Skye Aubrey; her son; 5 grandchildren; and a great-grandson.

NEIL TRAVIS (Herbert Neil Travis), 75, Los Angeles-born film editor, who won the Academy Award for his work on the 1990 film *Dances with Wolves,* died at his home in Arroyo Grande, CA, on March 28, 2012. His other credits include *The Cowboys, Hot Stuff, The Idolmaker, Cujo, The Philadelphia Experiment, No Way Out* (1987), *Cocktail, Deceived, Patriot Games, Clear and Present Danger,*

Outbreak, Stepmom, The Sum of All Fears, and *Premonition.* Survived by his wife; a son; and a daughter.

SUSAN TYRRELL (Susan Jillian Creamer), 67, San Francisco-born actress, who received an Oscar nomination for playing the drunken Oma in the 1972 film *Fat City,* died in her sleep on June 16, 2012 at her home in Austin, TX. Her other films include *Been Down So Long it Looks like Up to Me, The Steagle, Catch My Soul, Zandy's Bride, The Killer Inside Me* (1976), *Islands in the Stream; I Never Promised You a Rose Garden; September 30, 1955; Fast-Walking, Night Warning, Angel, Tapeheads, Big Top Pee-wee, Far from Home, Cry-Baby, Powder,* and *Masked and Anonymous.* She is survived by her mother; two sisters; a half-brother; and a niece.

GORE VIDAL (Eugene Luther Gore Vidal), 86, West Point, NY-born writer who first gained notoriety with one of the groundbreaking gay novels, *The City and the Pillar,* and later wrote such best-sellers as *Lincoln* and *Myra Breckinridge,* died at his home in the Hollywood Hills on July 31, 2012 of complications from pneumonia. He authored such plays as *Visit to a Small Planet* and *The Best Man* (which he adapted into a movie in 1964), while his screenplays included *The Catered Affair, I Accuse!, Suddenly Last Summer, Is Paris Burning?,* and *Caligula.* He also acted in such films as *Bob Roberts, With Honors, Shadow Conspiracy, Gattaca,* and *Shrink.* Survivors include a half-sister and half-brother.

GARRY WALBERG, 90, Buffalo-born character actor, best known for playing Lt. Frank Monahan on the NBC series *Quincy M.E.,* died on March 27, 2012 in Northridge, CA, of chronic pulmonary obstruction and congestive heart failure. His films include *Gangster Story, Charro!, The Maltese Bippy, Tell Them Willie Boy is Here, They Call Me Mister Tibbs!, The Organization, When the Legends Die, Two-Minute Warning, King Kong* (1976), and *MacArthur.*

SIMON WARD, 70, British actor, best known for playing Winston Churchill in the 1972 biopic *Young Winston,* died in Somerset, England, on July 20, 2012 after a long illness. His other movies include *If…, Frankenstein Must Be Destroyed, Hitler: The Last Ten Days, The Three Musketeers* (1974; as the Duke of Buckingham), *Aces High, Zulu Dawn,* and *Supergirl,* Survivors include his wife and his three daughters, one of whom is actress Sophie Ward.

ANDY WILLIAMS (Howard Andrew Williams), 84, Iowa-born singer who helped make popular such Oscar-winning songs as "Moon River" and "Days of Wine and Roses," died on September 25, 2012 at his home in Branson, MO, following a long battle with bladder cancer. While best known for his countless records, concert appearances, and for starring on several variety shows, he was seen singing in the feature films *Janie, Ladies' Man,* and *Something in the Wind* (along with his brothers), and had a sole acting assignment, in the 1964 comedy *I'd Rather Be Rich.* He is survived by his second wife; his three children from his marriage to singer-actress Claudine Longet; six grandchildren; and two brothers, Don and Dick, with whom he once performed (the fourth brother, Bob, passed away in 2003).

DICK ANTHONY WILLIAMS, 77, Chicago-born actor died on Feb. 16, 2012 in Van Nuys, CA, following a long illness. His movies include *The Lost Man, The Anderson Tapes, The Mack, Five on the Black Hand Side, Dog Day Afternoon, The Deep, An Almost Perfect Affair, The Jerk, The Star Chamber, Summer Rental, Tap, Mo' Better Blues, Edward Scissorhands,* and *The Rapture.* Survived by two daughters and a son.

NICOL WILLIAMSON, 75, Scotland-born actor, whose notable screen roles include Sherlock Holmes in *The Seven Per-Cent-Solution* and Merlin in *Excalibur,* died of esophageal cancer on December 16, 2011 in Amsterdam, Holland. His movies include *The Bofors Gun, Inadmissible Evidence* (repeating his stage role), *Laughter in the Dark, Hamlet* (1969; in the title role), *The Wilby Conspiracy, Robin and Marian, The Seven-Per-Cent Solution, The Goodbye Girl, The Cheap Detective, The Human Factor, Venom, I'm Dancing as Fast as I Can,*

Return to Oz, Black Widow (1987), *The Advocate, The Wind in the Willlows,* and *Spawn.* Survived by his son.

WILLIAM WINDOM, 88, New York City-born actor, whose busy career in film and television included winning an Emmy for the series *My World and Welcome to It,* died of congestive heart failure at his home in Woodacre, CA, on August 16, 2012. Following his 1962 debut as the prosecuting attorney in the classic drama *To Kill a Mockingbird,* he was seen in such other films as *Cattle King, One Man's Way, The Americanization of Emily, Hour of the Gun, The Detective* (1968), *The Gypsy Moths, Brewster McCloud, The Mephisto Waltz, Escape from the Planet of the Apes, Fools' Parade, The Man* (1972), *Grandview U.S.A., She's Having a Baby, Uncle Buck, Sommersby, Miracle on 34th Street* (1994), and *True Crime.* On television he also was seen on such series as *The Farmer's Daughter* and *Murder, She Wrote.* Survived by his fifth wife; four children; and four grandchildren.

AUDREY YOUNG, 89, Los Angeles-born actress-singer, the widow of filmmaker Billy Wilder, died on June 1, 2012. Mainly a bit player, she was seen in such films as *Lady in the Dark, Salty O'Rourke, The Affairs of Susan, Out of This World,* *George White's Scandals, Follow That Woman, Blue Skies, The Wistful Widow of Wagon Gap, Easy Living* (1949), and *Love Me or Leave Me.* She and Wilder married in 1949.

RICHARD D. ZANUCK, 76, Los Angeles-born film producer and executive, who won the Academy Award for producing the 1989 Best Picture winner *Driving Miss Daisy,* died of a heart attack at his home in Beverly Hills on July 13, 2012. The son of 20th Century Fox mogul Darryl F. Zanuck, he received his first producer credit on the 1959 film *Compulsion,* served as head of production at Fox from 1962 to 1970, and then formed (with David Brown) the Zanuck/Brown Company. His other credits as producer/executive producer include *The Chapman Report, Sssssss, The Sugarland Express, The Eiger Sanction, Jaws* (Oscar nomination), *The Verdict,* (1982; Oscar nomination), *Cocoon, Rich in Love, Mulholland Falls, Deep Impact, Road to Perdition, Big Fish, Charlie and the Chocolate Factory, Sweeney Todd: The Demon Barber of Fleet Street, Alice in Wonderland* (2010), and *Dark Shadows.* In 1991 he and Brown were recipients of the Irving G. Thalberg Memorial Award. He is survived by his third wife; two sons, and nine grandchildren.

Index